Media Voices

Pacific
WITHDRAWN
University

Media Voices

An Historical Perspective

An Anthology Edited by
Jean Folkerts

The George Washington University

PACIFIC UNIVERSITY LIBRARY
FOREST GROVE, OREGON

Macmillan Publishing Company
New York

Maxwell Macmillan Canada
Toronto

Editor: David Chodoff
Production Supervisor: George Carr
Production Manager: Paul Smolenski
Cover Designer: Blake Logan
Cover photos: (*left*) UPI/Bettmann
(*right*) The Bettmann Archive

This book was set in Palatino by V & M Graphics, Inc.
and was printed and bound by Book Press.
The cover was printed by Book Press.

Copyright © 1992 by Macmillan Publishing Company,
a division of Macmillan, Inc.

Printed in the United States of America.

All rights reserved. No part of this book may be reproduced or transmitted in any form or by any means, electronic or mechanical, including photocopying, recording, or any information storage and retrieval system, without permission in writing from the Publisher.

Macmillan Publishing Company
866 Third Avenue, New York, New York 10022

Maxwell Macmillan Canada, Inc.
1200 Eglinton Avenue East
Suite 200
Don Mills, Ontario M3C 3N1

Library of Congress Cataloging-in-Publication Data
Media voices: an historical perspective: an anthology / edited by
Jean Folkerts.
p. cm.
Includes index.
ISBN 0-02-338645-2 (paper)
1. Mass Media—United States—History. I. Folkerts, Jean.
P92.U5M454 1992 90-26958
302.23'0973—dc20 CIP

Printing: 1 2 3 4 5 6 7 Year: 2 3 4 5 6 7 8

COPYRIGHT NOTICES AND ACKNOWLEDGMENTS

DAVID D. HALL, "The World of Print and Collective Mentality in Seventeenth Century New England," reprinted with permission from Johns Hopkins University Press, *New Directions in American Intellectual History*, John Higham and Paul Conkin, eds., Baltimore. Copyright © 1980.

E. JENNIFER MONAGHAN, "Literacy Instruction and Gender in Colonial New England," reprinted with permission from the American Studies Association, copyright © 1988, *American Quarterly*, vol. 40.

DAVID PAUL NORD, "A Republican Literature: A Study of Magazine Reading and Readers in Late Eighteenth Century New York," reprinted with permission from the American Studies Association, copyright © 1988, *American Quarterly*, vol. 40.

LIONEL C. BARROW JR., "'Our Own Cause:' *Freedom's Journal* and the Beginnings of the Black Press," reprinted with permission from Lionel C. Barrow and *Journalism History*, vol. 4, copyright © 1978.

"Preface" from *Emergence of a Free Press* by LEONARD W. LEVY. Copyright © 1985 by Leonard W. Levy. Reprinted by permission of Oxford University Press, Inc.

STEPHEN BOTEIN, "Printers and the American Revolution," reprinted with permission from The American Antiquarian Society, *The Press and the American Revolution*, Bernard Bailyn and John B. Hench, eds., Worcester, Mass., copyright © 1980.

JEFFERY A. SMITH, "Public Opinion and the Press Clause," reprinted with permission from Jeffery Smith and *Journalism History*, vol. 14, copyright © 1987.

RICHARD B. KIELBOWICZ, "Modernization, Communication Policy, and the Geopolitics of News, 1820–1860," reprinted with permission from the Speech Communication Association, copyright © 1986, *Critical Studies in Mass Communication*, vol. 3.

DONALD LEWIS SHAW, "At the Crossroads: Change and Continuity in American Press News, 1820–1860," reprinted with permission from Donald Shaw and *Journalism History*, vol. 8, copyright © 1981.

JOHN C. NERONE, "The Mythology of the Penny Press," reprinted with permission from the Speech Communication Association, copyright © 1987, *Critical Studies in Mass Communication*, vol. 4.

DAVID PAUL NORD, "The Public Community: The Urbanization of Journalism in Chicago," reprinted with permission from Sage Publishing Co., copyright © 1985, *Journal of Urban History*, vol. 11.

JEAN FOLKERTS, "Functions of the Reform Press," reprinted with permission of Jean Folkerts and *Journalism History*, vol. 12, copyright © 1985.

TED CURTIS SMYTHE, "The Reporter, 1880–1900: Working Conditions and Their Influence on the News," reprinted with permission from Ted Curtis Smythe and *Journalism History*, vol. 7, copyright © 1980.

RICHARD L. McCORMICK, "The Discovery that Business Corrupts Politics: A Reappraisal of the Origins of Progressivism," reprinted with permission from Richard McCormick and the American Historical Association, *American Historical Review*, copyright © 1981.

MAURINE BEASLEY, "The Women's National Press Club: Case Study of Professional Aspirations," reprinted with permission from Maurine Beasley and *Journalism History*, vol. 15, copyright © 1988.

JERZY ZUBRZYCKI, "The Role of the Foreign-Language Press in Migrant Integration," reprinted with permission from Population Investigation Committee of the London School of Economics, *Population Studies*, vol. 12, copyright © 1958.

ROLAND MARCHAND, "Two Legendary Campaigns," *American Heritage*, permission granted by the University of California Press, copyright © 1985, The Regents of the University of California. The article is comprised of excerpts from *Advertising the American Dream: Making Way for Modernity, 1920–1940*.

CATHERINE L. COVERT, "'We May Hear Too Much': American Sensibility and the Response to Radio, 1919–1924," permission granted by Syracuse University Press, from *Mass Media Between the Wars*, copyright © 1984.

MARY S. MANDER, "The Public Debate About Broadcasting in the Twenties: An Interpretive History," reprinted by permission of the Broadcast Education Association, copyright © 1984, *Journal of Broadcasting*, 28:2.

ROBERT W. McCHESNEY, "Franklin Roosevelt, His Administration, and the Communications Act of 1934," reprinted with permission of *American Journalism*, copyright © 1988, vol. 4.

GREGORY D. BLACK, "Hollywood Censored: The Production Code Administration and the Hollywood Film Industry, 1930–1940," reprinted with permission from Hemisphere Publishing Corporation, New York, *Film History*, vol. 3, no. 3, 1989.

PATRICK S. WASHBURN, "J. Edgar Hoover and the Black Press in World War II," reprinted with permission of Pat Washburn and *Journalism History*, copyright © 1986, vol. 13.

GERALD J. BALDASTY and BETTY HOUCHIN WINFIELD, "Institutional Paralysis in the Press: The Cold War in Washington State," reprinted with permission of *Journalism Quarterly*, vol. 58, copyright © 1981.

JAMES L. BAUGHMAN, "Television in the 'Golden Age': An Entrepreneurial Experiment," reprinted with permission of Phi Alpha Theta, copyright © 1985, *The Historian*, XLVII:2.

DANIEL C. HALLIN, "The Media, the War in Vietnam, and Political Support: A Critique of the Thesis of an Oppositional Media," reprinted from *The Journal of Politics*, vol. 46, no. 1 (February 1984) by permission of the author and the University of Texas Press.

JAMES BOYLAN, "Declarations of Independence," reprinted with permission of the author and the *Columbia Journalism Review*, November/December, copyright © 1986.

Dedicated to Leroy,
Sean, and Jenny

Preface

This book is designed for students of media history. I hope that it will become a valued item in individual libraries, a useful supplementary text for undergraduate media history classes, and a stimulating set of readings for graduate seminars. It is designed to encourage the questioning of historical interpretation rather than the mastery of pat historical answers.

I believe the articles collected here represent the value of diligent, creative research, which too often remains hidden to general view, buried in the pages of journals read only by colleagues in the field.

I want to express my gratitude to the authors of the individual articles reproduced here. They have cooperated in a most gracious way in allowing these articles to be reproduced. I would also like to thank Lucy Cocke, Anne Emery, Ruth Duvall, and Diana Bradley of Eckles Library at Mount Vernon College, who helped secure copies of many of the articles. I would like to thank the members of the Department of Journalism at The George Washington University for their support. Martha McLemore assisted with copying and typing of the manuscript. I would also like to thank Professor Dwight Teeter of the University of Wisconsin at Milwaukee, Professor James L. Baughman at the University of Wisconsin at Madison, Professor David Paul Nord at Indiana University, and Professor Elaine Berland of Webster University, who provided valuable suggestions and encouragement. Susan Henry, editor of *Journalism History*, was most gracious in her support. My friends, Anthony and Agnes Scinta, read proof and provided moral support. The manuscript was reviewed by Steven Knowlton, Pennsylvania State University; Ted Smythe, California State University at Fullerton; John Nerone, Institute of Communications Research, University of Illinois; Roy Atwood, University of Idaho; Clarrisa Myrick-Harris, University of Georgia; Mary Ann Weston, Medill School of Journalism, Northwestern University; and Hazel Dicken-Garcia, University of Minnesota. David Chodoff, of Macmillan Publishing Company, provided encouragement and guided the development of the manuscript. My husband, Leroy Towns, supported the project even while the dining room table was stacked high with manuscript materials.

J.F.

Introduction

In the mid-1960s, when Elizabeth Eisenstein was "provoked" by Marshall McLuhan's *Gutenberg Galaxy* into examining the role of communication as an agent of change in early modern Europe, she found almost no historical literature on the subject. McLuhan, a popular English professor and pop culture devotee of the 1960s, and a fellow—although more complex and more cautious—Canadian, Harold Adams Innis, were among the few who contemplated the effects of communication on society rather than viewing communication forms as isolated elements within individual cultures.[1]

But whereas McLuhan and Innis focused on the differing impacts of oral and written communication, Eisenstein became one of the first to examine the change in written forms, or the impact of the printing press on what she terms the "Commonwealth of Learning." Her work provides a penetrating analysis of the shift from scribal to print-shop culture.

Eisenstein's work, which focuses on print and the Renaissance, the Reformation, and the Scientific Revolution, is dramatically important because it shifts the emphasis from the history of the book and the printing press to the history of the impact of print within a culture. She found, for example, that the print shop "served as a kind of institute for activity . . . which rivaled the older university, court, and academy and which provided preachers and teachers with opportunities to pursue alternate careers." She notes that the "point of departure . . . is not the invention of one device in one Mainz shop but the establishment of many printshops in many urban centers throughout Europe over the course of two decades or so. This entailed the appearance of a new occupational culture associated with the printing trades. New publicity techniques and new communication networks also appeared."[2]

Just as Eisenstein moved beyond the history of the printing press to investigate the impact of print on the culture of early modern times, the essays in this book treat the media not as one monolithic institutional structure with a singular history, but as myriad messages and forms of messages that precipitated, reflected, and interacted with other forces in determining cultural, political, economic, and intellectual life in the United States. Eisenstein's approach implies that we must ask different questions. We must go beyond asking how the newspaper, or radio, or television developed and probe for the interplay between media and culture. The media become participants as well as observers and mirrors in the patterns of historical development.

Asking such questions requires a broad view of both the media and their audiences. Only a few decades ago most historians were male—products of graduate schools dominated by middle- to upper-class men. Those men generally asked questions about how superior men in the past had conceived ideas and how they had structured nations and policies—and the media—around those ideas. In the post-1960 world, as women and minorities attended graduate school in increasing numbers, they began to ask questions about their own counterparts' roles in the past. Slowly, the picture of the past, as well as the ideologies of those creating the picture, changed. These changes have been reflected in approaches to journalism history. Until recently, journalism history has been dominated by the progressive approach, which entails viewing the past as a linear progression, an evolution of progress, a series of time-bound events, and a discrepancy between principles and practices. In this regard, journalism history has lagged behind other historical perspectives. Consensus histories, focusing on enduring qualities and continuity, and New Left approaches, emphasizing systems of power, are notably absent or in the minority.[3] In recent years, however, scholars have attempted to look at a broader "communications" history and to incorporate cultural and social history perspectives into the study of media and communications.

The movement toward cultural history in journalism can perhaps be traced most directly to James W. Carey's 1974 essay "The Problem of Journalism History," in which Carey argued that "cultural history is not concerned merely with events but with the thought within them. Cultural history is, in this sense, the study of consciousness in the past." He further argued that "the press should be viewed as the embodiment of consciousness."[4] Although Carey's challenge has certainly helped to broaden the concept of journalism history, it has, unfortunately, resulted more in *writing about* cultural studies than in *producing* them. In addition, there have been challenges to the cultural studies approach. David Paul Nord, in a 1988 article, "A Plea for *Journalism* History," has suggested that although it is "comforting to speak of interpretation, significance and meaning without reference to underlying causes and structures," it may also be inadequate for the study of mass media. Nord argues that institutional history is essential if it is cast in terms of "a careful exploration of the structure and exercise of power in and through journalism in the past."[5]

Each section of the book poses competing research viewpoints about a given issue as well as competing strains within the society during a specific period. Part I focuses on varying interpretations of communication audiences in early America. Were readers elite and male? Can we measure literacy by writing only, which excludes the possibility of an expanding female audience, or should we measure it by reading, which yields the possibility of a broadened audience? Do traditional concepts of audience endure when a subscription list is examined that indicates merchant and artisan readership? Does the existence of a black audience as early as 1827 alter our conception of early American media consumers? Do the answers to these questions alter our conception of American political and cultural life?

Although each section centers on a specific topic, the varying issues remain as undercurrents in subsequent sessions. Studying the concept of press freedom in the eighteenth century assumes the existence of an audience. In Part II, for example, Jeffery A. Smith comments on public opinion and the press clause, and Stephen Botein in an analysis of the economic impact of printers' political positioning denotes colonial printers' awareness of their audience. Leonard W. Levy, Botein, and Smith do not agree on their interpretations of press freedom in early America. To some degree, they ask different questions. One emphasizes law, one practice, and one theory. All consider what the others have to say, but each reaches substantially different conclusions. But whether we, as readers, support one conclusion or another, their combined efforts enlighten us about aspect of law, practice, and theory that contribute to an understanding of a cultural and intellectual climate of freedom versus suppression.

The concept of free expression in the twentieth century is treated in Part VI. Readers may want to study it there, as Part VI, where it fits chronologically, or they may want to compare it more directly to Part II. In it, the focus is on the interplay of media self-censorship, the pressure of public opinion and reporter values, industry self-interest in action, and government intimidation and regulation. Part II, on the eighteenth century, more directly defines freedom of expression as the right to criticize government, whereas Part VI, on the twentieth century, broadens the scope to include expression that may offend the audience's moral sensibilities, political values, and concepts of racial equality, as well as affect the electronic media industry's ability to derive profits from the market.

One does not move from provincial newspapers in the eighteenth century and their demands for freedom of expression to a mass market of print and electronic media without the development of a mass press. In Part III the reader discovers that congressional leaders in the early 1800s debated whether mass communication should emanate from metropolitan areas or whether localized, regional voices better supported a democratic society. Although the debate centered on communication policy, it reflected a conviction that communication affected political and social policy as well. The focus on modernization, urbanization, mass manufacturing, and city news competed with values grounded in local government and traditional ritual. Did the press of the nation promote a jazzy, modern national tone or did it work to preserve traditional values? Change across the nation did not necessarily parallel change in New York, Baltimore, and Philadelphia. Despite the 1830s advent of the penny press in the city, newspaper content across the nation reflected continuity. Simultaneously, newspapers also reflected technological development in the speed with which they covered the news. Part III carefully examines characteristics traditionally associated with the penny press as well as causes for its development.

What was the nature of the mass press during the second half of the nineteenth century? As business, communication, and transportation networks spanned the continent, did the penny press of the 1830s provide a model that survived the nineteenth century? Or were there competing models? In Part IV we discover that even within an urban area such as Chicago variation occurs. The high-circulation Chicago newspapers did not reflect or generate identical ideas about economics, politics, or metropolitan development. The differences among the newspapers were not superficial; they represented different structural views of society, and different ideas about the roles of voluntary associations, civic leaders, and government. So even the mass, daily newspaper press was not monolithic. Competing with these daily deliverers of news were more specialized publications, aimed at agrarian, labor, and female audiences. Such newspapers provided information, built a sense of community, and helped legitimize movements that seemed too far outside the mainstream for city dailies to comment on respectfully. The mass magazines at the turn of the century also added a voice, challenging the corruption that suddenly seemed to threaten the republic itself. Throughout the period, reporters, treated more as laborers than as professionals, sought professional status.

The emphasis in Part V shifts slightly to concentrate once more on the audience, in particular on audience response to massive change. The cultural anxiety often associated with the 1920s and 1930s translates easily to audience anxiety. The role of women in journalism as a profession, the introduction of radio, the expanding numbers of immigrants as media audiences, and the advent of advertising heralded much change, both promising and frightening. Advertising copywriters capitalized on the fears, providing products that would eliminate causes of anxiety and reward the embracing of modernity. Terminology common to the old century—concepts of transportation, newspapers as primary media, and public utilities—dominated the regulatory debate about radio, but the popular debate, spiritual and religious in tone, reflected fear of radio's cultural power. Audiences embraced the new technology in various ways—as amateur radio operators and as consumers or listeners—but the embrace was cautious, optimistic, and tentative.

Part VII reflects a twentieth-century concern with media as big business and the impact of corporate monoliths on media content, and thus on institutional and political culture. But the concern with corporate control or influence was not relegated to media criticism. Criticism of the corporate state was magnified by the New Left, a radical student movement that challenged authority and institutional control, championed civil rights, and protested the Vietnam War. By 1960, in the early stages of the movement, television had already disillusioned those who viewed it as the medium that would convert popular culture to a higher plane. The popular anthologies and spectaculars described as essential to television's "Golden Age" had disappeared, to be replaced by situation comedies and weekly series. Certainly, such entertainment contained little that could be said to contribute to an oppositional culture. Nevertheless, television and newspaper newsrooms were not sequestered from the world of dissent, and politicians and businesspeople alike challenged the integrity of news content. As a new generation assumed control of major newspapers and yet another generation filled the reporter slots in the television and newspaper newsrooms, criticism of U.S. policy abroad assumed new importance. Did coverage of the war cause defeat in Vietnam? Did the news reflect a deliberate attempt on the part of reporters and editors to oppose authority? Did television news bring into living rooms pictures that were too brutal to be acceptable? Or did the news reflect a growing oppositional culture within mainstream institutions? Was there a burgeoning independence among reporters? And if there was, did it last?

The analyses presented here are a tribute to the scholars who asked the questions and meticulously and creatively sought the answers. Each study brings us closer to a broad theoretical perspective of how media in the United States contribute to, reflect, or draw from political and cultural life. One can begin to examine the broad currents over time. We need to examine further the competing struggles to secure, preserve, and inhibit freedom of expression; the conflicts presented by media as business and media as critics of business; the cultural dilemmas of preserving the past and confronting the future; the role of mass versus specialized media. The answers to these questions enhance the understanding of media as creators, mediators, and disseminators of popular culture and information.

Endnotes

1. See Harold Adams Innis, *Empire and Communications* (1950; reprint ed. Toronto: University of Toronto press, 1972) and *Bias of Communication* (1951; reprint ed., Toronto: University of Toronto Press, 1971). For a short but comprehensive analysis of the influence of Innis and Marshall McLuhan, see "Metahistory, Mythology, and the Media: The American Thought of Harold Innis and Marshall McLuhan," chapter 6 in Daniel Czitrom's *Media and the American Mind: From Morse to McLuhan* (Chapel Hill: University of North Carolina Press, 1982) and "The 'Skeptical' Adversaries," part 10 in J. Herbert Altschull's *From Milton to McLuhan: The Ideas Behind American Journalism* (New York: Longman, 1990). A belief in communication as the cohesive force in society was also the subject of study for those identified with the Chicago School. See the works of John Dewey, Robert Park, and Charles Cooley. Most of this work was sociological. Eisenstein's work, on the other hand, grounded through historical research the concept of communication as an agent of change.

2. See Elizabeth L. Eisenstein, "In the Wake of the Printing Press," *Quarterly Journal of the Library of Congress* 35:3 (June 1978), 183–197.

3. See John D. Stevens and Hazel Dicken Garcia, *Communication History* (Beverly Hills: Sage Publications, 1980), 33–47.

4. James W. Carey, "The Problem of Journalism History," *Journalism History* 1:1 (Spring 1974): 3–5, 27.

5. David Paul Nord, "A Plea for *Journalism* History," *Journalism History* 15:1 (Spring 1988): 8–15.

Contents

I

Communication Audiences in Early America

It is often tempting, when using a modern framework to view the past, to collapse the more than two centuries that represent the colonial period of the United States into a narrow framework depicting political outcasts from England inhabiting a new land, rejecting the old political traditions, and creating a universally popular revolution that separated the new society from the old. The notion advanced in public education systems has been one of a homogeneous group of pilgrims, or Puritans, who sought religious freedom and abided by a Protestant work ethic. Historians' selection of ministers as the spokesmen for colonial society has contributed to this view. Media historians have been, perhaps, among the most guilty in perpetuating this one-dimensional view of colonial America, focusing on printers' entrepreneurial development of newspapers as the dominant communications product, which championed the cause of revolution and democracy.

This emphasis on the political role of the newspaper ignores not only many other aspects of colonial communication but also the multidimensional character of the colonists' world. Those who arrived during the early 1600s relied primarily on ideas and information exchanged at town meetings and in coffeehouses and taverns. Official documents and ship captains' letters that were distributed to only a few of the elite subsequently became sources of conversation. By the late 1600s newspapers from England circulated more widely.[1] Public speaking, sermons, and other traditional styles of oral communication combined with and based on printed documents completed the sphere of communications. The colonies represented heterogeneity—in terms of national origin, language, culture, custom, religion, social class, and race. By the end of the colonial period the new nation was attempting to unify a country composed of former Englishmen, French Protestants, Germans, Scotch-Irish, and African slaves.

A recognition of the new nation as a complex cultural system involving many traditions and communication styles has led historians to examine more carefully the layers of society during not only the colonial period but the early national period as well. Such analysis leads to questions about how individuals, or groups, in this multicultural society communicated, and the answers give life and character to colonial peoples. Suddenly a nation comes to life, with women and men of different cultures and backgrounds creating a multidimensional society. In the four articles presented here, historians look at the interplay between elite and popular culture, at the participation of women in learning and teaching reading and writing, at the involvement of artisans in the written culture of the new nation, and at the first black newspaper, which appeared during the latter part of the early national period. These articles indicate the complexity of the culture by acknowledging the existence of social class, gender, and race. This acknowledgment allows a broader view of oral and written communication styles and an understanding of the availability of information to individuals and social groups within a developing nation.

David D. Hall, in "The World of Print and Collective Mentality in Seventeenth-Century New England," emphasizes the blending of print and oral culture and the relationship between books and collective popular belief. He notes that there was a continuum between print and oral modes of communication. He also notes that, although the English markets were dominated by religious books, publishers catered to the buying public with popular romances and history as well—a pattern that developed similarly in the colonies, which relied on British imports throughout most of the seventeenth century. Hall notes the interaction of the local press with the marketplace and cites recurring themes that appeared in books, iconography, street rituals, and on gravestones, thus documenting the blurred lines of demarcation between oral and print culture.

E. Jennifer Monaghan, in "Literacy Instruction and Gender in Colonial New England," disputes the traditional method of determining who in seventeenth- and eighteenth-century America was literate.[2] Traditional historians long have associated the ability to sign one's name with the ability to read. Not so, notes Monaghan, citing evidence that many women read without learning to write. Monaghan analyzes the colonial reading curriculum and concludes that even reading teachers, many of whom were women, did not know how to write. Writing, considered a craft, was more often taught by male writing masters who occupied a higher status than reading teachers, and the rather costly writing texts were imported from England. The expectation of colonial town leaders was that all children would be able to read, for religious, economic, and political reasons, but that writing was a job-related skill, unnecessary for most women. This information expands our concept of who in colonial America was literate, and therefore expands the concept of the audience for printed products as well.

David Paul Nord, who looks at the 1790s in "A Republican Literature: A Study of Magazine Reading and Readers in Late Eighteenth-Century New York," shows that magazine reading in the period was a more democratic activity than historians generally have supposed. Analyzing the subscriber list to the *New-York Magazine,* Nord notes that although the readership of the magazine was decidedly wealthier than the population as a whole, about half the subscribers were shopkeepers and artisans. The "elite" readers were mostly successful merchants. The content of the magazine was highly eclectic, but it emphasized the necessity for public virtue in the early Republic, expressed a suspicion of luxury, and argued for the power of knowledge within the democracy. Although the *New-York Magazine* was not popular literature produced by and for the masses, it reached beyond the elite, providing a republican literature affirming traditional values.

Lionel C. Barrow Jr., in "'Our Own Cause': *Freedom's Journal* and the Beginnings of the Black Press," describes the content and circulation of this first black newspaper. Although he notes that probably about one-third of the readership was white, he also points to problems in determining black literacy rates and circulation figures. Census statistics for black literacy are not available until 1850, and those figures were based on the ability to write.

After reading Monaghan's description of the differences between the ability to read and to write, one might want to question government literacy figures for the early 1800s.

These authors indicate that the audience during the colonial and the early national period was extensive, not only in numbers but in variation of class and gender. By looking at patterns between oral and print culture, by reexamining what it meant to sign one's name, and by analyzing subscriber lists and probable circulations, these authors extend the understanding of communication in the colonial period.

Endnotes

1. Ian K. Steele, *The English Atlantic, 1675–1740: An Exploration of Communication and Community* (New York: Oxford University Press, 1986).

2. For discussions of literacy, see Carolyn Marvin, "Constructed and Reconstructed Discourse: Inscription and Talk in the History of Literacy," *Communication Research* 11:4 (October, 1984): 563–594 and Harvey J. Graff, "The Legacies of Literacy," *Journal of Communication* 32 (Winter, 1982): 12–26.

The World of Print and Collective Mentality in Seventeenth-Century New England

David D. Hall

A twelve-year-old boy, precociously alert to the literary marketplace, writes a ballad (in "Grub-street" style) on the capture of a pirate. Printed as a broadside, the poem is hawked in the streets of Boston and sells "wonderfully." An old man retells a family legend of how, in the persecuting times of "Bloody Mary" more than two centuries earlier, his ancestors hid their Protestant Bible in a stool. A young minister, ambitious as a writer, dreams of hiring a peddler who will carry cheap religious tracts from town to town.[1]

These are gestures that draw us into the world of print as it was experienced by Americans in the seventeenth century. I begin with this world because it is a useful starting point for rethinking the limitations and possibilities of intellectual history. A starting point, but not the means of answering every question, because the world of print is an imperfect mirror of intellectual experience, a partial reflection of all that is thought and believed. My evidence is taken from the seventeenth century, but I mean to contribute to a more general debate. This is the debate between social and intellectual historians about the distance that exists between elites or intellectuals and other groups; between "high" culture and that which is usually described as "popular"; between books and collective belief.

If we feel uneasy with the intellectual history of seventeenth-century New England, the explanation is our renewed sense of distance in any or all of these forms. It is the felt distance of the ministers from the rest of society that limits them to being spokesmen for an elite. It is the distance between the ministers, who live in the world of print, and the mass of the people, who retain "peasant" ways of thinking.[2] This last distinction has been enormously reinforced by the work of Keith Thomas, which shows that in seventeenth-century England formal systems of religious belief competed with alternative, more "primitive" beliefs, and, more generally, by the work of French historians of *mentalité*, which uncovers for early modern France a mental world of superstition and folk belief apparently quite separate from the mental world of the literate.[3] In effect, the discovery of collective mentality is being used as a weapon against intellectual history, a means of restricting it within narrow boundaries.

In taking up the world of the book, I mean to explore the possibilities for extending these boundaries. There are many limitations to what can be accomplished by the history of the book, one of which is intrinsic in the complexity of any verbal statement: how much or what parts of that complexity is transmitted to any reader?[4] Many assumptions must be made, the chief one being that those books which sold in largest quantity reflect collective ways of thinking. Nonetheless, I want to use the history of print as a means for reappraising the relationship between the ministers and society as a whole in seventeenth-century New England, and in doing so, to point the way toward a broader understanding of intellectual history.

The world of print in seventeenth-century New England was broadly continuous with that of Europe. Shortly after the discovery of printing, the book in Europe assumed the form it would have for centuries to come, even as techniques for the book trade also became standardized. In the early years, and especially in England for much of the sixteenth-century, individual patrons played an important role in deciding what was published. Early and late, the state attempted to control the world of print by restrictive licensing and censorship. But every effort at restraint was undercut by the lure of the marketplace. Printers produced whatever readers would buy. One-third of the books published in sixteenth-century England were not entered in the Stationer's Register, and in France, taking into account both what was printed within its borders and what was made available from outside, the actual world of print was far larger than any official version.[5] The entrepreneur reigned. What Robert Darnton says of publishers in Paris on the eve of the French Revolution, though colored by legal conditions, reflects the situation everywhere:

> *"Innovation" came through the underground. Down there, no legalities constrained productivity, and books were turned out by a kind of rampant capitalism. . . . foreign publishers did a wild and wooly business in pirating [books officially licensed in France]. . . . They were tough businessmen who produced anything that would sell. They took risks, broke traditions, and maximized profits by quantity instead of quality production.*

Almost as soon as printing began, printer-publishers were reaching out for the widest possible audience.[6]

The printing technology of the day was amazingly responsive to demands for quantity and speed.[7] But speed and innovation were not the only rhythms of the marketplace. For every Nathanael Butter (a London printer of the early seventeenth century who specialized in domestic intelligence, murders, cases of treason, and adventure stories, all requiring rapid publication before they fell out of date),[8] there was a printer who catered to needs that seemed unchanging, a printer who marketed the same product year in and year out. Provincial booksellers in eighteenth-century France published catechisms, liturgical handbooks, books of devotion, and similar steady sellers in far greater quantity than anything else; these were books, moreover, for which the copyrights had lapsed.[9] Their lack of glamour should not betray us into ignoring the significance of such steady sellers and the audience they served. In effect two major rhythms crisscrossed in the marketplace: one of change, the other of repetition. A constant recycling of tried and true literary products accompanied the publication of new styles and genres.

These rhythms offer clues to the relationship between modes of print and modes of thinking. But before pursuing them further, we must turn to evidence about literacy and book ownership in order to gain a clearer understanding of the marketplace. Figures on literacy vary from country to country and within each country by region. National averages can conceal the crucial difference in France between the North (literate) and the South (illiterate). What seems true of early modern Europe is that each country had its "dark corners of the land," regions in which the book was rare, few printers set up shop, and illiteracy (at least in the national language) was high. These were regions, moreover, where cosmopolitan travelers could barely make themselves understood.[10] In more integrated communities, literacy and book ownership varied with social and economic rank. By the early seventeenth century, professionals (clergy, lawyers) in England were completely literate, the aristocracy nearly so, with the rate descending to approximately 50 percent for yeomen and small tradesmen. Thereafter the decline is rapid, to a low of a few percent for laborers.[11] As for book ownership in England, a careful study of probate inventories in three towns in Kent has shown that by the early seventeenth century, between 40 and 50 percent of males owned books. This figure conceals immense variances: no laborer owned any books, but close to all professionals did.[12]

These estimates for literacy and book distribution are perplexing. It is possible to interpret them as meaning that a chasm separated the culture of the elite, who lived in the world of print, from that of the poor, who did not. Since the printed book was something new in European culture, historians have also argued that a "traditional oral" culture remained intact among "peasants" even as the world of print came into being in urban areas and among the upper classes.[13] But the evidence about literacy and reading may really indicate that these categories of elite and nonelite are too limiting. Every social group contained a certain percentage of persons who could read, even if their doing so defies our expectations. To us there is a mystery about the ways and means by which a French peasant in the sixteenth century taught himself to read the Bible he had acquired. Yet it happened.[14] In the sixteenth- and seventeenth-century Cambridgeshire towns Margaret Spufford has studied, books were read with extraordinary care by persons of every description, including many women. Her evidence, which goes beyond quantitative estimates of literacy to consider how print was put to use, indicates that social, economic, and sexual boundaries all yielded to the book.[15] As for "oral" culture, it too was entwined with the world of print. The culture of the European peasant may be likened to a river full of debris. That debris had various origins and qualities. Some of it arose from communal experience and was therefore "folk" in nature. But much of the rest of it is easily recognized as bits and pieces of literary culture extending from Christianity as far back as classical civilization. By the early seventeenth century this accumulation of materials effectively meant that there was nothing immaculate about "oral" culture. We must speak instead of a continuum between print and oral modes.[16]

That the boundaries of print were fluid and overlapping is apparent from books themselves. The reach of some books in the early modern period was extended visually by the woodcuts that embellished broadsides, primers, almanacs, emblem books, and the like. Collectively these pictures transmitted ideas beyond the reach of print. Iconography carried ideas downward into social milieux where the book may not have widely penetrated. It also seems true that certain kinds of books circulated in ways that touched even the apparently illiterate—the Bible, naturally, but also the cheapest of pamphlet literature, such as the "many old smokie paperbacks" on astrology complained of by a late-sixteenth-century English writer, and the equally inexpensive "Bibliotheque Bleue" of Troyes, a series of books designed to be read aloud.[17] We must also bear in mind that the illiterate participated in communal gatherings (fairs, festivals, church services) that functioned as occasions for the exchange of knowledge among different social groups. For all of these reasons it should be "obvious that illiteracy does not mean stupidity or mental blankness." The illiterate in early modern France, Pierre Goubert has observed, "are Christians, if unaware of the controversies over the nature of grace; . . . all of them receive an oral culture and even a bookish culture, by way of a reader or story-teller, since there is a whole printed literature designed especially for them." In England the same fluidity prevailed. There as elsewhere, illiteracy cannot be equated with a "peasant" mentality cut off from the world of print.[18]

To be sure, some boundaries do cut through

the world of print. Most of the literate could not read Latin, but a large (though after 1600, a steadily decreasing) percentage of books were published in that language. In some sense books in Latin bespoke a separate culture. But as translations multiplied in the late sixteenth century,[19] and as the classics were redacted in popular formats, Latin lost most of its significance as a carrier of ideas or as a cultural code. Meanwhile printer-entrepreneurs were responding to the needs of professional groups, publishing law books and manuals of church practice that had little circulation beyond their immediate audience.

But over all such categories of books stand others that, to judge from the number of editions and the quantities produced, reached a general audience. That such books bear witness to shared beliefs and common ways of thinking seems apparent from two kinds of evidence. One is the marketplace rhythm of long duration, the continuous production of certain literary genres and formulas over centuries. The other is evidence about quantity: the sheer number of books that were printed. Together, these types of evidence point to three major categories as dominant in the marketplace.[20] Let me consider each in turn.

Religious books outnumber all other kinds. This fact, like others in the history of print, may perplex historians who think of religion solely as a system of doctrine. H. S. Bennett, describing the situation in pre-Reformation England, brings us closer to actuality:

> *The religious houses required works of spiritual instruction and consolation in the vernacular. . . . The reader of pious legends, such as those contained in that vast compilation,* The Golden Legend, *or in smaller collections, . . . was catered for. Volumes of pious stories; handbooks of practical help in church worship; books of systematized religious instruction; volumes of sermons and homilies; allegorical and lyric poems. . . .*

Still closer is the anecdote repeated by Keith Thomas of an "old woman who told a visitor that she would have gone distracted after the loss of her husband but for the *Sayings* of the Puritan pastor John Dod, which hung in her house." Similarly, the wife of John Bunyan thought so much of Arthur Dent's *The Plaine Mans Pathway to Heaven,* a book that went through twenty-five editions between 1601 and 1640, that she included it in her dower, together with Lewis Bayly's *Practice of Piety.* Such devotional manuals flourished beneath the level of doctrinal controversy. Medieval *fabula* reappeared in Protestant guise, just as emblems were freely exchanged between Catholic and Protestant moralizing tales. Given this intermingling, it comes as less of a surprise that in 1667 a printer in Cambridge, Massachusetts, published an edition of Thomas a Kempis's *Imitation of Christ.*[21]

Romances—fairy stories, chivalric poems, light fiction—tell of "'Superman': the Paladin who splits Saracen skulls with a single blow; the crusader knight on his way to liberate Jerusalem and pausing to do the same for 'Babylon'; . . . the good giant Gargantua, coolly removing the bells of Notre-Dame; the artful righters of wrongs, straight or comic, Lancelot or Scaramouche; the invincible good enchanters and powerful fairies whose miracles almost outshine the saints'." A recurring thematic structure of danger and rescue can be said to have appealed to the wish to escape. In the "Bibliotheque Bleue," a paradigm of the literature of escapism, there is nothing of everyday reality, no poor people, no artisans, merely the sensation of entering, however briefly, a glittering world of miracle and magic. Allied to these romances were those kinds of print, especially broadsides, which played upon spectacular events such as murders and acts of treason. In Protestant England and Catholic France the genre was identical. The London printer Nathanael Butter printed news sheets and broadsides catering to "the public's innate curiosity in the strange, the supernatural, the gruesome, the intrepid and the splendid." Meanwhile in France the news sheets were telling of "juicy crimes sung in interminable lays, one *sou* per sheet, incendiarism, maned stars, weird, contagious ailments," all perhaps serving, as one historian has suggested, to provide "useful employment for the bemused minds of the . . . poor."[22]

Books of history range from travel narratives that verge on being sensational to the most ponderous of chronicles. Little of what passed as history was critical, in the sense of detaching legend from fact. Rather, legend was the stuff of historical writing. Most of these legends had to do with the history of the Christian church or the Christian community. The great example in English is Foxe's *Book of Martyrs*. Its structure as myth, providing a sacred interpretation of community origins and community destiny, together with its symbolism of light (the saints) warring against dark (the devil), were characteristic of popular history as a whole, though in any particular example the symbolism was adapted to partisan purposes.[23]

Books of history, romance, and religion as I have described them constituted a special kind of literary culture. The rhythms of this culture were slow, for what sold in the marketplace were formulas that did not need changing. Equally slow was the pace of reading, as the same books were read and reread. This practice may be designated "intensive," in contrast to the "extensive" style of persons wanting novelty and change.[24] Some readers in early modern Europe wanted new ideas from books or regarded them as objects of fashion, valuable for a season but then falling out of style. Not so the booksellers and their patrons in provincial France who sought books that had long since passed out of copyright. Not so the Franklin family or John Bunyan's wife, for whom Scripture and books of devotion gained in meaning as time went by. Such examples suggest the power of a world of print in which certain formulas had enduring significance.

Let me call this the "traditional" world of print. By doing so, I mean to emphasize the continuities between oral and print modes of culture, and among social groups. Class is certainly a factor in the making of the world of print, but the literary formulas that comprised "traditional" culture had appeal across class lines. I find it interesting that many of the stories in the "Bibliotheque Bleue" of Troyes, a true peddlers' literature, were derived from classical authors, or from "high culture" authors of a century earlier. Motifs, both literary and iconographic, seem to circulate among milieux and levels, some starting "high" and descending, others starting "low" and moving upward. What this means I do not know, but it surely suggests that all readers in early modern Europe, and many of the illiterate, participated in a common culture.[25]

Keith Thomas and Robert Mandrou argue differently. In *Religion and the Decline of Magic*, Thomas says that the reach of Protestantism extended only so far in post-Reformation England, leaving untouched an area of culture that included belief in magic, astrology, and witchcraft in ways that were contrary to orthodox religion. Adapting the view of Christoper Hill, Thomas suggests that this clash of cultures links up with the hostility between the middle class and social groups placed beneath it. An aggressively Protestant middle class preferred rationality, while groups lower in the social scale, suffering from dispossession and never in control of things, turned to magic and astrology for their world view. This world view is a survival from earlier times; it is "traditional" in the sense of having been around for ages, and also in not depending on books (though manifesting itself in the world of print) for transmittal. A kindred argument is made by Robert Mandrou, who believes that "French popular culture of the ancient regime constituted a separate category of culture, characterized by a literature of colportage portraying an unchanging wonderland of magic and miracles."[26]

These efforts to describe the mental world of the lower classes may help to correct the distortions inherent in labels like the "Age of Reason," and they teach us to take seriously the most casual of literary productions. But in the case of French popular culture an alternative interpretation is easily available, as I have already indicated.[27] And in the case of Thomas's "traditional" culture, the argument depends upon a sociology of religion (that marginal groups, or groups hard pressed by the environment, turn to "magic" for relief), or on assumptions about "ritual" (meaning a more "primitive" form of religion, appealing to lower classes) that cannot be borne out. Nor does the concept of a "rational" middle class take adequate account of the sloppy reading tastes of the literate, at once serious and sentimental, realistic and escapist. The case for separate and segregated cultures is yet to be made.[28]

The exception may be the milieu of the urban avant-garde. Here, two worlds of print coexist: the world of slow and repetitious rhythms, and that concerned with the new and critical. In ways we perhaps know little of, this latter had its own formulas and rituals bound up with distinctive cultural agencies (the literary salon, the Royal Society) and distinctive modes of communication (the *Journal des Savants*, the *Proceedings* of the Royal Society).[29] Yet the line between readers of these journals and readers of "traditional" books cannot be drawn too sharply. There was always an intermediary group interpreting the one to the other. And there came moments when the need for reassurance could only be satisfied by returning to the formulas that never changed.

In the storybook version of New England history, every one in Puritan times could read, the ministers wrote and spoke for a general audience, and the founding of a press at Cambridge in 1638 helped make books abundant.[30] The alternative, argued most strenuously by Kenneth Lockridge, is that illiteracy shackled half of the adult males and three-fourths of the women, with consequences for the whole of culture.[31] Any of these statistics is suspect. More to the point, they do not really define the relationship between the colonists and the world of print. In thinking about that broader problem, it is important to recognize that the "dark corners of the land" that figure in the European landscape failed to reappear in New England. A considerable number of seventeenth-century Europeans had to contend with three languages: Latin, a formalized version of the vernacular, and a local dialect. In New England these distinctions became insignificant. While allowing for minor variations, we can say that a common language linked all social groups. We can also say that the colonists lived easily in the world of print. In part this was owing to Puritanism, a religion—and here I repeat a cliché—of the book. In part this sense of ease was merely a consequence of the times, for by the mid-seventeenth century the book had lost its novelty. But whatever the reasons, the marketplace of print in New England was remarkably complex and mature.

Throughout the seventeenth century the colonists depended upon imports for the bulk of their reading. In buying from abroad, these Puritans acted much like the typical patron of print in early modern Europe. Religious books dominated, forming nearly half of the imports of Hezekiah Usher, a Boston bookseller, in the 1680s. Schoolbooks, the staple of many a bookseller then and now, ranked second. Aside from books in law, medicine, and navigation, all of which catered to professional needs, the next largest category was belles-lettres—romances, light fiction, modern poetry.[32]

Already, then, we know from Hezekiah Usher's records that two of the three basic types that made up the "traditional" world of print recurred in New England. And once printer-entrepreneurs began to publish locally, their imprints round out a picture of remarkable continuity between old world and new. In its early years the Cambridge press was responsive to state patronage, publishing books for the Indians, law codes, and public documents. But by the 1640s the imprint list was reflecting the entrepreneurial instincts of printers and booksellers. Almanacs and catechisms (all written locally) made their appearance.[33] History became important, as did a closely related literature of disasters. *The Day of Doom* struck a popular nerve, an edition of 1800 copies selling out within a year. Other popular books followed, like Mary Rowlandson's captivity narrative and Cotton Mather's execution sermon for the pirate Morgan. That the American marketplace was like the European in catering to "intensive" readers and the rhythm of long duration is stunningly suggested by the reprinting in 1673 of John Dod's *Old Mr. Dod's Sayings; or, a posie out of Mr. Dod's Garden*. Here too it must have become a familiar household object as, sixty years before, it had been in England.

The Cambridge press did not publish any romances, but almost from the outset included works of history in responding to colonial needs. A familiar structure reappears in the history published locally. All of these books taught either a generalized version of the Protestant myth or a version tied more closely to the founding of the colonies. Some of this literature dealt with the millennium and the Last Judgment (for example, Samuel Whiting's *Discourse of the Last Judgment*); some of it was about enemies of the saints, not only Catholics, but also those Protestant groups who wandered from the truth.[34] Local publications, chiefly election- and fast-day sermons, drew the colonists themselves into the drama of a chosen people warring against their enemies.

Judging by the qualities of what sold and the interaction of the local press with the marketplace, the world of print in seventeenth-century New England bespeaks collective mentality. As in Europe, the "traditional" literary culture reached out to and engaged every social group. There is other evidence as well of how certain ways of thinking extended across the levels of society. The case is clearest, perhaps, with anti-Catholicism, always a "popular" form of belief, and one that found expression in the iconography and rites of street festivals such as the celebration of Guy Fawkes Day.[35] The iconography of gravestones is something of a parallel case, for various of the symbols circulated from emblem books through poetry to carvings done by untrained artists.[36] The extraordinary publishing history of *The Day of Doom* grows out of the fact that all the basic themes of the "traditional" marketplace converged in a single text, a text that also borrowed its literary form from the ballad by which current events ("sensations") were announced to a popular audience. The event itself is sensational, the return of Christ to earth amid thunder and convulsions of the natural world. And in Wigglesworth's vivid pictures of heaven and hell his readers could find the excitement of adventure and assurance that the faithful would triumph over pain, disorder, and their enemies. All these forms of sustenance recur in Mrs. Rowlandson's captivity narrative. The book as artifact, the literary marketplace, the "intensive" reader, and collective ways of thinking all are joined in the history and substance of such texts.

What, then, of the ministers and their relationship to collective mentality? It is worth noting that no New England minister ever complained of having parishioners who could not understand his diction. The "dark corners of the land" in England and France were alien territory to persons speaking the English or French of the city. By comparison, the whole of New England constituted a reasonably uniform language field, a circumstance that helps us understand how deeply the culture was bound up with print as a medium of communication.[37]

We err greatly in thinking of the ministers as intellectuals, if by that we mean they formed a coterie, dealt in abstractions, and were interested in new ideas or criticism. Leaving aside all the other ways in which the ministers mingled with a general audience, their relationship to the literary marketplace would alone disprove this view. The ministers who entered the marketplace as writers offered a wide range of fare, from almanacs and poetry to works of history and popular divinity. They published in every size and format, from the cheapest broadside to the folio. Some of their publications sold well, others poorly. In nearly all, the contents were conventional, as were their intentions. The author in seventeenth-century New England did his writing in harmony with the modes of collective mentality. A "traditional" relationship, one ensuring the widest possible audience, existed between the ministers and the world of the book.

Two brief examples must do as illustrations of this argument: Cotton Mather and the Antinomian controversy.

Mather, like Franklin, seems to have arrived in the world with a full-blown awareness of the literary marketplace. The intensity of his life as reader and writer is obvious from the extraordinary number of books he owned, and equally from the number he wrote. The *Diary* makes it clear that this intensity flowed in traditional channels.[38] The marketplace in Mather's Boston was competitive (nineteen booksellers and seven printers were at work by 1700), pluralistic, and patterned to meet certain kinds of cultural needs. When Mather began his career as a minister, each week preaching sermons to an audience in Second Church, he simultaneously launched himself as a writer who with each book felt his way toward a popular audience. The two roles of minister and writer were really one. As minister-writer he spoke to and for collective needs, appropriating in his turn the formulas and genres of the traditional marketplace. Like the precocious Franklin, a youthful Mather took advantage of the formulas of "sensation" literature in his first publication, *The Call of the Gospel*, a sermon preached "to a vast Concourse of People" prior to the execution of the criminal James Morgan in 1686. Here is Mather speaking for himself about his literary endeavors and the marketplace: "Now it pleased God, that the people, throughout the Country, very greedily desired the Publication of my poor Sermon. . . . The Book sold exceedingly; and I hope did a World of Good. . . . There has been since, a second Edition of the Book, with a Copy of my Discourse with the poor Malefactor walking to his Execution, added at the End." That is, Mather told the world the conversation he had had with Morgan as the criminal walked to the scaffold. This mating of morality with sensation, one that endures into our own day, was thereafter a formula Mather used frequently, and, unfortunately, he used it when it came to witchcraft. The literature of remarkable providences and the literature of captivity narratives are related formulas, which he and his father produced in abundance and with excellent success in the marketplace. Cotton Mather was a popular writer alertly responsive to audience needs and audience tastes.[39]

At a certain point every student of the Antinomian controversy comes to appreciate John Winthrop's rueful remark that no one at the time could understand what separated the parties in terms of doctrine. Winthrop's point is really that the controversy had become rhetorical, a controversy that revolved around popular catchwords more than issues of Christian doctrine. Although the controversy included both, my purpose is to suggest why it expanded outside the circle of ministers to engage the anger and interests of all the colonists. The explanation lies in the rhetoric of the controversy. It is a rhetoric built around simple contrasts that invoke the symbolism of collective identity. On the part of the Antinomians, the basic pairing is that of light (Christ, the gospel, free grace, freedom) against dark (Adam, the law, bondage, captivity), a pairing that John Wheelwright, in a fast-day sermon that is a remarkable example of popular speech, applied to the nature of history: the ultimate struggle between the children of light and the children of darkness is occurring right here and now in New England. The "legal" preachers, Wheelwright made clear, were threatening figures, not because they misinterpreted the exact position of faith in the order of salvation, but because they represented, they were agents of, a gigantic conspiracy against the saints. The "legal" preachers were equally rhetorical in linking Anne Hutchinson with the Familists, a shadowy but monstrous group, as though "free love" were really at issue in 1637. But the ministers themselves on either side of the controversy could conceive of the situation in no other terms. Their rhetoric was not a matter of expediency, but was intrinsic to a collective mentality they shared with ordinary people. The Antinomian controversy had its roots in and drew energy from ways of thinking that united ministers and laymen.[40]

I do not mean to simplify the position of the ministers. University educated and at ease in the world of Latin, they stood apart from the general population. As writers and readers they participated in a wider range of literary culture than most of their parishioners, moving from formulas and proverbs that are very nearly "folk" in character to more esoteric prose, and back again. The contradictions in Cotton Mather's character exaggerate but also accurately reflect the complexity of roles: at once a pedant and a popularizer, Mather was also a man who eagerly read new books while continuing to publish in old forms. After this complexity is acknowledged, however, the fact remains that Mather was primarily engaged with the formulas of popular religion, and with the forms of print most suited to them.[41]

Leaving aside the ministers and their relationship to the "traditional" world of print, I want again to warn against the presumption that ordinary people think in different ways, or possess a separate culture, from the modes of an "elite." It does us little good to divide up the intellectual world of seventeenth-century New England on the basis of social class, or even, for that matter, of literacy. Rather, we can move from the world of print, with its fluid boundaries and rhythms of long duration, to an understanding of intellectual history as itself having wider boundaries than many social historians seem willing to recognize. How precisely to describe the formulas, the assumptions, that comprise collective mentality in seventeenth-century New England is a task that lies ahead. Another task is to locate the breakdown of "traditional" literary culture, a process that may well have been underway in Mather's time, and that was certainly occurring in the eighteenth century as upper-class groups began to detach themselves from popular culture.[42] But change came slowly. It is really the continuities that impress. In taking them seriously, we free ourselves from distinctions that seem to have restricted the scope and significance of intellectual history.[43]

Endnotes

1. *The Autobiography of Benjamin Franklin* (New Haven, Conn.: Yale University Press, 1964), pp. 50, 59–60; *The Diary of Cotton Mather,* 2 vols., ed. W. C. Ford (New York: Frederick Unger, n.d.), 1:65.
2. Kenneth Lockridge, *Literacy in Colonial New England* (New York: W. W. Norton, 1974). Important arguments correcting Lockridge appear in Lawrence Cremin, "Reading, Writing and Literacy," *Review of Education* 1 (November 1975): 517–21.
3. Keith Thomas, *Religion and the Decline of Magic* (London: Weidenfeld and Nicolson, 1971); Robert Mandrou, *De la culture populaire aux xvii and xviii siècles: La Bibliotheque Bleue de Troyes* (Paris: Stock, 1964).
4. "Mais à propos de chaque image et de chaque theme reste posée la question pour qui étaient-ils comprehensibles?" Georges Duby, "Histoire des mentalités," in *L'Histoire et Ses Méthodes,* ed. Charles Samaran (Paris: Gallimard, 1961), p. 923.
5. H. S. Bennett, *English Books & Readers, 1475 to 1557* (London: Cambridge University Press, 1969); idem, *English Books & Readers, 1558 to 1603* (Cambridge: At the University Press, 1965), referred to hereafter as Bennett, *English Books &*

Readers, 1, and Bennett, *English Books & Readers,* 2. The importance of patronage is argued in Bennett, *English Books & Readers,* 2, ch. 2, and the figure concerning the Stationer's Register is given in Bennett, *English Books & Readers,* 2, p. 60. The situation in eighteenth-century France is described in the essays brought together in *Livre et Societe dans La France du xviii siècle,* 2 vols. (Paris: Mouton, 1965, 1970). See also Lucien Febvre and Henri-Jean Martin, *The Coming of the Book* (Atlantic Highlands, N.J.: Humanities Press, 1976).

6. Robert Darnton, "Reading, Writing, and Publishing in Eighteenth-Century France: A Case Study in the Sociology of Literature," in *Historical Studies Today,* ed. Felix Gilbert (New York: W. W. Norton, 1972), pp. 261–62.

7. Bennett, *English Books & Readers,* 2, p. 244.

8. Butter's career is described in Leone Rostenberg, *Literary, Political, Scientific, Religious & Legal Publishing, Printing & Bookselling in England, 1551–1700* (New York: Burt Franklin, 1965), ch. 3.

9. Julien Brancolini and Marie-Therese Bouyssy, "La vie provinciale du livre à la fin de l'Ancien Régime," in *Livre et Société,* 2: 3–37.

10. Thomas, *Religion and the Decline of Magic,* p. 165; Eugen Weber, *Peasants into Frenchmen: The Modernization of Rural France, 1870–1914* (Stanford: Stanford University Press, 1976), pt. 1, especially chs. 1 and 6 (on language).

11. John Cressy, "Literacy in Seventeenth-Century England: More Evidence," *Journal of Interdisciplinary History* 8, no. 1 (Summer 1977): 141–50; Lawrence Stone, "Literacy and Education in England, 1640–1900," *Past and Present* 42 (February 1969): 69–139. The methodological limitations in reckoning literacy on the basis of signatures are underscored in Cremin's review of Lockridge, "Reading, Writing and Literacy," and in Margaret Spufford, *Contrasting Communities: English Villagers in the Sixteenth and Seventeenth Centuries* (Cambridge: At the University Press, 1974). Spufford demonstrates that persons who signed their wills with an *x* had written out their names on other documents (ch. 7).

12. Peter Clark, "The Ownership of Books in England, 1560–1640: The Example of Some Kentish Townsfolk," in *Schooling and Society,* ed. Lawrence Stone (Baltimore, Md.: The Johns Hopkins University Press, 1976), pp. 95–111. The situation in sixteenth-century France is touched on in Natalie Zemon Davis, *Society and Culture in Early Modern France* (Stanford: Stanford University Press, 1975), pp. 195–197. Probate inventories record holdings at the time of death, not the flow of experience with print over time. Since books get used up and discarded, the inventories are at best a partial record of encounters with the world of print. That no copies survive of the first edition of *The Day of Doom* or of any of the *New England Primer* published before 1729 are cases in point of books that were widely owned and used but that do not often turn up in inventories simply because they perished from so much use.

13. Davis, *Society and Culture,* ch. 7. Davis (and also Kenneth Lockridge) invokes the work of the anthropologist Jack Goody in drawing a sharp line between oral and literate experience. But how useful is this distinction when applied to European culture two millennia after the emergence of writing? Goody's point of view is presented in *Literacy in Traditional Societies* (Cambridge: At the University Press, 1968). But see the review by Daniel McCall, "Literacy and Social Structure," *History of Education Quarterly* 11 (Spring 1971): 85–92.

14. Davis, *Society and Culture,* p. 203.

15. Spufford, *Contrasting Communities,* pt. 2, ch. 8; pt. 3.

16. The most substantial demonstration of this point is Peter Burke, *Popular Culture in Early Modern Europe* (New York: Harper Torchbooks, 1978). The "oral" culture of the French peasants who proved impervious to Protestantism was rich in Catholic ideas and images; see Davis, *Society and Culture,* pp. 203–8.

17. Bennett, *English Books & Readers,* 2, p. 204; Mandrou, *De la culture populaire.*

18. Pierre Goubert, *The Ancien Regime* (New York: Harper Torchbooks, 1974), p. 263, generalizing from Mandrou, *De la culture populaire.* "If it is true that the parish meeting did not yet involve the kind of collective guidance of the community's spiritual life which it became at the end of the seventeenth century, the parish was nevertheless alive in the form of the Sunday gathering for mass, when for a long time the priest . . . com-

muned with his flock" (Robert Mandrou, *Introduction to Modern France, 1500–1640: An Essay in Historical Psychology* [New York: Harper Torchbooks, 1976], p. 91).

19. Bennett, *English Books & Readers,* 2, ch. 4.
20. There are tables quantifying production by types in *Livre et Société,* 1: 14–26. Less precise information is in Bennett, *English Books & Readers,* 1 and 2.
21. Bennett, *English Books & Readers,* 1, p. 8; Thomas, *Religion and the Decline of Magic,* p. 82; Spufford, *Contrasting Communities,* p. 210.
22. Goubert, *Ancien Regime,* pp. 267–68, relying on Mandrou, *De la culture populaire;* Genevieve Bolleme, "Littérature populaire et littérature de colportage au xviii siècle, in *Livre et Société,* 1: 61–92; Rostenberg, *Literary Publishing, Printing & Bookselling,* p. 78.
23. William Haller, *Foxe's Book of Martyrs and the Elect Nation* (London: Jonathan Cape, 1963).
24. This distinction between types of reading was drawn to my attention by Norman Fiering. The original source is Rolf Engelsing, *Analphabetentum und Lekture: Zur Sozialgeschichte des Lesens in Deutschland zwischen feudaler und industrieller Gesellschaft* (Stuttgart: J. B. Metzler, 1973). It is Fiering's view that the experience of reading romances and other fiction was not like the experience of reading devotional manuals, the difference being the novelty of successive works of fiction.
25. Duby, "Histoire des mentalités," p. 923. I am sympathetic to Alan Gowan's argument that "no consistent pattern of styles related to social class can be ascertained; in every one of these [American nineteenth- and twentieth-century] popular arts every sort of form can be found, from the most abstract to the most photographically literal." Gowans, *The Unchanging Arts* (Philadelphia: Lippincott, 1970), p. 53.
26. Thomas, *Religion and the Decline of Magic,* pp. 76, 111–12, 145, and *passim;* Robert Mandrou, "Cultures ou niveaux culturels dan les sociétés d'Ancien Régime," *Revue des études Sud-Est européenes* 10, no. 3, pp. 415–22, as summarized in Traian Stoianovich, *French Historical Method* (Ithaca, N.Y.: Cornell University Press, 1976), p. 170n.
27. See the work of Genevieve Bolleme on the "Bibliotheque Bleue" in "Littérature populaire."
28. Hildred Geertz, "An Anthropology of Religion and Magic, I," *Journal of Interdisciplinary History* 6, no. 1 (Summer 1975): 71–89; Mary Douglas, *Natural Symbols* (New York: Vintage Books, 1973), ch. 1. The most impressive demonstration of the circulation of motifs and the wholeness of popular culture (meaning without class boundaries) is Burke, *Popular Culture in Early Modern Europe.*
29. See Jean Ehrard and Jacques Roger, "Deux périodiques francais du xviii siècle: 'le Journal des Savants' et 'des Mémoires de Trévoux,' Essai d'une étude quantitative," *Livre et Sociéte,* 1: 33–59.
30. As found in Samuel Eliot Morison, *The Intellectual Life of Colonial New England* (New York: New York University Press, 1956).
31. Lockridge, *Literacy in Colonial New England.* Apart from its methodological limitations, Lockridge's argument proceeds in complete disdain of what was printed and read in New England, and the relentless opposing of "traditional" or "peasant" modes of thinking to others, which are denoted "modern," can only be regarded as a sad case of being trapped in abstract categories. For further comments, see my "Education and the Social Order in Colonial America," *Reviews in American History* 3 (June 1975): 178–83.
32. Worthington C. Ford, *The Boston Book Market, 1679–1700* (Boston: Club of Odd Volumes, 1917); books are analyzed according to subject categories in James D. Hart, *The Popular Book: A History of America's Literary Taste* (New York: Oxford University Press, 1950, p. 8.
33. The early almanacs were commissioned by the first Boston bookseller, Hezekiah Usher.
34. For example, a translation of a French history of the Anabaptists, published in 1668 as the Baptists in Boston were challenging the orthodoxy.
35. "Samuel Checkley's Diary," *Publications* of the Colonial Society of Massachusetts 12 (1908–9): pp. 288–90.
36. As demonstrated in Allan Ludwig, *Graven Images* (Middletown, Conn.: Wesleyan University Press, 1966).
37. Lebvre and Martin, "Printing and Language," in *The Coming of the Book,* pp. 319–32.

38. It is also true that Mather and his father were attracted to, and tried to create in New England, an urban avant-garde culture, their model being the Royal Society.

39. *The Diary of Cotton Mather,* 1:54,65,106,122–123.

40. David D. Hall, ed., *The Antinomian Controversy: A Documentary History* (Middletown, Conn.: Wesleyan University Press, 1968), *passim.*

41. Burke, *Popular Culture in Early Modern Europe,* pp. 133–36.

42. Ibid., chs. 8 and 9.

43. I am indebted to James McLachlan for a number of the references in this paper, and to Norman Fiering, James Henretta, James McLachlan, Elizabeth Reilly, and Harry Stout for thoughtful advice.

Literacy Instruction and Gender in Colonial New England

E. Jennifer Monaghan

Hanna Newberry, the most prominent mortgage-holder in Windsor, Connecticut, for most of the second quarter of the eighteenth century, was unable to sign the many documents to which she affixed her name. Instead, she subscribed her mark, the initials HN. Her case illustrates, according to Linda Auwers, "the widespread fact of female illiteracy among women born in the seventeenth century and the difficulty in relating literacy to social class."[1]

Literacy historians have used signatures and marks as indicators of, respectively, the literacy and illiteracy of ordinary people in the seventeenth and eighteenth centuries, in Europe and America.[2] For colonial New England, the best-known study remains that by Kenneth Lockridge, who tabulated the signatures/marks made on over 3,000 wills. He found that the proportion of males able to sign their own wills increased from 60 percent in the 1660s to 85 percent by 1760, and almost 90 percent by 1790. Female signing rates were much lower throughout the entire period. Some 31 percent of the women signed their wills before 1670; this average increased, but only to 46 percent by the 1790s.[3] Three later studies have found a higher rate of signing than Lockridge did, in part by using deeds and other sources in addition to wills, so accessing a larger and/or less decrepit population.[4] One of these is the study by Auwers, who allocated her signers/markers into birth cohorts and found that the proportion of women in Windsor who could sign their own names to deeds rose from 27 percent (for the cohort born between 1650 and 1669) to 90 percent for the 1740–49 cohort.[5]

The equation of literacy-possession with signing rests on the assumption that signing ability is roughly equivalent to fluent reading. As reading was taught before writing, the argument runs, the ability to write (as indicated by a signature) also indicates the ability to read. Carl Kaestle has recently summarized the arguments for and against this position, and—after warning us that the relationship between signing and reading may vary by gender, class, place and period—finally suggests that signature counts indicate roughly the "minimum number of people who were minimally literate."[6]

Although scholars have varied in their interpretations of what a signature implies, there has been more general agreement about the mark: it has been viewed as a valid indicator of illiteracy. Lockridge's figures have therefore contributed to the widely held belief that in New England and elsewhere females were dramatically less literate than males throughout the colonial period, reaching roughly half the literacy level of males.

Several scholars, however, have raised the possibility that some people—particularly women—could read but not write. Margaret Spufford and Victor Neuburg have provided examples of this in the context of seventeenth-

and eighteenth-century England.[7] The thesis of the present study is that this was also true of colonial New England. When we examine the contexts in which literacy instruction was conducted, paying close attention to the role played by gender, it will become apparent that the mark cannot be considered an infallible indicator of illiteracy, particularly in the seventeenth century.

The evidence to be presented is qualitative in nature, scattered and fragmentary; it is also skewed toward the seventeenth century. Further research will be necessary to see if the conclusions to be drawn will stand. Nonetheless, the bits and pieces of the puzzle seem to form a remarkably coherent picture across time and place. In order to support my contention, I first discuss how reading and writing were taught and by whom, then turn to examine how the colonists themselves viewed literacy from the legal and economic standpoints. Next follows an elaboration of the relationship between schooling and gender. Basic to the entire discussion is the concept that literacy was considered by the colonists to be comprised of a deliberately imparted set of skills, taught in ways that were both widely accepted and precise.

The Reading Curriculum

The colonial reading curriculum was of course brought over to the New World, along with so much else, from England. The seventeenth-century curriculum followed the outline sketched by John Locke, who in 1693 characterized it as the "ordinary road of the Horn-book, Primer, Psalter, Testament, and Bible."[8]

There is plenty of evidence that the colonists followed this "ordinary road" in the early days of settlement and throughout the seventeenth century. The hornbook formed the novice's introduction to reading. Its name derived from its single page (originally covered with transparent protective horn) tacked onto a little wooden paddle and presenting the alphabet, the first few lines of the syllabarium (*ab eb ib ob ub*) and the Lord's Prayer. Often mentioned in the same context as primers, hornbooks turn up here and there in the sources over the course of the seventeenth century, and advertisements for primers and both gilt and plain hornbooks have been found in Philadelphia newspapers as late at 1760.[9] The hornbook was used in dame schools—private schools for small children run by a woman in her own home—as the child's first "text." Samuel Sewall mentioned one in just such a context. He recorded in his diary on April 27, 1691 that he had sent his little son Joseph, not yet three years old, to school. "This afternoon had Joseph to school to Capt. Townsend's Mother's, his cousin Jane accompanying him, carried his Hornbook."[10]

Hornbooks were apparently never manufactured on American soil, but were imported.[11] Primers, the next step in the reading curriculum, were also imported very early into the colonies. They must have been a standard item in any village store. One example of their widespread availability is documented for New Haven, in 1645, only seven years after it was founded as a separate colony. That year, a Captain Turner was accused by Mistress Stolion before the New Haven Colony court of having reneged on a deal in which he had promised to give her two cows in exchange for six yards of cloth. Not to be outdone, the captain accused Mrs. Stolion in turn of price gouging: he claimed that "she sold primmers at 9^{d} [nine pence] apeece which cost but 4^{d} here in New England."[12]

Primers were such essential texts for instruction in both reading and religion, however, that their publication on American presses is documented early in the colonial adventure. The oldest extant American primer was composed by John Eliot as part of his efforts to convert the Massachuset Indians. Written in the Massachuset dialect of the Algonquian language, and published in 1669 on the Cambridge, Massachusetts press, the primer admirably sums up, in its title, the dual role it, like the hornbook, played in both reading and religious instruction. The English version reads: *The Indian Primer; OR, the Way of Training up of Our Indian Youth in the Good Knowledge of God, in the Knowledge of the Scriptures and in an Ability to Read.*[13]

Primers as a genre became a publishing staple in New England and the middle colonies as presses increased in number. The *New England Primer*, the most famous of colonial textbooks, has a publishing history that runs from 1690, when it was already in its second impression, to long after the American Revolution. (Its sales up to 1830 have been estimated at between 6 and 8 million copies.) It contained several pages of instructional material, presenting the syllabarium and words of increasing length, from monosyllables to words of six syllables. Its popularity was enhanced by the inclusion of a catechism.[14] In addition to the *New England Primer*, there were numerous other primers in the marketplace.[15]

The next text in both the religious and reading curriculum was the Psalter (the Book of Psalms). Psalters too were extensively printed on American presses. They were generally published without the addition of any reading instructional material, but we do know of one 1760 Philadelphia edition which indicated that it had been "Improved by the addition of a variety of lessons in spelling. . . . Likewise, rules for reading. . . . The whole being a proper introduction, not only to learning, but to the training of children in the reading of the holy scriptures in particular."[16]

One incident that revealed the Psalter's status as a reading instructional text occurred in the context of writing instruction. John Proctor, master of the town-financed North Writing School in Boston from 1731 to 1743, was summoned in 1741 before the Boston selectmen to answer what seems to have been a parental complaint: he was accused of having refused to admit boys from "Families of low Circumstances" to his school. Proctor replied that he had "refus'd none of the Inhabitants Children, but such as could not Read in the Psalter."[17] Clearly, the Psalter was being used as a kind of minimum competency test of reading ability.

The final two stages in the reading curriculum consisted of mastering first the New Testament and then the entire Bible (both Old and New Testaments). Because it was illegal to print these on American presses (John Eliot's *Indian Bible* being a specialized exception), English Bibles were imported until after the American Revolution.

The use of the Scriptures as the climax of the reading curriculum is well known. Two seventeenth-century instances occur in the records of New Haven. The first illustrates the seventeenth-century assumption that reading instruction was supposed to have begun before a child entered the town school. The job description for a New Haven schoolmaster, hired in 1651, was to "perfect male children in the English, after they can reade in their Testament or Bible, and to learne them to wright," and to bring them on to Latin, if he could.[18] The second involved a school for girls. That same year, the daughter of a Captain How was brought before the New Haven court and charged with misconduct that included speaking in a blasphemous way of the Scriptures. The girl's mother claimed that her daughter had picked up some of her bad habits at "Goodwife Wickams" where she went to school. Witnesses testified that they had seen the girl look in a Bible, turn over a leaf, and say that "it was not worth reading." It is not too far-fetched to assume that young Miss How had reached the stage of reading the Bible at her school.[19]

Not included in Locke's characterization of the "ordinary" road was the spelling book. In a major pedagogical shift that cannot be documented here in any detail, the spelling book was introduced to schools, perhaps fairly early in the eighteenth century, as an important introductory text for reading instruction.[20] In the rise of the speller we see the demands of religious content taking second place to the requirements of methodology, in a continuation of a process begun when the first alphabet was added to the primer.[21]

Spelling books as a genre appear at least as early as Edmund Coote's *The English Schoole-Maister*, published in London in 1596, and reprinted 54 times by 1737.[22] Moreover, spellers were printed very early on colonial presses: an unidentified speller came off Stephen Daye's press in Cambridge, in the Bay Colony, in about 1644.[23] It was not, however, until the eighteenth century that the speller's ascendancy as a school text began. An important clue to its popularity is the frequency with which English spellers were reprinted on American presses. (Unlike primers, some of which reflected colonial circumstances, American spellers were all reproduced verbatim from English copies until after the American Revolution.) When Benjamin Franklin in 1747 reprinted Thomas Dilworth's *A New Guide to the English Tongue*, he ushered onto the American scene a spelling book that would enjoy tremendous popularity in the second half of the eighteenth century ("the nurse of us all," as one user put it), until ousted by Noah Webster's speller after 1783.[24]

The name "spelling book" was a reflection of the prevailing methodology: spelling was the key to reading. After mastering the letters of the alphabet, the novice reader's next task was to spell out, orally, syllables and words (broken into syllables) from the printed page. Spelling books incorporated exactly the same methodology—the alphabetic method—as primers did. Although some spellers included secular content, a key difference between primers and spellers was that the latter presented the reading curriculum in a more elaborated and systematic fashion. The tables of words were greatly increased in number, and were followed by "lessons"—reading material based, in part, on vocabulary already introduced.[25]

One key aspect of the alphabetic method was that reading instruction was conducted entirely orally, without requiring the child to write. Progress in learning to read could therefore be gauged simply by listening to the child's oral spelling. As Edmund Coote had put it in the 1596 preface to his speller, addressing the purchaser of his book, he or she could sit at the loom or needle, "and neuer hinder thy worke, to heare thy scholers, after thou hast once made this little booke familiar vnto thee."[26]

Comprehension was virtually ignored, pedagogically speaking. It would probably be fairer to say that comprehension of the text was assumed. After all, the seventeenth-century reading curriculum was in essence a course in Christianity: the texts used were basic to the religion itself. Not until the spelling books of the eighteenth century would any reference be made to such matters as how easily a child could learn the material.

In sum, the task of the reading teacher throughout the entire colonial period was clearly laid out. Both methodology and content were agreed upon; the curriculum was, in effect, standardized. Moreover, no qualifications for teaching reading were necessary other than being able to read oneself. Not only did the child not write in the course of learning to read; as a matter of fact the teacher did not need to know how to write either.

The Reading Teacher

Because the task of the reading teacher was so well defined, and considered, rightly or wrongly, to be easy, the teaching of reading was more often than not considered to be a female province. In the context of family education, it is significant that in those rare cases when we know who taught the child to read at home, it is the mother who is singled out. A pious mother was particularly motivated to teach her child to read. The Boston minister Increase Mather was born in Dorchester, Massachusetts, in 1639, nine years after the town was founded. He wrote that he "learned to read of my mother" whom he described as a "very Holy praying woman." (Significantly, it was his father who taught him to *write*.) Richard Brown, born in 1675, also had a "pious and prudent" mother who endeavored to instill in him "the principals of Religion and Holiness." After "she had caused me to read well at home, she sent me to school."[27]

It appears, however, that early in the colonial period children began attending a school to learn to read, either as well as, or instead of, learning from their mothers. Such schools were called "dame schools" or "reading schools." The dame school is well documented for England in the seventeenth and eighteenth centuries.[28] A woman would take small children, boys and girls, into her own home for a few hours. While no doubt her major contribution was to afford an overworked mother a few hours of respite from her three- and four-year olds, ostensibly the dame's purpose was to introduce her charges to reading. On the other hand, some dame schools taught a substantial amount of reading. John Barnard, born in 1681, recalled that when he was less than six years old his school mistress "made me a sort of usher, appointing me to teach some children that were older than myself, as well as smaller ones; and in which time I had read my Bible through thrice."[29]

The dame, or reading, school was not funded by the town, but was a private venture. It represented, of course, a most useful source of income for a woman. We find women as paid teachers of reading in unexpected contexts. The Commissioners of the United Colonies of New England, who disbursed monies sent over from England for missionary work among the Indians, not only employed a woman to teach the Indians to read, but even gave her a raise. As their letter said, in 1653, "The wife of William Daniell of Dorchester hath for this three yeares last past bestowed much of her time in teaching seuerall Indians to Read and that shee hath onely Receiued the summe of six pounds towards her paines; [we] thought fitt to allow her nine pound more for the time past."[30]

Women are notoriously invisible in colonial records. Even though most townships (Boston, for instance) required private school teachers to obtain permission from the town before they were allowed to teach, private women teachers do not appear in the Boston records until the 1730s. In the seventeenth century, therefore, most of our evidence comes from those rare cases in which women teachers were involved with the law, as happened to Goodwife Wickham of New Haven. One can only guess how many women must have earned a few pennies a week as private teachers of reading throughout that century. As we shall see, in the following century women would be called upon to ply their skills in the public arena as well.

Writing Instruction

Writing was defined, in the colonial context, as penmanship.[31] In only a few respects did writing instruction resemble reading instruction. Just as "good" reading was considered to be accurate oral reading, so "good" writing seemed to be viewed entirely in terms of fine letter formation. Composition seems rarely to have been discussed at all. Similarly, mastery was to be attained by rote and repetition: by the careful reproduction by the learner of the "copy" set for him by the writing master. As was the case in reading instruction, mastery of the individual letters of the alphabet was the first step in the writing curriculum. Later the learner would copy, five or six times, pithy moral sentences, and then work his way up to copying poems or texts reproduced for him by his master from the traditional copybooks such as George Bickham's *The Universal Penman* (1743).[32]

In other respects, however, the contrast between the teaching of the two literacy skills could hardly have been greater. Writing was considered a craft, subject to all the limitations of access that that implied. The gender bias implicit in the term "penmanship" was not fortuitous: writing was largely a male domain. This was particularly true as it related to the gender of the instructor: men taught writing. The writing master, analogous to the scribe of earlier times, was the possessor of a fairly arcane skill. The most telling evidence that his knowledge was considered specialized was that he had usually had to attain it through the apprenticeship route.[33]

Moreover, unlike textbooks for reading instruction, which were early reproduced on American presses, the texts for writing instruction were, for technical reasons, not reprinted on American presses but imported. Although the successful reproduction of different kinds of "hands" (scripts) had been made much easier by the invention of copperplate engraving, engraving was not only costly but demanded a great deal of skill; in fact, the best engraving was undertaken by penmen themselves. (George Bickham, for instance, personally engraved the work of some 25 masters for his *Universal Penman.*) The closest Americans came to reproducing scripts was in a text like George Fisher's *The Instructor: or, Young Man's Best Companion,* which included a few pages of scripts in its American versions from 1748 on. Not until after the American Revolution would there be copybooks penned by Americans and printed on American presses.[34]

Again unlike reading texts, which could be purchased in any colony for mere pennies and were probably in most households, copybooks were costly to purchase and the prized possessions of the writing master. It was clearly not in the best interests of the profession to encourage the notion that anyone could learn from a book, rather than a person.[35] Writing, in short, unlike reading, was considered a specialized skill, and colonial access to instructional writing texts was far more limited than to reading texts.

Who would be taught penmanship was even more important than its usefulness as a specialized skill. Writing was a male job-related skill, a tool for ministers and shipping clerks alike. When the Boston town meeting voted in 1682 to open a town writing school, Bostonians were acknowledging the importance of Boston as a thriving commercial and mercantile center. Hundreds of boys a year passed through the three writing schools that Boston had established by 1720. They mastered the English round hand that had become the international script for commerce, routing the old secretary hand of the seventeenth century.[36] At a time when all clerical and bookkeeping work was a male stronghold, every young man with business aspirations needed to know how to form a legible script. Writing was also, of course, useful for agrarian concerns. Farmers who wanted to sell surplus produce needed to write in order to keep accounts. Penmanship was therefore both a hallmark of the well-educated and the servant of commerce.

Sequence of Instruction

The order, then, of the different components of the literacy curriculum followed the sequence implicit in the "Three R's," a term still glossed today as "reading, 'riting and 'rithmetic." There is nothing accidental about this universal phrase: its wording faithfully reflected the actual order of instruction during the colonial period. Reading instruction preceded, and was independent of, writing instruction. That this was possible was a function of its methodology—reading instruction was, as we have seen, conducted entirely orally. Arithmetic, which involved the endless writing of rules and examples, in turn presupposed the mastery of writing.[37]

It may be difficult for the modern reader/

writer to believe reading instruction could be conducted without having the child write. A few examples will have to suffice. In 1660, a master in New Haven was asked whether he had seen to his apprentice's education, as he was legally obliged to do. He responded that the apprentice "could read pretty well, and that he was now learning to write." Two years later, one William Potter, who had been accused of (and was subsequently hanged for) the crime of bestiality, was asked by the New Haven court if he had been educated. "He answered, well, and was taught to reade." Had he also been taught to write, he would undoubtedly have said so.[38]

Precisely a century later, in 1762, Samuel Giles of New York City advertised his private writing and arithmetic instruction at his evening school. After stating firmly that teaching small children the rudiments had taken up too much of his time, he said that "for the Future, no Children will be taken but such as have already been taught to Read, and are fit for Writing." Finally, there is an advertisement that appeared in a Boston newspaper in 1755. In it, the advertiser promised to teach "persons of both sexes from twelve to fifty years of age, who never wrote before, to write a good hand in five weeks, at one hour per day, at his house in Long Lane."[39]

Literacy and the Law

The dissenters who had made their way over hazardous seas to settle in New England saw themselves as part of a literate culture. At a time when paper itself was scarce and precious, the meticulous records of the early town secretaries stand as a self-explanatory tribute to a new settlement's belief in the power of the written word to safeguard the new laws passed by these settlements.

The greater importance placed by colonial Americans on the ability to read rather than to write is well exemplified by the legislation passed in 1642 by the colony of Massachusetts. Religious and political motives are explicit in this law; economic motives are implicit. The law empowered the colony's elected representatives, the selectmen, to enquire into the "calling and implyment" of all children, "especially of their ability to read and understand the principles of religion and the capitall lawes of this country." Children who were not being trained to a skill nor taught to read were liable to be removed from their parents and apprenticed to someone else for such instruction.[40] While the provisions in the law for "putting out" indigent children to apprenticeship were borrowed from English precedents, the educational provisions were unique to the colonies. As Lawrence Cremin has put it, the statute was part of "a vigorous legislative effort to increase the political and economic self-sufficiency of the colony."[41]

The Massachusetts law that required that children be taught to read was quickly replicated by other colonies. Connecticut passed such a provision in 1650, New Haven (then a separate colony) in 1655, New York in 1665, Plymouth in 1671, and Pennsylvania in 1683.[42] The colony of New Haven was unusual in adding, in 1660, a writing requirement to the law. Significantly, only one of the sexes was to be taught this skill:

> *To the printed law, concerning the education of children, it is now added, that the sonnes of all the inhabitants within this jurisdiction, shall (under the same penalty) be learned to write a ledgible hand, so soone as they are capable of it.*[43]

The only other colony to require writing initially was Pennsylvania, which in its 1683 ordinance mandated that parents and guardians should ensure that children "may be able to read the Scriptures and to write" by the age of twelve.[44]

The 1642 law on reading was taken seriously by at least several Massachusetts townships. When the Dorchester selectmen called in Timothy Wales and his sons in 1672, they examined the boys and found that they were unable to read. The following year Salem conducted its own investigation, found several families in violation of the law, and initiated—although it may not have carried out—the process of finding persons to whom the children could be apprenticed.[45] Watertown, Massachusetts, in particular, made a consistent effort over successive decades to keep parents up to the mark. The first recorded Watertown inspection occurred in 1661. Upon surveying their fellow townsmen to see whether they fulfilled the law which required "the knowledg of God and exercising reading to the advancing of Catachising," the selectmen discovered that four families, with eighteen children among them, had failed in this respect. All the families were poor (so providing an early example of a correlation between poverty and illiteracy).[46]

Successive versions of what came to be called the Massachusetts Poor Laws continued to authorize the removal of children, without the consent of their parents, if the latter were considered unable to maintain them. A 1703 supplement to earlier acts reaffirmed the need to provide apprentices with an education by stipulating that the masters should provide "for the instructing of children so bound out, to read and write, if they be capable." Clearly, as both sexes could be apprenticed, both sexes were to be taught reading and writing. It turned out, however, that the legislators had not intended this: in 1710, an amendment was passed that altered the order to: "males to read and write, females to read." The act was repeated in the same form once a decade until 1741, when the requirement of "cyphering" was added to the regulations for males. Finally, in 1771, the legislation was changed once again, and the legislation for children apprenticed under the Poor Laws now stipulated, "males, reading, writing, cyphering; females, reading, writing."[47]

In other words, it was not until 1771 that Massachusetts considered the ability to write to be an essential minimal educational necessity for girls. This is particularly significant because the whole purpose of apprenticing these children was to provide them with a skill with which they could eventually support themselves, and not be a burden on the town like their indigent parents. Boys needed to be able to write; girls did not.

Literacy and Employment

If legislation on involuntary apprenticeship reveals that children's gender made a difference to the kind of literacy instruction they were required to receive, so too do the terms of apprenticeship agreements that were completely voluntary. In a study of apprenticeship in seventeenth-century Massachusetts, Judith Walter identified 267 apprentices, of whom 32 were girls. For only 31 of all the apprentices was some kind of educational provision specified. For boys, the indenture usually stipulated that the boy be taught to read, write, and cypher. James Chichester, for example, when apprenticed at the age of ten, was to be sent to school "until he can write a leagable hand." The 1658 indenture of Hopestill Chandler, who was being apprenticed to a blacksmith, required that he be taught to read the Bible and "to write enough to keep book for his trade." In contrast, the educational provisions made in 1674 for Sarah Joye of Salem were that she be taught her catechism, and "to read English, [and] the capital laws of the country," while Sarah Braibrok of Watertown was apprenticed in 1656 to a couple who were to teach her "to reade the English Tongue" and provide her with religious instruction. In not one case does Walter report finding a writing provision for female apprentices.[48]

The explanation lies in colonial perceptions of the function of writing. Writing was a job-related skill. Because girls were not being trained to hold jobs, but to be successful homemakers, penmanship was an irrelevant acquisition for them. The skill that corresponded, for girls, to what writing was for boys, was the ability to sew. In the study just cited, Walter identified some 40 different crafts and trades which the boys were to learn during their apprenticeships. There was no indication, however, that girls were to learn anything other than housewifery and, in two cases, sewing or knitting and spinning.[49]

Further evidence on the relationship between jobs and literacy comes from court rulings. In 1655, the Hartford Court ordered the administrators of Thomas Gridley's estate to educate his children, "learning the sons to read and write, and the daughters to read and sew well." The next year, the same court interpreted the provisions of Thomas Thomson's will that related to education as follows: "the sons shall have learning to write plainly and read distinctly in the Bible, and the daughters to read and sew sufficient for the making of their ordinary linen."[50]

More evidence of sewing as the advanced skill to be acquired by girls in lieu of writing is provided by contemporary records from across the Atlantic. They are particularly instructive because both sexes were being educated in the same institution. Orphaned or needy children between the ages of five and fifteen were admitted to the Great Yarmouth Children's Hospital, which was in effect a charitable workhouse. The master of the hospital was expected to see to the children's education, and kept a register of their educational attainments upon entering and leaving the hospital. David Cressy has tabulated the notes in the hospital register on 132 boys and 85 girls admitted to the hospital between 1698 and 1715. The register reveals that several boys were taught to write before they left the hospital. In contrast, "none of the girls reached the stage of writing," according to Cressy. Their "highest achievement was to sew well and to read in the testament or Bible."[51]

The fact that none of the girls was taught to write should, however, surely be interpreted differently. As eleven of the girls were already in either their Testament or Bible on entering the hospital, they were as ready as were the 36 boys, similarly prepared, for further instruction. That not even these relatively accomplished readers were taught to write suggests that writing instruction was withheld from them because of their gender, not because they had not "reached the stage of writing." Mary Clark, for instance, had entered the hospital at the age of nine with the comment, "can't read at all." Four years later, she was characterized as reading "in her testament but indifferently and hath gone through her sampler."[52] If girls were to form letters, it would be through the medium of thread, not ink.

No wonder Anne Bradstreet, whose first book of poetry appeared in London in 1650, felt that she was incurring odium by stepping outside the role prescribed by society for women, in exchanging her needle for a pen:

I am obnoxious to each carping tongue
Who says my hand a needle better fits,
A Poets pen all scorn I should thus wrong.
For such despite they cast on female wits.[53]

Nor should gender restrictions on writing instruction be considered simply a seventeenth-century feature. Apprenticeship indentures for sixty poor children "put out" by the Newbury selectmen between 1743 and 1760 reveal precisely the same differentiation. Forty-nine boys were apprenticed to learn a range of skills from blacksmithing to making periwigs. The eleven girls, however, were only to learn "women's work" or "housewifery." All the apprentices were promised reading instruction, but only the boys were to be taught writing and arithmetic.[54]

There are several cases in which masters of apprentices were hauled into court for not fulfilling their educational obligations toward their apprentices. We have already noted the New Haven master, who in 1660 was brought to court for his alleged failure to teach his apprentice his craft, and who was examined on how much literacy education his apprentice had received. A telling instance is provided about a century later by John Adams. In 1761, Adams remarked on the case of Daniel Prat, "a poor, fatherless Child," who was suing his master Thomas Colson. The terms of the apprenticeship had required Colson to teach Prat to read, write and cypher, and to teach him the trade of a weaver. He had done none of these. Adams felt strongly that Prat, as a child without a male parent, was to be favored in the case, "Because the English Law greatly favours Education. In every English Country, some sort of Education, some Acquaintance with Letters, is necessary, that a Man may fill any station whatever."[55]

From the earliest days of settlement, then, and throughout the colonial period, the colonists expected that all children ought to be able to read, no matter how low their station or how poor their circumstances.

Schooling and Gender

As we have seen, in 1642 the Bay Colony had legislated reading without any mention of either schools or writing. Five years later, in striking contrast, a new law mentioned writing and a schoolmaster in the same breath: in 1647, Massachusetts passed its first schooling law. Every township of over fifty families was required to engage a master to "teach all such children as shall resort to him to write and reade," while towns of over one hundred families were to provide a (Latin) grammar school.[56]

The relationship between writing instruction and schooling is exemplified by Watertown, Massachusetts, which erected its first schoolhouse in 1649 and soon thereafter hired Richard Norcross as its first schoolmaster. The job description spelled out that he was responsible "for the teaching of Chilldren to Reed and write and soe much of Lattin . . . as allso if any of the said towne, haue any maidens, that haue a desire to learne to write that the said Richard, should attend them for the Learning off them; as allso that he teac[h]e such as desire to Cast acompt."[57] The clear implication of this wording is that girls would attend the school only if they wished to learn writing and arithmetic. Obviously, they were supposed to have learned to read at home.

Norcross' contract is also an example of the ambiguity of the word "children." To modern ears, the word indicates children of both sexes. In the colonial period, there was a strict separation of roles in the home and workplace by gender, and it was the males who held all the positions of responsibility and power.[58] Male children, therefore, were the prime targets of any town's educational efforts. As a result of this bias, the word "children" meant, in effect, male children, even though it always retained its broader meaning of children of both sexes. (In discussions of Boston schools, for example, the town records habitually refer to the students of their free schools as "children." Yet free schooling in the Boston system was restricted exclusively to males until 1789.)[59]

While "reading" is indeed included in Norcross' job description, as we saw earlier, children were supposed to have mastered initial reading before they reached the town school. The school was expected to "perfect" them in reading, not introduce them to it. Moreover, girls were often not admitted to town schools, particularly if such schools had any aspirations toward teaching Latin (the hallmark of the true grammar school). The rules and regulations of the Hopkins Grammar School, opened by New Haven in 1684, provide a case in point. They insisted that "noe Boyes be admitted into the said Schoole for the learning of English Books, but such as have ben before taught to spell their letters well and begin to Read, thereby to perfect theire right Spelling, and Reading, or to learne to write, and Cypher . . . and that all others either too young and not instructed in letters and spelling, and all Girles be excluded as Improper and inconsistent with such a Grammer Schoole. . . ."[60]

Walter Small, in his study of some two hundred schools in the colonial period, reported finding only seven schools which definitely admitted girls, and another five which might have. Rehoboth, Massachusetts, was among the seven. In 1699, Robert Dickson contracted with the Rehoboth selectmen "to do *his* utmost endeavor to teach *both sexes* of boys and girls to read English and write and cast accounts." Similarly, Deerfield, in northwestern Massachusetts, obviously allowed girls to enter its town school in 1698, because it warned parents that all heads of families with children between the ages of six and ten, whether male or female, should pay a poll tax to the school, "whether they send such children or not." Five years later the town made a similar motion, but this time changed the ages of admission. Families of "boys from four to eight, and girls from four to six years old," were to pay their proportion of £10 for the ensuing year.[61]

The comparatively late dates at which these and similar provisions were enacted is significant: they suggest that on the boundaries of settlement, as the seventeenth century drew to a close, the town school had two characteristics. In the first place, it did not attempt any education fancier than the three R's, and in the second, it chose not to restrict its education to boys. Indeed the experience of the frontier settlement of Hatfield may prove, with further research, to be characteristic. From 1695 to 1699 there were no girls in Hatfield's town school; in 1700 there were four girls and 42 boys during the winter term; nine years later there were 16 girls in a total of 64 schoolchildren.[62]

Nevertheless, there were many towns that stood firm against the admission of girls to the master's school throughout the entire seventeenth and even the eighteenth century. Farmington, Connecticut, for example, voted in 1686 to devote £20 to a town school, "for the instruction of all such children as shall be sent to it, to learn to read and write the English tongue." Some parents of daughters, it seems, interpreted this too broadly, for the following year the town issued a clarification: "*all* such children as shall be sent is to be understood only *male* children that are through their horning book [hornbook]." Small found many instances of town schools—Salem, Medford, Haverhill, Gloucester, Hingham and Charlestown—which, shortly before or even well after the American Revolution, were only just beginning to open their doors to girls. And in these cases, the girls were only being admitted for a couple of hours a day (presumably for writing instruction). As one witness put it, remembering his schooling in Lynn, Massachusetts, "In all my school days which ended in 1801, I never saw but three females in public schools, and they were there only in the afternoon to learn to write."[63]

School Dames

A new feature in colonial town schooling can be detected as the seventeenth century drew to a close: the towns' formal sponsorship of women to teach reading. One presumes that private dame school instruction had continued for decades in New England; after 1670, however, we see towns actively seeking for female teachers to teach reading to small children. These women were paid a few pennies per week per child, and substantially less than their male colleagues.

Walter Small collected numerous references to such "school dames." Among Massachusetts towns, Woburn paid ten shillings to two women in 1673, and the same sum to another in 1686. Cambridge reported in 1680 that "For English, our schooldame is Goodwife Healy; at present but nine scholars." Two years later, Springfield made an agreement with Goodwife Mirick that, in order to "encourage her in the good work of training up of children and teaching children to read," she should have three pence per child a week.[64]

After 1700, mention of school dames increases. Small found references to them in records running from 1700 to 1730 for, among others, Waterbury and Windsor in Connecticut, and for Weymouth, Lexington, Charlestown, Salem and Falmouth, all in Massachusetts. A few of these, as was the case for Charlestown, only involved the town in paying women for the instruction of poor children who could not otherwise attend school. Yet increasingly in the eighteenth century there seems to have been a definite shift in the direction of employing women to teach reading on a regular basis, in specific parts of town, with funds allocated for that purpose from the town treasury. Framingham had voted as early as 1713 to appoint selectmen to "settle school dames in each quarter of the town." Worcester in 1731 decided that, because small children could not walk to the school in the center of town, up to five school dames should be hired "for the teaching of small children to read," and placed in different parts of the town. Wenham, two years later, made an arrangement with its schoolmaster which permitted him to delegate some of his teaching responsibilities to others: he was to be "allowed to teach little children to read by suitable women, in the several parts of the town, that he shall agree with, by the approbation of the selectmen; also to teach to write by another man in another part of town."[65]

Marriage was no obstacle for a woman in teaching reading. In fact, there were those who taught for almost the whole of their adult lives. When Abigail Fowler died in Salem, Massachusetts, in 1771, her death was reported affectionately: "Widow Abigail Fowler, a noted school dame, finished her earthly labors. She was in her 68th year, and began to teach children before she was 18, and continued so to do till her decease, with the exception of a few years after she was married."[66]

The reason for the towns' new eagerness to employ women seems to have been the continuing failure of parents to carry out their legal responsibility to teach their children to read. For example, at the turn of the century Marblehead undertook a survey on the number of boys who could not read, and who could therefore not be admitted to the master's school. The town found a total of 122 such boys.[67]

Note that there were children who still read too poorly for the master's school despite the fact that standards for admission appear to have been lowered in many schools as the decades progressed. Whereas formerly schoolmasters had expected children to be in their Testament or Bible (still the case in Boston's three elite writing schools, as the incident with John Proctor revealed), now the admission requirement was, for the New Haven grammar school in 1684, only to "have been taught to spell the letters well and begin to Read," or, for Farmington, Connecticut, two years later, that boys should be through their hornbook.

For many women, the chance to earn money from the town must have been most welcome. Others, as the eighteenth century lengthened, were able to use the newspapers successfully to advertise their private literacy instruction.

Conclusion

The arguments made up to this point are as follows:

1. Reading was considered easy to teach, and reading instruction unaccompanied by writing instruction was the province of women, both at home and at school (private or town-sponsored). Texts for reading instruction were cheap and easy to obtain.
2. Writing was considered a craft, difficult to teach, and taught by men. Texts for writing instruction were comparatively expensive and difficult to obtain.
3. Reading instruction preceded, and was independent of, writing instruction, because of the oral alphabet method.

4. Because reading was considered to be important for religious, political and economic reasons, legislation was passed that required it of all children.
5. Because writing was considered a job-related skill, society only required that it be taught to boys.
6. Writing was one of the key components of the curriculum of the town schools, which were taught by men and in many cases restricted to boys. Girls won access to some, but by no means all, of the masters' schools from the 1690s on.
7. Towns began to employ women (school dames) to teach reading to small children of both sexes from the 1680s on.

These statements generate further conclusions:

8. Because reading was required to be taught, and because people could and did learn to read without also learning to write, we cannot assume that all those—particularly women—who only marked documents were totally illiterate.
9. Because educational standards in New England were raised over time, however, marks have to be interpreted in context.

In the seventeenth century, class, gender, and rural location all militated against obtaining writing instruction. In terms of class, the children whose apprenticeships have been mentioned above were at the bottom of the social heap, as were the orphans admitted into the Great Yarmouth Children's Hospital. Even at this low social level, it is clear that boys were offered both reading and writing instruction, but girls were only expected to know how to read and sew. If such girls could not sign when grown women, it was because no one had ever taught them to write.

Of course, then as now, low social class combined with poverty often correlated with illiteracy in reading as well as writing. It is surely no coincidence that the eighteen children found to be unable to read in Watertown in 1661 all came from impoverished families, and that the boys who could not read the Psalter, and who were therefore refused admittance to one of the Boston writing schools in 1741, were the children of "Families of low Circumstances."

As we would also expect, high social standing, when combined with an urban setting, was able to erase the restrictions on female access to writing instruction. In cities, the daughters of the higher ranks learned to write because their parents sent them off for private instruction. In Boston, for instance, even in the seventeenth century, girls were taught by private entrepreneurs like the writing master who taught Hannah Sewall (wife of Samuel Sewall) to write. In the eighteenth century, girls could also attend publicly financed town masters who taught fee-paying female students "out of hours."[68] The fact that during the early colonial period rural women, even when wealthy, signed at a lower rate than urban women is surely to be explained by the exclusion of girls from the town school and the relative paucity of private male teachers in rural areas. But in cities private teachers abounded: at least twenty private writing masters have been documented for Boston during the colonial period.[69]

It is the girls of modest social standing, however, who are of the most importance to my argument. Even in the seventeenth century, access to reading instructional materials was easy, and the teaching of reading was considered a female domain. There is every reason to believe that reading at some level was taught widely to girls by women, whereas writing, for a long time considered a male teaching preserve, was not.

Around the turn of the century, several strands were coming together, all of them favoring increased education in general, and female education in particular. One that should not be ignored is domestic tranquility, bought at considerable cost to both whites and Indians. King Philip's short but bloody war (1675–76) spelled the end of the political and military power of the Indians. Slaughter and disease had thinned their ranks, and surviving Indian communities passed into obscurity.[70] The colonists were therefore freer to concentrate less on defense and more on such matters as education.

As we have seen, after 1680 women were increasingly incorporated into town educational systems, hired for their skill in teaching beginning reading. (Such women would have had to be taught to write, for they needed to be able to keep school records.) Girls were also winning access to some of the masters' town schools, and so to writing instruction.

There are several other factors that no doubt made their contribution, although proof of these lies beyond the scope of this essay. For instance, eighteenth-century instructional texts in reading improved, thanks to the advent of the spelling book. Similarly, the switch from the secretary hand of the seventeenth century to the eighteenth-century round hand would appear to have made penmanship easier. The expansion during the course of the eighteenth century in the availability of secular reading material, including chapbooks and, at the end of the century, novels, was undoubtedly significant.

These speculations aside, it is still possible to take a fresh look at the supposed illiteracy of those who made marks instead of signatures. First, a comment on the mark itself. When we talk today about making a "mark" on a document, what springs to mind is the traditional "X." That is not, however, how most colonists marked documents. When the information is available, marks often turn out to be initials, like the HN used by Hanna Newberry. These initials indicate, at the least, an acquaintance with the alphabet.[71]

We can now reinterpret some of the detailed information provided by Auwers for Windsor, Connecticut. What puzzled Auwers was that she found no correlation between social class and the signatures ("literacy") of Windsor women born before 1690: many rich women, like Hanna Newberry, only made marks. We can now explain this as a function of gender, which impeded access to writing instruction. Surely Hanna could read: her socio-economic status alone makes it very unlikely that she would have been truly illiterate.

Windsor forms a useful example in other ways. In 1717 the town employed its first school dame: Sarah Stiles was hired to teach reading in the summer; schooling opportunities improved.[72] The dramatic increase that Auwers found in the percentage of women able to sign their names, as the decades passed, suggests that the right of girls to write in Windsor had been permanently won by the 1740s.

And what of the female will-markers in Lockridge's study, cited so often in defense of claims of massive female illiteracy in colonial New England? The figures from these women are misleading, I believe, in several respects. For one, as Lockridge is the first to point out, the sample of females is small, representing under 15 percent of his total sample and only 5 percent of the population he was investigating.[73] Just as important is the fact that wills were Lockridge's only source. Some women may have been able to sign but chose not to. People often make their wills late in life, and when a mark was as legal as a signature, initialing a will if you were old and ill may have seemed more appealing than struggling to sign. Auwers' study, for instance, identified 31 women who had affixed their names to both deeds and wills. Eight of these (26 percent) signed their deeds but marked their wills; only one did so in reverse. (This could also be interpreted, with Auwers, as evidence of the marginality of female signing skill.)[74] We can speculate that no stigma would have attached to a woman who chose not to sign her name. In contrast, because society increasingly expected them to write, men by the early eighteenth century might have felt more deeply about the social cachet attached to signing.[75] Even more important is the age at which a person subscribed his or her will. A mark in the 1760s may represent the absence of writing instruction as much as 40 or 50 years earlier.

Be that as it may, it is, in any case, likely that many of Lockridge's female will-markers could read, at least to some extent. Further research, ideally using Linda Auwers' birth cohort approach, is likely to produce evidence of higher female signing rates in the eighteenth century similar to those found by Auwers and, later in the century, by William Gilmore.[76]

How well could someone read who could read but not write? The colonists themselves were aware that there were differing levels of literacy. Experience Mayhew, discussing in 1727 the literacy of the Christian Indians who could read books published in their own language, said that such Indians read and wrote only at the "rate that poor Men among the English are wont to do."[77] Probably, many nonwriters read familiar material without too much trouble. This would have been particularly true of the Scriptures: their advantage was that the ministers and heads of households were constantly reading from them aloud. Nonwriters would also have been able to decipher writings such as the notes—like those asking for information on strayed animals—that were so often tacked onto the doors of meeting houses.[78] They surely could not, however, as Cathy N. Davidson points out, have been able to read the works of John Locke.[79]

On the other hand, we should not underestimate the pleasure that even a limited reading ability can bring. For a colonial woman, reading must have provided one of the very few sources of satisfaction that was not dependent upon those outside herself. In virtually all of the roles identified by Laurel Thatcher Ulrich, whether as housewife, deputy husband, consort, mother, mistress of servants or neighbor, a woman was looking out for the welfare of others.[80] When she was reading, she was doing something for herself. Above all, if she were a Christian (another of the roles posited by Ulrich), her reading would have been an important and meaningful part of her private devotions.[81] For those who were called upon to teach reading to others, their reading ability transformed itself into a measure of independence. These were small treasures of the mind and spirit that we should not despise.

There is no reason to suppose that the conclusions drawn here for New England are very different from those to be drawn for other parts of colonial America—except, perhaps, for the South. A poem penned by a judge in Philadelphia at the end of the seventeenth century shows that differentiation of schooling by gender was not exclusive to New England:

Here are schools of divers sorts,
To which our youth daily resorts,
Good women, who do very well
Bring little ones to read and spell,
Which fits them for writing, and then,
Here's men to bring them to their pen,
And to instruct and make them quick,
In all sorts of arithmetick.[82]

ACKNOWLEDGMENTS

This research was supported in part by grant number 6-64048 from the PSC-CUNY Research Award Program of the City University of New York.

Endnotes

1. Linda Auwers, "Reading the Marks of the Past: Exploring Female Literacy in Colonial Windsor, Connecticut," *Historical Methods* 13 (1980): 209.
2. See Carl F. Kaestle's summary of literacy studies in his "The History of Literacy and the History of Readers," *Review of Research in Education,* vol. 12, ed. Edmund W. Gordon (Washington, D.C., 1985): 11–53.
3. Kenneth A. Lockridge, *Literacy in Colonial New England: An Enquiry into the Social Context of Literacy in the Early Modern West* (New York, 1974), 128 n. 4, 13, 38–42, 140 n. 57.
4. Auwers, "Reading the Marks of the Past"; Ross W. Beales Jr., "Studying Literacy at the Commu-

nity Level: a Research Note." *Journal of Interdisciplinary History* 9 (1978): 93–102. The largest study to date is that by William Gilmore, who surveyed 10,467 documents dated between 1760 and 1830 from the Upper Connecticut Valley, and found almost universal male signing levels by the 1770s, while female signing began at two-thirds in the late 1770s and rose thereafter: William J. Gilmore, *Elementary Literacy on the Eve of the Industrial Revolution: Trends in Rural New England, 1760–1830* (Worcester, Mass., 1982), 98, 114.

5. Auwers, "Reading the Marks of the Past," 204–05.
6. Kaestle, "The History of Literacy and the History of Readers," 21.
7. E.g. Kaestle, ibid., 21, 29; Margaret Spufford, *Small Books and Pleasant Histories: Popular Fiction and Its Readership in Seventeenth-Century England* (Cambridge, England, 1981), 22, 27, 29, 34–35; Victor E. Neuburg, *Popular Education in Eighteenth Century England* (London, 1971), 55, 93; Gerald F. Moran and Maris A. Vinovskis, "The Great Care of Godly Parents: Early Childhood in Puritan New England," in *History and Research in Child Development*, ed. Alice Boardman Smuts and John W. Hagen, *Monographs of the Society for Research in Child Development* 50: 4–5 (1985): 34. Lockridge himself raises the possibility: *Literacy in Colonial New England*, 127.
8. James L. Axtell, ed., *The Educational Writings of John Locke: A Critical Edition with Introduction and Notes* (London, 1968), 260; Lawrence A. Cremin, *American Education: The Colonial Experience, 1607–1783* (New York, 1970), 277. I would like to acknowledge here my indebtedness to Professor Cremin's bibliography.
9. George A. Plimpton, *The Hornbook and Its Use in America* (Worcester, 1916), 9. Plain and gilt hornbooks were listed in the book inventories of a Boston bookseller in 1700: Worthington C. Ford, *The Boston Book Market, 1679–1700* (rpt. New York, 1972), 177–78.
10. Quoted in Andrew W. Tuer, *History of the Horn Book* (London, 1897; rpt. New York, 1979), 133.
11. Plimpton, *The Hornbook and Its Use in America*, 9.
12. Charles J. Hoadly, ed., *Records of the Colony and Plantation of New Haven, from 1638 to 1649* (Hartford, 1857), 176. *Note*: for ease of reading, I have silently expanded all the abbreviations in this and other quotations (e.g., "y^e," "y^t," and "$Testam^t$," appear as "the," "that" and "Testament"), but preserved the spelling, punctuation and capitalization of the originals.
13. John Eliot, *The Indian Primer* . . . (Cambridge, Mass., 1669).
14. Paul L. Ford, *The New-England Primer: A History of Its Origin and Development with a Reprint of the Unique Copy of the Earliest Known Edition* (New York, 1897); Richard L. Venezky, "A History of the American Reading Textbook," *Elementary School Journal* 87:3 (1987): 249.
15. Charles F. Heartman, *American Primers, Indian Primers, Royal Primers, and Thirty-Seven Other Types of Non-New-England Primers Issued Prior to 1830* (Highland Park, N.J., 1935).
16. Quoted in Nila Banton Smith, *American Reading Instruction* (Newark, Del., 1965), 17–18.
17. Boston, Registry Department, *Records Relating to the Early History of Boston*, vol. 15, *A Report of the Record Commissioners of the City of Boston, Containing the Records of Boston Selectmen, 1736 to 1742* (Boston, 1886), 288.
18. Franklin B. Dexter, ed., *New Haven Town Records, 1649–1662* (New Haven, 1917), 97.
19. Ibid., 88.
20. For spelling books in Britain, see Neuberg, *Popular Education*, 65–91; R. C. Alston, *A Bibliography of the English Language from the Invention of Printing to the Year 1800, Vol. 4, Spelling Books* (Bradford, 1967); Ian Michael, *The Teaching of English: From the Sixteenth Century to 1870* (Cambridge, England, 1987). For spelling books in the American colonies, see Raoul N. Smith, "Interest in Language and Languages in Colonial and Federal America," *Proceedings of the American Philosophical Society* 123 (1979): 36–38.
21. Venezky, "A History of the American Reading Textbook," 248.
22. William R. Hart, *"The English Schoole-Maister* (1596) by Edmund Coote: An Edition of the Text with Critical Notes and Introductions," diss. Univ. of Michigan, 1963, 8.
23. Robert F. Roden, *The Cambridge Press, 1638–1692: A History of the First Printing Press Established in*

English America, Together With a Bibliographical List of the Issues of the Press (New York, 1905), 36.

24. E. Jennifer Monaghan, *A Common Heritage: Noah Webster's Blue-Back Speller* (Hamden, Conn., 1983), 31–34; quotation, 26. There were 76 editions of Dilworth by 1801, of which 43 were printed before 1787: Smith, "Interest in Language and Languages in Colonial and Federal America," 36.

25. Monaghan, *A Common Heritage,* 33–34; Smith, *American Reading Instruction,* 25–31.

26. Edmund Coote, *The English Schoole-Maister . . .* (London, 1596), A3, in Hart, *"The English Schoole-Maister,"* 129.

27. M. G. Hall, ed., *The Autobiography of Increase Mather* (Worcester, Mass., 1962), 278; Richard Brown is quoted in James Axtell, *The School Upon a Hill: Education and Society in Colonial New England* (New Haven, 1974), 174–75. Cf. M. T. Clanchy, "Learning to Read in the Middle Ages and the Role of Mothers," *Studies in the History of Reading,* ed. Greg Brooks and A. K. Pugh (Reading, England, 1984), 33–39.

28. Spufford, *Small Books,* 35–36; J. H. Higginson, "Dame Schools," *British Journal of Educational Studies* 22:2 (1974): 166–81, and D. P. Leinster-MacKay, "Dame Schools: A Need for Review," *British Journal of Educational Studies* 24:1 (1976): 33–48, in Joan N. Burstyn, "Women in the History of Education," paper presented at the annual meeting of the American Educational Research Association, Montreal, April 1983.

29. "Autobiography of the Rev. John Barnard," *Collections of the Massachusetts Historical Society* 3:5 (1836): 178. Cf. "The Commonplace Book of Joseph Green," *Publications of the Colonial Society of Massachusetts* 34 (1943): 236.

30. David Pulsifer, ed., *Records of the Colony of New Plymouth, in New England. Acts of the Commissioners of the United Colonies of New England, Vol. 2, 1653–1679* (Boston, 1859), 106.

31. E. Jennifer Monaghan and E. Wendy Saul, "The Reader, the Scribe, the Thinker: A Critical Look at the History of American Reading and Writing Instruction," in *The Formation of School Subjects: The Struggle for Creating an American Institution,* ed. Thomas S. Popkewitz (New York, 1987), 88.

32. George Bickham, *The Universal Penman, Engraved by George Bickham, London 1743* (New York, 1954). For the writing curriculum, see E. Jennifer Monaghan, "Readers Writing: The Curriculum of the Writing Schools of Eighteenth-Century Boston," *Visible Language* (in press).

33. Ray Nash, *American Writing Masters and Copybooks: History and Bibliography Through Colonial Times* (Boston, 1959), 13.

34. George Fisher, *The Instructor; or, American Young Man's Best Companion,* 30th ed. (Worcester, Mass., n.d.); Nash, *American Writing Masters and Copybooks,* 25–34.

35. At least one copybook, however, proclaimed (in 1656) that it was *Set forth for the benefit of poore Schollers, where the Master hath not time to set Copies:* see Nash, *American Writing Masters and Copybooks,* 21–22.

36. Monaghan, "Readers Writing."

37. Cremin, *American Education,* 501–03; Patricia Cline Cohen, *A Calculating People: The Spread of Numeracy in Early America* (Chicago, 1982), 120–22.

38. Dexter, *New Haven Town Records, 1649–1662,* 438; Charles J. Hoadly, ed., *Records of the Colony or Jurisdiction of New Haven, from May 1653, to the Union, Together With the New Haven Code of 1656* (Hartford, 1858), 443.

39. Robert F. Seybolt, *The Evening School in Colonial America* (Urbana, 1925), 23; advertisement quoted in Walter H. Small, *Early New England Schools* (Boston, 1914); 317.

40. Nathaniel B. Shurtleff, ed., *Records of the Governor and Company of the Massachusetts Bays in New England, Vol. 2, 1642–1649* (Boston, 1853), 6–7.

41. Cremin, *American Education,* 125.

42. Ibid.

43. Hoadly, *Records of the Colony or Jurisdiction of New Haven, from May 1653, to the Union,* 376.

44. Quoted in Cremin, *American Education,* 125.

45. Dorchester Antiquarian and Historical Society, *History of the Town of Dorchester, Massachusetts* (Boston, 1859), 223–24; Salem, Mass., *Town Records of Salem, Massachusetts, Volume II, 1659–1680* (Salem, Mass., 1913), 180.

46. Watertown, Mass., *Watertown Records Comprising the First and Second Books of Town Proceedings*

(Watertown, Mass., 1894), 71. Subsequent inspections occurred in 1665, 1670, 1672, 1674, 1679, 1680, and later: ibid., 86, 104, 113, 121, 137, 145.

47. Robert F. Seybolt, *Apprenticeship and Apprenticeship Education in Colonial New England and New York* (New York, 1917), 46–47.

48. Judith Walter, "Apprenticeship Education and Family Structure in Seventeenth Century Massachusetts Bay," M.A. thesis, Bryn Mawr, 1971, 33–34, 42–43.

49. Ibid., 34.

50. Walter H. Small, "Girls in Colonial Schools," *Education* 22 (1902): 534.

51. David Cressy, *Literacy and the Social Order: Reading and Writing in Tudor and Stuart England* (Cambridge, 1980), 30–34; quotation, 34.

52. Ibid., 34. For girls taught only reading and sewing in England, see Spufford, *Small Books,* 34–35.

53. Quoted in Thomas Woody, *A History of Women's Education in the United States, Vol. I* (1929; rpt. New York, 1966), 132.

54. Laurel Thatcher Ulrich, *Good Wives: Image and Reality in the Lives of Women in Northern New England, 1650–1750* (New York, 1982), 43–44.

55. L. H. Butterfield, ed., *Diary and Autobiography of John Adams, Vol. 1, Diary 1755–1770* (Cambridge, Mass., 1961), 219.

56. Shurtleff, *Records of the Governor and Company of the Massachusetts Bay,* 2: 203.

57. *Watertown Records Comprising the First and Second Books,* 18, 21.

58. Lyle Koehler, *A Search for Power: The "Weaker Sex" in Seventeenth-Century New England* (Urbana, 1980).

59. See, for example, the proposal in 1682 to open a free school for the "teachinge of Children to write & Cypher": Boston, Registry Department, *Records Relating to the Early History of Boston,* vol. 7, *A Report of the Record Commissioners of the City of Boston, Containing the Boston Records from 1660 to 1701* (Boston, 1881), 158.

60. *American Journal of Education* 4 (1857): 710.

61. The shorter time span for girls suggests that they were to leave school at the point when they were supposed to be able to read, having reached the age for instruction in writing that they would not receive. Small, "Girls in Colonial Schools," 532–33. Small used primary sources such as town records for his study, but did not document his sources. Where I have been able to crosscheck them, I have found them accurate.

62. Ibid., 533.

63. Ibid., 533–37; quotations on 533–34.

64. Small, *Early New England Schools,* 168, 165.

65. Ibid., 165–170; quotations on 179, 168, 170.

66. Ibid., 169.

67. Ibid., 167.

68. Robert F. Seybolt, "Schoolmasters of Colonial Boston," *Publications of the Colonial Society of Massachusetts* 27 (1928): 137; for an example of female instruction by a writing master, see Alice Morse Earle, ed., *Diary of Anna Green Winslow: A Boston School Girl of 1771* (1894; rpt. Williamstown, Mass. 1974), 12, 92–94.

69. Seybolt, "Schoolmasters of Colonial Boston."

70. William C. Sturtevant, ed., *Handbook of North American Indians, Vol. 15, Northeast,* ed. Bruce G. Trigger (Washington, 1978), 177.

71. For initials as marks, see, for example, Joseph Underwood's V in 1684 as his mark set to an agreement to teach his male apprentice to read and write: *Watertown Records Comprising the First and Second Books,* 129.

72. Auwers, "Reading the Marks of the Past," 204.

73. Lockridge, *Literacy in Colonial New England,* 128.

74. Auwers, "Reading the Marks of the Past," 207.

75. I am indebted to Ross W. Beales Jr. for this insight.

76. Auwers, "Reading the Marks of the Past"; Gilmore, *Elementary Literacy on the Eve of the Industrial Revolution.*

77. Experience Mayhew, *Indian Converts: Or, Some Account of the Lives and Dying Speeches of a Considerable Number of the Christianized Indians of Martha's Vineyard, in New-England* (London, 1727), xxiii.

78. See, for example, the complaint in 1687 about such notes: Watertown, Mass., *Watertown Records Comprising the Third Book of Town Proceedings and the Second Book of Births Marriages and Deaths to End of 1737* (Watertown, 1900), 31.

79. Cathy N. Davidson, *Revolution and the Word: The Rise of the Novel in America* (Oxford, England, 1986), 59.

80. Ulrich, *Good Wives,* 9–10.

81. Charles E. Hambrick-Stowe, *The Practice of Piety: Puritan Devotional Disciplines in Seventeenth-Century New England* (Williamsburg, Va., 1982), 157–61.

82. Quoted in Carl Bridenbaugh, *Cities in the Wilderness: The First Century of Urban Life in America, 1625–1742* (1938; rpt. Oxford, England, 1971), 283–84.

A Republican Literature: A Study of Magazine Reading and Readers in Late Eighteenth-Century New York

David Paul Nord

President George Washington was a subscriber. So were vice president John Adams, Chief Justice John Jay, and New York Mayor Richard Varick. With such a distinguished readership, it is little wonder that the publishers of *The New-York Magazine; or, Literary Repository* decided to publish a list of subscribers to their first volume in 1790. Like all eighteenth-century magazine publishers, Thomas and James Swords were proud of their association with gentlemen of character, stature, and literary taste.[1] Yet men such as Washington and Adams were not the only readers of *The New-York Magazine*, as the standard magazine histories seem to suggest.[2] There were women on the list, and barbers, bakers, butchers, and boardinghouse proprietors. These are the forgotten readers of *The New-York Magazine*, and of late-eighteenth-century magazines in general. Who were these people? How did they make a living? Where did they live? What were they like? Were they different from nonsubscribers? What kinds of material did they read? This article seeks to answer these questions. It is, in effect, a magazine readership survey; and its purpose is to contribute to our understanding of the history of reading—especially among the shopkeepers and artisans of New York City—during the first years of the American republic.

As Carl Kaestle has recently pointed out, we have learned a great deal in the past twenty years about the demographics of simple literacy in the past, but we have only begun to develop a genuine social history of reading—that is, a history of the *uses* of literacy. This is hardly surprising, for as Kaestle says, it "is very difficult to trace printed works to their reader."[3] This paper tries to do both, though with more confidence about the former than the latter. It is a study of both the subscribers and the content of *The New-York Magazine* in 1790.

The main argument is that magazine reading in this era seems to have been a more broadly democratic activity than has usually been supposed. At first glance, the magazine's content would seem to be evidence of a rather elite audience; and this has been the supposition of most historians. Yet the subscriber list shows a more varied readership. Considered together, the subscriber list and the content may offer some insight into the social function of reading in this era. They suggest the importance of reading as a form of participation in the new social order of post-Revolutionary America. Edward Countryman has recently argued that "radical politics and nascent class consciousness foundered on electoral participation and on the spirit of voluntary association" in the 1780s.[4] In other words, the radicalism of the small shopkeepers and urban artisans lost its urgency as those groups began to participate more fully in a political culture that had once been closed to them. Similarly, the magazine might be viewed as another arena for popular participation, in this case participation in the formerly elite culture of science and education, arts and letters, virtue and honor, cultivation and character. The values of the magazine were traditional; it was the participation of the working class that was new. In short, this was a republican readership and a republican literature.

The Setting

"Republican" was a thoroughly commonplace term in the American political vocabulary of 1790, yet its ubiquity was probably matched by its ambiguity. Historians still disagree, rather warmly, over what Americans in the late eighteenth century meant when they talked about republicanism. One stream of scholarship, growing from the pathbreaking work of Bernard Bailyn and J. G. A. Pocock, emphasizes the classical republican tradition—that is, the tradition of Aristotle and Cicero, filtered through Italian Renaissance humanism and the radical whig thought of the English "country" politicians of the late seventeenth and early eighteenth centuries. In this tradition, the basis for republican government was civic virtue, the sacrifice of individual interests to the common good.[5] Another stream of scholarship emphasizes the liberal dimension of American republicanism. Though current historians such as Joyce Appleby have rejected the one-dimensional Lockean perspective of Louis Hartz, they still argue that the mainstream of American political thought in the late eighteenth century was liberal—that is, committed to private property and individualism. In this tradition, virtue and the sources of human happiness lay largely outside government in a natural economy and self-regulating society.[6] A third stream of scholarship owes much to the classical republican perspective, in that it finds even among the common people of the Revolutionary era a devotion to the ideas of civic virtue and commonwealth. But there are differences of emphasis. Growing more from social history than from the history of political thought, this literature stresses the equal rights or radical egalitarian aspects of American republicanism. Historians working in this stream are usually more interested in the actual political participation of working-class Americans than they are in abstract political theory.[7]

Of course, *all* of these (and still other) meanings of "republicanism" were current in American thought in the 1790s. As Joyce Appleby says: "It would be surprising if scholars were able to agree upon the meaning of a word that contemporaries themselves used in such disparate contexts." People clearly used the vocabulary of republicanism, but they used new vocabularies as well, and they used the old words in new ways, as circumstances changed.[8] Linda Kerber has recently suggested that the language and values of classical republicanism remained more meaningful, more vital, for some Americans than others, depending upon their place in the new liberal order that was rapidly emerging. Historians must be alert to how real people shaped political ideas to make sense of their own lives in a complex, modern world.[9]

New York City in 1790, for example, was an enormously complex social, political, and economic universe. At one extreme, the city was still the domain of the Livingstons, the Schuylers, and the Stuyvesants–a traditional aristocracy that continued to influence public life in the post–Revolutionary era. Furthermore, New York was the American capital in 1789–90, the gathering place for a new aristocracy of founding fathers and federal officials, who attended to the business of the country by day and to the balls, dinners, and receptions of New York high society by night. At the other extreme, New York was home to the desperately poor—cartmen, mariners, common laborers; the sick, the helpless, the chronically unemployed.[10] It would be remarkable indeed if these diverse New Yorkers shared the same notions of what it meant to be a citizen of the new republic.

Most of the citizens of New York, however, fell between these extremes, and their story is central to my story about reading in the late eighteenth century. A sample from the 1790 city directory suggests that nearly two-thirds of the city's heads of household were artisans or shopkeepers (see Table 1). Other historians have come up with roughly comparable figures. Certainly the largest group of working people in New York and in other large cities in this era were artisans—that is, master craftsmen and their journeyman employees.[11]

What it meant to be an artisan (or even a shopkeeper) was changing in 1790. The traditional relationships among master, journeyman, and apprentice had already begun to break down. Some masters were becoming retailers, manufacturers, or incipient capitalists. Some journeymen were becoming wage workers, with little hope of achieving the traditional status of independent master. Many shops were hiring untrained boys, without any commitment to the obligations of apprenticeship. The whole ancient system was shifting, very gradually, with the rising tide of laissez-faire.[12]

But though the economic world was changing, many of the values of the eighteenth-century artisan culture remained strong. In fact, some of these values were reinforced by the experience of the Revolution. During the Revolution and the decade of crisis that preceded it, the artisans and shopkeepers had become active participants in the political culture—first in crowd action, then in electoral politics. That commitment to politics would not subside.[13] Yet political equality and political participation were not the only components of "artisan republicanism," as Sean Wilentz has recently explained it. The tradesmen of New York and other American cities also embraced an older ideology that tied together a devotion to craft and to commonwealth. The artisans believed in equality and independence, but not as ends in themselves, for independence should free men "to exercise virtue, to subordinate private ends to the legislation of the public good."[14] Certainly, the artisans and small shopkeepers of New York City stood for individual initiative, for economic progress, and for the rights of private property. In this sense they were liberals. Yet, as Wilentz puts it, they also stood for something else:

> *With a rhetoric rich in the republican language of corruption, equality, and independence, they remained committed to a benevolent hierarchy of skill and the cooperative workshop. Artisan independence conjured up, not a vision of ceaseless, self-interested industry, but a moral order in which all craftsmen would eventually become self-governing, independent, competent masters. . . . Men's energies would be devoted, not to personal ambition or profit alone, but to the commonwealth; in the workshop, mutual obligation and respect—"the strongest ties of the heart"—would prevail; in more public spheres, the craftsmen would insist on their equal rights and exercise their citizenship with a view to preserving the rule of virtue as well as to protecting their collective interests against an eminently corruptible mercantile and financial elite.*[15]

Gordon Wood has argued that the grand achievement of the founders in the 1780s was to move political thought from a classical to a romantic or liberal conception of republicanism. In the classical republican vocabulary, virtue and commonwealth were the key terms. For a republic to survive, individual aspirations must be wedded to the common good. This was the language of 1776. By 1787, the old words had taken on new meanings. The republic devised by Madison and his colleagues was a system that would not depend upon the virtue of the people. In the Federalist scheme, the traditional vices of republican government—individualism and self-interest—became strengths. The commonweal would emerge automatically in the competition of private interests.[16] While Wood's study brilliantly illuminates the changing political thought of the founding elites, it obscures the continuity, the complexity, and the contradictory nature of the political thought of those men and women of the "middling classes." Urban artisans, especially, felt the steady pull of liberalism, yet they also harbored great misgivings about the new economic order that seemed to lie ahead. For them, the commitment to classical republican values remained strong, well into the nineteenth century. Just what sort of commonwealth or republican order they envisioned was not always clear or consistent. What was unmistakably clear, however, was their insistence that they be recognized as full-fledged participants in that order, whatever it may be.[17] The most obvious arena of participation was politics. Another was reading.

The Magazine

It was into this milieu that *The New-York Magazine* was born. It wasn't the first attempt to start a magazine in New York in the postwar era. Just three years earlier, in 1787, Noah Webster had brought out *The American Magazine*. After only a year, however, he abandoned the project, mainly for financial reasons. " I will now leave writing and do more lucrative business," Webster said. "I am happy to quit New York."[18] Thomas and James Swords hoped for a better fate as they offered to the public the first issue of *The New-York Magazine* in January of 1790. Though New York had been devastated economically by the war, the city was bustling again by 1790. The population passed 30,000 in 1789, and during the 1790s the city climbed to first rank as the commercial metropolis of America.[19] The Swords brothers often complained that the city's prosperity never trickled down to them ("the horizon remains dark and gloomy," they liked to report to their readers). But they did manage to stay in business eight full years—the longest run of any eighteenth-century American magazine.[20]

Part of the reason for the magazine's early success was its association with "a society of gentlemen," a local group of patrons of the arts and would-be "literary men," who began to work with the Swords brothers on the March issue. Their aim was to provide the magazine with "literary support" and editorial direction, and to promote "the pen of virtue and morality, science and taste." Clearly, *The New-York Magazine* represented the aspirations for culture and refinement of the American elite. The magazine's price was somewhat aristocratic as well—$2.25 per year, at a time when 50 cents a day was a common wage for a New York workingman.[21] In this sense, *The New-York Magazine* was not unlike similar magazines in the United States and Britain. Its model was *The Gentleman's Magazine* of London, the great pioneer of the general interest magazine in English. Like *The Gentleman's*, *The New-York Magazine* was impartial, restrained, stolid—not in the least critical of the culture of "the rich, the well-born, and the able," as subscriber John Adams described the new social elite of New York.[22]

Yet neither the editors nor the "society of gentlemen" viewed the enterprise as elitist. In an "Introductory Essay" published with the April issue, they proclaimed their commitment to the republican ideal of "equal liberty," especially equal access to *knowledge*. Following a eulogy to the democratic science of Benjamin Franklin, the editors described their vision of the purpose of a magazine:

> *A well conducted magazine, we conceive must, from its nature, contribute greatly to diffuse knowledge throughout a community, and to create in that community a taste for literature. The universality of the subjects which it treats of will give to every profession, and every occupa-*

tion, some information, while its variety holds out to every taste some gratification. From its conciseness, it will not require more time for its perusal than the most busy can well spare; and its cheapness brings it within the convenient purchase of every class of society.[23]

Was *The New-York Magazine* the province of the elite, as the magazine's tone suggests, or of "every class of society," as its editors declared? Fortunately, the answer to that question need not be pure guesswork, for the subscribers were listed by name in the 1790 volume.

The Readers

In 1790, *The New-York Magazine* had 370 subscribers, a small but respectable number for that time.[24] (Historians have generally assumed that each copy of a newspaper or magazine in this era was read by quite a few people.) About 80 percent of the subscribers lived in New York City (Manhattan). About 5 percent lived in Albany; another 5 percent lived in other New York state towns; and the rest were scattered from Nova Scotia to Antigua. The vast majority of subscribers were men (98 percent), though surely many of their subscriptions were intended for wives and children as well. Seven women were subscribers in their own names. I located 90 percent (269 of 298) of the New York readers in city directories and/or other biographical sources. For 265 of these I was able to secure information on occupations and street addresses. For comparison, I also drew a random sample of 400 entries from the 1790 city directory. (The nature and limitations of the city directory are discussed in Appendix A.)

The readership of *New-York Magazine* was indeed more "up-scale" than the general population of the city (see Table 1). While nearly 50 percent of the readers were professionals or merchants, only 15 percent of the random sample fell into these two categories. Moreover, the most common professional occupation among the readers was lawyer, while among the general population the most common professional jobs were somewhat lower in prestige: local government official and school teacher. The difference between the two groups at the bottom of the scale is even more striking. In the random sample, 17 percent fell into the "nonskilled" category. Most of these were cartmen, laborers, and mariners. In the subscriber group, only four individuals were classified as "nonskilled": a gardener, a nursery man, a washer, and a widow. The first two would certainly fall higher on a measure of skill than laborers or cartmen, and they may not even belong in this category.

Table 1 *Occupational Status of Subscribers to* The New-York Magazine *and a Random Sample from the New York City Directory, 1790*

Occupation Category	Subscriber %	Random Sample %
1. Professional	20.0%	6.6%
2. Merchant	29.1	8.5
3. Shopkeeper	21.5	26.5
4. Artisan	27.9	41.4
5. Nonskilled	1.5	17.0
TOTAL % (N)	100.0% (265)	100.0% (377)
Occupation information missing (n)	(33)	(23)

The same might be said of widows. The one widow subscriber, for example, was a Beekman, one of the leading families of the city. The washer also was a woman; and she, too, may have been a member of social class higher than her occupation suggests. (The other two women subscribers that I was able to trace were a teacher and a glover.) In short, it might be said that virtually no one from the very bottom of the socio-economic scale—the truly poor—subscribed to *The New-York Magazine*.[25]

Though the proportions at the top and bottom of the occupational scale for the two groups look quite different, the middle range proportions are much less disparate. About half of the subscribers were shopkeepers or artisans, compared with the two-thirds of the random sample. While this is a significant difference, of course, I would argue that 50 percent is still a substantial proportion. If it is important that half the readers of *The New-York Magazine* were merchants and professionals, it is equally important that the other half were artisans and shopkeepers. Both groups deserve a closer look.

Who were the elite readers? Most were merchants. More than one-quarter of the total list of subscribers identified themselves simply as merchants. The range of wealth and income within this category was large. Some "merchants" were doubtless no more than hopeful or pretentious shopkeepers; others were the leading commercial operators of the city and of the nation. Whether large or small, most merchants of that era were somewhat unspecialized, working on commission and handling a variety of goods. For example, one of *The New-York Magazine* subscribers advertised in a local newspaper a stock of Madeira wine, Carolina indigo and rice, China tea, a house and lot on Queen Street, thirteen acres near Harlem, and "a neat post chaise with harness." Another subscriber advertised imported cloth, buttons, buckles, glass, and "continental certificates"—and he was willing to barter for "country produce."[26]

If the prestige of an address reflects status, the merchants in the subscriber group may not have been much more well-to-do than merchants generally. Forty-two percent of the merchant readers held addresses on the most important business streets of the city: Queen (now Pearl), Water, and Hanover Square. But 37 percent of the merchants in the random sample also had addresses on these same streets. In both samples, only a scattering of individual merchants lived in the more distant sections of the city—north of what is now Fulton Street or west of Broadway.

Though many of the merchant readers were small-scale operators, some were the leaders of the mercantile elite. The names of Beekman, Kip, Livingston, Roosevelt, Van Rensselaer, and Verplank—old families and old money—dot the list.[27] Another subscriber, William Duer, is an example of a new-money man who read *The New-York Magazine*. Duer was perhaps the leading speculator of the day in land, securities, government contracts, and manufacturing ventures. He had made one fortune during the war, and he was hard at work on another in 1790. Besides the big merchants, some of the most prominent lawyers and politicians of the city were subscribers. Egbert Benson, one of the leading conservative assemblymen of New York in the 1780s, was on the list. So was James Duane, former Congressman and mayor of New York. And, of course, Washington, Adams, *et al.* Little wonder that the Swords brothers had such high hopes for their little magazine.[28]

But half the readers were not so wealthy or so prominent. Half were shopkeepers and artisans. Most of the shopkeepers, about 60 percent of them in both the subscriber group and the random sample, were listed simply as shopkeepers, storekeepers, or grocers. The others represented a variety of specialties: taverns, livery stables, bookstores, paint stores, hardware stores, tobacco shops, and so on. The main street for shopkeeper subscribers was Broadway, an up-and-coming business and residential street in New York in 1790. Others lived throughout the city. The artisans were a larger and even more varied group. Altogether, thirty-nine different trades were represented on the subscription list, compared with forty-eight trades in the random sample.

What kinds of artisans were likely to read *The New-York Magazine*? The quick answer seems to be: all kinds. The range of trades is striking, with many crafts represented by a single subscriber. (See Appendix B. The only woman artisan subscriber, for example, was also the only glover on the list.) Yet some patterns may be discerned (see Table 2). By far, the three leading trades in the general population were shoemaker, carpenter, and tailor, which account for nearly 37 percent of the artisans in the random sample. These three trades were not the leading trades among the artisan subscribers, however, though they were well represented. The top three trades among the subscribers were carpenter, printer, and sea captain. This is an interesting comparison, for no printers or sea captains turned up at all in the random sample. Obviously, these were not common artisan occupations; yet they were relatively common on *The New-York Magazine*'s subscription list. Conversely, two crafts—blacksmith and blockmaker—appear in the top ten artisan occupations in the random sample, but not at all on the subscription list.

Why printers and sea captains (but not blacksmiths and blockmakers) would subscribe to a magazine seems fairly obvious. Their trades and their life-styles were clearly more associated with reading. The same might be said for the barbers, whose customers loitered around the shops then just as they do today. But what of the coppersmiths and cutlers, the saddlers and sailmakers? The street addresses of the artisans provide a clue. The magazine subscribers were somewhat more likely than other artisans to live and work in the commercial heart of the city. This difference should not be exaggerated, however; the artisan subscrib-

Table 2 *The Ten Leading Occupations of Artisan Subscribers to* The New-York Magazine *and Artisans in a Random Sample from the New York City Directory, 1790*

Subscribers		Random Sample	
Occupation	% of Artisans	Occupation	% of Artisans
1. Carpenter	9.5%	1. Shoemaker	14.7%
2. Printer*	9.5	2. Carpenter	11.5
3. Sea Captain*	6.8	3. Tailor	10.3
4. Barber	5.4	4. Cooper	5.8
5. Cabinet Maker	5.4	5. Ship Carpenter	3.8
6. Shoemaker	5.4	6. Hatter	3.2
7. Baker	4.1	7. Blacksmith**	2.6
8. Clock/Watchmaker	4.1	8. Blockmaker**	2.6
9. Cooper	4.1	9. Chairmaker	2.6
10. Tailor	4.1	10. Gold/Silversmith	2.6
TOP TEN TOTAL % (n)	58.1% (43)		59.6% (93)
ALL ARTISANS % (N)	100.0% (74)		100.0% (156)

*These trades do not appear at all in the random sample.
**These trades do not appear at all on the subscriber list.

Table 3 *The Five Leading Street Addresses of Artisan Subscribers to* The New-York Magazine *and Artisans in a Random Sample from the New York City Directory, 1790*

Subscribers		Random Sample	
Street	% of Artisans	Street	% of Artisans
1. Queen	13.5%	1. Queen	12.8%
2. Hanover Square	8.1	2. Fair	5.1
3. Water	8.1	3. Water	4.5
4. Broadway	5.4	4. Chatham	3.8
5. King	5.4	5. Ann	3.2
TOP FIVE TOTAL % (n)	40.5% (30)		29.5% (46)
ALL ARTISANS % (N)	100.0% (74)		100.0% (156)

ers were spread out among thirty-four different streets in the city. Yet the artisans in the random sample were spread out even more widely on sixty-seven different streets, including some of the newer and less-built-up areas around Bowery Lane on what was then the far northeast side of town.

The artisan subscribers were more concentrated on the same streets as the merchant subscribers: Queen, Water, and Hanover Square. King Street (now Pine) was another prominent street in this same area. Again, this concentration should not be overstated; the artisans from the random sample were also heavily represented on Queen and Water. But the other main streets for them—Fair (now Fulton), Ann, and Chatham (now Park Row)—were several blocks farther north on the outskirts of the commercial center of the city in 1790 (see Table 3).

Because little is known about most of the individual artisan subscribers, it is difficult to say what sort of men they were. But at least some of them were clearly men of stature and influence, both within their crafts and in the larger public culture. Some were on their way to becoming manufacturers and capitalists. For example, White Matlock, a brewer on Chatham Street, was vice president of the New York Manufacturing Society, which was headed by the well-known merchant-politician Melancthon Smith. The aim of this society was precisely to move manufacturing from handicraft to factory.[29] Other artisan subscribers, on the other hand, were just as clearly devoted to the craft tradition. The chairman and deputy chairman of the General Society of Mechanics and Tradesmen were both readers of *The New-York Magazine*. Anthony Post was a carpenter; James Bramble was a whitesmith (tinned or galvanized iron). The General Society, founded in 1785, was a revival of the radical mechanics' committee of the 1770s, which had been instrumental in recruiting the city's working class to Revolutionary politics. It was an organization of substantial, ambitious, and politically active master tradesmen. By 1796, for example, Anthony Post owned property valued at 3,500 pounds. But it was also a group devoted to the traditions of craft work and to the values of artisan republicanism.[30]

The Content

The content of *The New-York Magazine* did not impress William Loring Andrews, one of the earliest of the few historians who have written about the magazine. His enthusiasm was expended on the copperplate engravings that formed the frontispiece of each issue. Of the rest of the content, he wrote:

> *Aside from the record of marriages and deaths and a few local items of some slight historical importance, there is nothing in the literature of* The New-York Magazine *that, if it had been totally destroyed, would have proved a serious loss to posterity or to the world of letters.*[31]

In a sense, Andrews was right. Except for some early poetry by William Dunlap, the literature of *The New-York Magazine* is of little interest to "the world of letters."[32] But it is of great interest to the social historian of reading, for here we can see what the merchants, shopkeepers, and artisans described above actually read in 1790.

Through a simple content analysis and a close reading of the 1790 volume, I discovered that many of the conventional notions about late-eighteenth-century American magazines are true of *The New-York Magazine*.[33] The magazine was highly eclectic—in subject matter, in style, and in source of material. In this sense, American magazines were like their English counterparts. The prototypical and highly successful English magazine, *The Gentleman's Magazine*, was perhaps most famous for its orderly but miscellaneous character. In fact, largely because of the influence of *The Gentleman's*, "magazine" became almost synonymous with "miscellany."[34] An article on the history of magazines that appeared in *The New-York Magazine* in 1790 was almost exclusively about *The Gentleman's*. A proper magazine, the article declared, should have two characteristics: it should be "very various and extensive" in its coverage and commentary, and it should unite "utility and entertainment, . . . instruction with pleasure."[35]

Certainly *The New-York Magazine* took the idea of instruction very seriously. Though few of its articles and essays dealt directly with government or politics, many were highly didactic on the subject of public virtue. In many ways, the content of *The New-York Magazine* was very much devoted to what have been called the "didactic arts," those arts and sciences considered useful to the cultivation of virtue and character, the essential ingredients of republican men and women (see Table 4).[36]

While a good deal of the content of *The New-York Magazine* was given over to discussions of

Table 4 *Proportions of Items Devoted to Various Subject Categories in* The New-York Magazine, 1790

Content Category	Proportion of Items
1. Politics and Government	15.3%
2. Manners & Morals	46.8
3. Religion	4.9
4. Science & Health	3.9
5. Household Advice	1.0
6. Humor	4.2
7. Commentary on Art, Music & Letters	3.9
8. "American Muse" (poetry)	3.9
9. "Intelligence" (news briefs)	3.6
10. "Marriages," "Deaths," & other Vital Statistics	12.6
ALL ITEMS TOTAL % (N)	100.1% (308)

Table 5 *Proportions of Items Devoted to Various Subjects* Within *the General Subject Category "Manners & Morals" in* The New-York Magazine, *1790*

"Manners & Morals" Sub-Category	Proportion of Items
1. Romance (love, seduction, etc.)	24.3%
2. Education	9.7
3. Virtue (morality, wisdom, etc.)	29.2
4. Description (travel, exotica, slice of life, etc.)	36.8
ALL "MANNERS & MORALS" ITEMS % (N)	100.0% (144)

specific topics in politics, religion, or science, the largest proportion of the articles fell into a more nebulous area that I have labeled "manners and morals" (see Table 5). Many of these pieces were romances—usually sentimental stories of love lost or found, seduction resisted or embraced. Many were simple expositions on virtue—with titles such as "Vanity," "Avarice," "On Idleness," "The Benefits of Temperance," or simply "On Virtue." Many were purely descriptive pieces—travelogues, anecdotes on manners and customs, sundry tales of exotica. Counting all the prose pieces for 1790, about two-thirds were written in descriptive or expository style; one-third were narratives. About one-eighth were set in New York City; seven-eighths were set elsewhere or had no specific locale.

What were these stories and articles like? A closer look at some of the regular features and some of the long-running serials provides some insight. Three of the most frequent contributors to *The New-York Magazine* in 1790 were "Philobiblicus," "Juvenis," and "The Scribbler." They rather nicely represent the range of material in the magazine, from the arcane to the mundane.

"Philobiblicus" falls into the arcane category. He contributed a piece each month on scriptural matters, especially issues in Biblical translation. The more subtle the philology, the more complex the etymology, the better "Philobiblicus" liked it. His aim, he said in his first piece, was to be "both instructing and entertaining" particularly through the use of "fine language and elegance of expression."[37]

"Juvenis" was more practical. Virtually all of his many pieces were little homilies on virtue. In a variety of ways, he preached a simple sermon: "that happiness results from the constant practice of virtue." On his list of the important virtues were the traditional ones. "The very ideas of justice, truth, benevolence, modesty, humility, mildness, and temperance please and beautify the mind," he wrote.[38]

"The Scribbler" was considerably more down to earth, even earthy, than either "Philobiblicus" or "Juvenis." Writing was his avocation; he was an artisan by occupation, though in what craft he does not say. In his first contribution he tells the story of how excited he had been as a young man to see his first piece of writing appear in a newspaper. He began to daydream and to imagine himself a great writer and a great man:

> *In my reflections upon it next day, I beheld myself wielding a pen with all the force of a furious and animated combatant, until reaching to supply it with ink, I overturned one of the implements of my profession. The noise brought me to my proper recollection, and, strange metamorphosis! I found myself in my master's workshop, busied in the execution of a design which my extraordinary avocation had destroyed, and surrounded by my fellow apprentices, who were looking at my actions with astonishment, and*

picking up the remains of the valuable instrument which I had thrown down, and which was broken to pieces. For this piece of mischief I was severely corrected by my master, but the disaster did not prevent me in the prosecution of my favorite hobby horse. I continued to wield the goose-quill, and I every day saw myself rising into consequence by the respectable figure Mr. Scribbler made in the newspapers.[39]

"The Scribbler['s]" contributions continued to touch on the lives of the "middling classes" of New York City.

The long-running serials in 1790 also reflect the range of material in *The New-York Magazine*. In this category, the most arcane may have been the series called "Observations on the Utility of the Latin and Greek Languages," which ran for eight months beginning in April. In this series, "T.Q.C." summarized in copious detail all the various arguments supporting the study of the ancient languages—ranging from the needs of Christianity to physiology.[40] Another prominent monthly feature was the serialization of John Adams' *Defense of the Constitutions of Government of the United States*, a book that explored and promoted English constitutional theory as much as American.[41] A third serial that ran for many months was "The History of the Dutchess de C____," a romance of passion, power, intrigue, confinement, cruelty, terror, outrage, and calamity among the rich and well-born of Europe.[42]

The other material in the magazine shows a similar diversity. For example, many of the articles and stories were aimed at women. Though only seven women were subscribers in their own names, it is clear that the readership was heavily female. The first issue, for example, carried a letter from a local woman praising the editors for launching such an important literary enterprise. She promised that she and all her friends would subscribe, and she hinted that Noah Webster's *American Magazine* had perished largely because the *men* of the city had failed to support it. About 11 percent of the articles in 1790 either had a woman as the main character or had a clearly identified female author, and many more were obviously aimed at and probably written by women. This is clearly true of the romances and sentimental fiction, generally considered at that time, as Linda Kerber has pointed out, to be the province of the woman reader.[43]

Some of the pieces aimed at women were simply conventional reflections on traditional feminine virtues: "How much more pure, tender, delicate, irritable, affectionate, flexible, and patient is woman than man?" Or: "The female thinks not profoundly; profound thought is the power of the man. Women feel more. Sensibility is the power of woman."[44] In their "Introductory Essay," the editors said that they expected their women readers to submit "many a poetic wreath," for poetry "seems peculiarly the province of that sex, whose sweetest ornament is the mild tear that trembles in the eye of sensibility."[45] The magazine also carried advice pieces for women: "On the Choice of a Husband," or "On the Virtue of Acorn Coffee" ("to cure the slimy obstructions in the viscera"), or on how to behave in company (no "sitting cross-legged, straddling, spitting, blowing noses, etc., etc.").[46] Some were parables of seduction and lost virtue, such as the sad story of "Frivola," who became so obsessed with luxury that she ended her wasted life in Europe, the slave of "every species of polite dissipation."[47] The emphasis on the supposed sensibility and sentimentality of the woman reader was characteristic of popular thought in England as well as in America.[48]

Yet some of the articles directed toward women were less conventional. These included tales of women's heroism, calls for women's education, and articles by women sensitive to women's concerns. An example of the latter was a piece criticizing men for always talking about women's vanity.[49] In this, *The New-York Magazine* seems to have been similar to other American magazines of the time. Mary Beth

Norton has found that magazines were often in the forefront of a new approach to women, an approach that emphasized a more active and equal participation of women in family life, household management, and the education of children. This new approach still placed woman's sphere within the home and family. But home and family had now taken on a somewhat larger and more political role in the nurture of the new republic.[50]

Despite all the diversity, however, several important themes recur. Virtue, for example, was commonly portrayed as *public* virtue. The golden rule was taken very seriously by the contributors to *The New-York Magazine*. "Amongst the number of public virtues we may note love to our country, zeal in promoting the good of society, seeking the good of our neighbor in all our conduct," wrote the author of a piece called "On Virtue." Similarly, even the deeply religious "Juvenis" stopped far short of arguing that virtue is a private matter between a man and God. If a man is virtuous, he wrote, "he has sacrificed his own interest rather than wrong his neighbor. He has been benevolent to his fellow men. The children of poverty and affliction he has assisted and consoled."[51] Women's virtue was usually portrayed as a more private matter of "morality and piety," but the relationship between women's virtue and the welfare of the community was sometimes suggested—for example, in an essay on women's education by a Philadelphia school girl in the magazine's first issue.[52] In short, the connection between virtue and commonwealth was vividly clear in the pages of *The New-York Magazine*.

Another recurrent theme was suspicion of luxury. On this theme, the aphorisms abounded: "Luxury and idleness are similar in their effects—By the former, families are reduced to indigence, and are involved in misery and ruin; by means of the latter, they are prevented from arriving at a comfortable situation in life." The parables and allegories were equally common. In one, "Wealth" and "Poverty" meet each other on life's road at the end of their journeys. In a piece called "On Avarice," the author argued that "the avaricious man regards nothing but his purse; the welfare and prosperity of his country never much employs his thoughts. . . . He is a stranger to public spiritedness." The theme was always that luxury is self-defeating because it is self-serving.[53] "Juvenis" perhaps expressed it most clearly: the virtuous man "has never indulged himself in luxury or any kind of excess, and used every exertion to promote the welfare of society."[54]

A third recurrent theme was the power and democracy of knowledge. In America, everyone had a right and a duty to participate in the life of the mind. Some writers put this theme rather bluntly. In a paean to science, one writer declared:

> *It is indeed questionable whether an ignorant people can be happy, or even exist, under what Americans call a free government. It may be also doubted, whether a truly enlightened people were ever enslaved. Science is so meliorating in its influence upon the human mind, that even he who holds the reins of power, and hath felt its rays, loses the desire of a tyrant, and is best gratified in the sense of public love and admiration. Liberty is a plant which as naturally flourishes under this genial light, as despotism is engendered by the horrors of intellectual darkness.*[55]

In more subtle form, this theme ran through many of the articles in *The New-York Magazine* in 1790. Women, for example, were urged "to attend to the cultivation of letters"—and not simply because of the obligations of "republican motherhood." One writer advocated education for women partly for their own "happiness." In old age, when their traditional feminine pleasures had faded, they could take "refuge in the bosom of knowledge."[56] Even "Philobiblicus," the master of erudition, argued that instruction in Latin and Greek should be central even to a "republican education," for in a republic every man should be and could be a scholar.[57]

In this, the magazine reflected a widespread belief in America that diffusion of knowledge was beneficial for republican government and for the virtue of the people. Though classical republican thinkers were sometimes rather skeptical of education for the masses, Americans were almost wholly for it.[58] Benjamin Rush, Noah Webster, Thomas Jefferson and many others argued passionately that education must be the foundation of republican government. But they went further than simply praising education. They stressed the broadest possible diffusion of knowledge through universal participation in public schools. As Rush put it, "a free government can only exist in an equal diffusion of literature." To this end, Rush proposed not only public schools and state universities, but also a wider diffusion of libraries and newspapers. "I consider it possible to convert men into republican machines," he declared in a now-famous quotation. "This must be done if we expect them to perform their parts properly in the great machine of the government of the state."[59] Of course, these men supported the diffusion of education and knowledge precisely because they believed it would have a conservative, a stabilizing, influence on the nation. The fear of mass education per se, which was widespread in England, never took root in America.[60] In American republican ideology, everyone had the right and the duty to participate in the life of the mind.

Public virtue, suspicion of luxury, and the power and democracy of knowledge—these were republican themes, and they were freighted with meaning for eighteenth-century Americans, perhaps especially American artisans. Of course, these themes did not appear in every story and article in *The New-York Magazine*. But they were common enough to run like brightly colored threads through the great diversity of material, from heavy political discourse to ethereal romance. This, then, was what the readers of *The New-York Magazine*—the shopkeepers and artisans, as well as the merchants and politicians—were reading in 1790.

Conclusion

In its first issue in January 1790, *The New-York Magazine* published an article titled "On the Means of Preserving Public Liberty." It is a nice summary of what might be called a republican ideology of magazine reading. "Information," the article said, had been the mainspring of the Revolution, and it must now be the wellspring of the new republic. The author continued:

> *A few enlightened citizens may be dangerous; let all be enlightened, and oppression must cease, by the influence of a ruling majority; for it can never be their interest to indulge a system incompatible with the rights of freemen. Those institutions are the most effectual guards to public liberty which diffuse the rudiments of literature among a people. . . . A few incautious expressions in our constitution, or a few salaries of office too great for the contracted feelings of those who do not know the worth of merit and integrity, can never injure the United States, while literature is generally diffused, and the plain citizen and planter reads and judges for himself. . . . Disseminate science through all grades of people, and it will forever vindicate your rights.*[61]

This sentiment, of course, was not confined to America. The claim to equal access to knowledge, as well as to political power, was central to the new revolutionary spirit of Europe. The old regimes of both France and England were notoriously fearful of the power of information and reading, as Richard Altick and Robert Darnton have made clear.[62] The American elites were likewise impressed by the power of information, but they tended to be less fearful of reading—perhaps because so much reading matter remained fundamentally supportive of the values of American republicanism. The literature of *The New-York Magazine*, for example, was not a popular, democratic literature produced by or even directed toward the lower classes. This kind of modern mass media would not emerge in the United States until the nineteenth century.[63] Yet neither was this an aristocratic literature accessible only to the elite. The readership was broader than this. It was instead a kind of republican literature with a republican purpose. It affirmed the traditional values, while inviting all (except the truly poor) to take part. Like politics, it was an arena in which artisans and shopkeepers could participate in public life—in this case the cultural life—of the new nation. And participation, not social revolution, was what artisan republicanism was all about.

Appendix A

Notes on Method

As far as I have been able to determine, this study is the first readership research based upon the subscription list of an eighteenth-century magazine. The methods that I used were fairly simple. I started with the list of 370 subscribers published in *The New-York Magazine; or, Literary Repository* (New York: Thomas and James Swords, 1790), 1:iii–vi. The list itself identified 298 of these as residents of New York City. I located information on 265 of these New Yorkers in city directories or, in a few cases, in the biographical sources cited in the footnotes. The directories I used were *The New-York Directory and Register* (New York: Hodge, Allen, and Campbell, 1789 and 1790) and *The New-York Directory and Register* (New York: T. and J. Swords, 1791 and 1792). I also drew a random sample of 400 entries from the 1790 directory. These two groups—the subscriber census and the random sample—provided the data for the reader analysis.

Of course, some people do not appear in these directories. Women, for instance, appear only if they were heads of households. In my random sample, only 7.8 percent were women, and almost all of them were identified by occupation (58 percent) or listed as widows (35 percent). Furthermore, historians have usually assumed that common laborers, especially mariners, were substantially under-represented and that vagrants and transients were not listed at all. Yet I also found the opposite to be true as well—that is, a few of the wealthy merchants on the subscription list did not appear in the city directories. I identified them from other biographical sources. Since I was able to trace only well-to-do people, not poor people, in these other sources, my survey of subscribers may be even more upwardly biased. On the other hand, because some of the incipient manufacturers in New York in 1790 still sometimes listed themselves as artisans, there is a countervailing downward bias in the survey as well. Overall, I tend to agree with Carl F. Kaestle that the New York directories from the 1790s probably provide a fairly reliable representation of the range of occupations in the city. See Carl F. Kaestle, *The Evolution of an Urban School System: New York City, 1750–1850* (Cambridge, Mass., 1973), 31–32. I'm confident partly because I was able to trace all but 33 of the New York subscribers. Moreover, if there is an upper-class bias in my survey, that would, of course, have a conservative effect upon the conclusions of the study, undercounting those at the lower end of the economic scale. This also gives me some confidence in my suggestion that shopkeepers and artisans made up about 50 percent of the readers of the magazine.

The classification of occupations in Table 1 and Appendix B is based largely upon my own understanding of late-eighteenth-century employment, but it does not differ radically from the schemes used by other historians, such as Carl Kaestle and Howard Rock. (See also Michael B. Katz, "Occupational Classification in History," *Journal of Interdisciplinary History* 3 [Summer 1972]: 63-88.) Several of the occupations in the "professional" category (such as clerk and local government official) are perhaps out of place there. Similarly, gardener, and nurseryman, and widow may not belong in the "nonskilled" category. But these involve so few individuals that I don't believe that the argument is distorted. Furthermore, the identical classification scheme was used for both the subscriber census and the random sample, so the comparative statements should be fairly reliable.

For the content analysis, I simply classified articles by topic. The unit of analysis was the individual article or story, though certain standard groupings of items were counted only once per issue. These included "American Muse," a collection of poems in each issue; "Intelligence," a monthly collection of short news items; "Marriages," and "Deaths"; and "Congressional Affairs," excerpts from the proceedings of Congress (coded as "politics"). I did not code the copperplate engravings at the beginning of each issue. I did not code advertisements, because in 1790 there were none. Fine distinctions among categories are not important for the argument. The aim was simply to get a general idea of the manifest content of the editorial matter in the magazine. The simple inter-coder reliability coefficient for the content analysis was approximately .85, with most of the ambiguity within the "manners and morals" category (Table 5).

Appendix B

Occupation List of Subscribers

1. PROFESSIONAL:
   - attorney
   - benevolent society
   - clerk
   - college
   - federal government official
   - local government official
   - military officer
   - minister
   - physician
   - college student
   - teacher

2. MERCHANT:
   - banker
   - broker
   - insurer
   - merchant

3. SHOPKEEPER:
   - boarding house
   - bookstore
   - grocer
   - ironmonger
   - jewelry store
   - livery stable
   - paint and glass store
   - porter house
   - ship chandler
   - store or shopkeeper
   - tavern
   - tobacco store
   - vendue master

4. ARTISAN:
   - baker
   - barber
   - bookbinder
   - brewer
   - butcher
   - cabinet maker
   - carpenter
   - carver and gilder
   - chairmaker
   - chandler
   - clock and watchmaker
   - coach painter
   - cooper
   - copperplate printer
   - coppersmith
   - cutler
   - dancing master
   - distiller
   - furrier
   - glover
   - gold and silver smith
   - hatter
   - mason
   - mathematical instrument maker
   - nail maker
   - pewterer
   - pilot
   - printer
   - saddler
   - sailmaker
   - sea captain
   - ship carpenter
   - ship joiner
   - shoemaker
   - tailor or mantua maker
   - tanner or currier

type founder	weaver
upholsterer	whitesmith

5. NONSKILLED:

gardener	washer
nurseryman	widow

Endnotes

1. "Preface," *The New-York Magazine; or, Literary Repository*, vol. 1 (New York: Thomas and James Swords, 1790), viii. Mathew Carey, proprietor of *The American Museum* magazine in Philadelphia, was similarly proud of the respectability and character of his subscribers. See "Preface," *The American Museum*, vol. 2 (Philadelphia: Mathew Carey, 1787).
2. Frank Luther Mott, *A History of American Magazines, 1741–1850* (Cambridge, Mass., 1930), 115–16; James Playsted Wood, *Magazines in the United States*, 3rd ed. (New York, 1971), 26.
3. Carl F. Kaestle, "The History of Literacy and the History of Readers," in *Review of Research in Education*, vol. 12, ed. Edmund W. Gordon (Washington, D.C., 1985), 45.
4. Edward Countryman, *A People in Revolution: The American Revolution and Political Society in New York, 1760–1790* (Baltimore, 1981), 294.
5. Bernard Bailyn, *The Ideological Origins of the American Revolution* (Cambridge, 1967); J. G. A. Pocock, *The Machiavellian Moment: Florentine Political Thought and the Atlantic Republican Tradition* (Princeton, N.J., 1975). For recent reviews of this literature see Linda Kerber, "The Republican Ideology of the Revolutionary Generation," *American Quarterly* 37 (Fall 1985): 474–95; Robert E. Shalhope, "Republicanism and Early American Historiography," *William and Mary Quarterly* 39 (April 1982): 334–56; Lance Banning, "Jeffersonian Ideology Revisited: Liberal and Classical Ideas in the New American Republic," *William and Mary Quarterly* 43 (January 1986): 3–19.
6. Louis Hartz, *The Liberal Tradition in America* (New York, 1955); Joyce Appleby, *Capitalism and a New Social Order: The Republican Vision of the 1790s* (New York, 1984); John Patrick Diggins, *The Lost Soul of American Politics: Virtue, Self-Interest, and the Foundations of Liberalism* (New York, 1984). For a recent review of this literature, see Joyce Appleby, "Republicanism in Old and New Contexts," *William and Mary Quarterly* 43 (January 1986): 20–34. See also Joyce Appleby, "Introduction: Republicanism and Ideology," *American Quarterly* 37 (Fall 1985): 461–73.
7. Eric Foner, *Tom Paine and Revolutionary America* (New York, 1976); Gary B. Nash, *The Urban Crucible: Social Change, Political Consciousness, and the Origins of the American Revolution* (Cambridge, Mass., 1979); Dirk Hoerder, *Crowd Action in Revolutionary Massachusetts, 1765–1780* (New York, 1977). See also Alfred F. Young, ed., *The American Revolution: Explorations in the History of American Radicalism* (DeKalb, Ill., 1976); and Dorothy Ross, "The Liberal Tradition Revisited and the Republican Tradition Addressed," in *New Directions in American Intellectual History*, ed. by John Higham and Paul K. Conkin (Baltimore, 1979).
8. Appleby, "Republicanism, 21; idem, "Introduction," 469. See also Shalhope, "Republicanism," 337.
9. Kerber, "Republican Ideology," 492–95.
10. Sidney I. Pomerantz, *New York: An American City, 1783–1803* (New York, 1938), 24–25, 460–61; Frank Monaghan and Marvin Lowenthal, *This Was New York: The Nation's Capital in 1789* (Garden City, N.Y., 1943), 33–34; Martha J. Lamb and [Mrs.] Burton Harrison, *History of the City of New York: Its Origins, Rise, and Progress*, vol. 3 (New York, 1896), 11. The most detailed account of day-to-day events in New York City during this era is I. N. Phelps Stokes, *The Iconography of Manhattan Island*, vol. 5 (New York, 1926).
11. See Table 1. See also Sean Wilentz, *Chants Democratic: New York City and the Rise of the American Working Class, 1788–1850* (New York, 1984), 27; Carl F. Kaestle, *The Evolution of an Urban School System: New York City, 1750–1850* (Cambridge, Mass., 1973), 31. For a discussion of my sampling and classification methods, see Appendix A.
12. Pomerantz, *New York*, 209–25; Wilentz, *Chants Democratic*, 24–35. See also David Montgomery, "The Working Classes of the Pre-Industrial American City, 1780–1830," *Labor History* 9 (Winter 1968): 3–22.

13. Countryman, *A People in Revolution*, 292–94. See also Staughton Lynd, "The Mechanics in New York Politics, 1774–1785," in *Class Conflict, Slavery, and the United States Constitution: Ten Essays* (Indianapolis, 1967).

14. Wilentz, *Chants Democratic*, 14.

15. Ibid., 102. See also Foner, *Tom Paine*.

16. Gordon S. Wood, *The Creation of the American Republic, 1776–1787* (New York, 1972), 606–15. See also Kerber, "Republican Ideology," 494.

17. Wilentz, *Chants Democratic*, 95. See also Howard B. Rock, *Artisans of the New Republic: The Tradesmen of New York City in the Age of Jefferson* (New York, 1979).

18. Webster quoted in Monaghan and Lowenthal, *This Was New York*, 147. See also Gary Coll, "Noah Webster, Magazine Editor and Publisher," *Journalism History* 11 (Spring/Summer 1984): 26–31.

19. Pomerantz, *New York*, 19–21, 155–59, 199–200; Thomas E. V. Smith, *The City of New York in the Year of Washington's Inauguration, 1789* (New York, 1889), 5–7.

20. Quote from "Preface," *New-York Magazine*, vol. 2 (1791), iv. Little has been written about *The New-York Magazine*. For brief sketches, see Mott, *History of American Magazines*, 114–116; William Loring Andrews, "The First Illustrated Magazine Published in New York," in *The Old Booksellers of New York, and Other Papers* (New York, 1895); Kenneth Scott and Kristin L. Gibbons, eds., *The New-York Magazine Marriages and Deaths, 1790–1797* (New Orleans, 1975); Mary Rives Bowman, "Dunlap and 'The Theatrical Register' of the *New-York Magazine*," *Studies in Philology* 24 (July 1927): 413–25. Incidentally, Isaiah Thomas's *Massachusetts Magazine* also survived eight years.

21. Editorial Announcement, *New-York Magazine* 1 (March 1790): unnumbered page. See also Mott, *History of American Magazines*, 34; Pomerantz, *New York*, 216.

22. *New-York Magazine* 1 (May 1790): 256–58; C. Lennart Carlson, *The First Magazine: A History of The Gentleman's Magazine* (Providence, 1938). Adams quote from Monaghan and Lowenthal, *This Was New York*, 34.

23. *New-York Magazine* 1 (April 1790): 197. I have modernized eighteenth-century spelling and capitalization.

24. By comparison the new nation's largest circulating magazine, *The American Museum*, had about 1,250 subscribers. See the subscription list published with *The American Museum* 2 (1787). See also Mott, *History of American Magazines*, 101.

25. Of course, some of the 33 subscribers that I couldn't trace may have been from the bottom occupational groups. If Table 1 is biased, it seems likely that it is biased upward. See Appendix A for a discussion of this issue. For a complete list of subscriber occupations, see Appendix B.

26. Smith, *City of New York*, 99. The ads are from Monaghan and Lowenthal, *This Was New York*, 52–53, 71. See also Pomerantz, *New York*, chap. 4.

27. Information on prominent individuals came from several biographical sources, including Margherita Arlina Hamm, *Famous Families of New York*, 2 vols. (New York, 1901); Lyman Horace Weeks, ed., *Prominent Families of New York*, rev. ed. (New York, 1898); James Grant Wilson, ed., *Memorial History of the City of New York*, vol. 5 (New York, 1893).

28. On Duer, see Pomerantz, *New York*, 181. On Benson and Duane, see Countryman, *A People in Revolution, passim.*

29. Smith, *City of New York*, 108; Pomerantz, *New York*, 197.

30. *The New-York Directory and Register* (New York, 1789), 117; Smith, *City of New York*, 107; On the General Society, see Wilentz, *Chants Democratic*, 38–39 and *passim*. On Anthony Post, see Lynd, "The Mechanics," 82, 107–08.

31. Andrews, "First Illustrated Magazine", 60.

32. L. Leary, "Unrecorded Early Verse by William Dunlap," *American Literature* 39 (March 1967); 87–88.

33. For notes on the content analysis method, see Appendix A. For a general description of the content of eighteenth-century magazines, see Mott, *History of American Magazines*, chap. 2.

34. Carlson, *First Magazine*, vii, 58. The passion for a wide variety of factual, scientific information in magazines had its counterpart in eighteenth-century European book publishing, most notably the success of the *Encyclopedie* in France. See Robert Darnton, *The Business of Enlightenment: A*

Publishing History of the Encyclopedie, 1775–1800 (Cambridge, Mass., 1979).

35. *New-York Magazine* 1 (May 1790): 257–58.

36. Wood, *Creation of the American Republic,* 104. See also Neil Harris, *The Artist in American Society: The Formative Years, 1790–1860* (New York, 1966).

37. *New-York Magazine* 1 (Jan. 1790): 4.

38. Ibid. 1 (Aug. 1790): 442. See also ibid. 1 (Feb. 1790); 104–06.

39. Ibid. 1 (Jan. 1790): 21. See also ibid, 1 (Feb. 1790): 104–06.

40. Ibid. 1 (April 1790): 212–18; 1 (Aug. 1790): 467–69.

41. The first segment is explicitly on the British constitution. See ibid. 1 (Jan. 1790): 41–47. On Adams and this book, see Wood, *Creation of the American Republic,* chap. 14; and Diggins, *Lost Soul*, chap. 3.

42. This tale begins in *New-York Magazine* 1 (Jan. 1790): 10–15; it ends in ibid. 1 (July 1790): 385–87. This is a translation of a romance by Madame la Comptesse de Genlis, a popular French writer of sentiment and sensation.

43. *New-York Magazine* 1 (Jan. 1790): 9; Linda K. Kerber, *Women of the Republic: Intellect and Ideology in Revolutionary America* (Chapel Hill, N.C., 1980), 235–36.

44. *New-York Magazine* 1 (June 1790): 335–36.

45. Ibid. 1 (April 1790): 198.

46. Ibid. 1 (Jan. 1790): 16–17, 51; 1 (March 1790), 160.

47. Ibid. 1 (Jan. 1790): 22–23; 1 (March 1790): 160–161; 1 (Nov. 1790): 646–48.

48. Richard D. Altick, *The English Common Reader* (Chicago, 1957), 45.

49. *New-York Magazine* 1 (Sept. 1790): 515–16; 1 (Oct. 1790): 563–65; 1 (Feb. 1790): 90; 1 (Dec. 1790): 694–95.

50. Mary Beth Norton, *Liberty's Daughters: The Revolutionary Experience of American Women, 1750–1800* (Boston, 1980), 246–50. See also Kerber, "Republican Ideology," 484–85; Kerber, *Women of the Republic,* 11–12; and Karen K. List, "Magazine Portrayals of Women's Role in the New Republic," *Journalism History* 13 (Spring 1986): 64–70.

51. *New-York Magazine* 1 (March 1790): 152–53; 1 (Aug. 1790): 442.

52. Ibid. 1 (Jan. 1790): 40–41.

53. Ibid. 1 (Jan. 1790): 28–29; 1 (March 1790): 159, 162; 1 (Jan. 1790): 18; 1 (Feb. 1790): 113.

54. Ibid. 1 (Aug. 1790): 442.

55. Ibid. 1 (May 1790): 295.

56. Ibid. 1 (Feb. 1790): 90.

57. Ibid. 1 (Feb. 1790): 89–90; 1 (Oct. 1790): 585–86.

58. Eugene F. Miller, "On the American Founders' Defense of Liberal Education in a Republic," *Review of Politics* 46 (Jan. 1984): 65–90. See also Eva Brann, *Paradoxes of Education in a Republic* (Chicago, 1979).

59. Benjamin Rush, "A Plan for the Establishment of Public Schools and the Diffusion of Knowledge in Pennsylvania," 1786, reprinted in *Essays on Education in the Early Republic,* ed. Frederick Rudolph (Cambridge, Mass., 1965), 3, 8, 17. See also Daniel Calhoun, *The Intelligence of a People* (Princeton, N.J., 1973), chap. 2; and Wilson Smith, ed., *Theories of Education in Early America, 1655–1819* (Indianapolis, 1973).

60. Altick, *English Common Reader,* chap. 3; Carl F. Kaestle, *Pillars of the Republic: Common Schools and American Society, 1780–1860* (New York, 1983), 33–34.

61. *New-York Magazine* 1 (Jan. 1790): 24–25.

62. Altick, *English Common Reader,* chap. 3; Robert Darnton, "Reading, Writing, and Publishing in Eighteenth-Century France: A Case Study in the Sociology of Literature," *Daedalus* 100 (Winter 1971): 243–44.

63. David D. Hall, "The Uses of Literacy in New England, 1600–1850," in *Printing and Society in Early America,* ed. William L. Joyce et al. (Worcester, Mass., 1983); David Paul Nord, "The Evangelical Origins of Mass Media in America, 1815–1835," *Journalism Monographs* No. 88 (May 1984); Michael Schudson, *Discovering the News: A Social History of American Newspapers* (New York, 1978), chap. 1. The same might be said of England, France, and Germany. See Altick, *English Common Reader;* and Darnton, "What is the History of Books?" *Daedalus* 111 (Summer 1982): 78–79. See also Paul J. Korshin, ed., *The Widening Circle: Essays on the Circulation of Literature in Eighteenth-Century Europe* (Philadelphia, 1976).

"Our Own Cause": Freedom's Journal *and the Beginnings of the Black Press*

Lionel C. Barrow Jr.

I

On March 16, 1827, the first issue of a new weekly newspaper called *Freedom's Journal* was published in New York City. This paper, the first published by blacks in the United States, had a front page article entitled "To Our Patrons." In it the editors, the Rev. Samuel Cornish and John Russwurm, announced:

> *We wish to plead our own cause. Too long have others spoken for us. Too long has the publick been deceived by misrepresentations, in things which concern us dearly, . . .*

The primary purpose of this article is to examine, briefly, the causes and consequences, form and content of the *Journal,* which lasted two years. Several other aspects of the publication, including some of the previous scholarship on the *Journal,* also will be examined in the process.

II

Background. President John Quincy Adams, elected in 1824, was in the last year of his first and only term of office and the shadow of Andrew Jackson was already on the land. The Erie Canal, which opened November 4, 1824, was ushering in an important phase of New York's commercial history. The Denmark Vessey slave revolt (1822) had probably passed out of the memory of most people—black and white—and Nat Turner's better known uprising was still four years away (1831).

March, 1827 could have been a time of preparation for a great celebration by blacks in New York state. Slavery in the state (in law if not in fact) was about to end on July 4, 1827,[1] as a result of a law passed on March 31, 1817, which in turn replaced one passed in 1797. The law, however, did not immediately end slavery for all persons. Smith indicates that only persons over 40 were to be free on July 4, 1827. This may have been true of the 1797 law but the 1817 one was more liberal.[2] As a result of this law, the number of slaves in New York state dropped from 10,088 in the 1820 census to 75 in the 1830 census.[3] Smith also states that as a result of the 1797 law, "for some time it had been illegal to transport slaves out of the state."[4] This, however, did not stop white slave-owners from doing so. Smith chronicles the details of one such case involving the son of Isabella Baumfree, later known as Sojourner Truth, who was sold by his owner to the wife of an Alabama plantation owner.[5]

In addition:

1—As Dann points out, "the state was still a happy hunting ground for kidnappers" as a result of the 1793 Fugitive Slave Law.[6]

2—Slavery was still legal just across the Hudson in New Jersey, which had 200 slaveholding families and 236 slaves as late as 1850 and still reported 18 slaves in the 1860 census.[7]

3—The American Colonization Society, organized in December, 1816, "was supported by some abolitionists and most proslavery men," and was actively promoting its program.[8]

4—As DuBois points out, free blacks in the early history of the South and North had the right to vote. This right was gradually being restricted or withdrawn in virtually every state in the union. While the concept of universal suffrage had been established in New York state in 1824, there was a "for white males only" sign on it. Black males, who had voted in New York in the 18th Century, according to DuBois, then were disfranchised, were "permitted to vote with a discriminatory property qualification of $250."[9]

With reference to the journalistic environment, there were, according to Chase and Sanborn, 843 newspapers being published in 1828, 161 of which were in New York state.[10] The vast majority of the 843 newspapers were weeklies, supported in large part by political parties, with circulations averaging 1,000 per week. Benjamin H. Day's New York *Sun,* the first successful penny daily, didn't begin until 1833. The New York *Herald* of James Gordon Bennett appeared in 1835 followed by Horace Greeley's New York *Tribune* in 1841 and Henry J. Raymond's New York *Times* in 1851. The friendly voice of the abolitionist press was not to get its start until William Lloyd Garrison started the *Liberator* in Boston in 1830. In addition, according to Detweiler, a local paper published in New York City was making "the vilest attacks on the Afro-American."[11]

Thus, far from being a time for rejoicing, March, 1827, probably was a time of great concern and some despair for free blacks who decided that if their views of slavery and of people-of-color were to be heard they would have to do it themselves. And so they did under the leadership of the Rev. Samuel Cornish, pastor of the African Presbyterian Church in New York City, and John Russwurm, born in Jamaica and one of the first blacks to graduate from college (Bowdoin College, Maine).

III

Format and Finance. Freedom's Journal originally had a four-page, four-column format. Its one-column headlines, typical of the papers of the day, had captions such as "To Our Patrons," "Memoirs of Paul Cuffee," "Common Schools in New York" and "The Effects of Slavery." This was changed with the start of Volume 2 (April 4, 1828) to a three-column make-up with eight pages. There were, obviously, no pictures in the paper, but drawings started to appear in the September 21, 1827, issue (Vol. 1, No. 28).

The paper was supported by its circulation and by advertising. There is no mention in the paper of the size of its circulation. Gross,[12] however, indicates that its successor, *Rights of All,* had 800 subscribers and *Freedom's Journal's* circulation should have been equal to or greater than that number, which would have made its circulation close to the weeklies of its time. The paper cost $3 a year "payable yearly in advance."

With reference to circulation, the first issue of the paper listed 14 agents from Portland, Maine, to Washington, D.C., who helped sell the publication. Some of them also wrote articles (letters actually) that were printed in the *Journal* and some may well have sent in other material for publication.

Issue number six listed advertising rates for the first time:

1. 50 cents for the first insertion of an ad of 12 lines and under.
2. 25 cents for every repetition of the above (or "of do," meaning ditto, as they stated in the *Journal*).

3. 75 cents for first insertion of an ad over 12 lines but not exceeding 22.
4. 38 cents "for each repetition of do."
5. Proportional prices for advertisements which exceed 22 lines.

On May 4, 1827 (Vol. 1, No. 8), the editors listed a "15 percent deduction for those persons who advertised by the year; 12 for 6 mos.; and 6 for 3 mos."

IV

Content of the Paper. In the first issue Russwurm and Cornish announced:

> *We wish to plead our own cause. Too long have others spoken for us. Too long has the publick been deceived by misrepresentations, in things which concern us dearly, . . . it shall ever be our duty to vindicate our brethren, when oppressed, and to lay the case before the publick. We shall also urge upon our brethren (who are qualified by the laws of the different states) the expediency of using their elective franchise, and of making an independent use of the same. . . . Useful knowledge of every kind, and every thing that relates to Africa, shall find a ready admission into our columns; and as the vast continent becomes daily more known, we trust that many things will come to light, proving that the natives of it are neither so ignorant nor stupid as they have generally been supposed to be. . . . From the press and the pulpit we have suffered much by being incorrectly represented. Men, whom we equally love and admire have not hesitated to represent us disadvantageously, without becoming personally acquainted with the true state of things, nor discerning between virtue and vice among us. . . .*

The editors started making good on their promises in the very first issue, which contained news from Haiti, Sierra Leone and such other items as the first installment of "Memoirs of Captain Paul Cuffee" (a black Bostonian who owned a trading ship staffed by free blacks), a 16-stanza poem on "The African Chief" (by Bryan), and an advertisement for the "B.F. Hughes' School of Colored Children of Both Sexes." Later issues had articles on Toussaint L'Ouverture, liberator of Haiti, on poet Phyllis Wheatley and articles on and by Bishop Richard Allen.

The paper took issue with the local press time after time. For example, on May 11, 1827 (Vol. 1, No. 9), the paper took issue with the editor of the New York *Evening Post* who praised slavery and concluded that free blacks ("people of colour") were better off as slaves "when they had a good master and mistress to provide for them," than they are in their "present precarious condition of emancipation and dependence." In the August 17, 1827, issue (Vol. 1, No. 24), "Mordecai" attacked the editor of the New York *Inquirer*, whom he said stands "foremost on the list" of those "whose object it is to keep alive the prejudice of the whites against the coloured community" of New York City.

The paper constantly rebutted the reasons given by advocates of colonization. An article published on March 30, 1827 (Vol. 1, No. 3), tore into a sermon preached in Newark, New Jersey, on behalf of the American Colonization Society in which the speaker stated that three-fourths of all free blacks "are proverbially idle, ignorant and depraved, and, therefore, should be sent back to Africa." The article points out that there was only "one coloured pauper (in New York City) to every 115, leaving the advantage vastly to our side." He felt the same was true for moral character and ventured to say that "the coloured man's offence, three times out of four, grows out of circumstances of his condition, while the white man's, most generally is premeditated and vicious."

The *Journal* printed (according to Aptheker[13]) the first report of a lynching published in the United States; ran campaigns to purchase and free slaves from sympathetic owners; held meetings with its subscribers to discuss their satisfaction or dissatisfaction with the content of the paper; ran editorials on colonization and others on "self-interest" (in which it took "persons of colour" to task for betraying black runaways and in which it urged such runaways not to trust even their most intimate friends on a subject "in which they are so deeply interested"); printed land offers for the formation of black communities; and ran notices of births, deaths, marriages and social events in the black community.

The paper foundered on the issue of colonization. Initially both Russwurm and Cornish were opposed to sending free blacks back to Africa and their editorials reflected this. Russwurm became sole editor in September, 1827, but he did not announce any change in his views until February 14, 1829.

Until December, 1828, all editorials on colonization were negative, although favorable views of the matter were published in the paper. In January, 1829, news items entitled "Expedition to Liberia" began to appear. On February 4, 1829, Russwurm announced he no longer was opposed, that he now was "a decided supporter of the American Colonization Society." However, he acknowledged that "a majority of our readers" were not so inclined and expanded on his views on the topic—in an obvious effort to change their minds—in three subsequent issues (February 21, 1829, p. 370; March 7, 1829, p. 386; and March 14, 1829, p. 394).

On March 28, 1829, Russwurm announced that he was no longer going to be editor of the paper, and that Rev. Cornish was assuming the editorship. This is the last issue on microfilm,[14] and, according to Dann,[15] the publication ceased with that issue. It resumed publication two months later with a new editor, Samuel Cornish, and a new name, *Rights of All*, on May 29, 1829. *Rights of All* probably did not last a year. Pride indicates that the last extant issue was published on October 9, 1829.[16]

V

On Samuel Cornish and David Walker. Several scholars have printed what the author considers to be erroneous statements about the involvement of Samuel Cornish and David Walker with *Freedom's Journal*. Bryan[17] indicates that the *Journal* opposed colonization only during the first six months of its publication and says that "Russwurm and Cornish disagreed over this issue, with the results that on September 27, 1827, Cornish resigned to return to his Presbyterian ministry, leaving Russwurm with full responsibility, and the Journal's position on colonization was reversed." Wolseley makes the same error.[18] He says:

> *The two men disagreed over the question of colonizing blacks, Cornish opposing and Russwurm favoring. As a result, six months after they had launched* Freedom's Journal *Cornish resigned, and Russwurm ran it alone.*

Russwurm didn't announce his change of views until February, 1829, considerably after the change in editorial leadership. The paper continued to publish anti-colonization material until February, 1829. On September 14, 1827, an article signed by Samuel Cornish appeared in which Rev. Cornish, the senior editor, announced that "our connection in the 'Journal' is this day dissolved, and the right and perogatives exclusively vested in the Junior Editor, J.B. Russwurm." Rev. Cornish praised Russwurm and gave "health and interest" as his reasons for resigning.

This announcement was immediately followed by the following "Notice":

> *As Mr. Cornish will be travelling through different parts of the country he has agreed to accept of a General Agency for the 'Journal,' and is hereby authorized to transact any business relating to it.*

This notice was repeated in the next issue, No. 28, September 21, 1827. In issue No. 29, September 28, 1827, the Rev. Samuel E. Cornish was listed as "General Agent" above the list of 23 "Authorized Agents." This listing remained throughout the life of the newspaper, which also frequently ran notices of weddings he performed and ads by him for the sale or purchase of land.

In addition, it does not appear that Cornish and Russwurm were in any argument over the merits of colonization at the time Cornish resigned from the editorship. In that issue (September 14, 1827) Russwurm did start printing articles supporting colonization (many by a white Philadelphian, John H. Kennedy, originally identified only by his initials) along with others in opposition. He did so, he said, "to see the subject fully discussed," even though he opposed the Society. Had Russwurm publicly changed his mind at that time, it probably would have been Russwurm who would have resigned—not Cornish. Thus, while Cornish did relinquish his position as senior editor, in my opinion it was due more to his belief that his activities better suited him for the business side of the paper. He apparently did a pretty fair job of lining up additional agents. Twenty-three were on board when he became the "General Agent" in September. The last issue (dated March 28, 1829) lists 37 agents.

David Walker, the paper's Boston agent, was author of an "Appeal" urging that slaves rise up and fight for their own freedom. There are several mentions of this early black hero in *Freedom's Journal* in addition to his weekly listing as an agent. The first issue gives information on a meeting "of the People of Colour of the City of Boston" held at his house which resulted in a resolution supporting the *Journal* and pledging "to use our utmost exertions to increase its patronage." On April 25, 1828 (Vol. 2, No. 5), Walker was mentioned as one of the speakers in a meeting in Boston that took place on March 16, 1828. The meeting was called to discuss "whether the *Freedom's Journal* had been conducted in a manner satisfactory to the subscribers and to the coloured community at large." On October 3, 1828 (Vol. 2, No. 27), he is mentioned as giving money to a fund "for the purchase of George M. Horton of North Carolina," an on-going project of the paper. On December 19, 1828 (Vol. 2, No. 90), the paper published an "Address, delivered before the General Colored Association at Boston by David Walker."

This address stressed the need for unity of colored people throughout the United States and urged the formation of a general body "to protect, and assist each other to the utmost of our power." It did not, however, call for a slave revolt and was not a synopsis of his "Appeal," which according to Wiltse,[19] was not published until September, 1829. In the earlier 1828 work, Walker praised whites who were working for the elimination of slavery but urged blacks to unite for their own salvation. Bryan says Russwurm printed David Walker's "Appeal" in 1828.[20] If he did, he didn't do it in *Freedom's Journal* since there is no record of such a printing. Dann[21] says the "Appeal" was published by Cornish in *Rights of All*. The author has been unable to obtain copies of that publication.

VI

The Readership of the Paper. Wolseley calls *Freedom's Journal* a "little paper" that "must have been aimed mainly at white readers, since the literacy rate of blacks in the early part of the 19th Century was low."[22] Murphy echoes this when she states that the chief audience of the *Journal* "was white, since only a small percentage of blacks could read."[23] The paper was little by today's standards but not by the standards of its own day as we have pointed out earlier in this article.

My rationale for doubting that the readership was primarily white takes a bit more explaining. First of all, free blacks, North and South but particularly in the North, were anxious to obtain an education and to learn to read and write. *Freedom's Journal* itself published a number of articles on the subject. In one (Vol. 2, No. 25, September 12, 1828), it announced the opening of a new school in New York City by the Manumission Society, which stated it was their desire "that every child of color should learn to read and write at least." The article also indicates that there were "2,500 coloured school-age children" at that time and deplored the fact that only 600 of them were attending any school (thus the need for the new school). Unfortunately, the earliest statistics on literacy are in the 1850 census. By that time there were 128,998 free blacks (10 or older) who were able to "write in some language" (the government's definition of "literacy"). This represented 49.8% of all free blacks counted in the census. 71,047 (or 67.1%) of the 105,891 free blacks in the North were classified as "literate." Even if the percentage had been considerably lower in 1827 than it was in 1850, there still should have been enough to support the paper's circulation of 800–1,000 subscribers.

Aptheker[24] says that 1,700 of the 2,300 persons who subscribed to Garrison's *Liberator* as late as 1834 were black and that the *Liberator* probably would not have survived without black patronage. Surely if 1,700 could subscribe to the *Liberator*, half that number could have purchased—and read—*Freedom's Journal*. The above, coupled with the fact that the paper held meetings to discuss "whether the *Freedom's Journal* had been conducted in a manner satisfactory to the subscribers and to the coloured community at large," indicates Wolseley and Murphy might be mistaken.

VII

Conclusion. Freedom's Journal gave blacks a voice of their own and an opportunity not only to answer the attacks printed in the white press but to read articles on black accomplishments, marriages, deaths, that the white press of its day ignored. Slavery is no longer here, but its vestiges are and today's reporters and publishers—black and white—could do well to study the *Journal*, adopt its objectives and emulate its content. Blacks still need to "plead our own causes," and will need to do so for sometime to come.

Endnotes

1. Bryan, Carter R., "Negro Journalism in America Before Emancipation," *Journalism Monographs*, No. 12 (September, 1969), 10.
2. Smith, Grace Ferguson, "Sojourner Truth—Listener to the Voice," *Negro History Bulletin*, 36:3 (March, 1973), 64. The 1817 law was complicated. A *Freedom's Journal* report indicated that all slaves born between July 4, 1799, and March 31, 1827, "shall become free, the males at 28, and females at 25 years old, and all slaves born after the 31st of March, 1817, shall be free at 21 years old, and also all slaves born before the 4th day of July, 1799, shall be free on the 4th day of July, 1827." See *Freedom's Journal*, April 27, 1827, p. 26.
3. U.S. Department of Commerce, *Negro Population in the United States 1790–1915* (N.Y.: Arno Press, 1968), p. 57.
4. Smith, *op. cit.*, p. 64.
5. *Ibid.*, p. 64. With the help of an attorney, Baumfree was able to get her son back from Alabama.
6. Dann, Martin E., ed., *The Black Press, 1827–1890* (N.Y.: Capricorn Books, 1972), p. 15.
7. U.S. Department of Commerce, *op. cit.*, pp. 56–57.
8. Dann, *op. cit.*, p. 15.
9. DuBois, W.E. Burghardt, *Black Reconstruction* (N.Y.: S.A. Russell Co., 1935), p. 8.
10. Chase, Henry and C.H. Sanborn, *The North and the South* (Westport, Conn: Negro Universities Press, 1970), pp. 106–107. (Originally published Boston: John P. Jewett & Co., 1857.)
11. Detweiler, Frederick G., *The Negro Press in the United States* (Chicago: Chicago University Press, 1922), p. 56.
12. Gross, Bella, "Freedom's Journal and the Rights of All," *Journal of Negro History*, 17:3 (July, 1932), 250. This is probably the most extensive and scholarly review of *Freedom's Journal* available.

13. Aptheker, Herbert, ed., *A Documentary History of the Negro People in the United States* (N.Y.: The Citadel Press, 1951), p. 86.
14. Bryan in a footnote gives March 21, 1828, as the date for the last issue on microfilm, and states that that is the date "when the name was changed to *Rights of All*." This is, obviously, a typographical error.
15. Dann, *op. cit.*, p. 13.
16. Pride, Armistead S., "A Registered History of Negro Newspapers in the United States: 1827–1950." Unpublished Ph.D. dissertation. Northwestern University 1950, p. 5. Also see Pride's article on *Rights of All* in this issue of Journalism History.
17. Bryan, *op. cit.*, p. 9.
18. Wolseley, Roland, *The Black Press, U.S.A.* (Ames, Iowa: Iowa State University Press, 1971), p. 18.
19. Wiltse, Charles M., ed., *David Walker's Appeal to the Coloured Citizens of the World, But in Particular, and Very Expressly, to those in the United States of America* (N.Y.: Hill and Wang, 1967), p. vii.
20. Bryan, *op. cit.*, p. 9.
21. Dann, *op. cit.*, p. 17.
22. Wolseley, *op. cit.*, p. 18.
23. Murphy, Sharon, *Other Voices: Black, Chicano and American Indian Press* (Dayton, Ohio: Pflaum/Standard, 1974), p. 79.
24. Aptheker, *op. cit.*, pp. 108–109.

II

Press Freedom in Eighteenth-Century America

The Constitutional Convention, meeting behind closed doors in Philadelphia in 1787, created the controversial document that was adopted during the following year as the Constitution of the United States. Ten states ratified the Constitution, but Virginians expressed grave reservations about the lack of a bill of rights to protect individual liberty against the power invested in the new government. James Madison, who argued that public opinion and state legislatures were greater threats than was the federal government, nevertheless drafted the Bill of Rights, which the states ratified in December 1791 with little recorded debate.

Because the Bill of Rights, which included the guarantee of press freedom, was not incorporated into the original governing document, and because it was adopted with little recorded debate, historians have long argued over the original intent of the framers of it and of the Constitution. Shaping those arguments have been debates over theory, law, and practice. Much of the discussion has focused on whether colonial printers actually had freedom in practice, whether they were free from laws of seditious libel, and whether the framers of the Constitution had a clearly developed theory of freedom of the press.

The impetus for much of the debate was generated by the 1960 publication of Leonard W. Levy's classic study of press freedom, *Legacy of Suppression: Freedom of Speech and Press in Early American History*. In the introduction to that volume, Levy countered the traditional view advanced by Zechariah Chafee, Jr., that the framers of the Constitution clearly intended to destroy the common law of seditious libel and to make further prosecutions for criticism of government forever impossible in the United States. Levy argued that "the generation which adopted the Constitution and the Bill of Rights did not believe in a broad scope for freedom of expression, particularly in the realm of politics." As he recounted later (1985) in the preface to his revised volume (retitled *Emergence of a Free Press*), his argument was not well received in the political and cultural climate of the 1960s. Initially underwritten by The Fund for the Republic, Levy's work on the press clause, begun in 1957, was rejected by fund director Robert M. Hutchins, who had headed the 1942–1947 Hutchins' Commission on the Freedom of the Press. Historians of the time worried that Levy's findings would give ammunition to those, such as Senator Joseph McCarthy, who sought to restrict freedom of expression.[1]

Scholars initially countered Levy's thesis by arguing that journalistic performance demonstrated more freedom than the law accounted for. Writing in a 1961 review of Levy's work, Merrill Jensen noted that scholars were well aware of the "vast amounts of some of the bitterest, most dishonest (and seditious) writing in American political history" published by the Pennsylvania papers between the time of the Declaration of Independence and the adoption of the Articles of Confederation. Many other writers focused on actual press practice in various colonies.[2]

The work examining journalistic practice was accompanied by studies of the origins of republican theory in England and the colonies and an exploration of the influence of "radical Whig" philosophy on colonial intellectuals.[3] Further, scholars began to examine the occupational ideology of colonial printers. In a slight departure from the debate over press freedom and political principle, Stephen Botein in 1975 argued that printers were motivated more from economic necessity than from political ideology.[4] In a subsequent article reprinted here, "Printers and the American Revolution," Botein carries his analysis into the revolutionary period. He argues that printers "were by training mechanics, without full legitimacy as men of independent intellect and creed." As businessmen, Botein claims that printers lived on the edge of poverty and faced the problem of pleasing all of the readers all of the time: the rhetoric of impartiality was merely a defense of a trade strategy designed to keep a printer in favor with all parties, and the attempt to be impartial actually prohibited full and free discussion because impartiality was defined as the "absence of polemics."

After the passage of the Stamp Act of 1765, printers found themselves in a much changed environment, Botein claims, and found that impartiality reduced their popularity. In this time of political turbulence, printers who gambled on the side of the patriots profited economically. Therefore, during the Revolution, Botein writes, printers abandoned the rhetoric of trade neutrality and reclaimed the ideology that they had espoused before they became tradesmen—that printers "were not 'mere mechanics,' but men of independent intellect and principle." Such printers derided the concept of printing for profit and argued instead the importance of principle. As they adapted to this period of political turbulence, Botein writes, they "seemed assured of recognition as major figures in the political life of the republic." As technology accelerated specialization during the 1830s in America, as it had in London a century earlier, printers once again became businessmen—capitalist publishers who hired other printers, or "hireling editors," who replaced the printer who claimed status as an intellectual.

In 1985, as noted earlier, Leonard Levy continued this discussion with a revision of his earlier work, the preface to which is included here. The new title, *Emergence of a Free Press*, which supplanted *Legacy of Suppression*, reflected some changes in Levy's thinking, but the work retained many of his previous assertions. Levy agreed with many of his critics that the American journalistic experience was indeed broader than he had originally maintained, but he continued to insist that the realm of theory was narrow and that a theory of free expression was not developed until after the passage of the Sedition Act of 1798. The Bill of Rights, Levy still maintains, was no more than a lucky political accident, and the first amendment reflected the principles of federalism (national rights superseding states' rights) rather than the principles of libertarianism.

Reclaiming the focus on political culture, disagreeing with Levy's assumption that free-press theory did not exist, and challenging Botein's assumption that printers hampered full discussion of issues leading toward independence, Jeffery A. Smith argues that colonial journalists followed a radical Whig tradition of distrust of government and belief in the principles of liberty in proclaiming "their independence of factions" and declaring "the importance of their serving as checks on government." Smith acknowledges that the editorial policies of printers were overturned during periods of strife but claims that the "occupational ideology itself was deeply entrenched." He argues that newspapers regularly challenged government long before the passage of the Stamp Act. Although Smith's elaboration of the influence of republican principles is outlined fully in his 1988 book, *Printers and Press Freedom: The Ideology of Early American Journalism*, the piece presented here focuses more specifically on the demonstrations, jury verdicts, legislative decisions, and popular support for freedom of the press that led to the Bill of Rights.[5]

The varying points of view presented here represent the complexity of the full nature of the colonial press experience. Republican theory, journalistic practice, legal rulings, and the public response to those rulings, as they were incorporated in the Constitution and the Bill of Rights, resulted in, as James Morton Smith so eloquently states, "a democratic form of republican rule that placed limitations on simple majoritarianism to preserve individual liberty while creating a more powerful general government and a more perfect Union."[6]

Endnotes

1. Zechariah Chafee, Jr., *Free Speech in the United States* (Cambridge: Harvard University Press, 1948), 21. See also Leonard W. Levy, *Legacy of Suppression: Freedom of Speech and Press in Early American History* (Cambridge, Mass: Belknap Press of Harvard University Press, 1960) and *Emergence of a Free Press* (New York: Oxford University Press, 1985).

2. See Merrill Jensen, review of *Legacy of Suppression, Harvard Law Review* 75 (1961): 457; Dwight L. Teeter, "A Legacy of Expression: Philadelphia Newspapers and Congress During the War for Independence, 1775–1783" (Ph.D. diss., University of Wisconsin, 1966); MaryAnn Patricia Yodelis, "Boston's Second Major Paper War: Economics, Politics, and the Theory and Practice of Political Expression in the Press, 1763–1775" (Ph.D. diss., University of Wisconsin, 1971); and Gerald J. Baldasty, "Toward an Understanding of the First Amendment: Boston Newspapers, 1782–1792," *Journalism History* 3:1 (Spring 1976): 25–30, 32.

3. For studies of political culture, see Bernard Bailyn, *The Ideological Origins of the American Revolution* (Cambridge: Belknap Press of Harvard University Press, 1967); and Gordon S. Wood, *The Creation of the American Republic, 1776–1787* (Chapel Hill: University of North Carolina Press for the Institute of Early American History and Culture, 1969).

4. Stephen Botein, "'Meer Mechanics' and an Open Press: The Business and Political Strategies of Colonial American Printers," *Perspectives in American History* 9 (1975): 140–150.

5. New York: Oxford University Press, 1988.

6. James Morton Smith, "The Great Rights of Mankind," *Colonial Williamsburg* (Autumn 1989): 28. See also Smith's *Freedom's Fetters: The Alien and Sedition Laws and American Civil Liberties* (Ithaca, N.Y.: Cornell University Press, 1956).

Preface to Emergence of a Free Press

by Leonard W. Levy

When this book was first published in 1960, I called it revisionist history. What was then a heresy became a new orthodoxy and, like any orthodoxy, generated dissent. I myself have long had a dissident view of the 1960 book. In a letter of 1976 to a friend, Max Lerner, I remarked that I had exaggerated the thesis and wanted to rewrite the book after an extended examination of newspaper sources. *Emergence of a Free Press,* a substantially expanded and revised version of *Legacy of Suppression,* is the result. This new edition, sixty percent larger than the original, is also revisionist history: I am revising myself. I no longer believe that history supports some of my original conclusions. Although I continue to endorse others, including the major conclusion, I prefer to mute the sledgehammer phrasing of some. Having done additional research, found new evidence, and listened to criticism, I reject the provocative thesis expressed in the original title and therefore have had to scrap that title for a neutral one.

Legacy of Supression was not a book I had planned to write. It was the result of chance and, I regret to say, spite. In 1957 I had a Guggenheim fellowship for the purpose of exploring the origins of the Fifth Amendment, specifically, the right against compulsory self-incrimination. But, at that time an opportunity presented itself to write for money—$1000 for about six weeks of work. That seemed an enormous amount because the Guggenheim, the sole source of my support, then paid $4000 for the year. Thanks to Henry Steele Commager's influence, The Fund for the Republic Inc., which later called itself The Center for Democratic Institutions, commissioned me to write a memorandum on the original meanings of the First Amendment's clauses.

Robert M. Hutchins, who headed The Fund, liked to hold formal conferences with the nation's leading intellectuals on urgent problems of the times, and he thought that a scholarly memorandum on the historical background of the First Amendment would be useful to have at hand in the event that a historical question arose in the course of some discussion. My own opinion was that Zechariah Chafee's *Free Speech in the United States* and Anson Phelps Stokes's *Church and State in the United States* provided all the data needed to resolve a question concerning the intentions of the Framers of the First Amendment. But, Hutchins preferred a more convenient packaging of the information based on a fresh look at the primary sources. Despite my strong liberal opinions on the First Amendment, I felt obligated to give an objective statement of the evidence and of the conclusions that they dictated. I wrote a memorandum of about seventy-five pages, two-thirds of which dealt with the clauses on religion and bore out what all liberals knew, namely, that the Framers intended a high wall of separation between church and state and guaranteed liberty of conscience even for non-Christians and non-believers; but the twenty-five pages or so on the free speech–free press clause flatly contradicted liberal assumptions and their champions such as

Chafee and Justices Oliver Wendell Holmes, Louis D. Brandeis, Hugo L. Black, and William O. Douglas. To my surprise, I discovered that the Framers had a constricted view of the scope of permissible political expression.

The Fund was enthusiastic about my work on the church-state and religious liberty clauses, but not the rest. I was summoned to New York for a discussion. Officials of The Fund wanted me to polish the work on the religion clauses, and they would publish it as a handsome pamphlet in their series called Basic Issues. But, Hutchins clearly disapproved of my work on the speech-press clause. He made it clear to me that the pamphlet would not include that section of the work.

Perhaps I was overly sensitive, but I felt that I was being subjected to censorship by one of the nation's foremost strongholds of civil liberties. My fellow liberals seemed to be suppressing scholarship that did not support their presuppositions. I was angry and decided to strike back by giving what I thought would be maximum publicity to the material that The Fund rejected. Deferring my research on the book that became *The Origins of the Fifth Amendment*, I decided to write an article of approximately fifty pages on the original meaning of the free speech–press clause. I planned to submit it to the *Harvard Law Review*.

I deepened my research on that clause and wrote the article, but before submitting it for publication I sent copies to Commager and to Mark Howe at Harvard Law School, a masterly legal historian. Commager, who was distressed by my findings, worried whether they provided scholarly ammunition for misuse by McCarthyites. Above all, however, he thought I should not rush into print; he argued that if I continued digging into the sources I very likely would find countervailing evidence that would support the Holmes-Chafee traditional liberal position.

Howe too believed that I should continue my research. He asked me questions about matters that I had not explored, about colonial English backgrounds that I had slighted, and about assumptions underlying some of the positions which I had taken. In effect he was asking me to expand the article.

So I went back to further research, and instead of producing a law review article I found myself writing a book, which turned out to be *Legacy of Suppression: Freedom of Speech and Press in Early American History*. In my acknowledgments I maliciously thanked The Fund for the Republic for having helped make the book possible, and it was not until 1972, in a book collecting various of my own essays, that I published for the first time the piece called "No Establishment of Religion: The Original Understanding," which constituted the rest of the original memorandum The Fund had liked. Thus I wrote *Legacy of Suppression* to spite Hutchins and The Fund and as a result of a chance opportunity to explore the subject.

The title I chose and the rather strong theme I developed in that book reflected both my shock at discovering the neglected evidence and my indignation at Hutchins and The Fund for attempting to suppress my work. As a result I overdid it. I had a novel position, which I overstated. I summarized my findings as follows in the 1960 preface.

> *This book presents a revisionist interpretation of the origins and original understanding of the First Amendment's clause on freedom of speech and press. I have been reluctantly forced to conclude that the generation which adopted the Constitution and the Bill of Rights did not believe in a broad scope for freedom of expression, particularly in the realm of politics.*
>
> *I find that libertarian theory from the time of Milton to the ratification of the First Amendment substantially accepted the right of the state to suppress seditious libel. I find also that the American experience with freedom of political expression was as slight as the theoretical inheritance was narrow. Indeed, the American legisla-*

tures, especially during the colonial period, were far more oppressive than the supposedly tyrannous common-law courts. The evidence drawn particularly from the period 1776 to 1791 indicates that the generation that framed the first state declarations of rights and the First Amendment was hardly as libertarian as we have traditionally assumed. They did not intend to give free rein to criticism of the government that might be deemed seditious libel, although the concept of seditious libel was—and still is—the principal basis of muzzling political dissent. There is even reason to believe that the Bill of Rights was more the chance product of political expediency on all sides than of principled commitment to personal liberties. A broad libertarian theory of freedom of speech and press did not emerge in the United States until the Jeffersonians, when a minority party, were forced to defend themselves against the Federalist Sedition Act of 1798. In power, however, the Jeffersonians were not much more tolerant of their political critics than the Federalists had been.

I was wrong in asserting that the American experience with freedom of political expression was as slight as the conceptual and legal understanding was narrow. Indeed, elsewhere in the 1960 preface I contradicted myself when more accurately stating that the common law did not in fact "actually prevent the widespread discussion of affairs of state by the common people." At several points in the book, but only in passing, I noted the discrepancy between theory and practice. Chapter One, for example, concluded with the observations that an "astonishing degree" of open political discussion existed, considering the legal restraints, and that "the law in the books and the law in life" must be distinguished. At best I was inconsistent. From a far more thorough reading of American newspapers of the eighteenth century I now know that the American experience with a free press was as broad as the theoretical inheritance was narrow.

My original interest lay with law and theory; I had paid little attention to press practices. I had searched the newspapers only for statements on the meaning of freedom of the press and had ignored the nearly epidemic degree of seditious libel that infected American newspapers after Independence. Press criticism of government policies and politicians, on both state and national levels, during the war and in the peaceful years of the 1780s and 1790s, raged as contemptuously and scorchingly as it had against Great Britain in the period between the Stamp Act and the battle of Lexington. Some states gave written constitutional protection to freedom of the press after Independence; others did not. Whether they did or did not, their presses operated as if the law of seditious libel did not exist. To one whose prime concern was law and theory, a legacy of suppression came into focus; to one who looks at newspaper judgments on public men and measures, the revolutionary controversy spurred an expanding legacy of liberty.

If the press freely aspersed on matters of public concern for a generation before 1798, the broad new libertarianism that emerged after the enactment of the Sedition Act formed a continuum linking prior experience with subsequent theory. If a legacy of suppression had existed at all, the realms of law and theory had perpetuated it, not the realm of practice. In effect the concern for freedom of political expression continually evolved, as the American reaction to the Sedition Act illustrated. In England, Fox's Libel Act of 1792, which merely allowed a jury to decide the criminality of a defendant's words, met with popular acclaim and enjoys the historical reputation of having been a libertarian reform. England did not, however, allow a defendant in a criminal libel case to plead truth as a defense until Lord Campbell's Act of 1843. By comparison the Sedition Act of 1798 should resonate as a truly libertarian achievement because it represented the final triumph of the principles of the Zenger case: it emulated Fox's Libel Act and preceded Lord Campbell's by forty-five years, and additionally, it required proof of malice. Its reformist character notwithstanding, the Sedition Act had a notorious reputation in its own time as well as during the subsequent course of American history, showing that Americans respected freedom of political expression far more than theoreticians and legalists had acknowledged before 1798.

I disagree with *Legacy of Suppression* in one other respect. In several places I gave the misleading impression that freedom of the press meant to the Framers merely the absence of prior restraints. Similarly, I sometimes declared that they shared Blackstone's view, as I still deliberately do. Whether referring to that oracle of the common law or to freedom of the press as freedom from prior restraints, I mean, first, that the criminal law held people responsible for abuse of that freedom. Second, I mean not to exhaust the meanings of freedom of the press by identifying it as, at the least, freedom from prior restraint. The Supreme Court was right when declaring in 1936, "It is impossible to concede that by the words 'freedom of the press' the framers of the first amendment intended to adopt merely the narrow view then reflected by the law of England that such freedom consisted only in immunity from previous censorship; for this abuse had then permanently disappeared from English practice."[1] The test for the criminal abuse of freedom of the press constituted the real problem, not the imposition of subsequent punishment for that abuse. In any case, freedom of the press merely began with its immunity from previous restraints.

Freedom of the press also meant that the press had achieved a special status as an unofficial fourth branch of government, "the Fourth Estate," whose function was to check the three official branches by exposing misdeeds and policies contrary to the public interest. Additionally, freedom of the press had come to mean that the system of popular government could not effectively operate unless the press discharged its obligations to the electorate by judging officeholders and candidates for office. The relationship between the press and the electoral process had become so close that popular government and political parties depended upon the existence of a free press. Some theorists even contended that a free press, by virtue of its watchdog function, also served as the matrix for the perpetuation of all other personal liberties protected by the Bill of Rights.

I am still convinced, however, that the revolutionary generation did not seek to wipe out the core idea of seditious libel, that the government may be criminally assaulted by mere words; that the legislatures were more suppressive than the courts; that the theory of freedom of political expression remained quite narrow until 1798, except for a few aberrant statements; that English libertarian theory was usually in the vanguard of the American; that the Bill of Rights in its immediate history was in large measure a lucky political accident; and that the First Amendment was as much an expression of federalism as of libertarianism. I also still contend that tarring and feathering a Tory editor because of his opinions showed a rather restricted meaning and scope of freedom of the press. Indeed, one may ask whether there was free speech during the revolutionary era if only the speech of freedom was free. And one may receive the same answers from people as different as Herbert Marcuse[2] and Richard Buel[3] that only truth deserves a right to be broadcast, or that those who oppose the truth don't deserve freedom of speech, or that if truth's enemies control the government, extralegal means including violence may justifiably be employed by

[1]*Grosjean v. American Press Co.*, 297 U.S. 233, 248 (1936).

[2]Marcuse, "Repressive Tolerance," in Robert Paul Wolff *et al.*, *A Critique of Pure Tolerance* (Boston, 1965), 81–117.

[3]Buel, "Freedom of the Press in Revolutionary America: The Evolution of Libertarianism, 1760–1820," in Bernard Bailyn and John B. Hench, eds., *The Press and the American Revolution* (Worcester, Mass., 1980), 59–98.

truth's out-of-power advocates. I regard anyone who takes that viewpoint as hostile to free political discussion.

My principal thesis remains unchanged. I still aim to demolish the proposition formerly accepted in both law and history that it was the intent of the American Revolution or the Framers of the First Amendment to abolish the common law of seditious libel. James Madison himself, the "father" of the Constitution and of the Bill of Rights, explicitly argued that proposition,[4] and it has been reiterated in our own time by our greatest judges, as well as by distinguished constitutional scholars.

Justice Holmes, for example, with Justice Brandeis concurring, declared, "I wholly disagree with the argument . . . that the First Amendment left the common law as to seditious libel in force. History seems to me against the notion."[5] Subsequently Justices Black and Douglas stated, "But the First Amendment repudiated seditious libel for this country."[6] More recently Justice William Brennan for a unanimous Court asserted that by the verdict of subsequent history the Sedition Act of 1798 was unconstitutional on First Amendment grounds.[7] The scholarship upon which the Holmesian view rests derives from the original and influential essay on freedom of the press in the United States by Henry Schofield, who noted that under the English common law many political publications in the colonies before the American Revolution were considered seditious and even treasonable. "One of the objects of the Revolution," Schofield concluded, in a statement quoted with approval by the Supreme Court, "was to get rid of the English common law on liberty of speech and of the press."[8] Justice Black for the Court added, "There are no contrary implications in any part of the history of the period in which the First Amendment was framed and adopted."[9] Professor Chafee, the author of the classic work on freedom of speech, alleged, "The First Amendment was written by men to whom Wilkes and Junius were household words, who intended to wipe out the common law of sedition, and make further prosecutions for criticism of the government, without any incitement to law-breaking, forever impossible in the United States of America."[10] Numerous others supported the same proposition.[11] They have, however, in

[4]"Madison's Report on the Virginia Resolutions" (1799–1800), in Jonathan Elliot, ed., *The Debates in the Several State Conventions on the Adoption of the Federal Constitution . . . and Other Illustrations of the Constitution* (Philadelphia, 1941, 2nd ed. rev.), 4:561–67.

[5]*Abrams v. United States*, 250 U.S. 616, 630 (1919).

[6]*Beauharnais v. Illinois*, 343 U.S. 250, 272 (1951). See also the opinion of Justice Jackson in the same case at 289.

[7]*New York Times Co. v. Sullivan*, 376 U.S. 254 (1964).

[8]Henry Schofield, *Essays on Constitutional Law and Equity* (Boston, 1921), 2:521-22, reprinting the essay, "Freedom of the Press in the United States," originally published in *Proceedings* of the American Sociological Society, II: 67–116 (1914).

[9]For the opinion of the Supreme Court, see *Bridges v. Cal.*, 314 U.S. 252, 264 (1941). Justice Black's remark followed a quotation from Madison's Report of 1799–1800 which argued the unconstitutionality of the Sedition Act. One might think that the statute constituted a "contrary implication."

[10]Zechariah Chafee, Jr., *Free Speech in the United States* (Cambridge, Mass., 1948), 21.

[11]See, for example, Theodore Schroeder, *Constitutional Free Speech* (New York, 1919), 98; Leon Whipple, *Our Ancient Liberties* (New York, 1927), 93–94; Giles J. Patterson, *Free Speech and a Free Press* (Boston, 1939), 101–2, 125–28; Osmond K. Fraenkel, *Our Civil Liberties* (New York, 1944), 64–65; Francis Biddle, *The Fear of Freedom* (New York, 1951), 55–56; James Morton Smith, *Freedom's Fetters: The Alien and Sedition Laws and American Civil Liberties* (Ithaca, 1956), 427–31; John Kelly, "Criminal Libel and Free Speech," *Kansas Law Review* 6 (1958): 310; and C. Herman Pritchett, *The American Constitution* (New York, 1959), 430. For a similar view by an older and very eminent authority, Judge Thomas M. Cooley, see his *Treatise on the Constitutional Limitations Which Rest Upon the Legislative Power of the States*, ed. V.H. Lane (Boston, 1903, 7th ed.), 613–15. Such views became infrequent after the publication of *Legacy of Suppression*. For explicit disagreements, see George Anastaplo, review of *Legacy of Suppression*, in *New York University Law Review* 39(1964):735–41, and in George Anastaplo, *The Constitutionalist: Notes on the First Amendment* (Dallas, 1971), consult index for entries under my name and under the heading

Mrs. Malaprop's phrase, "anticipated the past" by succumbing to an impulse to re-create it so that its image may be seen in a manner consistent with our rhetorical tradition of freedom, thereby yielding a message that will instruct the present. The evidence suggests that the proposition is suppositious and unprovable.[12]

Sedition; David A. Anderson, "The Origins of the Press Clause," *U.C.L.A. Law Review* 30(1983):456–540; and William T. Mayton, "Seditious Libel and the Lost Guarantee of a Freedom of Expression," *Columbia Law Review*, 84(1984): 91–142, which I read in typescript. After publication of *Legacy*, most authors who had occasion to pass judgment on the question whether the First Amendment superseded the common law of seditious libel chose to ignore the question as antiquarian or irrelevant. Thomas I. Emerson, in his magnificent book *The System of Freedom of Expression* (New York, 1970), noted the difference between Chafee and Levy and asserted that an "ambiguity" exists about the meaning of the First Amendment because of "historical dispute" on the question whether the Framers intended to abolish "the English law of seditious libel." Emerson, who is not strong on history, did not even get Fox's Libel Act correct (Emerson, p. 99). Edward G. Hudon, *Freedom of Speech and Press in America* (Washington, D.C., 1963), took higher ground; he listed *Legacy* in a bibliography to his preface and thereafter ignored it, thus avoiding altogether the need to cope with it. More characteristic were the responses of those who deprecated the values of history on learning that the Framers did not support their arguments. Alexander Meikeljohn, for example, in "The First Amendment Is an Absolute," *1961 The Supreme Court Review* (Chicago, 1961), 263–64, tolerantly accepted *Legacy* but declared that it did not deal with First Amendment problems "which now especially concern us." More crudely, Martin Shapiro, *Freedom of Speech: The Supreme Court and Judicial Review* (Englewood Cliffs, N.J., 1966), 93, dismissed *Legacy* as "irrelevant. As with all other constitutional provisions, it is not the founders' intentions but our intentions that count."

[12]A few older writers, whose articles were forerunners of *Legacy of Suppression*, agreed with this conclusion, but their differences with the Holmes-Chafee-Schofield thesis seem equally presuppositious because they offered no or slight evidence to support their view. See Edward S. Corwin, "Freedom of Speech and Press under the First Amendment: A Resumé," in *Selected Essays on Constitutional Law*, Douglas B. Maggs et al., ed. (Chicago, 1938), 2:1060–63; W.R. Vance, "Freedom of Speech and of the Press," *Minnesota Law Review* 2(1918):259; and Thomas F. Carroll, "Freedom of Speech and of the Press in the Federalist Period: The Sedition Act," *Michigan Law Review* 18(1920):636–37, 649–50.

We may even have to confront the possibility that the intentions of the Framers were not the most libertarian and their insights on the subject of freedom of expression not the most edifying. But this should be expected because the Framers were nurtured on the crabbed historicism of Coke and the narrow conservatism of Blackstone, as well as Zenger's case. The ways of thought of a lifetime are not easily broken. The Declaration of Independence severed the political connection with England but the American states continued the English common-law system except as explicitly rejected by statute. If the Revolution produced any radical libertarians on the meaning of freedom of speech and press, they were not present at the Constitutional Convention or the First Congress, which drafted the Bill of Rights. Scholars and judges have betrayed a penchant for what John P. Roche called "restrospective symmetry," by giving to present convictions a patriotic lineage and tradition[13]—in this case, the fatherhood of the "Framers." But this is no reason to be distressed. We may miss the comforting assurance of having the past's original intentions coincide with present preferences. Yet the case for civil liberties is so powerfully grounded in political philosophy's wisest principles, as well as the wisest policies drawn from experience, that it need not be anchored to the past. What passed for wisdom in the era of the Framers may very well have passed out-of-date with the growth of libertarianism in America.

My acknowledgment that the press of the new nation functioned as if the law of criminal libel hardly mattered is not entirely graceful. I refuse to *prove* the existence of unfettered press practices by giving illustrations of savage press criticisms of government policies or vicious character assassinations of American politicians. I am not intent on measuring the degree of free-

[13]Roche, "American Liberty: An Examination of the 'Tradition' of Freedom," in M. R. Konvitz and C. Rossiter, eds., *Aspects of Liberty* (Ithaca, 1958), 130.

dom that Americans enjoyed. I am interested, to use an analogy, in defining the concept of crime, and therefore do not find crime-rate statistics to be helpful. In our own time, obscenity is still illegal, though we live in a society saturated by it and witness few prosecutions; their paucity does not illumine the meaning of obscenity. So, too, the rarity of prosecutions for seditious libel, and the existence of an unfettered press do not illumine the scope and meaning of freedom of the press or the law on freedom of the press. The argument that freedom of political expression existed as a fact and therefore undermined the old thesis of a legacy of suppression is an odd one in some respects. That argument seems to be on all fours with the proposition that the existence of so many heretics during the reign of Bloody Mary proves there was a great degree of freedom of religion, despite the fires at Smithfield; or, that there was freedom of the press, a century later, because Lilburne, while in prison for his political opinion, was able to smuggle out a series of seditious tracts for publication. More to the point, perhaps, would be the experience of the Jeffersonian press during the Sedition Act period. The fact that the Philadelphia *Aurora* appeared regularly while William Duane, its editor, was under indictment for violation of the Act, strikes me as poor evidence that freedom of the press, as a matter of practice, was really secure at the time. Although the *Aurora* never ceased its scathing comments on the Administration, I believe that the prosecution of its editor for his opinions demonstrated a stunted concept of a free press; and I cannot accept the view that freedom of the press was safe despite the Sedition Act.

James Morton Smith lent his authority to the view that a wider degree of freedom existed than I originally indicated.[14] He was right. Professor Smith, in his own closely related study that I think is first-rate even if wrong at points, quotes approvingly Sir James Fitzjames Stephen's observation that the enforcement of the *law* of seditious libel in England "was wholly inconsistent with any serious public discussion of political affairs." Smith concludes: "As long as it was recognized as the law of the land, any political discussion existed by sufferance of the government."[15] I agree and maintain that the law of seditious libel, which was not superseded by either the Revolution or the First Amendment, made political discussion in this country dependent upon government sufferance. I find it difficult to believe that meaningful freedom of the press could exist in that condition. That so many courageous and irresponsible editors daily risked imprisonment amazes me.

I wrote *Legacy of Suppression* and this revision in the unshakable belief that the concept of seditious libel and freedom of the press are incompatible. So long as the press *may* be subjected to government control, whether or not that control is exercised, the press cannot be free—or is not as free as it should be. Freedom of the press cannot thrive as it should if closeted with a time bomb, the concept of seditious libel, ticking away in the law. The number or frequency of detonations does not matter. The Sedition Act of 1798, the Sedition Act of 1918, and the Smith Act of 1940, together with the prosecutions under them, are unendurable. One case is too many. Harry Kalven best made the point when he wrote:

> *The concept of seditious libel strikes at the very heart of democracy. Political freedom ends when government can use its powers and its courts to silence its critics. My point is not the tepid one that there should be leeway for criticism of the government. It is rather that defamation of the government is an impossible notion for a democracy. In brief, I suggest, that the presence or ab-*

[14]James Morton Smith, review of *Legacy of Suppression*, in *William and Mary Quarterly* 20(1963):156–59.

[15]James Morton Smith, *Freedom's Fetters: The Alien and Sedition Laws and American Civil Liberties* (Ithaca, 1956), 425.

sence in the law of the concept of seditious libel defines the society. A society may or may not treat obscenity or contempt by publication as legal offenses without altering its basic nature. If, however, it makes seditious libel an offense, it is not a free society no matter what its other characteristics.[16]

I believe that and am therefore puzzled by the paradox in the following pages of nearly unfettered press practices in a system characterized by legal fetters and the absence of a theory of political expression that justified those press practices.

The publication of *Legacy of Suppression* appalled some liberals. I myself was a little apologetic about it for fear, as Henry Commager predicted, that the wicked forces of reaction might capitalize on the discovery that the Framers gave their paternal blessing to suppressive impulses. "No citizen," I sonorously intoned, "and certainly no jurist worthy of his position, would or should conclude his judgment on either a constitutional question or a matter of public policy by an antiquarian examination of the original meaning of the freedom of speech-and-press clause."[17] Justice Hugo L. Black, the passionate and self-proclaimed absolutist on free speech and press issues, who was innocent of history when he did not distort it or invent it, assigned one of his law clerks to check out every fact and investigate every source in his search for errors in the book. Years later, in 1976, the clerk told me he had spent an entire summer on the task but found no mistakes. Justice Black, who heavily annotated his copy of the book, told me that he refused to read my next book, because of its subtitle: "The Darker Side." A close friend of Black, Professor Edmond Cahn of New York University Law School, tried to persuade him that *Legacy of Suppression* had some merit. Cahn had reviewed the book very favorably[18] and recommended it to Black. In the first draft of his reply to Cahn, Black wrote of *Legacy*, "In brief my judgment is that it is probably one of the most devastating blows that has been delivered against civil liberty in America for a long time." I am not sure whether Black ranked me above or below Joe McCarthy as an enemy of civil liberty. Probably below because he regretted that Levy, "a great libertarian" according to Cahn, had "seen fit to take this completely reactionary view of the First Amendment's purposes." Cahn sought to assure Black that First Amendment libertarianism would survive my book, but the justice moodily replied, "I hope you are right but I am afraid you are not in believing that Dean Levy's book has done no damage to the First Amendment."

Justice Black believed that the book would provide an armory of support for people who wanted the Amendment to mean less than he and Professor Cahn thought that it meant. As proof, Black wondered if Cahn had read the favorable review of the book in the *New Republic* by Alexander Bickel of Yale Law School, who was closely associated with Frankfurter, Black's antagonist on the Court.[19] Black's view of the book showed how selectively and very subjectively one can read. If Black had not read with his absolutist convictions dominating his understanding, he would have seen why Cahn and Commager could appreciate the book, though not necessarily agreeing with all of it. Black would have seen how it was possible for Willmore Kendall and Walter Berns to assault the book from the right.[20] Incidentally, though the

[16] "The New York Times Case: A Note on 'The Central Meaning of the First Amendment,'" *1964 The Supreme Court Review*, ed. Philip Kurland (Chicago, 1964), 205.

[17] Commager wrote a handsome review of the book, *New York Times Book Review*, Nov. 13, 1960.

[18] *New York Herald Tribune Book Section*, Oct. 16, 1960.

[19] *New Republic*, July 18, 1960.

[20] Kendall's weird review of *Legacy*, in his *Willmore Kendall: Contra Mundum*, Nellie D. Kendall, ed., 290–92, appeared originally in the *Stamford Law Review* for May 1964 and purported to be a review of my *Jefferson and Civil Liberties*. Citations to Berns's three essays on *Legacy* may be

book has been cited in several Supreme Court opinions, not even conservative judges have used it to support the results that Black so strongly feared.

On the contrary, I find delicious irony in the fact that the Supreme Court, speaking through Justice William Brennan, relied on *Legacy* to reach one of its foremost libertarian decisions in a 1964 free-press case. In a turgid yet critical passage, Brennan declared, "If neither factual error nor defamatory content suffices to remove the constitutional shield from criticism of official conduct, the combination of the two elements is no less adequate. This is the lesson to be drawn from the great controversy over the Sedition Act of 1798, 1 Stat. 586, which first crystallized a national awareness of the central meaning of the First Amendment. See Levy *Legacy of Suppression* (1960) at 258 *et seq.*"[21] Brennan said nothing about the Revolution or the First Amendment overturning the common law of seditious libel. His point, rather, was that the First Amendment protected mistaken opinions and even defamation of public officials, and that the proof consisted in the later emergence of a broad new libertarianism which repudiated the Sedition Act. The original intentions of the Framers and the original meaning of the First Amendment meant nothing to the Court; what counted in giving the Amendment content was subsequent opinion: "The central meaning" of the Amendment undermined the Sedition Act because "the attack upon its validity has carried the day in the court of history."[22] Another irony is that the Sedition Act, which played the villainous role here, was far more libertarian than the *Croswell* test,[23] which really carried the day in the court of history until *New York Times v. Sullivan*.

found below, in the bibliography; see index under Berns for discussion.

[21] *N.Y. Times Co. v. Sullivan*, 376 U.S. 254 at 273.

[22] *Ibid.*, 276. Justices Goldberg and Douglas, concurring, agreed, *ibid.*, 298 n.1.

[23] On the *Croswell* test, see below, pp. 338–39.

Printers and the American Revolution

Stephen Botein

I. Introduction

Among the miscellaneous material that Isaiah Thomas appended to his exhaustive *History of Printing in America* was a list of more than 350 American newspapers published in 1810. All but approximately 50 were classified according to political affiliation, Federalist or Republican.[1]

Reflected in this information was a powerful new trend in American journalism. As the Reverend Samuel Miller had observed at the start of the century, the newspapers of republican America were "immense moral and political engines" that advanced opinions as well as reported occurrences.[2] The press had become capable at once of greater good and more serious mischief, depending on the perspective of readers, than in the colonial period. To a nostalgic conservative like James Fenimore Cooper, writing from the vantage point of midcentury, this seemed to be a development as inevitable as it was ruinous. Not the least of the evils to undermine the island paradise that Cooper imagined in *The Crater* was the press. "Fortunately," in the happy early days of Cooper's fictional community, "there was yet no newspaper, a species of luxury which, like the gallows, comes in only as a society advances to the corrupt condition; or which, if it happens to precede it a little, is very soon to conduct it there." Eventually, after a newspaper had been introduced, this utopian experiment collapsed.[3]

It was almost as if Cooper meant to confirm or vindicate the fearful predictions of British authorities in the very infancy of American society. In a declaration of 1671 that has won him much historical notoriety, Gov. William Berkeley of Virginia had been moved to "thank God" that his colony lacked a press—which he associated with "disobedience," "heresy," "sects," and "libels against the best government."[4] For almost a century, Berkeley's alarm had appeared unjustified. In Virginia and the other mainland British colonies of the eighteenth century, it proved difficult to prevent the establishment of printing houses, many of which published newspapers; but these were normally innocent of controversial matter. By the time Isaiah Thomas wrote his *History*, however, virulent political partisanship had become characteristic of American journalism.

Drawing on the personal experience of its author, that pioneering chronicle focused knowingly on the crucial period and process of transformation. Although the political press of the early nineteenth century was a product of contemporary party conflicts, the origins of contro-

[1]Isaiah Thomas, *The History of Printing in America*, 2 vols. (Worcester, Mass., 1810), 2: 517–52; citations throughout are to the original version of this work, but see also Marcus A. McCorison's 1-volume annotated Imprint Society Edition (Barre, Mass., 1970).

[2]Quoted in Thomas, *History of Printing*, 2: 403. Earlier, according to Miller, newspapers had been mostly restricted to "mere statement of *facts*."

[3]James Fenimore Cooper, *The Crater*, ed. Thomas Philbrick (Cambridge, Mass., 1962), pp. 374–75, 432–38.

[4]Thomas, *History of Printing*, 2: 139.

versial journalism in America could be traced back to the decade of Revolutionary turmoil that preceded Independence. In the changing business and political strategies of printers, who ran the eighteenth-century press, were registered the circumstances that accounted for the new partisan practices. Revealingly, as an aside in his bitter narrative of the "American Rebellion," the loyalist Peter Oliver had called the art of printing "black," adding that Benjamin Franklin—for one—had made it "much blacker."[5] Many others were of the opinion, at the time, that the behavior of the trade as a whole had aggravated divisiveness and violence, thus hastening the movement of events toward war. Printers, reported one Pennsylvanian at the outset of the crisis, "almost without exception, stuffed their papers weekly . . . with the *most inflammatory pieces* they could procure, and *excluded every thing that tended to cool the minds of the people.*"[6] However exaggerated, this pointed quite accurately to those who were responsible for the unprecedented level of partisan controversy in American journalism during the Revolutionary years.

Throughout, too, Benjamin Franklin played a central part, as Oliver understood. It was a part more characteristically ambiguous, however, than angry loyalist feelings would allow. Franklin's career and reputation as a printer were illustrative of traditional practices in the colonial trade as well as the new patterns that emerged in the Revolution. By examining not only printers as a group but the curiously complicated role of Franklin as their most prominent "brother type," it is possible to appreciate some of the larger forces reshaping the public forum of a provincial society convulsed by political crisis. It is possible, furthermore, to understand how that crisis ultimately reshaped the self-imagery, or "occupational ideology,"[7] of the printing trade. For it was the figure of Franklin, already legendary, that loomed most impressively in the rhetorical efforts of American printers after Independence to affirm and honor the contribution of the press to the Revolutionary movement. Appropriately or not, he became the symbol of a new identity that they formulated for themselves in the new republic. This identity they would continue to promote even in the face of contrary realities, as they struggled with deteriorating business conditions in the early decades of the next century.

2. Colonial Habits

It was Franklin's custom, in later years, to speak fondly of the craft that he had practiced as a young man but abandoned in middle age. For one of his grandsons, he predicted, printing might be "something to depend on," an independent source of income that happened to have been "the original Occupation of his Grandfather." Meanwhile, at Passy, "Benjamin Franklin, Printer," would amuse himself with a private press, in emulation of aristocracy.[8]

If the inverted snobbery of this ritual pleased Franklin, it was pardonable. That the most illustrious American of the eighteenth century was also a printer, at least by training, seemed incongruous by European norms. Franklin's re-

[5] *Peter Oliver's Origin & Progress of the American Rebellion*, ed. Douglass Adair and John A. Schutz (San Marino, Calif., 1963), p. 79.

[6] John Hughes to Stamp Office Commissioners, Oct. 12, 1765, as reprinted in *Pennsylvania Journal*, Sept. 4, 1766; appointed to the office of stamp distributor in Philadelphia, Hughes was unable to put the new Stamp Act into practice.

[7] By "occupational ideology" is meant the general system of values and beliefs espoused by printers, arising out of but not limited to trade activities. See Vernon K. Dibble, "Occupations and Ideologies," *American Journal of Sociology* 68 (1962–63): 229–41.

[8] Franklin to Richard Bache, Nov. 11, 1784, *The Writings of Benjamin Franklin*, ed. Albert Henry Smyth, 10 vols. (New York, 1907), 9: 278–79; Franklin to Madame Brillon, Apr. 19, 1788, ibid., pp. 643–45; John Clyde Oswald, *Benjamin Franklin, Printer* (Garden City, N.Y., 1917), chap. 15.

markable career can only be appreciated in the distinctive context of American social and economic realities, particularly as found in the conditions of the colonial printing trade. Despite limitations on the status that printers could claim in the social hierarchy, the circumstances of the American trade encouraged upward mobility. Probably Franklin could never have achieved his most spectacular successes in the face of the harsh business realities that increasingly threatened the self-esteem of the printing fraternity in London.[9]

By the middle of the eighteenth century, it was no longer common for printers in the capital city of the empire to function as the major entrepreneurs of the publishing business; for the most part, others had usurped that lucrative and influential role. Initially, printers had controlled the principal stages of production in the English book world. Because they alone could actually put a manuscript into print, they were able to demand the exclusive right to profit by its sale. But as the book business grew and required more capital, in response to an expanding middle-class market for print, its separate stages of manufacture and distribution became more specialized. The bookseller, who dealt in the craftsman's product, emerged as the person who laid out capital in a publishing enterprise and then gathered in the benefits.[10] As early as 1663, a dissident group of printers launched an unsuccessful rebellion against the booksellers who dominated the Stationers' Company in London. Protesting that they were now "yok'd to the Booksellers," who once were "but as an Appendix to the Printers," the insurgents charged that their rivals had grown "bulkie and numerous" from the "several other Trades" that they had absorbed and were "much enriched by Printers impoverishment."[11]

A few printers in eighteenth-century London—among them William Strahan, Franklin's friend and correspondent—ran large businesses that generated sufficient profit to permit investment in copyright, with which they might hope to "emancipate themselves from the Slavery in which the Booksellers held them."[12] But they were exceptional figures. To most of their brethren in the trade, the times seemed hard. In 1750 an eccentric master printer named Jacob Ilive—whom Franklin had known, and remembered for his bizarre religious speculations—addressed a general meeting of the trade in London. "Where is the Man," he declaimed, "be he *Divine, Astronomer, Mathematician, Lawyer, Physician,* or what else who is not beholden to Us?" What a "great Pity," he lamented, that printers "do not meet with an *adequate Encouragement,* suitable to the Labour and Pains they take in the Exercise of it; but this verifies the old Proverb, '*That true Merit seldom or never meets with its Reward.*'" It is certain "from the present Situation of Affairs," he concluded, "that in *Our Case,* it never CAN, nor ever WILL."[13]

The difficulty was not simply a matter of economics. Many of the first European printers had been accomplished scholars, and this distant heritage seems to have shaped the ambitions of eighteenth-century London printers like Ilive. As their economic importance dimin-

[9]For more elaborate documentation of what follows, in part 2, see Stephen Botein, "'Meer Mechanics' and an Open Press: The Business and Political Strategies of Colonial American Printers," *Perspectives in American History* 9 (1975): 130–211.

[10]Marjorie Plant, *The English Book Trade: An Economic History of the Making and Sale of Books*, 2d ed. (London, 1965), pp. 59–62, and see generally A. S. Collins, *Authorship in the Days of Johnson* (London, 1927).

[11]*A Brief Discourse Concerning Printing and Printers* (London, 1663), pp. 4–5; Cyprian Blagden, *The Stationers' Company: A History, 1403–1959* (Cambridge, Mass., 1960), pp. 147–48.

[12]Strahan to David Hall, July 15, 1771, Miscellaneous Collections, Historical Society of Pennsylvania, Philadelphia, and see generally J. A. Cochrane, *Dr. Johnson's Printer: The Life of William Strahan* (Cambridge, Mass., 1964).

[13]*The Papers of Benjamin Franklin*, ed. Leonard W. Labaree et al. (New Haven, 1959–), 17: 315–16n. (hereafter cited as *Franklin Papers*); *The Speech of Mr Jacob Ilive to His Brethren the Master-Printers* (London, 1750), pp. 4, 6–7.

ished, so did the credibility of their original reputation as men of independent intellect and learning. The dissident printers of 1663, lamenting their subservience to booksellers, had given early voice to what would later be a common anxiety among London's printers—that they would be considered mere manual laborers. In England, the dissidents said, printers "have so light an esteem" that they fail to "finde like respect or care with the meanest of Occupations." Specifically, they complained of an argument used against them by booksellers in the internal struggles of the Stationers' Company. The printers were "the Mechanick part of the Company," it ran, "and so unfit to rule." By way of contrast, reported the insurgents, printers in France *"are above Mechanicks, and live in the suburbs of Learning."*[14] At stake were traditions that had sustained the pride and prestige of the English trade. Despite isolated literary achievements by members of the fraternity eager to establish credentials that would distinguish them from the ordinary run of skilled workers, printers as a group failed to make these traditions plausible in eighteenth-century London.[15]

Pre-Revolutionary American printers had some reason to hope that they might rank higher in general public esteem, despite prevailing social conventions to the contrary. Theirs was a delicately ambiguous role, however, the strengths and weaknesses of which were determined to a great extent by the structure of business life in an underdeveloped colonial economy.

Compared with the larger printing offices of London, even the most successful firms in the American colonies were modest enterprises. The decisive difference between American printers and those at the top of the London trade was that the former seldom had occasion or incentive to print books of substantial size, because demand for such items in the colonies was unsteady and oriented toward English products.[16] As a result, colonial printers could not expect to prosper from their craft alone, and poverty was often more than a remote contingency.

In order to compensate for limited printing business, however, it was the normal policy of a colonial printer to expand the scope of his work to include enterprises that were no longer or never had been associated with the craft in London. Like printers in provincial England, perhaps their closest counterparts, printers in the colonies participated in a relatively unspecialized trade that reflected the conditions of an inadequate market.[17] Although they lacked the volume of printing business engrossed by major figures in the London trade, they were in practice far from simple mechanics. The very slenderness of the living that they might expect to earn from their skill led them to diversify and thus play more varied roles in their communities than was customary for their brethren in London.

Colonial printers usually sold whatever they could get their hands on. It was not extraordinary to find a general store appended to a printing house; available there, along with the usual selection of dry goods and other imports, might be a wide assortment of the best books that the mother country had to offer. Not only was the colonial printer often a bookseller as well, unlike a printer in London, but quite possibly he also owned and edited a newspaper, which was a convenient place for him to advertise his vari-

[14] Plant, *English Book Trade*, p. 32; *Brief Discourse*, pp. 18, 15, 23.

[15] Samuel Richardson, author of *Pamela*, was the most celebrated literary printer in the mother country; see William M. Sale, Jr., *Samuel Richardson: Master Printer* (Ithaca, N.Y., 1950). A less ambitious figure was Samuel Palmer, an employer of Franklin and author of *The General History of Printing* (London, 1732).

[16] "All publications of consequence, in point of size and expence," wrote an English observer as late as 1789, "are executed in Europe." *Bibliotheca Americana* (London, 1789), p. 14.

[17] On provincial English printers, see Geoffrey Alan Cranfield, *The Development of the Provincial Newspaper, 1700–1760* (Oxford, 1962); Roy M. Wiles, *Freshest Advices: Early Provincial Newspapers in England* (Columbus, Ohio, 1965).

ous wares and insert himself into the intimate daily dealings of his town. Otherwise, too, printers in America were habitually at the center of things. Many staffed the colonial post office; some were clerks in the governments for which they printed laws and currency. By the sum of such activity, a colonial printer might well become a prominent man, unavoidably involved in a broad range of local affairs.[18]

Yet if prominent, he was also vulnerable, enjoying no more status—based conventionally on his occupation—than a printer in the mother country. However lofty his aspirations or diversified his business, it was inescapable that a colonial printer had been brought up to work with his hands. Isaiah Thomas neatly summed up the problem in a capsule memoir of Franklin's nephew, Benjamin Mecom. "He was handsomely dressed," recalled Thomas, "wore a powdered bob wig, ruffles and gloves; gentlemanlike appendages which the printers of that day did not assume—and, thus apparelled, would often assist, for an hour, at the press."[19] In the colonies, as in both London and the provinces, printers had to face the hard, discouraging fact that in the eyes of many neighbors, especially those who claimed to be "gentlemen," they were by training mechanics, without full legitimacy as men of independent intellect and creed.

The discrepancy here between social convention and occupational reality was ironical but easily ignored. One reason Franklin had chosen to be a printer, rather than a soapmaker like his father, was to satisfy his "Bookish Inclination." And certainly his own experience confirmed the advice he gave William Strahan in 1754, as Strahan's oldest son was learning the business in London. "If, with the Trade," Franklin wrote, "you give him a good deal of Reading and Knowledge of Books, and teach him to express himself well on all Occasions in Writing, it may be of very great Advantage to him as a Printer."[20] Although Franklin cited "some Instances" in England to prove his point, it was more frequently the colonial printer, so often a newspaper editor too, who needed and acquired literary facility. More plausibly than their brethren in London, whose work had felt the impact of specialization, printers in America might still take pride in the intellectual dimensions of their craft. Nevertheless, conventional social prejudices tended to persist. A colonial printer was not commonly expected to possess a mind of his own, and this expectation was likely to undercut whatever efforts he made to influence his neighbors.[21]

Even Franklin, perhaps the finest prose writer in the colonies, could not hope to transcend effortlessly the prevailing public image of his occupation. In 1740, when a lawyer in Philadelphia proposed to edit *The American Magazine* for Franklin's chief competitor in the printing trade, Franklin responded to the challenge by claiming that the scheme was originally his; the scornful reply was that Franklin's involvement in the periodical had never been projected "in any other capacity than that of a *meer* Printer."[22] Before the decade was over, Franklin had decided to disengage from work that ultimately impeded realization of the very ambitions it stimulated. A managing partner "took off my Hands all Care of the Printing-Office," he wrote in his *Autobiography*. Thus re-

[18]The best general account of the American trade is still Lawrence C. Wroth, *The Colonial Printer*, 2d ed. (Portland, Me., 1938); on diversity of enterprise, see esp. chap. 9.

[19]Thomas, *History of Printing*, I: 351.

[20]*The Autobiography of Benjamin Franklin*, ed. Leonard W. Labaree et al. (New Haven, 1964), p. 58; Franklin to Strahan, Nov. 4, 1754, *Franklin Papers*, 5: 439–40.

[21]Thus, in 1753, when Hugh Gaine attempted to defend himself against opponents of his *New-York Mercury*, he felt compelled to apologize for his audacity. It was a departure, he conceded, "to appear in print in any other Manner, than what merely pertains to the Station of Life in which I am placed." *New-York Mercury*, Sept. 3, 1753.

[22]*American Weekly Mercury*, Nov. 20, 1740. The literary dimension of Franklin's printing career is discussed in James A. Sappenfield, *A Sweet Instruction: Franklin's Journalism as a Literary Apprenticeship* (Carbondale, Ill., 1973).

leased, "I had secur'd Leisure during the rest of my Life, for Philosophical Studies and Amusements."[23] Only after ceasing to practice his craft could Franklin become a scientist and statesman.

Thus released, too, Franklin was no longer as vulnerable as he had been to the pressures of powerful men and competing interests in his community. A further weakness in the position of the colonial printer, working as he did in an undeveloped local market where he needed all the business he could get, was that he had to take pains to please all customers at all times. As often in the English provinces, but not in London, a printer in America might face no competition but still have few clients, because local demand for his product was apt to be slight. Usually unable to rely for a living on the favor of any one group among his neighbors, including those who wielded political power, a colonial printer by custom labored to serve diverse interests in his community. Unlike London, where large profits were sometimes to be had by making partisan commitments to one well-financed faction or another, colonial America was a place for printers to be studiously impartial.[24]

Upon occasion they explained and justified this trade strategy in elevated terms, professing devotion to "liberty of the press," as they chose to understand that phrase.[25] A press was "free," in this formulation, only if it was "open to all parties." A printer, in other words, should offer everyone the "liberty" of his press, without favoring one set of opinions over the rest. Whatever the social utility may have been of equalizing access to every colonial press, printers were attracted to the principle because it suited their business interests to serve all customers. Often they frankly admitted as much, in language that ignored the traditional learned pretentions of the English trade; at times, indeed, they sought to take rhetorical advantage of their conventional social standing as mechanics. "Governour, it is my imploy, my trade and calling," Pennsylvania's first printer had argued in 1689, finding himself in trouble for printing an unauthorized edition of the colony's charter, "and that by wch I get my living, to print; and if I may not print such things as come to my hand, which are innocent, I cannot live." Printing, he insisted, was "a manufacture of the nation," not an instrument of faith or ideology.[26]

By far the best known and most sustained colonial argument for an impartial press was Franklin's "Apology for Printers," first published in a 1731 issue of the *Pennsylvania Gazette*, after the wording of an advertising handbill produced in his shop had given offense to the local clergy. "Printers are educated in the Belief," Franklin insisted, "that when Men differ in Opinion, both Sides ought equally to have the Advantage of being heard by the Publick." Here was a principle consistent with advanced eighteenth-century doctrines of the public good, defined in terms of free competition by individuals or interests, but Franklin was quick to ground such considerations in business pragmatism. Printers "chearfully serve all contending Writers that pay them well" he explained, "without regarding on which Side they are of

[23]*Autobiography of Franklin*, pp. 195–96.

[24]See Cranfield, *Development of the Provincial Newspaper*, p. 118; Wiles, *Freshest Advices*, pp. 33–34, 292. The London pattern is illustrated in Sale, *Samuel Richardson*, pp. 54–59, and treated more generally in Laurence Hanson, *Government and the Press, 1695–1763* (London, 1936).

[25]The literature on liberty of expression in the colonies is vast but mainly tangential to the point here, since most of what has been written does not take into account the perspectives of printers. A useful overview of some general issues raised by the secondary literature may be found in Leonard W. Levy's preface to the paperback edition of his *Legacy of Suppression*, published as *Freedom of Speech and Press in Early American History: Legacy of Suppression* (New York, 1963). For a view that differs from what follows, see Lawrence H. Leder, *Liberty and Authority in Early American Political Ideology, 1689–1763* (Chicago, 1968), chap. 1.

[26]John William Wallace, *An Address Delivered at the Celebration . . . of the Two Hundredth Birth Day of Mr. William Bradford* (Albany, N.Y., 1863), pp. 49–52.

the Question in Dispute."[27] This was precisely the modest, self-denying role—so exclusively "mechanical"—that some members of the trade in London found disagreeable. Although literary craft traditions seemingly accorded more with reality in the colonies than in the mother country, Franklin's "Apology" offered on behalf of printers a formulation of principles usefully congruent with the trade strategies required by an underdeveloped economy. One man's right to be heard might be another man's employment.

The chief difficulty, as Franklin knew well, was to persuade one's neighbors to recognize the legitimacy of this strategy. It might be acceptable enough in normal circumstances, but in times of bitter controversy—when powerful men in the community turned to print to gain advantage in their quarrels with one another—its usefulness became less certain. Because "the Business of Printing has chiefly to do with Mens Opinions," Franklin observed, printers had to live with "the peculiar Unhappiness" of "being scarce able to do anything in their way of getting a Living, which shall not probably give Offence to some and perhaps to many."[28] Possibly because disharmony in the public forum was at odds with traditional norms of political behavior, many colonists still held a printer responsible for the sentiments he set in type and seem to have been unprepared to tolerate him if, caught in the middle of intense conflict, he wished to publish both sides.

When attitudes polarized, a printer sometimes had to work for a single faction; otherwise he might antagonize everyone. That this solution might be at least briefly lucrative, as well as unavoidable, is evident from the experience of such printers as John Peter Zenger and Franklin's brother James. Publications like the *New-York Weekly Journal* and the *New-England Courant* reflected temporary calculations by their printers that more was to be gained and little could be lost in periods of political turmoil if they abandoned neutrality and served those who insisted on and were willing to pay for partisanship. In quieter times Zenger or James Franklin might hope to maintain the "liberty" of their presses to different opinions, but this was a policy that did not always promise to be advantageous for a printer, especially if he were less than fully established in the trade. To pursue it rigorously could subject him to severe and contrary pressures when the political scene became agitated.[29]

To avoid trouble, the potential for which was greatest in the conduct of a newspaper, probably it was best in the long run to abstain from publishing polemics altogether, or as much as possible. Frequently, therefore, printers would qualify their dedication to the principle of an "open press" not by expressing veiled partiality to any one side but by trying to exclude the more censorious effusions of all parties. The result was not receptivity but even-handed aversion to diverse and forceful opinions. Although in his "Apology" Franklin wished to persuade people to tolerate the publication of polemical matter without blaming its printer, he also affirmed that printers did "continually discourage the Printing of great Numbers of bad Things,

[27]*Pennsylvania Gazette*, June 10, 1731. Whether or how a newspaper contributor was expected to pay is unclear, but the possibility was certainly contemplated in the well-known "Stage Coach" metaphor to which Franklin referred in his autobiography. (Anyone willing to pay had "a Right to a Place." *Autobiography of Franklin*, p. 175) On the other hand, there is no evidence to suggest that in practice printers of colonial newspapers routinely received payments from contributors or that they gave weight to the prospect of such payments in their business calculations. (Accusations that they did were rarely made before the Revolutionary period.) By accepting or rejecting controversial articles, they figured that they might gain or lose subscribers or—and this was doubtless more important—other kinds of printing business.

[28]*Pennsylvania Gazette*, June 10, 1731.

[29]See generally Livingston Rutherford, *John Peter Zenger, His Press, His Trial, and a Bibliography of Zenger Imprints* (New York, 1904); Harold Lester Dean, "The *New-England Courant*, 1721–1726: A Chapter in the History of American Culture" (Ph.D. diss., Brown University, 1943).

and stifle them in the Birth." Returning to the subject in his *Autobiography*, he was even more emphatic. "In the Conduct of my Newspaper," he recalled, "I carefully excluded all Libelling and Personal Abuse."[30]

Pre-Revolutionary trade habits of neutrality, it seems, did not always promote that disputatious "liberty of the press" advocated by such libertarian authors as Trenchard and Gordon. Instead, sometimes citing Addison, colonial printers repeatedly indicated their reluctance to open their presses—their newspapers especially—wide enough to allow a full range of controversial matter into the public forum.[31] Most commonly, by filling the columns of their papers with anecdotal news of European war and diplomacy, colonial printers tried to avoid becoming embroiled in local struggles. Accordingly, the contents of most colonial papers were unrelievedly bland—*"dull and flat,"* as James Franklin would tacitly concede in a late subdued phase of his career.[32]

If it is true that the political language and thought of pre-Revolutionary America were often curiously unrevealing, highly sensitive perhaps to the shared concerns of local elites but not to the issues that made for divisions among both powerful and common people, the trade strategies of printers may have been partially responsible. Unaccustomed to a politics in which partisan activity was fully legitimate, they acted in such a way as to retard the development of a public forum where conflicts could be thoroughly and continuously articulated. Only during the prolonged crisis of the Revolutionary period did printers as a group begin to act in ways that promoted a politics directly expressive of tension and dissent.

3. Franklin and His Friends

In the first major political contest of the Revolutionary years, the controversy over the Stamp Act, colonial printers had a substantial economic interest. David Ramsay was later to suggest that printers, never lacking in "attention to the profits of their profession," had united to oppose legislation that "threatened a great diminution" of their income as well as an abridgement of American liberty.[33] At the time the act was passed, Franklin—serving as a colonial agent in London—realized immediately that it would place a heavy economic burden on his former profession. "I think it will affect the Printers more than anybody," he wrote early in 1765 to his managing partner in Philadelphia, "as a Sterling Halfpenny Stamp on every Half Sheet of a Newspaper, and Two shillings Sterling on every Advertisement, will go near to

[30]*Pennsylvania Gazette*, June 10, 1731; *Autobiography of Franklin*, p. 165. From one point of view, James Morton Smith, *William and Mary Quarterly*, 3d ser. 20 (1963): 157–59, is probably correct in arguing that in practice—regardless of prevailing legal doctrine—there was considerable freedom in the American colonies from official coercion of the press. Self-censorship on the basis of business strategy, however, made the colonial press far less "radical" than Gary B. Nash suggests in "The Transformation of Urban Politics, 1700–1765," *Journal of American History* 60 (1973–74): 606, 616–18.

[31]On the influence of political writers like Trenchard and Gordon, see Gary Huxford, "The English Libertarian Tradition in the Colonial Newspaper," *Journalism Quarterly* 45 (1968): 677–86, but the argument there ignores an important contrary tradition; see, for example, Elizabeth Christine Cook, *Literary Influences in Colonial Newspapers, 1705–1750* (New York, 1912), p. 125.

[32]The convenience of foreign news has been noted with regard to the provincial English press by Cranfield, *Development of the Provincial Newspaper*, p. 67; the point applies equally well to America. *Rhode-Island Gazette*, Nov. 23, 1732.

[33]Ramsay's observations were cited approvingly by Arthur M. Schlesinger, *Prelude to Independence: The Newspaper War on Britain, 1764–1776* (New York, 1958), which greatly elaborated on the theme; a more recent discussion along the same lines is provided by Francis G. Walett, "The Impact of the Stamp Act on the Colonial Press," in Donovan H. Bond and W. Reynolds McLeod, eds., *Newsletters to Newspapers: Eighteenth-Century Journalism* (Morgantown, W. Va., 1977), pp. 157–69. An abbreviated version of the analysis that follows, through part 5, appeared in Botein, "'Meer Mechanics' and an Open Press," pp. 211–25.

knock up one Half of both. There is also Fourpence Sterling on every Almanack."[34]

There was ample precedent in England for taxing printed matter, novel as it was of Parliament to apply such a plan to the empire. For over half a century, a stamp tax had been in force in the mother country, and the system was not generally regarded as intolerable.[35] It had caused occasional distress in the provinces, however, and previous experience with local stamp duties in New York and Massachusetts had suggested that a tax on paper, payable by the printer in advance, might damage the colonial trade. Like their provincial brethren, but unlike publishers in London, printers in the colonies sold mostly on credit, some of which inevitably turned out to be bad. Understandably, then, they were fearful that much of the new tax could not be passed on to their customers.[36]

The first reaction of David Hall, Franklin's Philadelphia partner, was that it might not be worthwhile to continue the *Pennsylvania Gazette* at all. "The Case betwixt you and us, with respect to News Papers," Hall explained to Wiliam Strahan in London, "is very different—your Hawkers are ready to take yours all off, and pay the Ready Money for them." James Parker, a key Franklin associate in New York, predicted that his days in the trade were numbered, since "the fatal *Black-Act*" with its "killing Stamp" would surely turn printing into a business of "very little Consequence."[37]

No doubt this was unduly alarmist; both Franklin and Strahan tried to encourage Hall with a variety of optimistic suggestions.[38] But by the beginning of summer it was apparent that the dimensions of the problem had changed. Well before they had the opportunity to formulate business strategies that would minimize the threat of the Stamp Act to their livelihoods, printers in the colonies were faced with the more urgent challenge of coping with unprecedented political turbulence. For some—often "the more opulent," as Isaiah Thomas recalled[39]—traditional habits of political caution prevailed; among the hesitant were Franklin's associates in the trade. Such was the magnitude of the transatlantic crisis, however, that their customary business strategies failed to provide reliable guidelines for behavior.

David Hall, for one, had never been inclined to meddle rashly in controversy; but this instinct, so often useful in the past, seemed inappropriate or even imprudent in the radically altered circumstances. In June 1765, he reported to Franklin with some bewilderment that the *Gazette*'s customers were already "leaving off fast" in anticipation of the Stamp Act. For the most part, it was not that they lacked the extra shillings; it was a question of principle. Their resolution, Hall said, was "not to pay any thing

[34]Franklin to David Hall, Feb. 14, 1765, *Franklin Papers*, 12: 65–67.

[35]On English experience, which suggested that the "vent" of newspapers depended less upon price than upon "circumstances of the times exciting more or less curiosity," see Frederick S. Siebert, "Taxes on Publications in England in the Eighteenth Century," *Journalism Quarterly* 21 (1944): 12–24; Edward Hughes, "The English Stamp Duties, 1664–1774," *English Historical Review* 56 (1951): 234–64.

[36]On the problems of printers in provincial England, see Cranfield, *Development of the Provincial Newspaper*, pp. 44–47, 237–40; Wiles, *Freshest Advices*, pp. 98–103. Colonial experience is discussed by Mack Thompson, "Massachusetts and New York Stamp Acts," *William and Mary Quarterly*, 3d ser. 26 (1969): 253–58. The distress of printers in Massachusetts is mentioned by Thomas, *History of Printing*, 2: 186n, 232, 238–41. The effects of similar legislation in New York, "like to a killing Frost," were vividly described at the time in a printer's broadside; "James Parker *versus* New York Province," ed. Beverly McAnear, *New York History* 22 (1941): 321–22, 326–28, 330n. Parker's reaction to the new parliamentary statute, illustrated below, was perhaps predictable.

[37]Hall to Strahan, May 19, 1765, David Hall Papers, American Philosophical Society, Philadelphia; Parker to Franklin, Apr. 25, June 14, 1765, *Franklin Papers*, 12: 111–13, 174–76.

[38]Their basic assumption was that Hall would be able to add the tax to his prices and inaugurate a policy of payment in advance. Franklin to Hall, June 8, 1765, *Franklin Papers*, 12: 170–72; Strahan to Hall, July 8, 1765, David Hall Papers.

[39]Thomas, *History of Printing*, 2: 189.

towards that Tax they can possibly avoid; and News Papers, they tell me, they can, and will, do without." Evidently uncertain himself as to the constitutional implications of the new law, Hall perceived the temper of the colonies with apprehension. "In short," he observed privately, "the whole Continent are discontented with the Law, think their Liberties and Privileges, as Englishmen, are lost, and seem, many of them, almost desperate.—What the Consequences will be, God only knows." Hall's own fear was that there would be "a great deal of Mischief."[40]

Unquestionably, considered from the perspective of his trade, the Stamp Act was a "horrid Law" that would "knock up" most printers in America. But Hall was in no hurry to oppose it publicly. From the first, he told Franklin, exaggerating somewhat, "all of the Papers on the Continent, ours excepted, were full of Spirited Papers against the Stamp Law, and . . . because, I did not publish those Papers likewise, I . . . got a great Deal of Ill-will." Hall had hoped to ride out the storm, but after a while came to realize that he had been "much mistaken" as to his proper course of action. The *Gazette*'s silence, zealous patriots warned, would injure the cause of the people. "And, I have been told by many," Hall explained, "that our Interest will certainly suffer by it." It would be best "to humour them in some Publications, as they seem to insist so much upon it." Yet he hesitated to rush into the fray, "the Risk being so great" if he pursued a course of outright defiance.[41] Eventually, like many of his colonial brethren, he made the most of a disagreeable situation by publishing his paper without his name on it. Uneasily and with circumspection, he became and would remain a patriot—less ardent than his chief business rival, William Bradford III, but forthright enough at least to avoid being accused of Toryism.[42]

Further to the south, Charleston's Peter Timothy was even more circuitous in his response to the issues of the Revolutionary period. Since he was an official in the imperial postal system, his loyalties were suspect from the very beginning of the crisis. Naturally, he abhorred "Grenville's hellish Idea of the Stamp-Act," but he was reluctant to join the resistance movement. Acting in concert with most of his southern brethren, he elected to suspend his *Gazette* temporarily rather than to continue publication in overt disregard of the new law. Furthermore, he declined "to direct, support and engage in the most violent Opposition"—so he later explained to Franklin, a former business associate—and this thoroughly "exasperated every Body." The result was that within a short time he found himself reduced from "the most *popular*" to "the most *unpopular* Man in the Province." Especially humiliating was the decision of local patriots to help Charles Crouch, his brother-in-law and once his apprentice, to set up a new *South Carolina Gazette* that would represent the cause of American liberty more boldly than either Timothy's or the even more timorous *Gazette* of Robert Wells. For a time, Crouch's paper prospered, as its warm criticism of the Stamp Act attracted patriot readers. Having missed his chance, Timothy seemed unable to restore his credit with the more hot-blooded spirits of Charleston. "Ruduced [*sic*] to this situation," he advised Franklin in 1768, "I have not been myself since Nov. 1765. Nor shall I recover, unless I quit the Post-Office when some other Occasion offers to distinguish myself in the Cause of America."[43]

[40]Hall to Franklin, June 20, 1765, *Franklin Papers*, 12: 188–89; Hall to Strahan, Sept. 6, 1765, David Hall Papers.

[41]Hall to Strahan, Sept. 19, 1765, David Hall Papers, Hall to Franklin, Sept. 6, Oct. 14, 1765, *Franklin Papers*, 12: 255–59, 319–21. See generally Robert D. Harlan, "David Hall and the Stamp Act," *Papers of the Bibliographical Society of America* 61 (1967): 13–37.

[42]Schlesinger, *Prelude to Independence*, pp. 77–78.

[43]Timothy to Franklin, Sept. 3, 1768, *Franklin Papers*, 15: 199–203; Hennig Cohen, *The South Carolina Gazette, 1732–1775* (Columbia, S.C., 1953), p. 142; Schlesinger, *Prelude to Independence*, pp. 78–79; Thomas, *History of Printing*, 2: 160–61, 370–71.

When opportunity next beckoned, Timothy was somewhat more alert to the perils of hesitation. In 1770 he distinguished himself as the only southern printer to mark the Boston Massacre with black newspaper borders. Just the year before, however, he had printed William Henry Drayton's caustic criticisms of the nonimportation agreement in force at Charleston, and as late as 1772 his interest in politics seemed to lapse. He had "suffered, by never being lukewarm in any Cause," he told Franklin then, and so—his eyes "almost worn out"—he was prepared to accept a comfortable retirement post in the British imperial administration. As it happened, nothing was immediately forthcoming, and soon afterward Timothy's patriotic ardor revived, carrying him to the prestigious peak of his lengthy career. In the following years, as he proudly informed Franklin in 1777, he was "continually in Motion," as secretary to the second Provincial Congress and a member of various political committees. Briefly imprisoned by the British in 1780, he died two years later, assured of his reputation as a patriot.[44] To reach that point, however, had required a long and somewhat roundabout journey.

For James Parker—temporarily in New Jersey when the Stamp Act passed, having left his New York office under the management of a Virginian named John Holt—even a lukewarm commitment was to be avoided. Much as he loathed the new tax, he could not seriously contemplate resistance. Sometimes, he wrote to Franklin in June 1765, "the true Old English Spirit of Liberty will rise within me, yet as there is a Necessity to acquiesce in the Chains laid on me, I endeavour at a patient Resignation." Fortunately, it appeared, he was at a distance from the arena of conflict—"or perhaps the Impetuosity of my Temper would have plunged me deep one way or the other." Impetuous or not, he plainly had no stomach for popular agitation and disorder. As tensions mounted in the fall of 1765, it seemed to him that the people were "running Mad," and would speedily bring "an End to all Government" by their "dreadful Commotions."[45]

The next year, returning to New York, Parker continued to lament the insubordinate "Spirit of Independence" that inflamed the populace. He had moved back at the urging of Franklin, who wanted him there to serve more effectively as general comptroller of the colonial post office; as an additional incentive to relocate, Franklin provided a minor customs post in the city. Predictably, like Peter Timothy in Charleston, Parker soon became implicated in the bitter political divisions of the time. The Sons of Liberty, he told Franklin, "carry all before them." Their favorite printer, John Holt, was emboldened to harass Parker by refusing to relinquish management of the New York office, although Parker was unquestionably its sole proprietor. Eventually Holt yielded the title of Parker's old paper, the *New-York Gazette*, renaming his own after John Peter Zenger's famed *Journal*, but Parker was still obliged to "launch into Business" anew, without his former clientele and even some of his office equipment.[46]

[44]Cohen, *South Carolina Gazette*, pp. 13, 244–47; Schlesinger, *Prelude to Independence*, pp. 126–27. Timothy to Franklin, Aug. 24, 1772, *Franklin Papers*, 19: 283–85; June 12, 1777, in "The Correspondence of Peter Timothy, Printer of Charlestown, with Benjamin Franklin," ed. Douglas C. McMurtrie, *South Carolina Historical and Genealogical Magazine* 35 (1934): 128–29.

[45]Parker to Franklin, June 14, Sept. 22, Oct. 10, Nov. 6, 1765, *Franklin Papers*, 12: 174–76, 274–77, 308–10, 355. Parker's eagerness to avoid trouble may have been heightened as a result of his apparently inadvertent connection with the notorious *Constitutional Courant*, an extraordinary one-issue journal of radical propaganda that William Goddard—then associated with John Holt—seems to have printed on Parker's press at Woodbridge, presumably without Parker's permission. See ibid., pp. 287–88n, and Ward L. Miner, *William Goddard, Newspaperman* (Durham, N.C., 1962), pp. 50–52. Schlesinger, *Prelude to Independence*, p. 111, misleadingly groups Parker with Holt as "devoted patriots."

[46]Parker to Franklin, June 11, May 6, Oct. 25, 1766, *Franklin Papers*, 13: 300–312, 262–66, 472–76.

Most damaging was the decline that his political reputation had suffered in the course of the previous year. "Mr. *Holt*," he noted in a bitter broadside, "seems to insinuate . . . that in the late Troubles I was no Friend to Liberty." This was probably unfair of Holt, but Parker's public record was indeed ambiguous. In spite of his antipathy to the Stamp Act, he had done what he could to insure compliance with the law, evidently considering this to be the unavoidable duty of a royal official. One consequence, apparently, was "a little Sour Looking, and perhaps some Contempt." More serious was the widespread feeling, nurtured carefully by Holt, that Parker's crown offices—his customs appointment in particular—had compromised his personal integrity. In 1768, the customs job may well have cost him the patronage of the New York Assembly.[47]

Evidently it was difficult for Parker to abandon the old trade ways and plunge into controversy with enough zeal to please the emerging leadership of the patriot movement. John Holt had no trouble out-maneuvering his former employer and business associate. In 1768 Parker's fortunes rose as he began to run the "American Whig" essays of the Livingstonian party in his *Gazette*; within a short time he had gained more than 200 new subscribers, while losing only 70 Anglicans. Holt quickly pirated the series, though, and it became doubtful whether Parker's recently acquired customers would stay with him. Once again, late in 1769, he chose to try his hand at polemical politics by printing an anonymous broadside libel written by Alexander McDougall; then, threatened with a legal proceeding and dismissal from the post office, he backed down and identified the author. Not long afterward Parker died, having made a few last-minute efforts to atone for this treachery by publishing on behalf of McDougall's cause.[48]

Perhaps this indicated where his true sympathies lay; possibly he was in the process of beginning to commit himself aggressively—as Timothy would—to the Revolutionary position. Nevertheless, considered as a whole, Parker's politics in the crucial years after passage of the Stamp Act had been unhappily inconsistent. No American printer had been more vehement in his criticism of colonial stamp duties than Parker, but his perceptions of economic self-interest had not made him into a Son of Liberty. The lasting strength of old trade ways, in spite of new political realities, was revealed in Parker's continuing attempts to shun conflict long after it might have been apparent that this strategy was unwise. By trying to avoid one kind of trouble, Parker invited another.

One reason Hall, Timothy, and Parker were unequipped to deal with the abnormal pressures of a Revolutionary situation was Franklin, their long-time patron and associate in the trade. More than anyone else, even while on assignment as a colonial agent in London, he could claim influence among American printers; over the years, especially south of New England, he had accumulated business connections that to some observers looked dangerously like a transatlantic propaganda network. "Depend upon my doing every Thing in this Affair for the Printers and Papermakers," he had promised Hall at the time of the Stamp Act, "as zealously as if I were still to be concerned in the Business."[49] Unfortunately for those who followed his cues, Franklin's political judgment at

[47]Beverly McAnear, "James Parker *versus* John Holt," *Proceedings of the New Jersey Historical Society* 59 (1941): 88–95, 199. Parker to Franklin, Sept. 11, Oct. 11, 1766, *Franklin Papers*, 13: 409–13, 454–59; Jan. 21, 1768, ibid., 15: 27–28.

[48]Parker to Franklin, April 18, 1768, ibid., 15: 100–102; May 30, 1769, ibid., 16: 137–40. Thomas, *History of Printing*, 2: 479–83; Schlesinger, *Prelude to Independence*, pp. 114–15.

[49]Franklin to Hall, June 8, 1765, *Franklin Papers*, 12: 170–72. The charge that Franklin used his trade connections for political advantage became especially pointed as a result of his role in the Hutchinson letters controversy. *Writings of Franklin*, 6: 286–88, and see more generally *Benjamin Franklin's Letters to the Press*, ed. Verner W. Crane (Chapel Hill, 1950).

the beginning of the Revolutionary crisis was unsure, not least because at some level of consciousness—despite his retirement from active business life—he remained a colonial printer. His practice of imperial politics represented with curious exaggeration the habitual trade policy of neutrality, elevated to the sphere of statecraft. Much has been written of Franklin's passion for conciliation and his extraordinary diplomatic skill; interpretations based on political and even psychoanalytic theory have been suggested. Viewed from a different perspective, however, Franklin's public behavior in London during the period before Independence may be understood as an extension of the business and political strategies that he and his brethren in the colonial trade had followed for decades preceding the Revolutionary crisis.[50]

Thus, as an agent, he tried to act the part not of an advocate but of a reporter—an "impartial historian of American facts and opinions." With some of the instinctive distaste for controversy that characterized newspaper publishers in the colonies, Franklin also set out to mute transatlantic political debate. "At the same time that we Americans wish not to be judged of, in the gross by particular papers written by anonymous scribblers and published in the colonies," he wrote to his son in 1767, "it would be well if we could avoid falling into the same mistake in America of judging of ministers here by the libels printed against them." His self-assigned task was not only to report impartially the arguments of both sides, each to the other, but also to discount all extreme, offensive statements of opinion—"to extenuate matters a little," as he explained.[51]

If in the past this approach to imperial affairs had worked well, it was ill suited for a period of intense political turmoil. Hoping to please both his colonial employers and British officialdom, Franklin found it difficult to satisfy either side. It "has often happened to me," he wrote shortly after his subtle involvement in the Hutchinson letters uproar had been exposed, "that while I have been thought here too much of an American, I have in America been deem'd too much of an Englishman."[52] Both compromised and compromising, Franklin played a role in London—so typical in its essentials of a colonial printer—that diminished his credibility with patriots as well as English officials, and therefore reduced his usefulness to long-time associates like Hall, Timothy, and Parker.

Most troublesome to patriots was the lingering memory of his initial acquiescence in the Stamp Act. With pardonable ambivalence, Hall wrote that he wished his famous partner could have provided daily counsel "on the Spot" instead of three thousand miles away. Yet, added Hall, "I should be afraid of your Safety, as the Spirit of the People is so violent against every One, they think has the least concern with the Stamp Law, and they have imbibed the Notion, that you had a Hand, in the framing of it." Nowhere were the distortions of Franklin's outlook more evident than in the congratulations he conveyed to Hall for trying to exclude criticism of the Stamp Act from the *Pennsylvania Gazette*. "Nothing has done America more Hurt here," he explained, "than those kind of Writings; so that I should have been equally averse

[50]See, for example, Gerald Stourzh, *Benjamin Franklin and American Foreign Policy* (Chicago, 1954); Richard Bushman, "On the Uses of Psychology: Conflict and Conciliation in Benjamin Franklin," *History and Theory* 5 (1966): 227–40. Another interpretation of Franklin's outlook as a printer–which does not take into account the habits of a provincial tradesman—is to be found in Lewis T. Simpson, "The Printer as a Man of Letters: Franklin and the Symbolism of the Third Realm," in J. A. Leo Lemay, ed., *The Oldest Revolutionary: Essays on Benjamin Franklin* (Philadelphia, 1976), pp. 3–20.

[51]*Franklin's Letters to the Press*, p. xxxvii. Benjamin Franklin to William Franklin, Nov. 25, Dec. 29, 1767, *Franklin Papers*, 14: 322–26, 349–51.

[52]*Writings of Franklin*, 6: 260. This observation appeared in an apologetic tract of 1774 that went unpublished during his lifetime. To English radicals like Thomas Hollis, too, Franklin was a "doubtful Character." See, for example, Franklin to Thomas Brand Hollis, Oct. 5, 1783, ibid., 9: 103–5.

to printing them if I had held no Office under the Crown."[53]

Whether or not Franklin really was "a dangerous Person," as John Holt would later complain in private to a fellow printer, it was plain enough—within the trade as well as without—that in the early years of the imperial crisis he lacked his usually shrewd sense of political direction. His decision to abandon the middle ground and espouse the colonial cause was gradual and far from enthusiastic. "I assure you," he wrote in 1772 in answer to Peter Timothy's request for a job, "it is not in my Power to procure you that Post you mention or any other, whatever my Wishes may be for your Prosperity." His explanation reflected resignation more than patriot ardor. "I am now thought here too much of an American," he pointed out, "to have any Interest of the kind." Ultimately, like Timothy but on a much grander scale, Franklin emerged from the Revolutionary turmoil with honor, even glory; but this happened at least in part because in 1774 the British ministry moved against him so heavy-handedly for his complicity in the Hutchinson affair.[54] Until then, still the colonial printer, he had persisted in his reluctance to engage in overt partisan politics, continuing perilously late to value the benefits of official British patronage.

4. Reluctant Partisans

Similar doubts and hesitation were characteristic of other colonial printers, although they were not as close to Franklin as Hall, Timothy, or Parker. Unused to the violently polarizing effects of a Revolutionary conflict, they tried to temporize, often to their eventual regret. Willingly or not, sooner or later most printers in the colonies gave up neutrality to choose sides. More than twice as many, it appears, opted for the patriots as for the Tories. No exact count is possible, however, since some switched parties and others were so tepid in their commitments as to elude meaningful classification.[55] Reluctant to advertise themselves as full-fledged partisans, many printers tried in public to claim the middle of the road, steering one way or another only when obliged.

Some, like Franklin and his associates, managed in the end to establish themselves convincingly as patriots. In North Carolina, for example, James Davis and Adam Boyd were able to take a patriot line while continuing to avoid excessive partisanship, as were James Adams in Delaware and Jonas Green in Maryland.[56] Outside the southern colonies, however, this was less usual, on account of competition from more energetically patriot presses. For a patriot printer who wished seriously to persist in the old ways, the most effective solution may have been that adopted by the Fleet brothers, Thomas, Jr., and John, who published Boston's *Evening-Post*. Although it was known that their personal sympathies lay with the American cause, their policy as printers was to maintain at least a semblance of impartiality. According to

[53]Hall to Franklin, Sept. 6, 1765, *Franklin Papers*, 12: 255–59; Franklin to Hall, Sept. 14, 1765, ibid., 12: 267–68. Indeed, Franklin's custom of publishing softened versions of his opinions in London—which were then reprinted in colonial newspapers—was especially damaging to his reputation at home; see ibid., p. 207n. Of course, his position at the head of the colonial post office and the political ambitions of his son also complicated his role in London.

[54]Miner, *William Goddard*, pp. 163–64; Franklin to Timothy, Nov. 3, 1772, *Franklin Papers*, 19: 362; and see David Freeman Hawke, *Franklin* (New York, 1976), chaps. 29–30.

[55]Sidney Kobre, *The Development of the Colonial Newspaper* (Pittsburgh, 1944), pp. 147–48, lists 39 newspapers as patriot, 18 as Tory—which is probably as useful a ratio as any, since it was mainly by the contents of their papers that colonial printers signalled their loyalties.

[56]Charles Christopher Crittenden, *North Carolina Newspapers before 1790* (Chapel Hill, 1928), pp. 36–38; D. L. Hawkins, "James Adams, The First Printer of Delaware," *Papers of the Bibliographical Society of America* 28 (1934): 45–46; David K. Skaggs, "Editorial Policies of the *Maryland Gazette*, 1765–1783," *Maryland Historical Magazine* 59 (1964): 346.

one querulous Tory, the Fleets restricted comments by pro-American "Dirt-casters" to "the Holes and Corners and other private Purlieus" of their paper, whereas "all the Pages and Columns" of the fiery *Boston Gazette* were filled with inflammatory propaganda against the mother country. As late as the early months of 1775, the Fleet brothers were still promising that the *Evening-Post* would be "conducted with the utmost Freedom and Impartiality," and would always, "as usual, be open for the Insertion of all Pieces that shall tend to amuse or instruct, or to the promoting of useful Knowledge and the general Good of Mankind." The next month, they published a letter from a self-styled moderate commending their editorial policy, and another—on the duty of obedience—that hailed their "well known impartiality." A week later, without prior notice, the last issue of the *Evening-Post* appeared, with a brief note from the printers explaining that they had decided to suspend publication until matters were "in a more settled State." Since matters only became more unsettled, the *Evening-Post* never revived. Without sacrificing other printing business, the Fleets were thus able to remain faithful to old trade ways in a stridently patriot community.[57]

More commonly, however, lukewarm Toryism became the only realistic option for a printer determined to stay neutral in the face of strenuous patriot pressures. Georgia's James Johnston, for one, veered inconsistently as he responded to both threats and incentives; eventually, because he was not enough a patriot, he became a Tory, was declared by patriots to be guilty of treason, and was banished. Among other printers who were forced by this logic to back slowly into Toryism were such prominent figures as Robert Wells of Charleston and Boston's Richard Draper. Strict political neutrality, which had never been easy to achieve in a time of conflict, became highly implausible during a revolution. In 1775, Philadelphia's James Humphreys, Jr., founded the *Pennsylvania Ledger* with the naively stated intention of keeping it authentically open to all sides. When this proved futile, he became known by default as a Tory. "The impartiality of the Ledger," Isaiah Thomas commented laconically, "did not comport with the temper of the times."[58]

How Revolutionary pressures within the printing trade could transform an uneasy patriot into an easy Tory was revealed painfully in the careers of Daniel and Robert Fowle, in New Hampshire. Perhaps because of his previous unhappy involvement in a "famous Cause" of New England's political history, Daniel Fowle was disinclined to make a firm commitment in the Revolutionary crisis. Although he associated himself with Wilkes to support the longstanding lawsuit that he had brought after his false imprisonment by the Massachusetts House in 1754, for allegedly printing the notorious *Monster of Monsters*, otherwise his deportment reflected habits of prudence befitting a public printer who also served as a magistrate. His *New-Hampshire Gazette*, which he conducted with his nephew Robert, "was not remarkable in its political features," according to Isaiah Thomas. If "its general complexion was favorable to the cause of the country," mild patriotism was not enough in time of stress. "Some zealous whigs," Thomas recalled, "who thought the Fowles were too timid in the cause of liberty, or their press too much under the influence of the officers of the crown," encouraged one Thomas Furber to establish the *Portsmouth Mercury* early

[57]Thomas, *History of Printing*, 2: 333–34; Schlesinger, *Prelude to Independence*, p. 93; *Boston Evening-Post*, Mar. 6, Apr. 10, 17, 24, 1775. Mary Ann Yodelis, *Who Paid the Piper? Publishing Economics in Boston, 1763–1775* (Lexington, Ky., 1975), pp. 11–13, indicates that the Fleets' general printing business did not suffer especially before the outbreak of war; it was their newspaper that was vulnerable.

[58]Alexander A. Lawrence, *James Johnston: Georgia's First Printer* (Savannah, 1956), pp. 10–22; Philip Davidson, *Propaganda and the American Revolution, 1763–1783* (Chapel Hill, 1941), pp. 304–7; Thomas, *History of Printing*, 2: 333–34.

in 1765. Although the upstart paper began with a customarily cautious promise "to print Nothing that may have the least Tendency to subvert Good Order," it went on to assert that "neither Opposition, arbitrary Power, or publick Injuries" would be "screen'd from the Knowledge of the People, whose Liberties are dearer to them than their Lives."[59]

Furber himself proved so disappointingly prudent that the Fowles were able to outdo him in patriot spirit by the end of the Stamp Act controversy, but in the long run their *Gazette* was still insufficiently partisan. In 1772 Benjamin Edes and John Gill, printers of the *Boston Gazette*, accused Robert Fowle of scheming to obtain a customs house appointment—a charge that Fowle merely dismissed as "premature and founded in a Mistake." Furthermore, he told his readers, it was "more honorable to hold any Post under the Government, than to spend his Time in libelling and railing at the Rulers of the People," as Edes and Gill did. Two years later, following the neutral logic of pre-Revolutionary printers, the *New-Hampshire Gazette* reprinted the opposing views of "Novanglus" and "Massachusettensis" in parallel columns, along with advice from the printers that people "*read both Sides with an impartial Mind*." Daniel Fowle was subsequently reprimanded by the New Hampshire legislature for his willingness to publish an argument against American independence; Robert, less fortunate, came to be known unequivocally as a Tory and was forced to flee, eventually finding consolation as a British pensioner.[60]

Most Tory printers waited as long as they dared before abandoning fully the trade principle of neutrality. This was especially so in Boston, where patriot feeling was a stern discouragement to those interested in printing for the cause of crown and Parliament. Because Richard Draper was insufficiently enthusiastic in his attachment to the mother country, despite his appointment as printer to the governor and king, it was necessary for Thomas Hutchinson and his friends to cast about for more adventurous figures in the trade. To find the right men proved difficult. John Green and Joseph Russell, in business together since 1755 and printers to the Assembly, were apparently prepared to risk the displeasure of patriots and accept the lucrative contract that Governor Bernard secured for them in 1767, to serve the new Board of Customs Commissioners in Boston. It also seems that when John Dickinson's *Farmer's Letters* first attracted local notice, partisans of the mother country privately urged Green and Russell "by no means to print the same." Heeding this advice, they promptly fell out of favor with the House of Representatives and most of their former clientele. "Mind, Green, who will get most at the winding up of Affairs," Bernard supposedly said by way of cajolery, "Edes and Gill or you."[61] This was not enough to reassure the anxious partners, however, so Massachusetts Tories were forced to seek out other printers.

John Mein and his partner John Fleeming, recent immigrants from Scotland, had been quick to serialize the *Farmer's Letters* in their *Boston Chronicle*, professing eagerness that the paper "always, when any dispute claims general attention, give both sides of the question, if they can be obtained." But evidently the prospect of customs patronage persuaded them instead to try specializing in "the partial Praise of a Party," as Edes and Gill scornfully explained. Mein, it seems, was altogether too choleric to survive in Boston. After exposing local violators of the nonimportation agreement, assaulting John Gill, and drawing a pistol on a hostile mob, he

[59]Clyde Augustus Duniway, *The Development of Freedom of the Press in Massachusetts* (New York, 1906), p. 172; Thomas, *History of Printing*, 2: 281–84, I: 434.

[60]Ibid., 2: 283–84; *New-Hampshire Gazette*, Nov. 20, 1772; Schlesinger, *Prelude to Independence*, p. 221; Ralph H. Brown, "New Hampshire Editors Win the War," *New England Quarterly* 12 (1939): 35–51.

[61]Thomas, *History of Printing*, I: 347–48; O. M. Dickerson, "British Control of American Newspapers on the Eve of the Revolution," *New England Quarterly* 24 (1951): 455–59.

hastily made his way to England, where he became a hack writer for the North ministry. Left behind, his associate Fleeming struggled on for a time, only to be supplanted by a new Tory team consisting of two young printers—John Hicks, formerly an apprentice of Green and Russell, and Nathaniel Mills, who had been trained by Fleeming. Hicks, who originally had been something of a patriot, was said to have been involved creditably in the circumstances of the Boston Massacre. But, observed Isaiah Thomas, "Interest too often biasses the human mind." Although his own father was killed by English troops at the very beginning of the Revolutionary War, Hicks became a Tory.[62]

To the south, only New York offered Tories adequate printing facilities. By 1774, according to an indignant out-of-town newspaper reader, Hugh Gaine and James Rivington were brazenly publishing anyone who would "sneer at, and deduct from the merit of the most ascertained and sacred Patriots." Nevertheless, both printers persisted in justifying themselves in accordance with traditional trade rhetoric. "Gaine," Isaiah Thomas would recall, "seemed desirous to side with the successful party; but, not knowing which would eventually prevail, he seems to have been unstable in his politics." Perhaps because of his previous connections with New York's Anglican community, his *Mercury* appeared to be leaning in the direction of Toryism by the early 1770s, but not irrevocably so. Nor was Rivington's bias especially obvious when in 1773 he began to publish his highly successful *Gazetteer*. Promising to avoid "acrimonious Censures on any Society of Class of Men," Rivington announced that it was his goal to be "as generally useful and amusing as possible." In the circumstances, this would have required remarkable diplomatic talent. "When so many Persons of a vast Variety of Views and Inclinations are to be satisfied," the *Gazetteer* conceded in a shrewder vein, "it must often happen, that what is highly agreeable to some, will be equally disagreeable to others."[63]

What stamped both Gaine and Rivington as Tory sympathizers by 1774 was not so much their public political sentiments as their apparent determination to maintain the traditional neutrality of the trade. In contrast to Philadelphia's patriot printers, who were said to refuse to publish the Tory viewpoint because of their "unaccountable delicacy," Gaine and Rivington claimed to understand what a "free press" should be. The "TRUE SONS OF LIBERTY," Rivington suggested in his *Gazetteer*, were those who printed without showing partiality. A few issues later, he quoted with approval an article from a London newspaper that caustically described the efforts of American patriots to abridge "freedom of the press" by preventing printers from "daring to publish on both sides." Fortunately, noted Rivington, there were some courageous souls who could withstand such pressure. "The printer of a newspaper," he declared, "ought to be neutral in all cases where his own press is employed." He himself would definitely publish all views in his paper, and also all pamphlets submitted to him, "whether of the Whig or Tory flavour."[64]

Privately, too, Rivington did his best to resist

[62]Joseph T. Buckingham, *Specimens of Newspaper Literature*, 2 vols. (Boston, 1850), I: 213; John E. Alden, "John Mein: Scourge of Patriots," *Publications of the Colonial Society of Massachusetts* 34 (1937–42): 582–83, and 571–99 in general; "The Letter-Book of Mills & Hicks," ed. Robert Earle Moody and Charles Christopher Crittenden, *North Carolina Historical Review* 14 (1937): 39–41; Thomas, *History of Printing*, I: 389–91.

[63]*Pennsylvania Journal*, Oct. 19, 1774. Thomas, *History of Printing*, 2: 300; *The Journals of Hugh Gaine, Printer*, ed. Paul Leicester Ford, 2 vols. (New York, 1902), I: 51–52; *Rivington's New-York Gazetteer*, Apr. 22, 1773. Rivington's goals may have been quite conventional at the outset. According to Thomas, *History of Printing*, 2: 315–16, no American paper was "better printed, or more copiously furnished with foreign intelligence" than the *Gazetteer*.

[64]*New-York Gazette; and the Weekly Mercury* (the formal title of Gaine's paper after 1768), July 25, 1774; *Rivington's New-York Gazetteer*, July 14, Aug. 11, Dec. 8, 1774.

a premature commitment to Toryism, despite his own personal and business ties to the mother country, from which he had emigrated a decade earlier. In 1774 he assured Philadelphia's Charles Thomson that he would listen to the latter's "excellent moral Counsell" against antagonizing patriot colonists, and would be careful to "give no more offence on the score of Impurity." Most certainly, he would be happy to publish the opinions of American partisans in Philadelphia — "and I will use every endeavor to please all my patrons." Through Henry Knox, his Boston correspondent, he also seems to have tried to let John Hancock know that he had meant no harm whatsoever, but had acted merely out of "a necessity," in publishing a letter critical of his conduct. Any appropriate reply, he indicated, would be graciously received and promptly put into print.[65]

That this was an untenable strategy to follow in an era of revolution was tacitly conceded by Rivington in a *Gazetteer* of December 1774, which presented a brief poetic summary of the printer's plight:

> Dares the poor man impartial be,
> He's doom'd to want and infamy.

A week later, a correspondent commended Rivington for following the policy of "a true whig," by remaining "open to all doctrines," but admitted that this could be accomplished "only at the hazard of your fortune and your Life." Circumstances were forcing Rivington to become a partisan. Toryism, after all, might bring its own rewards, which Isaiah Thomas considered "sufficiently apparent" to be left unspecified. Circulating rumors mentioned the sum of £500 as a possible incentive. A boycott was organized against Rivington, and he was hanged in effigy; angry patriots went so far as to threaten his personal safety.[66]

Well into 1775, however, both he and Gaine were still equivocating. Much to the irritation of Lieutenant Governor Colden, Gain refused to include in his *Mercury* a Tory account of what had happened at Lexington and Concord, and Rivington — who in March had begun to serialize Burke's "Speech on American Taxation" — published two contradictory narratives. For a time, the latter even seemed to make his peace with some of the local patriots. Agreeing that he had "given great Offence to the Colonies," Rivington vowed publicly to make amends, explaining that he had been acting simply in deference to his notions of "the Liberty of the Press" and his "duty as a Printer." Having conformed, he was exonerated by the Provincial Congress, only to lose all of his equipment to a destructive mob, apparently unimpressed by his show of penance. In 1776, he returned to England; Gaine, just before English troops occupied the city, left for Newark.[67]

Both would be back, though. Eventually, war — and the comforting presence of the British army — brought vacillating printers like Gaine and Rivington into the Tory ranks. Once there, they had little choice but to declare their loyalties with a forthrightness that their brethren of an earlier day would have considered

[65]Rivington to Thomson, June 24, 1774, Bradford Papers, Historical Society of Pennsylvania, Philadelphia; Rivington to Knox, Apr. 20, 1774, in "Henry Knox, Bookseller," *Proceedings of the Massachusetts Historical Society* 61 (1927–28): 279–81. See generally Leroy Hewlett, "James Rivington, Loyalist Printer, Publisher, and Bookseller of the American Revolution, 1724–1802" (Ph.D. diss., University of Michigan, 1958), chap. 2.

[66]*Rivington's New-York Gazetteer*, Dec. 8, 15, 1774; Thomas, *History of Printing*, 2: 113; Hewlett, "James Rivington," chap. 3. Further information about Rivington, for these and subsequent years, may be found in *Rivington's New York Newspaper: Excerpts from a Loyalist Press, 1773–1783*, Collections of the New-York Historical Society, vol. 84 (New York, 1973), pp. 1–27; Robert M. Ours, "James Rivington: Another Viewpoint," in Bond and McLeod, eds., *Newsletters to Newspapers*, pp. 219–33.

[67]*Journals of Hugh Gaine*, I: 52, and see generally Alfred Lawrence Lorenz, *Hugh Gaine: A Colonial Printer-Editor's Odyssey to Loyalism* (Carbondale, Ill., 1972), chaps. 6–10. *Rivington's New-York Gazetteer*, Mar. 16, 23, Apr. 27, June 1, May 4, 1775.

most unbusinesslike. Gaine, it seems, deliberated and finally decided that "the strongest party" was encamped in New York; accordingly, he recrossed the Hudson and resumed trade there. Then, in October 1777, Rivington "surprised almost every Body," as Gaine recorded in his journal, by reestablishing himself in the city with new equipment and the title of King's Printer. Plainly, this was bad news for Gaine, although he professed to welcome it; soon he had to take second place to Rivington. Always, Rivington announced in a new version of the *Gazetteer* brought out under the royal arms, he had labored "to keep up and strengthen our Connection with the Mother Country, and to promote a proper Subordination to the Supreme Authority of the British Empire." He hoped that "his former Friends" would recall his services and patronize his office. Having belatedly discovered a firm sense of political principle underlying his previous conduct, Rivington proceeded to make the most of it.[68]

Like Gaine and Rivington, other printers in the colonies moved along the same circuitous route to Toryism, becoming unequivocally one-sided printers as much from military circumstance as from political principle or connection. Such camp followers in the trade included John Howe, the Robertson brothers, Mills and Hicks, and James Humphreys, Jr. Once they had made their decisions, they could not easily retrace their steps. No one "can wish more ardently than myself for a peace with America," wrote John Hicks from Charleston in 1782, "but rather than Great Britain should Stoop to acknowledge ye independency of this country I would sacrafice every farthing of my property & then my Person to oppose them." Having been forced to leave Boston, Hicks had tried his hand at a number of different printing jobs and then—after being reunited with his partner Mills, who had spent two intervening years in England—he had opened a luxury import shop in British-controlled South Carolina. By the close of 1782, as the two men told their London supplier, they could only "dread" a parliamentary surrender to American demands.[69]

In the end, like several of their fellow craftsmen who had come to favor the cause of the mother country, Mills and Hicks moved to Nova Scotia.[70] Toryism had been a gamble for them, and they had lost. More generally, traditional trade strategies had proven ineffective in Revolutionary conditions, incapable of protecting and sustaining those American printers who had tried to maintain the "freedom" of their presses to Tory points of view.

5. New Commitments

As the prospects of some colonial printers became uncertain after 1765, with passage of the Stamp Act, those of others looked brighter. Seemingly, what was required was a knack for exploiting the political situation. Benjamin Mecom, Franklin's nephew, was as quick as anyone to see the possibilities of the crisis, although—as always—he lacked the talent to achieve success. Despite the economic burden that the new stamp duties threatened to place on printers, he proposed to establish a newspaper of his own. This was to be a staunchly patriot revival of the *Connecticut Gazette*, aimed at zealous Whigs in New Haven. Rival printers soon moved into town and took away his business by putting out a superior paper, but Mecom had acted in terms of the same strategy followed by Charleston's Charles Crouch and

[68]Thomas, *History of Printing*, 2: 103–4; *Journals of Hugh Gaine*, 2: 50; *Rivington's New-York Gazette*, Oct. 13, 1777 (title varied afterward); Hewlett, "James Rivington," chap. 4.

[69]Schlesinger, *Prelude to Independence*, pp. 291–92. Hicks to Thomas Dickenson, Jr., May 27, 1782, in "Letter-Book of Mills & Hicks," p. 62; Mills and Hicks to Champion and Dickenson, Dec. 9, 1782, ibid., pp. 68–69; and see ibid., pp. 41–44.

[70]Schlesinger, *Prelude to Independence*, pp. 257–58.

New Hampshire's Thomas Furber, in trying to profit from the partisan fervor of the moment.[71] Especially for a printer of middling prosperity or less, the crisis could be interpreted as an opportunity to get ahead, by riding the waves of political emotion.

Correctly or not, many colonial printers appear to have made optimistic business calculations in response to the political troubles of the 1760s and 1770s, disregarding the economic discouragements first of the Stamp Act and later of the tax on paper included in the Townshend Act.[72] Before war physically disrupted the colonies, the Revolutionary period was a time of expansion in the American printing trade. From 1763 to 1775 the number of master printers at work in colonial America increased from forty-seven to eighty-two, while the number of newspapers that they published doubled, from twenty-one in 1763 to forty-two in 1775.[73] Conditions were such that many men in the trade were ready to try their luck and reach for entrepreneurial success. At least to some, however, it seemed that success was not to be achieved by following traditional routes. The vicissitudes of transatlantic conflict, non-importation in particular, constricted the profits that printers could expect to derive from such allied enterprises as imported books and stationery. At the same time, newspaper circulation increased markedly, reflecting the heightened polemical temperature of colonial journalism. In the circumstances, it was natural enough for some printers to conclude that partisan commitments might prove advantageous. Although it is unclear whether or to what extent purely political printing grew to become a significant business of its own during the Revolutionary years, it was obvious that the political loyalties of printers could be crucial in determining who would be their customers, or readers, and who would not.[74]

Compared with their Tory brethren, many patriot printers saw reason to react to the Revolutionary crisis by making early and relatively unambiguous political moves, accompanied by ardent expressions of high constitutional principle. Their cause, after all, was generally popular —hence likely to be profitable as well. Although some decorated their newspapers with variations on the slogan "Open to ALL Parties, but Influenced by NONE," this was now an empty gesture recalling a policy no longer relevant to the realities of American political controversy.[75]

Despite the persistence of conventional rhetoric, there was emerging a rudimentary alternative to the familiar trade understanding of "liberty of the press." Some of the inevitable

[71]Ibid, p. 75, and see James Parker to Benjamin Franklin, Dec. 24, 1767, *Franklin Papers*, 14: 345–48. It was a sign of Parker's own political obtuseness that he failed to appreciate Mccom's reasons for undertaking the project.

[72]Schlesinger, *Prelude to Independence*, p. 86, and Wroth, *Colonial Printer*, pp. 142–43, present the paper duties as onerous for the trade, but there is no evidence to suggest that printers perceived a serious economic threat. See, for example, Robert D. Harlan, "David Hall and the Townshend Acts," *Papers of the Bibliographical Society of America* 68 (1974): 19–38.

[73]Figures for printers are based on Charles Frederick Heartman, *Checklist of Printers in the United States from Stephen Daye to the Close of the War of Independence* (New York, 1915), which derives from a variety of standard bibliographical sources. As far as possible, Heartman has been corrected in the light of more accurate available information. Figures for newspapers are from Davidson, *Propaganda*, p. 225.

[74]See, for example, Harlan, "David Hall and the Townshend Acts," pp. 31–37; Schlesinger, *Prelude to Independence*, appendix A. Peter J. Parker, "The Philadelphia Printer: A Study of an Eighteenth-Century Businessman," *Business History Review* 40 (1966): 38; but cf. Yodelis, *Who Paid the Piper?*, pp. 19–23, 42–43, and passim, where it is suggested that the volume of purely political printing business did not become large enough to be the only or decisive consideration. It should be noted, too, that calculations made by patriot printers before 1776 would not necessarily assure them of success in the turbulent years that followed Independence.

[75]Schlesinger, *Prelude to Independence*, pp. 137, 165, gives examples of the old trade rhetoric that may have reflected confusion during a period in which habits were being altered; see also Davidson, *Propaganda*, p. 304.

verbal confusion accompanying this shift in meaning was evident in an issue of the *Pennsylvania Journal* that appeared in September 1766. Its printers, William Bradford III and his son Thomas, came forward to answer a harsh attack by the local stamp distributor, John Hughes, provoked by their exposé of his political correspondence. In threatening to start a lawsuit, they claimed, Hughes was trying "to demolish the liberty of the Press." But what precisely was that? Although the elder Bradford was a leading Son of Liberty and his paper had firmly opposed the Stamp Act, the Bradfords went on to recite a customary trade refrain. "We are only the printers of a free and impartial paper," they argued, "and we challenge Mr. Hughes and the world, to convict us of partiality in this respect, or of even an inclination to restrain the freedom of the press in any instance." Then, abruptly, they altered their emphasis. "We can appeal to North-America not only for our impartiality as printers," they said, "but also for the great advantages derived to us very lately from the unrestrained liberty, which every Briton claims of communicating his sentiments to the public thro' the channel of the press. What would have become of the liberties of the British Colonies in North-America, if Mr. Hughes's calls on Great Britain had been heard, to restrain the printers here from publishing, what he is pleased to stile *inflammatory pieces?*" Here was a subtle indication that "freedom" might become a word without implications of political neutrality. Like Zenger's paper in an earlier day, the *Pennsylvania Journal* could be considered "free" because it made a stand for "liberty" against the supposedly tyrannical designs of those in power.[76]

A similar distinction was suggested that same year by developments in Virginia. Alexander Purdie was naturally anxious to reassure readers that his new *Virginia Gazette*—unlike its "closed" predecessor—would be "as free as any publick press upon the continent," ready to publish the views even of those parties at odds with the authorities for whom he was official printer. But impartiality was not what would satisfy "some of the hot Burgesses," as Governor Fauquier called them, so William Rind was procured to print a second *Virginia Gazette*. This impressed Thomas Jefferson as truly a "free paper." Although its masthead bore a motto making the familiar promise of openness to all sides, Rind's practical understanding of "freedom" differed from Purdie's. Anticipating in his first issue what would later become more obvious, Rind hinted that he was particularly "free" from the influence of Tories, and highly receptive to patriot viewpoints. In publishing a piece of propaganda put out by the local Sons of Liberty, he also printed their monitory suggestion that by so doing he would give "an early Instance" of his determination to conduct his press with due respect for principles of freedom.[77]

One further indication of a new trade ethic came in 1774, when John Holt chose to respond to accusations in Rivington's *Gazetteer* that the fiery partisanship of his *New-York Journal* was "a flagrant perversion" of "Liberty of the Press." Was he a biased printer, "wholly employed in prosecuting Party Designs"? Holt's reply was not strictly a denial. He was indeed trying "to make the people in general sensible of their just Rights," and to warn them of "the great Danger of losing them." Had he sold himself to those able to offer the most? The ministry, noted Holt, "could bid higher than any Body else, nor are they without Mercenaries even more contemptible than myself"—a jab at Rivington. If "the Public in general" was what the words "highest Bidder" meant, added Holt, then to be sure he was guilty as charged. In fact, just re-

[76] *Pennsylvania Journal*, Sept. 11, 1766, and see John William Wallace, *An Old Philadelphian: Colonel William Bradford, the Patriot Printer of 1776* (Philadelphia, 1884), chap. 13.

[77] Thomas, *History of Printing*, 2: 146; *Virginia Gazette* (Purdie), Mar. 28, Nov. 6, 1766; Schlesinger, *Prelude to Independence*, p. 79; *Virginia Gazette* (Rind), May 16, 1766.

cently his patriot editorial line had brought the *Journal* more than 200 new subscribers. Nevertheless, unwilling to leave the subject on that note of self-interest, Holt proceeded to emphasize a different set of motives; he was himself personally devoted to the American cause. "In short," he concluded, "I have endeavoured to propagate such political Principles . . . as I shall always freely risk my Life to defend." Disingenuous or not, this was a statement that would have been unthinkable for a colonial printer before the Revolutionary era.[78]

Although the old standards and assumptions of the colonial printing fraternity were losing their force, the process of change was uneven and individuals pursued unclear or contradictory objectives. An instructive case is that of Isaiah Thomas, whose original contribution to the American cause was neither prompt nor enthusiastic. Recalling the first appearance of his *Massachusetts Spy* in 1770, he later explained that he had intended the Boston paper to "be free to both parties, which then agitated the country, and, impartially, lay before the public their respective communications." He soon found, however, that "this ground could not be maintained" in the passionate atmosphere of the period. For a few weeks, in accordance with a policy of "openness" proclaimed in its masthead, the *Spy* published some opinion favorable to the claims of the mother country, but not enough to satisfy hard-line Tories in the vicinity. As a result, they turned against Thomas, boycotted his paper, and used the powers of imperial officialdom to harass him. Supported by John Hancock, Joseph Greenleaf, and others whose politics were warm, Thomas with reluctance converted the *Spy* into a stridently one-sided organ of opinion. In "a general commotion of the state," one of his correspondents observed in 1771, "there should be *no neuters*." Though unavoidable and seemingly much to the advantage of the *Spy*, the circulation of which soon exceeded that of any other New England paper, this policy was not altogether to Thomas's liking. The next year, he contemplated abandoning the high road of patriotism in Boston and moving to the West Indies. Because a printer in Boston "must be either of one party or the other (he cannot please both)," he wrote to an acquaintance in Bermuda, "he must therefore incur the censure and displeasure of the opposite party." And "to incur the censure and displeasure of any party or persons, though carressed and encouraged by others," he added, "is disagreeable to me."[79]

Very gradually, despite such uncertainties of purpose and practice, there arose from the Revolutionary experience a revised understanding of what it was to be an American printer. Responding to and perhaps also promoting a new belief that sharply antagonistic opinions might properly be articulated in the public forum, printers in America began to discard their neutral trade rhetoric, in order to behave aggressively and unapologetically as partisans. At the same time, reflecting the more intense ideological content of Revolutionary politics, American printers began to revive the ancient trade refrain of their English forebears. Once again it was insisted that printers were not mere "mechanics" but men of independent intellect and principle.[80]

[78]*Rivington's New-York Gazetteer*, Aug. 11, 1774; *New-York Journal*, Aug. 18, 1774.

[79]Thomas, *History of Printing*, 1: 378–79, 2: 250; Buckingham, *Specimens of Newspaper Literature*, 1: 232–33; William Coolidge Lane, "The Printer of the Harvard Theses of 1771," *Publications of the Colonial Society of Massachusetts* 26 (1924–26): 9; Thomas to (Joseph Dill?), Mar. 18, 1772, Isaiah Thomas Papers, American Antiquarian Society, Worcester, Mass.; Clifford K. Shipton, *Isaiah Thomas: Printer, Patriot, and Philanthropist, 1749–1831* (Rochester, N.Y., 1948), chap. 2.

[80]How gradual and uncertain the process of change would be is evident from Dwight L. Teeter, Jr., "Decent Animadversions: Notes Toward a History of Free Press Theory," in Bond and McLeod, eds., *Newsletters to Newspapers*, pp. 237–45. Like most Americans for a long time to come, printers were inclined and expected to justify partisanship in terms of the general public interest. It should be

That this new understanding agreed with the spirit of the time is apparent from the response of patriot wits to the conduct of printers who sided with the mother country. Whether or not their motives were any more mercenary than those of their patriot brethren, Tory printers could not devise a rationale for their business strategies that drew effectively on the prevailing popular creed of "liberty." As one Philadelphian observed in 1774, it was difficult for anyone to print a Tory sentiment without exposing himself to the charge that he had been subsidized by the Treasury in London. Rivington, in particular, was the object of vicious diatribe. He was "not actuated by any Principles" but worked simply as "a tool" of officialdom, in implicit contrast to dedicated patriot printers. "I am . . . literally hired"—so went one parody of his position—"to wage open war with Truth, Honour and Justice." According to a "MIRROR for a PRINTER," submitted in 1774 to John Holt's *Journal* by an anonymous local poet, Rivington operated

> Without one grain of *honest* sense,
> One virtuous view, or *just* pretence
> To patriotic flame;
> Without a patriotic heart or mind.[81]

Most vulnerable to such satire were those Tory printers who, loath to go into exile, managed to rehabilitate themselves after their cause had failed. Rivington was perhaps acting as a double-spy by 1781, whereby he may have earned permission to remain in New York and carry on his trade after the war. By means of skillful but less desperate footwork, Hugh Gaine was able to rescue his reputation and stay on. Elsewhere, Georgia's James Johnston and Pennsylvania's Benjamin Towne were also able to negotiate abrupt reversals. Towne's political loyalties were more spectacularly erratic than those of any other colonial printer. Originally associated with Joseph Galloway and his friends, he later became a stout Whig and drove James Humphreys, Jr., from Philadelphia by prematurely branding him a Tory. Once British troops had taken over the city, Towne switched sides—and was promptly attainted as a traitor by the patriots. After Philadelphia had been retaken, he changed his colors again, and succeeded in escaping prosecution.[82]

New York's two outstanding examples of unpunished fickleness inspired Philip Freneau to compose biting doggerel. "As matters have gone," he had Hugh Gaine say of his initial decision to join the Tories,

> it was plainly a blunder,
> But *then* I expected the whigs must knock under,
> And I always adhere to the sword that is
> longest,
> And stick to the party that's like to be strongest.

A comparable calculation underlay Rivington's subsequent desertion of King George:

> On the very same day that his army went hence,
> I ceas'd to tell lies for the sake of his pence;
> And what was the reason—the true one is best;
> I worship no suns that decline to the west;
> In this I resemble a Turk or a Moor,
> The day star ascending I prostrate adore.[83]

understood, of course, that printers were not the only occupational group to show the effects of politicization during the years of Revolutionary crisis; see, for example, Charles S. Olton, *Artisans for Independence: Philadelphia Mechanics and the American Revolution* (Syracuse, N.Y., 1975). As custodians of the press, however, their trade response to Revolutionary conditions had unique impact on the nature of American public discourse.

[81] *Rivington's New-York Gazetteer*, Sept. 2, 1774; "To the Publick" (New York, Nov. 16, 1774); *Pennsylvania Journal*, Mar. 8, 1775; *New-York Journal*, Sept. 15, 1774.

[82] Charles M. Thomas, "The Publication of Newspapers during the American Revolution," *Journalism Quarterly* 9 (1932): 372; Catherine Snell Crary, "The Tory and the Spy: The Double Life of James Rivington," *William and Mary Quarterly*, 3d ser. 16 (1959): 61–72; *Journals of Hugh Gaine*, I: 63–64; Lawrence, *James Johnston*, pp. 24–27; Dwight L. Teeter, Jr., "Benjamin Towne: The Precarious Career of a Persistent Printer," *Pennsylvania Magazine of History and Biography* 89 (1965): 316–24.

[83] Freneau's poems are reproduced in Thomas, *History of Printing*, 2: 483–95.

Lack of principle, it seems, was the major offense committed by these two men, and the charge itself was a sign that expectations concerning the responsibilities of American printers were being reshaped by the Revolutionary conflict.

This change was revealed strikingly in John Witherspoon's prose satire upon Benjamin Towne's last political conversion. Towne's conduct, according to Witherspoon, was due to nothing more than "desire for gain," since he was utterly indifferent to the content of what he published. "I never was, nor ever pretended to be a man of character, repute or dignity," conceded Witherspoon's lampoon version of the capricious Philadelphia printer. Echoing a pre-Revolutionary formula of the American trade, Witherspoon had Towne explain that he was "neither Whig nor Tory, but a printer."[84] The disarmingly self-deprecatory style of Franklin's "Apology" had become the stuff of satire.

There would still be printers—New Jersey's Isaac Collins, for one—who continued to follow the traditional strategy, claiming that they hoped to please as many people as possible even during the most heated political struggles. For some, on the other hand, it became almost obligatory to assert their own principles. In 1770, when William Goddard wrote and published a lengthy defense of his stormy partnership with Joseph Galloway and Thomas Wharton, the old role and the new were balanced uneasily. In 1766, soon after printing an emphatically patriot *Constitutional Courant* in Woodbridge, New Jersey, Goddard had showed up in Philadelphia—"on speculation," as he put it. As it turned out, he was "misled" by Galloway's promises of support into forming an unnatural alliance with men whom he later came to regard as "enemies to their country." Explaining his decision to strike out on a more independent path, Goddard relied in part on trade custom. It was his policy, he said, to act "in the most impartial and just manner" in order to promote his own interest "without becoming a party in any disputes." Being implacable party men, Galloway and Wharton would not permit their printer to be true to the traditions of his craft. At the same time, Goddard offered another, less conventional apology for quarreling with his employers. Against Galloway's wishes, he had printed Dickinson's *Farmer's Letters* because he thought "they deserved the serious attention of all *North-America*." Apparently this initiative took his partners by surprise. "Mr. *Galloway*," Goddard remembered, "ridiculed my notions about liberty and the rights of mankind."[85]

Such ridicule was understandable enough. Unlike the European founders of their craft, printers in colonial America had neither professed nor been expected to have notions of any sort; they were supposed to make and sell their product indifferently, to suit this or that customer. During and after the Revolution, expectations came to differ. It was in the war years, for example, that the printer of Hartford's *Courant*, George Goodwin, first explicitly identified himself as an "editor." In Massachusetts, glossing over his reluctance to deviate from neutral trade policies, Isaiah Thomas subsequently insisted that he had given the *Spy* "a fixed character" consistent with his own patriot beliefs.[86]

In 1785, when the state of Massachusetts attempted to raise a revenue for itself by imposing stamp duties, the printing trade was piously indignant. The new tax, it was said, would lead to "the ruin of a set of artisans" whose exertions

[84]Ibid., pp. 453–58: "The Humble Confession, Declaration, Recantation, and Apology of Benjamin Towne, Printer in Philadelphia."

[85]Richard F. Hixson, *Isaac Collins: A Quaker Printer in Eighteenth-Century America* (New Brunswick, N.J., 1968), pp. 97–98; William Goddard, *The Partnership: or the History of the Rise and Progress of the Pennsylvania Chronicle &c* (Philadelphia, 1770), pp. 5, 17, 8–9, 16, and see generally Miner, *William Goddard*, chaps. 4–5, 7.

[86]J. Eugene Smith, *One Hundred Years of Hartford's Courant* (New Haven, 1949), p. 15; Thomas, *History of Printing*, 1: 379.

in the Revolutionary movement should have guaranteed them "a more liberal fate." Thomas's paper registered special outrage. "Generous Reader," it made a point of stressing, "the services rendered by the SPY to the Publick, were not for the sake of sordid gain, but from *Principle*."[87]

Late in the century, Benjamin Edes—a former Son of Liberty—would conjure up an image of himself standing forth as "an undaunted Centinel in those times which 'tried men's souls' . . . , when the hope of gain could not be considered as the lure to pretended Patriotism." However self-serving, his words did reflect the new rhetoric of ideological commitment that had entered the trade during the Revolutionary years. With that commitment went pride. The newspapers of colonial America, John Holt told Samuel Adams in 1776, had first received "Notice of the tyrannical Designs formed against America," and generated a response "sufficient to repel them."[88]

When Virginia's Governor Dunmore seized the patriot Norfolk press of John Holt's son, in 1775, there was an appropriate echo of the past in the words with which he justified the action. Thus would be suppressed "the means of poisoning the minds of the people," and arousing "the spirit of rebellion and sedition."[89] More than 100 years had passed since Governor Berkeley had warned of the disastrous consequences that would accompany the introduction of printing into Virginia. Alarmist as Berkeley's reaction had been, it had pointed to a distant future. For much of the eighteenth century American printers had followed business and political strategies that impeded the flow of diverse and dissident opinion into the public forum. But during the Revolutionary years the trade adapted to a new politics of controversy. By so doing, printers seemed assured of recognition as major figures in the political life of the republic. Presiding over a press transformed by the pressures of the Revolution, they would be free to report basic conflicts and disputes as well as remote "occurrences"; they would be expected not only to register events but to make and modify them.

6. '76 in Retrospect

Long after Independence, as the machinery of the new American party system came to be elaborated at both national and state levels, printers continued to express satisfaction at the expanding importance of the press. Newspapers "exert a controlling influence on public opinion, and decide almost all questions of a public nature," boasted one Boston printer before a gathering of his brethren in the third decade of the new century. Partisan journalism was a well-established feature of American politics.[90]

Undeniably powerful as the press had become, however, this was not to say that nineteenth-century American printers had succeeded in realizing the promise of the role fashioned for them during the Revolutionary years. Gradually, in a sequence of developments that in some respects resembled what had happened to the London trade more than a century before, printers in republican America had to withdraw from entrepreneurial activities previously associated with their craft skills. The

[87]Duniway, *Development of Freedom of the Press*, p. 136n; Buckingham, *Specimens of Newspaper Literature*, I: 241–42.

[88]Rollo G. Silver, "Benjamin Edes, Trumpeter of Sedition," *Papers of the Bibliographical Society of America* 47 (1953): 265; Holt to Adams, Jan. 29, 1776, in Victor Hugo Paltsits, *John Holt, Printer and Postmaster, Some Facts and Documents Relating to His Career* (New York, 1920), pp. 10–15.

[89]Paltsits, *John Holt*, p. 10.

[90]Jefferson Clark, *Address Delivered at the Anniversary Celebration of the Franklin Typographical Society* (Boston, 1826), p. 14. On the development of partisan journalism at the beginning of the nineteenth century, see generally Donald H. Stewart, *The Opposition Press of the Federalist Period* (Albany, N.Y., 1969), chap. 1.

trend in American publishing—accelerated by the introduction of costly new technology that opened up larger markets—was toward specialization. A "publisher" with capital would hire printers and others to produce the goods he wished to sell.[91] An exceptionally enterprising printer like Isaiah Thomas could count himself among the ranks of leading publishers, much as the London printer William Strahan had done in the eighteenth century, by investing capital in copyright and book production. But it soon came to appear that only in the "yet almost uncorrupted West" could the average printer still realistically plan to build the diversified business and act the prominent part in his community characteristic of the trade in colonial days. So, early in the century, one New Yorker with "utopian expectations" reportedly resolved to go west "to give elevation to the art of Printing." Remaining in the settled sections of the country, a printer might well have to relinquish his hopes of becoming a publisher as well.[92]

From the perspective of most printers, unprepared and unwilling to adjust to such changes, the conditions of the trade had deteriorated alarmingly. Like other artisans of the period, they turned to verse and song at their fraternal gatherings to share and perhaps alleviate their experiences of hardship. Pervading the folklore of post-Revolutionary American printers, whose "sorrows, sufferings, cares and strife" followed them "like their shadows . . . through life," was a bitter sense of economic ruin. "Sheriff," went one seriocomic poem,

> . . . spare that press;
> Touch not a single type;
> Don't put me in distress,
> To stick to me through life.
>
> 'Tis all in all to me;
> If lost, what shall I do?
> Then why not let it be,
> Oh, sheriff, boo hoo hoo.[93]

For journeymen, grievances multiplied early in the century and soon prompted organized protest. Their wages were said to be lagging behind those of other mechanics; new machinery seemed to threaten some jobs, while employers tried to cut costs by hiring foreign or inadequately trained native labor. According to one estimate of 1809, the situation in New York was so bleak that nearly half of those who completed their apprenticeships as printers were forced eventually to abandon their trade altogether and look for other kinds of work. Chief among the villains, as journeymen in Philadelphia viewed matters about the same time, were "the gang of pettifogging master printers," whose dedication to the welfare of the trade as a whole was appreciably less heartfelt than their individual desires for gain.[94]

Over time, the intensity of this particular antagonism seems to have subsided, to be replaced by a broader range of complaint with which many employers as well as employees in the trade could sympathize. Again and again, most regularly in the 1830s, public expressions of protest focused not on exploitation of journeymen by master printers but on exploitation of the entire craft by outside entrepreneurs. Such people, "speculating on the labor of print-

[91]See, for example, Rollo G. Silver, *The American Printer, 1787–1825* (Charlottesville, 1967), pp. 40–62; Milton W. Hamilton, *The Country Printer, New York State, 1785–1830* (New York, 1936), p. 46; Ethelbert Stewart, *A Documentary History of the Early Organizations of Printers* (Indianapolis, 1907), pp. 5–41. Of course, this trend in publishing was one element in a more general process of industrialization that affected other American craftsmen in the first half of the nineteenth century.

[92]Shipton, *Isaiah Thomas,* chap. 4; Stewart, *Documentary History,* p. 134; David Bruce, "Recollections of New York City" (c. 1810), Miscellaneous Manuscripts, New-York Historical Society, New York, N.Y.

[93]Robert S. Coffin, *The Printer and Several Other Poems* (Boston, 1817), p. vii; *A Collection of Songs of the American Press and Other Poems Relating to the Art of Printing,* ed. Charles Munsell (Albany, N.Y., 1868), p. 45.

[94]Stewart, *Documentary History,* pp. 11, 28–29, 43, 21, 14.

ers," were out to reduce everyone in the trade to poverty, according to some contemporaries. Perhaps most damaging to the traditional craft pride of American printers, long accustomed to function as newspaper proprietors, was the appearance of "professional" or "hireling" editors, who worked under contract to entrepreneurial publishers. Usually these new editors were lawyers. By midcentury, it had become rare for a printer in an urban center to edit a paper of his own.[95]

Like their English brethren of a previous era, many American printers in the early nineteenth century declined to accept passively the implications of the new economic order. Summoning up legends of learned Europeans in the trade, they began to affirm with an insistence unknown before in America that printers had contributed significantly and uniquely to the progress of western civilization. The art of printing, according to one of its New York practitioners in 1801, "is the parent of every other"—"an Art, the adoption of which has, in some degree, banished baleful superstition from the world, and in its stead reason and philosophy have found sanctuary in the mind of man." Another New York printer some years later called it "an art truly divine," without which the human intellect forever "might have slumbered in the lap of ignorance."[96]

The irony beneath this fulsome oratory, applied specifically to the situation of American printers, was obliquely acknowledged in the wordplay of one printer's song:

> Though I'm not skill'd in Greek or Latin lore,
> Nor ancient Hebrew in days of yore,
> With due submission I inform my betters,
> That I can boast I am a man of *letters*.

But others in the trade were less inclined to admit so humorously the discrepancy between their intellectual aspirations and reality. In the glorious career of Benjamin Franklin, above all, they found inspiration. As one printer in Boston chose to interpret the biographical facts, Franklin had made of printing "the instrument of his own fame," rising through his craft to become "a scholar, statesman, and philosopher." Despite discouraging trade conditions, Franklin's successors had only to follow in his footsteps to redeem their fraternal heritage. "The next in rank," continued the same Boston printer, ". . . is ISAIAH THOMAS."[97]

Thomas, indeed, emulated "learned" European predecessors not only by writing his *History* but by founding the American Antiquarian Society. His natural successor was Boston's Joseph Buckingham, whose career epitomized the post-Revolutionary sensibilities of the trade. Born just a few years after Independence, he had been impressed as a young man with the "dignity and importance" of printing a newspaper, and so determined to learn the craft. Like Franklin, he read voraciously, stressing grammar in his self-education. "I foresaw that it would be useful to me, as a printer," he later explained, "but indispensable as an editor,—a profession, to which I looked forward as the consummation of my ambition." From the beginning, he recalled, "I found it difficult to repress my aspirations to display my intellectual as well as my industrial and mechanical abilities." Eventually, having satisfied himself by building a reputation as a journalist with a mind of his own, he assumed "the character and pursuits of a scholar" to edit a sequel to Thomas's *History*, a two-volume historical anthology called *Specimens of Newspaper Literature*, published in 1850.[98]

[95]Ibid., pp. 59 and n, 131–32; Hamilton, *Country Printer*, pp. 150–51.

[96]John Clough, *An Address . . . before the Franklin Typographical Association* (New York, 1801), pp. 10–11; Adoniram Chandler, *An Oration, Delivered before the New-York Typographical Society* (New York, 1816), p. 9.

[97]*Collection of Songs of the American Press*, p. 113; John Russell, *An Address, Presented to the Members of the Faustus Association* (Boston, 1808), pp. 20–21.

[98]Shipton, *Isaiah Thomas*, chap. 6; Thomas, *History of Printing*, 1: 10, had undertaken his chronicle of the trade de-

Other American printers, too, refused to limit their intellectual prerogatives and be demoted to mere mechanics. In 1808, Boston's Society of Printers—of which Buckingham was a leading member—went so far as to change its name to the Faustus Society, because the old name was "too narrow and confined to embrace the higher branches of our profession, which are not *mechanical*, nor bounded by rules, but which soar to improvements as valuable to science and humanity as those which have immortalized the discovery of Faustus." The New-York Typographical Society, for its part, included men of recognizable "intellectual, moral, and social worth," not least its one-time president Peter Force, later an active antiquarian and editor of historical documents.[99]

"I have heard old journeymen claim that it was a Profession," William Dean Howells wrote of printing at the very end of the century, "and ought to rank with the learned professions." Himself the son of a printer, Howells remembered well one youth who had entered his father's shop "with the wish to be a printer because Franklin had been one, and with the intent of making the office his University." Such purposefulness may not have been uncommon in the nineteenth-century trade. "Let it not be to any a subject of special wonder," announced the preface to a mid-century collection of literature written by printers, "that they who have so often assisted in ushering into the world the productions of others should now in turn venture to originate ideas of their own, and appear before the public in the ambitious character of Authors." In fact, several of the century's most distinguished American writers—Walt Whitman and Mark Twain as well as Howells among them—had worked as young men in printing shops.[100]

Some notable political personalities, too, began their careers as members of the trade, often entering politics through journalism. "Printers should never lose sight of the dignity of their profession," observed a member of the fraternity, "for the most eminent men have embraced it." One was the Republican politician Thurlow Weed, who made a point in his memoirs of emphasizing that several of his journeymen acquaintances in the trade had been endowed with "decided literary taste and acquirements." Another was Horace Greeley, for whom entry into the trade had marked the beginning of his escape from the *"mindless monotonous drudgery"* of farming. Governors, legislators, diplomats, mayors—printers were pleased to record that among their brethren were occupants of the highest offices in the land.[101]

These of course were uncommon men, but ordinary printers could and did also claim a place of special importance in public life. Out of their Revolutionary heritage, they tried to assert a role less prominent but perhaps ultimately more rewarding. "Among the gloriously congenial effects, produced by the ART OF PRINTING," declaimed a patriotic speaker in 1802 at the Boston Franklin Association, "no one is so conspicuous on the roll of fame, as the FOURTH OF JULY, 1776!" Throughout the early decades of the nineteenth century, similar

spite a feeling that the task might have been better performed by "some person distinguished for literature." Joseph T. Buckingham, *Personal Memoirs and Recollections of Editorial Life*, 2 vols. (Boston, 1852), 1: 21, 27–28, 53.

[99]Silver, *American Printer*, p. 88; *Autobiography of Thurlow Weed*, ed. Harriet A. Weed (Boston, 1883), p. 58.

[100]William Dean Howells, *The Country Printer* (Norwood, Mass., 1919), p. 36; *Voices of the Press; A Collection of Sketches, Essays, and Poems, by Practical Printers*, ed. James J. Brenton (New York, 1850), p. iii. The link between printing and authorship remained, of course, journalism; see S.M. Lipset, M.A. Trow, and J.S. Coleman, *Union Democracy: The Internal Politics of the International Typographical Union* (Glencoe, Ill., 1956), pp. 29–30, where the role of printers editing the modern labor press is noted.

[101]Charles Turrell, "Longevity of American Printers," in *The Typographical Miscellany*, ed. Joel Munsell (Albany, N.Y., 1850), pp. 82–83; *Autobiography of Thurlow Weed*, p. 44; Horace Greeley, *Recollections of a Busy Life* (New York, 1868), pp. 60–61.

sentiments were repeatedly expressed by printers before assemblages of their brethren. According to the prize-winning ode at a July 4th celebration of the New-York Typographical Society in 1811,

> . . . Heaven decreed
> That Columbia be freed,
> And *Printing* and valour accomplish'd the deed.
> The banner of war was by Justice unfurl'd,
> And Freedom by Printing proclaim'd to the
> world.[102]

It was in this self-congratulatory spirit that at one banquet of printers a toast was offered to the Declaration of Independence—"From the *"Press* of Franklin and Company." As late as 1834, a grandson of the famed patriot printer William Bradford III could argue feelingly that his father, the printer Thomas Bradford, was entitled to a Revolutionary war pension because publication of the *Pennsylvania Journal* had been *"of more value to the cause of American freedom than if he had for six years commanded a regiment in the field."* Isaiah Thomas probably did more than anyone else to sustain such affirmations, having labored over his hagiographical *History* to demonstrate as fully as possible that the press "had a powerful influence in producing the revolution."[103]

Faithful to the relatively recent political traditions of the trade, it was understandable if a printer in the new republic should want to refer hyperbolically to the press as "one of the most deadly engines of destruction that can possibly be arrayed against the encroachments of despotic power." Especially in America, where newspapers were so widespread as to be considered among "the necessaries of life," printers had awesome public responsibilities. Since a "free press" was "the people's surest safeguard," it was vitally important for printers to "support the right, and wrong attack"—and "tweak the despot's nose."[104]

As custodians of the public welfare, too, printers could hope to make an unusually forceful case in protesting the very economic conditions that had conspired to diminish their livelihoods and undermine their social standing. The narrow interests of the trade, it seemed, were linked to the well-being of the larger American public. For if printers were the "natural guardians" of a free press, it was their duty as citizens and the duty of the general citizenry as well to resist usurpation by "hireling editors," subservient to combinations of wealthy individuals. To retain control of the press, thereby preserving its integrity, would require of printers much the same degree of "jealous regard and sleepless vigilance" that had marked their Revolutionary forebears—the generation memorialized by Isaiah Thomas.[105]

Appropriately, "independence" was a key word in the vocabulary of socioeconomic complaint by printers in early nineteenth-century America. As with other struggling mechanics at the time, *independence* signified desirable conditions of work and unoppressive structures of economic life; most emphatically for printers, the word also brought to mind crucial political experiences of a previous era. In 1826, at the Franklin Typographical Society in Boston, current aspirations and historical memories mingled revealingly in an elaborate toast:

> *Getting under weigh*—the good ship *Typographical*, Captain *Franklin*, with a *true hearted crew*, *bound on a voyage* of *charity*, *sailing* in the *current*

[102]William Burdick, *An Oration on the Nature and Effects of the Art of Printing* (Boston, 1802), p. 20; Asbridge, *Oration*, p. 26. Other groups of mechanics continued to celebrate the Revolution, but without as specific a sense of participation; see Howard B. Rock, "The American Revolution and the Mechanics of New York City: One Generation Later," *New York History* 52 (1976): 367–82. The 4th of July, of course, was the favored occasion for expressing such sentiments.

[103]Clark, *Address*, p. 21; Thomas Bradford, Jr., to Samuel McKean, May 7, 1834, Bradford Manuscripts, Historical Society of Pennsylvania, Philadelphia; Thomas, *History of Printing*, 1: 15.

[104]Asbridge, *Oration*, p. 12; Clark, *Address*, p. 14; *Collection of Songs of the American Press*, p. 21.

[105]Stewart, *Documentary History*, pp. 147–48.

> *of public opinion,* with *favourable breezes,* and taking the correct *course* of *truth, honesty,* and *sobriety;* keeping out of the *calm latitudes* of *idleness* and *gulph* of *intemperance;* avoiding the *rocks* of *dissipation; steering clear* of the *shoals* of *poverty,* and *touching* at the *port* of *benevolence,* may she *finally arrive* in *safety,* in the *harbour* of INDEPENDENCE.[106]

They have been called "intellectuals of the working class." Whatever the merits of that designation, printers in early nineteenth-century Europe joined the ideological vanguard of the first workingmen's movements. That this was so in America as well, despite the bland politics of the eighteenth-century trade, reflected the strong impact of the Revolution upon their occupational identity.[107]

Historical ironies aside, which might have been grimly pleasurable to a loyalist like Peter Oliver, it was peculiarly fitting that in 1856 the 150th anniversary of Benjamin Franklin's birth should have been celebrated in the city of Boston by a huge self-assertive parade of patriotic mechanics, in which the printing fraternity was separated from most other groups of mechanics by being designated as one of the "mechanical professions."[108] Franklin himself had been more of a mechanic than sometimes he had cared to admit, and less of a Revolutionary; for American printers by the middle of the nineteenth century, the meaning of both experiences had been redefined, and fused symbolically in his name.

[106]Clark, *Address,* p. 22. On the relationship of the American and Industrial Revolutions, see generally Alan Dawley, *Class and Community: The Industrial Revolution in Lynn* (Cambridge, Mass., 1976).

[107]Lipset et al., *Union Democracy,* p. 30.

[108]*Memorial of the Inauguration of the Statue of Franklin* (Boston, 1857), pp. 146–87.

Public Opinion and the Press

Jeffery A. Smith

When the United States Constitution was offered for ratification, many Americans reacted with alarm to the absence of a bill of rights and, in particular, to the lack of an explicit guarantee for liberty of the press. In New York a newspaper essayist insisted the proposed document would end journalistic freedom entirely and thereby "give our new masters an opportunity to rivet our fetters the more effectually."[1] In Philadelphia, "John Humble" told readers of the *Independent Gazetteer* that they could renounce all claim to the right forever and would have to "be perfectly contented if our *tongues* be left us to lick the feet of our well born masters."[2] Another Philadelphian, "Centinel," observed that designing and tyrannical men "have ever been inimical to the press, and have considered the shackling of it, as the first step towards the accomplishment of their hateful domination."[3]

In the final week of the Constitutional Convention, none of the states had voted in favor of a motion to form a committee to prepare a bill of rights. A motion was then made to insert a declaration "that the liberty of the Press should be inviolably observed," but it failed seven states to four.[4] After voicing fears about the powers given to the federal government and the dearth of explicit protections for civil liberties, several delegates refused to sign the document. Similar doubts were expressed as the states began ratifying the Constitution. The Antifederalists were assured that the national government would not have the authority to suppress basic freedoms and that to list some liberties would imply that others were not protected. Prominent Federalists initially depicted the movement for a bill of rights as demagoguery, but the demands grew more compelling. The ratifying conventions of key states demanded a bill of rights and three of the most populous—Virginia, New York, and North Carolina—specifically requested a press guarantee.[5]

The Federalists accordingly found themselves in retreat on the issue. Alexander Hamilton asked the readers of the *Federalist* how press freedom could be defined in a way that could not be evaded. He argued that "its security, whatever fine declarations may be inserted in any constitution respecting it, must altogether depend on public opinion, and on the general spirit of the people and of the government."[6] Reacting to Thomas Jefferson's desire for a federal bill of rights with a press guarantee, James Madison observed that such protections, while desirable, had proven to be mere "parchment barriers" in state constitutions. "The restrictions however strongly marked on paper will never be regarded when opposed to the decided sense of the public," he wrote, "and after repeated violations in extraordinary cases they will lose even their ordinary efficacy."[7] With prodding from Jefferson and eventually from voters when he ran for a seat in the House of Representatives, Madison altered his position and proposed a bill of rights in the First Congress. The Bill of Rights approved by Congress—with its guarantee for the press— was ratified in the states with little recorded debate.[8]

The press clause of the First Amendment was thus added to the Constitution not only because of a strong desire to preserve journalistic rights, but also with serious doubts about the willingness of the public to support freedom of expression. Historians have, in fact, found ample evidence of unfavorable attitudes toward journalists in eighteenth-century America. In his study of revolutionary-era newspapers, Arthur Schlesinger, Sr., considered the treatment of loyalist writers and concluded that the patriots "simply contended that liberty of speech belonged solely to those who spoke the speech of liberty."[9] In a survey of freedom of expression cases in early America, Leonard W. Levy has gone as far as to maintain that the idea colonists cherished freedom of expression "is an hallucination of sentiment that ignores history."[10] Schlesinger examined a period in which a revolutionary rather than a libertarian theory of the press might be expected to prevail temporarily[11] and Levy has admitted that journalists were more free in practice than he once thought,[12] but the work of both scholars does point out that public opinion—at least as displayed in particular incidents—could be intolerant when sensitive religious or political convictions were challenged.[13]

Instances of popular adherence to liberty of the press were, however, at least as striking and as common. Although personal and political emotions sometimes ran deeper than a commitment to the right, press freedom was regularly and dramatically defended in public displays of support. The demand for a press guarantee was preceded by a century and a half of popular demonstrations for writers and journalists in England and America. The support may have been neither universal nor based exclusively in selfless devotion to liberty, but it did appear at critical junctures and made the press difficult if not impossible for government to control. Thus, by the end of the eighteenth century, James Madison was able to condemn the Sedition Act of 1798 by observing that the "freedom exercised by the press and protected by public opinion" had far exceeded the limitations of the common law in England and the United States, that the meaning of press freedom had been established in its vigorous practice rather than in outmoded precedents.[14]

I

The Americans who insisted on the press clause were familiar with the long history of the British government's attempts to suppress publications and with the equally long history of popular efforts to defeat such exercises of authority. At the beginning of the English Revolution, the Long Parliament released three Puritan pamphleteers from prison. William Prynne, Henry Burton, and John Bastwick were subsequently cheered by London crowds exasperated at the "personal rule" of Charles I and the religious innovations of Bishop Laud. Ten thousand persons met Prynne and Burton as they entered the city and had flowers and herbs strewn in their path. Bastwick was given a similar reception.[15] Three years earlier, in 1637, the Star Chamber had found the three guilty of seditiously libeling the church hierarchy and sentenced them to lose their ears in the pillory, to be fined £5,000, and to be imprisoned for life.[16] The case was periodically recalled by writers advocating freedom of expression. An essay published in the *Boston Gazette* in 1755 suggested that the true cause of the English Revolution was suppression of the press and that "had not *Prynne* lost his *Ears*, K. *Charles* would have never lost his Head."[17]

Prynne's punishment was not so portentous an event, but a seditious libel case in 1688 was closely tied to the downfall of James II in the Glorious Revolution. Apprehensive that the king was attempting to propagate Roman Catholicism, the archbishop of Canterbury and six other bishops presented him with a petition questioning his authority in religious matters. The seven bishops were tried for seditious libel, but were acquitted by the jury.[18] Shouts of approval resounded through the courtroom, church bells rang, and bonfires were lighted as the news spread. That evening, seven prominent Englishmen, who represented a wide spectrum of opposition to James, met and dispatched a letter to William of Orange inviting him to land an army in England. The invitation was accepted, James fled to France, and Parliament reached a settlement which gave the crown to William and Mary.[19]

The specific actions taken on behalf of the three Puritans and the seven Anglican bishops may have been more political and religious statements than calculated efforts to champion freedom of expression, but reasoned justifications for the right were being made in the seventeenth century. During the English Revolution, pamphlets began to appear which argued for expanded liberty of the press. The most powerful and lasting of these was John Milton's classic *Areopagitica*.[20] By the time of the Glorious Revolution, support was beginning to emerge in government. Two of the four judges who presided at the trial of the bishops took the position that any writing critical of authority could be punished, but Justice Holloway stated that every subject had a right to petition and Justice Powell told the jury that the king's attorney had not shown that the writing was false, malicious, or seditious and therefore a libel.[21] In 1694 the House of Commons refused to renew the Regulation of Printing Act which had required licensing of the press. In 1695 the Commons voted to approve a statement prepared by John Locke which described the licensing system as arbitrary, unjust, and oppressive.[22]

In eighteenth-century England, juries repeatedly showed their willingness to frustrate seditious libel prosecutions. In 1729 a jury acquitted Richard Francklin, the printer of Bolingbroke's opposition organ, *The Craftsman*. It took the seating of a "special jury" packed against Francklin to obtain a conviction in 1731.[23] The periodical *The Political State of Great-Britain* reported that a "vast Crowd of Spectators of all Ranks and Conditions" gathered around Westminster Hall for preliminary proceedings in the second trial and that when William Pulteney, one of the *Craftsman*'s patrons, left the court he was "loudly huzza'd by the Populace" outside. "Which," the journal concluded, "shews the Fondness of the People of *England* for the Liberty of the Press."[24]

At the next major seditious libel trial in England, that of bookseller William Owen in 1752, the jury ignored the judge's instructions and found the defendant not guilty. A cheer rang out and the participants began leaving the courtroom. The jury members were called back, however, and questioned on their verdict, but they would only repeat it without comment. "Upon which the Court broke up; and there was a prodigious shout in the hall," said the report of the trial. "The attorney-general desired more questions might be asked, but the judge would not, nor would the noise permit it."[25]

Rioting over a dozen years by supporters of John Wilkes was another indication of public sentiment in favor of a right to publish. In the spring of 1763, Wilkes was promoting and consciously testing press freedom as he used the pages of his paper, the *North Briton*, to attack the policies of the king's favorite, the Earl of Bute. When Wilkes took aim at George III himself in the *North Briton* No. 45, a general warrant was issued to apprehend the authors, printers, and publishers of the paper. The arrest of Wilkes and dozens of others prompted mass demonstrations in London. Released on a writ of habeas corpus, Wilkes joined some of those charged in successfully challenging the legality of general warrants and convincing juries in a series of cases that they were entitled to damages for wrongful arrest and seizure of papers. The episode may have cost the government as much as £100,000. Wilkes himself was awarded £1,000.[26]

Enough votes were found in the two houses of Parliament late in 1763 to declare the *North Briton* No. 45 a seditious libel and to order that it be burned by the common hangman. A mob of more than 500 persons met the hangman, however, and retrieved the copy intended for the flames. Two sheriffs were showered with dirt and wood and one had his coach smashed.[27] Wounded in a duel with a political adversary, Wilkes left England for the safety of France, but neither his supporters nor his opponents would let matters rest. Early in 1764, Wilkes was expelled from his seat in the House of Commons and convicted *in absentia* of seditious libel by the Court of the King's Bench.[28] One of the publishers of No. 45, John Williams, was tried in July and later sentenced to the pillory, a fine, and six months in prison. As more than 10,000 people watched the pillorying, elaborate demonstrations were staged against the government, more than £200 was collected for the printer, and slogans were shouted for Wilkes and liberty of the press.[29]

Another round of confrontations began when Wilkes returned to England in 1768 and was again elected to Parliament. In a political system where public offices were often obtained through bribery and personal connections, the Wilkes phenomenon bespoke popular disenchantment with the British oligarchy.[30] Crowds celebrated for two days in London and demonstrations took place around the country. Benjamin Franklin, who was in London as a colonial agent, wrote to his son that the city was illuminated for two nights, that coaches and doors were marked with the number 45, and that mobs were requiring passing ladies and gentlemen to shout for Wilkes and liberty. "The damage done and the expence of candles has been computed at £50,000," Franklin noted. "It must have been great, though probably not so much." Wilkes was nevertheless sentenced to 22 months in jail and was fined £1,000 for the earlier libel conviction.[31]

Support for Wilkes, meanwhile, swelled to new proportions. Mobs menaced the prison where he was confined and scattered rioting took place. On May 10, 1768, guards fired into a crowd numbering in the tens of thousands and killed 11 men and women.[32] Among the journalists who took up the Wilkite cause in discussing public affairs and championing freedom of the press was the acerbic, pseudonymous writer who called himself "Junius." Publishers who sold his barbed "Letter to the King" written in 1769 were brought to trial, but obstinate juries thwarted the prosecutions.[33] According to the report of the trial of John Miller, one of the publishers, a "vast" crowd received news of his acquittal with "the loudest huzzas."[34] After his release from prison in 1770, Wilkes and his cohorts managed a successful and sometimes riotous campaign for the freedom of publishers to print the proceedings of the House of Commons.[35] In America, cities and children were named after Wilkes, funds were raised to support his activities, and colonists heading toward revolution toasted him and No. 45.[36]

II

Eighteenth-century Americans did not, of course, have to look across the Atlantic to find patterns for their support of dissenting journalists. Colonial authorities were continually frustrated in their attempts to punish writers and publishers who were critical of their actions. In what may have been America's first criminal trial concerned with press freedom, Pennsylvania printer William Bradford was charged with printing a seditious pamphlet for a Quaker faction led by George Keith. Arrested in 1692, Bradford demanded a jury trial and during the proceedings insisted, contrary to prevailing legal doctrine, that the jurors should not only determine the fact of publication, but should also decide on the law itself. The jury deadlocked and could not reach a verdict.[37] At a second trial, according to one version, Bradford was released after one juror accidentally or on purpose tipped over the frame that held the types being used as evidence.[38] Thomas Maule, a Massachusetts Quaker, similarly asked a jury to decide the law in 1696 after being accused of writing a tract slandering the government and subverting religion. The judge sought a guilty verdict, but Maule was acquitted. The foreman explained that the jury considered the case a religious rather than a civil matter.[39]

Sustained political journalism did not appear in the colonies until Massachusetts writers began debating the merits of paper money and other issues during the administration of Samuel Shute, an inflexible and quarrelsome royal governor determined to have the legislature and press under his control.[40] One of the publishers who risked official displeasure was Benjamin Gray, a Boston bookseller. In 1721 the governor's Council decided that Gray should be prosecuted for publishing a pamphlet decrying the province's currency problems.[41] Gray reacted by advertising that he had "all" recent pamphlets for sale in his shop and by lampooning the Council's action with the publication of another pamphlet, *News from the Moon*.[42]

Enraged by such effrontery, Gov. Shute asked the legislature for a licensing law to use against the "many Factious & Scandalous papers printed, & publickly sold at Boston, highly reflecting upon the Government, & tending to disquiet, the minds of His Majestie's good Subjects."[43] The Council passed "An Act for preventing Libel & Scandalous Pamphlets & punishing the Authors and Publishing thereof,"[44] but the House of Representatives did not concur. Instead the House issued a statement saying that in considering licensing, no one could foresee "the innumerable inconveniencies and dangerous Circumstances this People might Labour under in a little time."[45] Gray's case was brought before a grand jury, but he was not indicted.[46]

Later in 1721, James Franklin began publishing the *New-England Courant* in Boston. The *Courant*'s writers, dubbed the "Hell-Fire Club" by their adversaries, brought a daring and sometimes vicious approach to colonial journalism. With satirical essays on city life, accounts of immorality and improper electioneering, and sharp ridicule of Puritan ministers and government officials, the *Courant* made enemies. Increase Mather issued a statement admonishing the public not to read the "Wicked Paper"[47] and his son Cotton stopped the printer on the street and lectured him on the perils of serving Satan.[48]

In 1722, the two houses of the General Court took notice of the paper's insults and jailed Franklin for a month for breach of legislative privilege, but the lower house refused to agree to a Council measure placing the *Courant* under government censorship.[49] The publisher and his younger brother Benjamin, who edited the paper while James was imprisoned, answered with radical Whig essays on the right and responsibility of the press to expose wrongdoing in government. Upon his release, James Franklin printed letters questioning the legality of the proceedings against him. A mocking front-page poem portrayed an appearance he made before the Council and said:[50]

> And truly 'tis a fatal Omen,
> When Knowledge, which belongs to no Men
> But to the Clergy and the Judges,
> Gets in the Heads of common Drudges.

After further taunting from the *Courant*, the House early in 1723 narrowly approved a measure to place Franklin under prior restraint,[51] but the printer did not comply with the restrictions. Letters to the paper condemned the actions taken against him and recalled the Salem witch trials and the Spanish Inquisition.[52] Franklin's case was eventually brought to a grand jury which did not indict him. The failure to suppress the *New-England Courant* put an end to any realistic hope of formal censorship in Massachusetts.[53]

The *Courant*'s brand of journalism had proven

popular. The paper was able to claim that it had a "far greater " circulation than its two competitors in Boston and was "more generally read by a vast Number of Borrowers" who did not subscribe.[54] Among its supporters was the only colonial newspaper outside of Boston, Philadelphia's *American Weekly Mercury*.[55] At one point in Franklin's tribulations, a Portsmouth reader noted speculation that New Hampshire would prohibit reading the *Courant* because it "sometimes sets for the Rights and Liberties of Mankind." A *Courant* writer responded that if their representatives wanted to enslave them, they should elect better ones. A month later the paper reported that the high sheriff of New Hampshire had seized and burned a copy of the issue with the *Courant*'s reply "fearing it might infect the Inhabitants with a Desire of Liberty."[56]

The most celebrated seditious libel case of the eighteenth century occurred in New York in 1735. Disgusted by Gov. William Cosby's avarice and political indiscretions, a coalition headed by attorney James Alexander used John Peter Zenger's *New-York Journal* to depict the governor as a pompous tyrant and to promote liberty of the press as the means of exposing "the glaring Truths of his ill Administration."[57] Cosby and his minions tried unsuccessfully to obtain the cooperation of grand juries, the Assembly, and the city's Common Council in taking action against the publication. Finally, Zenger was arrested and tried for seditious libel. Defense lawyer Andrew Hamilton of Philadelphia urged the jury to decide the law of the matter and to accept truth as a defense. A verdict in favor of Zenger brought "three Huzzas" to the courtroom. Hamilton was honored with a dinner at the Black Horse Tavern that evening and was saluted by the guns of several ships in the harbor as he departed the next day. The Common Council presented him with the freedom of the city and a gold box purchased with voluntary contributions.[58] Gouverneur Morris later remarked that the Zenger trial was "the germ of American freedom—the morning star of that liberty which subsequently revolutionized America."[59]

Zenger was apparently the last colonial printer to be tried in court on a charge of seditious libel.[60] Subsequent attempts to bring legal actions against journalists were typically met with indignation. In 1747 a Charleston grand jury rejected an anonymous request that Peter Timothy, editor of the *South-Carolina Gazette*, be presented for publishing sarcastic remarks about Gov. James Glen's efforts to enforce Sabbath laws. The eighteen grand jurors signed a statement saying the request was "*destructive* of THE LIBERTY OF THE PRESS, a *Privilege* we *enjoy*, and has been so *justly contended for* by our Ancestors, and we hope *will* be *preserved* to *our latest Posterity*."[61] In 1750 and 1751, attempts were made to indict Timothy for printing a pamphlet critical of the governor's handling of Indian affairs, but both attempts failed.[62]

III

After mid-century, as political debate intensified in America, signs of strain began to appear in public support for the press. Printers sometimes found it necessary to remind irate readers of the value of press freedom. "How common is it to see a Shoemaker, Taylor, or Barber, haranguing with a great deal of Warmth on the publick Affairs?" complained a letter to the *New-York Post-Boy* in 1756. "He will condemn a General, Governor, or Province with as much Assurance as if he were of the Privy Council, and knew exactly wherein they had been faulty:—He gets his Knowledge from the News-Papers, and looks upon it undoubtedly true because it is printed." The writer suggested that controversies in the press were undermining the unity needed to fight the French and Indian War and expressed a wish "that some Expedient could be found out to curb the Liberties of the Press, without infringing on the Freedom of the English Nation." The letter merely suggested that the public ignore divisive writings, but the editors of the paper, James Parker and William Weyman, expressed dismay at finding an Englishman with so little respect for liberty. They therefore covered most of the issue's front page with an essay on the role of the press in spreading knowledge to the common people and warding off tyranny.[63]

As the stakes grew in colonial politics, legislatures took steps to punish their critics and to back their friends in journalism. Rev. William Smith, for instance, was arrested in contempt of the Pennsylvania Assembly in 1758 after years of attacking the personal reputations of Benjamin Franklin and other popular politicians in the province. Smith, a supporter of proprietary interests in Pennsylvania, made a rousing speech for personal liberty and freedom of expression which was loudly applauded by a hundred onlookers, but the Assembly was ready for revenge and voted to jail him for a protest against the legislature he had arranged to have published in a German-language newspaper.[64] The protest, which concerned the Assembly's efforts to punish a justice of the peace for misconduct, had earlier been printed in David Hall's *Pennsylvania Gazette* without any action having been taken. Hall had consulted with three members of the Assembly before publishing the piece and they had assured him that he would not want to appear to be failing to preserve a free and open press.[65] In spite of its action against Smith, the Assembly formally expressed its appreciation to the three members who advised Hall for the care they had taken "to guard against any Encroachment on so useful a Privilege as the Liberty of the Press."[66]

The increasingly revolutionary spirit of the colonies did help several printers overcome legislative threats. In 1754, the Massachusetts House jailed Daniel Fowle for publishing a pamphlet denouncing an excise tax designed to raise funds for the colony. After being held for five days, Fowle was released at night in an apparent attempt to avoid any demonstration of support by his friends. He then published a pamphlet declaring that he had been denied due process of law and filed a suit for £1,000.[67] Fowle fought the case for 12 years. The legislature, apparently influenced by the Wilkes phenomenon and the Stamp Act crisis, finally relented and decided to pay Fowle's expenses in 1764 and £20 in damages in 1766.[68]

In 1768, the Massachusetts House blocked an attempt by Gov. Francis Bernard to take action against the leading radical organ, the *Boston Gazette*. Angered by a *Gazette* correspondent who had portrayed him as a cruel and malicious administrator, Bernard asked the legislature to punish the paper. The House displayed its patriot proclivities by voting 56 to 18 to reject the request and by issuing a message insisting on its duty to defend freedom of the press as "a great Bulwark of the Liberty of the People."[69] The chief justice of the province, Thomas Hutchinson, then took the case to a grand jury and delivered a charge admonishing them to remember their oaths and to consider the perils of the "licentious Abuse of Government."[70] When the jurors returned no bill, patriot writers rejoiced. Samuel Adams wrote in the *Gazette* that nothing was "so justly TERRIBLE to tyrants, and their tools and abettors, as a FREE PRESS" and that the paper had shown the people "their danger and their remedy." Later in the month, on the anniversary of the repeal of the Stamp Act, a celebration in Boston included flag displays, cannon fire, and toasts to the *Gazette*, the House, and the "worthy and independent Grand Jurors."[71]

Boston newspapers again blazed with rhetoric on press freedom in 1771 after the Massachusetts Council summoned printer Isaiah Thomas for publishing a letter in the *Massachusetts Spy* depicting Gov. Thomas Hutchinson as a monster and usurper.[72] Three times the governor and his Council sent a messenger to the printer's shop and three times he refused to appear. Thomas coolly replied that he was too busy.[73] The Council then directed the attorney general to prosecute the printer for seditious libel. Crowds milled in the court house from day to day as the case was considered by the grand jury. Thomas was not indicted and subsequent efforts to punish him also failed. The Ministry eventually told Hutchinson that the temper of the times made prosecutions futile.[74]

The temper in other colonies was also fervent. In 1770, New York authorities arrested and imprisoned Alexander McDougall, a Son of Liberty, for writing an angry broadside protesting the Assembly's willingness to contribute to the costs of quartering royal troops in the colony. McDougall was soon hailed in the press as America's Wilkes and treated to festive demonstrations by hundreds of citizens. Recalling the number of the issue of the *North Briton* which led to the Wilkes case, 45 men went to the jail on the 45th day of the year and consumed 45 pounds of steak. In March, 45 "virgins" reportedly walked in a procession to the jail and sang the 45th Psalm.[75] In April, McDougall was indicted for seditious libel by a grand jury carefully packed by the aristocratic De Lancey faction responsible for the Assembly actions his broadside had attacked. McDougall posted bail and was escorted to his home by 600 supporters.[76] After repeated delays and the death of a key witness, the attorney general decided not to prosecute the case. McDougall was, however, called before the Assembly where he gave defiant answers and was arrested for breach of privilege. He was held in custody until the legislative session ended 82 days later.[77]

A breakdown occurred in South Carolina politics after the Commons House of Assembly voted in 1769 to allocate £1,500 sterling to a civil liberties fund which was helping to pay the debts of John Wilkes. The Council opposed the grant and, as a result, no annual tax bill was passed in the colony after 1769 and no other bills after February 1771.[78] In 1773, as the struggle between the two houses continued, the Council jailed the editor of the *South-Carolina Gazette*, Thomas Powell, for breach of privilege for publishing a protest against some of its actions. Powell was, however, granted a writ of habeas corpus by two members of the Commons who were justices of the peace. The Council objected vehemently, but the Commons insisted the action taken against Powell was unconstitutional and oppressive and it awarded the *Gazette*'s printers the sole right to publish its proceedings. "Thus was defeated," the paper concluded, "the most violent Attempt that ever had been made in his Province, upon the Liberty of the Subject." The *Gazette* reminded its readers that press freedom was "one of the most valuable Blessings that can be enjoyed by Britons, it being the best Alarum to rouze us against the Attacks of Arbitrary Power."[79]

In the same year, a grand jury in Rhode Island refused to indict John Carter, editor of the *Providence Gazette*, after his paper berated a member of the Assembly's committee of correspondence for testifying before a commission of inquiry investigating the mob destruction of a British ship, the *Gaspee*. "This very extraordinary Attempt to destroy the Liberty of the Press became a Matter of great Expectation, and did not fail to alarm the Friends of Freedom," the *Gazette* reported, "their Apprehensions however soon subsided, the honest Jury having returned the Bill IGNORAMUS."[80]

IV

The generation that produced the Bill of Rights spoke often of the importance of press freedom. Moreover, steps were taken to ensure that the concept was officially recognized. In 1774 the Continental Congress listed press freedom as one of the five "invaluable rights" Americans were seeking in the struggle with Britain.[81]

Nine of eleven revolutionary-era state constitutions had language stating that liberty of the press should be inviolable or ought never to be restrained.[82]

In practice, however, the political passions of the Revolution sometimes prevailed over press theory. Printers were periodically threatened by patriots and some, such as the arch-loyalist James Rivington, were subject to mob actions.[83] The British could also resort to force as Virginia's governor, Lord Dunmore, demonstrated in 1775 when his soldiers confiscated the printing equipment of John Hunter Holt, the editor of the *Virginia Gazette, or, the Norfolk Intelligencer*. Dunmore, who cared little for Holt's published insults or his insistence on liberty of the press, then began publishing a paper of his own aboard a ship off the coast of Virginia. When the mayor, aldermen, and common council of Norfolk protested the seizure as "a gross violation of all that Men and Freemen can hold dear," Dunmore suggested that instead they be pleased to be deprived of a "means of poisoning the minds of the people, and exciting in them a Spirit of Rebellion and Sedition."[84]

In the early years of the war, states began adopting treason laws and establishing penalties for Americans who expressed adherence to the king.[85] Yet government tended to take a forbearing approach to journalistic carping. Congress in 1776 took note of the presence of "uninformed people" in the states who had been "deceived and drawn into erroneous opinions respecting the American cause," but it resolved that the friends of liberty should "treat all such persons with kindness and attention" and "view their errors as proceeding rather from a want of information than want of virtue or public spirit." It recommended to the legislatures that they distribute copies of patriot writings and Congressional proceedings to the public "to elucidate the merits" of the American position.[86]

Some patriots, of course, favored more direct methods of persuasion. "I wish most heartily we had Rivington & his ministerial Gazetteers for 24. hours in this place," James Madison wrote to William Bradford in 1775. "Execrable as their designs are, they would meet with adequate punishment." Madison went on to express apparent approval of a Virginia man being "lately tarred & feathered for treating one [of] our county committees with disre[s]pect."[87]

The fury of the mob and the calming influence of government were particularly evident in a series of incidents involving a Maryland printer, William Goddard. In the February 25, 1777, issue of the *Maryland Journal*, he published a letter giving sarcastic praise to the king and Parliament for their peace overtures to America. Not appreciating the irony, Baltimore's Whig Club, a patriot organization, seized the printer and ordered him to leave the city. Goddard rode to Annapolis and complained to the legislature about "a lawless ambitious *knot*" that was "violently invading the Liberty of the Press." The Assembly's Committee of Aggrievances considered the episode and issued a report declaring that the action had been a manifest violation of the state's Constitution and Declaration of Rights. Goddard returned to Baltimore, but was soon trading published insults with the Whig Club. A mob of his tormentors broke into his shop on March 25 and again ordered his departure. This time the Assembly rounded up all the members of the Whig Club who could be found and brought them to the state capitol where they were chastised for their conduct and forced to admit their mistakes.[88] In 1779, Goddard was back at Annapolis after a mob forced him to publish an apology for a letter he had printed criticizing George Washington. Hearings were held at the capitol and he returned to Baltimore to recant the apology and to see that the *Journal* raise the issue of press freedom and blast the city's zealous patriots as ruffians and outlaws.[89]

In Philadelphia, press freedom was tested repeatedly. Thomas Paine was forced to resign his post as secretary to the Committee on Foreign Affairs in 1779 for writing a *Pennsylvania Packet* article revealing that Congress had been receiving secret aid from France, but he was not prosecuted. Later that year the *Packet* published accusations by Dr. Benjamin Rush that Congress was incompetent in its handling of the currency and in its ability to deal with government fraud and corruption. Elbridge Gerry moved that John Dunlap, the publisher of the paper, be summoned to Congress for interrogation. All the other members opposed the motion, however, and Dunlap was not asked to appear. Instead, delegates made arguments which hailed liberty of the press and noted the popularity which had accrued to writers like John Wilkes when faced with government action.[90]

In 1782 another Philadelphia printer, Eleazer Oswald, published scathing remarks about the judicial conduct of Pennsylvania's chief justice, Thomas McKean. The grand jury was given a bill of indictment by the attorney general, but voted 16 to 3 against approving it. In the face of severe newspaper criticism, McKean continued to seek an indictment, an action which provoked the grand jurors to publish a statement saying they retained "their unshaken zeal for the liberties of their country."[91]

As the ratification of the Constitution was being fiercely debated in the press, printers were harassed and boycotted. In some cases, the tensions led to defamatory writings and to violence.[92] A New York City mob attacked the home and shop of Antifederalist editor Thomas Greenleaf in the summer of 1788, breaking down the door and smashing windows. Greenleaf fired pistols into the crowd and escaped, but his office was ransacked and many of his types destroyed. After quickly resuming publication, the editor attributed the incident to deluded enemies and reminded his readers that "the FREEDOM of the PRESS, has hitherto been conceived the 'PALLADIUM of LIBERTY,' in America."[93]

Public demands for a press clause in the Constitution were, nevertheless, given a halfhearted reception by some noted political figures. Benjamin Franklin, who had been depicted in Eleazer Oswald's newspaper as a senile fool for backing ratification,[94] was a printer by trade but did not make any stirring pleas for liberty of the press. Instead, he wrote in his autobiography and in a letter to the *Pennsylvania Gazette* that the press had abandoned itself to false personal accusations and that it presented a disgraceful picture of the country to the rest of the world.[95] In an essay published in the *Federal Gazette* in 1789, Franklin wondered why the discussion of checks and balances in the Constitution had not included consideration of a check on the "Court of the Press" which he said operated like the Spanish Inquisition in dealing with individuals. He said that he could not think of any solution that would not infringe upon "the sacred *liberty of the Press*" except allowing the "*liberty of the Cudgel*" to go with it for those whose personal reputations were harmed—a solution he admitted would disturb the peace. Franklin explained that he was for as much freedom as people desired in the publication of opinions on public matters, but resented the ability of newspapers to condemn honest citizens and then to portray them as enemies to press freedom if they objected. "It seems indeed somewhat like the *liberty* of the *press* that felons have by the common law of England before conviction," Franklin remarked, "that is, to be either *pressed* to death or hanged."[96]

V

Through popular support in the form of demonstrations, jury verdicts, and legislative decisions, the press had, in fact, achieved a remarkable degree of freedom by the last decade of the eighteenth century. Official control of the press had all but vanished. Yet, freedom of expression remained vulnerable to public pressure. Popular sentiment, as Hamilton had observed in the *Federalist,* seemed to determine how much liberty of the press would actually exist. Laws made little difference. The public appeared to be both the best friend and worst enemy of expression, but most writers on the topic were still concerned with past battles against government. Like the many newspaper essayists who clamored for a constitutional protection for journalism, Thomas Jefferson concentrated on a need to preserve the press as a check on wrongdoing in office. He recognized that it might be difficult to define the limits of such rights, but he wrote to Madison in 1788 that it was better to establish them "in all cases" than not to do it in any.[97]

Madison responded to Jefferson's concerns about government incursions on liberties by stating that the danger of oppression in reality came from "overbearing majorities" in the states and that Virginia's declaration of rights had been "violated in every instance where it has been opposed to a popular current." He told Jefferson that in America "the real power lies in the majority of the Community, and the invasion of private rights is *chiefly* to be apprehended, not from acts of Government contrary to the sense of its constituents, but from acts in which the Government is the mere instrument of the major number of the constituents." Madison did see the value of a federal bill of rights, however. "The political truths declared in that solemn manner acquire by degrees the character of fundamental maxims of free Government," he wrote, "and as they become incorporated with the national sentiment, counteract the impulses of interest and passion."[98]

Jefferson answered a list of standard Federalist objections Madison supplied by admitting that a declaration of rights would not always work as desired, but he said that the good would outweigh the bad. "A brace the more will often keep up the building which would have fallen with that brace the less," he wrote. Jefferson chided Madison for ignoring "the legal check which it puts into the hands of the judiciary" which, if independent, would disregard the frenzy of citizens seeking what is wrong.[99] In his correspondence at the time, Jefferson promoted the position that the press could be held liable for printing false statements of fact damaging to personal reputation,[100] but he recognized free presses as one of "certain fences which experience has proved peculiarly efficacious against wrong, and rarely obstructive of right, which yet the governing powers have ever shewn a disposition to weaken or remove."[101]

Madison moved beyond the conventional republican depiction of official power menacing liberty[102] and recognized that the public was a threat as well. When he introduced his proposed Constitutional amendments to Congress in 1789, Madison noted that English law did not secure "those rights, respecting which the people of America are most alarmed," that the "freedom of the press and rights of conscience, those choicest privileges of the people, are unguarded in the British Constitution." The purpose of a bill of rights, he said, was to stand against the abuse of government and community power "or, in other words, against the majority in favor of the minority." Although he acknowledged that "paper barriers" might be thought too weak, Madison said that courts would compel observance of them and that the declarations would impress the nation and tend "to establish the public opinion in their favor."[103]

The First Amendment, which stated that Congress shall make no laws abridging freedom of the press, was ratified in 1791. In an essay published in the *National Gazette* shortly after the adoption of the Bill of Rights, Madison commented on the importance of a free press in facilitating communication and thereby preserving liberty. Governors would both obey and influence public opinion, he said, and the Bill of Rights would become part of public opinion and would assure that the people would have an influence on government. "Public opinion sets bounds to every government," he wrote, "and is the real sovereign in every free one."[104]

More than a century of demonstrations of popular support for freedom of expression preceded the press clause of the Constitution. Public demands were responsible for the drafting and ratification of the First Amendment. Still, American political theorists saw a need to shield rights such as liberty of the press from the public. The principle of journalistic freedom was easy to advocate for oneself, but sometimes difficult to uphold for opponents in the course of partisan confrontation. Madison told Congress that the Bill of Rights would have to serve an educational role and would have to be enforced by an enlightened and independent judiciary if it was to safeguard fundamental liberties. The experience of printers and journalists had suggested that freedom of the press would not only be one of the "choicest" liberties, but also one of the most precarious ones.

Endnotes

1. *New-York Journal,* November 8, 1787.
2. [Philadelphia] *Independent Gazetteer,* October 29, 1787.
3. [Philadelphia] *Freeman's Journal,* October 24, 1787.
4. John P. Kaminski and Gaspare J. Saladino, eds., *Commentaries on the Constitution, Public and Private* (Madison: State Historical Society of Wisconsin, 1981—), 1: 197–99.
5. Robert A. Rutland, *The Ordeal of the Constitution, The Antifederalists and the Ratification Struggle of 1787–1788* (Norman: University of Oklahoma Press, 1966); David A. Anderson, "The Origins of the Press Clause," *U.C.L.A. Law Review* 30 (February 1983): 466–75.
6. Alexander Hamilton, "The Federalist No. 84," in Jacob E. Cooke, ed. *The Federalist* (Middletown, Conn.: Wesleyan University Press, 1961), p. 580.
7. James Madison to Thomas Jefferson, October 17, 1788, in *The Papers of Thomas Jefferson,* ed. Julian P. Boyd et al. (Princeton: Princeton University Press, 1950), 14: 19, 20.
8. Anderson, "The Origins of the Press Clause," pp. 475–86.
9. Arthur M. Schlesinger, *Prelude to Independence, The Newspaper War on Britain, 1764–1776* (New York: Alfred A. Knopf, 1958), pp. 189, 297.
10. Leonard W. Levy, *Emergence of a Free Press* (New York: Oxford University Press, 1985), p. 16.
11. For a discussion of the revolutionary theory of the press, see William A. Hachten, *The World News Prism, Changing Media, Clashing Ideologies* (Ames: Iowa State University Press, 1981), pp. 69–72.
12. Jeffery A. Smith, "Legal Historians and the Press Clause," *Communications and the Law* 8 (August 1986): 69–80.
13. Public opinion is, of course, not a monolithic entity. It is rather the diverse reactions to an issue at hand. The term is applied here to varied responses made in particular situations involving the exercise of press freedom.
14. "Report on the Resolutions," 1799–1800, in *The Writings of James Madison,* ed. Gaillard Hunt, 9 vols. (New York: G.P. Putnam's Sons, 1900–1910), 6: 388.
15. Brian Manning, *The English People and the English Revolution, 1640–1649* (London: Heinemann, 1976), pp. 2–3; Edward, Earl of Clarendon, *The History of the Rebellion and Civil Wars in England Begun in the Year 1641,* 6 vols. (Oxford: Clarendon Press, 1888), 1: 265–70.
16. Proceedings Against John Bastwick, Henry Burton, and William Prynn, 3 *Howell's State Trials* 711 (1637).
17. *Boston Gazette, or Country Journal,* June 2, 1755.
18. The Trial of the Seven Bishops, 12 *Howell's State Trials* 183 (1688).
19. Maurice Ashley, *The Glorious Revolution of 1688* (London: Hodder and Stoughton, 1966), pp. 195, 199–202; *John Miller, James II, A Study in Kingship* (Hove, East Sussex, England: Wayland Publishers, 1977), pp. 182–87; Roger Thomas, "The Seven Bishops and their Petition, 18 May

1688," *Journal of Ecclesiastical History* 12 (April 1961): 56–70.

20. Jeffery A. Smith, "Freedom of Expression and the Marketplace of Ideas Concept from Milton to Jefferson," *Journal of Communication Inquiry* 7 (Summer 1981): 48–53.
21. The Trial of the Seven Bishops, 12 *Howell's State Trials* at 425–28.
22. *Journals of the House of Commons*, 11: 305–6.
23. Laurence Hanson, *Government and the Press, 1695–1763* (London: Oxford University Press, 1936), pp. 23, 67–68; The Trial of Richard Francklin, 17 *Howell's State Trials* 625 (1731).
24. Abel Boyer, ed., *The Political State of Great-Britain*, 60 vols. (London: Printed for T. Cooper, 1710–1740), 42: 88.
25. The Trial of William Owen, 18 *Howell's State Trials* 1203 at 1228, 1229 (1752).
26. Robert R. Rea, *The English Press in Politics, 1760–1774* (Lincoln: University of Nebraska Press, 1963), pp. 28–69; George Rudé, *Wilkes and Liberty, A Social Study of 1763 to 1774* (Oxford: Clarendon Press, 1962), pp. 17–36.
27. Rea, *The English Press in Politics*, pp. 75–77; Rudé, *Wilkes and Liberty*, pp. 33–34.
28. Rea, *The English Press in Politics*, pp. 77–82; Proceedings in the Case of John Wilkes, 19 *Howell's State Trials* 1075 (1763–1770).
29. Rea, *The English Press in Politics*, pp. 82–86; *Annual Register* 7 (1764): 87, 108; ibid., 8 (1765): 59, 65; *London Magazine* 34 (February 1765): 108–9; *Gentleman's Magazine* 35 (February 1765): 96.
30. On the Wilkes phenomenon, see John Brewer, *Party Ideology and Popular Politics at the Accession of George III* (Cambridge: Cambridge University Press, 1976).
31. Benjamin Franklin to William Franklin, April 16, 1768, in *The Papers of Benjamin Franklin*, ed. Leonard W. Labaree, William B. Wilcox, et al. (New Haven: Yale University Press, 1959—), 15: 98–99; Rea, *The English Press in Politics*, pp. 153–61.
32. Rudé, *Wilkes and Liberty*, pp. 37–56.
33. Rea, *The English Press in Politics*, pp. 174–87.
34. The Trial of John Miller, 20 *Howell's State Trials* 869, at 895 (1770).
35. Peter D.G. Thomas, "The Beginning of Parliamentary Reporting in Newspapers, 1768–1774," *English Historical Review* 74 (October 1959): 623–36; Peter D.G. Thomas, "John Wilkes and Freedom of the Press (1771)," *Bulletin of the Institute of Historical Research* 33 (1960): 86–98.
36. Pauline Maier, "John Wilkes and American Disillusionment with Britain," *William and Mary Quarterly*, 3rd ser., 20 (July 1963): 373–95; Richard J. Hooker, "The American Revolution Seen Through a Wine Glass," *William and Mary Quarterly*, 3rd ser., 11 (January 1954): 52–57.
37. [George Keith], *New England's Spirit of Persecution Transmitted to Pennsilvania* ([New York, 1693]), pp. 32–38.
38. Isaiah Thomas, *The History of Printing in America*, ed. Marcus A. McCorison (New York: Weathervane Books, 1970), pp. 354–55.
39. [Thomas Maule], *New-England Persecutors Mauld With their own Weapons* ([New York, 1697]), pp. 52–62; Lawrence W. Murphy, "Thomas Maule: The Neglected Quaker," *Journalism Quarterly* 29 (Spring 1952): 171–74; Clyde A. Duniway, *The Development of Freedom of the Press in Massachusetts* (New York: Longman, Green, & Co., 1906), pp. 70–73.
40. Leo P. Bradley, Jr., "The Press and the Declension of Boston Orthodoxy, 1674–1724" (M.A. thesis, University of Washington, 1977), pp. 97–117.
41. *Boston News-Letter*, March 6, 1721.
42. *Boston Gazette*, March 6, 1721; [Daniel Defoe], *News From the Moon. A Review of the State of the British Nation* ([Boston: James Franklin, 1721]).
43. General Court Records, Massachusetts Archives, Boston, Mass., 11, p. 113.
44. Council Records, Massachusetts Archives, 7, p. 252.
45. *Boston News-Letter*, April 3, 1721.
46. Duniway, *The Development of Freedom of the Press in Massachusetts*, pp. 93–96; Thomas Hutchinson, *The History of the Colony and Province of*

Massachusetts-Bay, ed. Lawrence Shaw Mayo, 3 vols. (Cambridge: Harvard University Press, 1936), 2: 174–208.

47. *Boston Gazette*, January 29, 1722.

48. *New-England Courant*, December 4, 1721. On the *Courant*, see Arthur B. Tourtellot, *Benjamin Franklin, The Shaping of Genius, The Boston Years* (Garden City, N.Y.: Doubleday & Co., Inc., 1977), pp. 197–436.

49. General Court Records, 11, pp. 319–20, 370.

50. *New-England Courant*, September 17, 1722. For examples of the *Courant*'s controversial articles and discussions of press freedom, see ibid., August 7, 14, 21, 28, September 4, 11, October 16, November 20, December 4, 1721; January 22, February 5, 12, April 16, 30, May 14, 28, June 11, July 9, 1722. On the sporadic and largely ineffectual use of legislative privilege against the colonial press, see Jeffery A. Smith, "A Reappraisal of Legislative Privilege and American Colonial Journalism," *Journalism Quarterly* 61 (Spring 1984): 97–103, 141.

51. General Court Records, 11, pp. 491–93; Council Records, 7, pp. 452–53; Suffolk County Court Files, Boston, Mass., 146, No. 16480; Records of the Superior Court of Judicature, Boston, Mass., 1721–1725, p. 119.

52. *New-England Courant*, January 14, 21, 28, February 4, May 6, 13, 1721.

53. Duniway, *The Development of Freedom of the Press in Massachusetts*, pp. 102–3.

54. *New-England Courant*, February 11, 1723.

55. *American Weekly Mercury*, February 26, 1723.

56. *New-England Courant*, December 18, 25, 1721; January 22, 1722.

57. *New-York Weekly Journal*, November 12, 1733.

58. James Alexander, *A Brief Narrative of the Case and Trial of John Peter Zenger, Printer of the New York Weekly Journal*, ed. Stanley N. Katz, 2nd ed. (Cambridge: Harvard University Press, 1972); Livingston Rutherford, *John Peter Zenger, His Press, His Trial* (New York: Dodd, Mead, 1904); Cathy Covert, "'Passion is Ye Prevailing Motive': The Feud Behind the Zenger Case," *Journalism Quarterly* 50 (Summer 1973): 3–10; *Journals of the Votes and Proceedings of the General Assembly of New York*, 2 vols. (New York: Printed by Hugh Gaine, 1766), 1: 671–72.

59. The remark by Morris is quoted in William Dunlap, *History of the New Netherlands, Province of New York, and State of New York, to the Adoption of the Federal Constitution*, 2 vols. (New York: Printed for the author by Carter & Thorp, 1839–1840), 1: 302.

60. On the apparent lack of seditious libel trials in colonial courts after 1735, see Harold L. Nelson, "Seditious Libel in Colonial America," *The American Journal of Legal History* 3 (April 1959): 170.

61. *South-Carolina Gazette*, January 5, 19, February 9, March 30, 1747.

62. R. Nicholas Olsberg, ed., *The Journal of the Commons House of Assembly, 23 April 1750–31 August 1751* (Columbia, S.C.: University of South Carolina Press, 1974), pp. 7–12; Jeffery A. Smith, "Impartiality and Revolutionary Ideology: Editorial Policies of the *South-Carolina Gazette*, 1732–1775," *Journal of Southern History* 49 (November 1983): 519–21.

63. *New-York Post-Boy*, November 8, 1756.

64. *Pennsylvania Journal*, February 23, 1758; *American Magazine* 1 (January, February, April 1758): 199–200, 210–27, 308; Edward Shippen, Jr., to Edward Shippen, January 28, 1758, Balch Papers, Historical Society of Pennsylvania.

65. *Pennsylvania Gazette*, December 1, 1757; Examination of David Hall, January 18, 1758, Penn Manuscripts, Wyoming Controversy, Smith and Moore vs. Assembly, Historical Society of Pennsylvania, 5: 223–25.

66. Gertrude MacKinney and Charles F. Hoban, eds., *Pennsylvania Archives*, 8th ser., 8 vols. (Harrisburg: State Printers, 1931–1935), 6: 4707. On the case, see Ralph L. Ketcham, "Benjamin Franklin and William Smith: New Light on an Old Philadelphia Quarrel," *Pennsylvania Magazine of History and Biography* 88 (April 1964): 142–63; Peter C. Hoffer, "Law and Liberty: In the Matter of Provost William Smith of Philadelphia, 1758," *William and Mary Quarterly* 38, 3rd ser. (October 1981): 681–701.

67. Daniel Fowle, *A Total Eclipse of Liberty* (Boston, 1755); *Journals of the House of Representatives of Massachusetts, 1754–1755* (Boston: Massachusetts Historical Society, 1956), pp. 63–64, 67, 72.

68. Duniway, *The Development of Freedom of the Press in Massachusetts*, pp. 115–19, 171–73; General Court Records, 25, pp. 268–91; 26, p. 340. For background, see Paul S. Boyer, "Borrowed Rhetoric: The Massachusetts Excise Controversy of 1754," *William and Mary Quarterly*, 3rd ser., 21 (July 1964): 328–51.

69. *Boston Gazette*, February 29, March 7, 1768; *Journals of the House of Representatives of Massachusetts, 1767–1768* (Boston: Massachusetts Historical Society, 1975), pp. 206–210.

70. Josiah Quincy, Jr., *Reports of Cases Argued and Adjudged in the Superior Court of Judicature of the Province of Massachusetts Bay, Between 1761 and 1772* (Boston: Little, Brown, & Co., 1865), pp. 262–78.

71. *Boston Gazette*, March 14, 21, 1768.

72. *Massachusetts Spy*, November 14, 1771.

73. Thomas, *A History of Printing in America*, pp. 165–68, 174–75, 267–72.

74. Schlesinger, *Prelude to Independence*, pp. 140–42, 147–48.

75. *New York Journal*, February 15, March 22, 29, 1770.

76. Ibid., March 22, 29, April 5, 12, 1770; *New-York Post Boy*, January 29, February 19, March 19, 26, April 2, 9, 1770; William Smith, *Historical Memoirs, From 16 March 1763 to 9 July 1776*, ed. William H.W. Sabine (New York, 1956), pp. 71–76, 81.

77. Thomas Jones, *History of New York During the Revolutionary War*, ed. Edward F. De Lancey, 2 vols. (New York: New York Historical Society, 1879), 1: 24–33; Roger J. Champagne, *Alexander McDougall and the American Revolution in New York* (Schenectady, N.Y.: Union College Press, 1975), pp. 24–43.

78. Jack P. Greene, "Bridge to Revolution: The Wilkes Fund Controversy in South Carolina, 1769–1775," *Journal of Southern History* 29 (February 1963): 19–52.

79. *South-Carolina Gazette*, September 2, 6, 13, 15, 1773; Smith, "Impartiality and Revolutionary Ideology," pp. 524–25.

80. *Providence Gazette*, July 3, 1773; Schlesinger, *Prelude to Independence*, pp. 154–56.

81. "To the Inhabitants of the Province of Quebec," October 26, 1774, in Worthington C. Ford, et al., eds. *Journals of the Continental Congress, 1774–1789*, 34 vols. (Washington, D.C.: U.S. Government Printing Office, 1904–1937), 1: 108.

82. Bernard Schwartz, ed., *The Bill of Rights: A Documentary History*, 2 vols. (New York: Chelsea House, 1971), 1: 235, 266, 278, 284, 287, 300, 335, 342, 378.

83. Dwight L. Teeter, "'King' Sears, the Mob, and Freedom of the Press in New York, 1765–76," *Journalism Quarterly* 41 (Autumn 1964): 539–44.

84. Brent Tarter, ed., *The Order Book and Related Papers of the Common Hall of the Borough of Norfolk, Virginia, 1736–1798* (Richmond: Virginia State Library, 1979), pp. 192–94. See generally, Brent Tarter, "'The Very Standard of Liberty: Lord Dunmore's Seizure of the Virginia Gazette, or the Norfolk Intelligencer," *Virginia Cavalcade* 25 (Autumn 1975): 58–71.

85. Claude H. Van Tyne, *The Loyalists in the American Revolution* (New York: Macmillan Co., 1902), pp. 66, 198–201, 327–29.

86. Ford et al., eds., *Journals of the Continental Congress*, 4: 18–19.

87. James Madison to William Bradford, [Early March 1775], in *The Papers of James Madison*, ed. William T. Hutchinson and William M.E. Rachal (Chicago: University of Chicago Press, 1962—), 1: 73.

88. [William Goddard], *The Prowess of the Whig Club* (Baltimore, [1777]); Ward L. Miner, *William Goddard, Newspaperman* (Durham, N.C.: Duke University Press, 1962), pp. 150–62.

89. Ibid., pp. 168–73.

90. Dwight L. Teeter, "Press Freedom and the Public Printing: Pennsylvania, 1775–83," *Journalism Quarterly* 45 (Autumn 1968): 445–51.

91. *Independent Gazetteer*, October 15, 19, November

9, December 7, 14, 21, 28, 31, 1782; January 4, 11, 18, 1783; *Pennsylvania Gazette,* January 8, 15, 22, 1783; Dwight L. Teeter, "The Printer and the Chief Justice: Seditious Libel in 1782–83," *Journalism Quarterly* 45 (Summer 1968): 235–42, 260; G.S. Rowe, *Thomas McKean, The Shaping of an American Republicanism* (Boulder: Associated University Press, 1978), pp. 182–88.

92. John P. Kaminski, "Newspaper Suppression during the Debate over the Ratification of the Constitution, 1787–1788," paper presented at the Midwest Mass Communication History Conference, School of Journalism and Mass Communication, University of Wisconsin—Madison, April 23, 1982.

93. *New York Journal, and Weekly Register,* August 7, 1788.

94. *Independent Gazetteer,* October 5, 1787.

95. *The Autobiography of Benjamin Franklin, A Genetic Text,* ed. J.A. Leo Lemay and P.M. Zall (Knoxville: University of Tennessee Press, 1981), pp. 94–95; "To the Editors of the *Pennsylvania Gazette,*" 1788, in *The Writings of Benjamin Franklin,* ed. Albert H. Smyth, 10 vols. (New York: Macmillan Co., 1905–1907), 9: 639.

96. *Federal Gazette,* September 12, 1789.

97. Thomas Jefferson to James Madison, July 31, 1788, in *The Papers of Thomas Jefferson,* 13: 442.

98. James Madison to Thomas Jefferson, October 17, 1788, in ibid., 14: 19, 20.

99. Thomas Jefferson to James Madison, March 15, 1789, in ibid., 14: 659, 660.

100. See, e.g., Thomas Jefferson to James Madison, July 31, 1788, in ibid., 13: 442; "Draft of a Charter of Rights," 1789, in ibid., 15: 168; Thomas Jefferson to James Madison, August 28, 1789, in ibid., p. 367.

101. Thomas Jefferson to Noah Webster, Jr., December 4, 1790, in ibid., 18:132.

102. For a review of recent scholarship on republican theory, see Linda K. Kerber, "The Republican Ideology of the Revolutionary Generation," *American Quarterly* 37 (Fall 1985): 474–95.

103. "Amendments to the Constitution," June 8, 1789, in *The Writings of James Madison,* 5: 380, 381, 382, 385.

104. [Philadelphia] *National Gazette,* December 19, 1791.

III

Development of a Mass Press

The development of a mass-circulation press in the United States traditionally is dated to 1833, the year that Benjamin Day introduced the *New York Sun*. In the first issue Day wrote that the object of the paper was to "lay before the public, at a price within the means of every one, ALL THE NEWS OF THE DAY, and at the same time afford an advantageous medium for advertising." Day's newspaper challenged the established commercial newspapers that catered to New York's elite and provided an alternative to the highly partisan newspapers that preceded it. As Day's penny idea was adopted by other metropolitan editors, it gained a reputation as a revolutionary journalistic endeavor characterized by cheap street sales, human interest content, reliance on advertising revenues, and an emphasis on "news" rather than "views." Editors began to hire reporters and to emphasize speed in collecting the news. Such an emphasis helped to generate new technologies that provided ever faster capabilities for producing and distributing newspapers. Police court stories and criminal trial reports took precedence over editorial matter.

The development of the mass press coincided with a developing market economy and a political climate that professed to champion egalitarianism. Congress expressed its continuing concern about the relationship of rural to urban communities through the interest it took in how newspapers would be distributed through the postal system, even as the city newspapers broadened their appeals to new classes of readers.

The mass-circulation press coincided with Andrew Jackson's presidency (1829–1837), an era that has undergone a variety of interpretations by historians. Jackson, or "Old Hickory" as he was fondly known by Westerners, represented the end of a Virginia–Massachusetts domination of the presidency. Contemporary historians regarded Jackson as vulgar, uneducated, and power-hungry, although they agreed with many of his policies, including his emphasis on a sound currency, his laissez-faire philosophy, and his nationalistic stance. They condemned him for introducing the spoils system and for acting out of political expediency rather than from principle.

During the first half of the twentieth century Jackson's reputation improved. Progressive historians from diverse economic and geographic backgrounds characterized the Jacksonian period as one of progress and democratization and regarded Jackson as the champion of the people against the special interests.[1] In 1945, with the publication of Arthur M. Schlesinger, Jr.'s Pulitzer Prize-winning book *The Age of Jackson*, historians began to examine the class conflicts inherent in the Jacksonian period. Schlesinger posed the Jacksonian conflict as one between liberalism and conservatism, a conflict between those who sought to ally business with government and those who sought to minimize the influence of business. Although Schlesinger viewed Jackson as a champion of the masses, Jackson's critics accused him of supporting middle-class entrepreneurs who resisted economic and governmental regulation; thus the debate centered on whether Jackson supported the poor and the downtrodden or championed liberal capitalism on the part of the middle class.

Historians writing after 1945 often challenged the interpretations that had come before. Emphasizing continuity and consensus in the American experience, some regarded Jackson as attempting to preserve a simple agrarian society in the face of industrialization. Others simply denied that the variety of local reform endeavors during the Jacksonian period ever constituted an organized, cohesive political movement.[2] New Left historians have challenged not only whether the Jacksonian period constituted a political movement but also whether equality was even a goal. Others, such as Sean Wilentz, have integrated political and social aspects of the period, with an emphasis on class conflict and class formation.[3]

Although journalism historiography has not followed a path identical to that of general American histories, scholars have employed many similar interpretations in explaining the penny press. Writing in 1881, S. N. D. North characterized the penny press in terms of its progression from the partisan newspaper's sorry state, claiming that in the penny press "the political connection was properly subordinated to the other and higher function of the public journal—the function of gathering and presenting the news as it is, without reference to its political or other effect upon friend or foe."[4] Willard G. Bleyer, director of the School of Journalism at the University of Wisconsin, wrote in 1927 that the political party organs had emphasized political and economic issues—rather than news—for the mercantile and professional classes.[5] The penny press was the cheap, popular newspaper designed for the masses. Writing uncharacteristically for a historian of the period, Bleyer pointed to "growing class consciousness of the workers, both in England and in America" as a cause for penny press development.[6] He discussed demands for the ten-hour day, higher wages, and better working conditions. In a vein more reflective of 1920s historiography, he also cited efforts to secure voting rights for a greater majority of the populace. Bleyer viewed the penny press as a sound business proposition that increased advertising volume and provided sensational material to the masses.

Subsequent journalism historians continued to characterize the penny press in terms used by Bleyer. Alfred McClung Lee, writing in 1937, cited class consciousness and efforts to expand voting rights as issues taken up by the penny press; he also added that growing literacy made the product popular. In 1941, Frank Luther Mott, in a journalism history text that remained popular for more than twenty years, emphasized the elements of progress, dubbing the political party press "The Dark Ages of Partisan Journalism" and the penny press "Sunrise." However, although Mott described the penny press as revolutionary, he cautioned readers to remember that it did not "immediately cause a sharp break with the past in American journalism," and that mercantile and political newspapers exceeded the penny press in both numbers and influence. He noted that, rather than abandoning politics, newspapers such as the *Sun* gave less weight to political news and incorporated more "breezy" items: they emphasized local news, human interest stories, sensational crime, and sex. Mott measured the press by presentist standards, lamenting that "modern reporting by no means sprang into full vigor upon the inauguration of the penny papers, however. At first, names and details were sadly lacking. News accounts were full of editorializing . . . the novel concept of the news made its way slowly."[7] Reflecting consensus historiography, Mott emphasized the entrepreneurial quality of the penny editors and the advent of the machine and downplayed class division. He noted that "a new economic level of the population" was added "to the newspaper audience," and that the penny paper was "a phase of that widespread transformation of the industrial system and upset of class relationships and traditional ideas which go by that name."[8]

In 1954, with the first edition of *The Press and America,* Edwin Emery and Henry Ladd Smith abandoned the concept of class and adopted progressive rhetoric used to describe Jacksonian democracy, designating the new class of readers as "the common man." "Before long," they wrote, "some of the penny newspapers began to attract readers from other social and economic brackets. And the common man, as his literacy skill improved, also demanded a better product. Within a decade after the appearance of the first penny paper, the press of the common man included respectable publications that offered significant information and leadership." Smith and Emery emphasized penny press characteristics such as "news" over "views" and, echoing Mott, labeled the period the "sunrise of a new journalism."[9]

The progressive interpretation of the penny press held sway until the late 1970s, when a new group of historians and sociologists began to question standard interpretations of press developments of the 1830s. Although early historians had made references to Jacksonian democracy, expanding literacy, technology, and natural evolution, Michael Schudson was the first to systematically analyze these explanations of the development of the penny press. Schudson dismissed the technological argument as facilitating the rise of the penny press, but not explaining it; he noted that although literacy was on the rise during the Jacksonian period, rising literacy in other countries did not precipitate a penny press elsewhere; and he argued that the concept of natural evolution based on inevitability does not constitute solid ground for theory building.[10] Schudson chose to reemphasize the Age of Jackson as an egalitarian movement characterized by expanded public education, a mass press, and equal opportunity, and he described the revolution as middle class in orientation. "The founding of the penny papers," Schudson wrote, "is evidence of the new kind of entrepreneur and the new type of enterprise the 1830s encouraged. The qualities contemporaries admired or detested in these papers—relative independence from party, low price, high circulation, emphasis on news, timeliness, sensation—have to do with the rise of an urban middle class."[11]

Writing only a few years later, Dan Schiller took issue with Schudson's emphasis on the middle class. Schiller focused exclusively on New York City and argued that the audience for the penny press was a group of downwardly mobile artisans shouting their last battle cry, rather than a rising middle class. He claimed that an expanding economy moving toward national distribution was forcing local artisans to compete with out-of- town producers, and that even the legal system was changing, with a focus on protecting business and making sure that law and order reigned among the working class. The penny press, argued Schiller, "reanimated the core political beliefs of the artisans and mechanics" of New York.[12]

The essays presented here examine several issues that have been debated concerning the exact nature of the Jacksonian period and the development of a mass-circulation press. Richard B. Kielbowicz's article, "Modernization, Communication Policy, and the Geopolitics of News, 1820–1860," examines congressional debate over postal policy during the period. Postal policy, Kielbowicz maintains, was related to congressional belief that communication was an agent of modernization. The Jacksonians' attempt to structure postal policy to foster the development of a localized, face-to-face society boldly challenged the Whig desire for easy transmission of urban and commercial values. Kielbowicz's article integrates the arguments about development of a mass-circulation press into the political discourse of the times.

Donald Lewis Shaw, writing in 1981, during the same year as Dan Schiller, examines the same forty-year period covered by Kielbowicz. Shaw's article, "At the Crossroads: Change and Continuity in American Press News, 1820–1860," reexamines characteristics usually assigned to the penny press and measures the degree to which they permeated American society. Shaw concludes that the penny press was not a model for the entire nation, and although types of content changed little during the period, stories written by reporters became more prominent and speed in reporting news increased dramatically. In terms of content, the story is one of continuity; in terms of sources used and places covered, the story is one of change.

John C. Nerone, in the final piece here, "The Mythology of the Penny Press," examines the scholarly productivity about the penny press. He concludes that much of the analysis is myth, and the myth has "provided historical legitimacy for current practices and ideas." Nerone takes Schiller and Schudson to task for overemphasizing urban newspapers, particularly those of New York, and discusses in detail each attribute that has been assigned as a characteristic of the penny press.

Schudson, Schiller, Shaw, and John Pauly responded to Nerone's essay. Schudson and Schiller reemphasized their original positions; Shaw, who analyzed newspapers throughout the country, noted that to a degree historians had rightfully emphasized the urban press of the 1830s because the population was moving to the cities. John Pauly praised Nerone for his examination of penny press historiography and challenged historians to look further for explanations. Writing from a cultural studies perspective, Pauly emphasized that instead of merely accepting words and their meanings it is important to analyze meanings that were current at the time. For example, he pointed out that in the nineteenth century the term *independence* could suggest not only journalism freed from overt party control but also freed of "outmoded European customs, inspired by ideas of self-reliance, sympathetic to a laissez-faire economy, scientifically objective in its reports about the world, supportive of particular styles of occupational identity, emotionally disinterested and aloof in its everyday operations."[13] For the journalism historian, Pauly wrote, "the penny press is less an evolutionary than a dramatic stage, upon which are played all our protracted confrontations over capitalism, democratic politics, machine technology, social class and status, urbanism, and reportorial identity."[14] No doubt historians will continue to examine the press of the 1830s, looking not only at the penny press of the metropolis but at the country newspapers and other vehicles of communication that competed for audience attention with the mass press. Whether the 1830s developments did set the stage for modern journalism will continue to be a fundamental question.

Endnotes

1. Gerald N. Grob and George A. Billias, *Interpretations of American History: Patterns and Perspectives* (New York: Free Press, 1967) 2 vol.
2. The preceding discussion relies heavily on Grob and Billias' introduction to essays on Jacksonian America; see 367–381.
3. Sean Wilentz, *Chants Democratic: New York City and the Rise of the American Working Class, 1788–1850* (New York: Oxford University Press, 1984).
4. S. N. D. North, *History and Present condition of the Newspaper and Periodical Press of the United States* (Washington, D.C.: U.S. Census Bureau, 1881), 91.
5. Willard G. Bleyer, *Main Currents in the History of American Journalism* (New York: Houghton Mifflin Co., 1927), 152.
6. Bleyer, 155.
7. Frank Luther Mott, *American Journalism* (New York: Macmillan Co., 1947 [reprint of 1941 edition]), 243–244.
8. Mott, p. 215.
9. Edwin Emery and Henry Ladd Smith, *The Press and America* (Englewood Cliffs, N.J.: Prentice Hall, 1954), 214–218.
10. Michael Schudson, *Discovering the News: A Social History of American Newspapers* (New York: Basic Books, 1978), 31–43.
11. Schudson, 49–50.

12. Dan Schiller, *Objectivity and the News: The Public and the Rise of Commercial Journalism* (Philadelphia: University of Pennsylvania Press, 1981). See also Schiller, "Critical Response: Evolutionary Confusion," *Critical Studies in Mass Communication* 4:4 (December, 1987); 409.

13. John J. Pauly, "Critical Response: The Rest of the Story," *Critical Studies in Mass Communication* 4:4 (December, 1987): 415–419.

14. Pauly, 418. See also David L. Eason," Review Essay: The New Social History of the Newspaper," *Communication Research* II (January, 1984): 141–151.

Modernization, Communication Policy, and the Geopolitics of News, 1820–1860

Richard B. Kielbowicz

As nations modernize, traditional attachments of family, birthplace, and community are increasingly supplemented by supralocal affiliations. Communication plays a central role in the process of drawing people into national communities; face-to-face communication gives way, at least in part, to impersonal, mediated relations (Rogers, 1969). Consequently, many of the signs—and strains—of modernization are visible in a nation's communication system and the policies governing it.

In the mid-nineteenth century, roughly the 1820s to 1860s, the United States was undergoing modernization. Subsistence agriculture was being commercialized; manufacturing shifted from homes and small shops to factories where specialized laborers produced standardized products; the economy was developing regional specializations that necessitated increased trade; and various social institutions—religious sects, reform groups, political parties, and occupational associations—were coalescing in national communities. Modernization, however, proceeded unevenly. Some regions, notably the South, as well as districts within regions, lagged behind the rest of the country. This unevenness created a number of tensions, and federal policy had to accommodate the differences (Brown, 1976).

Communication was a major agent of modernization, and through the mid-1800s the nation's communication network was built on the operations of the post office. The mails provided the mechanism by which information circulated throughout a sprawling, developing country before the telegraph and press associations began furnishing similar services at mid-century.[1] Those in and out of Congress who sought to influence the nature of the growing communication network, and thereby affect the pace of modernization, concentrated their efforts on shaping postal policy. One of the most divisive complaints recurring throughout debates was that postal policy favored urban publications, especially a handful in the largest Northeastern cities, at the expense of their smaller rural counterparts. Debate occurred on several levels, but most fundamentally the struggle over newspaper postal policy was part of a larger contest to decide which conceptions of community would prevail in the nation's formative decades.

The tension was essentially between interests trying to promote a national culture, and those trying to protect regionalism or localism. For the most part, the former favored a communication system in which information flowed rapidly with few impediments, often from urban centers, while the latter strived to protect local and regional media voices. There was more at stake than simply the structure of the communication system, for policymakers perceived that lines of political, economic, and cultural influence followed lines of transportation and communication. Whether this perception was accurate (many scholars agree that it was [Deutsch, 1953; Odum & Moore, 1938, p. 119; Park, 1929; Pred, 1973]), it figured prominently in the debates over the earliest U.S. communications policy.

The mails, by carrying periodicals, forged links among scattered and diverse people, an essential step in modernization. The postal system exhibited some of the contradictory tendencies of the much broader communication revolution that Carey (1969) has so aptly characterized. On the one hand, improvements in communication had a centripetal or unifying tendency by bringing disparate groups into contact; a leading example would be the symbols of nationalism communicated to the country across social and geographic lines. On the other hand, it had a centrifugal effect, that is, the few individuals with kindred interests in each of thousands of communities developed large-scale national associations; reform movements of the mid-1800s are good examples. Although Carey rightly calls these tendencies contradictory, they share one overriding trait: they both represented supralocal communication. Both, moreover, are characteristic of modernization. The mails abetted these contradictory tendencies by conveying information that cut across narrow groups and bound the nation into a whole, while simultaneously carrying publications that endowed specialized groups with their separate identities.

In an exegesis of Innis' (1951) work, Carey (1981) explains that the U.S. "policy of improving communication over long distance" aided the "shift from local and regional units to national and international ones, though not without considerable struggle and conflict. Individuals were linked into larger units of social organization without the necessity of appealing to them through local and proximate structures" (p. 84).

Struggles over newspaper postage, therefore, can be understood as part of the debate over modernization, the transition from a traditional society, in which local affiliations predominate, to a nation-state. Those who welcomed the changes wrought by modernization tended to be relatively cosmopolitan with information flowing from distant centers. Those who preferred a traditional society, in which local ties take precedence, resented supralocal communication because it threatened the authority of those in the immediate community. To some extent, the lines of contention were urban versus rural, North versus South. But such dichotomies are a bit too facile since many individuals are cosmopolites or localites regardless of their place of residence (Rogers, 1969, pp. 146–168).

This essay argues that contemporaries' orientations—local or regional versus those that were primarily national—affected the way postal policy governing newspapers was structured. These geopolitics, in turn, grew out of the strains and anxieties associated with modernization. Most of the evidence presented here was derived from remarks made during debates over newspaper postage, with some supplemental analysis of data on publications sent through the mails.

Newspaper Postage in the Age of Jackson

The first administrations and Congresses believed that building a postal network and underwriting the circulation of information through the press would keep the western territories faithful to the federal government (Bretz, 1909; Kielbowicz 1982, 1983). Chambers (1963, p. 42) notes that partisan papers, which relayed intelligence by post, "constituted a major force for fractional or party cohesion, communicating partisan information and views from the centers of power to the outlying communities."

Few attempts were made to restructure newspaper postal policy during the first three decades of the nineteenth century. But in 1832 Congress seriously considered the ultimate postal privilege for newspapers—the abolition of postage. The ensuing debates, which occupied a great deal of the Senate's time, provide the best insights into the geopolitics of news during the Jacksonian period.

The proposal to abolish newspaper postage was offered by George Bibb of Kentucky, a one-time Jacksonian who had turned against the President in 1828 (*Register of Debates*, 1832, p. 875). Most of the backers were Whigs and other anti-Jackson Senators who contended that the abolition of newspaper postage was necessary to put all papers on the same footing as those enjoying the patronage of the Executive departments (*Register of Debates*, 1832, p. 882). Many arguments dealt with the economics of abolishing newspaper postage and its impact on partisan newspapers, but much of the debate centered on its consequences for the urban and rural press.

Most Jacksonian Senators opposed the move to abolish newspaper postage, in part because they believed that it would "annihilate at least one-half of our village newspapers" (*Register of Debates*, 1832, p. 912). The post office committee, headed by Felix Grundy, a staunch Jackson supporter, asserted that, if postage was eliminated, "a prevailing curiousity in the interior to see and read the papers which are published in the large cities" would displace the local press (U.S. Senate, 1832, p. 5). They forecast dreadful results:

> *The city editors, by fixing agents in the different towns and villages to receive and circulate their papers, will depress, and eventually supplant, the smaller establishments.*
>
> *A monopoly of influence in the large cities, whose political atmosphere is not always most congenial to a spirit of independence, will be the consequence. That freedom, that manliness of spirit, which has always characterized the great body of the common people of our country, and which constitutes the safeguard of our liberties, will gradually decline.* (U.S. Senate, 1832, p. 5)

Rural legislators preferred to have country editors mediate the flow of news; "all the useful intelligence" in the city papers could be selected from the exchanges, reprinted, and circulated "with but a few hours delay, through the medium of the local press" (U.S. Senate, 1832).

John Holmes, a Whig from Maine, refuted this claim, countering with a more cosmopolitan conception of American journalism: "The idea that news should not come to the people from abroad [out-of-town] or if it does, that it should be first fashioned, fitted, and pruned by a village editor, before it would be safe to see it, is a caprice so bordering on the ridiculous, that I can hardly treat it seriously" (*Register of Debates*, 1832, p. 887). Large city papers and small country ones not only competed, Holmes recognized, but the coverage of one also complemented the other. "Both have different offices to perform," he remarked.

At the close of a seven-day debate, the motion to abolish newspaper postage failed by a 23 to 22 vote. An analysis of the voting reveals that it divided along party lines; the administration's supporters favored retaining newspaper postage, those generally opposed to Jackson voted for the postage-free conveyance of newspapers.[2] "Not a single Jackson man . . . voted for the abolition," the *Boston Evening Transcript* (1832) snapped. "And pray what has Jacksonism to fear from the universal diffusion of intelligence?"

The defeat of the amendment to abolish newspaper postage did not discourage its most tenacious proponents. The amendment lost on May 10, the post office bill passed on May 14, and the next day Holmes introduced a bill specifically designed to repeal newspaper postage, which was referred to the post office committee headed by Grundy (Parks, 1940; *Register of Debates*, 1832, p. 930). The committee reported against the bill (*Register of Debates*, 1832, pp. 933–934). Other measures introduced in the House and Senate in 1832 were also defeated because policymakers believed they would give city publications too large a share of the market (*Register of Debates*, 1832–1833, pp. 927–930, 943).

The 1832 debates held the close attention of Congress because the outcome affected the fortunes of partisan papers, the major form of journalism at the time. Not surprisingly, partisan concerns pervaded the deliberations. Subsequent debates, however, increasingly focused on how postal policies affected the newer brand of journalism, mass-circulated city dailies.

City v. Country in Postal Policy

One of the most stalwart Jacksonians, Amos Kendall, served as postmaster general from 1835 to 1840. He consistently opposed any measure that would increase the long-distance circulation of city papers. Believing that "there is justice and good policy in graduating the postage on newspapers according to the size and weight of the matter to be conveyed," Kendall proposed a slightly higher rate for large papers. His plan, offered in 1836, would have increased from 1½ to 2 cents the charge for large papers (Postmaster General, 1836, p. 542). In 1838, Kendall pressed his case more vigorously in a letter to the House post office committee. He pointed out that the New York *Courier and Enquirer*, weighing 1.75 ounces, could be mailed anywhere in the country for 1½ cents. But a letter of the same weight would be charged $1.75—116 times as much as the paper. The postmaster general also discounted the value of the large city papers that traveled great distances, "three-fourths of which are filled with matter of no utility to the distant reader" (U.S. House of Representatives, 1838, pp. 3–4). Not until the 1840s, however, did Congress seriously consider graduating newspaper rates according to size and distance.

In 1836, Kendall lobbied successfully for the establishment of postal expresses because he believed that they would free readers from dependence on the large dailies published in a few Eastern cities. With the advent of the expresses, "the editors [in the South and West] will have the advantage of being the original dispensers of the news to their subscribers; and the people will obtain it through their own papers, without postage five or six days sooner than it can reach them in the New York papers, with postage" (Postmaster General, 1836, p. 544). Editors along the express routes obtained most of their news from slips— digests or proofs of important stories. Previously, editors had culled their news from the major dailies with which they exchanged postage-free (Kielbowicz, 1982). The exchanges had come in the same coaches that brought city papers to subscribers, and since postage never exceeded 1½ cents, there was little to deter readers from taking distant publications, depriving local editors of sales and the opportunity to mediate the flow of news. Editors in the West and South, of course, resented having to compete with the leading metropolitan dailies, and the expresses promised to give them an edge in getting nonlocal news to readers in their communities.

One of the Jacksonians' most persistent objections to the modest postage charged newspapers was that it encouraged city papers to circulate widely through the mails. Only scanty data bearing on this issue remain, but they all support the contention that cities were responsible for a disproportionate share of newspapers entered in the mails. In 1832, a group of Boston publishers estimated that 1,275,000 newspapers were mailed yearly from their city. Of these, 525,000 circulated within 100 miles at 1 cent postage and 750,000 traveled beyond, paying 1½ cents (U.S. House of Representatives, 1832).

Six years later, the postmaster general asked his deputies in five large cities to keep a count of matter mailed from their offices during one week. The post offices at New York, Philadelphia, Baltimore, Washington, and Richmond accepted for mailing a total of 44,468 lbs. of newspapers, 8,857 lbs. of other periodicals, and

1,916 lbs. of letters. As a rough estimate, these five cities probably accounted for half of the papers mailed in 1838.[3] Many of these papers circulated substantial distances. The postmaster general estimated in 1838 that New York City sent southward about one and a half tons of printed matter each day (U.S. House of Representatives, 1838, p. 12).

Taking advantage of the low newspaper postage, publishers in the cities actively courted subscribers in the country. Dailies discovered that readers in their hinterlands prized news from the cities, and they began offering special editions for circulation in the country, issued once, twice, or three times a week, and compiled from the columns of the daily. By 1820, at least 20 country editions emanated from New York, Philadelphia, and Baltimore, while more came from Boston, Albany, Alexandria, Lynchburg, Norfolk, Richmond, Charleston, Savannah, Mobile, St. Louis, and New Orleans (Lee, 1937, pp. 381–384, 714; Pred, 1973, pp. 61–62). The mails that brought country editors their city exchanges carried competing sheets directly to subscribers. A Goshen, New York editor analyzed the plight of country journalism in 1827:

> *It is well known that post roads and post offices have increased rapidly within a few years; and that almost every person can have convenient access to papers by mail; and printers know, that the New York papers, designed for circulation in the country, are made up twice a week from the daily papers, and published at less expense than we can publish our country papers—hence they can afford them at a lower price, in proportion to the news they contain, than we can publish our papers in the country; and thus in consequence of the facility of the mails, and the cheapness of the city papers, the circulation of our country papers is rapidly diminishing, and ere long many of them must be consigned to oblivion. . . . And if this system is to continue, and increase as it has done of late years, we shall by and by have very few country papers published, and the poorer class of our population will be doomed to remain ignorant, like the same class in the monarchies of the old world.* (cited in Hamilton, 1936, pp. 236–237)

The most notable such paper, Horace Greeley's *Weekly Tribune*, begun in 1841, eventually attained a huge national following, perhaps a million readers (Hale, 1950, p. 227). Subscriptions to the country editions cost little—one dollar a year for the weekly edition of the New York *Courier and Enquirer*—plus modest postage (Crouthamel, 1969, p. 87).

The country press mounted a counterattack. In the mid-1820s, as the encroachment of country editions grew more threatening, editors in rural areas began reporting local news missing from city publications. Earlier, most newspapers had featured international, national and state capital news; thus country papers increased coverage of news in their communities, distinguishing their coverage from that of the city press (Birdsall, 1959, pp. 206–209; Russo, 1980, pp. 6–8).

During the Jacksonian period, abolitionist publications suffered abuse at the hands of postmasters. The controversy provoked by the abolitionists' use of the mails raised questions of communication and regional culture (Eaton, 1964, pp. 196–215; Nye, 1945, 1972, pp. 41–85; Savage, 1938). The censorship of antislavery publications by postal authorities and mobs was a reaction to a massive public information campaign launched in 1835. About one million pamphlets were distributed in that year alone. This, of course, triggered the well-known backlash, in part because Southerners feared the incendiary literature would spark a slave revolt. More significantly, the resentment derived partly from the source of the information—Northern cities. Southerners invariably observed that the perpetrators directed their propaganda war from remote cities with an alien culture. The underlying concern, according to Richards (1970, p. 61), "was the fear that social control was shifting from local elites to organizations and metropolitan centers."

The South's antipathy for abolitionist publications had many of the same roots as the Jacksonians' repugnance for city papers. This marked the first time that a social movement coupled cheap printing technology with the delivery system afforded by the post office to launch a nationwide public information campaign. Previously, political factions and religious groups had used the mails extensively to disseminate their organizations' information among the faithful. But beginning in the 1830s, reform groups, notably abolitionists, went a step further and combined cheap printing and minimal postage to proselytize among people who abhorred their views. Alexis de Tocqueville, in his observations of American society in the 1830s, noted the symbiosis between reform movements and the periodical press — that communication was essential in uniting widely dispersed individuals who shared some concern (Tocqueville, 1835/1966, pp. 489–491). The abolitionists, though the most aggressive and abrasive reform movement using the mails, were hardly alone. Evangelical maternal associations were among the other antebellum movements that exploited the potential of cheap printing and cheap postage (Meckel, 1982).

Nationalism v. Localism in Antebellum Newspaper Postal Policy

In the first major revision of newspaper postage in half a century, the Post Office Act of March 3, 1845, Congress adopted two provisions affecting the press. First, newspapers could pass in the mails free within 30 miles of the office of publication. Second, postage remained unchanged for all newspapers under 1900 square inches, but those exceeding 1900 square inches were assessed at higher magazine rates.

Some characterized free circulation within 30 miles as a boon for the urban and New England press. "This bill comes before us merely to cheapen postage to the inhabitants of the great cities," said Representative William L. Yancey (*Congressional Globe* appendix, 1845, pp. 307–308). This was also a New England bill, Representative William Payne claimed; Yancey and Payne, both Democrats, represented Alabama. Nearly all the inhabitants of New England could receive a newspaper postage-free from within 30 miles of the residence. "Not so in the South or West," Payne complained. Fewer than one-fourth of the people in these regions lived within the 30-mile free-postage radius (*Congressional Globe* appendix, 1845, p. 339). A minority of the House post office committee, one Democrat and two Whigs all from the Northeast, had framed that provision (U.S. House of Representatives, 1844).

But free local circulation was not solely the product of regional chauvinism. As with most legislation, it reflected compromises. Reacting to agitation for cheap postage, Congress eliminated postage on newspapers distributed in the vicinity of the office of publication. Regardless of which regions benefited, free circulation within 30 miles enhanced the competitive position of local publications while making it relatively more costly for subscribers to take distant ones. An across-the-board reduction in newspaper postage, as advocated by some, would have brought city papers into direct competition with the country press. The interests of the people were best served by preserving local outlets for news and opinion, some policymakers argued (*Congressional Globe*, 1844, p. 423).

The provision for free local circulation was withdrawn two years later (Post Office Act of March 3, 1847), primarily because of lost revenues, but it kept reappearing in proposals as Congress worked on further revisions of postal policy (*Congressional Globe*, 1847, p. 57). In 1848, the Senate debated the merits of restoring the 30-mile free-postage zone. Again, it revived the argument of whether such a policy benefited country papers more than those issued from cities. In the less developed parts of the country, it was noted, few subscribers lived within a 30-mile radius of a newspaper. Thus, the Senate considered extending the area of free circulation to 50 miles, or even the entire state in which a paper was published. The latter proposal was found defective by some because it would have made it easier for the weekly editions of city dailies to circulate in the rural areas of their own state. Despite such objections, the Senate accepted an amendment to permit weekly papers to circulate free in their own states. The Thirtieth Congress failed to agree on other parts of the post office bill, however, and adjourned its first session without any changes in newspaper policy (*Congressional Globe*, 1848, pp. 1059, 1065–1066).

By the early 1850s, policymakers were considering the implications of the telegraph for the flow of news through the mails. As a House report observed:

> *It was formerly thought that the support of the country press demanded a tariff upon the city papers, but the establishment of telegraph lines has superseded this necessity; for whilst their circulation has been circumscribed, new dailies are constantly springing up in every portion of the country, so that when the papers from the city arrive, their chief news has been several days anticipated upon the wings of the lightning.* (U.S. House of Representatives, 1850, p. 6)

In other words, the telegraph enhanced the competitive edge of country papers in relation to those from cities, and the committee therefore concluded that a buffer zone of free local postage was no longer needed.

Congress in December 1850 resumed debating the postal status of newspapers, this time in earnest. Three months later Congress adopted the most revolutionary change in newspaper postage—and the most complex rate schedule since the founding of the United States. The Post Office Act of March 3, 1851, restored the privilege of postage-free circulation in the vicinity of the office of publication. The 1845 law had a 30-mile postage-free zone, but the new bill permitted free circulation in the county where the paper was published. This section of the new post office law arose in the House where the free in-country privilege received the fullest explication. Most of those who spoke on behalf of the provision remarked that it was necessary to insulate the country press from the aggressive city sheets using the mails to circulate throughout the nation. Representative Abraham W. Venable, a Democrat from North Carolina, offered the most extreme opinion on the subject:

> *The poisoned sentiments of the cities, concentrated in their papers, with all the aggravations of such a moral and political cesspool, will invade the simple, pure, conservative atmosphere of the country, and, meeting with no antidote in a rural press, will contaminate and ultimately destroy that purity of sentiment and of purpose, which is the only true conservatism. Fourrierism, agrarianism, socialism, and every other ism, political, moral, and religious, grow in that rank and festering soil; and if such influence and such channels of communication are to be the only ones felt and employed, the press would be the greatest calamity instead of the greatest blessing. We desire our country papers for our country opinions, our provincial politics, the organs of our conservative doctrines, and to assert the truth, uninfluenced by the morbid influences of city associations.* (*Congressional Globe*, 1850, p. 74)

After those intemperate remarks, others who supported the idea of free local circulation took pains to emphasize that they respected the city press, but felt that it was unfair to put rural papers in competition with those from the cities. The city papers were produced at lower unit costs because of their massive circulations, and, through the agency of the post office, they circulated widely for minimal postage.

Orsamus B. Matteson, a Whig from New York, provided an illustration of this unjust arrangement. When at home in Utica, Matteson said, he was kept apprised of developments in Washington by the local dailies. But dailies twice the size could be obtained from New York City, 250 miles away, at the same postage that it cost to take a paper carried only 4 or 40 miles from Utica. "Is not this gross injustice?" he asked. "Ought these country or inland papers thus be compelled to submit not only to fair competition, but to struggle on with the aid of the Government extended virtually to the city journals against them in this manner?" (*Congressional Globe*, 1851, p. 220). As a privilege extended to the country press, free local circulation simply counterbalanced the privileges accorded city publications, proponents argued (p. 220).

Even among those who shared these views there was disagreement over the dimensions of the free-postage buffer zone. Congressmen debated the various merits of free conveyance within 30 miles of the office of publication, within 40 and 50 miles, anywhere in the county where published, in the Congressional district, or in the state. Each variation had certain drawbacks. There were two problems with in-county free circulation, the option finally adopted. Counties varied greatly in size; those in the West and Southwest tended to be much larger than those in New England, which meant that those regions benefited more from this provision. In addition, a newspaper published near the county border would have circulation restricted in that direction (*Congressional Globe*, 1851–1852, pp. 76, 84–93, 140, 166–167, 218, 220, 236, 240, 243, 245).

Only a few Congressmen spoke out against free local circulation. Joseph M. Root, a Whig from Ohio, noted that the telegraph gave local papers an effective edge in competition with city papers carried into their communities by post. By the time the city papers reached the country, he explained, local publications already had received and printed the important national and international news (*Congressional Globe*, 1851, p. 170).

The House not only dwelled on the free in-county provision, but it also formulated an entirely new rate schedule for all publications. The final House version fixed a 1-cent rate for newspapers of 2 ounces or less for carriage anywhere in the country, plus 1-cent for each additional ounce. Papers circulating outside the county but still within the state of publication could pass at half the regular rates. The low, uniform rate sparked little discussion in the House. Paradoxically, the House bill lowered the barrier protecting local papers by encouraging subscribers to take publications from distant cities; if a paper came from outside the state, its postage would be the same regardless of distance (*Congressional Globe*, 1851, pp. 252–253, 261, 264).

In contrast, the newspaper postal policy devised by the Senate and ultimately signed into law only faintly resembled the version passed by the House. Free in-county delivery was the one House provision that also prevailed in the Senate, though it occasioned much less discussion. The Senate post office committee, chaired by Thomas J. Rusk, a Texas Democrat, reported a bill that had been drafted in consultation with the postmaster general and his assistants. Most of the bill that passed, insofar as it affected newspapers, originated in the Post Office Department (*Congressional Globe*, 1851, p. 370).

The heart of the bill as reported by the Senate committee called for graduating newspaper postage according to the distance conveyed, in sharp contrast to the House's nearly uniform postage. It created six zones in addition to the one within the county of publication. A weekly paper paid quarterly postage of 5 cents for transport outside the county but less than 50 miles; 10 cents for 51 to 300 miles; 15 cents for 301 to 1,000 miles; 20 cents for 1,001 to 2,000 miles; 25 cents for 2,001 to 4,000 miles; and 30 cents for distances over 4,000 miles. Dailies paid five times the preceding rates, and postage for all newspapers was half if prepaid at the office of mailing or delivery. As enacted, the bill deviated from the version sanctioned by the postmaster general in only a few respects (*Congressional Globe* appendix, 1851, pp. 257, 263–265; New York *Herald*, 1851).

In both its major features—free in-county delivery and a postage scale graduated to distance conveyed—the Senate bill erected hurdles to the long-distance circulation of public information through the press and post office. It was by far the most complicated newspaper schedule ever enacted to that time. Since 1792, there had been only two zones, plus, between 1845 and 1847, free delivery within a 30-mile radius of the office of publication. Senator William H. Seward, a New York Whig who preferred the flat rate adopted in the House, observed that graduated rates would have a tendency "to denationalize this Union."

> *This bill very ingeniously adopts a tariff which will limit the circulation of the papers in the eastern States to the Atlantic coast, and the circulation of the papers published on the Pacific coast to the borders of the Pacific ocean, and which will confine the papers of Alabama and South Carolina to their borders, or nearly so, and the papers of New Hampshire and Maine to their borders. What is the object? These newspapers are the political lungs of the Republic. They ought to have free play. They ought to play vigorously, and therefore they ought to be kept in health. But, sir, the effect of this whole system, in my opinion, will be to make such discriminations between them that we shall be divided and classified into states and communities destitute of the means of maintaining communication and sympathy with each other.* (*Congressional Globe appendix*, 1851, p. 266)

The newspaper policy was an anomalous part of the 1851 law. For letters, the law reduced a variety of zones to one flat rate; for newspapers, on the other hand, a long-standing nearly uniform rate was expanded to six zones (Post Office Act of March 3, 1851).

For a bill that had its origins in the cheap postage movement, with simplicity and uniformity of rates as its principal tenets, the newspaper provisions were an unlikely outcome. And they did not last long. Within a year, Congress overhauled the newspaper rate schedule.

The policy reflected in the Post Office Act of August 30, 1852, was diametrically opposed to that represented by the 1851 law. The new legislation provided that a newspaper of three ounces or less could circulate anywhere in the United States for 1 cent postage. For every additional ounce another cent was charged. The law retained free in-county delivery and permitted papers of 1½ ounces or less to circulate within the state of publication for half the regular rates.

Debate over the free in-county provision was relatively muted this time. Indeed, only the standard weight limit occasioned much discussion. Two and a half ounces would have permitted all but a few of the largest New York City dailies to pass through the mails at the lowest rates, according to Edson B. Olds, an Ohio Democrat and chairman of the House post office committee. James Brooks, a Whig representing New York City, objected strongly. The Senate amended the House version to fix the standard limit at three ounces so such papers as the New York *Journal of Commerce* and *Courier and Enquirer* could be mailed anywhere in the nation for 1 cent. (Like the 1851 law, this rate was halved if prepaid at the office of mailing or delivery.) This reform proceeded smoothly because, before debates commenced, the House and Senate post office committees had conferred with the postmaster general to outline a newspaper policy that was acceptable to all (*Congressional Globe*, 1852, pp. 1663, 1711–1713, 1725–1727, 1743, 1764–1766, 2268, 2271, 2389).

In short, the new law greatly simplified newspaper rates and made them more nearly uniform. The free in-county provision of the 1851 law had been retained, but under new provisions any paper could now traverse the continent for a fairly modest rate. Two New York papers, the *Herald* (1852) and the *Times* (1852), welcomed the new law. The former noted that it could now be mailed to the Pacific Coast for 1 cent instead of 6 cents, and the latter observed that yearly postage for its daily edition would be reduced to $1.56. Thus, one part of the law, the virtually flat rate for newspapers, abetted the nationalizing influence of the press while another provision, free circulation in the county of publication, protected local, provincial interests.

Flow of News on Eve of Civil War

The mails were the mechanism by which diverse publications flowed into thousands of towns and cities. The quantity and variety of public information transmitted by post is evident from the lists of periodicals mailed to Crown Point, New York, in 1846–1847 and 1857–1860 (Barker, 1950), and Stockbridge, Massachusetts, in 1852 (Jones, 1854). Both towns, in the hinterland of New York City, took more periodicals from that publishing center than any other place. Even more revealing, virtually no publications came from south of Washington, DC, or west of the Alleghenies, underscoring the concentration of the publishing business in the Northeast.

Data from Crown Point and Stockbridge, though not representative of the country, point to the dominance of New York City as a source of communication messages. Two analyses of more representative data suggest that Northeastern cities generally and New York in particular were the sources of much of the printed matter circulated by mail through the country. In a content analysis of American newspapers published between 1820 and 1860, Shaw (1981) traced the origins of news and the paths of circulation. In terms of the first place of publication, New York tended to dominate. For example, in the period 1847–1860, 7 percent of the stories published in a national sample first appeared in New York papers—the same share claimed by all the papers of the South. Shedding even more light on the flow of news were Shaw's findings about the second place of publication. Of all the stories picked up for republication in the decade before the Civil War, one-fourth had their second incarnation in the New York City press. New York's share had declined from 37 percent since 1820, but the country had also grown enormously in the meantime.

Tackling the same problem from a different angle, Pred (1971, 1973, 1980) reached similar conclusions. For the period between the invention of the telegraph and the Civil War, Pred's (1980) work "has left little doubt that major [urban] centers either strengthened their previously existing advantages and spatial biases with respect to the procurement and exchange of specialized economic information, or that they acquired new advantages and biases" (p. 156). As in the pre-telegraphic period, papers in Southern cities generally obtained more economic information from New York than from other cities in their own region. Pred also found that, at least in terms of economic information, a city's press mentioned other urban centers more frequently than towns in its own hinterland, though the latter type of information was still fairly prominent (1980, pp. 159–165). Shaw's and Pred's studies thus seem to add weight to the perception of many Congressmen that the mails brought a disproportionate amount of information from a few Eastern cities.

Conclusion

Policymakers of the early and mid-nineteenth century appreciated communication's role as an agent of modernization, which to some meant its capacity to undermine the foundations of traditional society. Even before 1800, federal officials believed that the diffusion of information from the federal capital to state capitals and ultimately to county seats tended to nationalize a loosely-knit society. Low newspaper postage rested in part on this assumption.

After the 1820s, when the urban media took advantage of the government's transmission system, it fostered resentment of a seeming cultural imperialism. Social change occurred most rapidly in large cities, the headwaters in the flow of information, and urban news and symbols permeated the entire society. Subcultures less receptive to modernization objected, and their representatives tried to structure postal policy to insulate them from messages of change that they found threatening.

The Jacksonians and their successors, the Democrats, "championed a quiet, stable, localized, face-to-face society, simple in form and manageable," a leading historian of political culture has written (Kelley, 1979, p. 160). In contrast, their opponents, the Whigs, felt more comfortable in the increasingly commercial and cosmopolitan environment of the modernizing United States (Kelley, 1979, p. 162; Ladd, 1970, pp. 68–72). With a few exceptions, these divisions were mirrored in the debates over newspaper postage.

On a more general level, a few scholars have hypothesized that a growing communication system tends to break down localism while heightening regionalism and nationalism (Odum & Moore, 1938, p. 131; Russel, 1928; Turner, 1922/1961, p. 152). These tentative conclusions remain to be proven in the context of the nineteenth century United States, but some contemporaries seemed to intuitively arrive at the same understanding, and proceeded to shape postal policy accordingly. This produced, at times, a bifurcated postal policy linked to contradictory social goals. Some features fostered a cosmopolitan or nationalistic outlook by facilitating the widespread circulation of public information through low rates and a few zones. But other policies protected provincial interests through such provisions as free local circulation.

Endnotes

1. Private express companies did not appear until the 1830s, and their services were too limited and too expensive for most users; messages could be entrusted to travelers, but such delivery was haphazard; and newspapers gathered information (usually through the mails), but could not circulate widely without the services of the post office (Mott, 1962, pp. 153–156, 194–198, 244–248).
2. Pro-Jackson Democrats (20) were uniformly against the amendment to abolish newspaper postage; two Senators identified as Whigs were also opposed, as was one Senator whose affiliation cannot be determined. In favor of the amendment were six non-Jackson Democrats, seven Whigs, four National Republicans, three with other party allegiances, and two whose political preferences are unknown (*Biographical Directory of the American Congress*, 1961; *Register of Debates*, 1832, p. 919).
3. This estimate was made as follows: Assuming that newspapers weighed about two ounces each, and that the sample week was average for that year, about 18 million papers were mailed from the five cities. This was about half of the estimated 38 million papers mailed in the country (Dill, 1928; Postmaster General, 1840, p. 490).

References

Barker, E. E. (1950). What Crown Printers were reading one hundred years ago. *New York History, 31*, 31–40.

Biographical directory of the American Congress, 1774–1961. (1961). Washington, D.C.: U.S. Government Printing Office.

Birdsall, R. D. (1959). *Berkshire county: A cultural history*. New Haven, CT: Yale University Press. *Boston Evening Transcript*. (1932, May 16).

Bretz, J. P. (1909). Some aspects of postal extension

into the West. In *American Historical Association Report*, 141–150.

Brown, R. D. (1976). *Modernization: The transformation of American life, 1600–1865*, New York: Hill and Wang.

Carey, J. W. (1969). The communications revolution and the professional communicator. *Sociological Review Monograph, 13*, 23–38.

Carey, J. W. (1981). Culture, geography, and communications: The work of Harold Innis in an American context. In W.H. Melody, L. Salter, & P. Heyer (Eds.), *Culture, communication, and dependency: The tradition of H. A. Innis* (pp. 73–91). Norwood, NJ: Ablex.

Chambers, W. N. (1963). *Political parties in a new nation*. New York: Oxford University Press.

Congressional Globe. (1843–1873). (Vols. 1–109). Washington, DC: Blair and Rives.

Crouthamel, J. L. (1969). *James Watson Webb*, Middletown, CT: Wesleyan University Press.

Deutsch, K. W. (1953). *Nationalism and social communication*. New York: Wiley

Dill, W. A. (1928) *Growth of newspapers in the United States*. Lawrence: University of Kansas Bulletin.

Eaton, C. (1964). *The freedom-of-thought struggle in the old South* (rev. ed.). New York: Harper & Row.

Hale, W. H.(1950). *Horace Greeley: Voice of the people*. New York: Harper & Bros.

Hamilton, M. W. (1936). *The country printer: New York state, 1785–1830*. New York: Columbia University Press.

Innis, H. A. (1951). Technology and public opinion in the United States. In H. A. Innis, *The bias of communication* (pp. 156–189). Toronto: University of Toronto Press.

Jones, E. F. (1854). *Stockbridge, past and present*. Springfield, MA: Samuel Bowles & Co.

Kelley, R. (1979). *The cultural pattern in American politics: The first century*. New York: Knopf.

Kielbowicz, R. B. (1982). Newsgathering by printers' exchanges before the telegraph. *Journalism History, 9*, 42–48.

Kielbowicz, R. B. (1983). The press, post office, and flow of news in the early republic. *Journal of the Early Republic, 3*, 255–280.

Ladd, E. C., Jr. (1970). *American political parties: Social change and political response*. New York: W. W. Norton.

Lee, A. M. (1937). *The daily newspaper in America: the evolution of a social instrument*. New York: Macmillan.

Meckel, R. A. (1982). Educating a ministry of mothers: Evangelical maternal associations, 1815–1860. *Journal of the Early Republic, 2*, 403–423.

Mott, F. L. (1962). *American Journalism* (3rd ed.). New York: Macmillan.

New York Herald. (1851, March 2, 3, 4).

New York Herald. (1852, September 2).

New York Times. (1852, September 2).

Nye, R. B. (1945). Freedom of the press and the antislavery controversy. *Journalism Quarterly, 22*, 1–11.

Nye, R. B. (1972). *Fettered freedom: Civil liberties and the slavery controversy, 1830–1860*. Urbana: University of Illinois Press.

Odum, H. W., & Moore, H. E. (1938). *American regionalism: A cultural-historical approach to national integration*. New York: Henry Holt and Co.

Park, R. E. (1929). Urbanization as measured by newspaper circulation. *American Journal of Sociology, 35*, 60–79

Parks, J. H. (1940). *Felix Grundy: Champion of democracy*. Baton Rouge: Louisiana State University Press.

Postmaster General. (1823–1860). *Annual Report*. Washington, DC: Various publishers.

Post Office Act of March 3, 1845. *U.S. Statutes at Large. 5*, 733.

Post Office Act of March 3, 1847. *U.S. Statutes at Large. 9*, 202.

Post Office Act of March 3, 1851. *U.S. Statutes at Large. 9*, 588.

Post Office Act of August 30, 1852. *U.S. Statutes at Large. 10*, 38–39.

Pred, A. R. (1971). Urban systems development and the long-distance flow of information through preelectronic U.S. newspapers. *Economic Geography, 47*, 498–524.

Pred, A. R. (1973). *Urban growth and the circulation of information*. Cambridge, MA: Harvard University Press.

Pred, A. R. (1980). *Urban growth and city-systems in the United States*. Cambridge, MA: Harvard University Press.

Register of debates in Congress. (1825–1837). (Vols. 1–29). Washington, DC: Gales and Seaton.

Richards, L. L. (1970). *"Gentlemen of property and standing": Anti-abolition mobs in Jacksonian America* New York: Oxford University Press.

Rogers, E. M. (1969). *Modernization among peasants: The impact of communication*. New York: Holt, Rinehart and Winston.

Russel, R. R. (1928). A revaluation of the period before the Civil War: Railroads. *Mississippi Valley Historical Review, 15*, 341–353.

Russo, D. (1980). The origins of local news in the U.S. country press, 1840s–1870s. *Journalism Monographs, 65*, 1–30.

Savage, W. S. (1938). *The controversy over the distribution of abolition literature, 1830–1860*. Washington, DC: Association for the Study of Negro Life and History.

Shaw, D.L. (1981). At the crossroads: Change and continuity in American press news, 1820–1860. *Journalism History, 8*, 38–50.

Tocqueville, A. de (1966). *Democracy in America*. (J. P. Mayer & M. Lerner, Trans). New York: Harper & Row. (Original work published 1835)

Turner, F. J. (1961). Sections and nation. In F. Turner (Ed.), *Frontier and Section* (pp. 136–153). Englewood Cliffs, NJ: Prentice-Hall. (Original work published 1922)

U.S. House of Representatives. (1832, February). *Petition of some citizens of Boston*. Document 116, 22, 1.

U.S. House of Representatives. (1838, May). *Letter postage*. Report 909, 25, 2.

U.S. House of Representatives. (1844, May). *Franking privilege and rates of postage*. Report 483, 28, 1.

U.S. House of Representatives. (1850, July). *Reduction of rates of postage*. Report 411, 31, 1.

U.S. Senate. (1832, May). *Postage on newspapers*. Report 147, 22, 1.

At the Crossroads: Change and Continuity in American Press News, 1820–1860

Donald Lewis Shaw

The years before the Civil War were important for the American press. Technology enabled newspapers to reach for a mass audience with timely telegraph news. Technology also decentralized the power of the widely clipped Washington, D.C., press and likewise accelerated the development of a new position in the newsroom, the position of reporter. As newspapers became one of the nation's first mass-produced products, reporters were needed to ensure that publishers had enough timely information for the voracious news appetites of newspapers now on the edge of expansion in physical size and, after the Civil War, in numbers of pages.

Likewise, the press in this period began to exchange a traditional benefactor, the political party, for new ones, the general audience and advertisers, with an accompanying popularization of content. Stories about weddings, horse races, local meetings, deaths, court actions and other kinds of everyday activities began to find space in the newspapers.

Adjusting to technological changes and enlarged potential audiences, the American newspaper charted a course in 1820–1860 in some ways still followed today. This study attempts to outline these changes, to chart the types of information carried, and to trace the amount of time and routes which news and other types of information took in their journey to inform Americans in all corners of their rapidly expanding nation.

The data, based upon a content analysis of the press of the period, finds a story of both continuity and change for the newspapers which in the 1820–1860 years were at an historical crossroads. As we shall see, the content and style of the press remained constant in the period, contrary to what some historians have argued, while news more often began to be gathered by reporters, to be delivered more rapidly, and to focus more upon the home community. That is, of course, as historians have argued.[1]

STUDY QUESTIONS

This study focused upon some historical observations made about the United States press of the 1820–1860 years. The author formulated several specific questions to ask, using content analysis, of a large sample of newspapers of the period. These questions can be grouped by areas.

Political versus Social Content? Did the penny press of the 1830s provide a model for the American press in general? If so, as the press widened audiences, newspapers should reflect a more diverse picture of the communities in which they were published. Social and cultural events should push against the space allocated to politics and economics. But, as we shall see, that was not the case.

Furthermore, in style, we would expect this news and other information to be written more from the point of view of a popular than elite audience. Journalism historians often have cited the readable style of the first successful American penny newspaper, the New York *Sun*, and one would expect use of this style in more newspapers, especially those in larger cities with large numbers of citizens, particularly immigrants, with marginal reading skills. Likewise, this did not happen during the 1820–1860 years. The press in news style in general was unresponsive to growing urban audiences which otherwise were changing the nature of our cities in particular and nation in general.

At the same time, in news coverage, the areas of the country and world most covered should emerge clearly. Scholar Richard Merritt argues that increased emphasis upon local events during the 18th Century reflected a growing national over colonial consciousness.[2] By analogy, one would expect that 19th Century national concerns would appear, as shadows, in the news coverage patterns of the American press. After all, the nation soon was to fragment into sections to fight one of the most devastating civil wars of human history.

Yet, as we will see, the North emerged as the dominant news source region. This was because for trade and technological reasons (such as the spread of the telegraph), the North was better situated to export an important and profitable new national product, "news," not because the region sought national dominance. The reason for this seemed due more to trade than politics. At the same time, *all* national eyes remained consistently focused upon news from the center of federal power, Washington City. From many states, indeed, a national power was emerging, with of course a powerful regional challenge to confront in 1861.

The Journalist as Active Information Gatherer? News during the 1820–1860 period should reflect more use of reporters as journalism staked ground as a profession and news became a mass produced product. Conversely less use should be made of news clipped from other newspapers. In this study, the evidence supports the generalization that active means of gleaning information edged out the more passive methods of the 18th Century. The journalist as reporter emerged.

Did Time between Event and Reader Shorten? Finally, the historical literature argues that news should come to the newspaper more rapidly as technological developments shortened time between event and publication. That expectation fully is borne out by the data, which are explored in the following section.

Findings

The Emergence of the Journalist. There is evidence that the 1820–1860 years were ones of development of the role of the reporter as professional. In the early part of those years reporters accounted for about one story in 10 but by the end for one in five (20%). See Table 1. Likewise editors inserted more of their points of view into newspapers, from 13% of the stories in the early years to 25% in the 1847–1860 period. However intrusive this might seem from our point of view, at least editors refused to serve as mere conduits for stories. Editors inserted an interpretative point of view; apparently they must have considered this part of their responsibility. The social responsibility theory of the press would not emerge for decades.

Decline of the 18th Century. As newspapers more actively undertook news gathering there was an accompanying decline in use of news and features clipped from other newspapers, from 54% to 30% across the 1820–1860 period. These changes, plus an increase in rapidly delivered telegraph news, represented an impor-

Table 1 *Who Wrote the News?*
News Sources for Dailies and Nondailies, 1820–1860[1]

Sources	Periods			
	1820–1832	1833–1846	1847–1860	1820–1860
Local Reporter	12%	13%	20%	15%
Local Editor	13	23	25	21
Correspondent	7	8	10	8
Letter to Newspaper	10	7	6	7
Clipped News	54	46	30	42
Telegraph	0	*	8	3
Other	4%	2%	2%	3%
Total%	100%	99%**	101%**	99%**
Total N	983	1,066	1,224	3,273

*Less than .5%.
**Does not sum to 100% because of rounding.
1. On sources, daily and nondaily newspapers correlated (Spearman's rho) in the following way: 1820–1832, .97 (<.001); 1833–1846, .95(<.001); 1847–1860, .96(<.001); and 1820–1860, .97(<.001).

tant movement in American journalism, the triumph of speed.

On the other hand, it also represented a decline in relative power of those newspapers which, such, as Niles' *Weekly Register*, because of their location, were able to provide a window (often tinted) through which the nation could examine events in Washington. Widely respected and generally factual, albeit permeated with a point of view, the *Register*, for example, favored tariff protection for fledgling American industries. If a newspaper elsewhere wanted to carry government news—and government news most often meant state or national news[3]—it would have to clip it from a newspaper close enough to cover the government. For distant newspapers it was difficult to throw out the bathwater of protectionism while keeping the baby of news; it was part of one package. There was little alternative.

But the growth of telegraph news, up to nearly one story in 10 (8%) by the 1847–1860 period, provided a way to obtain rapid factual information while bypassing the traditional Washington party press. Wire news was distributed to newspapers of all political beliefs and it apparently soon became clear that facts were more safely marketed than opinion.

At any rate, in this period, facts and context separated and, in the latter part of the 19th Century, finally divorced, in regular news columns at least.[4] From one point of view, the dark ages of partisan journalism finally were coming to an end. From another, facts began to triumph over context. Facts would have to speak for themselves. In the future truth would have to emerge from the clash of facts unfreighted by political party interpretations. Newspapers began to shift to readers the awesome challenge of finding the wheat buried in the chaff.

News Content. If the content of news was settling into a predictable format, as Russo argues,[5] the content of the sample newspapers was reasonably predictable throughout the 1820–1860 period. See Table 2. Stories about government accounted for about one story in four across the period. Obviously the American newspaper deeply was involved in politics throughout the entire 1820–1860 period.

Although the Civil War lay behind the veil of the future, news and comment of growing sec-

Table 2 *News Topics*
Subjects Carried in Dailies and Nondailies, 1820–1860[1]

Topics	Periods			
	1820–1832	1833–1846	1847–1860	1820–1860
Government				
Elections and Politics	6%	9%	10%	9%
General Government	16	19	14	16
Sectional Problems				
Slavery	1	2	3	2
Sectional Differences	1	1	4	2
Territories	3	5	5	4
Economic Related				
Economic News	10	15	10	12
Science and Technology	5	4	4	4
Social and Intellectual				
Social Activities	22	21	24	23
Intellectual and Cultural	13	14	13	13
Education	2	2	2	2
Foreign Relations	20%	8%	10%	13%
Total %	99%*	100%	99%*	100%
Total N	983	1,066	1,224	3,273

*Does not sum to 100% because of rounding.
1. On subjects, daily and nondaily newspapers correlated (Spearman's rho) in the following way: 1820–1832, .79(<.02); 1833–1846, .89(<.003); 1847–1860, .86(<.007); and 1820–1860, .93(<.001).

tional problems increased steadily during the period, from 5% of the coverage in the early years to 12% by the end.[6]

In the wonderful age of steam engines, perhaps it is little surprising that stories of science and technology maintained a steady, if relatively small, amount of attention. As we have seen, editors on occasion issued panegyrics about technological change.[7] Across the entire 1820–1860 period about one story of every six (16%) focused on technology or economic matters. Tariffs and the issue of a national bank were important economic news issues.

If, as historians have argued, the New York *Sun* and other penny newspapers discovered that the activities of ordinary people and feature news could garner an audience, that discovery also was made by newspapers of the period in general, not just the urban or the penny press. As Table 2 indicates, nearly one of every three stories was about such social activities as weddings, local meetings, funerals, births, or included such cultural material as novels, features or diversionary matter of other kinds.

All the American press—not just the popular urban press—diverted as well as informed. In a period in which states were debating the pros and cons of publicly supported education, newspapers devoted a consistent, if small (2%), amount of news to that topic. But the penny press did not discover social news although it certainly may have exploited it more than other newspapers.

A Shrinking World? Newspapers discovered and covered their own cities and states during the 1820–1860 years. News also sometimes traveled diverse paths to readers. See Tables 3 through 5. These tables require a note of explanation.

The "Location of the Event" (Table 3) refers to

Table 3 *Where the News Happens*
Locations of News Events, 1820–1860

Dates	Locations									Total	
	City	State	Washington, D.C.	South	North	New York	Boston	West	Foreign	%	N
1820–1832	20%	9%	19%	9%	7%	5%	1%	2%	28%	100%	701
1833–1846	22%	14%	19%	11%	10%	6%	2%	3%	14%	101%	800
1847–1860	28%	16%	12%	8%	6%	6%	1%	5%	18%	100%	967
1820–1860	24%	13%	16%	10%	7%	6%	1%	3%	19%	99%*	2,468

*Does not sum to 100% because of rounding.

Table 4 *Where the News Starts*
Locations of Newspapers Where the News was First Published in 1820–1860

Dates	Locations									Total	
	City	State	Washington, D.C.	South	North	New York	Boston	West	Foreign	%	N
1820–1832	34%	6%	15%	10%	5%	8%	2%	1%	21%	102%*	673
1833–1846	44%	9%	12%	11%	6%	7%	1%	2%	8%	100%	781
1847–1860	49%	8%	9%	7%	4%	7%	2%	4%	11%	101%*	952
1820–1860	43%	8%	12%	9%	5%	7%	2%	3%	13%	102%*	2,406

*Does not sum to 100% because of rounding.

the geographic place at which something specific occurred. To be included, an "event" actually had to have taken place within the past five years; most "events" of course occurred within the past few days before publication. This operational definition seems to include the century's more leisurely way of approaching events while excluding historical excerpts and topics. Fiction and feature accounts therefore also were excluded.

But editorials which focused upon a specific event were included as "events." In all there were 2,468 specific event stories which could be sorted from the total 3,273 stories. The remaining 805 stories were not about specific events. The study sought to discover in what parts of the country and world these 2,468 events occurred.

"Where the News Starts" (Table 4) refers to the first location at which these stories were published. For example, a fire in Syracuse, N.Y., the location of the event, for some reason may first have been publicized in a New York City newspaper, the first point of news origination. Many of these same stories later might have been reprinted in (at least) another newspaper ("Where the News Traveled Next," Table 5), or even others before, finally, being republished in our sample newspaper. Hence one can follow the "route" of many stories, along with the time taken during the journey from event to sample newspaper, in this way: location of event → location of first publication → location of second publication.

For many stories, such as travelogues, fiction,

Table 5 *Where the News Traveled Next*
Locations of Newspapers Where the News was Published Second

Dates	Locations									Total	
	City	State	Washington, D.C.	South	North	New York	Boston	West	Foreign	%	N
1820–1832	9%	3%	12%	13%	7%	37%	4%	1%	12%	98%*	121
1833–1846	30%	5%	9%	10%	10%	20%	7%	3%	6%	100%	118
1847–1860	30%	5%	4%	19%	3%	25%	1%	3%	9%	99%*	161
1820–1860	24%	4%	8%	15%	6%	27%	4%	2%	9%	99%**	400

*Does not sum to 100% because of rounding.

and anecdotes, points of origin did not really relate to events and they were not included in this analysis. In calculating the first and second points of publication, local editorials about a specific event and clipped news which includes extensive editorial comment to "help" the reader are considered as originating in the city of newspaper publication, giving more weight to the comment than to the event itself (as did the editorialists), thus somewhat inflating that category because of the editorial tendency often to comment extensively on news events which happened elsewhere. Yet this comment was about specific events. Of the 2,468 stories about specific events, 2,406 could be located in terms of where the news was first published and, of these, 400 could further be traced to the second newspaper point of publication along the way. The study did not further follow stories.

Where the News Happens. Coverage of these 2,468 specific news events centered heaviest on the city of publication, 24% during the entire 1820–1860 period. See Table 3. Over each period, however, there was a definite increase in home coverage. Newspapers were finding news closer to home and that included a similar increase in state news.

Considering the growth of the federal government, one might have expected a steadily increasing focus upon Washington—that seems to have been true in recent years[8]—but that was not the case. From nearly one story of five (19%) in the early period, coverage of Washington events dropped to about one of 10 (12%), still a lot, by the end of the period. Coverage of events in New York and Boston remained about the same across the period.

Coverage of events in the South, the North and West remained about the same across the period. Coverage of events in the North and South is about even if New York City and Boston events are separated from other Northern events. Inclusion of these two cultural and trade centers, however, provided the North with a distinct advantage. From these cities, among others, American ships carried products all over the world,[9] as the United States began its move to become a major world commercial power. New York, particularly, maintained a powerful hold on national attention. That remains true today.

Apparently increases in local and state news came at the expense of foreign news. The latter declined from 28% of the coverage in the early period to 18% by the end. This probably reflected an increase in interest in local communities as they grew in size, a crystallizing sense of nationalism as the new country became home to millions and, over time, the old countries receded in importance in collective memory. It was, most likely, the emergence of an American community; one, however, which soon would tragically fragment.

Where the News Starts. Increasingly, also, news was filed from the city of publication. See Table 4. This represents a stronger trend than where events were located because sometimes reporters and editors wrote about distant events but clearly (from the internal evidence of the stories) were not present where the events actually happened. In that period, distance certainly was no barrier to comment. Editors were not shy; they apparently relished the role of commentator.

Even so, the North, counting New York City and Boston, predominated in terms of where the news first appeared, with news filed less often from locations in the South and far less often from the West. As the South was dependent upon the North for "products of Yankee mills and Yankee colleges, of Yankee commercial houses and Yankee publishing houses, of Yankee ships and Yankee textbooks,"[10] it also was dependent upon the North for much of its news, especially if one includes the news from New York City and Boston.

Throughout the period, one of every six stories (14%) was launched from a Northern newspaper. Although the location remained important, news decreasingly saw first publication in Washington, D.C., true also of foreign locations.

Far more than for other U.S. sections, news was a Northern product exported to other regions. News to Southerners often seemed to arrive in an abolitionist package. "All reform thus acquired a Yankee tint."[11] For the South this had important implications for the gathering storm ahead.

Where the News Traveled Next. Those news stories which were published in still another newspaper, 400 of the original 2,468 stories, continued their journey. Here New York City newspapers emerged as enormously important, accounting for nearly four of 10 stories (37%) in the early period and holding strong at one of four (25%) by the closing years of the 1820–1860 period. Clearly New York City dominated the Northern states (which, as a group, actually declined in importance as an interchange point by the end of the period to 3%) as a communications relay center.

Presumably, although the study did not further chart it, as these stories traveled on their way to a final destination in the sampled newspapers, much of the news moved via these urban centers, particularly in the North. By the end of the period the Washington, D.C., press had declined dramatically in importance as a secondary travel point along the way. Such, likely, was the considerable power of the telegraph to decentralize.

The News: How Long in Transit? The time needed to gather and move this news across the nation dramatically declined during the 1820–1860 period. See Tables 6 and 7. These tables show time "lags" in four ways and need a word of explanation.

"Newsgathering: Event to Newspaper" reports the amount of time, on the average, taken by reporters from gathering and writing the facts to the first published newspaper story.

"Across America" records the average amount to time in transit for a newspaper story first appearing in an American newspaper, such as Niles' *Register*, to be clipped and published in another American newspaper.

"Event to Reader" is the average total time lapse between the time the event happened to the report in the sample newspaper. This encompasses all other time lags. Not all time lags could be computed for each sample story, accounting for the different number of sample stories for each of the different lag computations. In other words, the Ns will not sum up.

Finally, "Across the Ocean" reports the average time taken by a story which first appeared in a European newspaper to appear in an American newspaper. For dailies, this could be computed only for 66 stories across the total period, a small number which requires caution in interpretations. This is even more true for the 35

Table 6 *How Long?*
Time Lapse from Event to Reader, Dailies, 1820–1860

Periods and Days	Time Lags			
	Newsgathering	Across America	Across the Ocean	Event to Reader
1820–1832				
1–3 days	55%	27%	*	21%
4–7 days	22%	35%	*	24%
8 days–1 month	14%	31%	7%	28%
More than 1 month	9%	7%	93%	28%
Total %	101%**	100%	100%	101%**
Total N	141	83	27	170
1833–1846				
1–3 days	67%	28%	*	41%
4–7 days	20%	29%	*	22%
8 days–1 month	10%	41%	36%	24%
More than 1 month	3%	2%	64%	13%
Total %	100%	100%	100%	100%
Total N	205	68	14	242
1847–1860				
1–3 days	74%	69%	*	57%
4–7 days	16%	16%	*	19%
8 days–1 month	9%	10%	88%	17%
More than 1 month	1%	5%	12%	8%
Total %	100%	100%	100%	101%**
Total N	347	134	25	366
1820–1860				
1–3 days	68%	47%	*	44%
4–7 days	18%	25%	*	21%
8 days–1 month	10%	24%	44%	21%
More than 1 month	3%	5%	56%	14%
Total %	99%**	101%**	100%	100%
Total N	693	285	66	778

*The Ns are too low to compute for the short periods.
**Does not sum to 100% because of rounding.

Table 7 *How Long?*
Time Lapse from Event to Reader, Nondailies, 1820–1860

Periods and Days	Time Lags			
	Newsgathering	Across America	Across the Ocean	Event to Reader
1820–1832				
1–3 days	34%	5%	*	7%
4–7 days	32%	13%	*	18%
8 days–1 month	25%	52%	4%	34%
More than 1 month	8%	29%	96%	42%
Total %	99%**	99%**	100%	101%**
Total N	111	75	28	168

Periods and Days	Time Lags			
	Newsgathering	Across America	Across the Ocean	Event to Reader
1833–1846				
1–3 days	39%	14%	*	15%
4–7 days	34%	19%	*	20%
8 days–1 month	23%	60%	33%	47%
More than 1 month	4%	8%	67%	18%
Total %	100%	101%**	100%	100%
Total N	95	52	3	132
1847–1860				
1–3 days	50%	26%	*	23%
4–7 days	34%	35%	*	36%
8 days–1 month	13%	29%	75%	30%
More than 1 month	4%	11%	25%	11%
Total %	101%**	101%**	100%	100%
Total N	119	55	4	130
1820–1860				
1–3 days	41%	14%	*	14%
4–7 days	33%	21%	*	24%
8 days–1 month	20%	47%	14%	37%
More than 1 month	6%	18%	86%	25%
Total %	100%	100%	100%	100%
Total N	325	182	35	430

*Ns are too low to compute for the short periods.
**Does not sum to 100% because of rounding.

stories which appeared in the nondaily sample newspapers during the 1820–1860 period.

These different time lags are illustrated in the following figure:

Four Types of News Lags, 1820–1860

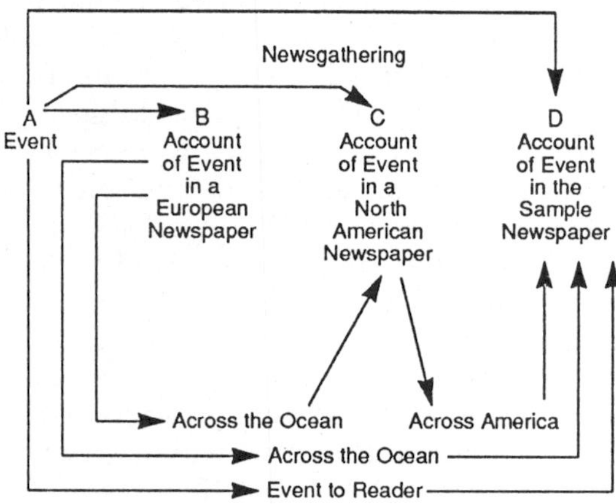

For any given sample news story, the "Newsgathering" time lag is: B–A, C–A, or D–A but only one of these. Similarly, the "Across America" lag is D–C. The "Across the Ocean" time lag is C–B or D–B, but only one was counted for a given story. Finally, the "Event to Reader" lag is D–A. Obviously the total lag could be computed for more stories than could any other type of lag.

The Reporter Gathers the Facts. The decreasing amount of time needed to gather and present news is evident for both dailies and nondailies. For dailies, in the early period, more than half (55%) of the stories were about events occurring within the past thee days but nearly three of four (74%) were about events happening within three days by the end of the 1820–1860 span. For nondailies, the trend was similar. If an entire week is considered, dailies edged out nondailies in newsgathering speed by only a little. Newsgathering speed did not really differentiate daily and nondaily newspapers in 1820–1860, at least by much.

This increase in speed parallels the use of reporters, as we have seen, and is further evidence of the competition to present information fast—the rise of "news"—and the growing importance of someone to gather that news, the reporter. For some publishers and readers an exciting new world was coming. For other publishers, distressed by the popularizations of the urban press, technology linked the beauty of the press with the beast (to them) of a mass audience.

Stretching Across the Nation. The time needed to move the news across the nation also dramatically declined during the period.

In the early years, one daily newspaper story of every four (27%) took only one to three days to move from its point of first newspaper publication to the next newspaper but nearly seven of 10 (69%) moved that rapidly by the end of the 1820–1860 years. By these later years of course railroads and telegraph greatly had enhanced the ability of newspapers to obtain information rapidly, particularly by newspapers in Northern and, to some extent, Western states.

For nondailies, the same trend emerged, although less dramatically. In the early years, 5% of the stories were about a news event published within the previous three days while that figure swelled to 26%, one in four, by the end of the period. If an entire week is considered, however, dailies were only slightly better able to republish news within a week of first publication.

Why Was the Speed Increasing? This rapid movement of information across the nation doubtless represented the combined forces of what journalism historian Frank Luther Mott called the miracles of 19th Century communication—"the steamship, the railroad, the magnetic telegraph."[12] A canal building craze began in 1817 and by 1840, more than 3,000 miles had been dug. Not all canals were as financially successful as the famous Erie Canal, but all reduced travel time and reduced shipping costs.[13]

Not only did canals facilitate movement of goods and information, the miles of surfaced roads jumped from 10,000 in 1820 to 88,000 in 1860. Stage coaches improved. In 1820 it took a stagecoach 78 days to bump along from Washington, D.C., to Little Rock, Arkansas, but by 1830 the time for this trip dropped to 14 days.[14]

Post offices were quick to take advantage of the improved interior means of transportation. The number of post offices expanded from some 4,500 in 1820 to more than 28,000 by 1860.[15] During the same period, post roads expanded from more than 72,000 to more than 240,000 miles.[16]

Steam meanwhile conquered inland waterways. Robert Fulton built the Clermont which in 1807 putted successfully up the Hudson River from New York to Albany. The trip took 32 hours. In 1811 the first steamer left Pittsburg at eight miles an hour to arrive in New Orleans about two months later.[17] By 1843, a diarist of the period expressed surprise at the "greenness" of a man he met who never had been on a steamboat.[18] How fast technology conquers.

In 1830, 23 miles of railroad were built to bring the nationwide total to 40. In 1860, 1,500 miles were added to the nation's network of more than 30,000 miles.[19] From the railroad's carnival-like start in 1830 when Peter Cooper's Tom Thumb raced a horse between Baltimore to nearby Ellicott City— the machine fated to lose that first race—an empire on steel had begun spreading.[20] Little wonder editors could be ecstatic.

In this rapid expansion, historian Lee Benson sees a country of continental proportions undergoing the changes in transportation and communication necessary to achieve national potential. As we have seen, no one knew how large a nation could become without crumbling at the outer edges.[21] Except for Russia, European states were comparatively small. In the Benson thesis, "the boom in transportation and the dynamic expansion of the economy acted as powerful stimulants to movements inspired by the egalitarian ideals of the Declaration of Independence."[22]

Whatever else, these inventions played their part in bringing information quickly across the nation. It also is evident that for stories for which the time lapse could be determined, the transportation improvements of the period resulted in more rapid contact with Europe.

Across the Ocean. As speed conquered the nation it helped bring world events closer. For stories about European events for which the time lapse could be determined it seems evident that the transportation improvements of the period resulted in more rapid contact with Europe.

In the 18th Century that contact often took months, depending upon the season, wind and weather. Although in this study the small number of stories about foreign events for which the time lapse could be calculated requires a cautious period-by-period comparison, for the 1820–1860 period as a whole, it was about a month (44% of the stories) between most European events and their report in an American daily newspaper. Somewhat slower, in nondailies, about one story in six (14%) about European events appeared within a month or less of the event. Although the Ns are low, Table 6 and 7 show that the time needed for news to cross the Atlantic steadily declined.

This change in speed reflected a period of dramatic change in ocean-going traffic. In the first week of January 1818, the ship James Monroe set sail from New York and headed for Liverpool while the ship Courier headed westward from Liverpool to New York. With this, the Black Ball Line opened the first regularly scheduled monthly sailing between two distant ports.[23]

As early ships gave rise to the beautifully streamlined clipper ships, world sailing times declined rapidly. The average time from Liverpool to New York during 1818–1822 was 39.0 days but this dropped to 33.3 days in 1848–1852.[24]

But as so often happens in a technological age, beauty retreated before utility as one of the miracles of the age, the steam engine, found its way aboard. Operating first on America's great rivers—steamship transportation increased one hundredfold from 1820 to 1860[25]—steam-operated vessels soon braved the open sea. Steamships operating between England and New York in 1839 averaged 17 days on the westward trip and a bit over 15.4 days the other way.[26] By 1860 record trips were made in less than 10 days and transatlantic trips of more than 13 or 14 days were considered unusually slow.[27] Less glamorous than clippers, but more dependable, steamers took command of the sea. They remained there for decades.

Total Time Lapse. The total time lapse between events and publication in 1820–1860 declined. The total "Event to Reader" lag includes the total of all previous lags—"Newsgathering" and (where appropriate) "Across America" and "Across the Ocean" as well.

For dailies, on the average, one of five stories (21%) in the early part of the 1820–1860 years were about events which had occurred in the past three days. By the end of the 1820–1860 span, only one story of every 10 (8%) took a month to creep to public attention.

For nondailies the results are similar. In fact, nondailies demonstrated about the same ability to deliver news within a week of an event as could dailies throughout the period. Nondaily readers therefore never were very far behind daily newspaper readers and neither type newspaper trailed events very far by the end of the period.

Response to a Growing Popular Audience? Citing such sources as the New York *Sun* and *Herald*, journalism historians have found the 1820–1860 period one in which the press became more responsive to the enlarged urban audiences, composed in part at least of people with marginal reading skills. As the press devoted more space to a fuller range of human activities, not just politics, the press adopted a readable, popular style to fit all classes, historians have argued.[28]

For the press in general, however, this study does not substantiate this historical observation. If the level of readability can be taken as one important index of style, as this study argues, the press was not particularly responsive to its audience during the 1820–1860 years.

Using the Flesch formula,[29] readability measures were computed for each sample newspaper for those stories written by local reporters, local editors, or which came to the sample newspaper from another newspaper (clipped) or telegraph. For any given sample newspaper for a particular year, a maximum of four of each type was included in this computation. Normally there were fewer.

Audiences in Large vs. Small Towns. The analysis also divided the sample newspapers according to whether the newspaper was published in a "town" (here defined as a city under 30,000 population, according to the U.S. Census closest in time) or "city" (more than 30,000 population). The study reasoned, following the argument of journalism historians, that cities more likely would have larger numbers of readers with marginal reading skills. It was into these cities that large numbers of immigrants poured. To be responsive to these audience members, newspapers more likely would simplify the writing, as did the New York *Sun*; in that case, circulation growth demonstrated success.

Not Particularly Readable. But that was not the case. Across the 1820–1860 years the strongest finding is that there was little change, regardless of size of city of publication. See Table 8. Drawing an analogy to the Flesch scale, one story of six (15%) was judged "extra difficult" in both towns and cities, while one of 10 fell into the "easy" category.[30] By the end of the 1820–1860 period about one of 10 belonged to either the "extra difficult" or "easy" classification. Throughout the period the number of stories judged "difficult" or "average," about four of every 10 for each, remained the same. Size of city made little difference. Year made little difference. In news style as in news content the story of these historical data is one of continuity, not change.

Of course we must remember that what is "extra difficult" for us, at least as determined by the modern Flesch scale, might not have been for readers of that day, used as readers were to the flourishing oratorical style of the period. *But the point is that there was little change across the 41 years of the study.* As a group, American newspapers did not become more popular in style or more responsive to their readers during the 1820–1860 period. The New York penny press is not an accurate model of the American press in general during these years.

Technology diffuses more rapidly than ideas; perhaps the New York approach to news style was adopted later—certainly newspapers in general later became simpler in style by our standards. At any rate, these findings suggest that the press *may* initially be more responsive to technological than social change, a finding of some contemporary studies.[31]

Summary

In the 1820–1860 years American newspapers in many ways began to assume a contemporary shape. This study, a content analysis of more than 3,000 sample newspaper stories of the 1820–1860 press, substantiated some observations long ago made by historians about our press development.[32] But there are points of dif-

Table 8 *Response to Readers*
Readability of Daily and Nondaily Newspapers, 1820–1860

Periods and City Size	Level of Difficulty				Total%	Total N
	Extra Difficult	Difficult	Average	Easy		
1820–1832						
Towns	13%	39%	38%	10%	100%	240
Cities	17%	38%	35%	11%	101%*	314
Total %	15%	39%	36%	10%	100%	554
Total N	84	214	200	56		
1833–1846						
Towns	7%	38%	40%	16%	101%*	313
Cities	13%	42%	37%	8%	100%	301
Total %	10%	40%	38%	12%	100%	614
Total N	60	244	236	74		
1847–1860						
Towns	8%	38%	40%	14%	100%	254
Cities	8%	37%	43%	11%	99%*	474
Total %	8%	38%	42%	12%	100%	728
Total N	58	274	306	90		
1820–1860						
Towns	9%	38%	39%	14%	100%	807
Cities	12%	39%	39%	10%	100%	1,089
Total %	11%	39%	39%	12%	100%	1,896
Total N	202	732	742	220		

*Does not sum to 100% because of rounding.

ference also with earlier historical views. The historical story is one of both continuity and change.

For example, newspapers of the period did concentrate much attention upon politics. However, there also was evidence throughout the period that newspapers devoted major attention to the social and intellectual aspects of their communities and to economic concerns. And, relatively speaking, there was not much change in the space devoted to these types of information. Newspapers did not become less political and more social.

Newspapers were, as historians have argued, very political throughout the period. Likewise much attention was devoted to the activities of ordinary people. Social news, however, was not a type of news which erupted in the penny press in the 1830s, unlike earlier historical arguments. It already was there and it remained in about the same proportions throughout the 1820–1860 years. In terms of press content the story of the 1820–1860 period is one of continuity, not change.

But in terms of news sources used, the evidence is different. Stories written by reporters began to displace news clipped from another newspaper and, propelled by the development of the telegraph and other communication means, the location of a newspaper (such as in Washington) began to be less important than the ability to obtain news rapidly. As traditional newspaper leaders were less clipped and quoted, speed displaced interpretation, a process considerably speeded up by the end of the 19th Century, outside the period of this study.

During the 1820–1860 years, there was a dramatic decline in the time which elapsed between an event's occurrence and its report in a newspaper. As news established its market value, party support for newspapers, which continued until after the Civil War, began to recede in importance and publishers found steadier support in advertising and street sales. That process began during the 1820–1860 years.

As events and readers came closer in time so too did the topics of many stories. News came home. Over the period, the number of stories originating from the city of publication grew sharply. Perhaps, as Ben Bagdikian suggests,[33] cities demanded news interpreters as communities outgrew the bounds of interpersonal communications. Institutional press was louder than individual voice.

At any rate Boston and New York, important cultural and trade centers, retained a small but steady importance throughout the period as locations of stories which later were picked up by other newspapers. That influence, however, declined as culture and trade apparently were displaced by a new awareness of local community and local news began to command larger news space.

Stories from Washington, D.C., important throughout the period, began to decline in number as the Civil War edged closer. This focus upon Washington, however, the center of national power, apparently continues in our press and, in fact, recently may even be accelerating.[34] If so, following scholar Richard Merrit's argument that an American community emerged in the 18th Century,[35] in the 19th and 20th Centuries we are witness of an American federal community.

In terms of sources used and places covered, the historical evidence suggests change, not continuity. Newspapers began to gather their own news with reporters, more speed and their focus narrowed to home.

In viewing the press response to the growing audiences of the 19th Century, early historical observations need qualification. Data here suggest that newspapers as a group did not substantially alter their styles of writing in the 1820–1860 years. Stories proportionately were just as "difficult" or "simple" to read at the end of the period as at the beginning. Penny newspapers were atypical and continued historical focus upon their styles of writing as characteristic of all American newspapers is misleading. In style, the American press of the period did not adjust to the growing audiences.

Increase in speed of delivery, use of reporters, declining use of once heavily-clipped newspapers, and more attention to local news—all these were trends of the 1820–1860 years. In content, the press did not much vary during the period, with politics given heavy emphasis throughout the 1820–1860 years.

The contemporary press has continued to build upon this foundation. In a world being wound together by cable systems and with messages bouncing from satellite to earth, the press confronts awesome new challenges. The news topics and approaches seem most likely to remain; at least they are most resistant to change. Perhaps they are embedded in the basic needs of a social system. Recent evidence suggests enormous similarity of news topics across the world, regardless of political systems.[36] But the technology will alter ways of gathering, processing and delivering news, much as was true in the 19th Century.

While the past does not predict the future—history does not repeat itself—it does suggest paths of action, or paths to avoid. In terms of rapid news spread and employment of active news gatherers, the 1820–1860 press was modern, demonstrating a sharp break with the century before it. As was true in Europe, the press harnessed steam to absorb the exciting new technology and to produce one of the young nation's first truly mass produced products, newspapers. These newspapers served the rapidly enlarging and nationalizing audience of the United States. By focusing continuing (if declining, as the Civil War approached) attention on Washington, the press may even have enhanced the process of nationalization.

Endnotes

1. For background works related to this subject see Merle Curti, *The Growth of American Thought*, 2nd ed. (New York: Harper & Brothers, 1951); Glyndon G. Van Deusen, *The Jacksonian Era 1828–1848* (New York: Harper & Row, 1963); Edwin Emery and Michael Emery, *The Press and America*, 4th ed. (Englewood Cliffs, N.J.: Prentice-Hall, 1978); Frank Luther Mott, *American Journalism, A History: 1690–1960*, 3rd ed. (New York: MacMillan Company, 1962). Also see George Boyce, James Curran, and Pauline Wingate, eds., *Newspaper History from the Seventeenth Century to the Present Day* (Beverly Hills, Calif.: Sage Publications, 1978), especially Chap. 2 for a view of development of journalism in England. Also useful are David M. Potter and Thomas G. Manning, eds., *Nationalism and Sectionalism in America 1775–1877: Select Problems in Historical Interpretation* (New York: Holt, Rinehart, and Winston, 1949); and Daniel J. Boorstin, *The Americans: The National Experience* (New York: Vintage Books, 1965). The relationship between communication technology and national power is insightfully discussed in Harold A. Innis, *The Bias of Communication* (Toronto: University of Toronto Press, 1951), pp. 33–60 (in 1971 reprint). Also see his *Empire and Communications* (Toronto: University of Toronto Press, 1972), which is revised by Mary Q. Innis and contains a foreword by Marshall McLuhan.
2. See Richard L. Merritt, *Symbols of American Community 1735–1775* (New Haven: Yale University Press, 1966).
3. David J. Russo, "The Origins of Local News in the U.S. Country Press, 1840s–1870s," *Journalism Monographs*, No. 65, February, 1980, p. 19. Edited by Bruce H. Westley.
4. See Donald L. Shaw, "News Bias and the Telegraph: a Study of Historical Change," *Journalism Quarterly*, 44 (Spring 1967): 3–12, 31.
5. Russo, *Origins of Local News*, p. 21.
6. Not shown in this table, Southern newspapers particularly were aware of gathering war clouds. They carried more news focusing on sectional differences. This is explored in separate analysis.
7. Calder M. Pickett. "Technology and the New York Press in the 19th Century," *Journalism Quarterly*, 37 (Summer 1960), pp. 398–407.
8. See Christine Ogan, Ida Plymale, D. Lynn Smith, William H. Turpin, and Donald Lewis Shaw, "The Changing Front Page of the New York Times, 1900–1970," *Journalism Quarterly*, 52 (Summer 1975): 340–344.
9. See Boorstin, *The Americans*, Chapters 1–3.
10. Curti, *Growth of American Thought*, p. 451.
11. Boorstin, *The Americans*, p. 215.
12. Mott, *American Journalism*, p. 244.
13. Mary Elizabeth Junck, "Newsgathering in the Deep Southern Press, 1820–1860," M.A. thesis, University of North Carolina, 1971, p. 17. This source contains an excellent discussion of the influence on the press of early technological developments.
14. *Ibid.*
15. *Historical Statistics of the United States, Colonial Times to 1957: A Statistical Abstract Supplement* (Washington, D.C.: U.S. Bureau of the Census, 1960), p. 497.
16. Alfred McClung Lee, *The Daily Newspaper in America: The Evolution of a Social Instrument* (New York: MacMillan Company, 1937), pp. 745–746.
17. Junck, "Newsgathering in the Deep South," p. 13.
18. See George Templeton Strong, "Diary," in David Grimsted, ed., *Notions of the Americans 1820–1860* (New York: George Braziller, 1970), p. 273.
19. *Historical Statistics*, pp. 427–28.
20. Junck, "Newsgathering in the Deep South," pp. 14–15.
21. See Potter and Manning, eds., *Nationalism and Sectionalism*, p. 69.
22. Lee Benson, *The Concept of Jacksonian Democracy: New York as a Test Case* (New York: Atheneum, 1964), p. 13.
23. George Rogers Taylor, *The Transportation Revolution 1815–1860* (New York: Reinhart & Company, 1951), p. 106.
24. *Ibid.*, pp. 110–111.
25. *Ibid.*, p. 114.
26. *Ibid.*, p. 146.
27. *Ibid.*
28. See Emery and Emery, *The Press and America*, Chap. 10; Mott, *American Journalism*, Chap. 13.

29. See Rudolf Flesch, *The Art of Readable Writing* (New York: Harper & Row, 1949), especially pp. 147–156, 213–218.

30. The Flesch scale divided up categories in the following way: 0–30 on the readability measure was "very difficult"; 30–50, "difficult"; 50–60, "fairly difficult", 60–70, "standard"; 70–80, "fairly easy"; 80–90, "easy"; 90–100, "very easy." In this study the data were grouped differently in order (1) to take into account the distribution of the data, and (2), as far as possible, to make the data more representative of reading skills of the period. Hence, in this study, scores of 1–21 were judged "extra difficult" 22–41, "difficult"; 42–56, "average"; and 57–94, "easy." What we are calling "average" would be "fairly difficult" today but not likely then. What we are calling "easy" would include what we today call "standard." See Rudolph Flesch, "A New Readability Yardstick," *Journal of Applied Psychology* 32 (June 1948) 3: 221–33.

31. See for example Donald L. Shaw, "Surveillance vs. Constraint: Press Coverage of a Social Issue," *Journalism Quarterly*, 46 (Winter 1969): 707–712.

32. See especially Emery and Emery, *The Press and America*; Mott, *American Journalism*; and Willard Grosvenor Bleyer, *Main Currents in the History of American Journalism* (Boston: Houghton Mifflin Co., 1927).

33. Ben H. Bagdikian, *The Information Machines: Their Impact on Man and the Media* (New York: Harper & Row, 1971), p. 268.

34. See Christine Ogan, Ida Plymale, D. Lynn Smith, William H. Turpin, and Donald Lewis Shaw, "The Changing Front Page of the New York *Times*, 1900–1970," *Journalism Quarterly*, 52 (Summer 1975): 340–44.

35. See Merritt, *Symbols of American Community 1735–1775*.

36. See Robert L. Stevenson, Richard R. Cole, and Donald L. Shaw, "Patterns of World News Coverage: A Look at the UNESCO Debate on the 'New World Information Order,'" Paper presented to the International Communication Division, Association for Education in Journalism, Boston, August, 1980.

The Mythology of the Penny Press

John C. Nerone

One of the commonplaces of U.S. communications history is a mythology about the penny press of the 1830s and 40s. This mythology consists of a set of vivid characterizations that can be found in histories of every shade of opinion. With roots going back more than a century, the mythology of the penny press is part of the common sense about U.S. journalism.

The gist of the mythology is that a small number of daring innovators, working especially in New York City, revolutionized the content and style of American journalism by creating what was essentially the modern popular commercial newspaper. These penny papers were the first commercial papers, the first popular papers, the first politically independent papers, and the first "news" papers. They were the ancestors of contemporary U.S. newspapers.

These ideas provide a myth of origins for the contemporary press. As such, the mythology has been involved in the development of the institution it describes, providing historical legitimacy for current practices and ideas. The mythology originated in the self-characterizations of penny press operators, was adopted by the writers of the first journalism histories (generally designed as texts to be used in journalism schools), and has provided a genealogy for the contemporary culture of journalism.

The mythology of the penny press also serves to direct research into the history of the American press. Scholars seem to agree that a revolution in American journalism took place in the middle decades of the nineteenth century, and that the penny press wrought it, even though they disagree on the precise consequences and whether they were beneficial. Most surveys choose 1833, the year Benjamin Day's *New York Sun* demonstrated the viability of the penny press format, as the dividing point between two diametrically opposite periods of press conduct. While detailed research on either side of this divide may fail to invoke the epochal influence of the penny press, the mythology rarely has been challenged and always finds its way back into fresh syntheses.

Describing this set of beliefs as a mythology does not necessarily mean that it is factually false. Indeed, many of the facts invoked in the mythology of the penny press are true. What is characteristic of the mythology, however, is its system of organizing these facts around a heroic narrative with didactic effect. Because a mythology is a story organized around a set of values, it almost always involves an oversimplification of history. Mythology's shortcoming is not a falsification of facts but a misappropriation of facts.

In this article, I outline the main characterizations of the penny press and show how they constitute a set of beliefs with implications beyond the arguments or intentions of any particular scholar. To support this point, I then outline briefly the historiography of U.S. journalism, with special attention toward attitudes concerning the penny press. Finally, I present a detailed critique of conventional ideas about the penny press and propose some alternate characterizations of the history of its period.

The main points I make about the history are these: The expansion of the press in the United States was a result of ideas and expectations popularized in the period of the American Revolution. This change, beginning in the eighteenth century, was deeply affected by two grand developments in the nineteenth century: the rise of popular partisan politics and the appearance of a market economy. Two resulting trends are apparent in nineteenth century newspapers: politicization and commercialization. These twin processes were apparent in every sector of the press but shaped different classes of papers in different ways: Because of accidental factors in some of the major Eastern cities, politicization, or the integration of the press into the party system, and commercialization, or the integration of the press into the market economy, seemed to come into conflict with each other. This episode has given birth to the myth of a revolution in journalism.

I argue that the development of American journalism is more properly understood as an evolutionary development rooted in shifts in social and cultural environment. The penny press is properly understood as a mutation in one class or species of newspaper, rather than as a revolution in editorial policy and business strategy. The innovations associated with the penny press are functions of forces external to the papers themselves rather than the result of unique personal initiative. The strategies—editorial, political, and commercial—adopted by penny press operators were responses to changes in specific environments rather than discoveries of fundamental human truths (e.g., the people want news, not opinions) or of new principles (e.g., political independence). And changes in newspaper structures and techniques were more the products of processes of evolutionary change than the inventions of imaginative entrepreneurs. The same forces that produced the dramatic innovations in penny papers acted simultaneously on the press as a whole.

This point of view changes the emplotment of journalism history in the penny press era in key ways. It also promises to shift attention away from the usual characters and settings. The moral of the story should be different too. I begin with a review of the mythology of the penny press.

The Mythology

Conventional ideas credit the penny papers with revolutionizing U.S. newspapers in several areas. First, they revolutionized circulation by making papers cheaply available to the public. Second, they revolutionized content by declaring their independence from political parties and concentrating on news rather than opinion. And third, they revolutionized the newspaper business by introducing new technologies (such as the telegraph), new occupations (such as that of the reporter), and new sources of income (such as advertising). Put together, these characterizations in effect argue that the penny press transformed the U.S. newspaper from a tool of political privilege to a social instrument of popular democracy. It will be helpful to analyze each area in some detail.

Price and Circulation

The definitive innovation of the penny press was the introduction of a newspaper that sold daily for one cent. The cheapness of these papers made them accessible to new readerships.

The penny papers also introduced the cash system of circulation, which meant that the papers were sold for cash to distributors who then sold the papers to readers in whatever manner they deemed appropriate. Distributors are usually depicted as newsboys, "live lads" who "wrought the greatest change in journalism that had ever been made, for they brought the paper to the people" (O'Brien, 1928, p. 19). These newsboys are said to have concentrated on street sales rather than subscriptions, the traditional mainstay of newspaper circulation. Street sales dictated sensational content (Peterson, Jensen, & Rivers, 1965, p. 43) and different graphics created "better makeup and more readable type" (Emery and Emery, 1984, p. 143). All of these innovations—street sales, sensationalism, and graphics—made the paper more accessible to the working class.

Consequently, the penny papers are said to have achieved readerships radically larger than earlier papers. Indeed, the commonly discussed New York penny papers achieved unprecedented circulations. By 1836, for instance, the *Sun* claimed a circulation greater than that of its 11 six-penny competitors combined (*Sun*, 8/20/1836). The *Sun* later was rivalled by the *New York Herald* and the *New York Tribune*, the *Baltimore Sun*, and the *Philadelphia Public Ledger*, all with much larger circulations than the six-penny dailies that preceded them (Schudson, 1978, pp. 17–18).

It is claimed that the large circulations of penny dailies signalled a new emphasis on seeking out readers. Earlier papers are treated as exclusive and elitist: the special property of "the aristocrats" (Lee, 1923, pp. 204–205), of the "politician and entrepreneur" (Crouthamel, 1964, p. 95), and of the "mercantile and political elites" (Schudson, 1978, p. 15). Before the penny press, "metropolitan papers paid little attention to ordinary people" (Heren, 1985, pp. 36–37). Payne (1920, p. 243) calls the *Sun* the "first popular paper" and J. M. Lee (1923, p. 201) writes that, with the penny press, "for the first time journalism was brought directly to the people." More specifically, it is argued that the penny papers were the first U.S. newspapers to tap the working class. Thus Crouthamel (1964, p. 91) writes, "Newspapers priced moderately enough to be available to the average reader were unknown in the United States before the 1830s." The penny papers were papers for the masses, "the mechanics and servant girls" (Lee, 1923, p. 188; see also Bleyer, 1927, p. 155; Emery & Emery, 1984, p. 139; North, 1881, pp. 89–90; Peterson, Jensen, & Rivers, 1965, p. 42). They were, it is argued, deeply colored by artisanal consciousness and tapped the urban working class sources of radical Jacksonian democracy (Saxton, 1984; Schiller, 1981). Schiller (1981, chaps. 2 & 3) goes so far as to credit the penny press with inventing the appeal to the total public, as opposed to specific interests.

Most standard treatments of the penny press argue or imply that it created a mass readership and gave that readership a self-awareness of its political interests. Most quote with tacit acceptance a *Sun* editorial celebrating that paper's impact that reads, in part: "Already we can perceive a change in the mass of the people. They think, talk, and act in concert. They understand their own interest, and feel they have the numbers and strength to pursue it with success" (6/28/1838; cited in Hughes, 1940, p. 160; Payne, 1920, p. 246; Saxton, 1984, p. 225).

Content

The penny papers are said to have cultivated a new readership by capitalizing on striking innovations in content. Three main claims dominate the literature. First, the penny press initiated a policy of political neutrality. Second, it emphasized news over opinion, pioneering in sensationalism and human interest stories. Third, it simplified writing styles, making the American newspaper more readable. In some accounts, penny press operators are depicted as heroic agents of change. In others, they appear as the obedient servants of social forces. In both versions, though, the penny papers play a decisive and revolutionary role.

Before the penny press, it is argued, all papers were political. Thus Hudson (1873) designates the period 1783–1832 as the age of "The Political Party Press," and his label has been adopted by virtually every historian since. Mott (1950), for instance, in his chapter titles contrasts the "Dark Ages of Partisan Journalism" with the "Sunrise" of the penny press. Bleyer (1927, p. 152) refers to earlier newspapers as "primarily political party organs," and North (1881, p. 19) talks of "the emancipation of the American press from thralldom to party, under which it struggled for so many years, years in which its growth and usefulness seemed to stagnate. . . ." Since the time of the revolution, at least, the American press had been a partisan advocate and not a source of public enlightenment. Hudson (1873, pp. 410–414) again writes, "Every newspaper writer and every printer had been educated for half a century in the belief that no journal of any respectability could be established without the consent of politicians and the pecuniary aid of party." Thus the press was "the slave of the two political oligarchies."

The penny press, unlike its predecessors, was politically independent (Lippmann, 1931, p. 435; North, 1881, p. 91; Schiller, 1979; Schudson, 1978, p. 21). Because penny papers served readers and not politicians, they printed information of use to citizens rather than opinionated arguments on behalf of partisan interests. Thus North (1881, p. 91) asserts that the penny press "taught the higher-priced papers that the political connection was properly subordinated to the other and higher function of the public journal—the function of gathering and presenting the news as it is, without reference to its political or other effect upon friend or foe" (see also Crouthamel, 1964, p. 92; Emery & Emery, 1984, p. 143; Schudson, 1978, p. 22).

Commentators agree that the penny press was novel in capitalizing on the popular audience for news but are not precise in identifying news as a category. Consider the following:

> *The product sold to readers was "news," and it was an original product in several respects. First, it claimed to represent, colorfully but without partisan coloring, events in the world. Thus the news product of one paper could be compared to that of another for accuracy, completeness, liveliness, and timeliness.* (Schudson, 1978, p. 25)

> *But the commercial penny press substituted the market for the mission. Its object was to sell, not its influence, but the news, and its customers, therefore, were those who were more interested in the news than in the editor's interpretation of the news.* (Hughes, 1940, p. 7)

> *The* Sun *and its galaxy of imitators proved that the news was a valuable commodity, if delivered in a sprightly manner.* (Emery & Emery, 1984, p. 142)

> *James Gordon Bennett . . . created the idea that the newspaper is primarily a purveyor of news, not of editorial opinion.* (Peterson, Jensen, & Rivers, 1965, p. 43)

These statements are representative of characterizations of the novel nature of the news carried in the penny press.

What then are the novel characteristics of news? It is event oriented rather than issue oriented, for one. Thus a news item recounts an event rather than simply presenting an artifact from the event, such as a transcript of a speech. News then is more lively, or so it is claimed. And, because it is more lively, it is said to have a broader appeal and to be a marketable commodity. Further, news is said by its nature to be separate from opinion, and perhaps opposed to opinion. (For newspapers to consider news as their primary content they must reject, at least implicitly, a primary role as promoters of opinion.) Finally, when news becomes the chief content of a newspaper, new criteria for judging performance become possible, perhaps necessary. Accuracy, completeness, and timeliness are aspects of news that are foreign to newspapers of opinion.

By concentrating on news, it is argued, the penny press performed a function that conventional papers had ignored: it presented a picture of ordinary social life. Here is Schudson (1978, p. 22) on this issue:

> *For the first time the American newspaper made it a regular practice to print political news, not just foreign but domestic, and not just national but local; for the first time it printed reports from the police, from the courts, from the streets, and from private households. One might say that, for the first time, the newspaper reflected not just commerce and politics but social life. To be more precise, in the 1830s the newspaper began to reflect, not the affairs of an elite in a small trading society, but the activities of an increasingly varied, urban, and middle class society of trade, transportation, and manufacturing.*

So, not only did the penny press liberate the newspaper from partisan interest, it also made the newspaper into a medium of everyday life. The penny paper transformed the American newspaper from a political to a social instrument.

Part of this transformation was the introduction of the human interest story as a mainstay of news content. While earlier papers had carried such stories as filler material, the penny press is said to have specialized in human interest stories, particularly in the interest of selling newspapers (Hughes, 1940, p. 47). Hughes sees this as a case of the newspaper assuming a function that had traditionally been performed by gossip and folk tales; other commentators see it as a more fundamental change. Schudson (1978, p. 30) writes that "the new journalism of the penny press . . . ushered in a new order, a shared social universe in which 'public' and 'private' would be redefined." Whether the penny press created new concerns and styles of thought or catered to old ones, writers have agreed that the exploitation of human interest stories in newspapers was novel.

Just as common is the characterization of penny press content as sensational. It is generally assumed that the popularity of the penny press was directly tied to sensationalism. Thus Bleyer (1927, p. 164) writes, "The basis of the Sun's success is unquestionably to be found in its giving the masses what they wanted—sensational, 'human interest' news . . ." (Emery & Emery [1984, p. 146] agree; see also Crouthamel, 1974). Schudson (1978, p. 23) argues that sensationalism was one of the roots of the hostile reaction of conventional papers to penny papers.

Structure and Conduct

The penny press is usually credited with several dramatic innovations in structure and conduct. Among these are: mass readership and, along with it, a new reliance on advertising; a new occupational emphasis on news reporting and, along with it, a new interest in timely reporting; and because of these other factors, a new receptiveness toward new technologies.

The penny papers are said to have been the first papers run strictly as businesses. According to Hughes (1940, p. 15), "the whole complex of the penny press, its news and its marketing, signalized the commercialization of the newspaper." Schudson (1978, p. 25) agrees: "Until the 1830s, a newspaper provided a service to political parties and men of commerce; with the penny press, a newspaper sold a product to a general readership and sold the readership to advertisers." The penny paper was sold as a commodity to an undifferentiated public in the open market. It was a strictly commercial product.

As a consequence, penny papers became excellent advertising media. Commentators stress the new reliance on advertising revenue that resulted from mass readership (Bleyer, 1927, pp. 183–184; Emery & Emery, 1984, p. 142; Hudson, 1873, pp. 419–420). Schudson (1978, p. 20) argues further that, while earlier papers had limited advertising for noneconomic reasons—for instance, some had refused to carry patent medicine ads—the penny papers "appealed to the equal right of any advertiser to employ the public press, so long as the advertiser paid." The penny papers rationalized the business of newspaper advertising, in obedience to the market, so that "advertising, as well as sales, took on a more democratic cast" (p. 19).

In step with economic rationalization, the penny papers also refined the occupational structure of the newspaper. They hired reporters for the first time, an innovation that was considered shocking by some politicians (Schudson, 1978, pp. 23–24). At the same time, the new occupational structure and the new concern with the market of readers and advertisers bred new values.

It has been commonplace, for instance, to assume that the emphasis on timeliness in news was a creation of the penny papers and that these were the first papers to seek ways to speed up delivery of news (Heren, 1985, p. 39; O'Brien, 1928, pp. 90–98; Schudson, 1978, p. 26). In line with this novel emphasis on timeliness, the penny papers were uniquely supportive of new technologies, like the steam press and the telegraph, to the extent that such inventions might not have been developed without support from the penny papers (Czitrom, 1982, p. 15; Emery & Emery, 1984, pp. 142–143; Pickett, 1960; Schudson, 1978, pp. 33–35).

According to the mythology of the penny press, then, the contemporary newspaper is the direct descendant of the penny paper. It was the penny paper that invented modern systems of distribution, mass circulations, the modern concept of news, the occupational and business structure of the modern newspaper, and the technologies that produced the modern newspaper. All of these innovations were introduced over the active or passive opposition of a conventional newspaper establishment that was the servant of political parties and social elites. The rise of the penny press constituted the liberation of market forces and the triumph of democracy in the press.

Historiography of Journalism

In the preceding review, I draw freely from works with widely differing attitudes toward the press and press history. All of these works, I contend, are influenced by the mythology of the penny press, even though many of them work from points of view that are clearly at odds with the implications of this mythology. I now briefly review the historiography of U.S. journalism to broaden the context for this discussion.

U.S. journalism history has spawned several subgenres. Most numerous are biographical studies, treatments of the lives of famous editors or newspapers, often commissioned by individual papers and usually sympathetic to their subjects. Also common are studies of specific issues as treated in the press. Such issue-oriented studies, together with biographies, make up the bulk of monographic research in the area. These detailed studies, however, rarely propose broader syntheses. Indeed, this division of labor between synthetic and monographic works has been a major weakness in journalism history.

The work of synthesis has been carried out by a series of comprehensive histories, dating from Hudson's *Journalism in the United States* (1873) to the latest revision of Edwin and Michael B. Emery's *The Press and America* (1984). Usually designed in part as textbooks, these histories approach journalism from within. Their aims are to provide historical roots for an industry and a profession and to encourage appropriate behavior by presenting modern standards as the result of a long chain of progress. This latter goal encourages a concentration on the heroes of journalism, shapers of history and role models for the present and future. (This is especially true of the older studies of Hudson, Payne, Bleyer, and J.M. Lee.) Such treatments harmonize well with both biographical studies, which sympathetically highlight important papers and editors, and issue-oriented studies, which tend to emphasize the power of the press in shaping public opinion.

The first half of the twentieth century also saw the publication of a few classic works in the sociological history of the press. The key works here are A.M. Lee's *The Daily Newspaper in America* (1937), Hughes' *News and the Human Interest Story* (1940), and several essays by Robert Park, especially "The Natural History of the Newspaper" (1955). These works outline an ecological approach: Changes in environment, especially economic and demographic factors, encouraged through a process of natural selection an evolution of structures and behaviors, especially editorial policy. While notable for their theoretical bent, these works remain disappointing in terms of actual historical research. With the exception of Lee's massive accumulation of statistical data, these studies draw their history from the more anecdotal biographical and comprehensive studies. Also, perhaps because they were the products of sociologists whose interest in the past was ancillary to the study of contemporary institutions, these studies led to little historical research. They stand as isolated exceptions to the main styles of journalism history, at least until the past few years.

Dissatisfaction with prevailing styles of journalism history became vocal in the 1970s. A flurry of historiographical critiques appeared, calling for new styles of research and announcing the demise of the "Whig" or "Progressive" paradigm. (The most prominent examples are Carey [1974], Dicken Garcia [1980], and McKerns [1977].) In part, this was a reflection of controversies in the study of U.S. history in the 1960s; in part it also signalled a coming of age for communications history, which was no longer as closely tied to the interests of journalism education. It was time to write social and cultural histories of the press.

In recent years, several important monographs and at least one synthesis (Schudson, 1978) have offered alternative approaches. Often informed by a critical attitude toward the press, these social histories have directed attention to issues such as the influence of class structures, market concerns, and occupational ideologies on newspaper behavior.

Several features of this recent research reinforce themes from the received history of the penny press. First, there is a common concern with modernization; the mythology of the penny press easily can be made to fit the sociological scheme of modernization. Second, there is an interest in the social bases of ideological shifts (Kaul & McKerns, 1985); again, the received history of the penny press is opportune, combining as it does a change from partisanism to independence or objectivity with shifts in readerships and market strategies. Third, there is a general interest in conflict: of social groups, of ideologies, and of economic structures. Again, the mythology of the penny press is convenient, emphasizing as it does the conflict between penny papers with their constituencies and conventional papers with their traditional elite readerships.

Consequently, recent histories have not challenged the mythology of the penny press, even though they have reacted strongly against the Whig or Progressive tradition in journalism history. Rather, they have tended to accept as fact the raw material of traditional journalism history, even while proposing alternative interpretations. Thus it has been possible to quote recent histories alongside of traditional ones in reconstructing the mythology of the penny press. The mythology remains the common sense of journalism history and as such perpetuates errors of fact and interpretation.

The Mythology Revisited

In this section, I analyze standard characterizations of the penny press, showing where each misconstrues or is misleading.

Street Sales

It has been argued that in adopting the cash system of distribution the penny press shifted the crucial basis of newspaper support from subscriptions to street sales. There is truth in this characterization but also an element of exaggeration.

It is not clear that the cash system of distribution actually translated into street sales. Circulation records are very rare, and the self-reports of penny paper editors are probably unreliable, but what little hard evidence I have seen seems to indicate that subscription sales remained the overwhelming majority of newspaper sales. Benjamin Day's *New York Sun*, for instance, in 1835 reported that of more than 19,000 total sales, more than 16,000 went to regular subscribers in New York and Brooklyn while only 2,000 were sold in the streets. (The remainder were sent out of town, presumably on a subscription basis [O'Brien, 1928, p. 49].) Furthermore, these figures were from around the time of the celebrated moon hoax, which probably generated an uncommon number of street sales. A subscription list remained a most important ingredient for starting a newspaper, even a penny paper (see, for instance, Greeley [1868, pp. 139–140]).

There are sound practical reasons why steady subscription sales likely remained of crucial importance to newspaper conductors. An obvious reason was the importance of steady advertising revenue, for which penny papers competed vigorously: advertisers naturally sought to exploit the paper with the best-established readership, and that paper likely was the one with the most extensive subscription list. A second reason is the economic interest of the newspaper distributors, the newsboys who bought papers in bulk from the proprietor and sold them to readers. As newsboys paid cash for their papers, 67¢ per 100 copies, and as they probably operated with a rather small cash cushion, they probably preferred to deliver their papers to regular customers on a subscription basis. (Bleyer [1927, p. 161] refers to carriers delivering penny papers to "subscribers," though later writers concentrate exclusively on newsboys making street sales.)

It also is inaccurate to say that single-issue sales did not exist before the penny press. The London dailies were commonly sold on the streets, and in many ways the history of the New York press in the early nineteenth century is a recapitulation of the development of the London press. But it seems clear that other papers in the United States were sold on a single-issue basis before the mid-1830s, at least from time to time. This is indicated by the common practice of printing extras for late-breaking news, a practice that was particularly common among weekly and semiweekly papers.

It could be argued that the most significant contribution of the cash system of circulation was not single-issue sales, or even street sales, but the cash exchange itself. Hudson (1873, p. 425) treats the introduction of the cash system as a money-making reform that eliminated the common problem of unpaid subscriptions. The cash system should be looked upon as a separation of labor or a rationalization of the newspaper economy, one step in a continuous evolutionary process that included the separation of printing from editorial duties and would later include the creation of the position of managing editor and the consequent separation of business from editorial duties, and the introduction of publicly held newspaper companies.

While it seems clear that the penny papers did introduce a change in distribution, it is not clear how significant that change was. It does not seem fair to conclude from the existing evidence that, with the advent of the penny press, street sales suddenly became the crucial index of a newspaper's success. In the absence of hard data, speculations on the ways newspaper sales patterns changed must be considered tentative.

The Penny Press and the Cheap Press

In terms of cost, it seems accurate to say that a penny paper sold for a penny, and that this price marked a sharp departure from previous pricing for daily newspapers. Yet some background is called for here also.

Prior to the penny press, the typical American daily sold for 6¢. The typical American newspaper, however, was not a daily. In most parts of the country, and in most cities outside the major Eastern metropoles, daily newspapers were unknown or at best a novelty. Even in Eastern cities, a large readership existed for weekly papers. And, precisely because these were issued less frequently, the weekly papers were much cheaper on an annual basis than dailies. Thus while the introduction of penny papers constituted a sharp drop in prices for *dailies*, it is not clear that it marked a sharp drop in the price of newspapers.

Again, in the context of American newspapers taken as a whole, the introduction of penny papers was a step in a process of evolution, a process that might best be conceived of as the augmentation of the newspaper, or the addition of different newspaper formats: The sequential introduction of weeklies, biweeklies, triweeklies, and dailies was followed by the penny paper, and later the evening paper and the all-day paper. In each case the innovation was an augmentation and not a revolution (see Nerone, 1982, chap. 2).

It is unfortunate that New York City has been taken as the epitome of American journalism. Because in New York City where the six-penny dailies were particularly well established, a situation that was somewhat true for Boston and Baltimore and perhaps Philadelphia, the introduction of the penny paper was dramatic. But this is not true of other cities and certainly not true of nonurban areas where the transition to a commercial press was gradual.

The first penny papers sold for a penny, but the successful ones, like James Gordon Bennett's *Herald*, raised their price to 2¢ when it became clear that profits would not fall. The rule seemed to be that as a penny paper became more substantial as a newspaper it increased its price. The trend continued until, by the 1880s, the usual price for a daily was again up to 5¢, this despite the general deflation of the currency in the nineteenth century (Hudson, 1873, pp. 426–427; North, 1881, p. 90). There were still penny dailies; the earliest journalism historians, Hudson and North for instance, write of a "cheap press," but this is not the press that recent journalism historians describe as the penny press, namely the *New York Sun*, *Herald*, *Tribune*, and *The New York Times*. These latter successful papers quickly became an establishment themselves, enabling a new wave of penny papers, Pulitzer's *New York World* and Hearst's *New York Journal*, to appear as revolutionary in the 1880s and 90s. Emery and Emery (1984, pp. 139–140) identify a cyclical process of readers becoming more demanding while newspapers improve, until a new generation of unimproved readers calls forth a new popular press. But did the cheap press disappear when the *Herald* began charging 2¢?

It is clear that a class of "cheap" daily newspapers—as they were called by contemporaries—came into existence in the 1830s and that the well-known penny papers were among those cheap papers. But it also seems likely that the highly successful penny papers migrated away from their less prestigious cognates. It is possible that the cheap press proper constituted a class of newspapers separate from the penny papers that have been studied. It is a fact that a large number of cheap papers were founded in New York and in other major cities in the 1830s and 40s. (Emery and Emery [1984, p. 147] say 35 were established in New York in the 1830s; Hudson [1873, p. 425] says over 100 between 1833 and 1872; O'Brien [1928, pp. 84–85] says "a dozen a year" in New York in the 1830s. In Cincinnati 33 penny papers were begun before 1848 [Nerone, 1982, p. 80].) But this subclass of newspapers has not been studied, largely because it left no legacy for modern mainstream American journalism and also because records and surviving copies of these papers are very rare.

The price of the penny paper, like its method of distribution, is a complex matter. The qualities attributed to the cheap press cannot automatically be transferred to the penny papers commonly treated by journalism historians, which came in time to resemble the earlier six-penny dailies in terms of prestige and, perhaps, attitude. Cheap papers were of a different nature than the mighty *Herald* of the Bennetts. Horace Greeley (1868, pp. 141–142) himself recognized the distinction between cheap papers and the more substantial dailies when he remarked that "No journal sold for a cent could ever be much more than a dry summary of the most important or the most interesting occurrences of the day; and such is not a newspaper, in the higher sense of the term."

The Expansion of Readership

Standard treatments of the penny press claim a revolutionary expansion of newspaper readership, a claim that is usually supported by circulation figures for the *Sun*, *Herald*, and *Tribune* in New York. Again, qualifications are needed. First, these figures are only for the most successful papers in the largest cities. Less successful papers are not considered, and the penny papers of smaller cities are also ignored. While it can be determined that some penny papers achieved previously unimagined circulations, it cannot be concluded that penny papers as a whole expanded circulation by a radical amount. Second, even the figures given are suspect, since they are based on self-reports in editorial columns and are obviously biased toward self-promotion. The falsification of circulation data in the early to mid-nineteenth century is a well-known problem.

Even so, it seems fair to say that the circulation of penny dailies was larger than six-penny dailies. After all, the logic of economic necessity suggests larger circulations were needed to cover printing costs, and an increased emphasis on advertising income also suggests the need for increasing circulation. Expanded circulation therefore should be acknowledged.

Still, should expanded daily circulation lead us to accept the assertion that the penny press was the first popular press? On the contrary, there is every reason to believe that newspapers were popular before the penny press. Their basis of comparison makes the standard arguments misleading in this area. Penny dailies justifiably are shown to have larger circulations than six-penny dailies. The hidden and incorrect assumption, however, is that the six-penny dailies were characteristic of American journalism as a whole. But the typical American newspaper in the 1830s was not a metropolitan daily; the metropolitan daily was only one class of newspaper, and that was a minority class. Far more common were country weeklies and other nondailies with regional circulations, and these obviously had less restricted circulations than the six-penny dailies.

Impressionistic evidence concerning newspaper circulation before the penny press indicates that ordinary people habitually read newspapers. Foreign travelers like De Tocqueville (1954, chap. 11) and Trollope (1949, pp. 92–93) described newspaper readership as universal in the early 1830s, and it is clear that they were not referring to penny papers or metropolitan dailies.

One reason why the popularity of earlier newspapers is misunderstood is that higher circulation is translated into expanded readership in a direct and unambiguous manner. Earlier newspapers, however, usually had readership far in excess of circulation. There are several reasons for this: the durability of paper with high rag content; the tendency of higher prices to encourage sharing and saving papers; less-than-daily publication, which meant that an issue of a paper was current for a longer period of time; and dense content, which invited prolonged browsing. Historian Lawrence Cremin (1980, p. 188) puts the ratio of readers to copy of the typical early weekly as high as 20 to 1. That multiple readership was common practice is attested to by the example of a Cincinnati penny paper called the *Daily Microscope*, which claimed a readership 10 times its probable circulation (July 12, 1842). The *Microscope*'s magnification of its readership has the appearance of conventional wisdom: the established papers of the time probably did have 10 readers per copy. It is unlikely that penny dailies had that many readers per copy. Their very cheapness suggests that the penny papers were purchased as individual and disposable. This pattern of use is an interesting and suggestive change in American news habits and may indicate the advent of consumerism or heightened individualism. It is not fair to argue, however, that it indicates the first appearance of popular newspapers.

Earlier newspapers had reasons of their own to seek broad popular audiences. The "political" newspapers that the penny papers are said to have superseded were integral to a party system that was election oriented. These papers were designed to tap and organize an expanding electorate, to assist in gaining power by motivating voters. The second party system in the United States appeared in the 1820s, the decade immediately preceding the appearance of the penny press, and was novel in its appeal to mass voter support (Hofstadter, 1972; McCormick, 1966). The newspapers associated with the parties were self-consciously popular too. The six-penny dailies of the major Eastern cities, again the major source for scholarly comparisons of the penny press, are not representative of the partisan press.

It seems that a tremendous expansion of newspaper publishing began in the period following the American Revolution, and that this expansion was fueled by the consciousness of the implied necessity for effective communication in a nation to be governed by popular consent. This awareness is evident in the writings of Thomas Jefferson and in the formulation of early postal policies; it was apparently the common sense of the revolutionary and postrevolutionary generations.

Explosive growth in newspapers in America dated from the turn of the century and was fueled by the republican ideology of the revolution. What figures are available show a smooth increase in the number of papers published and in the total number of copies circulated through the first four decades of the nineteenth century (North, 1881, p. 47). It is true, as is commonly pointed out, that newspapers grew explosively in the United States in the 1830s, but it is also true that explosive growth had been characteristic of all the earlier years of that century. The circulations achieved by the successful penny papers were one aspect of a process of evolution then.

Working Class Readers

The penny papers are said to have tapped for the first time a massive audience of working class readers, an audience ignored by conventional six-penny dailies. This is a claim difficult to demonstrate in the absence of subscription lists and other concrete indicators of readership. Nevertheless, it seems obvious, both from impressionistic evidence and from indications in the newspapers' content, that the intended audiences were not elite, and it seems clear also that the subscribers to the six-penny dailies did belong to a mercantile elite. But again the comparison is only partly appropriate, as the six-penny dailies constituted only one part of the one class of American newspapers. Because other papers, particularly partisan weeklies and semiweeklies, did consciously appeal to the working classes, it is not accurate to portray the appeal to a total nonexclusive public to be an invention of the penny press as does Schiller (1981, chaps. 2 & 3).

The perception that penny papers were

oriented to the working class is based in most histories on the case of New York, an example that limits broader generalizations. While New York was becoming America's premier city at the time, that status tends to undermine its claim to being representative of U.S. political and social structures and patterns. New York was the exception, not the rule, and class consciousness in New York penny papers, which may indicate a working class uprising against dominant classes there, does not indicate a similar battle between elite and popular media elsewhere.

The evidence for class consciousness in New York's penny papers also is inconclusive. Schiller (1981, p. 46), for example, cites rhetoric of "equal rights, enlightenment, and political independence" as expressing an artisanal consciousness and considers this rhetoric to be a novel contribution, an innovation. The rhetoric of popular enlightenment and the appeal to the independent citizen, however, were integral to newspaper ideology from the time of the revolution onward. Saxton is more detailed, examining the early penny papers' positions on various issues to demonstrate their alignment with the political program of the left wing of the Jacksonians. But the sympathy of these papers with the working class, and the artisanal backgrounds of their operators, are of only local significance and do not demonstrate a national realignment of newspaper structures. And, in fact, Saxton and Schiller both note that artisanal control of the press quickly waned with the coming of the depression following the Panic of 1837.

Schudson (1978, pp. 52–60) sees the rise of the penny press as tied to the rise of a democratic market society. The crucial class in both phenomena was the middle class. Schudson supports this argument by discussing the intended audience of Bennett's *Herald*. While this line of analysis is attractive, it remains unclear whether the middle class that read the *Herald* differed in fundamental ways from readers of political papers. It seems likely that the sorts of people who bought the *Herald* in New York likely read partisan papers in other cities or regions. Was the *Herald*'s readership typical of all Eastern metropolitan penny papers? There remains insufficient evidence to link the penny press with the rise or fall of any particular class.

Partisanism

Perhaps the single most persistent characterization of the penny press describes it as the first impartial or nonpartisan class of newspaper. The penny press transformed the American newspaper by freeing it from the control of partisan interests. Here the mythology is most misleading.

It is not possible here to evaluate thoroughly the behavior of the press before the 1830s. Furthermore, it is doubtful that any general characterization would suffice to cover the highly diverse and essentially local newspapers of the early republic. It is unfair to talk of "the American newspaper" in that period, I think, because there really was no such thing. It is more meaningful, as I have suggested earlier, to refer to classes of newspapers.

The newspaper of opinion was one kind of newspaper in the early republic, and this newspaper tended to be partisan. Another class of newspaper existed, though, and was common; this class of newspaper espoused an ideology of impartiality and usually served a local readership. Newspapers of this class were frequently monopolies, often run by small printers and often edited by postmasters or other local authorities in a similar fashion to the colonial press (Botein, 1975). A third class of newspaper was the metropolitan daily, the immediate predecessor and rival of the penny paper.

All of these classes of newspapers tended to be political in focus, just as newspapers today are political in focus. On the other hand, they were not necessarily, and I think not usually, partisan. While it is true that the elite papers of the day were partisan in some way (they are studied because politicians read them), we should not focus exclusively on the elite papers to determine whether the American press in general was partisan.

While virtually all newspapers focused on politics, and it should be kept in mind that the expansion of the press in this period was fueled by a common belief that newspapers were essential for democracy, it is not true that common newspapers were as a rule partisan throughout the early national period. It is true that, upon careful scrutiny, a party preference can be found for most papers, but it is not true that this preference determined the content of the paper, nor is it true that such papers designed their content to function as propaganda for a political party. A political preference did not make a paper a party organ. (Isaiah Thomas' list of newspapers in 1810, which includes a party affiliation for most, is misleading because it does not indicate the *quality* of party affiliation. Surely we could assign party affiliations to most newspapers today, but it would hardly be acceptable to designate them as organs. Thomas' list, however, is frequently cited as evidence of the overwhelmingly partisan nature of the early American press [see, for example, North, 1881, pp. 38–45; Botein, 1975, p. 11].)

A simple designation of partisanism is far less important than an assessment of the quality of partisanism in a newspaper. It is here that the standard characterization of a "dark age" of partisan journalism that is associated with the mythology of the penny press has its most regrettable effect; it promotes the belief that the quality of partisanism was constant throughout the early national period. This is far from true.

Prevailing patterns of political involvement changed dramatically in the 1820s with the rise of the second party system. Before this time, newspapers espoused an ideology of impartiality and impersonality. Even newspapers that were involved in partisan promotion opposed in principle the exclusion of opposing arguments and claimed to be open to all parties. At the same time, the newspapers opposed "personalities" in political discourse; that is, personal attacks were to be excluded, and the force of an argument was to be based on intrinsic merit, not on personal authority. Newspapers should discuss measures, not men. This ideology of impartiality or rational liberty, as it was called, was embodied in certain newspaper conventions, such as the usual absence of any editorial voice and the habit of publishing letters over pseudonyms rather than actual names. This ideology is reflected, for instance, in the pseudonymous publication of the Federalist papers in the later 1780s in New York newspapers. In terms of information (as opposed to opinion), impartiality and rational liberty meant the publication of the raw stuff of political discourse: verbatim transcripts of important speeches, often printed in extras, and unbiased digests of debates and legislative actions, the sort of content for which the *National Intelligencer* was famous. While partisan designs no doubt lurked behind much of the impartial material and close reading of newspaper content in this period reveals subtle biases, the public commitment to impartiality moderated the tone of partisanism. In many cases, especially in smaller monopoly newspapers run by printers and not by professional editors, it seems that impartiality was actually pursued.

This style of press politics changed swiftly with the coming of the second party system. Candidates set up newspapers as part of their campaign strategy, and existing newspapers were co-opted into party organizations. Instead of being passive conveyors of fact and opinion, newspapers began to portray themselves as lawyers arguing a cause in the courtroom of public opinion or as military leaders organizing armies of voters. At the same time, newspapers came to concentrate on personality in candidates and to pursue readers as voters with increased zeal. (For an extended discussion of this transformation in a local context, see Nerone [1982, chaps. 3 & 4].)

The quality of partisanism in newspapers had changed. Against the backdrop of this new kind of electoral partisanism, the appearance of a penny press that claimed to be politically neutral was more a return to traditional values than an innovation in press ideology.

What, then, of the actual political stance of the penny papers? It is certainly true that the first penny papers, at least in New York, invoked political neutrality and paid less attention to political discourse, both opinion and information, than their conventional six-penny predecessors. But this was not novel. Rather it was a reaction against novelty, namely the novel partisanism of the press in the 1820s. In the course of the history of press political behavior, this episode in neutrality is neither unprecedented nor of enduring consequence.

Partisanism was never absent from penny papers, and it became more pronounced as the penny paper became more successful. Saxton (1984, pp. 224–234), for example, has shown that early penny papers backed the workingman's wing of the Democratic party on virtually every relevant issue. This makes sense, given those papers' conscious appeal to working class readers. Still, historians claim the penny papers were different and attribute a fledgling sense of objectivity to the penny papers.

There may be cause to consider the earlier penny papers to be different from other newspapers in their political purpose, though to do so, as I have argued, requires adopting a simplified view of the conventional press. For the later penny papers, however, political purposes were clearly present at the creation. The classic example here, of course, is Horace Greeley's *New York Tribune*, begun as an explicit Whig alternative to the less explicit Democratic thrust of earlier penny papers. As Greeley (1868, p. 138) himself explained:

> *I had been incited to this enterprise by several Whig friends, who deemed a cheap daily, addressed more specifically to the laboring class, eminently needed in our city, where the only two cheap journals then and still existing—the* Sun *and the* Herald*—were in decided, though unavowed, and therefore more effective, sympathy and affiliation with the Democratic party. Two or three had promised pecuniary aid if it should be needed. . . .*

The *Tribune*, then, was initiated by Whig politicos and launched with an explicit promise of cash support if needed. (Greeley's own editorial independence need not be questioned here; it should be noted, though, that some earlier partisan editors could also claim independence.) Independence of opinion is not the same as objectivity or political neutrality: the penny press did not invent political independence and did not institute neutrality or objectivity.

Penny press editors frequently used their papers as instruments of their own political ambitions. Bennett's and Greeley's intrigues in politics are well known. Emery and Emery (1984, pp. 152–153) also note the political ambitions of Henry Raymond of *The New York Times*, though they say his newspaper remained fair and impartial. Leonard (1986, p. 132) also notes the persistence of partisanism even while demands for factual accuracy increased.

What, then, can we make of the issue of partisanism in the American press? I have argued here that a process of politicization began in the 1820s and that this partisanism was essentially different from earlier partisanism. In this scheme, the initial political neutrality of the penny press was a temporary aberration from a long-term process of politicization of editorial policy. As organs of *opinion*, there is no doubt that the penny papers came to fit well into the scheme of ongoing politicization. North (1881, p. 37) remarked in the 1880s that "The great mass of the newspapers of the United States continued to be conducted in the interests of one or the other of the existing parties, and still continue to be so conducted, and they will so continue for an indefinite time to come." Partisanism remained the rule. As North concludes, "It is neither unnatural nor improper that this relationship should exist." It was and is one of the purposes of newspapers to facilitate political discourse, and it is to be expected that, when parties compete and when newspapers compete, newspapers will become aligned with parties. The penny papers may have fought this tendency, but only for awhile.

Another argument is made about the politics of the papers: namely that the penny press caused a shift in the balance of power between newspaper and party. Whereas earlier the newspaper was dependent on the party for support and therefore servile to the interests of politicians, it is argued, the penny papers became more dominant, and their editors acquired influence independent of party functionaries. While this argument correctly accords great prestige in political circles to men like Greeley, it incorrectly denies the prestige and authority exercised by other and earlier partisan editors. The newspaper wielded power in party circles *before* the penny press.

Political Information

There is another aspect of the penny press to be dealt with here, that is, the newspaper as a conveyor of information. Here there are two questions to be answered: Did the penny press offer a different or superior amount or style of political information? Did the penny press introduce new nonpolitical categories of news content? The first question can be dealt with briefly; the second will require deeper consideration.

According to standard characterizations in the mythology of the penny press, earlier partisan newspapers were devoted to persuasion. Because of their partisan connections, it is claimed, they were woefully inadequate in conveying information. They were all opinion and no fact.

The partisan papers *were* full of political information. Early newspapers had an ideological commitment to presenting the reader with all the raw material needed to make informed decisions on political issues, and consequently newspapers carried surprising amounts of the undigested stuff of politics—speeches and accounts of debates and verbatim copies of bills and huge tables of budgets and vote tallies. (Leonard [1986, pp. 63–66] sees an increase in the printing of political debate in the 1820s.) There was much political information in the partisan papers; it was the penny press, with its professed lack of concern with electoral politics, that took emphasis away from the transmission of political information.

The Penny Press and News

The penny press is said to have created a new notion of "news" as factual reports with marketable appeal that have no necessary public significance. Several points need to be made about this concept of news before we try to judge the role of the penny press in inventing it. First, besides the assertion of market appeal, there is nothing particularly *democratic* about news as opposed to other sorts of newspaper content. News does not necessarily promote popular interests, nor does it necessarily protect rights, nor does it necessarily enable citizens to participate more actively in governing processes. On all of these points, an argument can be made that the newspaper of opinion is more democratic. Second, the nineteenth century concept of news does not necessarily require the twentieth century concept of objectivity. The presentation of news can be as subjective and as partisan as any other type of newspaper content; if it were not so, the causes should be sought in the constellation of attitudes that surrounded the presentation of news. Third, it is clear that the notion of news attributed to the penny papers is actually based on the values of

American journalists in the twentieth century. Writers on the penny press, like many journalism historians in the United States, have a tendency to seek out the roots of contemporary journalism. Schiller (1979, 1981), for instance, argues that the penny press invented *objectivity* when it adopted political neutrality, an idea, I think, that is an anachronism.

What contribution did the penny press make to the evolution of the news content of U.S. newspapers? First, it is clear that news as a type of content preceded the introduction of the penny press. It is also clear that at least the well-known penny papers initially emphasized news over other kinds of content, but it is not clear that this was the rule, especially outside of New York City. It is also clear that the differences between penny papers and their conventional rivals regarding the balance of news and opinion decreased over time: the penny papers of the 1840s were less distinctive than those of the 1830s. The ultimate question is whether the news practices of penny papers signal a revolution in American newspaper content. The answer here is no. Content analysis does not reveal any revolutionary change in newspaper content in the period 1820–1860 (Shaw, 1981, p. 38). In a study of the Cincinnati press in the years 1793–1848, a gradual rise in the percentage of items in newspapers that might be categorized as news was found, but this rise was in no way revolutionary, nor was it initiated by penny papers (Nerone, 1982, chap. 2). Far too much has been made of the penny papers' substitution of news for editorial opinion.

Sensationalism

Scholars likewise have been too uncritical about the penny papers' pioneering exploitation of sensationalism and the human interest story, two topics which will bear examination in more detail. Two points should be made about the sensationalism of the penny press. First, the researcher expecting to find examples of modern tabloid sensationalism in the penny papers of the 1830s and 40s will be disappointed. Beyond an interest in remarkable or melancholy events, an interest, incidentally, also quite common in conventional papers, the penny papers were not lurid or scandalous either by modern standards or those of their own time. It was, however, very common for newspapers to accuse each other of licentiousness and it has been the habit of researchers to take these accusations at face value.

Second, the appeal to the sensations in penny papers was fundamentally moralistic. When sensational details were given, they were intended to arouse an appropriate moral response, one of revulsion or compassion, depending on the situation. This practice of appealing to readers' emotions by giving details of a sensational nature was not considered immoral or shameful unless it was excessive, and the penny papers claimed to be sensational only within proper moral bounds. The publication of police court reports, for instance, was explained as a method of exposing the evils of criminal life to discourage criminal behavior (Bleyer, [1927, chap. 6] presents copious evidence of the expressed concern of penny papers with mortality). In some cases, this moralizing function took the form of exposing the immorality of the well-to-do, as Schiller (1981, pp. 57–65) has shown in the case of the Robinson-Jewett murder trial (see also Saxton, 1984, p. 224).

Accusations of sensationalism were an attempt to capture the moral high ground in newspaper battles of the time. It is tempting to conclude that this moral posturing indicated a conflict between a commercial mentality and a moralistic set of attitudes toward the function of a newspaper in society, with the penny press adhering to the former and the conventional press to the latter, but the penny press was just as moralistic as conventional papers, and probably more so. Also, the moral battle lines were not as a rule drawn between penny papers and conventional papers. Penny papers joined in the moral war against Bennett's *Herald*, for instance, and the harshest critics of the morality of penny papers were often other penny papers.

The appeal to righteous emotional sentiments through sensational material was not a novel practice in American newspapers. Sensational items can be found in colonial newspapers and were common during the early national period. The content of the penny press in this regard was not revolutionary, nor did it institute a new trend. Rather it more resembled a conservative appeal to traditional values.

The Human Interest Story

It is true that the New York penny papers at least took a particular delight in printing items that we would characterize as human interest stories: that is, items whose compelling interest is rooted either in personality or in some fundamental illumination of the human condition. Such items seem to strike a stark contrast with the content of partisan newspapers, but too much can be made of this difference in content. Insofar as human interest stories signalled a preoccupation with personality, for example, they were not too much different from the personalities that appeared in the party press. It is possible that the concern with personality in the penny press was actually an extension of a style of news initiated by the partisan press and already quite common in the conventional papers.

On the other hand, it may be argued that the penny papers were radically different from conventional newspapers because they directed attention to ordinary people rather than to the holders of political authority. The penny papers of New York were more likely to print nonelite human interest stories than the six-penny dailies of New York. But did the penny papers initiate a similar trend in U.S. journalism as a whole? The evidence that they did is slim. Indeed, outside of New York, penny papers often reacted against the trend toward personality. Consider the comments of the editor of the *Cincinnati Commercial* who deplored the behavior of "vile and slanderous sheets that, engendered by the low and vulgar avarice of petty larceny knaves, pander to the sympathizing taste of scoundrels and harlots in the purlieus of our large cities" (October 19, 1843). It was not atypical that a penny paper should appeal to the sober guidelines of traditional U.S. press ideology. The rise of the *Sun* in 1833 did not signal a rush either to a new type of content or to a new set of values in U.S. journalism as a whole. The dramatic divisions of the New York daily press are misleading here.

Readability

It is claimed that the penny papers pioneered a more accessible style, a style calculated to appeal to ordinary people who lacked both leisure time and erudition. It is true that they tended to print shorter items with more of an emphasis on events than did conventional papers, and the contemporary researcher will detect a different flavor to the paper as a whole. It is not clear, however, that the penny papers were actually more readable to their contemporaries, and especially penny papers like the *Tribune* seem to have indulged as much in florid language and obscure allusions as conventional papers. Shaw's content analysis of U.S. newspapers in the period 1820–1860 concluded that "as a group, American newspapers did not become more popular in style or more responsive to their readers . . ." (1981, p. 49).

Given all these qualifications about standard interpretations of penny press content, it nevertheless should be recognized that newspaper content changed gradually throughout the period, and in ways that seem to give some support to the mythology of the penny press. News became more common as a category of newspaper content; personalities were also more common; and local news also seemed to become more common (Russo, 1980). Where the mythology errs is in delimiting the change to and assigning causes for it to the penny papers. Changes in content were not limited to penny papers; conventional papers too increased their news content and published more local news. While penny papers led this movement in New York, it is not clear that they did so in other parts of the country, even in other cities.

A further point should be made here about the practice of clipping and reprinting news items. It was common for papers that were not penny papers to copy items from the penny press, thereby amplifying the penny press audience. It seems likely that this practice enhanced the authority of the penny press, as well as the other elite news organs from which items were frequently clipped. It might be inferred further that the news values of the penny papers were transferred to the papers that clipped them. Was this the case? On the contrary, in actual practice, such clipped items were reprinted alongside items clipped from party or denominational organs and other sources, diluting their distinctiveness. Also, it was not necessarily the most important of the news items that were clipped, and the context for the item was changed, meaning that the producer of the item did not have the ability to set agendas for the nation's press as a whole. Because the clipping ultimately appeared in another newspaper under another aegis, frequently without attribution, it can be argued that the clipping enhanced the authority of the newspaper that printed it or, more generally, that of local newspapers. Although penny papers produced stories and information that reappeared in other formats throughout the country, they did not thereby have the power to impose novel news values on the nation's press as a whole. Again this is a topic that has not been sufficiently researched to permit conclusive evaluations.

Because changes in content were not restricted to and in many cases not initiated by the penny press, the causes of changes in content should be looked for outside of the penny press. I would like to suggest that the reason new types of news appeared in newspapers was that new types of organizations were producing news. To take the most obvious examples, the New York penny papers are frequently credited with inventing the printing of news about Broadway, Wall Street, and the police courts. Though the six-penny papers had included some news from these sources, the penny papers did actually greatly increase the concentration on such news. But the mythology of the penny press then leaves us with the impression that the editors of the penny press were the ones who created this news. Broadway, Wall Street, and the police courts actually were three news sources that had only come into their own in the decade or so before the penny papers: they had not lain neglected for ages, awaiting the astuteness of Day and Bennett. From this perspective, the penny press would seem more to have been the creature of novel news sources than the other way around. The evolution of the social organizations that produced news was an essential precondition for the news content of the penny press. By mythologizing the penny press, writers have tended to make it a heroic agent of social change rather than a product of social forces. Change in the medium was the result of changes in society and was reflected in conventional and penny papers alike.

The Penny Paper as Mass Medium

Commentators have argued that the penny papers were the first real mass media because they were the first media organized to sell to a mass or undifferentiated audience. Further, they have argued that the penny press subsequently transformed the American newspaper, making it a market-oriented business enterprise that relied on advertising revenue rather than on subscriptions or subsidies.

The major difficulties with this set of characterizations are a misattribution of causality and the projection of present-day patterns onto the past. While penny papers did tend to sell more copies and to carry what might be called more marketable content, neither development was as striking or revolutionary as has been claimed. The penny press did not create a mass readership in the modern sense of the word; the average circulation of daily newspapers was increasing regularly throughout this period but was still under 3,000 in 1850 (Saxton, 1984, p. 212). Furthermore, it is not clear what patterns of segmentation prevailed in newspaper readerships. Did daily papers pursue undifferentiated readerships, or were readerships segmented along lines of social or economic class, political or social attitudes, or cultural styles? There is no doubt that readership patterns varied widely from place to place, but it seems unfair to project modern mass readership back upon the 1830s and 40s, even if important changes were taking place in some cities.

Just as it is unclear that the penny papers were mass media, it is also unclear that they were radically modern in their pursuit of advertising revenue. It is true that new kinds of consumer product advertising appeared in the early to mid-nineteenth century, but here again, as in the case of certain kinds of news content, it seems that tradition has reversed cause and effect. New types of consumer goods were marketed in the 1830s and afterwards, the most notorious type being patent medicines, and these utilized newspaper advertising, in both penny papers and conventional papers. As consumer advertising became more prevalent, the importance of advertising revenue to a newspaper's financial security became more pronounced. This change, however, already was well underway by the advent of penny papers. The percentage of newspaper columns occupied by advertising matter had increased steadily; indeed, if there was a point of radical increase, it was in the jump from weekly to daily publication, not in the shift from six-penny to penny dailies. One of the frequent negative characterizations of six-penny papers by contemporaries is that three-fourths of the content was ads.

Nevertheless, penny papers had somewhat different rates and policies than conventional papers. They downplayed repeat advertising and made single daily insertions cheaper, changes that indicated more reliance on market forces and less on ongoing patronage. These subtle changes, however, were to be incorporated by conventional dailies also and are more indicative of how market forces were changing the newspaper business than of how newspaper policies were changing the marketplace.

In terms of business structure, long-term trends in newspapers can be summed up as the shift of the newspaper from a craft to an industry. This process involved sources of revenue, like advertising, and it also involved mechanisms of production, as we shall see. What was taking place in the long run was the integration of the newspaper into the market economy that itself was just coming of age in antebellum America. The changes in structure and conduct that the penny press introduced should be looked upon as features of this long-term process. The penny press did not revolutionize newspaper development. Rather, in most aspects of its business history, it advanced in a direction that had already been indicated by earlier dailies.

Concentration on the penny press has diverted attention from other significant moments in this long process of change. For instance, virtually no attention has been paid in standard U.S. journalism histories to incorporation in newspapers, though publicly held newspaper companies must have differed from privately held newspapers in many significant ways, including economic motivation and perhaps a sense of accountability. Perhaps standard histories ignore incorporation because they already have projected changes, erroneously I think, in economic structure back into the penny papers.

(Incidentally, J.M. Lee [1923, pp. 214–215] sees Greeley's distribution of stock in the *Tribune* to that newspaper's employees in 1849 as the beginning of joint-stock newspaper companies.)

By shifting attention from penny papers to the integration of the newspaper industry as a whole into the market economy, it is possible to see how many of the standard attributions of change to the penny papers are inappropriate. It becomes clear that changes said to have been initiated by penny papers were part of processes already in place and affecting all sectors of the newspaper industry. The expansion of advertising revenue was one such process. So were developments in occupational differentiation (i.e., the rise of the reporter) and technological sophistication.

The Professional Reporter

It is commonly claimed that penny papers transformed news reporting by paying people to do it, that is, by inventing the professional reporter. While it is true that, in New York at least, penny papers were the first to hire reporters to cover the police courts and so forth, this action marked neither a change in direction in the development of reporting nor a very considerable leap in its effectiveness. It already had become common for elite newspapers to pay political correspondents. Even among less elite newspapers, regular contributors performed reporting functions, and in many cases editors acted as reporters. Furthermore, the trend in newspaper operation was a continual one toward specialization. In fact, editorial work too had recently been separated from printing as the newspaper proprietor changed in status from craftsman to publisher. The rise of the editor might be seen as one of the peculiar contributions of the partisan newspaper, but this development should be seen as part of a larger trend of specialization that included the rise of the reporter, rather than as a trend in opposition to it. The mythology of the penny press, though, tends to depict the rise of the reporter and the rise of the editor as contradictory developments.

New Technology

The mythology also claims that because penny papers were the first to compete vigorously for news and readers they were responsible for the development and adoption of new technologies, especially the steam press and the telegraph. But this claim is incorrect: penny papers were not the only ones that competed for circulation, nor were they the only ones to feel a need to accelerate news transmission.

The drive to accelerate news transmission was well established before the advent of the penny press. Earlier newspapers printed extras and hired postriders to hustle information to the public as quickly as possible. O'Brien (1928, p. 65), for instance, records that it was the six-penny papers in New York that formed a combination to run a horse express line from Philadelphia in order to take Washington news more quickly to New York; afterwards, the penny *Sun* and *New York Transcript* set up a rival line. Crouthamel (1964, p. 93) refers to a news rivalry between the *Journal of Commerce* and the *Courier and Enquirer* in New York before the advent of the penny press. And outside of New York the relative contributions of conventional papers to the speeding up of news transmission were even more pronounced. This was also the case with other news technologies. In many cities, probably in most cities, it was the well-established conventional dailies that first introduced steam presses. (In Cincinnati, for instance, it was the *Cincinnati Daily Gazette*, a conventional paper, that installed the first steam presses [Nerone, 1982, p. 26].) And in inland cities, telegraph lines were built with funds underwritten by conventional and penny papers alike. While much has been made of the contribution of Moses Beach, a penny paper publisher, in promoting early telegraph construction, another important promoter was Amos Kendall, a Jacksonian partisan editor and politico.

In many cases, penny papers actually were technologically retrogressive. The earliest penny papers seemed to harken back to the days of craft production and artisan control rather than look forward to the modern newsroom. Benjamin Day, for example, began the *Sun* with a hand press and a few helpers. His entire operation was contained in a room that measured 12 by 16 feet (O'Brien, 1928, p. 4). The *Cincinnati Daily Times*, one of the earliest successful penny papers, began publication on an old Dickinson hand press, which it rented from the conventional *Republican* for $5 a month. For several years, the paper employed only two men (Coggeshall, 1851, p. 46). There seems to have been no inherent or exclusive relationship between advanced technology and penny papers, especially outside of New York City.

In terms of structure and conduct, then, it seems that penny papers followed trends but did not necessarily set them. Most of the trends were rooted in forces that operated on the newspaper establishment as a whole, not just penny papers, and some penny papers did not follow dominant trends.

Conclusion

I have reconstructed a set of characterizations of the penny press and evaluated their accuracy, but it remains to be seen how these characterizations operate as a mythology. I contend that the body of ideas I have discussed exist as the common sense of historical writing. As a mythology, it has an autonomous influence on thought beyond that of any particular work or writer. Many of the commentators I have drawn on, ironically, have argued against many of the implications I will now sketch out.

The received history of the penny press, I contend, operates as a myth of origins of present newspaper practices that serves to legitimate contemporary U.S. newspapers by presenting them as the heirs of papers that were popular and democratic and that overthrew a press establishment that was elite and privileged. Two commonplaces of the penny press mythology operate here: first, that the penny press was democratic and that democracy could not have flourished without it, and second, that the penny press is the direct ancestor of the contemporary U.S. newspaper.

Before the penny press, the argument goes, there were no democratic newspapers because all newspapers were instruments of restricted privilege (Payne, 1920, p. 255; Lippmann, 1931, p. 437). I already have shown that earlier newspapers did indeed circulate popularly and provide citizens with the political information necessary to make decisions on political issues, but there is another issue, that of the definition of democracy, that needs to be addressed. It is claimed that newspapers, at least until the 1820s, operated in a society that maintained ideas of privilege and deference and so could not have been democratic in the modern egalitarian sense of the word. It is necessary here to quote Schudson (1978, pp. 57–58) at length one more time:

> *By "democratic" I refer to the replacement of a political culture of gentry rule by the ideal and institutional fact of mass democracy. . . . The modern American system of bureaucratic, non-ideological parties. . . .*
>
> *But "democratization" was not solely political either in its causes or consequences. . . . A culture of the market became a more pervasive feature of human consciousness. And this culture, it is fair to say, was democratic. In the market there were no special categories and privileges.*

The penny papers were the unique spokespeople for this egalitarian market society:

> *These papers, whatever their political preferences, were spokesmen for egalitarian ideals in politics, economic life, and social life through their organization of sales, their solicitation of advertising, their emphasis on news, their catering to large audiences, their decreasing concern with the editorial.*
>
> *The penny papers expressed and built the culture of a democratic market society, a culture which had no place for social or intellectual deference.* (p. 60)

By its practices as well as by its ideals, the penny press was uniquely democratic. Two points must be made about this argument. First, it defines democracy in a particular way: Democracy is equality before market forces; that is, democracy is the absence of acknowledged special privilege. Stated this way, it is possible to agree that a commercial press is more democratic. Yet the word "democratic" means a great deal more. In its root, it means rule by the people, and this is something quite different from equality in the marketplace. The mythology of the penny press, however, substitutes the marketplace for the broader meaning of democracy (though certainly Schudson, Schiller, and Saxton do not agree with the thrust of this substitution). It thereby gives the impression that, without a specifically commercial structure, newspapers cannot enable rule by the people.

A second point to be made about the "democracy" argument is that it accepts as fact many things that are questionable and some that simply are not true. For instance, it accepts as fact that penny papers were mass circulation papers, and this is questionable. It also accepts as fact that earlier papers were exclusively special interest papers, and this is not true. And it accepts as fact that rebellion against privilege indicated a belief in equality, and this is highly questionable. It adopts the notion that Jacksonian America saw the creation of an equality of opportunity and an equality of condition that was unprecedented, but many historians have called this interpretation into question (e.g., Pessen, 1978).

One final point should be made here. Most writers on the penny press assume that the attack against privilege in the Jacksonian Era was led by adherents and leaders of the Democratic party in politics. If, however, the Democratic party was the spearhead of the attack on privilege, and if the new party system championed electoral democracy, then why should we regard the party press as a restricted, privileged, and antidemocratic press? Rather, if we are to look for the rise of equality and democracy in this period, should not we expect to find it first in the partisan press, and not exclusively in the penny press?

It is possible to argue that *commercial* papers are democratic in a specific way, and this is what Schudson in effect does. And it is also possible to argue that the rise of a market society in antebellum America led to the rise of a more specifically commercial press. But it is mythology to maintain that commercialization took place only in penny papers, and it is nearsighted to restrict democracy to that one class of commercial newspapers.

Finally, it is argued that the penny papers were the direct ancestors, the prototypes, of the contemporary American newspaper. Saxton (1984, p. 217) states that "they demonstrated the sorts of relationships that must prevail between publishers and readers, readers and advertisers, if mass circulation was to be achieved. In this sense they staked out the boundaries in which second, and ongoing, waves of daily newspapers would be obliged to operate." The penny press defined what would be possible for future American newspapers. And so the formula for success established by penny papers led directly to the current business structure of contemporary American newspapers, and the advance of democracy that the penny papers spearheaded, it might be concluded (though Saxton does not so argue), finds its current champions in modern American dailies.

The ancestor myth is largely true: the penny papers do seem more modern than their contemporary rivals. It is also clear that this ancestor myth acts as a powerful legitimation for modern practices and ideals, objectivity and commercial support, and so forth. To locate your roots in a glorious past is to clothe yourself in glory.

The ancestor myth too needs qualification. First, many of the qualities attributed to the penny press are read into it from present experience. For instance, the news values of penny papers are presented as similar to and sometimes identical with modern news values. Likewise, it is claimed that the same circulation patterns, the same divisions of labor, and the same production techniques were used. There was, however, a great deal in the penny papers that was nonmodern and actually antimodern, and there were sectors of the penny press that were distinctly backward-looking, both in ideals and practices. Thus I have argued that the political neutrality of some penny papers was nearer the impartiality of the papers of the early republic than it was to twentieth century objectivity. The same may be said for the concern with morality in human interest stories.

Second, contemporary American journalism is not monolithic. As journalism in the nineteenth century was, it is made up of classes of papers and segmented audiences. Much of American journalism today traces its roots not to the penny press but to weeklies and country papers and reform journalism. The mythology of the penny press oversimplifies the present just as it oversimplifies the past.

Third, the ancestor myth implies a gradual building up of successful ideals, the retention of the best of the past and the addition of the best that the present can supply. It implies a continual improvement both in practices and ideals. This attribution of moral superiority is clear in much of the mythology of the penny press: penny papers were superior insofar as they came to resemble contemporary papers, and modern papers are superior because they trace their lineage back to penny papers. The search for roots always tends to emphasize what is considered best in contemporary journalism. Just as it gives the impression that all of history conspired to create *The New York Times*, so it gives the impression that all American newspapers today are run like the *Times*. By claiming that political independence was initiated by penny papers, it leads us to believe that all newspapers today are politically independent. By saying that penny papers initiated democracy, it leads us to say that today's newspapers are democratic.

The concerns and ideals of contemporary journalists lie behind much of the mythology of the penny press. For the pioneering journalism historians were themselves journalists, and their motives for writing journalism history were to explain and justify themselves on the one hand, and to provide textbooks for the training of future journalists on the other. Later scholars inevitably relied on the facts if not the interpretations left by their journalistic predecessors.

In addition to legitimating contemporary press structures, the mythology of the penny press also serves to set limits on proposals for change. To give the most obvious example, the mythology of the penny press insists on a connection between the business structure and the political function of a newspaper: political independence and reliance on the marketplace were linked in the rise of the penny press. Consequently, a necessary theoretical relationship between commercialism and political independence is argued. But commercial newspapers actually remained partisan in editorial policy in many cases; there was no necessary relationship between commercialism and political neutrality. The initial historical argument is false, and the theoretical argument also may be false. Political neutrality and objective reporting may be perfectly possible in newspapers that have government subsidies. The experience of several Western nations attests to this possibility. Thus the mythology of the penny press exerts a significant inertia on attitudes toward the modern newspaper.

In this essay, I have argued indirectly that historical research into nineteenth century American newspapers would benefit from a redirection of focus. Instead of focusing on notorious or dramatic newspapers and editors, we should focus on the typical. Instead of focusing on the major Eastern metropoles, we should focus on smaller cities and towns. Instead of looking for a monolithic characterization of American journalism, we should talk about classes of newspapers and segmented audiences. Instead of looking at newspapers as independent actors in the historical arena, we should look for the long-term, broad-based social and cultural developments behind them.

All of this is not meant to deny the distinctiveness of the penny press, whether in New York or in other cities. Specifically, it should be acknowledged that historians of the penny press are correct in identifying its tone as lively, popular, and at times rebellious: the penny papers reflected much of the cultural ferment and social dislocation in Jacksonian cities. As creatures of their time, they stand out as discontinuous; they have a character that is not simply the product of evolutionary forces. We should also acknowledge the creativity of the penny press conductors. Men like Bennett and Greeley were more than just servants of historical processes; they were also agents of change, and there is more than a little truth to the common view that they were not only the most influential but also the best newspapermen of their age.

Acknowledging the distinctiveness of the penny press is also a way of putting limits on its historical significance. If, as Schiller, Schudson, and Saxton have agreed, the penny press was a unique creature of the social and cultural context of the cities of the 1830s, then it is cut off from subsequent history by the same measure as it is cut off from preceding years. Inasmuch as its unique features were not inherited from the past, by the same token they were not handed down to the future. Again, as Saxton in particular has argued, both the artisanal control of manufacture and the populist flavor to content tended to pass away. Distinctiveness faded with time.

The features of the penny press that persisted were evolutionary in nature. These features include developments in circulation and readership, in business and occupational structure, and in certain types of content, like news and the human interest story. But these features were not unique to the penny press, and these developments were not discontinuous. Evolutionary developments can be separated from unique features; one of the effects of mythologizing the history of the penny press conductors has been to confuse the two. Thus we have the persistent claim that the penny press invented the idea of the newspaper as a business or the idea of political neutrality or the human interest story.

There is no doubt that the unique culture of the penny press left a legacy for U.S. journalism as a whole. Nor is there doubt the leading conductors of the penny press served as role models for other and later journalists. But there is doubt as to whether the historical invocation of the penny press has served to accurately portray actual practice, or whether instead it has functioned as a kind of mystification of actual practice. This is a question that requires detailed research to answer. Though the argument is a compelling one, there is insufficient evidence that the actual practices of the penny press conductors were models for the actual practices of either their contemporaries or of subsequent generations of journalists.

Recognizing the uniqueness and distinctiveness of the penny press does not require that it be considered revolutionary. Successful penny papers were the most prosperous and the most widely circulated newspapers of their time. They were feared and respected by contemporary politicians and the news they carried was reprinted from newspaper to newspaper throughout the country. The penny papers were the newspaper elite of their day and were powerful indeed.

They were not, however, the first elite newspapers, nor were they necessarily different in their functioning from other elite papers. And here is another unfortunate result of the mythology of the penny press: It leads us to believe that the populist flavor of the early cheap papers also characterized the later function of the penny papers as elite newspapers. This is not necessarily true. And again it is important to distinguish the unique features of the penny press as cheap press from the characteristics that historical forces were producing in the leading newspapers of the day, the acceleration of information transmission and occupational differentiation in reporting and so forth. Even as elite newspapers, the contribution of the penny press was to develop an established trajectory of change rather than alter it.

The reason why the penny press has been so popular with historians, after all, is that it seems to represent a stage in the evolution of journalism. I propose that we study the evolution of journalism by studying the rise of components of journalism: the development of readerships and technologies, the rise of crime reporting or sensationalism, and the nature of working class readerships and the appeals to working class sensibilities. The fact that some of these components sometimes seem to have been combined in the penny press is frequently misleading.

References

Bleyer, W. G. (1927). *Main currents in the history of American journalism*. Boston: Houghton Mifflin.

Botein, S. (1975). "Meer mechanics" and an open press: The business and political strategies of colonial printers. *Perspectives in American History, 9,* 127–225.

Carey, J. (1974). The problem of journalism history. *Journalism History, 1,* 3–5, 27.

Coggeshall, W. T. (1851). *History of the Cincinnati press and its conductors.* Unpublished manuscript, Cincinnati Historical Society.

Cremin, L. (1980). *American education: The national experience, 1783–1876.* New York: Harper & Row.

Crouthamel, J. L. (1964). The newspaper revolution in New York, 1830–1860. *New York History, 45,* 91–113.

Crouthamel, J. L. (1974). James Gordon Bennett, the New York Herald, and the development of newspaper sensationalism. *New York History, 54,* 294–316.

Czitrom, D. (1982). *Media and the American mind: From Morse to McLuhan.* Chapel Hill: University of North Carolina Press.

De Tocqueville, A. (1954). *Democracy in America.* New York: Vintage Books.

Dicken Garcia, H., & Stevens, J. D. (1980). *Communication history.* Beverly Hills: Sage.

Emery, E., & Emery, M. B. (1984). *The press and America: An interpretive history of the mass media* (5th ed.). Englewood Cliffs, NJ: Prentice Hall.

Greeley, H. (1868). *Recollections of a busy life.* New York: J. B. Ford.

Heren, L. (1985). *The power of the press?* London: Orbis.

Hofstadter, R. (1972). *The idea of a party system: The rise of legitimate opposition in the United States, 1780–1840.* Berkeley: University of California Press.

Hudson, F. (1873). *Journalism in the United States, from 1690 to 1872.* New York: Harper.

Hughes, H. M. (1940). *News and the human interest story.* Chicago: University of Chicago Press.

Kaul, A. J., & McKerns, J. P. (1985). The dialectic ecology of the newspaper. *Critical Studies in Mass Communication, 2,* 217–233.

Lee, A. M. (1937). *The daily newspaper in America: The evolution of a social instrument*. New York: Macmillan.

Lee, J. M. (1923). *History of American journalism* (rev. ed.). Boston: Houghton Mifflin.

Leonard, T. C. (1986). *The power of the press: The birth of American political reporting*. New York: Oxford University Press.

Lippmann, W. (1931). Two revolutions in the American press. *Yale Review, 20,* 433–441.

McCormick, R. P. (1966). *The second American party*

system: Party formation in the Jacksonian era. Chapel Hill: University of North Carolina Press.

McKerns, J. (1977). The limits of progressive journalism history. *Journalism History, 4,* 88–92.

Mott, F. L. (1950). *American journalism: A history of newspapers in the United States* (rev. ed.). New York: Macmillan.

Nerone, J. C. (1982). The press and popular culture in the early republic: Cincinnati, 1793–1848. Unpublished doctoral dissertation, University of Notre Dame.

North, S. N. D. (1881). *History and present condition of the newspaper and periodical press of the United States.* Washington, DC: U.S. Census Bureau.

O'Brien, F. M. (1928). *The story of the Sun: New York, 1833–1928* (2nd ed.). New York: D. Appleton and Company.

Park, R. E. (1955). The natural history of the newspaper. *American Journal of Sociology, 29,* 80–98.

Payne, G. H. (1920). *History of journalism in the United States.* New York: Appleton–Century.

Pessen, E. (1973). *Riches, class, and power before the civil war.* Lexington, MA: D. C. Heath.

Peterson, T., Jensen, J., & Rivers, W. (1965). *The mass media and modern society.* New York Holt, Rinehart and Winston.

Pickett, C. M. (1960). Technology and the New York press in the nineteenth century. *Journalism Quarterly, 37,* 398–407.

Russo, D. J. (1980). The origins of local news in the U.S. country press, 1840s–1870s. *Journalism Monographs, 65.*

Saxton, A. (1984). Problems of race and class in the origins of the mass circulation press. *American Quarterly, 36,* 211–234.

Schiller, D. (1979). An historical approach to objectivity and professionalism in American news reporting. *Journal of Communications, 29* (49), 46–57.

Schiller, D. (1981). *Objectivity and the news: The public and the rise of commercial journalism.* Philadelphia: University of Pennsylvania Press.

Schudson, M. (1978). *Discovering the news: A social history of American newspapers.* New York: Harper.

Shaw, D. L. (1981). At the crossroads: Change and continuity in American press news, 1820–1860. *Journalism History, 8,* 38–53, 76.

Trollope, F. (1949). *Domestic manners of the Americans.* New York: A. A. Knopf.

IV

Competing Values at Century's Turn

In the years after the Civil War, expansion of the periodical press paralleled the expansion of business that characterized a modernizing society. Transportation and communication networks spanned the nation. Expanding telegraph lines created the possibility for instant news; transportation networks paved the way for centralization of industry and national distribution of manufactured goods. Rural people, black and white, flocked to the cities looking for work. By the end of the century business consolidation brought entire industries under the control of individual corporations. The political debate shifted from an examination of the relationship of rural America to its urban counterparts and focused instead on the relationship of business to government.

Forms of mechanization that affected the entire country also affected the periodical industry. The advent of the linotype and the perfection of high-speed presses accelerated the development of large-circulation city newspapers. Favorable postal rates, increasing numbers of American writers, and expanding incomes spurred the development of the magazine. At the same time that newspapers commented on the passing scene they became part of corporate development itself. In New York City, Joseph Pulitzer and William Randolph Hearst developed sensational newspapers designed to appeal to mass populations. Their circulations surpassed all that had gone before, reaching as high as 1.5 million copies the day after the McKinley-Bryan election.

Accompanying rapid modernization were continuing fears of political and business corruption and of the capitalistic structure that undergirded the development of large-scale enterprise. By 1904 a variety of citizens' groups and magazine writers (labeled "muckrakers" by President Theodore Roosevelt) challenged the renegade path of corporate business, arguing that progress did not always result from the development of private enterprise and that private interests did not always serve the public trust. During the first decade of the twentieth century, regulation was developed to control lobbying, campaign contributions, free passes, and utility and transportation companies. Some studies have characterized the regulatory development as a triumph of the people over government, whereas others have argued that regulation merely served to rationalize the role of business in stabilizing its own gains and protecting it against public interference.[1] Historians of the 1930s, writing in the midst of a depression that itself challenged the capitalistic structure, characterized the captains of industry as robber barons; only in the 1950s with the advent of business history did the industrial giants once again receive more favorable treatment as talented individuals who made "creative contributions to the economy."[2]

Early studies of turn-of-the-century newspaper development focused on two models: the sensational papers of Pulitzer and Hearst and the informational papers such as the *New York Times*. Writing in 1927, Willard Bleyer characterized the period in progressive terminology. He described the tremendous mechanical progress, the mass production and standardization of products, the increase of city populations, the speeding up of life and "consequent nervous tension" in society, the development of huge business organizations, and an attempt to create higher standards of business and professional ethics. Reflecting a common conception that the press lowered its ideals to serve the masses, Bleyer noted that sensational or "yellow" journalism "flourished in larger cities where the number of half-assimilated foreigners was greatest." Yet, he remarked, greater advances were made during the first quarter of the twentieth century than during the same length of time in any previous period. Although yellow journalism represented a negative side of journalistic development, Bleyer believed the overall growth represented progress.[3]

Edwin Emery and Henry Ladd Smith, writing in 1954, used the celebratory rhetoric common to consensus historians of the fifties, noting that the changes in industrialization, mechanization, and expansion were "the true nationalization of the United States, the achievement of economic and social interdependence." But they expressed sharp concern about the theory of individualism, the "unrestrained exploitation," and the concentration of wealth that occurred at century's turn. Newspapers, they contended, "believed in the news function as the primary obligation of the press; they exhibited independence of editorial opinion; they crusaded actively in the community interest; they appealed to the mass audience through improved writing, better makeup, use of headlines and illustration, and a popularization of their contents." Commenting on sensationalism in a fashion similar to Bleyer, they noted that "if popularization of the product gave rise to an overpowering and crude sensationalism, still the over-all result was a great expansion of the influence of the newspaper." E. W. Scripps and Joseph Pulitzer they viewed "as effective champions of progressive democracy" who, with others, "helped to develop a new main current of American thought and action, in keeping with the requirements and the wishes of the majority."[4]

In recent years, scholars have questioned this monolithic view of the grand progress of the American press and have begun to analyze individual newspapers to provide a more comprehensive view of the diversity of the press of the period. In the selections presented here, David Paul Nord analyzes three mainstream newspapers of the 1880s in Chicago, whereas Jean Folkerts focuses on nonmainstream media. Ted Curtis Smythe looks at journalistic employment and asks penetrating questions about whether reporters were treated as professionals in the late nineteenth century. Richard L. McCormick examines the history of concepts of corruption and evaluates the role of magazine muckrakers in the context of progressivism.

Nord's article, "The Public Community: The Urbanization of Journalism in Chicago," confronts many of the issues of urban communities in the 1870s and links his study of the newspapers to traditional beliefs in individual property rights and laissez-faire government policies that encountered an emerging sense of public community. In a recent essay, Nord categorized the article as cultural history, noting that it was a study of "how people lived and thought about living in a modern industrial city, and how the mass-circulation newspaper interacted with that life."[5] He describes the *Chicago Tribune* and the *Chicago Times*—newspapers that differed in levels of sensationalism, style, and substance—as newspapers that nevertheless held "similar commitments to private property and individualism and similar notions of what news should be in a big-city newspaper." But the newcomer to Chicago, the *Chicago Daily News*, he labels the first thoroughly urban newspaper, the first newspaper "to articulate a vision of public community." The *News*, unlike the other newspapers of Chicago, emphasized interdependence and sympathy, the potential of the voluntary association, and "formal public action through government." Nord notes that the *News* advocated, in particular, "increased government intervention in business and urban life," with the city and state assuming responsibility for city problems such as public health and safety.

Folkerts, in "Functions of the Reform Press," documents the vitality of newspapers outside the mainstream. Looking in particular at Populist newspapers, she develops a theory of performance that includes building a sense of community among rural peoples with similar economic and social interests, providing information about agricultural and political issues not treated by competing mainstream newspapers, and seeking legitimation of an agrarian movement that was derided by newspapers that labeled Populists as radical have-nots.

One feature of the period, often used to describe the turn-of-the-century press as progressive, was the formation of national journalistic organizations that advocated acceptable standards of behavior. The American Newspaper Publishers' Association of 1887, Chicago press clubs, and other similar metropolitan organizations, and the beginning of trade journals, such as the *Journalist*, which addressed industrywide issues, are activities that characterized a developing profession. In his analysis of trade journal content, "The Reporter, 1880–1900," Smythe notes that journalism was "more a way station on the highway to politics, business, literature or editorial work than a profession itself." Smythe documents the long hours, lack of stability, and low wages that characterized reporting.

Turn-of-the-century media included a viable magazine industry as well as an expanding newspaper press. During the first decade of the twentieth century inexpensive periodicals aimed at a mass audience flourished. Many allied themselves with Theodore Roosevelt's Progressive party, although it was Roosevelt who labeled those magazines "muckrakers" that wrote about social and economic ills. Richard L. McCormick's "The Discovery that Business Corrupts Politics: A Reappraisal of the Origins of Progressivism" notes that muckrakers demanded the removal of the "corrupt politico-business alliance" that characterized turn-of-the century politics. Why, asks McCormick, did the progressives feel so strongly about this issue when corruption had been a continuing fear and theme in American life from the time of the Revolution? Indeed, as early as the 1850s newspapers such as the *New York Times* had uncovered corruption in city politics and demanded the removal of corrupt politicians. McCormick notes, however, that before 1900 the chief means of influencing government was through partisan politics. After 1900, when voter turnout declined, voluntary associations and civic organizations began to exert nonelectoral means of influence. As Nord noted in Chicago, these civic organizations demanded government assistance in developing and regulating city services. Further, by citing specific examples across the nation, the muckrakers made corruption part of the national vocabulary. McCormick maintains that revealing the details of corruption, along with recognizing that it was a national pattern, not just an isolated incident, reawakened the fear that privileged business corrupted politics. This awareness, notes McCormick, forced people to look beyond replacing "bad" people and toward finding solutions that attacked problems resulting from "identifiable economic and political forces." The resulting difference between government in the nineteenth and the twentieth centuries, McCormick contends, was that twentieth-century forces of centralization, bureaucratization, and government action to adjust group differences superseded the nineteenth-century values of individualism. Nevertheless, many commissions created to regulate business in the end became captives of industry.

The issues of corruption, community, and the viability of capitalism dominated contemporary accounts at the turn of the century, and journalists' attempts to control their professional development as well as to comment on and participate in the passing scene reflected their personal and institutional roles in a modernizing society.

Endnotes

1. Historians have interpreted the progressive movement of the early twentieth century in a variety of ways. For analysis of progressivism as a nostalgic return to the past, see Richard Hofstadter, *The Age of Reform: From Bryan to F.D.R.* (New York: Vintage Books, 1955). George Mowry in *The California Progressives* (Berkeley, Calif: University of California Press, 1951) develops the thesis of the middle class in revolt against labor and capital, and Hofstadter assigns these men an anxiety about their own status. David P. Thelen in "Social Tensions and the Origins of Progressivism," *Journal of American History* 56:2 (September 1969), discusses the problems of assigning psychological motivation to reform movements and suggests that progressivism in Wisconsin was a cooperative consumer response to the depression of 1893–97 and to corporate arrogance. Samuel P. Hays in *The Response to Industrialism* (Chicago: University of

Chicago Press, 1957) and Robert H. Wiebe in *The Search for Order 1877–1920* (New York: Oxford University Press, 1975) examine the response of business to the needs of an industrializing nation and the attempt by the middle class to use scientific expertise in their search for order within society. Gabriel Kolko in *The Triumph of Conservatism: A Reinterpretation of American History, 1900–1916* (London: Free Press of Glencoe, Collier-Macmillan, 1963) cites a deliberate attempt by businessmen to preserve profits and power. See Vernon Parrington, *Main Currents of American Thought* (New York: Harcourt, Brace & World, 1927–1930), for a discussion of progressivism as a "liberal renaissance."

2. Grob, Gerald N. and George A. Billias, *Interpretations of American History: Patterns and Perspectives* (New York: Free Press, 1967), 77.
3. Willard G. Bleyer, *Main Currents in the History of American Journalism* (Boston: Houghton Mifflin Co., 1927), 390, 429.
4. Edwin Emery and Henry Ladd Smith, *The Press and America* (Englewood Cliffs, N.J.: Prentice-Hall, 1954), 338, 355, 480.
5. David Paul Nord, "A Plea for *Journalism* History," *Journalism History* 15:1 (Spring 1988): 12. See also Nord, "The Business Values of American Newspapers: The 19th Century Watershed in Chicago," *Journalism Quarterly* 61 (Summer 1984): 265–273. Nord describes this second article as institutional history, concerned with the nature of the newspaper *business*.

The Public Community: The Urbanization of Journalism in Chicago

David Paul Nord

Although newspapers have always resided in cities, they have not always lived in them—lived in the sense of understanding, embracing, and building an ethos of urbanism. The urbanization of the American newspaper was a late nineteenth-century phenomenon, and a prototype of this new "urbanized" popular press was the *Chicago Daily News*, founded in 1875.

The *Chicago Daily News* and newspapers like it represent a kind of second stage in the development of the modern, urban newspaper in America. Earlier big-city newspapers of mid-century were rather more modern than urban. They were modern not merely in their business and journalistic practice, but in their ready acceptance of the formal, contractual society and their enthusiastic promotion of capitalism, industrialism, and the justice and discipline of the marketplace. Their very modern economic and political views, however, were rooted in notions of private property rights, individualism, and laissez faire that were being challenged in the late nineteenth century by the imperatives and growing complexities of urban life. Like many city institutions built by individual entrepreneurs, big-city newspapers, even self-consciously popular ones, did not necessarily grasp what was happening to the collective life in the metropolis. Publishers were rather like Jeffersonian yeomen transplanted unthinkingly into capitalism. Their newspapers were the products of the "private city," and they remained private in outlook, thoroughly individualistic in editorial policy and news philosophy.[1]

Newspapers such as the *Chicago Daily News*, on the other hand, began in the 1870s and 1880s to develop a new vision of community life for this new kind of city—the modern metropolis. Theirs was a vision of community that was inspired less by nostalgic longing for the communal seventeenth century than by a fear of the very tangible social problems of the capitalistic, individualistic nineteenth. This was community forced by urban life and, it was hoped, suited to the inherent impersonality of large-scale urban existence. It was *public community*—that is, a kind of association founded on communitarian notions of interdependence and identity, of sentiment and sympathy, yet powered by formal organizations and activist government and guided by the new agencies of mass communication.

The important differences between the urban press of the late nineteenth century, such as the *Chicago Daily News*, and the big-city press of earlier decades were not what they are sometimes thought to have been. The *Daily News* was not the first sensational paper, the first politically independent paper, the first departmentalized paper, the first telegraph newspaper, the first multi-class paper, or the first screaming headline paper in Chicago. In short, it was neither the first popular nor the first modern newspaper in the city. But it was the first thoroughly urban one—that is, the first to articulate a vision of public community. What this vision was and how it differed from the philosophy and practice of the older-style popular press is the subject of this study.

II

The transformation of community life in American cities is currently a subject of intense and increasing interest in historical studies. The idea of community, of course, has always been central to both urban sociology and urban history. Until recently, however, both have tended to treat the concept rather ahistorically. Community traditionally has been discussed as an ideal type—sometimes lost, sometimes hoped for, but seldom explored in the intricacies of historical context. A long tradition of urban sociology developed around the dichotomous typologies of Ferdinand Tännies (Gemeinschaft versus Gesellschaft), Emile Durkheim (organic versus mechanical solidarity), and Max Weber (communal versus associative relationships). The essence of modernization was thought to have been the eclipse of community and the rise of impersonal, contractual, and mechanistic modes of association.[2] The parts of the dichotomies usually were seen as temporally sequential, and thus historical. The many empirical "community studies" of the 1920s and later, however, did not really test these theories in history so much as assume a history to fit the theory. "Community" became what the town had had sometime before the investigator arrived to find it gone. Oddly, historians often have been equally ahistorical. Steeped in the sociological tradition, they have assumed a priori that the march from traditional past to modern present meant the breakdown of community. And different American historians have found that time of breakdown in just about every decade from the 1650s to the 1920s.[3]

These traditions of ahistorical urban sociology and urban history, like the idealized vision of community they created, are now in decline. Increasingly, students of America's urban past and present have rejected the dichotomous and especially the sequential nature of Gemeinschaft and Gesellschaft, community and society. The materials of the past have reaffirmed what historians have always professed to believe, that the meaning of human life is complex and the direction of historical change ambiguous. Studies of nineteenth-century town and city growth and other aspects of modernization now more typically stress the persistence of traditional values and community structures. Some historians, such as Samuel Hays and Richard Jensen, continue to use dichotomous ideal types (e.g., modern versus traditional, cosmopolitan versus local), but they tend to link them with competing classes or groups within the same society at the same time.[4] Other historians, such as Thomas Bender, suggest that each individual person experiences *both* Gemeinschaft and Gesellschaft, both community and formal organization, in the complexity of modern life.[5]

Although reaffirming the complexities and ambiguities of the history of community life, scholars still tend to insist upon the distinction between public and private in their definitions of community. Community is seen as a private affair of family, kin, and face-to-face relationships. "Community," in the words of Robert Nisbet, "is founded on man conceived in his wholeness rather than in one or another of the roles, taken separately, that he may hold in a social order. It draws its psychological strength from levels of motivation deeper than those of mere volition or interest."[6] The public culture, on the other hand, is the sphere of roles, interests, organizations, contracts, and politics. In fact, the careless confusion of the public and private realms in the nineteenth century has caused many of our most serious modern problems, according to Richard Sennett, whose brilliant essay *The Fall of Public Man* is largely an extended effort to distinguish between the two.

Sennett argues persuasively that public life was eroded in the eighteenth and nineteenth centuries as people began to project private, psychological values and modes of thought into the public realm. "As a result, confusion has arisen between public and intimate life; people are working out in terms of personal feelings public matters which properly can be dealt with only through codes of impersonal meaning." Because people ceased to deal with one another in impersonal, formal, public ways, "community" became merely "shared personality" based on a common psychological fantasy of imagined but unachievable intimacy.[7] Thomas Bender makes a similar distinction. Although he argues that community need not involve geographical proximity, he does insist that community is a private affair that should be separate from the public sphere.[8]

If the malaise of the twentieth-century man is a product of the confusion of the public and private realms of life, then newspapers such as the *Chicago Daily News* surely contributed to it, for these papers directly challenged traditional ideas of private property and public action in the nineteenth-century city.[9] With great fervor and optimism, they urged a community spirit in what Sennett would define as the public realm. Furthermore, they provided their audience with a limited, organized, common frame of reference, so that diverse city dwellers could communicate with one another—communicate in the sense that they could think about the same things at the same time and thus share a vision of social reality. These newspapers saw in the fragmenting forces of urbanization the germ of public community.

III

The *Chicago Daily News* was born into a city that was becoming a giant metropolis. By the time of the great fire of 1871, nearly 300,000 Chicagoans crowded along the shores of Lake Michigan. The fire scarcely slowed the pace of growth. By 1880 Chicago was a city of 500,000; by 1890 more than one million.[10] Such rapid growth undermined traditional community life in Chicago. These many thousands of newcomers were a diverse lot, arriving from all parts of America and the world, and bringing with them their peculiar habits, institutions, and prejudices. By the 1870s neighborhoods, churches, social clubs, immigrant newspapers, mutual aid societies, patriotic associations, and political organizations were all fragmented and isolated from one another along class, ethnic, and linguistic lines. And the pot was slow to melt these disparate, wary, fearful peoples.[11]

Public institutions in Chicago in the 1870s also were fragmented and increasingly unable to cope with the growing problems of collective life in a large, modern city. The rapid concentration of industry and population created enormous environmental and social problems that defied solution by traditional means. Problems of sewerage, water supply, transportation, smoke abatement, crime and fire control, housing, unemployment, and scores of other matters of health, sanitation, and public welfare all grew more intense as the city grew more complex and congested. But neither public nor private institutions were well equipped to confront these crises of urbanization. After a brief spurt of concerted public spirit and action after the fire of 1871, Chicago's city government seemed to decline in power and effectiveness during the 1870s. Although population continued to rise, taxes and revenues fell and public works and services remained undone.[12] The depression of 1873–1877 was the chief culprit, but not the only one. The public philosophy of Chicago was as fragmented as the material life of the city. Chicago remained a "private city," with no consensus on what should be the public response to urbanization, no consensus on the place of public action in economic and social life, no consensus on the meaning of community in the modern metropolis.

In the early 1870s, before the *Daily News* entered this new urban world, the largest and most popular newspaper in Chicago was the *Chicago Times*, perhaps the apotheosis of modern, big-city journalism in mid-nineteenth-century America. Like the popular press of other large cities, the *Times* was sensational, irreverent, diverse in content, and quick in coverage. Its modern production practices influenced papers all over the country.[13] Yet while the *Times* was a paper that would sell in the city, it was never a paper *of* the city. Despite its popularity, the *Times* never developed a particularly urban outlook. Despite its cosmopolitan veneer, the *Times* remained committed to conventional values of individualism, private property, and small-scale, face-to-face community.

The *Times* was the creature of Wilbur F. Storey, a kind of nineteenth-century entrepreneur run amuck. Storey's most striking personal trait was his ferocious, idiosyncratic, absolutely rock-hard independence. He is remembered today, if he is remembered at all, as the journalistic nemesis of Abraham Lincoln, as the vitriolic Copperhead editor whose paper was shut down by General Ambrose Burnside for two days in 1863.[14] Yet despite his unwavering devotion to the Democratic Party during the Civil War, Storey broke with the party after the war because it failed to follow him. He was guided and he guided his paper by his own lights. The *Times* masthead declared simply: "The *Times* . . . by W. F. Storey."

Storey was notorious in Chicago in the 1860s and 1870s for what his long-time associate Franc Wilkie called the *Times*'s "glaring indecency . . . which reeked, seethed like a hell's broth in the *Times* cauldrons."[15] In the idiom of the era, the *Times* was salacious, licentious, scurrilous, vituperative, blasphemous, obscene, debased, debauched, depraved, and generally deplored. No American newspaper before the Hearst papers of the 1890s or perhaps even the jazzy New York tabloids of the 1920s was as dedicated as the *Times* to sensationalism.

Sexual violence was probably the *Times*'s favorite form of sensation, although either sex or violence separately served almost as well. Rapists, lechers, sadists, polygamists, arsenic fiends, and spouse roasters all clamored for coverage in the *Times*, and found room in the daily round-ups of "Heathenish Horrors," "Sin and Sorrow," "The Age's Abominations," "The Prevailing Putridity."[16] Executions always were hot news for the *Times*, and Storey's most famous headline was one that stood at the top of an account in 1875 of four murderers who had repented of their sins at the gallows: "Jerked to Jesus."[17]

By the time he died, Storey was heartily despised by the "better element" of Chicago, but he was also a millionaire. His genius lay in mingling sensation and scandal with solid news reporting. In its golden age in the 1860s and 1870s, no other newspaper west of New York carried so much news. Storey knew how to produce a paper with murder, suicide, and divorce on one page and the most extensive and complete market reports in town on another. By all accounts, the *Times*'s readership was wide, cutting across class lines and neighborhood boundaries, both within Chicago and throughout the Midwest.[18]

In its fascination with the sordid underworld of city life on the one hand and its devotion to the city's business world on the other, the *Chicago Times* would seem a decidedly urban institution. In a sense it was. But the *Times* had no vision of the collective life of Chicago. The city was merely a complex of marketplaces where individuals conducted their private affairs. Like its editor and many of its readers, the *Times* remained a wary stranger in the city, an outsider, an uneasy spectator. Its values remained private, individualistic, and these values shaped both the editorials and the news content of the paper.

For the *Times*, the city of Chicago meant the individual people and the private property in it. In editorials Storey spoke explicitly for the "owners of Chicago"; that is, the people who actually held title to the lots, the buildings, and the businesses. During the first half of 1876, when the new *Daily News* was just getting started in Chicago, the *Times* was tremendously agitated and outraged by what it saw as the depredations of local government "tax-eaters" upon these owners of the city.[19] The *Times* insisted that the "city" was merely individual people, and people must take care of themselves. Government must be small and weak; and only property owners should be allowed to vote and participate in it. Voluntary associations must be small and local and built on neighborhood relationships.[20]

Lower taxes, government retrenchment, and protection for property owners from corrupt office holders, these were Storey's chief local concerns in the 1870s. In the first six months of 1876, the *Times* carried 60 major editorials calling for drastic cutbacks in local government and taxes, and another 70 denouncing local government officials, editorials in which "tax-eating" was the common theme. This was fully half of all editorials on local subjects. In Storey's view government was an "irresponsible, corrupt devourer of property and industry" that had to be stopped. The *Times* urged individuals to take matters into their own hands, to resist taxes; and the paper heartily applauded those "patriots" who simply declined to pay.[21] "There is no way to compel the devouring monster called government to surrender and submit to the economic law, but to cut off the supplies."[22]

The *Times* did not shrink from the obvious logic that to cut off taxes meant to cut off government. The dismantling of government, except for the barest of necessities, was precisely what the paper proposed. At least two-thirds of the city government should be abolished, the *Times* declared, maybe all of it. The board of health, the fire department, the building inspector's office, the library, and other examples of "useless officialdom" should be killed outright. Other agencies, such as the police department and the public schools, should be saved but greatly reduced. On occasion the *Times* argued that even these should go.[23]

In place of an increasingly complex and, in the view of the *Times*, increasingly corrupt and paternalistic city government, the paper urged upon the citizens of Chicago the traditional virtues of self-help, self-sufficiency, and free enterprise. Abolish the fire department and the insurance underwriters would quickly organize private brigades. Abolish the police department and within 48 hours its place would be filled by an extension of the private night-watch services. Abolish the public works department and property owners would hire their own private contractors for sewer and street improvements. Abolish the public schools and people would be forced to spend their own money instead of someone else's on their own education.[24] The *Times* proposed to fragment the municipality into hundreds of small neighborhood subdivisions, each with its own "New England town meeting." These many meetings of neighbors could contract for their own police, fire, and community services. Only a skeleton central city government should be retained. Such a decentralized system would make government directly responsible to the individual taxpayers, the owners of Chicago.[25] It would allow each citizen to live his or her own private life, in but not of the metropolis.

Permeating the *Times*'s editorial philosophy was a firm belief in the morality and the efficacy of free markets, private enterprise, and competition. Monopoly, where it existed in railroads, public utilities, or other businesses, was the result of unnatural government regulation, the product of the "statute spawners." In scores of editorials in 1876, the *Times* railed against the tariff and currency policies of the federal government and against any kind of "special legislation."[26] Moreover, in arguments that echoed the social Darwinist philosophy of the day the *Times* carried its belief in laissez-faire beyond the business world to denounce charity and social reform and to embrace personal liberty for individuals in matters such as temperance and observance of the Sabbath.[27] The paper followed what Storey took to be the philosophy of Jefferson and Jackson, insisting that in this world individuals must make their own way. The rise of the city made no difference. Storey's image of Chicago was a marketplace in which individuals struck the best deal they could. If lighting gas prices are too high, switch to kerosene; if there are no jobs, move to the country.[28] Neither government nor charity could contravene the iron laws of the market and of individual responsibility.

The popularity of the *Chicago Times* undoubtedly did not rest upon its editorials. After its demise the paper was remembered for its editorials, but it was celebrated for its news.[29] Like most American newspapers from that era to our own, the *Times* emphasized the news of government, politics, and business. Major national government stories could dominate front-page coverage for months. But the most striking characteristic of the *Times*'s news coverage, taken as a whole, was its astonishing diversity.

In 1876, the *Times* was a daily extravaganza of information. Major stories, such as the Whisky Ring trials and the Hays-Tilden election, were covered in stupefyingly fine detail, frequently with long verbatim transcripts of legal proceedings, legislative debates, speeches, letters, and interviews. But more striking than the depth of the *Times* news coverage was its breadth. The paper was filled with column after column of tiny stories from everywhere on every conceivable subject. Many of these were unrelated one-or-two sentence items, grouped together under headings such as "Slices of News," "News Nebulae," or "Local Skimmings." Counting all of these little unconnected items along with the scores of longer stories, it was not uncommon for an eight-page paper to contain more than a thousand separate bits of news!

The "News Nebulae" column suggests the nature of this approach to news. One of these columns begins in the following way:

> *They have a chain gang in Fort Wayne.*
>
> *Terre Haute is going to have a soup house.*
>
> *An Indiana man has 17,000 cat skins for sale.*
>
> *Here comes Greencastle, Ind., with the smallpox.*
>
> *The crusaders of Keokuk will soon commence street work.*[30]

Some of the news bits were departmentalized, as in "The Religious World."

> *There are 77 Protestant Episcopal churches in New York.*
>
> *The death is announced of Rev. A.H. DeMora, a Protestant Episcopal minister, at Lisbon, Portugal.*
>
> *The report that Mr. Moody received a purse of $1,500 at Augusta, Ga., is denied on the best authority.*[31]

These examples are merely the first few items; each of these columns goes on and on. And columns such as these appeared daily throughout the paper.

This strange randomness of news was not confined to the special columns of miscellany. Although the longer stories usually were grouped and classified in a more orderly fashion, the tendency of the whole paper was toward the miscellaneous. Government news ranged from the doings of President Grant to the exact amount of fees collected yesterday at the Water Department; court news ranged from Supreme Court decisions to minor bankruptcies in distant cities; religious news from the health of the Pope to the number of Quakers in Iowa (there were 8,865); foreign news from the crisis in Turkey to an ice skating accident in France. In short, virtually any event from anywhere in the world could make the paper.

Storey's goal was to provide something for

everyone, individual items for individuals. This approach to news did not develop accidentally at the *Times*; it complemented the editorial philosophy of the paper. In the 1870s, the *Times* was a marketplace of the sort that Storey favored, filled with infinite choice. The news content of the *Times* was as diverse, fragmented, disorganized, and bewildering as the life of the city it served. The modern city scene portrayed in the news columns was an enormously complicated spectacle, spread out in disarray before the reader like the city itself.[32]

In the 1870s the chief competitor of the *Times* was the *Chicago Tribune*. Unlike the *Times*, the *Tribune* did not aspire to be a general circulation newspaper; nor did it pretend to appeal to the masses. It was, by its own declaration, "the businessman's newspaper," and it scoffed at the *Times* efforts to entice readers from the "slums and back alleys" of Chicago.[33] The *Tribune* prided itself on being part of the modern metropolis that Chicago had grown to be by the 1870s. The paper chided the *Times* for its lingering small-town ways. To the *Tribune*, the *Times'* endless, miscellaneous gossip from the local churches and neighborhoods "belongs to the worst class of newspaper enterprise of small towns, where everybody knows everyone else." The *Tribune* reminded Storey that "the mingled town and village aspects are gone. . . . The tendency is to the metropolitan in everything,—buildings and their uses, stores and their occupants. And village notions are passing away with them. . . . We are getting to be a community of strangers. No one expects to know and nod to half the audience at church or theatre, and, as to knowing one's neighbors, that has become a lost art."[34] Yet despite the *Tribune*'s mockery of the *Times'* outmoded vision of city life in Chicago, the two papers were not strikingly different in their understanding of either urban community or urban journalism.

After 1874, when he gained controlling interest, Joseph Medill was the editor and guiding light of the *Tribune* in much the same autocratic way as the *Times* was "by W.F. Storey." Storey hated Medill, and Medill hated Storey. They were antagonistic in almost every way—in politics, in business, in social circles, and in personal style. Yet beneath surface contrasts lay similar commitments to private property and individualism and similar notions of what news should be in a big-city newspaper. Medill was closer than Storey to the political and social elites of Chicago, but the values reflected in the editorials and in the news content of the *Tribune* remained, like the *Times'* values, private and individualistic.[35]

Because Medill was a political as well as a business and social insider, the *Tribune* harbored less suspicion than did Storey and the *Times* of government per se. Medill was an organizer of the Republican Party, a drafter of the Illinois state constitution of 1871, and mayor of Chicago from 1871 to 1873 in the aftermath of the great fire.[36] Through the *Tribune* Medill affirmed the necessity of urban government and branded the *Times'* call for complete tax resistance in 1876 "an infamous incendiary appeal." The *Tribune* argued simply that life would not be endurable in Chicago without tax-supported government to handle essential services such as water supply, sewerage, police, and fire protection.[37]

Medill believed that the range of government authority was broader than the *Times* perceived it to be, but that range was still quite limited. Although a party regular, Medill was in other ways in the philosophical tradition of the Liberal Republican and Mugwump movements of the 1870s and 1880s.[38] He believed that the end of government was the preservation of individualism in an urban environment, especially the individualism of private property and free business enterprise. Like Storey, Medill viewed Chicago essentially as a marketplace. The *Tribune* fought taxes because taxes encumbered property and hurt business. Private property and business, however, required a minimal level of public collective action. Commerce depended on paved streets, well-maintained bridges, and even schools and libraries.[39] As a former mayor elected on the "Union-Fireproof" ticket, Medill was especially concerned about fire protection. Fires were bad for businesses and fire insurance rates were sky high in Chicago after 1871.[40] For the *Tribune*, fire control was a clear case of an appropriate collective function; the protection of life and (as the editorials more typically suggested) property.

Government activities not directed toward these ends were inappropriate, in the opinion of the *Tribune*. The paper was especially opposed to the notion that government should serve a welfare function, except for orphans and the disabled who were without family. On this subject, the *Tribune* saw no difference between the industrial, metropolitan Chicago of 1876 and the village of Chicago 40 years before. People must take care of themselves. The government should be out of the charity business almost altogether, and even private philanthropy should be curtailed in order to preserve the character of the individual and the vitality of individualism in society.[41]

Even the appropriate functions of local government must be strictly limited to achieve salutary ends. The *Tribune* argued in 1876, for example, that the great public works of the city were largely done. The street grade had been raised to improve drainage, the main streets were paved, the water supply was supposedly pure and ample, the river was a bit less horrible. Now property owners could take care of their own street and sewer extensions and repairs without intrusion of government. The collective work of the city could now be limited to routine maintenance to the infrastructure that had already been built. Thus, the paper argued, government could be reduced significantly and taxes cut dramatically, all of which would increase the value of property and would enhance the true business of Chicago, which was business.[42]

Although it chastised the *Times* for rejecting government altogether, the *Tribune* was nearly as hostile as the *Times* to the continuing expansion of local government and to what it perceived to be corrupt domination of government by loafers, bummers, and tax-eaters.[43] In the first six months of 1876, the *Tribune* carried 115 major editorials pleading for retrenchment and lower taxes in local government and another 119 attacking local government officials, usually for extravagance and corruption. This adds up to nearly two-thirds of all editorials on local subjects. Like the *Times*, the *Tribune* brooded and fulminated over the "spendthrift, reckless demagogues who think that governments are instituted for no other purpose than to confiscate private property."[44]

The *Tribune* preferred that local government be run as an adjunct to the business culture of the city. The paper professed a belief in democracy, while at the same time it insisted that government should be the province of the "better classes" — "men of brains, wealth, and standing in the community."[45] Medill could openly favor aristocracy because he believed it was merely meritocracy, rule by a natural, free-market-generated elite. So convinced was the *Tribune* of the righteousness and efficiency of private enterprise and the free market in urban life that it saw no need, as the *Times* did, to limit democracy. Surely all rational people could be persuaded to support a business-oriented government, because what was good for business was good for Chicago.[46]

At the same time that it professed an abiding faith in democracy and American public institutions, the *Tribune* warned in 1876 that the country was rapidly sliding into a deep and general moral decline. The corruption of government, ranging from the Grant administration to the ward machines of Chicago, the *Tribune* traced to individual immorality. To solve the problem, the paper continually urged a return to old-fashioned honesty, frugality, simplicity, work, church, and family. Society was simply the gathering together of individual people and small-scale communal institutions, and "individual integrity and purity of life must be again recognized as among the highest requisites of social life."[47]

In 1876, Wilbur Storey bragged that the *Times* spent twice as much as the *Tribune* on news gathering, and that the *Tribune* was a decadent and decaying news medium.[48] The content of the two papers suggests otherwise. The *Tribune* was the rival of the *Times* in all departments of news and information. Medill's paper was less scandalous and sensational than Storey's, but the variety of subjects covered and the amount of space devoted to broad categories of subjects were virtually identical in the two papers, despite their differences in ideology, politics, and target audiences. Like the *Times*, the *Tribune* favored news of government, politics, and business. Moreover, the *Tribune* handled the news much as the *Times* did. Every day the paper contained hundreds of items of the most amazing diversity. Like the *Times*, the *Tribune* was a teeming marketplace of miscellaneous information.

The organization of this mass of information was not altogether random. Typically, it was well classified under headings such as "Foreign," "Washington," "The City," "The Court," "Criminal News," "Fires," and "Finance and Trade." Under any one of these broad categorical headings, the scores of items usually varied enormously and included much the same kind of trivia that filled the pages of the *Times*. For example, the *Tribune*'s "Washington" column was filled daily with stories, reports, statements, speeches, and the verbatim proceedings of Congress. The "City Hall" column listed virtually every official happening in city government, many in single-sentence briefs, from the day's water rent receipts to the number of buildings inspected. "The City" included personal gossip, real estate transfers, anything that could be written in the form of a brief statement of fact.[49] Like Storey, Medill proposed to print all the news of the day.

The *Tribune* in the 1870s called itself the businessman's newspaper, and so it was. But as a circulation leader, it was not unlike an aggressively popular newspaper, such as the *Chicago Times*. On the editorial page it stood for conventional values—individualism, private property, and free enterprise. In the news pages it conducted a marketplace of information with something for everyone—a spectacular bazaar that reflected more than interpreted the complexity and diversity, the individualism and privatism of the modern metropolitan city.

It was into this urban and journalistic milieu that the *Chicago Daily News* was born in December 1875. The *Daily News* succeeded almost from the start. By the early weeks of 1876, the paper claimed a larger circulation than other evening papers in Chicago, about 10,000 daily. This was probably an exaggeration. But by June of its second year the *Daily News* averaged about 20,000 per day, a figure surpassed in Chicago only by two giants, the *Times* and the *Tribune*.[50] By the 1880s the *Daily News* itself was the giant, with a circulation of more than 150,000. Whereas no other Chicago paper (except the *Record*, the morning edition from the *Daily News* shop) achieved a steady circulation of 100,000 before the twentieth century, the *Daily News* hit 200,000 by 1895. Publisher Victor Lawson boasted matter-of-factly in 1886 that nearly everyone who read English in Chicago read the *Daily News*.[51] This was exaggeration, to be sure, but not by much. The *Daily News* was the only approximation to a modern medium of mass communication in Chicago in the nineteenth century.

The *Daily News* was a newspaper quite unlike the *Times* or the *Tribune* or any other paper in Chicago. It was a "penny paper," a small-format, four-page sheet, selling for one cent instead of the usual four or five cents. In appearance alone, it was strikingly different. Everything was on a smaller scale—smaller format, fewer stories, and fewer departments; everything tightly edited and drastically condensed. But in a more subtle sense, its philosophy was as different as its look. Of course, the *Daily News* was a business enterprise, and its enterprising founders shared many of the business values of men like Wilbur Storey and Joseph Medill. The *Daily News* also reflected many of the social values of the dominant, Protestant, native-born elites of Chicago. Yet when it turned to concrete issues in the city of Chicago the *Daily News* seemed to recognize certain imperatives of collective life in the modern metropolis. Despite its general commitment to private enterprise, the paper promoted from the beginning a kind of community life much less dominated by rigid notions of private property and individualism. In both editorial philosophy and journalistic technique, the *Daily News* was an *urban* newspaper, an activist portrayer and promoter of the public community.

The founder of the *Daily News* was Melville E. Stone, a classic example of the self-made man, the son of a poor itinerant Methodist minister, destined to become one of the most prominent journalists of his time. Throughout his life Stone celebrated the homely virtues of his childhood on the Illinois frontier: family, honesty, hard work, conscience, equality.[52] As a young, energetic citizen of post-Civil War Chicago, Stone became an active participant in the associational life of the city, serving on the boards of a variety of government agencies and private organizations. In politics he was a Lincoln admirer and a Mugwump, or, as he liked to say, "a Republican with a conscience." He professed to believe that a newspaper should always be independent of party politics, devoted to the presentation of "facts" rather than the manipulation of public opinion.[53] Stone's partner almost from the beginning of the *Daily News* was Victor Lawson, a man much like Stone in personal background, political philosophy, and social vision. Lawson took over sole control of the *Daily News* in 1888 and continued Stone's editorial tradition, contributing his own special talent for the promotion of advertising and circulation.[54]

Although Stone and Lawson were probably somewhat more involved in voluntary organizations than most businessmen, they were in most respects not exceptional men in nineteenth-century America. Their biographies read much like those of other self-made businessmen, including newspaper publishers such as Storey and Medill. Their professed values were conventional. But the nature of their newspaper led Stone and Lawson, almost in spite of themselves, down a different path, away from an unexamined devotion to private property and individualism and toward a vision of collective life and community in the fragmented "private city" of the late nineteenth century. Stone's aim was not to publish a smorgasbord paper with some different thing for everyone in the style of the *Times* and the *Tribune* and other popular papers. His aim was to print a small newspaper, edited so that a majority of the content would appeal to a majority of the readers. Like the *Times*, the *Daily News* was to be a mass-audience paper aimed at all the citizens of Chicago. But rather than serve the individual tastes of individual readers, Stone sought out the common tastes of a community of readers.[55]

The image of Chicago evoked in *Daily News* editorials was one of community and family, rather than of individualism and marketplace. From the beginning, the editorial philosophy of the paper was much more attuned to the idea of interdependence than to the notion of individualism in the great metropolises of the late nineteenth century. The social obligations of Chicago to its people were frequent editorial themes. In a remarkable editorial during its first month of life, the *Daily News* argued that the city should provide public relief and employment for all in times of need, because hard times were much more difficult for the unemployed in a modern city than in the countryside or small town. Moreover, to care for the poor was to care for the whole community. Such a plan, of course, would cost money, the paper admitted; but in a larger sense "nothing would be lost, but simply capital would be removed from one pocket to another, to be circulated for the good of the community." And anyway, community spirit, not cost, should be the sole concern: "Are we, citizens of the boasted Queen of the West, the first in every enterprise, to pause to consider a question of dollars and cents when a great end is to be accomplished?"[56] The argument was based less on Christian charity and more on the practical requirements of life in a large city. "No class in society can afford to ignore another," the paper declared; "we are far too interdependent."[57]

To some extent, Melville Stone's editorial philosophy grew out of his own personal sense of place in Chicago. On one hand, Stone was part of the business and social elite of the city, relishing his membership and leadership in upper-class clubs and societies. On the other hand, Stone loved the "other half" of Chicago just as well. He seemed to attract and to support with great good humor a long line of drunks and vagabond reporters and editors on the staff of the *Daily News*. He proudly numbered among his friends drifters and burglars as well as business magnates and presidents. Fifty years later he recalled how he had loved it all, from top to bottom. "As Dean Swift would have said," he wrote, "we lived all the days of our life."[58]

More specifically, the Chicago fire of 1871 became an enormously important event and symbol for Melville Stone's understanding of Chicago and of urban life in general. During the unhappy winter of 1871–1872, Stone was one of the chief directors of relief efforts in the city, and he came away from the experience much impressed by the commonality of interests among residents of a large city, regardless of their class or occupation. "There was no shelter for the rich, none for the poor; for the time being the millionaire was no better off in the worldly goods than the pauper," Stone wrote on the fifth anniversary of the fire. In that fall of 1876, with the city in economic depression, Stone reminded Chicagoans that the whole community must rise together as it had five years before. "The poor shall not suffer, the sick shall not be neglected," he wrote, "and all must look forward to better times that are coming."[59] Stone, in effect, had accepted the idea that private property in a large city has social roots and community obligations—a view that he had not fashioned for himself through study and reflections, but one that had been forged for him in the fire of 1871.

Because of its belief in the interdependent nature of urban society, the *Daily News* was much less inclined than the *Times* or the *Tribune* to place the blame for social problems on the heads of individuals. Stone argued that the poor were poor because of hard times; prostitutes were prostitutes because they could find no honest work; bad boys were bad because of poor nurture in the schools and churches.[60] With such a view of the power of environment and community over the individual, it is not surprising that the *Daily News* was a strong advocate of charity and an early proponent of what would soon be called the Social Gospel. The paper urged the creation of all sorts of philanthropic organizations, including shelters for prostitutes and homeless waifs, public baths, soup kitchens, mutual aid building societies, and especially unemployment relief agencies.[61] Almost always, interdependence and sympathy were the key ideas, the organic city the key image. In calling for large-scale, organized charity for the approaching winter of 1876–1877, the *Daily News* rejected the idea that a person should have to be a property owner to be a part of the city. "It is enough for charitable people, for Christian people, for humane people, to know that a man is in need, whether he comes from Maine or California, from Illinois or Kentucky, from Germany, Ireland, or the Cape of Good Hope, he is still a man." But, as usual, Stone's reasoning was based as much on the practical interdependence of city life as on the moral obligations of Christian charity. Recalling again the aftermath of the fire, Stone reminded Chicagoans that "the man who would refuse to aid his fellow man this hard winter will, in all probability, find use for a soup house himself before he dies."[62]

While promoting voluntary association as a way to strengthen community life in the city, the *Daily News* also argued formal public action through government. In this respect, the *Daily News* early drifted from the individualistic and volunteeristic reform ideology of conventional Mugwump organizations such as the Chicago Citizens' Association, founded in 1874 as the city's first permanent municipal reform group.[63] Melville Stone was certainly no socialist, however, in the ideological sense. Like Medill and Storey, he complained about high taxes and governmental waste and corruption. He even sometimes spoke in the abstract of immutable laws of political economy.[64] But on most concrete cases the *Daily News* found itself advocating increased government intervention in business and urban life, and even arguing from time to time that taxes were not too high considering the social tasks at hand. In the first six months of 1876, the paper carried more than three times as many editorials calling for expansion of government activities as for retrenchment.[65] While the *Times* was calling for the dismantling of city government and the *Tribune* was carefully drawing the boundaries between the proper realms of public and private action, the *Daily News* was urging more government enterprise and more government regulation as the only way to make life liveable in a modern city.

The *Daily News* promoted government enterprise for two reasons. First, the paper argued that large-scale urban centers such as Chicago demanded large-scale public works. For simple reasons of health and safety streets must be repaired and extended, sewers and water works maintained, trash collected, schools and parks operated, public baths built, air pollution controlled, and hospitals improved.[66] In this the *Daily News* was not unlike the *Tribune*. But in its advocacy of public works, the *Daily News* went far beyond the *Tribune* and the business-dominated reform tradition in Chicago. The *Daily News* urged government enterprise not only because it was necessary to provide an economic infrastructure for private enterprise, but also as a way to provide work for the unemployed. In early 1876, the *Daily News* called upon the city to provide a job to every man who needed one. The paper believed that the community owed its most unfortunate members help in time of need, for their misfortune was no fault of their own and was the community's misfortune as well. While the *Times* was counseling the unemployed to get out of town, the *Daily News* was urging the town to take them in. In a traditional community this might have been accomplished by the private action of kin or clan. In the modern urban world such community building would require the formal, organized effort of government. It would require the public community.[67]

The *Daily News* promoted an expanded role for government in regulation as well as enterprise. The paper proposed that city and state governments take more responsibility for ensuring the health and safety of citizens through the control of railroad and wagon traffic, the regulation of food and drug quality, the enforcement of fire codes, the inspection of buildings, the abatement of smoke and foul odors, and the regulation and municipal ownership of public utilities.[68] The *Daily News* was much less doctrinaire about the rights of private property than were the *Times* or the *Tribune*. In the social scheme of Stone and the *Daily News*, business was meant to serve people, property to serve community. If business and property failed in this service, the people should intervene.

As a penny paper the *Daily News* gathered an audience that was heavily working class, and the paper sought to affirm its sympathies with the laborers of Chicago.[69] The *Daily News*, however, was not in any sense a socialist or labor paper. Its aim was to promote community across class lines and to appeal to common interests of all classes. While its calls for public works and government regulation of business may have been in the interest of the lower classes, the paper also favored social regulations, such as antigambling laws, liquor control, immigration restrictions, compulsory school and Sunday school attendance, and compulsory English language instruction.[70] This insistence of the *Daily News* on social control and conformity along with extensive economic regulation suggests that the paper's ideology was a transformation of older ideals of an ordered, organic community rather than an incipient class-based socialism. Although the *Daily News*'s program might be labeled socialistic, its goal was not radical social change; rather, it was social and community preservation against the storms of urbanism.[71]

If its editorial philosophy set the *Daily News* apart from the other leading newspapers of Chicago, its news policy was just as different. In a prospectus the first day of publication, Stone promised potential readers a compact newspaper that would cover a variety of news, but without the "never-ending miscellany" of the other popular Chicago papers. He said the paper would carry the latest telegraph news, plus the criminal, legal, social, religious, political, and trade news of Chicago. He also promised more of what might be called "urban consumer news," housekeeping tips and advice on insurance and other consumer purchases. And Stone promised more sporting news and a daily short story of "intense dramatic interests," "instructive as well as entertaining."[72]

Stone's philosophy of editing was to edit, rather than to print "all the news" in the custom of popular newspapers of the day. This, more than the content of the information, is the key to the paper's news policy. Stone believed that busy readers preferred the condensed format, and that they preferred to focus their attention on one big, continuing story at a time. Stone criticized newspapers such as the *Chicago Tribune*, which he said "was conducted upon the theory that it was justified in publishing whatever it believed the public would enjoy reading." Perhaps thinking of the *Chicago Times*, Stone said, "It is easy to edit a newspaper if one does no thinking. . . . He then labels all murders and suicides and hangings and prize fights and chicken fights as news, and his task is a simple one." Stone did not disapprove of sensationalism and human interest news. He merely felt that both good business and good morality required an editor to be highly selective in the shaping of his or her product. Rather than cater to the myriad interests of a complex city, he would seek the common interest; assuming, of course, that there was such a thing.[73]

In its first year the *Daily News* lived up only partly to its prospectus and to Stone's notions of good popular journalism. In general, the paper carried a smaller proportion of government news than the *Times* and the *Tribune*, and some what more consumer news and fiction. Stone regularly included household tips, medical advice, and scientific news, along with a few tersely written editorials. This material was what Stone had in mind when he talked of news of interest to the majority of readers. The *Daily News* carried quite a few crime and disaster stories as well as other human interest news, but the paper carried few purely private items, such as society gossip, church news, and other such "tittle-tattle," as Stone called it.[74]

The *Daily News* was so condensed in 1876, however, that its only real news page (Page 1) read almost like the miscellaneous shorts that Stone had renounced in his prospectus. Major stories usually were only one or two column inches long, and many items were single sentences. Neither Stone nor his staff favored the extreme condensation of the *Daily News* in its early years; they were forced by the financial needs to keep the paper small while accepting as much advertising as possible.[75]

Gradually, as the *Daily News* grew in size, it settled on investigative reporting and crusading as its chief strength. From the beginning Stone was fond of what he called "detective journalism," especially the "investigation of public wrongs." In 1877, for example, the *Daily News* began a crusade for state inspection and regulation of savings banks, as part of its interest in consumer protection. In the course of the investigation Stone exposed a crooked bank president, who fled to Canada and then to Europe. Stone personally gave chase and finally tracked him down in Germany. This was the first of many such investigative stories, and all of them provided just the sort of news that Stone preferred: stories of wide interest among all readers; stories that continued day after day, focusing the attention of the whole audience; stories that served the "betterment of readers"; and stories laced with drama and inherent sensation.[76]

The older popular city press, such as the *Chicago Times* and the *Chicago Tribune*, and the new metropolitan press, such as the *Chicago Daily News*, both had to confront the problems of the growing complexity and diversity in modern cities and the breakdown of traditional community life. To some extent all recognized and celebrated diversity; they had to in order to be broadly popular.[77] And all recognized that much of modern city life had become formal and impersonal. But in a more fundamental sense, their confrontations with complexity took quite different forms. The *Times* and *Tribune* conceived their function as serving essentially private interests. As proponents of laissez-faire, they drew a sharp distinction between public and private. Certainly they covered in great detail the chief public institution, government. But the public realm was strictly limited. The rest of the life of the city was simply the aggregation of private lives, and the task of the newspaper was to serve these private interests, diverse, discrete, and individual. The *Daily News*, on the other hand, conceived of a public of a few broadly shared interests. The *Daily News* understood that the denizens of the modern city did not share many strictly private interests, as did the members of traditional face-to-face communities. The populations of cities were, in fact, becoming increasingly heterogeneous, isolated, and private. Yet, paradoxically, the growing interdependence of life in the modern city made some private interests public, in the sense of being widely and deeply shared. For the *Chicago Daily News* the task was to locate and to serve these interests, to promote a new kind of public community.

The *Chicago Daily News* was not alone, and Chicago was not unique. In New York City, for example, the popular press was similarly transformed in ethos and ideology in the late nineteenth century. The penny press of the 1830s and 1840s began the modernization process, expanding the definition of "news" and developing a commercial product that would appeal to a wide audience. The successful penny papers of New York, however, were kin to the *Chicago Times*. They followed the smorgasbord model of something for everyone, and they generally remained committed to a traditional understanding of private property, free enterprise, and individualism.[78] It was the *New York World*, after Joseph Pulitzer took it over in 1883, that urbanized popular newspaper journalism in New York in the manner of the *Chicago Daily News*. It was the *World* that developed both an editorial and a news policy that played on and promoted common interests and a pragmatic, collectivist urban vision.[79] The pattern was repeated in other cities as well.[80]

IV

The history of Chicago and other large American cities suggests that the confusion between public and private was in some ways forced by the urbanization process in the late nineteenth century. Richard Sennett, Thomas Bender, and others have demonstrated that problems arose when public life came to be dominated by private values and individual psychology. But the forces of the city worked in the opposite direction as well, making private lives matters of public concern. Modern urban life, by its nature, blurred the distinction between private and public. Urbanization perforce created the paradox of people who were increasingly strangers but who also were increasingly dependent on one another and increasingly affected by one another's private behavior. Private issues became public issues and then private again. City dwellers breathed the same sooty air, drank the same poisoned water, slogged the same muddy streets, shared the same crowded streetcars and the same fatal diseases.[81] The peculiar terror of modern urban life was that it rewarded individualism, while making individualism untenable; it undermined traditional community, while making community ever more necessary for survival; it sharpened the distinction between public and private in some ways, while blurring it in other ways. The *Daily News* and its editors did not set out to sell a program for a collectivist urban utopia. But in their efforts to sell a newspaper that would appeal to some part of everyone in the city, they found such a program thrust upon them by the city itself.

Michael Frisch has suggested that community life in nineteenth-century cities was not eclipsed or necessarily perverted, but was transformed. He found that in Springfield, Massachusetts

> *the growing public functions of government and the accumulating results of rapid social and physical change were giving to the community a new meaning: it was becoming more important and comprehensive as a symbolic expression of interdependence. Community, in other words, was changing from an informal, direct sensation to a formal, perceived abstraction.*[82]

This new notion of community grew gradually and pragmatically, shaped by the historical force of urbanization. Like all abstractions and symbols, it grew in communication. Of course, some traditional forms of communication were lost in the urbanization process. In his effort to show how community became a matter of individual personality in the nineteenth century, Richard Sennett asks rhetorically, "If people are not speaking to one another on the street, how are they to know who they are as a group?"[83] In Springfield, Massachusetts they found new ways to communicate, including the medium of the *Springfield Republican*.

The broad thesis of this article has been that newspapers were part of the transformation of community life in nineteenth-century American cities. More specifically, I have argued that the major difference between the popular newspaper press of the mid-century and the urban press of the late nineteenth century—*Chicago Daily News* style—was that the latter believed, whether correctly or not, that modern urbanization had eroded the distinction between public and private. In some ways this was a return to an older tradition of communitarian thought. But it was a belief born not of nostalgia, but of practical necessity. While modern life had helped to distinguish the private from the public realm, urban life seemed now to require again a mingling of the two. I have called the urban vision of the *Daily News* a vision of public community—public because it was nontraditional, nonface-to-face, nongeographical, built on government, formal organization, and mass communication; *community* because it was rooted in shared private interests, common experience and sympathy, and a deep sense of interdependence.

Endnotes

1. The "enduring tradition of privatism" in American cities is described by Sam Bass Warner, Jr., *The Private City: Philadelphia in Three Periods of Its Growth* (Philadelphia, 1968). On the transformation of colonial cities from organic communities to impersonal marketplaces, see Gary B. Nash, *The Urban Crucible: Social Change, Political Con-*

sciousness, and the Origins of the American Consciousness, and the Origins of the American Revolution (Cambridge, MA, 1979).

2. See, for example, Roland Warren, *The Community in America* (Chicago, 1972); Maurice Stein, *The Eclipse of Community* (Princeton, NJ, 1972).

3. This literature is reviewed in Thomas Bender, *Community and Social Change in America* (New Brunswick, NJ, 1978), chap. 3. See also Richard R. Beeman, "The New Social History and the Search for 'Community' in Colonial America," *American Quarterly* 29 (1977), 422–443; Robert V. Hine, *Community on the American Frontier* (Norman, OK, 1980); and Park Dixon Goist, *From Main Street to State Street: Town, City and Community in America* (Port Washington, NY, 1977).

4. Samuel P. Hays, "A Systematic Social History," in George Billias and Gerald N. Grob, ed., *American History* (New York, 1971), 315–366; Samuel P. Hays, "The Changing Political Structure of the City in Industrial America," *Journal of Urban History* 1 (1974), 6–38; Richard Jensen, *Illinois: A Bicentennial History* (New York, 1978). See also Herbert G. Gutman, *Work, Culture, and Society in Industrializing America* (New York, 1976); Richard D. Brown, *Modernization: The Transformation of American Life 1600–1865* (New York, 1976).

5. Bender, *Community and Social Change*, 58–61. See also Don Harrison Doyle, *The Social Order of a Frontier Community* (Urbana, IL, 1978); Michael H. Firsch, *Town into City: Springfield, Massachusetts, and the Meaning of Community, 1840–1880* (Cambridge, MA, 1972).

6. Robert Nisbet, *The Sociological Tradition* (New York, 1966), 47–48.

7. Richard Sennett, *The Fall of Public Man* (New York, 1977), 5, 222–223.

8. Bender, *Community and Social Change*, 148.

9. On the changing meaning of private property in American thought, see William B. Scott, *In Pursuit of Happiness: American Conceptions of Property from the Seventeenth to the Twentieth Century* (Bloomington, IN, 1977).

10. U.S. Department of the Interior, Census Office, *Report on the Population of the United States at the Eleventh Census: 1890*, Part I, lxvii, 580–583, 670–673.

11. Bessie Louise Pierce, *A History of Chicago*, Vol. III: *The Rise of a Modern City, 1871–1893* (New York, 1957), chap. 2. On the growing fear of social disorganization in late nineteenth-century cities, see Paul Boyer, *Urban Masses and Moral Order in America, 1820–1920* (Cambridge, MA, 1978), 123–131.

12. Table on "Municipal Finances," in Pierce, *History of Chicago*, 536; see also chap. 9. Chicago's fiscal problems were like those of other cities of this era. See Morton Keller, *Affairs of the State: Public Life in Late Nineteenth Century America* (Cambridge, MA, 1977), 324–326.

13. Willis J. Abbot, "Chicago Newspapers and Their Makers," *Review of Reviews* 11 (1895), 650–651. See also Justin E. Walsh, *To Print the News and Raise Hell! A Biography of Wilbur F. Storey* (Chapel Hill, NC, 1968), chap. 1.

14. Walsh, *To Print the News*, chap. 7.

15. Franc B. Wilkie, *Personal Reminiscences of Thirty-Five Years of Journalism* (Chicago, 1891), 130.

16. These headlines are typical examples from the *Times* in late 1875 and early 1876. Although crime news helped to make the paper's reputation, it was actually not a large proportion of the news content.

17. *Chicago Times*, November 27, 1875.

18. Abbot, "Chicago Newspapers," 651; Walsh, *To Print the News*, 216–217. Determining the size and nature of a nineteenth-century newspaper's circulation is mainly guesswork, although sources seem to agree that the *Times*, along with the *Tribune*, held circulation leadership in Chicago in the 1870s—both in the 30,000 to 35,000 range. See, for example, George P. Rowell & Co., *American Newspaper Rate Book and Directory 1870* (New York, 1870); and George P. Rowell & Co., *American Newspaper Directory, 1879* (New York, 1879). For a typical 1870s newspaper donnybrook over rival circulation claims, see *Times*, April 29, May 2, 1876; *Chicago Tribune*, May 1, 1876.

19. The next few paragraphs are based on a reading of all major (headlined) editorials in the *Times*, January through June, 1876. This amounted to 935 editorials, an average of about five per day.

20. *Times*, January 2, 8, 10, 18, 23, February 26, May 11, 1876.
21. Ibid., January 11, February 19, March 7, July 23, 25, 1876.
22. Ibid., January 4, 7, February 2, March 25, 1876.
23. Ibid., February 2, 8, March 8, 14, July 5, 25, 1876.
24. Ibid., February 8, May 20, July 25, 1876.
25. Ibid., July 5, 1876.
26. See, for example, ibid., January 18, 20, February 19, 1876.
27. Ibid., January 18, 23, February 22, May 11, October 22, 1876.
28. Ibid., January 2, 23, March 30, May 23, 1876.
29. Abbot, "Chicago Newspapers," 651.
30. *Times*, January 24, 1876.
31. Ibid., July 23, 1876.
32. One of the few writers on journalism history who has tried to describe the metropolitan press as an urban institution is Gunther Barth. In my view, however, Barth is much too sweeping in his thesis that the metro press helped to make diversity "acceptable" and the city "comprehensible." A paper such as the *Chicago Times*, which Barth celebrates, was fearful of the city and as bewildered as its readers. Barth makes no clear distinctions among the "metropolitan" newspapers he mentions. See Gunther Barth, *City People: The Rise of Modern City Culture in 19th Century America* (New York, 1980), 97–98, 106–107.
33. *Chicago Tribune*, May 1, 1876. The *Tribune* and the *Times* were usually considered the largest circulating newspapers in Chicago in the 1870s (see Note 18).
34. *Tribune*, March 30, 1873.
35. The best accounts of Medill's career are Lloyd Wendt, *Chicago Tribune: The Rise of a Great American Newspaper* (Chicago, 1979); and John Tebbel, *An American Dynasty* (Garden City, NY, 1947). Wendt is almost entirely uncritical; Tebbel is almost entirely unsympathetic.
36. Wendt, *Chicago Tribune*, chaps. 10–11; Pierce, *History of Chicago*, vol. III, chaps. 9–10.
37. *Tribune*, March 19, July 3, 4, 6, 7, 1876. The next few paragraphs are based on a reading of all major (headlined) editorials in the *Tribune*, January through June 1876. There were 851.
38. John B. Spoat, *"The Best Men": Liberal Reformers in the Gilded Age* (New York, 1968), 159–160.
39 *Tribune*, January 24, March 5, May 20, July 7, 1876.
40. Ibid., April 7, May 7, 1876. The news columns also reflected the *Tribune*'s interest in fire control. Most fire stories were from out of town. When a Chicago fire was reported, the paper often played down the losses. See, for example, *Tribune*, March 8, 1876.
41. Ibid., January 30, March 2, June 25, 1876.
42. Ibid., January 9, March 12, July 2, 1876.
43. Ibid., January 4, 24, 1876.
44. Ibid., March 16, 1876.
45. Ibid., January 4, March 26, May 14, 1876.
46. Ibid., March 12, April 7, May 20, 1876.
47. Ibid., January 9, February 21, March 6, 10, July 4, 1876.
48. *Times*, May 2, 1876.
49. See, for example, *Tribune*, January 1, 2, February 2, 15, 1876.
50. *Chicago Daily News*, October 30, 1876; Rowell, *American Newspaper Directory: 1879*; Charles H. Dennis, *Victor Lawson: His Time and His Work* (Chicago, 1935), 33–34, 38–40.
51. Victor Lawson to Melville Stone, September 11, 1888, Victor Lawson Papers, Newberry Library, Chicago; *Daily News* advertising copy, April 14, 1–86, in Lawson Papers; N.W. Ayer & Son, *American Newspaper Annual* (Philadelphia, 1887, 1889 and 1895); Dennis, *Victor Lawson*, 139.
52. Melville E. Stone, *Fifty Years a Journalist* (Garden City, NY, 1921), 11–14. Stone left the *Daily News* in 1888. He became general manager of the Associated Press in 1892 and was an architect of AP's rise to world prominence.
53. Stone, *Fifty Years*, 35–36, 53–54, 76, 152–153. See also Gerald W. McFarland, *Mugwumps, Morals, and Politics* (Amherst, MA, 1975).
54. The best study of Lawson's stewardship of the *Daily News* is Donald J. Abramoske, "The Chicago *Daily News*: A Business History, 1875–1901"

(Ph.D. dissertation, University of Chicago, 1963). See also Dennis, *Victor Lawson*, chaps. 9–10.

55. Prospectus, *Daily News*, December 20, 1875; Stone, *Fifty Years*, 53–54, 56–57, 109–110. See also Donald J. Abramoske, "The Founding of the *Chicago Daily News*," *Journal of the Illinois Historical Society* 59 (1966), 341–353.
56. *Daily News*, January 18, 1876.
57. Ibid., April 1, 17, May 10, 1876. Comments on the *Daily News*'s editorial policy are based largely on a reading of all major editorials, January through June 1876. There were 340.
58. Stone, *Fifty Years*, 82 and passim.
59. *Daily News*, October 9, 1876. See also Stone, *Fifty Years*, 35–36.
60. *Daily News* January 11, February 1, 2, December 18, 1876.
61. Ibid., January 20, 24, July 15, October 26, 27, November 8, 1876. See also Graham Taylor, *Pioneering on Social Frontiers* (Chicago, 1930). Taylor, a vigorous advocate of the Social Gospel, became closely associated with the *Daily News* in the 1890s.
62. *Daily News*, Dec. 18, 1876.
63. On the Citizens' Association and Chicago newspapers, see David Paul Nord, *Newspapers and New Politics: Midwestern Municipal Reform, 1890–1900* (Ann Arbor, 1981), chap. 4.
64. *Daily News*, December 23, 1875, January 9, 10, July 13, 1876.
65. Ibid., January 18, February 10, 1876.
66. Ibid., February 4, April 10, June 24, July 26, 28, August 23, 31, September 11, 1876.
67. Ibid., January 18, 1876. On the mingling of formal organization with community-building efforts in nineteenth-century cities, see Thomas Bender, *Toward an Urban Vision* (Lexington, KY, 1975).
68. *Daily News*, January 7, 25, February 26, March 30, May 5, 8, 12, July 5, August 29, September 7, 1876.
69. Ibid., April 17, November 2, 1876; Dennis, *Victor Lawson*, 41–42. The best account of the *Daily News*'s views of labor is Royal J. Schmidt, "The *Chicago Daily News* and Illinois Politics 1876–1920" (Ph.D. dissertation, University of Chicago, 1957), 150–171.
70. *Daily News*, January 11, February 15, April 21, September 4, October 9, 1876.
71. The *Daily News* reflected many of the values typical of middle-class reformers. See Boyer, *Urban Masses*, 123–131.
72. *Daily News*, December 20, 1875. The prospectus is in all the early issues.
73. Stone, *Fifty Years*, 52–57, 77, 109–110, 114.
74. Ibid., 11. Statements in this paragraph (and throughout the article) about amounts of news content are based on a single content analysis of randomly selected, constructed weeks of issues of the three newspapers for the period January–July, 1876.
75. Dennis, *Victor Lawson*, 56.
76. Stone, *Fifty Years*, 77–82.
77. This is Gunther Barth's major thesis about the metropolitan press. It is partly true, but oversimplified. See Barth, *City People*, 106–109.
78. Dan Schiller, *Objectivity and the News: The Public and the Rise of Commercial Journalism* (Philadelphia, 1981), 71–75. See also Michael Schudson, *Discovering the News* (New York, 1978), chap. 1.
79. George Juergens, *Joseph Pulitzer and the New York World* (Princeton, 1966), chaps. 1 and 11.
80. For example, St. Louis, Kansas City, and Milwaukee. See Nord, *Newspapers and New Politics*, chap. 7.
81. The importance of shared experiences among city dwellers in the rise of progressivism is a major theme in David P. Thelen, *The New Citizenship: Origins of Progressivism in Wisconsin, 1885–1900* (Columbia, MO, 1972).
82. Frisch, *Town into City*, 247. See also Bender, *Toward an Urban Vision*, 131–132.
83. Sennett, *Fall of Public Man*, 222.

Functions of the Reform Press

Jean Folkerts

While the development of the Populist Party and the nature of agricultural and labor reform in 19th-Century American society have received considerable attention from historians, the reform press has been a neglected bedfellow of these highly controversial political movements.[1] This neglect represents not mere historical omission, but an emphasis on high-volume, metropolitan media as the accepted focus for historical and contemporary communication research.

The thesis of the article, which focuses on Farmers' Alliance newspapers of the 1880s, is that the reform press performed three important functions for its readers: it provided information that mainstream newspapers either neglected or chose to ignore; it formed the core of a communication network that helped Alliance men and women to develop a sense of community; and it presented the Alliance movement as a legitimate effort to oppose the dominant political and economic structure.

The Farmers' Alliance was organized first in Texas in 1877, then spread throughout the South and the midwest, ultimately forming the base for the Populist Party. Farmers formed cooperatives to combat the crop-lien system which bound Southern farmers to the furnishing merchant; in the Midwest the emphasis was on eliminating differential railway rates which hampered the shipment of crops.[2]

Significance

Analysis of the functions of the Alliance press refutes the common concept that late-19th-Century newspapers functioned for a mass, undifferentiated audience. It also reveals one type of pluralistic journalism which survived for almost a century after the commercialization of the penny press. Contributing to the neglect of newspapers such as those connected to the Farmers' Alliance has been the transitory nature of the reform press within the context of an underlying progressive interpretation of journalism history, an emphasis on the metropolitan press, and the identification of the reform press with political bias.[3] Contemporary journalists and businesspeople, as well as historians, readily discounted reform newspapers not only because they made no claim to objectivity, but because they were often financially less stable than more traditional newspapers.[4] The reform newspapers faced great financial difficulties, rarely developed innovative journalistic techniques, and almost never represented winning causes.

Despite these claims, the lack of credibility of the reform press is due largely to the fact that reform newspapers and editors represented a different cultural-political tradition than did their mainstream counterparts. This difference is far more important in explaining why reform newspapers have been neglected than are the old charges that the reform press was politically biased or tied to a party.

Historians accepted 19th-Century journalists' claims that the mainstream press addressed itself to a mass audience and ignored the fact that rural and town audiences had distinctly different special interests and communication needs. The attitude of the mainstream press which has thus been perpetuated is significant, particularly when the dominant Republican and Democratic orientation of the editors is considered. Bachrach and Baratz noted that mass media systematically promote "a set of predominant values, beliefs, rituals and institutional procedures" that operate to the consistent benefit of some and exclusion of others.[5] The Populists, many of whom did not adhere to predominant values and institutional procedures, and who challenged the two-party structure, were labeled deviant by the mainstream press.

The unfortunate aspect of this attitude is that the concept of deviance has been carried on in historical tradition. When historians began to reassess the Populist movement, they moved from an interpretation of the Populists as deviant, nostalgic complainers to a more accurate picture of a group of people who were fighting for economic and cultural survival. Nevertheless, historians retained their concept of the Populist press as distinctly not modern, biased, propagandistic and lacking all journalistic value. Reform editors have been described as nonprofessional, "confessedly propagandistic, and devoted to political causes rather than to journalism." Such labels have provided the ammunition to discount whatever influence these "unassuming little sheets" might have had.[6] In addition, more often than not these newspapers have been used as primary source material for studies of the Populist Party, but have been ignored as worthy of study as a journalistic institution or medium.

Information Function of the Reform Press

One of the best examples of the information function of reform newspapers in the late 19th-Century can be seen in their coverage of droughts in Texas and Kansas.[7] Reform newspapers printed stories that varied greatly from those printed by mainstream papers. In 1886, the Texas Alliance journal, the *Southern Mercury*, expressed concern about starving farmers in western counties in Texas. The *Mercury* requested that each Alliance act quickly to donate seed and food, and arrange to transport the donations to areas in need, because "already the depopulation of many sections of the west has begun, and trains of farm wagons with their freight of miserable, half-starved humanity is [sic] winding their way over the barren plains eastward in search of food." The State Alliance, in session at the beginning of August in Cleburne, donated the remaining $7,000 of its treasury to the drive.[8]

At the same time, the mainstream daily papers, most conspicuously the Dallas *Morning News*, expressed doubt about drought reports. Most of the reports focused on hardships to cattlemen, with little mention of farmers. The dailies' major concerns were beef prices and declining property values for land speculators, while the reform press was more interested in the effects of the drought on farmers.[9]

This promotional approach taken by the Dallas *Morning News* was not unique. Thirteen years earlier, when the drought of 1873 plagued much of southern and western Kansas, Marshall Murdock of the Wichita *Eagle* took what Robert Dykstra called a strictly urban viewpoint—that publicity of drought and crop failure damaged the community more than the drought hurt the farmer. The urban editor not only wrote articles blaming farmers for drinking too much whiskey and not being conscientious about farming, but he also, as a member of the state relief committee, convinced authorities there were no destitute people in Sedgwick County. Yet in the winter of 1874–75, about 2,000 of the 5,000 rural Sedgwick residents needed food and/or clothing.[10]

This attitude was common among mainstream frontier editors. Charles Scott, editor of the established Iola *Register*, said that for years Kansas editors had promoted the state as having "roses on every hillside," although "two-thirds of her territory was still branded on all maps as sandy desert."[11] The reform press—not the mainstream press—provided the most information about the drought and subsequently helped get relief for distressed farmers.

The reform press also provided basic agricultural information not carried in the mainstream newspapers. The Jacksboro *Rural Citizen*, probably the first Alliance newspaper in Texas, discussed crop diversification, planting and harvesting. "We need articles giving the experience of our farmers and stockmen in this and adjoining counties on stock raising and the cultivation of various crops," the editor wrote. The *Rural Citizen* believed "Scientific farming will pay."[12] Leonidas L. Polk, who later became president of the national Farmers' Alliance, started his North Carolina *Progressive Farmer* in 1886 primarily as an agricultural, rather than as a political, newspaper. He included practical instruction in up-to-date farming, discussions of ensilage and silos, potato culture, egg production and fruit canning.[13]

The mainstream press did not treat agricultural subjects in such depth but focused instead on conventional party politics, acquisition of Eastern capital and attraction of industry. William Allen White, nationally known editor of Kansas' Emporia *Gazette*, set an agenda for his readers that denied economic hardship of farmers from 1895–1900 because he disliked the institutional remedies they proposed, and he feared loss of both societal control by businesspeople and Eastern capital. He viewed outside capital as necessary for town development, and he opposed rural demands that retarded such growth.[14]

Community Function of the Reform Press

The role that specialized presses perform in developing a sense of community has been documented in studies of the suffrage press and the ethnic press.[15] The community function of the reform press is exemplified in the *Rural Citizen* and in the Kansas Alliance organ, the *Kansas Advocate*. Both newspapers assumed the role of uniting farmers who were attempting to gain more control over their economic situation. This sense of community extended beyond local geographical boundaries.[16] In examining the suffragist press, Steiner defined community as an "acknowledgement of common goals and shared interests, participation in cooperative activity, self-conscious emphasis on loyalty and commitment."[17] Similar community-building activity was promoted by the *Citizen*, which championed the Alliance cause in its first issue of September 24, 1880.

The editor, J.N. Rogers, created a forum in the newspaper by printing not only the platforms of the Alliance, but also by dedicating one page in each issue to correspondence among members of the various Alliances, particularly those in West Texas. Occasionally the writer was the president or secretary of a local Alliance, or even the president of the state Alliance, but office-holding was not a prerequisite for gaining space in the newspaper. The idea was one of communication *among* people, not communication to a group of people. In July 1885 a Denton County farm wife wrote, "Brothers and sisters, let us do everything in our power to bring about a feeling of equality, and brotherly love, in this part of the community, and may we live as one family."[18]

The northeastern *Kansas Advocate*, edited by

Stephen McLallin, viewed its community as a national one. McLallin's newspaper began several years after the *Citizen*, in 1889, when the Alliance was entering a stage of political involvement. McLallin printed correspondence from members of various Alliances, and the demand for space was so great that he published a notice telling his readers that if their letters were not included, it was not because they were not important; rather, he simply had no more space unless he enlarged the newspaper, which he could not do at the current price.[19]

Shortly before his newspaper was accepted as the official Alliance organ, McLallin wrote that an organizational newspaper was needed to cope with outside elements that were a detriment to the group, to provide common reading material for all members, and to uphold the sacred ties of the order. The *Advocate* contained a "rally round the flag" quality, with Alliance songs, requests for contributions and pep talks included. Columns from other state journals often were reprinted. If circulation claims are to be believed, the appeal of the *Advocate* was apparent, since by August 1890 it claimed to circulate to more readers than any other newspaper in Kansas.[20]

Legitimation Function of the Reform Press

The third area of Alliance newspaper activity—that of legitimizing the movement—is the most complex, and the most significant of the three. Recent political communication research indicates that the mass media are capable of discounting deviant political groups while legitimizing the status quo.[21] Earlier research established the ability of the media to act as agents of social control.[22] If the press viewed Alliance tenets as outside the social norm, or as aberrant, Populism would not have received consideration as a serious reform movement.

Impartiality and objectivity are closely tied to political consensus—"and the more radical the dissent, the less impartial and objective the media."[23] Media may depict a group as deviant by picturing it as making "single grievances with which a system can deal without altering its fundamental social relations." Such a picture negates a group's efforts to present a cohesive opposition to the current structure. The media "also may determine which events are legitimate news events," and report statements by authoritative figures who may also perceive a group as deviant. These approaches often make a group "seem eccentric and not to be taken seriously."[24]

Definitions of legitimacy currently are evolving, but for the purposes of this study Pollock's definition as developed in his study of U.S. Supreme Court decisions is adequate. Pollock defined newspaper articles as legitimizing if their content presented court positions as "legal, competent, cooperative, stable, peaceful, progressive, nonexploitive and/or model."[25] Populist newspapers presented farmers as reasonable, competent, cooperative, stable, peaceful and progressive members of society who worked through legal channels to achieve change. Mainstream newspapers viewed farmers as naive, unsophisticated, unintelligent troublemakers.

Hall's concept of the politics of signification can be used to further expand the importance of the role of reform newspapers in legitimizing Populist activity.[26] Hall suggested that when "events in the world are problematic . . . where powerful social interests are involved; or where there are starkly opposing or conflicting interests at play" the power of the media to signify events increases. Populist activity was defined by the mainstream press as threatening to the economic and social structure of the nation. In such a situation, Hall suggested, "such significations would construct or define issues of economic and industrial conflict in terms which would consistently favour current economic strategies . . . lending credence to the specific policies of government which seek to curtail the right to strike or to weaken the bargaining position and political power of the trade unions."[27]

The *Rural Citizen* and the Dallas *Morning News* provide the best comparison of attitudes taken by the reform press and the mainstream press. Both newspapers reported on the farmers' movement throughout 1885 and 1886, and by the end of 1886 both reached similar conclusions—that the Farmers' Alliance should remain a nonpolitical body and that it should not affiliate with striking laborers. Despite the similarity in conclusions, however, the two newspapers assigned different levels of legitimacy to agrarian activists.

The *Rural Citizen* viewed labor affiliation and political action as detrimental to the Alliance organization itself, while the *News* labeled the farmers as politically naive and ineffectual. The reform-minded *Citizen* stressed unity, cooperation and personal social growth among the members of its audience, while it encouraged individual farmers and family members to express their views. Such an attitude enhanced the self image of the *Citizen*'s subscribers and of the farmers' movement. In 1883 an Alliance member wrote that "farmers as a class must be freely qualified to fill any position or office in life before their occupation will command the respect of the world at large."[28] In February 1886 the paper printed comments from Joe Bigson of Ennis, Texas, who said, "it is compatible with and most assuredly the duty of the Alliance to bring forth from her ranks men to fill places of trust in our government . . . and yet we are told that it won't do for the farmer to dabble in politics, oh, no."[29] The *Rural Citizen*'s editor depicted farmers as serious, intelligent and motivated individuals who were struggling to secure their economic position in a changing world.[30]

The mainstream *News* with a town audience, promoted development in the form of increased manufacturing and transportation. Early in the newspaper's life, the editors put farmers in the same business group as residents of Dallas. But as the farmers began to assert political strength and challenge the existing economic structure, the newspaper's description of them changed. Words like "miscellaneousness" and "leopardian" crept into descriptions of the farmers' politics, and their organization was defined as a "dark-lantern political body." They were represented as naive individuals who acted not in their own best interest but spontaneously out of particular grievances.[31] The *News* did not have exclusive rights to deriding farmers, however. In the early 1890s when the Farmers' Alliance organized in Butler County, Kansas, William Allen White laughed at the farmers because the leaders were "mostly incompetents of one sort or another, sometimes moral misfits but more often just plain ne'er-do-wells."[32]

Because Populist newspapers circulated primarily to members of the Alliance and the party, their impact was limited. They were critical vehicles for legitimizing the movement to its members and in building self-esteem among farmers. However, the mainstream newspapers, which circulated to far wider audiences, obviously had greater access to society as a whole. The Alliance and Populist papers thus failed to legitimize the movement to the dominant society. They did, however, create an alternative to the dominant structure.

Conclusion

Despite the fact that reform newspapers provided needed and accurate information concerning rural and labor issues that mainstream newspapers either were ignorant of or denied, they have been regarded as simple propaganda tools of party leaders. The additional roles of the reform press—those of community building and legitimation of the Alliance movement—have not been considered. This author concludes that these newspapers and their editors have been denied a place in history because they represented a cultural tradition that did not identify with or praise the tradition of progress common to urban editors and other urban businesspeople. Mass circulations, financial success and journalistic recognition were not their goals. Rather, editors operated their newspapers to educate an audience in a tradition which provided a sense of community for economically depressed farmers and which challenged the business and political control of mainstream editors and their business compatriots.

This study is relevant to current communication theory research and to studies of political communication. The institutional emphasis of much of such research, with its focus on the two-party system and on major print and broadcasting systems, precludes adequate attention to the variety of media which serve special purposes.

To overlook the reform press is to overlook not only information about the time and societies in which it existed, but also to overlook a distinct journalistic tradition that should not be submerged in favor of the winning side. The neglect of the Populist press parallels the neglect of the socialist and much of the labor press as well, for these publications and editors no doubt represented grave challenges to dominant value systems and cultural traditions of the mainstream society and its editors.

Endnotes

1. Norman Pollack in *The Populist Response to Industrial America: Midwestern Populist Thought* (Cambridge: Harvard University Press, 1962) argues effectively for Populism as a class movement, with a broad base including intellectuals and urban labor. For a thorough description of Populist disaffection with the political system see Pollack's *The Populist Mind* (Indianapolis: Bobbs-Merrill Co., Inc., 1967). For comments on the return of prosperity and the decline of Populism, see John Hicks, *The Populist Revolt* (Minneapolis: The University of Minnesota Press, 1931) and Richard Hofstadter, *The Age of Reform: From Bryan to F.D.R.* (New York: Vintage Books, 1955). For efforts on the part of the corporate power structure to thwart Populist efforts, see Lawrence Goodwyn, *The Populist Moment* (Oxford: Oxford University Press, 1978). Other sources on Populism include Bruce Palmer's *"Man Over Money:" The Southern Populist Critique of American Capitalism* (Chapel Hill: University of North Carolina Press, 1980) and Stanley Parson's *The Populist Context: Rural Versus Urban Power on a Great Plains Frontier* (Westport, Conn.: Greenwood Press, Inc., 1973).
2. Goodwyn. The term "reform press" is used throughout this article in reference to the Farmers' Alliance and Populist press. The term was chosen because the farmers of these organizations chose that term for themselves when they organized the national Reform Press Association. Other terms were considered and rejected. The "rural press" too often has been used to describe small-town newspapers, which often did not represent reform politics of the 1880s and 1890s. "Advocacy" and "alternative" are terms often used to represent "underground" newspapers of the 1960s.
3. Edwin Emery and Michael Emery, *The Press in America*, 4th ed., (Englewood Cliffs, N.J.: Prentice-Hall, 1978); Frank Luther Mott, *American Journalism*, rev. ed. (New York: Macmillan, 1962). For an appeal for a different vision of journalism history see James W. Carey, "The Problem of Journalism History," *Journalism History* 1 (Spring, 1974); 3–5, 27.
4. Roscoe Martin, *The People's Party in Texas: A Study in Third Party Politics*, University of Texas Bulletin, No. 3308, 1933; Palmer.
5. P. Bachrach and M. Baratz, *Power and Poverty, Theory and Practice* (Oxford: Oxford University Press, 1970), pp. 3–4.
6. Martin, pp. 189, 191.
7. The Alliance/Populist newspapers chosen for study—the Dallas *Southern Mercury*, the Jacksboro *Rural Citizen* and the *Kansas Advocate*—represent some of the earliest Alliance and/or

populist newspapers in the two states most involved in the early stages of the movement. Mainstream newspapers in the same states were chosen because their geographical location corresponded to the Alliance/Populist papers studied and because they were well-known and well-accepted as mainstream newspapers.

8. *Dallas Southern Mercury*, 23 July; 6, 20, 27 August, 1886.
9. *Dallas Morning News*, July, August, 1886.
10. Robert R. Dykstra, *The Cattle Towns* (New York: Atheneum, 1979), pp. 193–195. See footnote, pp. 194–195.
11. Kansas Historical Collections 1888, vol. 4, p. 259, cited in Raymond Curtis Miller, "The Economic Basis of Populism in Kansas," (M.A. thesis, University of Chicago, 1923), p. 9.
12. *Jacksboro Rural Citizen*, 13 October 1881.
13. Stuart Noblin, *Leonidas LaFayette Polk: Agrarian Crusader* (Chapel Hill: University of North Carolina Press, 1949), p. 151.
14. Jean Folkerts, "William Allen White's Anti-Populist Rhetoric as an Agenda-Setting Technique," *Journalism Quarterly* 60 (Spring, 1983): 28–34.
15. Linda Steiner, "The Importance of Early Suffrage Papers in Creating a Community," paper presented to the Association for Education in Journalism, Michigan State University, 1981; Tamara K. Hareven, "Un-American America and the *Jewish Daily Forward*," *Yivo Annual of Jewish Social Science* 14 (1969): 234–250.
16. George A. Hillery, Jr., "Definitions of Community: Areas of Agreement," *Rural Sociology* 20 (June 1955): 111–123.
17. Steiner.
18. *Rural Citizen*, 30 July 1885.
19. *Kansas Advocate*, 16 April 1890.
20. *Kansas Advocate*, 27 August 1890.
21. R. Miliband, *The State in Capitalist Society* (London: Weidenfeld and Nicholson, 1969). See also Pamela J. Shoemaker, "The Perceived Legitimacy of Deviant Political Groups: Two Experiments on Media Effects," *Communication Research* 9 (April 1982): 249–285.
22. Paul Lazarsfeld and Robert Merton, "Mass Communication, Popular Taste and Organized Social Action," in Wilbur Schramm, ed., *Mass Communication* (Urbana: University of Illinois Press, 1960), pp. 492–512.
23. Miliband, p. 224.
24. Shoemaker, pp. 249–285.
25. J.C. Pollock, et. al., "Media Agendas and Human Rights: The Supreme Court Decision on Abortion," *Journalism Quarterly* 55 (Fall 1978): 544–548, 561.
26. Stuart Hall, "The Re-discovery of 'Ideology': Return of the Repressed in Media Studies," in Michael Gurevitch, Tony Bennett, James Curran and Janet Woolacott, eds., *Culture, Society and the Media* (London: Methuen, 1982), pp. 234–250.
27. *Ibid.*
28. *Rural Citizen*, 28 June 1883.
29. *Rural Citizen*, 4 February 1886.
30. Jean Folkerts, "The Role of the Populist Press in Agrarian Reform: The *Jacksboro Rural Citizen* and the *Dallas Morning News*," paper presented to the Association for Education in Journalism, Oregon State University, August 1983.
31. *Dallas Morning News*, 8 August 1886.
32. William Allen White, *The Autobiography of William Allen White* (New York: The Macmillan Co., 1946), p. 219.

The Reporter, 1880–1900: Working Conditions and Their Influence on the News

Ted Curtis Smythe

The rise of the reporter and the shifting content of the American newspaper from editorial to news, from opinion to fact, long has been noted by journalism historians. *When* the shift to news actually occurred and *when* the changing news values which accompanied the shift became well defined remain a subject of debate. There is little debate regarding the new prominence of the reporter. City dailies in 1880–1900 relied heavily upon large numbers of reporters to gather and report the news.[1]

Yet the particular role of reporters during this period remains ill-defined, fuzzy. What contributions, if any, did reporters make to the news? Were they the linchpins of journalism, who influenced the news values of the day? Richard Hofstadter claimed they "brought to the journalistic life some of the ideals, the larger interests, and the sense of public responsibility of men of culture." Did their increasing status and glamour indicate that "The reporter had come into his own." Or were they but menial factotums, commanded hither and thither at the whim of editor and publisher, with few rights and little standing except among peers? Were they nothing but clerks? Edwin Shuman claimed that the newspaper was like the department store. The publisher offered what the readers wanted, "just as a merchant gave his customers calico if they want[ed] it instead of silk. The reporter," Shuman concluded, "must hand the goods over the counter." Which was the reality, which the myth? Or were both correct?[2]

This study explores the importance of the reporter to the newspaper by examining employee-employer relationships, as defined by pay, tenure and status. It is assumed that the managerial system of rewards and recognition, of hiring and promoting reflected managerial concerns about the product which was produced—that the system was established for the task of securing the news. This is, therefore, a study of the influence of economics on news concepts and news practices.[3]

Working Conditions

Samuel G. Blythe, recounting in later years his first encounter with reporters who were covering a trial in his village, drew a rather romantic yet fairly accurate picture of newspaper working conditions in the early 1880s.

> *What an underpaid, happy-go-lucky, careless, and in the case of several, brilliant crowd it was! Not one of them had a cent, or expected to have one, except on payday. All lived from hand to mouth. All worked fourteen, sixteen, seventeen hours a day at the most grueling work, reporting*

> *on a paper in a small city where many yawning columns must be filled each day whether there is anything going on or not, and all loyal to the core to that paper, fighting its battles, working endlessly to put a scoop over on the opposition morning paper, laboring until four o'clock in the morning for from ten to fifteen dollars a week, doing anything that came along from a state convention to a church wedding.*[4]

This appears to be a reasonably accurate description of the reporter-tribe working on a daily newspaper in the small city or the metropolitan area. The hours may have been too long, even for a reporter, and the pay is certainly less than what one would or could earn on a metropolitan newspaper, but otherwise the description would apply there as well. All that is missing is the fear and despair that consumed many reporters as they plied their craft.

Salaries

Reasonably accurate figures on wages and salaries for many crafts may be found during this period; reporting, however, is not among them. Government census figures did not break out the reporter's salary from those of other employees on the paper, including the backshop personnel. S.N.D. North's special survey of the newspaper industry following the census of 1880 concluded that newspaper employees produced more per capita than comparable industries, yet they received far less per capita than did the personnel of other industrial categories. He suggested the reason wages were so low for newspapers as a group is that they included reporters! It is conceivable, of course, that the discrepancy was a result of publisher penuriousness. Whatever the data, there is good reason to believe that reporters did not earn good sums, especially in their first few years on the job.[5]

Since systematic study of reporter salaries was not undertaken during this period, there is a tendency to rely upon isolated salaries or upon informed but not necessarily accurate opinions. In 1884 *The Journalist* claimed that reporters averaged "fifteen to twenty-five dollars a week." It was speaking for general reporters in New York. Many other cities during the early 1880s paid less. Samuel Blythe recalled earning $10 a week when he began work on a daily newspaper in a community of about 100,000 people. Other reporters on his paper earned $12; one or two may have earned $15. Arthur Russell, after graduating from Bowdoin College in 1883, began as a telegraph editor on a Portland, Maine, newspaper at $4 a week, with a high of $15 possible in three years. The disparity in salaries between cities and even among newspapers in the same city was sometimes great.[6]

By the end of the period, during the late 1890s, salaries appear to have improved a little, but again only for the experienced reporters. Using data from two fairly precise although probably incomplete sources, we can conclude that from about 1895–1900, reporters were receiving the following:

In New York, the highest pay in the country, about $15 to $60 a week, according to Henry King. Walter Avenel, however, concluded that "Many assignment reporters get salaries of from $40 to $60 a week; copy editors, from $35 to $50; but hundreds of writers earn only from $20 to $30 a week, and even less." Other cities, especially as surveyed by King and Avenel, paid even less. According to King, Chicago reporters received from $15 to $35, with an average of $25; St. Louis, $12 to $35, with an average of $20; Boston, $10 to $35, with an average of $18 to $20; Philadelphia, about the same, but Baltimore and Washington were 10 to 15 percent less. Avenel, who surveyed 11 cities of medium size and collected data only from seven-day newspapers, found that the largest weekly salary for a city averaged $27.22; the lowest but $17.58.[7]

How did these salary levels compare with

other crafts for the same period? One cannot generalize too much, but journalists, including editors and rewrite men, seemed to fare better than most other crafts, especially in total income. Plumbers, using New York state data, averaged 57 hours a week of work and received $3.37 a day in 1880; this decreased to 50 hours a week in 1900 with only a slight decrease to $3.19 a day. Therefore, there was an improvement in their hourly compensation. Compositors in New York state also improved their position. In 1880 they averaged 60 hours a week at a daily wage of $3.28. In 1900 the average was only 54 hours at $3 a day.

One can see why reporters were frustrated over the perceived inequities. Working a minimum of 10 hours a day, and often 12 to 14, they may have averaged $2.93 to $4.53 a day at the end of the period. We cannot compare the figures, of course, because the data were not gathered the same way. In any case, reporters did not wish to compare themselves with the crafts; they wished to be compared with professionals, such as physicians, clergy, lawyers and teachers. Again we have a contradiction between King and Avenel. King felt the young person who entered journalism and had an aptitude would do better than lawyers, doctors or clergy! Avenel, in contrast, felt there were very few opportunities in journalism that would pay as well as law or medicine. "Clergyman's (sic) salaries harmonize more nearly with those of newspaper workers. . . ." But the clergyman's hours and housing did not. Shuman seemed to clarify the dichotomy: "Newspaper writing, in the essential qualifications required, is a learned profession; but in its exact comparative insecurity it more nearly resembles a trade."[8]

Space System

One reason for low salaries and indefinite figures was the spread of "space and time rates" to many of the positions on the reportorial side. S.N.D. North concluded, "Much of the editorial work of the modern newspaper is paid for by the piece, even when done by editors regularly employed, and this is more frequently the case with those engaged in the purely reportorial duties. . . ." This was, apparently, a trend growing out of the Civil War experience. *The Journalist* expressed surprise in 1884, claiming that "leading papers in the city [New York] are now paying by space and time, and salaries are rapidly going out of existence in the reporterial (sic) world." The editor claimed that the average salary, including all reporters, was only $25 a week. This practice of paying space rates continued beyond the period of this study.[9]

The space and time system worked as follows. Reporters received a fixed rate per column for any copy that was printed. If they were assigned to a story that did not materialize, they were paid an hourly rate for the time they had spent on the story. Stories printed were placed in a "string book" and the column inches totalled weekly. The practice, whenever it started, was widespread by 1880 and after. Will Irwin described his experience with the system in 1900 in San Francisco. He claimed that nearly all of the morning newspapers "paid their reporters on a system calculated to extract the last ounce of energy in return for the first dollar of wages. After you passed your apprenticeship, you worked on 'space and detail.' " (Detail was slang for assignment.) The reporter gathered news from the assignment then "wrote the story, including the headlines. That last was a device for economizing on help at the copy desk. This returned [the reporter] two dollars."[10] The San Francisco papers, along with some others, appeared to pay for "space" based on assignments rather than the column inch.

The rates per column and for time varied greatly. The New York *Herald* paid $8 a column. If the reporter, through no fault of his own, returned without a story after he had been assigned one, he was paid 50 cents an hour.

The New York *Tribune* paid $6 per column, but according to *The Journalist*, the *Tribune* had "the meanest city department of any local paper. Six dollars are paid for one solid column of nonpareil in these columns of extraordinary size." Since the older reporters were on salary the new reporters were most affected by the space system.[11] The New York *Sun* paid either $6 a column or $8 a column and 40 cents an hour. Whichever, it was a difficult paper on which to make money because of the tight editing and the small type. Nevertheless, the *Sun*'s columns contained about half as much copy as the *Tribune* so that reporters for the two newspapers received strikingly different wages for the same amount of copy.[12]

There is confusion as to how well the *World* paid under Pulitzer, especially during the 1880s. *The Journalist* contradicted itself, claiming in April 1884 that the paper did not pay especially good rates, while in June of the same year it claimed the paper paid as well as any paper in the city, although there was not a fixed rate per column. The emphasis was on "exclusive news." Theodore Dreiser, who attempted to break into New York journalism on the *World* in 1894 was appalled at the newspaper's practices. Although an experienced reporter, having worked in Chicago, St. Louis and Pittsburgh, among other cities, he was placed on space. He claimed, putting words years later into the mouth of a colleague, that the established writers and rewrite men received salaries and space because they would not "stand for the low salaries they pay here." The *World* paid $7.50 a column for space and 50 cents an hour for time, less than the *Herald* in 1884. Mott suggests that Pulitzer improved salaries and wages for New York reporters and reduced the abuses of the space rate system. On the record, it does not appear that he did much to improve working conditions for reporters.[13]

Other newspapers in New York paid generally lower rates. The *Star* paid space writers only $5 a column. Time rates also were generally lower. The *Commercial Advertiser* reportedly established a scale of prices in 1884 "which gave sixteen cents an hour for time work." Even that figure may have been too high. Charles Edward Russell, who started in New York journalism on the *Commercial Advertiser*, condemned the paper's pay practices for time. He claimed there was no pay at all for those reporters who returned from an assignment without a story. Russell related two incidents from his experience. He spent an entire day chasing around the marshes of Jamaica Bay looking for duck hunters who reportedly had been caught in a blizzard and were missing. After searching in bitter weather, he returned to find that they had been found safe. He received no pay, not even time pay, because there was no story. To add injury to injury, he was out $1 for expenses because the business office denied his bill for a carriage. Another time the rumor of an impending strike of the Belt Line street railroad caused the city editor, who had "an office full of men that he could employ without expense," to send many of them "to watch the line, each having a section of eight or ten blocks. What we were to watch for, I do not know," Russell noted sardonically, "but our instructions were to watch—possibly to see if the rails curled up in the heat." Russell and his co-laborers remained the entire day in the summer heat. He spent 40 cents. There was no strike. There was no story. He and the others not only did not receive pay for their day in the sun, they were out their expenses.[14]

Bill-Cutting

The space system lent itself to abuse on the part of penny-pinching business managers. There evidently was a practice of "bill-cutting" for a short period of time. Editors and business managers simply disallowed the total number of inches of published material which a reporter might accumulate during a pay period. The figure, even though accurate, might be cut by an editor. There was no logical or legal basis for doing so, but reporters often were in no position to vigorously complain; they needed their jobs.

Leander Richardson, an early editor of the *Journalist*, attributed the practice to William Henry Hurlburt of the New York *World*. "This editor employed a man to cut bills and do other work," Richardson alleged, "upon the understanding that he was to remove at least enough money from the reporters' incomes to save the amount of his own salary. This saved Mr. Hurlburt one salary, and gave him all his dramatic and musical criticisms for nothing." Richardson also criticized Sanderson of the *Star* for his bill-cutting practices, claiming: "His sole qualification for the position which he holds is his total lack of feeling in the matter of reducing the salaries of the men in his employ to the lowest possible minimum. He is a pawn broker gone wrong. A journalistic Shylock whose meanness has made the *Star* a by word (sic) and a reproach in the world of journalism." Richardson publicized incidents given to him by reporters on the paper. Sanderson claimed that the business office required economies.[15]

How widespread this practice was cannot be determined. The *Journalist* publicized the practice time and again during 1884–1885. Perhaps the publicity helped to reduce the problem.[16]

Other economies were exacted from the newsroom, many of them petty and mean; nearly all of them detracting from the news product. Business managers kept watchful eyes upon editorial payrolls. Nevertheless, expansion of the news budget was inevitable. Editors oftentimes had to choose between more reporters and additional facilities, on the one hand, and increases in the salaries of existing staff, on the other. There was not much choice; salaries suffered. Editorial savings were applied even in routine assignments. Reporters were reimbursed for expenses incurred in covering local stories, such as using a street car to get to the scene of an accident. However, minimum distances were established so as to avoid reimbursable expenses. "The paper paid our carfare when we were out on a story," Irwin reported, "but only if the trip was longer than eight blocks. This last piece was a piece of neat calculation. City Hall, the Hall of Justice, the city jail, and the morgue, the places where reporters went most often, lay about seven blocks away from the office." Other papers established a mile as the minimum.[17] Such a policy communicated to reporters that they were of less value than carfare. It is not surprising that reporting was considered a young man's game, since reporters often had to run or walk to news events in order to save the paper money.

Tenure of Reporters and Editors

The penurious pay system was supplemented by a hiring and firing system that kept reporters in fear of their jobs, ill-paying as some of them were. Because reporters were paid weekly and hired on a verbal order, it was easy to fire them when they received their pay for the week, even though they had done nothing that was actionable. In 1898 the *Fourth Estate* claimed that "The chief fault with journalism in the large cities is the insecurity felt by the workers in their positions. . . . Reporters are discharged upon the slightest pretexts. Desk men who have a reasonable right to believe their positions secure as long as they do conscientious work suddenly find themselves thrown out in the street without warning." Managing editors and city editors also had short tenures. Shuman suggested that the city editor was fearful of two things: "scoops" by rival editors and libel suits, since either could cost him his job. "It is as if Ulysses had been compelled to steer all his life between Scylla and Charybdis; sooner or later one or the other is pretty sure to wreck him or swallow him up."[18]

These pressures resulted in numerous changes when editors failed or could not bring about circulation gains overnight. When Moses Koenigsberg became city editor on the Chicago *Evening American* in 1903, he was the 27th person to occupy the editor's chair in 37 months. Changes in editors were most upsetting to reporters, for the changes not only created tension over the demands of a new man, they oftentimes were accompanied with cuts in salaries. Sometimes there were massive layoffs occasioned by the changes in editors. A few editors established reputations for fairness by keeping reporters and training them even after they had made one or two mistakes.[19] These editors were the exceptions, and they probably had the confidence of their publishers. Fearful editors resulted in fearful reporters.

Office Intrigue

One side of the editor-reporter relationship was the ever present "office politics." Some newspapers were more blatant than others. In New York, the *Herald* and the *World* were among the worst; the *Sun*, at least when Chester Lord was editing the paper, was probably one of the best. Lord "abominated 'knocking' and office politics," Will Irwin claimed, and he effectively kept it down by embarrassing those who attempted it.[20] Lord was one of the exceptions.

Office intrigue was widespread on other newspapers. James Gordon Bennett Jr. of the *Herald* was notorious for his "system of espionage." Elaborate reports were prepared and sent to the absent owner, all of which caused trouble for the staff. Reporters called the spies "white mice." Joseph Pulitzer followed a similar practice. He often had two men competing for the same position; reports regularly flowed to the owner. They had the effect of creating dissension and distrust among the reporters, editors and managing personnel. Charles Edward Russell started work on the *World* during a particularly hot conflict between the city editor and the news editor, who were "engaged in a savage attempt to ruin each other." Russell, because he was a newcomer, was assigned by the city editor to check out a "flaw" in an exclusive story which was under the direction of the news editor. Russell's responsibility was to track down the lad. He found that the story was incorrect. "In his joy over this triumph," Russell later reported, "the city editor . . . became aware of my existence." When an opening occurred in Chicago for a staff correspondent, "the grateful city editor pushed [Russell] into the opening." It was a system that had generally spotty results in creating a good journalism.[21]

Long Hours, Short Careers

One last point regarding working conditions should be made. Reporters and editors worked long hours at a furious pace under extreme pressure with little time off. Publishers did not provide attractive benefits in lieu of attractive pay. Vacations were few, even for salaried personnel. Reporters on space dare not take off a day or two for they received pay only when copy was published, or at least gathered. Sick reporters were sick reporters—they did not stay home unless bed ridden. Even editors operated under a high pressure system with little vacation or holiday time. When E.O. Chamberlin, managing editor of the *Evening World*, died at 38, *Fourth Estate* took the occasion to remind its readers of the rigors of the editorial chair:

> *Midnight often finds the man who began his day's toil at 8 a.m. still jogging away at his desk. He gets his meals at irregular hours. His night's sleep is often disturbed by the impatient ringing of the telephone bell at the head of his bed by some one of his assistants, who finds it necessary to consult with him upon some vital question that has arisen since he left the office. His time is never his own. His wife may find fault with him for his apparent neglect of her and*

the children, but he cannot help it. He is working for a master that is merciless, (sic) If he fails in the slightest measure he knows that another man will be put in his place. He must keep up the pace or lose his position.[22]

Difficult as it was for the editor, the reporter's lot was much worse. Blythe recounted that as one of seven reporters on a seven-day newspaper, he got one day off during the week. This meant that only six reporters were available to cover a city of approximately 100,000 people. He worked on a morning newspaper, reporting at 1 p.m. with his deadline for afternoon copy of 6 p.m. He would then have dinner, return for his night assignments by 7:30 p.m. and meet a deadline of 11 or 12 o'clock. All of the reporters stayed until the proofs were read and revised, which was usually until 1 or 1:30 a.m. "Then," Blythe added, "the long-watch man stayed until four, catching that assignment two or three times a week." It was the new man on the staff who received the long-watch assignment most frequently. Reporters had from 14 to 15 assignments a day, assignments which meant they had to go out and gather information *on each one*, whether or not it resulted in publishable material.[23]

Effects of Working Conditions Upon News Practices

Publishers and business managers followed the practices discussed above because they felt resulting economies were necessary to good business, or because they felt reporters and editors needed such stimuli to perform at high levels. The spy systems of Bennett Jr. and Pulitzer, for example, were put into practice for specific reasons. Bennett felt he would improve his newspaper by proving the loyalty of the men who worked for him; Pulitzer felt the competition and spying would improve both news output and creative levels.[24] Nevertheless, managerial attitudes and practices and the conditions which they fostered were dysfunctional. Indirectly, reporter performance was affected by long hours, arduous working conditions, lack of sick leave and vacation time, fear of job loss and lack of self-esteem. Determining the specific effects on reporter performance growing out of these conditions is not possible. There were, however, certain practices that did have direct influence on the news product. These are more easily traced: Reporters padded stories and expense vouchers to get them past "bill-cutters," they "moonlighted" and took "payola" because of low pay. But the more important influences on the news product were the resulting inaccuracies and sensationalism which grew out of (in part) editorial values, parsimonious news budgets and the space system of pay.

Bill-Cutting

The practice of bill-cutting and the general practice of paying space rates had the effect of causing reporters to "pad" their writing and to pad their bills. Reporters tended to write long rather than tightly and concisely. Thus it is that the *Sun* gained such a reputation in New York City for its tight writing, using an economy of words to express the gist of the story. The *Sun*'s practice grew out of Dana's conviction regarding news writing and his desire to restrict his newspaper to four pages. Most of the newspapers either increased in size by adding pages or by enlarging their sheet, both of which reflected an editorial decision as to whether stories should run long or tight and short.

Bill-cutting affected news style by causing reporters to cheat. One reporter for the New York *Times* became angry over the systematic cutting of his bills. Reportedly he had $9 cut one week, whereupon he decided to take action into his own hands and changed from "conscientious worker" to "a most ingenious shirk, and made out his bills each week so as to allow for cutting." In five weeks he left the newspaper, saying he was even with the *Times*, in the process getting back what he claimed they had "stolen as clearly as if they had picked my pocket." Whether reporters had first begun cheating the newspapers by padding their bills and column counts, or whether editors and business managers had begun the bill-cutting of legitimate space and expenses, the result was warfare between the reporting staff and the editorial and business offices of the newspaper. It follows that a loss of good news writing and coverage occurred for there was a general demoralization of the reporting staff on those newspapers that practiced bill-cutting.[25]

Moonlighting and Payola

Reporters responded to low salaries by earning additional sums through various forms of moonlighting. This was done partly because they had unique opportunities for sending news and information to other papers around the country and partly because they received relatively little pay. Many of the men needed the money for existence; some for luxuries. There were the usual sources of extra money which derived from articles written for magazines or for other newspapers, from news "letters" sent to metropolitan newspapers in other cities and from correspondence.

Some wrote advertisements while working as reporters; a few made a great deal of money at this. Walt McDougall claimed to have "made almost every newspaper illustration used by Barnum's Circus" from 1886 to 1906. Others "moonlighted" in government while serving on newspapers. Two men for one of the New York newspapers were stenographers in the city courts, holding down those fulltime jobs at $2,500 a year while also reporting for their newspapers. Until many of the dailies began their own Sunday editions, reporters could earn extra income by producing news and features for the independent Sunday papers, or, if done surreptitiously, for the opposition's Sunday editions.[26]

The potential for abuse in such a system was obvious. Since ethical standards were not fully developed, reporters and other staff members supplemented their incomes by dropping names into stories, by including product names in drawings of news events and cartoons and by assisting favored politicians who might return the favor at a later date. In fact, several commentators suggested that the future for the average journalist was to leave the field to continue a career elsewhere after having gained *experience* and *contacts* in newspaper work. This is not to suggest that reporters sold their souls for a few dollars; they appear to have been a remarkably clean group, especially given the temptations of the craft, the opportunities that came their way and the paltry sums they received.[27]

Combination Reporting

Two seemingly contradictory practices grew out of the management concepts of the day. One was combination reporting; the other, sensationalism. One required cooperation; the other often resulted from competition. They were actually complementary.

Reporters usually were required to cover a certain number of stories each day. They also had to avoid being beaten on important stories.

Whether it was a routine beat, or a chance meeting of several reporters covering a story, combination reporting reared its attractive head. Sometimes the technique grew into a thoroughgoing practice, as H.L. Mencken recounted in *Newspaper Days*. He and two reporters from opposition newspapers covered the South Baltimore beat by clubbing together on stories. This way they satisfied their editors as to their accuracy and protected themselves from being beaten on certain stories. This practice continued when Mencken moved into city hall reporting. It was widespread in the journalism of the day; most reporters practiced it to one degree or another. The reasons were many, including laziness, but they were far more economic in origin. Most newspapers did not hire enough staff to cover the city completely. Nevertheless, the editors made reporters responsible for all of the news from their beats. The only way reporters could protect themselves was to club together with the opposition by splitting news gathering duties and sharing their information. This was especially true of beat coverage. But even general news incidents which brought competing reporters together sometimes resulted in combination reporting if the assignment did not produce a newsworthy story or was too difficult for one reporter to cover. In those cases, reporters combined to help each other.[28]

It was partly because of editorial ambivalence toward combination reporting that the practice became so widespread. Editors verified names, addresses and facts of stories by checking the stories of the opposition newspaper.

For this reason reporters agreed together on addresses, spelling of names and data even if the facts were incorrect. Editors also covertly used the system to extend their own coverage without increasing the news budget. As one reporter asked: "If you double the man power on a job without increasing the employer's expense, who is the chief beneficiary?" While editors publicly frowned on the practice, it was only when the system broke down and the opposition scored a "scoop" or beat that editors reacted. The economic advantages otherwise were too important.[29]

The complementary nature of combination reporting and sensationalism was personified by Mencken. He and his cohorts on the South Baltimore beat not only combined to report the news, they "synthesized" it as well. By this Mencken meant exaggeration and creative embellishments—indeed, the creating of facts. There was pressure from editors for good, readable, exciting stories. Reporters gave them what they wanted, even if it meant faking the news. Even general assignment reporters sometimes clubbed together to provide editors with those exciting stories.[30]

Sensationalism in the News[31]

The cumulative impact of the system of pay, coupled with working conditions, fostered sensationalism in the press. When reporters received pay based on the number of column inches they printed, there was a powerful economic force at work which caused many of them—perhaps most of them—to fully capitulate to the news values of the day; they worked not for social ideals, with a sense of public responsibility, but rather for column inches. The *Journalist* claimed that "nine-tenths" of the exaggeration in news stories could be explained by the space system. If stories were given over to the facts of the case, they would be reduced in length and reporters would lose "many a column of space and many a consequent dollar—dollars which meant clothes, food, and extra home comforts." Allan Forman, the editor, was loath to blame the reporter:

> *It is easy for a man with an ample salary to say that a newspaper writer should state facts just as they are, with no exaggeration, but when the reporter knows that the plain "fire" is worth a dollar and the "conflagration" will make him a possible ten, the fire is very apt to conflagrate if ingenuity can persuade the city editor to allow it to do so. It is the natural result of the space system where the worker is paid not for work but frequently for padding.*[32]

Forman probably overstated the problem. There were many contributing causes to the exaggeration and sensationalism of the time.

These included competition among newspapers, general individual desire to be first with a story (the ego factor) and changing news values among editors and publishers. Yet, the pay system did contribute to sensationalism in the news. It honored and rewarded sensationalism, as against accurate, factual reporting.[33]

An example of such economic reinforcement was the extra pay given to reporters for exclusives or beats. Across the country during this period news staffs were "organized . . . urged and inspired to get exclusive news. . . . " Some newspapers "played up any big exclusive story out of proportion to its real news value." The pay scale reflected this editorial desire. As mentioned earlier, a one-column story in the New York *Herald* returned $8 to the reporter at prevailing space rates. An *exclusive* story returned $16 per column. Many metropolitan dailies paid double rates for exclusive stories. This economic incentive reinforced the natural competitiveness and generally fear-inspired news drive which existed among reporters and editors. It fostered an unnatural, extreme sensationalism without, however, being the sole cause of it.[34]

Charles Edward Russell, citing an incident from his own experience, placed in high relief the influence of the space system on the reporter. A woman and her two daughters were reported missing. Russell was assigned to the story. There was speculation that she may have jumped into the river. After several days coverage the *Herald* received a letter from a well known woman philanthropist, who reported that the missing wife and children were safe "and under the care of friends." Russell followed up, interviewing the society matron and forcing from her the mother's address. He then arranged a reunion. He acknowledged that the handling of the story "was highly unprofessional." His rationale? "The reporter got a column and three-quarters. It was an exclusive story. At sixteen dollars a column. And times were hard." What makes this incident unusual is that Russell related it and acknowledged the ethical problem as well as the economic imperative. His was not a unique case.

Other reporters recounted incidents of "unethical" methods in news gathering which were considered necessary, at the time, in order to get the story. Hapgood recounts, with appropriate guilt, the deceit he used to get a story from the mother of a son who was missing.[35] The competitive factors allied with psychic and monetary rewards, caused many reporters and editors to step even further across the ethical boundaries into illegal acts. Several examples follow:

1. Witnesses were "hired" and squirreled away from opposition and police. The perplexing death of a young woman in San Francisco caused the newspapers to pull all stops in an attempt to be first and loudest with the answer. Hearst's *Examiner*, when it found a witness, would "put him on salary [take] him to their shop and virtually [lock] him up." On the story in question, the "witness" was the victim's mother and brothers and sisters. The *Chronicle* tried something similar, but failed.

2. News events were created on paper, then were "authenticated." News bureaus and press associations in the cities, particularly in New York, actually created stories. Their reporters, who worked on space, sometimes went out on assignment to find a "hero" willing to "stand for" the story that was already written; that is, they were seeking someone who would agree that they had taken part in the fictitious incident, should the police or reporters follow up. The people who agreed were reported as heroes of the news story.

3. Reporters, misappropriating identities, came close to "entrapment." A New York *World* reporter and his colleague were introduced to the governor of Mississippi and his aides "as New York lawyers, who would act as guides." They showed the Mississippians a rousing good time in New York City, with only the governor returning to *his* hotel that night. The reporters wrote up the story and, "with picture, the story

filled a page of the Sunday paper. It was a shame to do it. It was a sort of Judas act—but it made a beautiful story. Echoes of it were heard from Mississippi for months afterward," the reporter concluded.

4. Reporters stole or secured criminal evidence which the police had in their possession. An example took place in 1892 when one of the top reporters in New York City, Isaac D. White of the New York *World*, discovered the identity of the man blown up in an attempt to assassinate Russell Sage. Using a button on two inches of cloth, White discovered the identity of the man. White received glorious praise from contemporaries and historians—the pertinent question was never asked: what was he doing with the physical evidence?[36]

It was, indeed, the approbation of editors and colleagues, reinforced by economic rewards and penalties, that perpetuated sensationalism, faking and even illegal acts. Editors praised or censured reporters on the basis of whether they had a story and how good it was, not on their own good deeds. Augustus Thomas, as a young reporter in St. Louis, was assigned to a missing girl story. He interviewed the weeping mother and then, through a fluke, found the girl. He returned her to her mother. His city editor's scorn, when Thomas related what he had done, perplexed him. A more experienced colleague explained how another reporter once had found a body in the street, hid it in a building, and then wrote stories about the missing man before finally "discovering" the body and reporting it. The editors had praised him for being able "to clear up the mystery which he had created."[37]

Conclusions

Reporting during the 1880–1900 period was more a way station on the highway to politics, business, literature or editorial work than a profession itself. Even practitioners and publishers felt general reporting was a deadend job. It was a job for the young man who still had his energy, enthusiasm and legs. Perhaps the economic inducements of the period reflected this perception. If reporting were not yet a profession, a long-term job for qualified men and women, then it was perfectly logical to pay inadequate salaries, especially for the majority of the staff, to use happenstance procedures in finding and hiring personnel, and to create a climate of tension and fear among employees in hopes that they would produce more copy and more interesting copy.

Pay was low, jobs were tenuous, hours were long and arduous. Reporters—with notable exceptions—knew they were not worth much to their publishers. Reporters, except for the truly talented, were treated as though they "were machines or privates in an ill-paid army to be thrown in any breach." Theodore Dreiser, when he expressed disillusionment "in the sharp contrast between the professed ideals and preachments of such a constantly moralizing journal as the [New York] *World* and the heartless and savage aspect of its internal economy," also expressed the thoughts of countless reporters.[38] After all, there were worse newspapers than the *World*.

Some reporters, but not all, were broken by the management practices and publisher attitudes. As a class, he, and the occasional she, adapted. When business managers cut bills for reasons of economy, reporters padded stories and expenses. When city editors saved money by hiring too few reporters to cover beats, reporters protected themselves by combining with the opposition. This provided the newspaper with greater coverage, but it also fostered inaccurate reporting. Names and events took on an added dimension—accuracy suffered and the tendency was great to fake or "synthesize" the news. Inadequate pay and long hours had a more subtle influence. Young legs—and inexperienced minds—often covered the court houses and police beats as well as general assignments. It is likely that errors caused by inexperience increased; that news was shaped by the exuberance of youth, which also may have contributed to sensationalism.

A more direct influence on the news grew out of the space rate system. Whether intended or not, the space system reinforced the reporter's natural tendencies toward sensationalism. It rewarded those who could gather and present exciting news; the time rate was so minimal that reporters were tempted to create stories when news was not generated in the normal course of events. Editors *expected* reporters to show ingenuity. The double rates for exclusive news, something the enterprising newspapers of the day greatly desired, spurred reportorial searches for such news. It was nice to have a few extra dollars in the pay envelope, even if professional and ethical standards took a beating in the process.

This is not to suggest that sensationalism was caused only by the pay system, nor even that the pay system was designed only to implement sensationalism. But there was a positive relationship between the system of rewards and the news gathering practice of the day, practices which included sensationalism. Thus, it seems reasonable to conclude that the managerial system shaped to some extent the news values of the press of 1880–1900.

Endnotes

1. For standard historical treatment, consult Frank Luther Mott, *American Journalism. A History of Newspapers in the United States Through 250 Years, 1690–1940* (New York: The Macmillan Co., 1941), pp. 384–85, 488–90; Edwin Emery and Henry Ladd Smith, *The Press and America* (Englewood Cliffs, N.J.: Prentice-Hall, Inc., 1954), especially pp. 386–91. I have used the first editions because they provide more detailed information than later editions. For insightful discussions of the development of news concepts during this period, consult Michael Schudson, *Discovering the News: A Social History of American Newspapers* (New York: Basic Books, 1978), especially chapters 2 and 3, and Bernard Roshco, Newsmaking (Chicago: The University of Chicago Press, 1975), especially chapter 3.
2. Richard Hofstadter, *The Age of Reform: From Bryan to F.D.R.* (New York: Vintage Books, 1955), pp. 190–91; Mott, pp. 488–89; Edwin L. Shuman, *Practical Journalism. A Complete Manual of the Best Newspaper Methods* (New York: D. Appleton and Co., 1903), p. 17.
3. This article is part of a larger study examining the influence of advertising on newspaper values and practices, especially as a result of the significant shift in advertising support which marked the press of this period. The base year of 1880 was used because it was the last reliable census before an explosion in newspapers and newspaper jobs took place. The only history of journalism which provides important information on the reporter and his social relationship to the newspaper is Alfred McClung Lee, *The Daily Newspaper in America. The Evolution of a Social Instrument* (New York: The Macmillan Co., 1937). Lee devotes two chapters to the news and editorial staffing of the press. Chapter 16 is most useful for this study. Lee did not attempt to relate compensation and working conditions to news concepts and performance during this period. His statistic-filled study is a gold mine of data for scholars who carefully trace the ore-laden veins from chapter to chapter. Daniel J. Leab, *A Union of Individuals: The Formation of the American Newspaper Guild, 1933–1936* (New York: Columbia University Press, 1970), provides little information on this period.
4. Samuel G. Blythe, *The Making of a Newspaper Man* (Philadelphia: Henry Altemus, Co., 1912), p. 4. The trial occurred when Blythe was a youth; his report of the incident came after long experience as a reporter. He may have been writing as much from his experience as from his perceptions of those youthful day.
5. S.N.D. North, *History and Present Condition of the Newspaper and Periodical Press of the United States With a Catalogue of the Publications of the Census Year* (Washington: Government Printing Office, 1884), p. 83; Franc B. Wilkie, *Personal Reminis-*

cences of Thirty-Five Years of Journalism (Chicago: F.J. Schulte and Co., Publishers, 1891). Wilkie recounts that Wilbur F. Storey of the Chicago *Times* economized by having his reporters and editors, most of whom wrote with pencils, use "tong-like arrangements which would clasp the end of a pencil" when it was worn too small to be held normally. P. 152.

6. "Outside Work," *Journalist*, No. 8 (May 10, 1884), p. 3; Blythe, pp. 30–32; A.J. Russell, *Good-Bye Newspaper Row* (Excelsior, Minn.: Minnetonka Record Press, 1943), pp. 9–10. When Russell went to the Minneapolis *Journal* in 1885 as a proofreader he received $15 a week.
7. Henry King, "The Pay and Rank of Journalists," *Forum*, 18 (January 1895), pp. 587–96, and Walter Avenel, "Journalism as a Profession," *Forum*, 25 (May 1898), pp. 366–74. For the specific figures, see King, p. 591, Avenel, pp. 367, 370. Avenel surveyed 11 cities: Baltimore, Cincinnati, Cleveland, Detroit, Milwaukee, Minneapolis, New Orleans, Omaha, Pittsburgh, St. Paul and Washington, D.C. Avenel's study appears to have been more rigorous than King's. I am inclined to accept Avenel's figures as being closer to the truth, especially when they are compared with reports from individual reporters who worked during this period. Other sources of data, not used in the body of this report but of some interest to researchers, include reports in trade journals and Eugene M. Camp, "What's the News?" *Century*, 18 (June 1890), pp.: 260–62. Camp claimed to have gathered statistics from editors and publishers for years. The indefinite time frame as well as vagueness regarding the kinds of newspapers covered make his data even less reliable than those of King, who did not provide information about his methods of gathering statistics either. Trade paper information can be secured from *The Journalist*, which several times offered surveys of salaries. Their quality is highly suspect. For early in the period, consult especially "Reporters' Pay," No. 4 (April 12, 1884), p. 3; "Outside Work," p. 3; Mathew Unit (pseud.?), "Editors Versus Reporters," 2 (Oct. 31, 1885), p. 1. for the end of the period, see "Reporters' Recompense," in *Fourth Estate*, 3 (April 4, 1895), p. 6, and Shuman, *Practical Journalism*. . . . Shuman claimed the average pay for all large cities in 1900 was about $30 a week; in Chicago reporters received about $14 to $40, pp. 26–27. He did not provide sources.
8. "History of Wages in the United States From Colonial Times to 1928," *Bulletin of the United States Bureau of Labor Statistics*, No. 604 (October 1929), Washington: Government Printing Office, 1934. Reprinted Gale Research Company. See Table B-22 for data on plumbers; Table K-12 for data on compositors. The reader should keep in mind that census data are gathered for entire states; most of the information on reporter salaries, inadequate though it be, is from large and medium cities. Avenel's data are used to develop comparisons. Daily wages were computed on a six-day week, although reporters were subject to call at any time. For compassion with professions, see King, p. 596; Avenel, p. 369, and Shuman, p. 25. Business probably paid much better. Moses Koenigsberg worked for the St. Louis *Chronicle* circa 1894, when wages were $32.50 a week for the top three reporters. This was the highest salary that had been paid in St. Louis. When Koenigsberg took the job he also took a *cut* in salary of $2.50 a week from his position as advertising manager of a jewelry firm. Moses Koenigsberg, *King News: An Autobiography* (Philadelphia: F.A. Stokes Co., 1941), pp. 212–13. For an interesting study of the movement toward professionalism see Dan Schiller, "An Historical Approach to Objectivity and Professionalism in American News Reporting," *Journal of Communication*, 29: 4 (Autumn, 1979), pp. 46–47.
9. North, p. 83; "Reporters' Pay," p. 3. Alfred McClung Lee contradicted North, claiming that by 1884 (when North's study was published) "payment by the line or inch for copy was impractical, except in the case of special correspondents." P. 629. Lee was incorrect. The space rate system was just getting into full swing. Schudson, citing the *Journalist*, noted that in 1898 in New York City, newspapers had "at least ten college graduates on their staffs, but that the reporter 'working on space,' rather than on salary, was practically extinct." p. 69. I am inclined to disbelieve the *Journalist*'s conclusion, as the text will illustrate. There may indeed have been a decline in space and time rates for well established reporters, although this cannot be verified. Using cen-

sus data supplied by Lee, Table 30, p. 750, one can see that there was a drop in wages from 1889 to 1899 of one percent, while the number of wage earners increased 10.5 percent. The number of salaried employees increased 40 percent during the same period; salaries increased 52 percent. These figures may reflect such changes late in the period, although one cannot be sure since the totals include nearly all personnel on the newspaper. Nearly all of the craft employees in the production end of the business were on a piece rate schedule or wages. David Stern, beginning as a cub reporter on the Philadelphia *Ledger* in 1908, demonstrated that the space rate system continued for quite some time. He began on space rates at $5 a column. During his second week on the job he ran into a streak of good luck, producing six straight stories that made the paper and returned him $40, which was a senior reporter's salary. He was promptly hired at $15 a week, no longer working on space. "What a cockeyed system," he related; "my first raise was a cut from forty to fifteen dollars." He claimed reporters worked from 1 p.m. to 1 a.m. six days a week for an average salary of $25, which earned them about thirty-five cents and hour. J. David Stern, *Memoirs of a Maverick Publisher* (New York: Simon and Schuster, 1962), pp. 33–34.

10. "Reporters' Pay," p. 3; Will Irwin, *The Making of a Reporter* (New York: G.P. Putnam's Sons, 1942), pp. 52–53; Chicago papers also followed the space system into the 20th century. William Salisbury worked on the Chicago *Tribune* about 1903. He and many other reporters worked on space; Salisbury claimed they were "on the bargain counter." Reporters might make up to $20 weekly, he wrote, but assignments often "netted us only half that." He asserted that $25 "was a good salary." William Salisbury, *The Career of a Journalist* (New York: B.W. Dodge and Co., 1908), p. 123. On the other hand, when Theodore Dreiser ran into the system on the New York *World* late in 1894, he wrote: "No reportorial staff with which I had ever been connected had been paid by space." Theodore Dreiser, *A Book About Myself* (London: Constable and Co., Ltd., 1929), p. 474. The American edition was published in 1922. Joseph Medill, publisher of the Chicago *Tribune*, testified in 1883 that the space rate had not yet been widely adopted in Chicago, although it was used to a limited extent. See pp. 985–86 in *Laboring Classes in the United States, Conditions of, etc., Testimony Relating to taken by Committee on Education and Labor,* 1885. This appears in the series *Labor and Capital, Senate Committee on Education and Labor, 1882–1887*. The testimony fills four volumes.

11. "Reporters' Pay," p. 3; "The City Departments," *Journalist*, 1 (June 28, 1884), p. 2. Willis Abbot also complained about the *Tribune*'s enormous columns. "As it paid the regular price per inch for reportorial work, the wide columns were a source of profit to the paper and a disaster to the reporter. I recall that working about fourteen hours a day my first week netted me some $2.85 by way of salary." Willis J. Abbot, *Watching the World Go By* (Boston: Little, Brown and Co., 1933), p. 29.

12. "The City Departments," p. 2; "Reporters; Pay," p. 3.

13. See *Journalist*, April 5, 1884, p. 3, and June 28, 1884, p. 2. The contradiction may have grown out of a change in ownership and editors of the *Journalist*. For Dreiser's comments, see Dreiser, pp. 474–78; Mott. p. 489. Abbot asserts that William Randolph Hearst "raised the general salary level probably twenty-five per cent" when he invaded New York. This too seems unlikely, based on the data. Any improvement probably came in the competitive bidding between Hearst and Pulitzer to top staff. It is unlikely that much of this "increase" filtered down to the general reporter or that it remained high over an extended period. There were large numbers of unemployed or little employed reporters in the New York market ready to step in when given an opportunity. John Livingston Wright, "Reporters and Oversupply," *Arena*, 20 (December 1898), pp. 614–15.

14. "Reporters' Pay," p. 3; Charles Edward Russell, *These Shifting Scenes* (New York: George H. Doran Co.), 1914, pp. 57–59, 71–73. Russell claimed that by working industriously and by writing filler for the Saturday edition, which went to six pages from the regular four, he was able "occasionally" to earn S12 a week. One reporter, he recalled, a university graduate of some ability and

character, who later gained fame as an art critic, covered the Yorkville police court for $6 weekly on the average! It was a vicious system. When Lincoln Steffens began reporting on the New York *Evening Post* in 1892, on space rates, the first week he earned $1.75. Soon he was earning about $20 a week plus extra from long weekly articles to the Sacramento *Record-Union*. See Justin Kaplan, *Lincoln Steffens* (New York: Simon and Schuster, 1974), pp. 47–48. Ray Stannard Baker began work on the Chicago *Record* in 1892, working 1 p.m. to midnight: " . . . my income did not at first average four dollars a week," he wrote. On his lowly pay, even after an increase, he could afford only "a hall bedroom in North State Street, where I had to do my reading standing on a chair under a single dim gas light." He later moved "to a more comfortable front room in a brick house . . . as befitted a man who had seen his salary shoot up from twelve dollars to fifteen dollars a week." Ray Stannard Baker, *American Chronicle. The Autobiography of Ray Stannard Baker* (New York: Charles Scribner's Sons, 1945), pp. 1–3.

15. "Cutting Bills," *Journalist*, No. 3 (April 5, 1884), p. 6: "Mr. Sanderson of the Star," *Journalist*, No. 11 (May 31, 1884), p. 3.
16. See, in addition to above issues, *Journalist* of April 26, 1884, p. 6; May 10, 1884, p. 4; Oct. 31, 1885, pp. 1 and 4; and Nov. 7, 1885, p. 1. No reference to the practice has been found in *Journalist* or *Fourth Estate* during the 1890s.
17. Koenigsberg, pp. 211–12; Irwin, p. 53; Blythe, pp. 28–29.
18. "Journalism's Chief Fault," *Fourth Estate*, 10 (Dec. 22, 1898), p. 6; "High Pressure Journalism," *Fourth Estate*, 10 (April 21, 1898), p. 6; Edwin Llewellyn Shuman, *Steps Into Journalism. Helps and Hints for Young Writers (Evanston, Ill.: Correspondence School of Journalism, 1894), p. 44.*
19. Koenigsberg, p. 19; Wright, pp. 614–15; "Journalism's Chief Fault," p. 6; "Keeps His Men," *Fourth Estate*, 10 (Sept. 15, 1898), 238: 3. Shuman, who was writing to inform potential journalists about conditions in the newspaper field, candidly pointed out that the "reporter is the individual who actually does the hardest hustling for the least pay, and whose tenure of office is so precarious that he is supposed never to pass the waste-basket without looking in to see if his head is there." Shuman, *Steps*, p. 21.
20. Irwin, p. 108.
21. Don C. Seitz, *The James Gordon Bennetts. Father and Son. Proprietors of the New York Herald* (Indianapolis: The Bobbs-Merrill Co., Publishers, 1928), pp. 220–21; Walt McDougall, *This is the Life!* (New York: Alfred A. Knopf, 1926), p. 266; W.A. Swanberg, *Pulitzer* (New York: Charles Scribner's Sons, 1967), pp. 168–70, 242–45; Russell, *Shifting Scenes*, p. 79; "Reporters' Pay," p. 3. Russell's experience was confirmed by Dreiser, who condemned the *World*'s management techniques. His view of Pulitzer deserves quoting:

> *. . . this man because of his vital, aggressive, restless, working mood, and his vaulting ambition to be all that there was to be of journalistic force in America, was making a veritable hell of his paper and the lives of those who worked for him. . . . Of managing editors, all slipping about and, as the newspaper men seemed to think, spying on each other, at one time as many as seven. He had so little faith in his fellow-man, and especially such of his fellow men as were so unfortunate as to have to work for him, that he played off one against another as might have the council of the Secret Ten in Venice, or as did the devils who ruled in the Vatican in the Middle Ages. Every man's hand, as I came to know in the course of time, was turned against that of every other. All were thoroughly distrustful of each other and feared the incessant spying that was going on. Each, as I was told and as to a certain extent one could feel, was made to believe that he was the important one, or might be, presuming that he could prove that the others were failures or in error. . . . Every man was for himself.* (Dreiser, pp. 469–70.)

Swanberg (p. 169) concludes that Pulitzer's methods worked. I disagree.

22. "Vacations," *Journalist*, 5 (Aug. 20, 1887), p. 8; "High Pressure Journalism," p. 6. A clear example of the kind of pressure that contributed to Chamberlin's death can be found in Swanson, p. 248. Both Swanson and Don C. Seitz, *Joseph Pulitzer. His Life and Letters* (Garden City, N.Y.: Garden City Publishing Co., Inc., 1927), p. 193,

spell his name as Chamberlin; *Fourth Estate* spelled it Chamberlain.

The work load of the average reporter was quite high; sometimes it became unbearable. Bill Hooker, who was a newsman in Milwaukee, recalled one day of his reporting life in 1884:

> *He reported a court trial in the morning, covered the Milwaukee City Hall in the afternoon, interviewed a temperance lecturer, covered the marine run, got the arrivals at the hotels, and had his copy on the city editor's desk at 6 p.m. Before calling it a day, he helped the editor edit several columns of country correspondence and at 10 p.m. found himself reporting a prize fight at a roadhouse six or seven miles from the office, whence he had walked. The fight wound up in a free-for-all scrap among the spectators at close to 1 a.m., and there being no telephone, he walked back to the office in a heavy snowstorm, wrote a column and just managed to make the city edition.*
>
> *As soon as this was finished, [Bill] Hooker was called to the managing editor's cubbyhole and handed a bundle of 150 or 200 exchanges, telling him to find 15 or 20 columns of time copy. It was close to daylight when this job was finished and the M.E. [managing editor] and the Colonel [as Hooker later was called] journeyed over to the Kirby House bar, so well known to the older generation of newspapermen, to relieve tired brain and taut nerves. And, as the Colonel was assigned to the police court at 9 a.m., he strolled from the Kirby bar to the single police station of the day in Milwaukee, and slept a few hours on the soft side of a wooden bench, then grabbed a cup of coffee that was intended for a prisoner and headed for the courtroom.*

Reminiscence recounted in "Today's Scribes Have It Easy Says Hooker," *Editor and Publisher* Golden Jubilee Number, Section 2 (July 21, 1934), p. 212. Hooker most likely did not have this as a regular routine, for he recalled this incident in his 78th year.

23. Blythe, p. 28. See also Dreiser, pp. 474–75.

24. Seitz, p. 224. According to Thomas G. Alvord, whom Seitz quotes, Bennett's capriciousness was designed to discover loyalty among his employees. If men stayed with the *Herald* after being mistreated, demoted without cause and having their salary cut, Bennett allegedly knew they could be trusted. McDougall was so piqued by the Pulitzer system and the fact he had been placed on space rates that he resigned as cartoonist of the *World*, despite an extremely good personal relationship with Pulitzer. McDougall, p. 266.

25. For the *Times'* incident, see "Reporters' Pay," p. 3. See also Truman A. DeWeese, "Journalism: Its Rewards and Opportunities," *Forum*, 26 (December, 1898), especially p. 450; "Cutting Bills," p. 4, "Editors Versus Reporters," p. 1, and Dreiser, pp. 476–78.

26. "Outside Work," p. 3; King, p. 594; "By-the-bye," *Journalist*, 5 (April 2, 1887), p. 9; McDougall, p. 57; "Office-Holders as Reporters," *Journalist*, No. 51 (March 7, 1885), p. 4; Joseph I.C. Clarke, *My Life and Memories* (New York: Dodd, Mead and Co., 1925), pp. 103–04; Baker, p. 47. Many of the metropolitan newspapers had enormous correspondent lists; the *Sun* reportedly had over 1,000 in 1887, while the *Herald* had over 3,000. But these were hardly money-making jobs. One of the St. Louis papers was credited with 1,500 correspondents with an annual outlay of $60,000. In the aggregate this appears to be rather astonishing. Broken down, however, it is less impressive. This is a $40-a-year average per correspondent, or 76 cents a week. See "By-the-bye," p. 9 and King, p. 594. One editor recommended that small town and country correspondents be paid from 75 cents to $1.50 a column! "The Value of the Correspondent," *Fourth Estate*, 2 (Sept. 20, 1894), p. 7.

27. Oliver Pilat, *Pegler, Angry Man of the Press* (Boston: Beacon Press, 1963), pp. 28–34; William A. Croffut, *An American Procession, 1855–1914. A Personal Chronicle of Famous men* (Boston: Little, Brown, and Co., 1931), pp. 164–65; McDougall, pp. 185–86, where he resists a "bribe" to put the name of the store into a drawing of a street scene, but see p. 196 where he often put the name of a champagne in a cartoon or scene, for which he received a case from friends. Pulitzer queried him about it but was not offended at the practice. It was a practice that many publishers and editors winked at for the incidental pay reduced pres-

sures from reporters for better salaries. Augustus Thomas compromised his ethical standards many times, once to get an exclusive story from a union, pp. 214–15, and again by probing inside information from a political opponent, which the mayor (a friend) used to turn around an election, pp. 217–22.

In 1887 the Philadelphia *Times* exposed the city editor of the Philadelphia *Daily News* because he was in the pay of gamblers. Editorializing, the *Times* wrote:

> *. . . the time has come when newspapers which long regarded gifts and courtesies of every sort as legitimate perquisites of the profession, understand that only the entirely clean newspaper can be respected, and that genteel professional mendicancy is even more disgraceful in journalism than in any other calling, as it involves the degradation of the great fountain of popular intelligence in our free government.*

Reprinted in "Clean Journalism," *Journalist*, 5 (April 2, 1887), p. 10.

One writer surveying the qualities of reporting in 1884, claimed that "It is to the credit of the craft . . . that few reporters, if any, ever throw the influence they have on the wrong side of wrong—at least in the courts." He explained how politicians could not understand the ethical probity of reporters, citing Frank Swift, a New York politician, who allegedly "sneeringly remarked to Curtis of the *Herald*: 'You reporters are damned fools. You are all the time making other men rich, but you never get rich yourselves.'" "Reporters' Pay," p. 3.

Reporters' ethics, while in need of elevation, still were remarkably high when one considers the examples of editors and publishers. Stern, after he bought the Camden (N.J.) *Courier* in 1919, found that the previous owner had earned 28 percent profit a year against the prevailing 10 percent average. He had done so by stringent economies, such as having reporters make long-distance phone calls from his office, which was two blocks away in city hall where he, the publisher, also was the city treasurer. This rule applied even to suburban calls, which cost only 10 cents. The five members of the editorial staff had jobs with the city and county government, as secretary to the mayor, clerk of the city council, etc. Stern, p. 126.

28. H.L. Mencken, *Newspaper Days, 1899–1906* (New York: Alfred A. Knopf Co., 1941, reissued 1955), pp. 260–66; Irwin, p. 52; Koenigsberg, p. 95; J.B. Montgomery-M'Govern, "An Important Phase of Gutter Journalism: Faking," *Arena*, 19 (February 1898), pp. 250–51.

29. Mencken, p. 263, explained how he and his two comrades in combination reporting "were sometimes commended for our accuracy." The fact they got together on names, numbers, addresses and other specific information before they wrote the story contributed to this "accuracy." See also Koenigsberg, p. 95, for the quote. As a city editor, Mencken spent his time trying to stamp out the practice.

30. Mencken, Chapter 18, "The Synthesis of News;" Salisbury, pp. 101–02.

31. Reporters; editors and critics knew that minor stories were blown out of proportion, stories were created from whole cloth, and reporters involved themselves in stories in such a way that they changed the news. The term as used here covers both the writing and the methods of gathering news. It does not refer only to larger headlines and lurid stories.

32. "The Space System," *Journalist*, 5 (Aug. 6, 1887), p. 8.

33. Ralph Pulitzer, writing in 1912, suggested that editors encouraged reporters in their "faking." When a newspaper does not discipline a reporter, he remarked, it "encourages that particular reporter to gain extra space rates by further faking of one-stick items into one-column stories [and] tempts other honest reporters to do likewise." He also pointed out that a reporter must work hard for accuracy, yet when he achieves it he receives no praise. "For an exclusive story he is rewarded, for a brilliantly written story he is praised, but for an accurately written story he receives no acknowledgment. For accuracy . . . is expected . . . as a matter of course." Ralph Pulitzer, *The Profession of Journalism. Accuracy in the News* (New York: The World, 1912). An address before the School of Journalism , Columbia University, New York, delivered at Earl Hall, Dec. 16, 1912, pp. 14, 15.

34. Irwin, p. 52; Russell, *Shifting Scenes*, p. 248.

35. Russell, *Shifting Scenes*, chapter 11, see pp. 210–11; Norman Hapgood, *The Changing Years* (New York: Farr and Rinehart, Inc., 1930), pp. 103–05.

36. Irwin, pp. 58–64; Montgomery-M'Govern, pp. 240–44; Salisbury, pp. 453–54; Russell, *Shifting Scenes*, pp. 298–300. Edwin Shuman, in his practical advice to budding journalists, made the rather startling admission that reporters and editors often used their imaginations to fill in missing details on many stories. " . . . to this has newspaper ethics come," he explained. He defended the practice if the details were unessential and there was an attempt to discover the truth—"the fact remains that all newspapers employ this method more or less. . . . " He was referring to stories on weddings, speeches, etc., in which the story was written in the past tense as though the writer were on the scene. He admitted that even this "mild form" could backfire. The standard to follow, he suggested, was "Truth in essentials, imagination in non-essentials, [which] is considered a legitimate rule of action in every office. The paramount object is to make an interesting story." Shuman, *Steps*, pp. 120–23. This dubious, although candid, advice was missing from the revised edition, titled *Practical Journalism*. I am indebted to Schudson for having noted this. Schudson, pp. 78–80.

37. Thomas, pp. 195–97; Salisbury, p. 166. This is not intended to be a catalog of illegal and unethical acts of the reporters, although such a study is needed. It is intended to demonstrate that reporters, in response to the competitive and economic pressures of their day, did just about anything to get the story. Dreiser, by the way, "created" a story which made the *World*'s front page. When he was sent on other stories, where he was expected to use a little creative imagination, he refused to do so. Dreiser, pp. 483–85. Lehan, his biographer, suggests he was not always so scrupulous. Richard Lehan, *Theodore Dreiser: His World and His Novels* (Carbondale and Edwardsville: Southern Illinois University Press, 1969), pp. 24–25.

38. Dreiser, p. 487. Admittedly, Dreiser had a biased view for he had failed to make a place for himself on the *World*. On the other hand, what has been presented in this paper confirms his viewpoint, not only for the *World* but for most metropolitan newspapers.

The Discovery that Business Corrupts Politics: A Reappraisal of the Origins of Progressivism

Richard L. McCormick

Almost any history textbook that covers the Progressive era and was written at least twenty years ago tells how early-twentieth-century Americans discovered how big business interests were corrupting politics in quest of special privileges and how an outraged people acted to reform the perceived evils. Commonly, the narrative offers ample anecdotal evidence to support this tale of scandal and reform. The autobiographies of leading progressives—including Theodore Roosevelt, Robert M. La Follette, William Allen White, Frederic C. Howe, and Lincoln Steffens, among others—are frequently cited, because all of them recounted the purported awakening of their authors to the corrupt politico-business alliance.[1] Muckraking journalism, not only by Steffens but also by David Graham Phillips, Charles E. Russell, Ray Stannard Baker, and numerous others, is often drawn upon too, along with evidence that the magazine for which they wrote achieved unprecedented circulation. Political speeches, party platforms, and newspaper editorials by the hundreds are also offered to buttress the contention that Americans of the early 1900s discovered the prevalence of illicit business influence in politics and demanded its removal. But all of this evidence would probably fail to persuade historians today that the old textbook scenario for progressivism is correct.

And for good reason. Every prominent interpretation of the Progressive movement now encourages us not to take the outcry against politico-business corruption too seriously. Some historians have seen progressivism as dichotomous: alongside the individualist, antibusiness strain of reform stood an equally vocal, and ultimately more successful, school that accepted industrial growth and sought even closer cooperation between business and government.[2] Other recent interpreters have described progressivism as a pluralistic movement of diverse groups, including businessmen, who came to-

[1]Although it is a common autobiographical convention to recount one's growth from ignorance to knowledge, it is nonetheless striking that so many progressive autobiographies should identify the same point of ignorance and trace a similar path to knowledge. See Roosevelt, *An Autobiography* (New York, 1913), 85–86, 186, 297–300, 306, 321–23; La Follette, *La Follette's Autobiography: A Personal Narrative of Political Experiences* (Madison, Wisc., 1960), 3–97; White, *The Autobiography of William Allen White* (New York, 1946), 149–50, 160–61, 177–79, 192–93, 215–16, 232–34, 325–26, 345, 351, 364, 428–29, 439–40, 465; Howe, *The Confessions of a Reformer* (New York, 1925), 70–72, 100–12; and Steffens, *The Autobiography of Lincoln Steffens* (New York, 1931), 357–627.

[2]Richard Hofstadter, *The Age of Reform: From Bryan to F.D.R.* (New York, 1955), 133; George E. Mowry, *The Era of Theodore Roosevelt, 1900–1912* (New York, 1958), 55–58; John Braeman, "Seven Progressives," *Business History Review*, 35 (1961): 581–92; and Sheldon Hackney, *Populism to Progressivism in Alabama* (Princeton, 1969), xii–xiii, 329–30.

gether when their interests coincided and worked separately when they did not.[3] Still other historians have seen businessmen themselves as the key progressives, whose methods and techniques were copied by other reformers.[4] Whichever view of the movement they have favored, historians have increasingly recognized the Progressive era as the age when Americans accommodated, rather than tried to escape, large-scale business organizations and their methods.[5] More often than not, the achievement of what used to be called reform now appears to have benefited big business interests. If our aim is to grasp the results and meaning of progressivism, the evidence in the typical textbook seems to lead in the wrong direction.

The currently dominant "organizational" interpretation of the Progressive movement has particularly little room for such evidence. Led by Samuel P. Hays and Robert H. Wiebe, a number of scholars have located the progressive impulse in the drive of newly formed business and professional groups to achieve their goals through organization and expertise. In a related study, Louis Galambos has described the progressive outcry against the trusts as merely a phase in the nation's growing acceptance of large corporations, and, with Hays and Wiebe, he has suggested that the rhetorical attack on business came to very little. The distinctive achievement of this interpretation lies in its account of how in the early twentieth century the United States became an organized, bureaucratic society whose model institution was the large corporation. Where reformers of the 1880s and 1890s had sought to resist the forces of industrialism, or at least to prevent their penetration of the local community, the progressives of the early 1900s accepted an industrial society and concentrated their efforts on controlling, ordering, and improving it. No interpretation of the era based on ideological evidence of a battle between the "people" and the "interests" can capture the enormous complexity of the adjustments to industrialism worked out by different social groups. Hays and Wiebe have succeeded better than any previous historians in describing and characterizing those adjustments and placing them in the context of large social and economic changes. In this light the progressives' claims to have discovered and opposed the corruption of politics by business seem to become a curiosity of the era, not a clue to its meaning, a diversion to the serious historian exploring the organizational achievements that constituted true progressivism, a suitable subject for old textbooks.[6]

[3]John D. Buenker, "The Progressive Era: A Search for a Synthesis," *Mid-America*, 51 (1969): 175–93; David P. Thelen, "Social Tensions and the Origins of Progressivism," *Journal of American History* [hereafter, *JAH*], 56 (1969): 323–41; and Peter G. Filene, "an Obituary for 'The Progressive Movement,'" *American Quarterly*, 22 (1970): 20–34.

[4]Robert H. Wiebe, *Businessmen and Reform: A Study of the Progressive Movement* (Cambridge, Mass., 1962); Gabriel Kolko, *The Triumph of Conservatism: A Reinterpretation of American History, 1900–1916* (New York, 1963); and Samuel P. Hays, "The Politics of Reform in Municipal Government in the Progressive Era," *Pacific Northwest Quarterly*, 55 (1964): 157–69.

[5]Samuel P. Hays, *The Response to Industrialism, 1885–1914* (Chicago, 1957); Robert H. Wiebe, *The Search for Order, 1877–1920* (New York, 1967); Louis Galambos, *The Public Image of Big Business in America, 1880–1940: A Quantitative Study in Social Change* (Baltimore, 1975); William L. O'Neill, *The Progressive Years: America Comes of Age* (New York, 1975); and David P. Thelen, *Robert M. La Follette and the Insurgent Spirit* (Boston, 1976).

[6]Louis Galambos provided a sympathetic introduction to the work of the "organizational" school; see his "The Emerging Organizational Synthesis in Modern American History," *Business History Review*, 44 (1970): 279–90. For another effort to place the work of these historians in perspective, see Robert H. Wiebe, "The Progressive Years, 1900–1917," in William H. Cartwright and Richard L. Watson, Jr., eds., *The Reinterpretation of American History and Culture* (Washington, 1973), 425–42. In addition to the works by Wiebe, Hays, and Galambos, already cited, several other studies by Hays also rank among the most important products of the organizational school: Samuel P. Hays, *Conservation and the Gospel of Efficiency: The Progressive Conservation Movement, 1890–1920* (Cambridge, Mass., 1959), "Political

Despite its great strengths, however, the organizational model neglects too much.[7] Missing is the progressives' moral intensity. Missing, too, are their surprise and animation upon discovering political and social evils. Also absent are their own explanations of what they felt and what they were doing. And absent, above all, is a description, much less an analysis, of the particular political circumstances from which progressivism emerged in the first years of the twentieth century. In place of these vivid actualities, the organizational historians offer a vague account of what motivated the reformers who advocated bureaucratic solutions and an exaggerated estimation of their capacity to predict and control events. Actually, progressive reform was not characterized by remarkable rationality or foresight; nor were the "organizers" always at the forefront of the movement. Often the results the progressives achieved were unexpected and ironical; and, along the way, crucial roles were sometimes played by men and ideas that, in the end, met defeat.

The perception that privileged businesses corrupted politics was one such ultimately unsuccessful idea of particular short-run instrumentality. Especially in the cities and states, around the middle of the first decade of the twentieth century, the discovery of such corruption precipitated crises that led to the most significant political changes of the time. When the crises had passed, the results for political participation and public policy were roughly those that the organizational interpretation predicts, but the way these changes came about is far from adequately described by that thesis. The pages that follow here sketch an account of political change in the early twentieth century and show how the discovery of politico-business corruption played this central, transforming role—though not with quite the same results that the old textbooks describe.

Admittedly, to interpret progressivism on the basis of its political and governmental side is a more risky endeavor than it once was. Indeed, a major thrust of contemporary scholarship has been to subordinate the Progressive era's political achievements to the larger social and economic changes associated with what Wiebe has called "the process of America's modernization."[8] From such a perspective, "developments in politics" became, as John C. Burnham has observed, "mere epiphenomena of more basic forces and changes."[9] But what if political behavior fails to fit trends that the rest of society seems to be experiencing? What conclusions are to be drawn, for instance, from the observation that American political rhetoric was preoccupied with attacking corporations at precisely the moment in the early twentieth century when such businesses were becoming ascen-

Parties and the Community-Society Continuum," in William Nisbet Chambers and Walter Dean Burnham, eds., *The American Party Systems: Stages of Political Development* (New York, 1967), 152–81, and "The New Organizational Society," in Jerry Israel, ed., *Building the Organizational Society: Essays on Associational Activities in Modern America* (New York, 1972), 1–15. Although Wiebe and Hays share the same broad interpretation of the period, their works make quite distinctive contributions, and there are certain matters on which they have disagreed. Some of Wiebe's most important insights concern the complex relationships between business and reform, while Hays has demonstrated particular originality on the subjects of urban politics and political parties. Concerning the middle classes, they have differing views: Wiebe has included the middle classes among the "organizers," while Hays has emphasized their persistent individualism. Compare Wiebe, *The Search for Order, 1877–1920*, chap. 5, and Hays, *The Response to Industrialism, 1885–1914*, chap. 4.

[7]For related comments on the organizational model's shortcomings, see William G. Anderson, "Progressivism: An Historiographical Essay," *History Teacher*, 6 (1973): 427–52; David M. Kennedy, "Overview: The Progressive Era," *Historian*, 37 (1975): 453–68; O'Neill, *The Progressive Years*, x, 45; and Morton Keller, *Affairs of State: Public Life in Late-Nineteenth-Century America* (Cambridge, Mass., 1977), 285–87.

[8]Wiebe, "The Progressive Years, 1900–1917," 429.

[9]John D. Buenker, John C. Burnham, and Robert M. Crunden, *Progressivism* (Cambridge, Mass., 1977), 4. For some disagreements among these three authors about how central politics was to progressivism, see *ibid.*, 107–29.

dant in economic and social life? One approach simply ignores the anomalous behavior or, at most, considers it spurious or deceptive. Another answer lies in the notions that American politics is fundamentally discontinuous with the rest of national life and that, as several political scientists have suggested, it has always retained a "premodern" character.[10] A better solution, however, rests upon a close study of the ways in which apparently anachronistic political events and the ideas they inspired became essential catalysts for "modernizing" developments. Studied in this manner, politics has more to tell us about progressivism than contemporary wisdom generally admits.

Shortly after 1900, American politics and government experienced a decisive and rather rapid transformation that affected both the patterns of popular political involvement and the nature and functions of government itself. To be sure, the changes were not revolutionary, but, considering how relatively undevelopmental the political system of the United States has been, they are of considerable historical importance. The basic features of this political transformation can be easily described, but its causes and significance are somewhat more difficult to grasp.

One important category of change involved the manner and methods of popular participation in politics. For most of the nineteenth century, high rates of partisan voting—based on complex sectional, cultural, and communal influences—formed the American people's main means of political expression and involvement. Only in exceptional circumstances did most individuals or groups rely on nonelectoral methods of influencing the government. Indeed, almost no such means existed within the normal bounds of politics. After 1900, this structure of political participation changed. Voter turnout fell, and, even among those electors who remained active, pure and simple partisanship became less pervasive. At approximately the same time, interest-group organizations of all sorts successfully forged permanent, nonelectoral means of influencing the government and its agencies. Only recently have historians begun to explore with care what caused these changes in the patterns of political participation and to delineate the redistribution of power that they entailed.[11]

American governance, too, went through a fundamental transition in the early 1900s. Wiebe has accurately described it as the emergence of "a government broadly and continuously involved in society's operations."[12] Both the institutions of government and the content of policy reflected the change. Where the legislature had been the dominant branch of government at every level, lawmakers now saw their power curtailed by an enlarged executive, and, even more, by the creation of an essentially new branch of government composed of administrative boards and agencies. Where nineteenth-century policy had generally focused on distinct groups and locales (most characteristically through the distribution of resources and

[10]Samuel P. Huntington, *Political Order in Changing Societies* (New Haven, 1968), 93–139; Walter Dean Burnham, *Critical Elections and the Mainsprings of American Politics* (New York, 1970), 175–93; and J. G. A. Pocock, *The Machiavellian Moment: Florentine Political Thought and the Atlantic Republican Tradition* (Princeton, 1975), 549.

[11]I have elsewhere cited many of the sources on which these generalizations are based; see my "The Party Period and Public Policy: An Exploratory Hypothesis," *JAH*, 66 (1979): 279–98. On the decline in turnout and the increase in ticket-splitting, see Walter Dean Burnham, "The Changing Shape of the American Political Universe," *American Political Science Review* [hereafter, *APSR*], 59 (1965): 7–28. On the rise of interest-group organizations, see Hays, "Political Parties and the Community-Society Continuum." For two studies that make significant contributions to an understanding of how the political changes of the early twentieth century altered the power relationships among groups, see J. Morgan Kousser, *The Shaping of Southern Politics: Suffrage Restriction and the Establishment of the One-party South, 1880–1910* (New Haven, 1974); and Carl V. Harris, *Political Power in Birmingham, 1871–1921* (Knoxville, 1977).

[12]Wiebe, *The Search for Order, 1877–1920*, 160.

privileges to enterprising individuals and corporations), the government now began to take explicit account of clashing interests and to assume the responsibility for mitigating their conflicts through regulations, administration, and planning. In 1900, government did very little in the way of recognizing and adjusting group differences. Fifteen years later, innumerable policies committed officials to that formal purpose and provided the bureaucratic structures for achieving it.[13]

Most political historians consider these changes to be the products of long-term social and economic developments. Accordingly, they have devoted much of their attention to tracing the interconnecting paths leading from industrialization, urbanization, and immigration to the political and governmental responses. Some of the general trends have been firmly documented in scholarship: the organization of functional groups whose needs the established political parties could not meet; the creation of new demands for government policies to make life bearable in crowded cities, where huge industries were located; and the determination of certain cultural and economic groups to curtail the political power of people they considered threatening. All of these developments, along with others, occurred over a period of decades—now speeded, now slowed by depression, migration, prosperity, fortune, and the talents of individual men and women.

Yet, given the long-term forces involved, it is notable how suddenly the main elements of the new political order went into place. The first fifteen years of the twentieth century witnessed most of the changes; more precisely, the brief period from 1904 to 1908 saw a remarkably compressed political transformation. During these years the regulatory revolution peaked; new and powerful agencies of government came into being everywhere.[14] At the same time, voter turnout declined, ticket-splitting increased, and organized social, economic, and reform-minded groups began to exercise power more systematically than ever before.[15] An understanding of how the new polity crystallized so rapidly can be obtained by exploring, first, the latent threat to the old system represented by fears of "corruptions"; then, the pressures for political change that had built up by about 1904; and, finally, the way in which the old fears abruptly took on new meaning and inspired a resolution of the crisis.

Long before 1900—indeed, since before the Revolution—Americans had been aware that governmental promotion of private interests, which became the dominant form of nineteenth-century economic policy, carried with it risks of corruption. From the English opposition of Walpole's day, colonists in America had absorbed the theory that commercial development threatened republican government in two ways: (1) by spreading greed, extravagance, and luxury among the people; and (2) by encouraging a designing ministry to conspire with monied interests for the purpose of overwhelming the

[13]McCormick, "The Party Period and Public Policy"; Robert A. Lively, "The American System: A Review Article," *Business History Review*, 29 (1955): 81–96; James Willard Hurst, *Law and the Conditions of Freedom in the Nineteenth-Century United States* (Madison, Wisc., 1956); Theodore J. Lowi, "American Business, Public Policy, Case-Studies, and Political Theory," *World Politics*, 16 (1964); 677–715; and Wiebe, *The Search for Order, 1877–1920*, 159–95.

[14]James Willard Hurst, *Law and Social Order in the United States* (Ithaca, 1977), 33, 36, and *Law and the Conditions of Freedom*, 71–108; and Grover G. Huebner, "Five Years of Railroad Regulation by the States," *Annals of the American Academy of Political and Social Science*, 32 (1908): 138–56. For a further account of these governmental changes, see pages 267–69, 271–74, below.

[15]Burnham, "The Changing Shape of the American Political Universe," and *Critical Elections and the Mainsprings of American Politics*, 71–90, 115; and Jerrold G. Rusk, "The Effect of the Australian Ballot Reform on Split-Ticket Voting, 1876–1908," *APSR*, 64 (1970): 1220–38. For a contemporary effort to estimate and assess split-ticket voting, see Philip Loring Allen, "Ballot Laws and Their Workings," *Political Science Quarterly*, 21 (1906): 38–58.

independence of the legislature. Neither theme ever entirely disappeared from American politics, although each was significantly revised as time passed. For Jeffersonians in the 1790s, as Lance Banning has demonstrated, both understandings remained substantially intact. In their belief, Alexander Hamilton's program of public aid to commercial enterprises would inevitably make an agrarian people less virtuous and would also create a phalanx of privileged interests—including bank directors, speculators, and stockjobbers—pledged to support the administration faction that had nurtured them. Even after classical republican thought waned and the structure of government-business relations changed, these eighteenth-century fears that corruption inevitably flowed from government-assisted commercial development continued to echo in American politics.[16]

For much of the nineteenth-century, as Fred Somkin has shown, thoughtful citizens remained ambivalent about economic abundance, because they feared its potential to corrupt them and their government. "Over and over again," Somkin stated, "Americans called attention to the danger which prosperity posed for the safety of free institutions and for the maintenance of republicanism."[17] In the 1830s the Democratic Party's official ideology began to give voice to these fears. Using language similar to that of Walpole's and Hamilton's critics, Andrew Jackson decried "special privileges" from government as dangerous to liberty and demanded their abolition. Much of his wrath was directed against the Second Bank of the United States. That "monster," he said, was "a vast electioneering engine"; it has "already attempted to subject the government to its will." The Bank clearly raised the question of "whether the people of the United States are to govern . . . or whether the power and money of a great corporation are to be secretly exerted to influence their judgment and control their decisions." In a different context Jackson made the point with simple clarity: "Money," he said, "is power." Yet Jackson's anti-Bank rhetoric also carried a new understanding of politico-business corruption, different from that of the eighteenth century. For the danger that Jackson apprehended came not from a corrupt ministry, whose tool the monied interests were, but from privileged monsters, acting independently from public authorities and presenting a danger not only to the government but also to the welfare of other social and economic groups ("the farmers, mechanics, and laborers") whose interests conflicted with theirs. Jackson's remedy was to scale down governmental undertakings, on the grounds that public privileges led to both corruption and inequality.[18]

Despite the prestige that Jackson lent to the

[16]Banning, *The Jeffersonian Persuasion: Evolution of a Party Ideology* (Ithaca, 1978); J.G.A. Pocock, "Virtue and Commerce in the Eighteenth Century," *Journal of Interdisciplinary History*, 3 (1972): 119–34, and *The Machiavellian Moment*, 506–52; Gordon S. Wood, *The Creation of the American Republic, 1776–1787* (Chapel Hill, 1969), 32–33, 52, 64–65, 107–14, 400–03, 416–21; Morton Keller, "Corruption in America: Continuity and Change," in Abraham S. Eisenstadt *et al.*, eds., *Before Watergate: Problems of Corruption in American Society* (New York, 1979), 7–19; and Edwin G. Burrows, "Albert Gallatin and the Problem of Corruption in the Federalist Era," *ibid.*, 51–67.

[17]Somkin, *Unquiet Eagle: Memory and Desire in the Idea of American Freedom, 1815–1860* (Ithaca, 1967), 24.

[18][Jackson] *Annual Messages, Veto Messages, protests, &c. of Andrew Jackson, President of United States* (Baltimore, 1835), 162, 165, 179, 197, 244. Numerous studies document the Democratic Party's use of the accusation that privileged business was corrupting politics: Lee Benson, *The Concept of Jacksonian Democracy: New York as a Test Case* (Princeton, 1961), 52–56, 96–97, 236; William G. Shade, *Banks or No Banks: The Money Issue in Western Politics, 1832–1865* (Detroit, 1972), 56–59; Marvin Meyers, *The Jacksonian Persuasion: Politics and Belief* (Stanford, 1957), 23–24, 30, 157–58, 196, 198; and Edward K. Spann, *Ideals and Politics: New York Intellectuals and Liberal Democracy, 1820–1880* (Albany, N.Y., 1972), 60, 68–78, 105–06. President Martin Van Buren's special message to Congress proposing the subtreasury system in 1837 contained accusations against the Bank similar to those Jackson had made, except that Van Buren expressed them more in "pure," eighteenth-century republican language; James D. Richardson, ed., *A Compilation of the Mes-*

attack on privilege, it was not a predominant fear for Americans in the nineteenth century. So many forms of thought and avarice disguised the dangers Jackson saw. First of all, Americans were far from agreed that governmental assistance for some groups hurt the rest, as he proclaimed. Both the "commonwealth" notion of a harmonious community and its successor, the Whig-Republican concept of interlocking producer interests, suggested that economic benefits from government would be shared throughout society. Even when differences emerged over who should get what, an abundance of land and resources disguised the conflicts, while the inherent divisibility of public benefits encouraged their widespread distribution. Especially at the state and local levels, Democrats, as well as Whigs and Republicans, freely succumbed to the nearly universal desire for government aid. Not to have done so would have been as remarkable as to have withheld patronage from deserving partisans.[19] Nor, in the second place, was it evident to most nineteenth-century Americans that private interests represented a threat to the commonweal. While their eighteenth-century republican heritage warned them of the danger to free government from a designing ministry that manipulated monied interests, classical economics denied that there was a comparable danger to the public from private enterprises that were independent of the government. Indeed, the public-private distinction tended to be blurred for nineteenth-century Americans, and not until it came into focus did new threats of politico-business corruption seem as real as the old ones had in the 1700s.[20]

As time passed, Jackson's Democratic Party proved to be a weak vehicle for the insight that privileged businesses corrupted politics and government. The party's platforms, which in the 1840s had declared a national bank "dangerous to our republican institutions," afterwards dropped such rhetoric. The party of Stephen A. Douglas, Samuel J. Tilden, and Glover Cleveland all but abandoned serious criticism of politico-business corruption. Cleveland's annual message of 1887, which he devoted wholly to the tariff issue, stands as the Gilded Age's equivalent to Jackson's Bank veto. But, unlike Jackson, Cleveland made his case entirely on economic grounds and did not suggest that the protected interests corrupted government. Nor did William Jennings Bryan pay much attention to the theme in 1896. Unlike his Populist supporters who charged that public officials had "basely surrendered . . . to corporate monopolies," the Democrat Bryan made only fleeting mention of the political influence of big corporations or the danger to liberty from privileged businesses.[21]

sages and Papers of the Presidents, 1789–1897, 10 vols. (Washington, 1896–99), 3: 324–46.

[19]McCormick, "The Party Period and Public Policy," 286–88. On the "commonwealth" ideal, see Oscar Handlin and Mary Flug Handlin, *Commonwealth—A Study of the Role of Government in the American Economy: Massachusetts, 1774–1861* (New York, 1947); and Louis Hartz, *Economic Policy and Democratic Thought: Pennsylvania, 1776–1860* (Cambridge, Mass., 1948). For a classic expression of the Whig concept of interlocking producer interests, see Calvin Colton, ed., *The Works of Henry Clay, Comprising His Life, Correspondence, and Speeches*, 5 (New York, 1897): 437–86; and, for a later Republican expression of the same point of view, see Benjamin Harrison, *Speeches of Benjamin Harrison, Twenty-Third President of the United States* (New York, 1892), 62, 72, 157, 167, 181, 197. For a discussion of the Republican ideology and economic policy, see Eric Foner, *Free Soil, Free Labor, Free Men: The Ideology of the Republican Party Before the Civil War* (New York, 1970), 18–23.

[20]Lively, "The American System," 94; Carter Goodrich, "The Revulsion against Internal Improvements," *Journal of Economic History*, 10 (1950): 169; and Hays, *The Response to Industrialism, 1885–1914*, 39–40. On the reluctance of state legislatures to prohibit their members from mixing public and private business, see Ari Hoogenboom, "Did Gilded Age Scandals Bring Reform?" in Eisenstadt *et al.*, *Before Watergate*, 127–31.

[21]Compare the Democratic platforms of 1840–52 with those for the rest of the century; see Donald Bruce Johnson and Kirk H. Porter, eds., *National Party Platforms, 1840–1972* (Urbana, 1973); for the People's Party platform of 1896, see *ibid.*, 104. For Cleveland's message of 1887, see Richardson,

From outside the political mainstream, the danger was more visible. Workingmen's parties, Mugwumps, Greenbackers, Prohibitionists, and Populists all voiced their own versions of the accusation that business corrupted politics and government. The Greenbackers charged that the major parties were tools of the monopolies; the Prohibitionists believed that the liquor corporations endangered free institutions; and the Populists powerfully indicted both the Democrats and the Republicans for trucking to the interests "to secure corruption funds from the millionaires." In *Progress and Poverty* (1879), Henry George asked, "Is there not growing up among us a class who have all the power . . . ? We have simple citizens who control thousands of miles of railroad, millions of acres of land, the means of livelihood of great numbers of men; who name the governors of sovereign states as they name their clerks, choose senators as they choose attorneys, and whose will is as supreme with legislatures as that of a French king sitting in a bed of justice."[22] But these were the voices of dissenters and frail minorities. Their accusations of corruption posed a latent challenge to an economic policy based on distributing privileges to private interests, but for most of the nineteenth century their warnings were not widely accepted or even listened to by the political majority.

The late 1860s and early and mid-1870s, however, offer an apparent exception. These were the years when the Crédit Mobilier and other scandals—local and national—aroused a furor against politico-business corruption. "Perhaps the offense most discredited by the exposures," according to C. Vann Woodward, "was the corrupting of politicians to secure government subsidies and grants to big corporations—particularly railroads." For several years, in consequence, there was a widespread revulsion against a policy of bestowing public privileges and benefits on private companies. Editorializing in 1873 on the Crédit Mobilier scandal, E. L. Godkin of the *Nation* declared, "The remedy is simple. The Government must get out of the 'protective' business and the 'subsidy' business and the 'improvement' and the 'development' business. It must let trade, and commerce, and manufactures, and steamboats, and railroads, and telegraphs alone. It cannot touch them without breeding corruption." Yet even in the mid-1870s, by Woodward's own account, it was possible for railroad and other promoters, especially in the South and Midwest, to organize local meetings that rekindled their fervor for subsidies in town after town. The fear of corruption that Godkin voiced simply was not compelling enough to override the demand for policies of unchecked promotion.[23]

Even the nineteenth century's most brilliant and sustained analysis of business and politics—that provided by the Adams brothers, Charles Francis, Jr. and Henry, in their *Chapters of Erie* (1871)—failed to portray the danger convincingly. Recounting the classic Gilded Age roguery of Jay Gould and Jim Fisk, including their corruption of courts and legislatures and

Messages and Papers of the Presidents, 1789–1897, 8: 580–91; and, for a compilation of Bryan's speeches of 1896, see his *The First Battle: A Story of the Campaign of 1896* (Chicago, 1896).

[22]Johnson and Porter, *National Party Platforms, 1840–1972*, 90; and George, *Progress and Poverty—An Inquiry into the Cause of Industrial Depressions and of Increase of Want with Increase of Wealth: The Remedy* (New York, 1880), 481. For examples of other late-nineteenth-century dissenters who recognized the corruption of politics and government by business interests, see H.R. Chamberlain, *The Farmers' Alliance: What It Aims to Accomplish* (New York, 1891), 12, 37–38; and Henry Demarest Lloyd, *Wealth against Commonwealth* (New York, 1894), 369–404.

[23]Woodward, *Reunion and Reaction: The Compromise of 1877 and the End of Reconstruction* (Boston, 1951), 65; and Godkin, "The Moral of the Crédit Mobilier Scandal," *Nation*, 16 (1873): 68. Also see Allan Nevins, *The Emergence of Modern America, 1865–1878* (New York, 1927), 178–202; and John G. Sproat, *"The Best Men": Liberal Reformers in the Gilded Age* (New York, 1968), 72–73. For the ebb and flow of public aid to private enterprise in this era, see Keller, *Affairs of State*, 162–96. For other expressions of Godkin's opinion, see the *Nation*, 16 (1873): 328–29, and 24 (1877): 82–83.

their influence on the president himself, the Adamses warned that, as Henry put it, "the day is at hand when corporations . . . —having created a system of quiet but irresistible corruption—will ultimately succeed in directing government itself." But the Adams brothers presented Gould and Fisk as so fantastic that readers could not believe that ordinary businessmen could accomplish such feats. Rather than describing a process of politico-business corruption, the Adamses gave only the dramatic particulars of it. Words like "astounding," "unique," and "extraordinary" marked their account. Writing of the effort by Gould and Fisk to corner the market on gold in 1869, Henry said, "Even the most dramatic of modern authors, even Balzac himself, . . . or Alexandre Dumas, with all his extravagance of imagination, never have reached a conception bolder or more melodramatic than this, nor have they ever ventured to conceive a plot so enormous, or a catastrophe so original." Far from supporting the Adamses' thesis, such descriptions must have undermined it by raising doubts that what Gould and Fisk did could be widely or systematically repeated.[24]

Expressed by third parties and by elite spokesmen like Godkin and the Adamses, the fear that business corrupted politics exerted only minor influence in the late nineteenth century. When they recognized corruption, ordinary people seem to have blamed "bad" politicians, like James G. Blaine, and to have considered the businessmen guiltless. Even when Americans saw that corruption involved the use of money, they showed more interest in how the money was spent—for example, to bribe voters—than in where it came from. Wanting governmental assistance for their enterprises, but only sporadically scrutinizing its political implications, most people probably failed to perceive what the Adamses saw.[25] Nor did they, until social and industrial developments created deep dissatisfaction with the existing policy process. Then, the discovery that privileged businesses corrupted politics played a vital, if short-lived, role in facilitating the momentous transition from the nineteenth-century polity to the one Americans fashioned at the beginning of the twentieth century.

By the 1890s, large-scale industrialization was creating the felt need for new government policies in two distinct but related ways. The first process, which Hays and Wiebe have described so well, was the increasing organization of diverse producer groups, conscious of their own identities and special needs. Each demanded specific public protections for its own endeavors and questioned the allocation of benefits to others. The second development was less tangible: the unorganized public's dawning sense of vulnerability, unease, and anger in the face of economic changes wrought by big corporations. Sometimes, the people's inchoate feelings focused on the ill-understood "trusts"; at other times, their negative emotions found more specific, local targets in street-railway or electric-power companies. Older interpretations of progressivism gave too much weight to the second of these developments; recently, only a few historians have sufficiently recognized it.[26]

Together, these processes created a political crisis by making people conscious of uncom-

[24]Adams and Adams, *Chapters of Erie* (reprint ed., Ithaca, 1956), 136, 107. Originally published as articles during the late 1860s and early 1870s, these essays were first issued in book form in 1871 under the title *Chapters of Erie and Other Essays* (Boston).

[25]For the vivid expression of a similar point, see Wiebe, *The Search for Order, 1877–1920*, 28.

[26]Hays, *The Response to Industrialism, 1885–1914*; and Wiebe, *The Search for Order, 1877–1920*. On the fear and anger of the unorganized, see Hofstadter, *The Age of Reform*, 213–69; Irwin Unger and Debi Unger, *The Vulnerable Years: The United States, 1896–1917* (Hinsdale, Ill., 1977), 102–08; and David P. Thelen, *The New Citizenship: Origins of Progressivism in Wisconsin, 1885–1900* (Columbia, Mo., 1972).

fortable truths that earlier nineteenth-century conditions had obscured: that society's diverse producer groups did not exist in harmony or share equally in government benefits, and that private interests posed a danger to the public's interests. The crisis brought on by the recognition of these two problems extended approximately from the onset of depression in 1893 until 1908 and passed through three distinct phases: (1) the years of realignment, 1893–96; (2) the years of experimentation and uncertainty, 1897–1904; and (3) the years of discovery and resolution, 1905–08. When the crisis was over, the American political system was different in important respects from what it had been before.

During the first phase, the depression and and alleged radicalism of the Populists preoccupied politics and led to a decisive change in the national balance of party power. Willingly or unwillingly, many former voters now ceased to participate in politics, while others from almost every social group in the North and Midwest shifted their allegiance to the Republicans. As a result, that party established a national majority that endured until the 1930s. Yet, given how decisive the realignment of the 1890s was, it is striking how quickly the particular issues of 1896—tariff protection and free silver—faded and how little of longstanding importance the realignment resolved.[27] To be sure, the defeat of Bryan and the destruction of Populism established who would not have control of the process of accommodating the nation to industrial realities, but the election of 1896 did much less in determining who would be in charge or what the solutions would be.

In the aftermath of realignment, a subtler form of crisis took hold—although several happy circumstances partially hid it, both from people then and from historians since. The war with Spain boosted national pride and self-confidence; economic prosperity returned after the depression; and the Republican Party with its new majority gave the appearance of having doctrines that were relevant to industrial problems. Soon, President Theodore Roosevelt's activism and appeal helped foster an impression of political command over the economy. However disguised, the crisis nonetheless was real, and, in the years after 1896, many voices quietly questioned whether traditional politics and government could resolve interest-group conflicts or allay the sense of vulnerability that ordinary people felt.

Central to the issue were the dual problems of how powerful government should be and whether it ought to acknowledge and adjust group differences. Industrialism and its consequences seemed to demand strong public policies based on a recognition of social conflict. At the very least, privileged corporations had to be restrained, weaker elements in the community protected, and regular means established for newer interest groups to participate in government. But the will, the energy, and the imagination to bring about these changes seemed missing. Deeply felt ideological beliefs help explain this paralysis. The historic American commitment, on the one hand, to weak government, local autonomy, and the preservation of individual liberties—reflected in the doctrines of the Democratic Party—presented a strong barrier to any significant expansion of governmental authority. The ingrained resistance, on the other hand, to having the government acknowledge that the country's producing

[27]The three most important studies of the electoral realignment of the 1890s are Paul Kleppner, *The Cross of Culture: A Social Analysis of Midwestern Politics, 1850–1900* (New York, 1970); Richard Jensen, *The Winning of the Midwest: Social and Political Conflict, 1888–1896* (Chicago, 1971); and Samuel T. McSeveney, *The Politics of Depression: Political Behavior in the Northeast, 1893–1896* (New York, 1972). A number of studies associate the realignment with subsequent changes in government policy: Walter Dean Burnham *et al.*, "Partisan Realignment: a Systematic Perspective," in Joel H. Silbey *et al.*, eds., *The History of American Electoral Behavior* (Princeton, 1978), 45–77; and David W. Brady, "Critical Elections, Congressional Parties and Clusters of Policy Changes," *British Journal of Political Science*, 8 (1978): 79–99.

interests were not harmonious—voiced in the doctrines of the Republican Party—presented an equally strong obstacle to the recognition and adjustment of group differences.[28]

Weighted down by their doctrines as well as by an unwillingness to alienate elements of their heterogeneous coalitions, both parties floundered in attempting to deal with these problems. The Democrats were merely more conspicuous in failing than were the Republicans. Blatantly divided into two wings, neither of which succeeded in coming to grips with the new issues, the Democrats blazoned their perplexity by nominating Bryan for president for a second time in 1900, abandoning him for the conservative Alton B. Parker in 1904, and then returning to the Great Commoner (who was having trouble deciding whether to stand for nationalizing the railroads) in 1908. The Republicans, for their part, were only a little less contradictory in moving from McKinley to Roosevelt to Taft. Roosevelt, moreover, for all of the excitement he brought to the presidency in 1901, veered wildly in his approach to the problems of big business during his first term—from "publicity" to trust-busting to jawboning to conspiring with the House of Morgan.[29]

While the national leaders wavered and confidence in the parties waned, a good deal of experimenting went on in the cities and states—much of it haphazard and unsuccessful. Every large city found it difficult to obtain cheap and efficient utilities, equitable taxes, and the variety of public services required by an expanding, heterogeneous population. A few, notably Detroit and later Cleveland and New York, made adjustments during the last years of the nineteenth and the first years of the twentieth centuries that other cities later copied: the adoption of restrictions on utility and transportation franchises, the imposition of new taxes on intangible personalty, and the inauguration of innovative municipal services. But most cities were less successful in aligning governance with industrialism. Utility regulation was a particularly difficult problem. Franchise "grabs" agreed to by city councilmen came under increasing attack, but the chaotic competition between divergent theories of regulation (home rule versus state supervision versus municipal ownership) caused the continuance of poor public policy.[30] In the states, too, the late 1890s and early 1900s were years of experimentation with various methods of regulation and administration. What Gerald D. Nash has found for California seems to have been true elsewhere as well: the state's railroad commission "floundered" in the late nineteenth century due to ignorance, inexperience, and a lack of both manpower and money. These were, Nash says, times of "trial and error." Antitrust policy also illuminates the uncertainty that was characteristic of the period before about 1905. By the turn of the century, two-thirds of the states had already passed antitrust laws, but in the great majority the provi-

[28]For a discussion of the major parties' ideological beliefs, see Robert Kelley, "Ideology and Political Culture from Jefferson to Nixon," *AHR*, 82 (1977): 531–62. And, for a brilliant account of the resistance to change, see Keller, *Affairs of State*.

[29]On the Democratic Party's doctrinal floundering in these years, see J. Rogers Hollingsworth, *The Whirligig of Politics: The Democracy of Cleveland and Bryan* (New York, 1963). For the Republican side of the story, see Nathaniel W. Stephenson, *Nelson W. Aldrich: A Leader in American Politics* (New York, 1930); and John M. Blum, *The Republican Roosevelt* (Cambridge, Mass., 1954). Roosevelt's doctrinal uncertainties can be traced in his annual messages as president; see Hermann Hagedorn, ed., *The Works of Theodore Roosevelt*, memorial edition, 17 (New York, 1925): 93–641. For a recent treatment of these matters, see Lewis L. Gould, *Reform and Regulation: American Politics, 1900–1916* (New York, 1978).

[30]Melvin G. Holli, *Reform in Detroit: Hazen S. Pingree and Urban Politics* (New York, 1969); Martin J. Schiesl, *The Politics of Efficiency: Municipal Administration and Reform in America, 1880–1920* (Berkeley and Los Angeles, 1977); Mowry, *The Era of Theodore Roosevelt, 1900–1912*, 59–67; Thelen, *The New Citizenship*, 130–201; and David Nord, "The Experts versus the Experts: Conflicting Philosophies of Municipal Utility Regulation in the Progressive Era," *Wisconsin Magazine of History*, 58 (1975): 219–36.

sions for enforcement were negligible. Some states simply preferred encouraging business to restraining it; others felt that the laxity of neighboring states and of the federal government made antitrust action futile; still others saw their enforcement policies frustrated by court decisions and administrative weaknesses. The result was unsuccessful policy—and a consequent failure to relieve the crisis that large-scale industrialization presented to nineteenth-century politics and government.[31]

In September 1899, that failure was searchingly probed at a conference on trusts held under the auspices of the Chicago Civic Federation. Attended by a broad spectrum of the country's political figures and economic thinkers, the meeting's four days of debates and speeches amply expressed the agitation, the uncertainty, and the discouragement engendered by the nation's search for solutions to the problems caused by large business combinations. In exploring whether and to what extent the government should regulate corporations and how to adjust social-group differences, the speakers addressed basic questions about the nineteenth-century American polity.[32] Following the conference, the search for answers continued unabated, for there was little consensus and considerable resistance to change. In the years immediately following, pressure to do *something* mounted. And roughly by the middle of the next decade, many of the elements were in place for a blaze of political innovation. The spark that finally served to ignite them was a series of disclosures reawakening and refashioning the old fear that privileged business corrupted politics and government.

The evidence concerning these disclosures is familiar to students of progressivism, but its meaning has not been fully explored. The period 1904–08 comprised the muckraking years, not only in national magazines but also in local newspapers and legislative halls across the country. During 1905 and 1906 in particular, a remarkable number of cities and states experienced wrenching moments of discovery that led directly to significant political changes. Usually, a scandal, an investigation, an intraparty battle, or a particularly divisive election campaign exposed an illicit alliance of politics and business and made corruption apparent to the community, affecting party rhetoric, popular expectations, electoral behavior, and government policies.[33]

Just before it exploded in city and state affairs, business corruption of politics had already emerged as a leading theme of the new magazine journalism created by the muckrakers. Their primary contribution was to give a national audience the first systematic accounts of how modern American society operated. In so doing, journalists like Steffens, Baker, Russell, and Phillips created insights and pioneered ways of describing social and political relationships that crucially affected how people saw things in their home towns and states. Since so many of the muckrakers' articles identified the widespread tendency for privilege-seeking businessmen to bribe legislators, conspire with party leaders, and control nominations, an awareness of such corruption soon entered local politics. Indeed, many of the muckraking arti-

[31]Nash, "The California Railroad Commission, 1876–1911," *Southern California Quarterly*, 44 (1962): 293, 303; Harry L. Purdy *et al.*, *Corporate Concentration and Public Policy* (2d ed., New York, 1950), 317–22; Hans B. Thorelli, *The Federal Antitrust Policy: Origination of an American Tradition* (Baltimore, 1955), 155–56, 265, 352–55, 607; and William Letwin, *Law and Economic Policy in America: The Evolution of the Sherman Antitrust Act* (New York, 1965), 182–247.

[32]Civic Federation of Chicago, *Chicago Conference on Trusts* (Chicago, 1900).

[33]For other analyses that indicate the importance of the year 1906 in state politics around the country, see Richard M. Abrams, *Conservatism in a Progressive Era: Massachusetts Politics, 1900–1912* (Cambridge, Mass., 1964), 131; and Dewey W. Grantham, Jr., "The Progressive Era and the Reform Tradition," *Mid-America*, 46 (1964): 233–35.

cles concerned particular locales—including Steffens's early series on the cities (1902–03); his subsequent exposures of Missouri, Illinois, Wisconsin, Rhode Island, New Jersey, and Ohio (1904–05); Rudolph Blankenburg's articles on Pennsylvania (1905); and C. P. Connolly's treatment of Montana (1906). All of these accounts featured descriptions of politico-business corruption, as did many of the contemporaneous exposures of individual industries, such as oil, railroads, and meat-packing. Almost immediately after this literature began to flourish, citizens across the country discovered local examples of the same corrupt behavior that Steffens and the others had described elsewhere.[34]

In New York, the occasion was the 1905 legislative investigation of the life insurance industry. One by one, insurance executives and Republican politicians took the witness stand and were compelled to bare the details of their corrupt relations. The companies received legislative protection, and the Republicans got bribes and campaign funds. In California, the graft trials of San Francisco city officials, beginning in 1906, threw light on the illicit cooperation between businessmen and public officials. Boss Abraham Ruef had delivered special privileges to public utility corporations in return for fees, of which he kept some and used the rest to bribe members of the city's Board of Supervisors. San Francisco's awakening revitalized reform elsewhere in California, and the next year insurgent Republicans formally organized to combat their party's alliance with the Southern Pacific Railroad. In Vermont, the railroad commissioners charged the 1906 legislature with yielding "supinely to the unfortunate influence of railroad representatives." Then the legislature investigated and found that the commissioners themselves were corrupt![35]

Other states, in all parts of the country, experienced their own versions of these events during 1905 and 1906. In South Dakota, as in a number of Midwestern states, hostility to railroad influence in politics—by means of free passes and a statewide network of paid henchmen—was the issue around which insurgent Republicans coalesced against the regular machine. Some of those who joined the opposition did so purely from expediency; but their charges of corruption excited the popular imagination, and they captured the state in 1906 with pledges of electoral reform and business regulation. Farther west Denver's major utilities, including the Denver Tramway Company and the Denver Gas and Electric Company, applied for new franchises in 1906, and these applications went before the voters at the spring elections. When the franchises all narrowly carried, opponents of the companies produced evidence that the Democratic and Republican Parties had obtained fraudulent votes

[34]The fullest treatment of the muckrakers is still Louis Filler's *The Muckrakers*, a new and enlarged edition of his *Crusaders for American Liberalism* (University Park, Pa., 1976). Filler's chronology provides a convenient list of the major muckraking articles; *ibid.*, 417–24. Steffens's initial series on the cities was published as *The Shame of the Cities* (New York, 1904). His subsequent articles on the states appeared in *McClure's Magazine* between April 1904 and July 1905; these essays were later published as *The Struggle for Self-Government* (New York, 1906). Blankenburg's articles on Pennsylvania appeared in *The Arena* between January and June 1905; Connolly's "The Story of Montana" was published in *McClure's Magazine* between August and December 1906. Other major magazine articles probing politico-business corruption include "The Confessions of a Commercial Senator," *World's Work*, April–May 1905; Charles Edward Russell, "The Greatest Trust in the World" [the meat-packing industry], *Everybody's Magazine*, 1905; and David Graham Phillips, "The Treason of the Senate," *Cosmopolitan Magazine*, 1906.

[35]Robert F. Wesser, *Charles Evans Hughes: Politics and Reform in New York, 1905–1910* (Ithaca, 1967), 18–69; Richard L. McCormick, *From Realignment to Reform: Political Change in New York State, 1893–1910* (Ithaca, 1981), chap. 7; George E. Mowry, *The California Progressives* (Berkeley and Los Angeles, 1951), 23–85; Spencer C. Olin, Jr., *California's Prodigal Sons: Hiram Johnson and the Progressives, 1911–1917* (Berkeley and Los Angeles, 1968), 1–19; Winston Allen Flint, *The Progressive Movement in Vermont* (Washington, 1941), 42–51; and the *Tenth Biennial Report of the Board of Railroad Commissioners of the State of Vermont* (Bradford, Vt., 1906), 25.

for the utilities. The case made its way through the courts during the next several months, and, although they ultimately lost, Colorado's nascent progressives derived an immense boost from the well-publicized judicial battle. As a result, the focus of reform shifted to the state. Dissidents in the Republican Party organized to demand direct primary nominations and a judiciary untainted by corporate influence. These questions dominated Colorado's three-way gubernatorial election that fall.[36]

To the south, in Alabama, Georgia, and Mississippi, similar accusations of politico-business corruption were heard that same year, only in a different regional accent. In Alabama, Braxton Bragg Comer rode the issue from his position on the state's railroad commission to the governorship. His "main theme," according to Sheldon Hackney, "was that the railroads had for years deprived the people of Alabama of their right to rule their own state and that the time had come to free the people from alien and arbitrary rule." Mississippi voters heard similar rhetoric from Governor James K. Vardaman in his unsuccessful campaign against John Sharp Williams for a seat in the U.S. Senate. Georgia's Tom Watson conjured up some inane but effective imagery to illustrate how Vardaman's opponent would serve the business interests: "If the Hon. John Sharp Williams should win out in the fight with Governor Vardaman, the corporations would have just one more doodle-bug in the United States Senate. Every time that a Railroad lobbyist stopped over the hole and called 'Doodle, Doodle, Doodle'—soft and slow—the sand at the little end of the funnel would be seen to stir, and then the little head of J. Sharp would pop up." In Watson's own state, Hoke Smith trumpeted the issue, too, in 1905 and 1906.[37]

New Hampshire, Rhode Island, New Jersey, Pennsylvania, Ohio, Indiana, North Dakota, Nebraska, Texas, and Montana, among other states, also had their muckraking moments during these same years. Although the details varied from place to place, there were three basic routes by which the issue of politico-business corruption entered state politics. In some states, including New York, Colorado, and California, a legislative investigation or judicial proceeding captured attention by uncovering a fresh scandal or by unexpectedly focusing public attention on a recognized political sore. Elsewhere, as in New Hampshire, South Dakota, and Kansas, a factional battle in the dominant Republican Party inspired dissidents to drag their opponents' misdeeds into public view; in several Southern states, the Democrats divided in similar fashion, and each side told tales of the other's corruption by business interests. Finally, city politics often became a vehicle for spreading the issue of a politico-business alliance to the state. Philadelphia, Jersey City, Cincinnati, Denver, and San Francisco all played the role of inspiring state reform movements based on this issue. Some states took more than one of these three routes; and the politicians and reformers in a few states simply echoed what their counterparts elsewhere were saying without having any outstanding local stimulus for doing so. This pattern is, of course, not perfect. In Wisconsin and Oregon, the discovery of politico-business corruption came earlier than 1905–06; in Virginia its arrival engendered almost no popular excitement, while it scarcely got to Massachusetts at all.[38]

[36]Herbert S. Schell, *History of South Dakota* (Lincoln, Neb., 1961), 258–61; Fred Greenbaum, "The Colorado Progressives in 1906," *Arizona and the West*, 7 (1965): 21–32; and Carl Abbott, *Colorado: A History of the Centennial State* (Boulder, 1976), 203–06.

[37]Hackney, *Populism to Progressivism in Alabama*, 257; Watson's *Weekly Jeffersonian*, July 25, 1907, as quoted in William F. Holmes, *The White Chief: James Kimble Vardaman* (Baton Rouge, 1970), 184; Dewey W. Grantham, Jr., *Hoke Smith and the Politics of the New South* (Baton Rouge, 1958), 131–46; and C. Vann Woodward, *Origins of the New South, 1877–1913* (Baton Rouge, 1951), 369–95.

[38]Geoffrey Blodgett, "Winston Churchill: The Novelist as Reformer," *New England Quarterly*, 47 (1974): 495–517; Thomas Agan, "The New Hampshire Progressives: Who

An anonymous Kansan, whose state became aware of business domination of its politics and government in 1905 and 1906, later gave a description of the discovery that also illuminates what happened elsewhere. When he first entered politics in the 1890s, the Kansan recalled, "three great railroad systems governed" the state. "This was a matter of common knowledge, but nobody objected or was in any way outraged by it." Then "an awakening began" during Roosevelt's first term as president, due to his "hammering on the square deal" and to a growing resentment of discriminatory railroad rates. Finally, after the railroads succeeded in using their political influence to block rate reform, "it began to dawn upon me," the Kansan reported, "that the railway contributions to campaign funds were part of the general game. . . . I saw they were in politics so that they could run things as they pleased." He and his fellow citizens had "really been converted," he declared. "We have got our eyes open now. . . . We have seen that the old sort of politics was used to promote all sorts of private ends, and we have got the idea now that the new politics can be used to promote the general welfare."[39]

State party platforms provide further evidence of the awakening to politico-business corruption. In Iowa, to take a Midwestern state, charges of corporation influence in politics were almost entirely confined to the minor parties during the years from 1900 to 1904. Prohibitionists believed that the liquor industry brought political corruption, while socialists felt that the powers of government belonged to the capitalists. For their part, the Democrats and Republicans saw little of this—until 1906, when both major parties gushed in opposition to what the Republicans now called "the domination of corporate influences in public affairs." The Democrats agreed: "We favor the complete elimination of railway and other public service corporations from the politics of the state." In Missouri, a different but parallel pattern emerges from the platforms. There, what had been a subordinate theme of the Democratic Party (and minor parties) in 1900 and 1902 became of central importance to both parties in 1904 and 1906. The Democrats now called "the eradication of bribery" the "paramount issue" in the state and declared opposition to campaign contributions "by great corporations and by those interested in special industries enjoying special privileges under the law." In New Hampshire, where nothing had been said of politico-business corruption in 1900 and 1904, both major parties wrote platforms in 1906 that attacked the issuance of free transportation passes and the prevalence of corrupt legislative lobbies. Party platforms in other states also sug-

and What Were They?" *Historical New Hampshire*, 34 (1979): 32–53; Charles Carrol, *Rhode Island: Three Centuries of Democracy*, 2 (New York, 1932): 676–78; Erwin L. Levine, *Theodore Francis Green: The Rhode Island Years, 1906–36* (Providence, 1963), 1–19; Arthur S. Link, *Wilson: The Road to the White House* (Princeton, 1947), 133–40; Ransom E. Noble, Jr., *New Jersey Progressivism before Wilson* (Princeton, 1946), 24–81; Eugene M. Tobin, "The Progressive as Politician: Jersey City 1896–1907," *New Jersey History*," 91 (1973): 5–23; Lloyd M. Abernethy, "Insurgency in Philadelphia, 1905," *Pennsylvania Magazine of History and Biography*, 87 (1963): 3–20; Hoyt Landon Warner, *Progressivism in Ohio, 1897–1917* (Columbus, 1964), 143–210; Clifton J. Phillips, *Indiana in Transition: The Emergence of an Industrial Commonwealth, 1880–1920* (Indianapolis, 1968), 93–100; Charles N. Glaab, "The Failure of North Dakota Progressivism," *Mid-America*, 39 (1957): 195-209; James C. Olson, *History of Nebraska* (Lincoln, Neb., 1955), 250–53; Alwyn Barr, *Reconstruction to Reform: Texas Politics, 1876–1906* (Austin, 1971), 229–42; Michael P. Malone and Richard B. Roeder, *Montana: A History of Two Centuries* (Seattle, 1976), 196–99; Robert S. Maxwell, *La Follette and the Rise of the Progressives in Wisconsin* (Madison, Wisc., 1956); Herbert F. Margulies, *The Decline of the Progressive Movement in Wisconsin, 1890–1920* (Madison, Wisc., 1968); Raymond H. Pully, *Old Virginia Restored: An Interpretation of the Progressive Impulse, 1870–1930* (Charlottesville, 1968); and Abrams, *Conservatism in a Progressive Era*.

[39]"How I Was Converted—Politically: By a Kansas Progressive Republican," *Outlook*, 96 (1910): 857–59. Also see Robert Sherman La Forte, *Leaders of Reform: Progressive Republicans in Kansas, 1900–1916* (Lawrence, Kansas, 1974), 13–88.

gest how suddenly major-party politicians discovered that business corrupted politics.[40]

The annual messages of the state governors from 1902 to 1908 point to the same pattern. In the first three years, the chief executives almost never mentioned the influence of business in politics. Albert Cummins of Iowa was exceptional; as early as 1902 he declared, "Corporations have, and ought to have, many privileges, but among them is not the privilege to sit in political conventions or occupy seats in legislative chambers." Then in 1905, governors across the Midwest suddenly let loose denunciations of corporate bribery, lobbying, campaign contributions, and free passes. Nebraska's John H. Mickey was typical in attacking "the onslaught of private and corporation lobbyists who seek to accomplish pernicious ends by the exercise of undue influence." Missouri's Joseph W. Folk advised that "all franchises, rights and privileges secured by bribery should be declared null and void." By 1906, 1907, and 1908, such observations and recommendations were common to the governors of every region. In 1907 alone, no less than nineteen state executives called for the regulation of lobbying, while a similar number advised the abolition of free passes.[41]

What is the meaning of this awakening to something that Americans had, in a sense, known about all along? Should we accept the originality of the "discovery" that monied interests endangered free government or lay stress instead on the familiar elements the charge contained? It had, after all, been a part of American political thought since the eighteenth century and had been powerfully repeated, in one form or another, by major and minor figures throughout the nineteenth century. According to Richard Hofstadter, "there was nothing new in the awareness of these things."[42] In fact, however, there was much that was new. First, many of the details of politico-business corruption had never been publicly revealed before. No one had ever probed the subject as thoroughly as journalists and legislative investigators were now doing, and, moreover, some of the practices they uncovered had only recently come into being. Large-scale corporation campaign contributions, for instance, were a product of the 1880s and 1890s. Highly organized legislative lobbying operations by competing interest groups represented an even more recent development. In his systematic study of American legislative practices, published in 1907, Paul S. Reinsch devoted a lengthy chapter to describing how business interests had developed a new and "far more efficient system of dealing with legislatures than [the old methods of] haphazard corruption."[43]

[40]*The Iowa Official Register for the Years 1907–1908* (Des Moines, 1907), 389, 393; *Official Manual of the State of Missouri for the Years 1905–1906* (Jefferson City, Mo., 1905), 254; and *Official Manual of the State of Missouri for the Years 1907–1908* (Jefferson City, Mo., 1907), 365. Also see State of New Hampshire, *Manual for the General Court, 1907* (Concord, N.H., 1907), 61–63. State party platforms for the early 1900s are surprisingly hard to locate. For some states, particularly in the Northeast and Midwest, the platforms were printed in the annual legislative manuals and blue books, but otherwise they must be found in newspapers. Of the ten states—Iowa, Missouri, New Hampshire, New York, New Jersey, Indiana, Pennsylvania, Illinois, Wisconsin, and South Dakota—for which I was able to survey the party platforms of 1900–10 fairly completely (using the manuals, supplemented when necessary by newspapers), only two fail to support the generalization given here: Wisconsin, where an awareness of politico-business corruption was demonstrated in the platforms of 1900 and 1902 as well a those of later years; and New Jersey, where the Democrats used the issue sparingly in 1901 and 1904, while the Republican almost completely ignored it throughout the decade.

[41]New York State Library, *Digest of Governors' Messages* (Albany, N.Y., 1903–09). This annual document, published for the years 1902–08, classifies the contents of the governors' messages by subject and permits easy comparison among them. For Mickey's and Folk's denunciations, see New York State Library, *Digest of Governors' Messages, 1905*, classifications 99 (legislative lobbying), 96 (legislative bribery).

[42]Hofstadter, *The Age of Reform*, 185.

[43]Reinsch, *American Legislatures and Legislative Methods*

Even more startling than the new practices themselves was the fresh meaning they acquired from the nationwide character of the patterns that were now disclosed. The point is not simply that more people than ever before became aware of politico-business corruption but that the perception of such a national pattern itself created new political understandings. Lincoln Steffens's autobiography is brilliant on this point. As Steffens acknowledged, much of the corruption he observed in his series on the "shame" of the cities had already come to light locally before he reported it to a national audience. What he did was take the facts in city after city, apply imagination to their transcription, and form a new truth by showing the same process at work everywhere. Here was a solution to the problem the Adams brothers had encountered in writing *Chapters of Erie*: how to report shocking corruption without making it seem too astounding to be representative. The solution was breadth of coverage. Instead of looking at only two businessmen, study dozens; explore city after city and state after state and report the facts to a people who were vaguely aware of corruption in their own home towns but had never before seen that a single process was at work across the country.[44] This concept of a "process" of corruption was central to the new understanding. Uncovered through systematic journalistic research and probing legislative investigations, corruption was now seen to be the result of concrete historical developments. It could not just be dismissed as the product of misbehavior by "bad" men (although that kind of rhetoric continued too) but had to be regarded as an outcome of identifiable economic and political forces. In particular, corruption resulted from an outmoded policy of indiscriminate distribution, which could not safely withstand an onslaught of demands from private corporations that were larger than the government itself.[45]

Thus in its systematic character, as well as in its particular details, the corruption that Americans discovered in 1905 and 1906 was different from the kind their eighteenth- and nineteenth-century forebears had known. Compared to the eighteenth-century republican understanding, the progressive concept of corruption regarded the monied interests not as tools of a designing administration but as independent agents. If any branch of government was in alliance with them, it was probably the legislature. In a curious way, however, the old republican view that commerce inherently threatened the people's virtue still persisted, now informed by a new understanding of the actual process at work. Compared to Andrew Jackson, the progressives saw big corporations not as monsters but as products of social and industrial development. And their activist remedies differed entirely from his negativistic ones. But, like Jackson, those who now discovered corruption grasped that private interests could conflict with the public interest and that government benefits for some groups often hurt others. The recognition of these two things—both painfully at odds

(New York, 1907), 231. On the history of party campaign funds, see James K. Pollock, Jr. *Party Campaign Funds* (New York, 1926); Earl R. Sikes, *State and Federal Corrupt-Practices Legislation* (Durham, N.C., 1928); and Louise Overacker, *Money in Elections* (New York, 1932).

[44]Steffens later commented insightfully on his own (and, by implication, the country's) process of "discovery" during these years; see his *Autobiography*, 357–627. Also see his *Shame of the Cities*, 3–26; and Filler, *The Muckrakers*, 257–59.

[45]Around 1905 a social-science literature emerged that attempted to explain the process of corruption and to suggest suitable remedies. In addition to Reinsch's *American Legislatures and Legislative Methods*, see Frederic C. Howe, *The City: The Hope of Democracy* (New York, 1905), and *Privilege and Democracy in America* (New York, 1910); and Robert C. Brooks, *Corruption in American Politics and Life* (New York, 1910). Several less scholarly works also analyze the cause of politico-business corruption; see, for example, George W. Berge, *The Free Pass Bribery System* (Lincoln, Neb., 1905); Philip Loring Allen, *America's Awakening: The Triumph of Righteousness in High Places* (New York, 1906); and William Allen White, *The Old Order Changeth: A View of American Democracy* (New York, 1910).

Table 1 *Selected Categories of State Legislation, 1903–1908*[1]

Type of Legislation	1903–1904	1905–1906	1907–1908	1903–1908
Regulation of Lobbying	0	2	10	12
Prohibition of Corporate Campaign Contributions	0	3	19	22
Regulation or Prohibition of Free Railroad Passes for Public Officials	4	6	14	24
Mandatory Direct Primary	4	9	18	31
Regulation of Railroad Corporations by Commission	5	8	28	41
Totals	13	28	89	130

Note: Figures represent the number of states that passed legislation in the given category during the specified years.
Source: New York State Library, *Index of Legislation* (Albany, N.Y., 1904–09).

with the nineteenth century's conventional wisdom—had been at the root of the floundering over principles of political economy in the 1890s and early 1900s. Now, rather suddenly, the discovery that business corrupts politics suggested concrete answers to a people who were ready for new policies but had been uncertain how to get them or what exactly they should be.

Enacted in a burst of legislative activity immediately following the awakening of 1905 and 1906, the new policies brought to an end the paralysis that had gripped the polity and constituted a decisive break with nineteenth-century patterns of governance. Many states passed laws explicitly designed to curtail illicit business influence in politics. These included measures regulating legislative lobbying, prohibiting corporate campaign contributions, and outlawing the acceptance of free transportation passes by public officials. In 1903 and 1904, there had been almost no legislation on these three subjects; during 1905 and 1906, several states acted on each question; and, by 1907 and 1908, ten states passed lobbying laws, nineteen took steps to prevent corporate contributions, and fourteen acted on the question of passes (see Table 1). If these laws failed to wipe out corporation influence in politics, they at least curtailed important means through which businesses had exercised political power in the late nineteenth and early twentieth centuries. To be sure, other means were soon found, but the flood of state lawmaking on these subjects, together with the corresponding attention they received from the federal government in these same years, shows how prevalent was the determination to abolish existing forms of politico-business corruption.[46]

Closely associated with these three measures were two more important categories of legislation, often considered to represent the essence of progressivism in the states: mandatory direct primary laws and measures establishing or strengthening the regulation of utility and transportation corporations by commission. These types of legislation, too, reached a peak

[46]The figures in this paragraph (and in the accompanying table) are based on an analysis of the yearly summaries of state legislation reported in New York State Library, *Index of Legislation* (Albany, N.Y., 1904–09). The laws included here are drawn from among those classified in categories 99 (lobbying), 154 (corporate campaign contributions), 1237 (free passes), 160 (direct nominations), and 1267, 1286 (transportation regulation). The legislative years are paired because so many state legislatures met only biennially, usually in the odd-numbered years; no state is counted more than once in any one category in any pair of years. The *Index of Legislation* should be used in conjunction with the accompanying annual *Review of Legislation* (Albany, N.Y., 1904–09).

in the years just after 1905–06, when so many states had experienced a crisis disclosing the extent of politico-business corruption. Like the laws concerning lobbying, contributions, and passes, primary and regulatory measures were brought forth amidst intense public concern with business influence in politics and were presented by their advocates as remedies for that problem. Both types of laws had been talked about for years, but the disclosures of 1905–06 provided the catalyst for their enactment.

Even before 1905, the direct primary had already been adopted in some states. In Wisconsin, where it was approved in 1904, Robert M. La Follette had campaigned for direct nominations since the late 1890s on the grounds that they would "emancipate the legislature from all subserviency to the corporations." In his well-known speech, "The Menace of the Machine" (1897), La Follette explicitly offered the direct primary as "the remedy" for corporate control of politics. Now, after the awakening of 1905–06, that same argument inspired many states that had failed to act before to adopt mandatory direct primary laws (see Table 1). In New York, Charles Evans Hughes, who was elected governor in 1906 because of his role as chief counsel in the previous year's life insurance investigation, argued that the direct primary would curtail the power of the special interests. "Those interests," he declared, "are ever at work stealthily and persistently endeavoring to pervert the government to the service of their own ends. All that is worst in our public life finds it readiest means of access to power through the control of the nominating machinery of parties." In other states, too, in the years after 1905–06, the direct primary was urged and approved for the same reasons that La Follette and Hughes advanced it.[47]

The creation of effective regulatory boards—progressivism's most distinctive governmental achievement—also followed upon the discovery of politico-business corruption. From 1905 to 1907 alone, fifteen new state railroad commissions were established, and at least as many existing boards were strengthened. Most of the new commissions were "strong" ones, having rate-setting powers and a wide range of administrative authority to supervise service, safety, and finance. In the years to come, many of them extended their jurisdiction to other public utilities, including gas, electricity, telephones, and telegraphs. Direct legislative supervision of business corporations was also significantly expanded in these years. Life insurance companies—whose corruption of the New York State government Hughes had dramatically disclosed—provide one example. "In 1907," as a result of Hughes's investigation and several others conducted in imitation of it, Morton Keller has reported, "forty-two state legislatures met; thirty considered life insurance legislation; twenty-nine passed laws. . . . By 1908 . . . [the basic] lines of twentieth century life insurance supervision were set, and thereafter only minor adjustments occurred." The federal regulatory machinery, too, was greatly strengthened at this time, most notably by the railroad, meat inspection, and food and drug acts of 1906.[48]

[47]Ellen Torelle, comp., *The Political Philosophy of Robert M. La Follette* (Madison, Wisc., 1920), 28; and Hughes, *Public Papers of Charles E. Hughes, Governor, 1909* (Albany, 1910), 37. Also see Maxwell, *La Follette and the Rise of the Progressives*, 13, 27–35, 48–50, 53–54, 74; Allen Fraser Lovejoy, *La Follette and the Establishment of the Direct Primary in Wisconsin, 1890–1904* (New Haven, 1941); Wesser, *Charles Evans Hughes*, 250–301; Direct Primaries Association of the State of New York, *Direct Primary Nominations: Why Voters Demand Them, Why Bosses Oppose Them* (New York, 1909); Ralph Simpson Boots, *The Direct Primary in New Jersey* (New York, 1917), 59–70; Grantham, *Hoke Smith and the Politics of the New South*, 158, 162, 172–73, 178, 193; Schell, *History of South Dakota*, 260; Olin, *California's Prodigal Sons*, 13; and Charles Edward Merriam and Louise Overacker, *Primary Elections* (Chicago, 1928), 4–7, 60–66.

[48]Huebner, "Five Years of Railroad Regulation by the States"; Robert Emmett Ireton, "The Legislatures and the Railroads," *Review of Reviews*, 36 (1907): 217–20; and Keller, *The Life Insurance Enterprise, 1885–1910: A Study in the Limits*

The adoption of these measures marked the moment of transition from a structure of economic policy based largely on the allocation of resources and benefits to one in which regulation and administration played permanent and significant roles. Not confined for long to the transportation, utility, and insurance companies that formed its most immediate objects, regulatory policies soon were extended to other industries as well. Sometimes the legislative branch took responsibility for the ongoing tasks of supervision and administration, but more commonly they became the duty of independent boards and commissions, staffed by experts and entrusted with significant powers of oversight and enforcement. Certainly, regulation was not previously unknown, nor did promoting commerce and industry now cease to be a governmental purpose. But the middle years of the first decade of the twentieth century unmistakably mark a turning point—that point when the direction shifted, when the weight of opinion changed, when the forces of localism and opposition to governmental authority that had sustained the distribution of privileges but opposed regulation and administration now lost the upper hand to the forces of centralization, bureaucratization, and governmental actions to recognize and adjust group differences. Besides economic regulation, other governmental policy areas, including health, education, taxation, correction, and the control of natural resources, increasingly came under the jurisdiction of independent boards and commissions. The establishment of these agencies and the expansion of their duties meant that American governance in the twentieth century was significantly different from what it had been in the nineteenth.[49]

The developments of 1905–08 also changed the nature of political participation in the United States. Parties emerged from the years of turmoil altered and, on balance, less important vehicles of popular expression than they had been. The disclosure of politico-business wrongdoing disgraced the regular party organizations, and many voters showed their loss of faith by staying at home on election day or by casting split tickets. These trends had been in progress before 1905–06—encouraged by new election laws as well as by the crisis of confidence in traditional politics and government—but in several ways the discovery of corruption strengthened them. Some reigning party organizations were toppled by the disclosures, and the insurgents who came to power lacked the old bosses' experience and inclination when it came to rallying the electorate. And the legal prohibition of corporate campaign contributions now meant, moreover, that less money was available for pre-election entertainment, transportation to the polls, and bribes.[50]

---

of Corporate Power (Cambridge, Mass., 1963), 257, 259. The manner in which the states copied each other's legislation in this period is a subject deserving of study; for a suggestive approach, see Jack L. Walker, "The Diffusion of Innovations among the American States," *APSR*, 63 (1969): 880–99.

[49]Among the best accounts of this transformation in policy are Herbert Croly, *Marcus Alonzo Hanna: His Life and Work* (New York, 1912), 465–79; Hurst, *Law and the Conditions of Freedom*, 71–108; and Wiebe, *The Search for Order, 1877–1920*, 164–95.

[50]The causes of the decline in party voting have been the subject of considerable debate and disagreement among political scientists and historians in recent years. Walter Dean Burnham began the controversy when he first described the early-twentieth-century changes in voting behavior and explained them by suggesting that an antipartisan industrial elite had captured the political system after the realignment of the 1890s; "Changing Shape of the American Political Universe." Jerrold G. Rusk and Philip E. Converse responded by contending that legal-institutional factors could better account for the behavioral changes that Burnham had observed; Rusk, "The Effect of the Australian Ballot Reform on Split Ticket Voting"; and Converse, "Change in the American Electorate," in Angus Campbell and Philip E. Converse, eds., *The Human Meaning of Social Change* (New York, 1972), 263–337. All three political scientists carried the debate forward—and all withdrew a bit from their original positions—in the September 1974 issue of the *American Political Science Review*. At present, the weight of developing evidence seems to indicate that, while new election laws alone cannot explain the voters' changed behavior, Burnham's

While the party organizations were thus weakened, they were also more firmly embedded in the legal machinery of elections than ever before. In many states the direct primary completed a series of new election laws (beginning with the Australian ballot in the late 1880s and early 1890s) that gave the parties official status as nominating bodies, regulated their practices, and converted them into durable, official bureaucracies. Less popular now but also more respectable, the party organizations surrendered to state regulation and relinquished much of their ability to express community opinion in return for legal guarantees that they alone would be permanently certified to place nominees on the official ballot.[51]

Interest organizations took over much of the parties' old job of articulating popular demands and pressing them upon the government. More exclusive and single-minded than parties, the new organizations became regular elements of the polity. Their right to represent their members before the government's new boards and agencies received implicit recognition, and, indeed, the commissions in some cases became captives of the groups they were supposed to regulate. The result was a fairly drastic transformation of the rules of political participation: who could compete, the kinds of resources required, and the rewards of participation all changed. These developments were not brand new in the first years of the twentieth century, but, like the contemporaneous changes in government policy, they derived impressive, decisive confirmation from the political upheaval that occurred between 1905 and 1908.

Political and governmental changes thus followed upon the discovery that business corrupts politics. And Americans of the day explicitly linked the two developments: the reforms adopted in 1907–08 were to remedy the ills uncovered in 1905–06. But these chronological and rhetorical connections between discovery and reform do not fully explain the relationship between them. Why, having paid relatively little heed to similar charges before, did people now take such strong actions in response to the disclosures? Why, moreover, did the perception of wrongdoing precipitate the particular pattern of responses that it did—namely, the triumph of bureaucracy and organization? Of most importance, what distinctive effects did the discovery of corruption have upon the final outcome of the crisis?

By 1905 a political explosion of some sort was likely, due to the accumulated frustrations people felt about the government's failure to deal with the problems of industrialization. So combustible were the elements present that another spark besides the discovery of politico-business corruption might well have ignited them. But the recognition of such corruption was an especially effective torch. Upon close analysis, its ignition of the volatile political mass is unsurprising. The accusations made in 1905–06 were serious, widespread, and full of damaging information; they explained the actual corrupt process behind a danger that Americans had historically worried about, if not always responded to with vigor; they linked in dark scandal the two main villains—party bosses and big businessmen—already on the American scene; they inherently discredited the existing structure of economic policy based on the distribution of privileges; and they dramatically sug-

notion of an elite takeover after 1896 is also inadequate to account for what happened; McCormick, *From Realignment to Reform*, chap. 9. What I am suggesting here is that the shock given to party politics by the awakening of 1905–06 played an important part in solidifying the new tendencies toward lower rates of voter participation and higher levels of ticket splitting. On the relative scarcity of campaign funds in the election of 1908, see Pollock, *Party Campaign Funds*, 37, 66–67; Overacker, *Money in Elections*, 234–38; and Brooks, *Corruption in American Politics and Life*, 234–35.

[51]Peter H. Argersinger, " 'A Place on the Ballot': Fusion Politics and Antifusion Laws," *AHR*, 85 (1980): 287–306; Merriam and Overacker, *Primary Elections*; and William Mills Ivins, *On the Electoral System of the State of New York* (Albany, 1906).

gested the necessity for new kinds of politics and government. That businessmen systematically corrupted politics was incendiary knowledge; given the circumstances of 1905, it could hardly have failed to set off an explosion.

The organizational results that followed, however, seem less inevitable. There were, after all, several other known ways of curtailing corruption besides expert regulation and administration. For one, there was the continued reliance on direct legislative action against the corruption of politics by businessmen. The lobbying, anti–free pass, and campaign-contribution measures of 1907–08 exemplified this approach. So did the extension of legislative controls over the offending corporations. Such measures were familiar, but obviously they were considered inadequate to the crisis at hand. A second approach, favored by Edward Alsworth Ross and later by Woodrow Wilson, was to hold business leaders personally responsible for their "sins" and to punish them accordingly. There were a few attempts to bring individuals to justice, but, because of the inadequacy of the criminal statutes, the skill of high-priced lawyers, and the public's lack of appetite for personal vendettas, few sinners were jailed. Finally, there were proposals for large structural solutions changing the political and economic environment so that the old corrupt practices became impossible. Some men, like Frederic C. Howe, still advocated the single tax and the abolition of all privileges granted by government.[52] Many more believed in the municipal ownership of public utilities. Hundreds of thousands (to judge from election returns) favored socialist solutions, but most Americans did not. In their response to politico-business corruption, they went beyond existing legislative remedies and avoided the temptation to personalize all the blame, but they fell short of wanting socialism, short even of accepting the single tax.

Regulation and administration represented a fourth available approach. Well before the discoveries of 1905–06, groups who stood to benefit from governmental control of utility and transportation corporations had placed strong regulatory proposals on the political agendas of the states and the nation. In other policy areas, the proponents of an administrative approach had not advanced that far prior to 1905–06, but theirs was a large and growing movement, supported—as recent historians have shown—by many different groups for varied, often contradictory, reasons.[53] The popular awakening to corruption increased the opportunity of these groups to obtain enactment of their measures. Where their proposals met the particular political needs of 1905–08, they succeeded most quickly. Regulation by commissions seemed to be an effective way to halt corruption by transferring the responsibility for business-government relations from party bosses and legislators to impartial experts. That approach also possessed the additional political advantages of appearing sane and moderate, of meeting consumer demands for government protection, and, above all, of being sufficiently malleable that a diversity of groups could be induced to anticipate favorable results from the new policies.[54]

[52]Ross, *Sin and Society: An Analysis of Latter-Day Iniquity* (Boston, 1907); John M. Blum, *Woodrow Wilson and the Politics of Morality* (Boston, 1956); John B. Roberts, "The Real Cause of Municipal Corruption," in Clinton Rogers Woodruff, ed., *Proceedings of the New York Conference for Good City Government*, National Municipal League publication (Philadelphia, 1905), 148–53; and Howe, *Privilege and Democracy in America*.

[53]For an astute analysis of which groups favored and which groups opposed federal railroad legislation, see Richard H. K. Victor, "Businessmen and the Political Economy: The Railroad Rate Controversy of 1905," *JAH*, 64 (1977): 47–66; and, for an excellent survey of the literature on regulation, see Thomas K. McCraw, "Regulation in America: A Review Article," *Business History Review*, 49 (1975): 159–83. The best account of the emergence of administrative ideas is, of course, Wiebe, *The Search for Order, 1877–1920*, 133–95.

[54]On the adaptability of administrative government, see Otis L. Graham, Jr., *The Great Campaigns: Reform and War in*

In consequence, the passions of 1905–06 added support to an existing movement toward regulation and administration, enormously speeded it up, shaped the timing and form of its victory, and probably made the organizational revolution more complete—certainly more sudden—than it otherwise would have been. These accomplishments alone must make the discovery of corruption pivotal in any adequate interpretation of progressivism. But the awakening did more than hurry along a movement that already possessed formidable political strength and would probably have triumphed eventually even without the events of 1905–06. By pushing the political process toward so quick a resolution of the long-standing crisis over industrialism, the passions of those years caused the outcome to be more conservative than it otherwise might have been. This is the ultimate irony of the discovery that business corrupts politics.

Muckraking accounts of politico-business evils suggest one reason for the discovery's conservative impact. Full of facts and revelations, these writings were also dangerously devoid of effective solutions. Charles E. Russell's *Lawless Wealth* (1908)—the title itself epitomizes the perceptions of 1905–06—illustrates the flaw. Published originally in *Everybody's Magazine* under the accusatory title, "Where Did You Get It, Gentlemen?," the book recounts numerous instances of riches obtained through the corruption of politics, but, in its closing pages, merely suggests that citizens recognize the evils and be determined to stop them. This reliance on trying to change how people felt (to "shame" them, in Steffens's phrase) was characteristic of muckraking and of the exposures of 1905–06. One can admire the the muckrakers' reporting, can even accept David P. Thelen's judgment that their writing "contained at least as deep a moral revulsion toward capitalism and profit as did more orthodox forms of Marxism," yet can still feel that their proposed remedy was superficial. Because the perception of politico-business corruption carried no far-reaching solutions of its own or genuine economic grievances, but only a desire to clean up politics and government, the passions of 1905–06 were easily diverted to the support of other people's remedies, especially administrative answers. Had the muckrakers and their local imitators penetrated more deeply into the way that business operated and its real relationship to government, popular emotions might not have been so readily mobilized in support of regulatory and administrative agencies that business interests could often dominate. At the very least, there might have been a more determined effort to prevent the supervised corporations themselves from shaping the details of regulatory legislation. Thus, for all of their radical implications, the passions of 1905–06 dulled the capacity of ordinary people to get reforms in their own interest.[55]

The circumstances in which the discovery of corruption became a political force also assist in explaining its conservatism. The passions of 1905–06 were primarily expressed in state, rather than local or national, politics. Indeed, those passions often served to shift the focus of reform from the cities to the state capitals. There—in Albany, or Madison, or Sacramento—the remedies were worked out in relative isolation from the local, insurgent forces that had in many cases originally called attention to the evils. Usually the policy consequences were more favorable to large business interests than local solutions would have been. State utility boards, for example, which had always been considered more conservative in their policies than comparable local commissions, now took the regulatory power away from cities and foreclosed experimentation with such alternatives

America, 1900–1928 (Englewood Cliffs, N.J., 1971), 50–51; and Wiebe, *The Search for Order, 1877–1920*, 222–23, 302.

[55]Russell, *Lawless Wealth: The Origin of Some Great American Fortunes* (New York, 1908), 30–35, 52–55, 274–79; and Thelen, "Lincoln Steffens and the Muckrakers: A Review Essay," *Wisconsin Magazine of History*, 58 (1975): 316.

as municipal ownership or popularly chosen regulatory boards. In gaining a statewide hearing for reform, the accusations of politico-business corruption actually increased the likelihood that conservative solutions would be adopted.[56]

Considering the intensity of the feelings aroused in 1905 and 1906 ("the wrath of thousands of private citizens . . . is at white heat over the disclosures," declared a Rochester newspaper) and the catalytic political role they played, the awakened opposition to corruption was surprisingly short-lived. As early as 1907 and 1908, the years of the most significant state legislative responses to the discovery, the messages of the governors began to exhibit a more stylized, less passionate way of describing politico-business wrongdoing. Now the governors emphasized remedies rather than abuses, and most seemed confident that the remedies would work. Criticism of business influence in government continued to be a staple of political rhetoric throughout the Progressive era, but it ceased to have the intensity it did in 1905–06. In place of the burning attack on corruption, politicians offered advanced progressive programs, including further regulation and election-law reforms.[57] The deep concern with business corruption of politics and government thus waned. It had stirred people to consciousness of wrongdoing, crystallized their discontent with existing policies, and pointed toward concrete solutions for the ills of industrialism. But it had not sustained the more radical, antibusiness possibilities suggested by the discoveries of 1905–06.

Indeed, the passions of those years probably weakened the insurgent, democratic qualities of the ensuing political transformation and strengthened its bureaucratic aspects. This result was ironical, but its causes were not conspiratorial. They lay instead in the tendency—shared by the muckrakers and their audience—to accept remedies unequal to the problems at hand and in political circumstances that isolated insurgents from decision making. Once the changes in policy were under way after 1906, those organized groups whose interests were most directly affected entered the fray, jockeyed for position, and heavily shaped the outcomes. We do not yet know enough about how this happened, but studies such as Stanley P. Caine's examination of railroad regulation in Wisconsin suggest how difficult it was to translate popular concern on an "issue" into details of a law.[58] It is hardly surprising that, as regulation and administration became accepted public functions, the affected interests exerted much more influence on policy than did those who cared most passionately about restoring clean government.

But the failure to pursue antibusiness policies does not mean the outcry against corruption was either insincere or irrelevant. Quite the contrary. It was sufficiently genuine and widespread to dominate the nation's public life in 1905 and 1906 and to play a decisive part in bringing about the transformation of American politics and government. Political changes do

[56]Nord, "The Experts versus the Experts"; and Thelen, *Robert M. La Follette and the Insurgent Spirit*, 50–51.

[57]Rochester *Democrat and Chronicle*, October 18, 1905; and New York State Library, *Digest of Governors' Messages, 1907, 1908*. In a number of states where politico-business corruption had been an issue in the party platforms around 1906, the platforms were silent on the subject by 1910.

[58]Caine, *The Myth of a Progressive Reform: Railroad Regulation in Wisconsin, 1903–1910* (Madison, Wisc., 1970), 70. Also see Mansel G. Blackford, *The Politics of Business in California, 1890–1920* (Columbus, Ohio, 1977); Bruce W. Dearstyne, "Regulation in the Progressive Era: The New York Public Service Commission," *New York History*, 58 (1977): 331–47; and McCraw, "Regulation in America." These and other studies cast considerable doubt on the applicability at the state level of Gabriel Kolko's interpretation of regulatory legislation; for that position, see his *The Triumph of Conservatism*. Commonly, the affected interests opposed state regulation until its passage became inevitable, at which point they entered the contest in order to influence the details of the law. Businessmen often had considerable, but not complete, success in helping shape such legislation, and they frequently found it beneficial in practice.

not, of course, embrace everything that is meant by progressivism. Nor was the discovery that business corrupts politics the only catalytic agent at work; certainly the rise of consumer discontent with utility and transportation corporations and the vigorous impetus toward new policies given by Theodore Roosevelt during his second term as president played complementary roles. But the awakening to corruption—as it was newly understood—provided an essential dynamic, pushing the states and the nation toward what many of its leading men and women considered progressive reform.

The organizational thesis sheds much light on the values and methods of those who succeeded in dominating the new types of politics and government but very little on the political circumstances in which they came forward. Robert H. Wiebe, in particular, has downplayed key aspects of the political context, including the outcry against corruption. Local uprisings against the alliance of bosses and businessmen, Wiebe has stated, "lay outside the mainstream of progressivism"; measures instituting the direct primary and curtailing the political influence of business were "old-fashioned reform."[59] Yet those local crusades, by spreading the dynamic perception that business corrupts politics, created a popular demand for the regulatory and administrative measures that Wiebe has claimed are characteristic of true progressivism; and those "old-fashioned" laws were enacted amidst the same political furor that produced the stunningly rapid bureaucratic triumph whose significance for twentieth-century America Wiebe has explained so convincingly. What the organizational thesis mainly lacks is the sense that political action is open-ended and unpredictable. Consequences are often unexpected, outcomes surprising when matched against origins. While it is misleading, as Samuel P. Hays has said, to interpret progressivism solely on the basis of its antibusiness ideology, it is equally misleading to fail to appreciate that reform gained decisive initial strength from ideas and feelings that were not able to sustain the movement in the end.[60] The farsighted organizers from business and the professions thus gained the opportunity to complete a political transformation that had been begun by people who were momentarily shocked into action but who stopped far short of pursuing the full implications of their discovery.

[59]Wiebe, *The Search for Order, 1877–1920*, 172, 180.

[60]Hays, "The Politics of Reform in Municipal Government."

V

Twentieth-Century Media as Cultural Artifacts

Although changes in communication styles and technologies have always generated public interest in the media, the social and political environment of the 1920s and 1930s engendered increased speculation about the role of communication in cultural change. The rapid technological changes of the late nineteenth century, both in the periodical industry and in society at large, caused critics to question how cultural values could be preserved within an urbanizing, industrializing country. With the advent of radio in the first decade of the twentieth century, critics expressed optimism that rapid, comprehensive communication would promote a sense of community, but simultaneously recognized that rapid change might create a sense of lost values. "By the time we reach the 1920s," wrote Warren Susman, "there is a sharpening and a focusing on the issue of culture and communications. Significant doubts flourish amid significant hopes. But all agree that there was a new world and that communications in large part had helped make it."[1] James W. Carey, analyzing the impact of the telegraph, wrote in 1983 that it had created new social interactions, a new conceptual system, new forms of language, and a new structure of social relations.[2]

The analysis of the impact of communication on the social structure dates as far back as the 1830s, when critics discussed the press's negative impact on public morals, but not until the 1890s did critics begin "the first comprehensive reckoning with modern communication in toto as a force in the social process."[3] The first studies reflected the optimism of progressive thought and connected the concept of communication to that of community. Charles Horton Cooley, John Dewey, and Robert Park "construed modern communication essentially as an agent for restoring a broad moral and political consensus to America, a consensus they believed to have been threatened by the wrenching disruptions of the nineteenth century: industrialization, urbanization and immigration."[4] Cooley argued that modern communication held promise for the possibility of a "truly democratic community," whereas Dewey noted that there was "more than a verbal tie between the words common, community, and communication. Men live in a community in virtue of the things they have in common; and communication is the way in which they come to possess things in common."[5] Park is probably best known for his work on the foreign-language press. He argued that such newspapers helped to establish reading habits among those who had not read before, to preserve "ethnic cultures," and to breed "new loyalties from the old heritages."[6]

Optimism pervaded the work of Cooley, Dewey, and Park, which was based on an assumption that communication could promote true unity in a technological society, although all three commented on the possibility that new forms of media could challenge traditional cultural beliefs. Nevertheless, they expressed the hope that the diffusion of knowledge through the media would improve the level of public discourse.[7] Susman's description of the cultural milieu of the 1920s is less sanguine. He notes that fascination with the concept of community defined in terms of a process of communication surged during the decade, but he describes the period as "a world come apart, a social order divided and confused."[8] A changing culture paved the way for the advent of advertising as the underlying financial structure of media. The conflict between an older culture, which demanded character, and a postcommunications revolution culture, which demanded personality and "emphasized being liked and admired," suggested a profound social and culture shift, wrote Susman.[9]

The articles included here do not overtly discuss the issues of culture and communication but rather depict a theme of amelioration between "old" and "new" styles. These articles reflect the role of the professional news organization, the foreign-language newspaper, the radio and its subsequent regulatory rhetoric, and advertising in adapting to a rapidly changing culture, community, and communications environment. Within each article are strains of tension common to the 1920s, with the concurrent strains of accommodation, resistance, and acculturation.

Maurine Beasley, in "The Women's National Press Club: Case Study of Professional Aspirations" (the club was organized in 1919), documents the efforts of women to organize to "enhance their self-images and advance the idea that they were true professionals" in a male-dominated world that either snubbed women or welcomed them only on the periphery. She connects the organizational efforts to the outgrowth of the women's club movement of the nineteenth century as well as to the suffrage drive. The organization changed its name in 1970 and admitted men, but not until a merger with the National Press Club in 1985 did the women's organization relinquish its female identity. Through the years the women's club organized events that heralded women's intellectual and occupational accomplishments and that challenged the prevailing cultural assumption that only men were capable of being journalistic professionals.

Jerzy Zubrzycki's article, "The Role of the Foreign-Language Press in Migrant Integration," does not focus particularly on the 1920s, but rather concentrates on immigration as experienced by a variety of migrants and host countries through the nineteenth and twentieth centuries. He describes the foreign-language press as bringing to immigrants news of the world, the home country, and group life and interests. He says that foreign-language newspapers educate the immigrants for citizenship and inculcate respect for the host country, while maintaining social cohesion of the immigrant group. The newspapers therefore, become important cultural bridges.

Roland Marchand's article, "Two Legendary Campaigns," reflects the tensions depicted in advertising copy and illustrations in the 1920s and describes advertising men as "missionaries of modernity." Products became palliatives for anxious citizens, Marchand writes. The leading man in advertising copy, he contends, is the businessman subject to stress, whereas the leading woman is the emotional figure who assumes responsibility for her husband's and her children's success. She alone, with the help of modern products, can relieve her husband's anxiety and improve her children's classroom performance. As the primary household purchaser, she is the direct target of advertising copy. Marchand brilliantly illuminates advertising themes of the decade that capitalize on the fears and hopes of modernization on the march.

Of all the articles reprinted here, "We May Hear Too Much: American Sensibility and the Response to Radio, 1919–1924," Catherine L. Covert's analysis of radio's "startling impact on sensibility," perhaps most directly addresses the issues of loss and progress. Concentrating on the years between 1919 and 1924, before radio becomes a corporate entity, Covert notes the euphoria in public anticipation of the medium, but also the ominous and foreboding messages that accompanied the excitement. The language that science inherited in discussing technological innovation such as the radio "bore religious or spiritual connotations," Covert suggests. The technological comparison was the telephone, and against the private nature of telephone communication early radio seemed markedly deficient. Throughout the period, as radio moved from the amateur operator in the garage to the family in the living room, the equipment was transformed from "a laboratory apparatus into a piece of furniture." Accompanying the transformation was a sense of listening, consuming, and domestication that also encouraged a feeling of loss of mastery. The active amateur operator—usually male—was turned into a passive recipient. Ambiguities were abundant, with a new reality of immediately experiencing a live event that was taking place miles away. Although the listener was in the company of millions, she also was solitary in her participation. Optimists viewed radio as fostering international and national ties, enhancing the democratic process, reviving family unity, and creating a new form of social control. Those not so convinced of radio's positive effects feared the separation of the populace from legal and political authority, the solitary effects of radio listening versus participation, and the negative effects of undiscriminating program content.

The last article in this section—the second that focuses on radio—extends the discussion to the creation of the Federal Radio Commission in 1927. In "The Public Debate About Broadcasting in the Twenties: An Interpretive History," Mary S. Mander characterizes the public debate about radio as one that borrowed from familiar concepts of the past to harness the unfamiliar. She notes the use of words such as " traffic cop" and "air paths" to connote the similarities between broadcast and transportation; the familiar concepts of public utilities and newspapers provided other terminology for the new phenomenon. Radio should be operated in the "public interest, convenience or necessity," read the Radio Act of 1927; newspaper models of private ownership that provided propaganda-free information became models for broadcast financing.

Endnotes

1. Warren Susman, "Culture and Communications," in *Culture as History* (New York: Pantheon Books, 1984), 260.

2. James W. Carey, "Reconceiving 'Mass' and 'Media,'' in *Communication as Culture* (Boston: Unwin Hyman, 1989), 70. This article originally appeared in *Prospects: The Annual of the American Studies Association*, vol. 8 (Cambridge: Cambridge University Press, 1983).

3. For analysis of criticism of the nineteenth-century press, see Hazel Dicken-Garcia, *Journalistic Standards in Nineteenth-Century America* (Madison: University of Wisconsin Press, 1989). For quotation, see Daniel Czitrom, *Media and the American Mind: From Morse to McLuhan* (Chapel Hill: University of North Carolina Press, 1982), 91.

4. Czitrom, 91.

5. Czitrom, 98–99; John Dewey, *Democracy and Education* (New York: Macmillan Co., 1915), 4, cited in Czitrom, 108.

6. Czitrom, p. 117. Park quotation from Robert Park, *The Immigrant Press and Its Control* (New York: Harper and Brothers, 1922), 468, cited in Czitrom, 117.

7. Czitrom, pp. 119–120.

8. Susman, 121.

9. Susman, xxii.

The Women's National Press Club: Case Study of Professional Aspirations

Maurine Beasley

In the fall of 1919, a group of independent minded women met in Washington, D.C., to further two goals: the elevation of women within their field and the advancement of their own careers by formal and informal means. On the surface their intent seemed rather modest—to form a club for women journalists and publicists (as practitioners of public relations then were called). Underlying the endeavor, however, lay motives that reflected the striving of women journalists for a sense of professional identification in the early 20th Century.

Their organizational meeting, which took place on September 27, 1919, led to the founding of the Women's National Press Club, a group that remained in existence until 1971. For half a century, the club provided a forum for members to address the specific problem of being women within a male-dominated occupation in which they were only marginally welcome. It offered more than a platform for protest because it facilitated a sense of solidarity that allowed members to enhance their self-images and advance the idea that they were true professionals. In this way it served to influence both their journalistic practices and perceptions of their own worth and dignity.To understand the importance of the organization, it is necessary to understand the background of its origin, its leadership and philosophy and the reasons for its ending.

Background

By the year 1919 press clubs in major cities were accepted features of the American journalistic scene. Their success stemmed from the desire of journalists to join together socially to seek both camaraderie and public approval of their occupation. Although journalists lacked the prestige of lawyers and doctors, who had to meet rigid educational and certification standards, the establishment of journalism schools and societies signified attempts by journalists themselves to elevate their field and to make it as respectable in the eyes of the public as the professions of medicine and law.[1] In their clubs they sought recognition of the importance of their roles. For example, the Chicago Press Club, founded in 1880, sought to integrate journalists into the power structure of the city by developing contacts with influential individuals as part of the club's activities.[2]

Women were excluded from the mainstream press clubs, often known for their bars and locker-room atmosphere, as a matter of course. Yet this did not stop them from forming their own associations, which were outgrowths of the women's club movement of the 19th Century that brought women together for both educational and social purposes. Significantly, Sorosis, the association that led the women's study club movement, was founded by Jane Cunningham Croly. A journalist who wrote fashion and other articles for women under the name "Jennie June," she started Sorosis in New York in 1868 after she was barred from a dinner given by the New York Press Club in honor of Charles Dickens.[3]

Segregated as the men's and women's clubs were, both represented aspects of an expanding climate for journalists at the start of the 20th Century. Journalism, which had started as a craft allied to printing, emerged as one of the new white-collar, middle-class occupations that advertised their technical competence and civic virtue. These occupations afforded opportunities to provide the specialized services necessary for a nation committed to the ideal of material progress. In the 30-year period before 1900, for example, the number of editors and journalists tripled while the number of dentists quadrupled and the number of architects quintupled.[4]

An astounding growth in publications created new opportunites for women journalists. At the start of the 20th Century, women's magazines like *Ladies' Home Journal, McCall's, Pictorial Review* and *Woman's Home Companion* achieved some of the top circulations among all American magazines. In 1919 *Ladies' Home Journal,* for instance, attained a circulation of 2 million and was the most valuable monthly magazine property in the world.[5] Newspapers expanded enormously, with the average circulation of dailies doubling in the period from 1892 to 1914.[6] This was due partly to efforts to gain new readers by instituting women's and society pages.[7] While male editors remained in firm control, women were hired to write material aimed at other women and housed in women's departments physically isolated from the offices used by men. Occasionally one or two women of exceptional tact and ability were allowed to work on city staffs with male journalists, but this was rare.[8]

Therefore clubs exercised particular importance in the lives of women journalists by providing an outlet for their professional development. By interacting with each other in club settings, the women were able to influence each other's aspirations and achievements. According to experts on professionalization, personal interaction is likely to affect behavior.[9]

In Washington, D.C., both male and female journalists tried to organize clubs before the turn of the century. In 1883 male reporters started a Washington Press Club that met in the back rooms of the *Baltimore American*'s office. It soon dwindled away in "unpaid bar bills" and "rent long in arrears," according to one account.[10] Two years later the more durable Gridiron Club, still a Washington fixture known for annual dinners that "roast" the President, came into existence. With membership limited to a select group of newspapermen, the Gridiron failed to serve the purpose of a general reporters' club. In 1891 a National Capital Press Club was started but soon ran into financial difficulties, prompting the auction of its assets—a bar, deep leather chairs, cuspidors and late-Victorian wall hangings.[11]

Women journalists predated men in their attempt to set up a formal club. On July 10, 1882, the Woman's National Press Association was started, with Emily Edson Briggs, a Washington correspondent who wrote under the pen name of "Olivia," as the first president. The group joined the National Federation of Women's Clubs in 1893 and started the D.C. Federation of Women's Clubs the following year. In 1895 it had 130 members doing literary or journalistic work and headquarters in Willard's Hotel where it welcomed visiting press women.[12]

A second organization of women journalists was begun in Washington, D.C. in 1897—the League of American Pen Women, later to become the National League of American Pen Women that continues today. The founders were Marion Longfellow O'Donoghue, niece of Henry Wadsworth Longfellow and a prolific writer of prose and poetry for Boston and Washington newspapers, Margaret Sullivan Burke, one of the few women to be accredited to the Congressional Press Gallery as a telegraphic correspondent in the 19th Century, and Anna Sanborn Hamilton, social editor of the *Washington Post.* Unlike press clubs, however, the league included women artists, dramatists, lecturers and composers as well as journalists and writers.[13]

The first successful general club for male Washington reporters did not get under way until 1908. In May of that year a group of newspapermen, aided by the chief of police, heaved a piano, bar, chairs and tables up the stairs to an apartment over a jewelry store and unceremoniously opened the doors of the National Press Club in downtown Washington. This time the bar was operated on a cash-only basis and the club survived.[14]

Sixty years later the club, still in the heart of the capital, has become a venerable institution in American journalism, visited by presidents, foreign dignitaries and virtually every public figure of importance. Through the years it has admitted members who are non-journalists, including lobbyists and representatives of trade associations. But until 1971 it refused to accept women, thereby setting the stage for the Women's National Press Club.

By the post-World War I era the Woman's National Press Association had failed to recruit new members and faded from the scene. It was replaced by a lively new group, the Women's National Press Club. In 1922 Mary S. Lockwood, a founder of the Daughters of the American Revolution and long-time president of the Woman's National Press Association, died at the age of 93.[15] The vice-president, Grace Porter Hopkins, did not hold a meeting and placed the association's records in a bank, making a notation, "most of the members having passed away."[16] Hopkins was a charter member of the Women's National Press Club, identified on the club rolls as a special writer.

Partly an outgrowth of the campaign for woman suffrage, the Women's National Press Club had six founders, three of whom were publicists for the National Woman's Party, the militant arm of the suffrage movement, and three of whom were newspaperwomen. The publicists were Florence Brewer Boeckel, Eleanor Taylor Marsh Nelson and Alice Gram Robinson. The newspaperwomen were Cora Rigby, chief of the Washington bureau of the *Christian Science Monitor* and the most distinguished woman journalist in Washington, Carolyn Vance Bell, a syndicated feature writer for the Newspaper Enterprise Association, and Elizabeth King (later Stokes), a reporter for the *New York Evening Post.*[17]

As Bell recalled years later, "The campaign to give women the vote was closely entwined with the beginning of the WNPC." After the passage of the suffrage amendment, Boeckel, Nelson and Robinson were "looking around for new worlds to conquer, establishing a partnership for doing what we call today 'public relations,'" Bell continued. "The idea of starting a woman's press club where they could peddle their wares enthused them." Bell recollected, however, that she herself suggested the idea of the press club to the publicists, who handled news for women's groups like the Visiting Nurses Association.[18] Robinson remembered late in life that the club began because "we needed to keep in close touch with the newspaper women, of course. It was good business for us and also they were our friends."[19]

The initial September meeting took place at the office of the Boeckel-Nelson-Robinson public relations firm.[20] About 40 women attended but only 28 joined, perhaps because some were unwilling to associate with publicity writers. As Vylla Poe, a newspaperwoman who later joined the club, put it, "We were suffragists ourselves and had nothing against the causes represented. Just wanted it to be more professional."[21] Bell herself did not go to the meeting because she was pregnant. "It was considered shameful for a woman to show herself in public when there was the slightest evidence of the blessed state," she recalled.[22]

The letter of invitation, signed by all of the founders except Robinson, went out to women in government publicity bureaus, news bureaus and local newspapers. The letter said nothing about efforts to bring together journalists and publicists, stating instead that "it might be both pleasant and profitable for the newspaper and magazine women of Washington to have some means of getting together in informal and irregular fashion."[23] It went on to say meetings would provide "an opportunity to hear more intimately than we otherwise could, prominent men and women who come to Washington."[24]

Such wording implied a protest against the discriminatory practices of the National Press Club, which refused to allow women to cover leading figures who spoke there. Shortly after the organizational meeting, for example, the Prince of Wales appeared at the National Press Club but no women reporters were invited to meet him.[25] As Bell recalled, "The [women's] club came into being because of the climate of the day with women demanding their rights on all sides."[26]

At the club's first luncheon-business meeting, held November 6, 1919, at a Washington restaurant, Rigby was chosen honorary president and *New York Times* correspondent Lily Lykes Rowe (later Shepard) active president for the year. Rigby, who took over as sole president from 1920 to 1926, saw the organization as offering women journalists mutual support in the face of male hostility. She said it was needed to combat "the conspiracy of men to keep women off the newspapers—or at least to reduce their number, wages, and importance to a minimum."[27]

At the suggestion of Bell, the WNPC confined itself chiefly to luncheon gatherings, patterned after similar events at the National Press Club that featured speeches by persons in the news. The luncheon speakers fulfilled two objectives: They provided news stories for members and they helped elevate the status of women journalists by agreeing to meet with them. The first guest was Margaret Bondfield, a British labor expert, who spoke at a luncheon on November 13, 1919. Shortly thereafter the WNPC heard Lowell Thomas, who told, for the first time in Washington, of his experience with the legendary Lawrence of Arabia.[28]

Unlike their male counterparts in the National Press Club, who put up their own imposing edifice near the White House, the women were not able to acquire a clubhouse. The National Press Club building offered not only meeting rooms, a restaurant and bar but also prime office space rented by news organizations that employed some of the women. As Winifred Mallon, WNPC president in 1935 and a correspondent for the *New York Times*, wrote, the women's club was "rich only in its associations and interests" and lacked its own "home."[29] Over the years it met in many different places in Washington—at restaurants, tea rooms, hotels and headquarters of women's groups like the American Association of University Women.[30]

Leadership and Philosophy

From the beginning it was clear that membership conferred social prestige, giving the women journalists entree to persons and places of importance in Washington. According to Bell, the WNPC was put "on the map" after Warren G. Harding was elected President in 1920. His wife, Florence, invited club members to sail down the Potomac River on the presidential yacht and honored them with a White House tea.[31] But while the women enjoyed social gatherings, the club wanted officials to take it seriously. This was not always the case. For example, William G. McAdoo, secretary of the treasury under President Wilson, talked down to club members at a luncheon. "He treated us as if we were debutantes to be flattered by pretty compliments instead of giving us at least some shreds of information about current affairs," one member recalled years later. "He left us deflated and resentful."[32]

From its original 28 members, the club grew to about 100 members by the late 1930s, taking in the most respected women journalists in the capital. It made no attempt to draw all women involved in Washington journalism, some of whom worked part-time, but defined eligibility strictly: "The active membership shall consist of reputable publishers, editors, writers, correspondents and reporters, actively engaged in Washington on well established newspapers, press associations or periodicals including government publications, and deriving there from all or the greater part of their income."[33]

It offered membership to women doing publicity work only "if engaged in such work professionally and deriving the greater part of their incomes from it, and maintaining direct and regular contact with the press."[34] Members who discontinued newspaper or publicity work automatically became ineligible for active membership but could remain in the club as non-voting, non-active members pending reinstatement if they renewed their press connections.[35]

The task of denying membership to those who did not meet the club's standard of professionalism demanded diplomacy. From the beginning the membership committee had a difficult job—"one requiring members who are smart sharp, and with backbone & tact," Lily Lykes Shepard, the first club president, explained in the 1960s.[36] She noted it was the committee's task to say "gently but firmly to a member why it cannot recommend for membership her friend Susy Doaks on the basis of Susy Doaks' nice letters from her Congressman to the committee telling how she sends back such interesting social items about the Congressman's wife, which appear in the Bingville Bugle."[37]

In the early years members disagreed over membership requirements and the orientation of the club to general rather than social news. Even though two presidents, Sallie V. H. Pickett of the *Washington Star*, elected in 1928, and Ruth Jones of the *Washington Herald*, who succeeded Pickett, were society editors, the organization continued to emphasize luncheons with serious speakers instead of social occasions. Socially prominent women sometimes attended these events as guests of society reporters who pressed to have the women admitted as lay members to foster relationships with their news sources. The majority of the group disagreed, holding that the club should remain an organization of journalists.[38]

In 1932 a group of society reporters withdrew and organized a rival Newspaper Women's Club. Unlike the WNPC, it offered associate membership to prominent women featured in women's and society sections. It also established an honorary membership category for women well known either in their own right or through their husbands. Co-founded by Margaret Hart and Katharine M. Brooks, both society reporters for the *Washington Star*, the new group staged parties and charitable benefits. It eventually purchased a clubhouse (perhaps a reason why the group remains in existence today as the American News Women's Club). In spite of initial hostility, the clubs eventually had considerable overlapping membership.[39]

The WNPC remained the dominant group exemplifying journalistic competence and dedication. Its roll served as a "Who's Who" of Washington women journalists and many of its presidents, in particular, qualified for the hard-won title of "front page girl." This was the name given to newspaper women of the period allowed the rare privilege of covering the same hard news as men—politics, courts, public affairs and other front-page topics—even though they were paid less. Among the presidents were Genevieve Forbes Herrick (1933), a correspondent for the *Chicago Tribune*, Doris Fleeson (1937), a political columnist for the *New York Daily News*, Ruby Black (1939) and Esther Van Wagoner Tufty (1941), both of whom operated their own news bureaus.[40] Women in publicity work were barred from serving as president and accepted only on the basis of one to every two journalists admitted so that the club would maintain its news orientation.[41]

Club members benefitted from the interest in women journalists taken by Eleanor Roosevelt as first lady from 1933 to 1945. Realizing that newspaperwomen needed to obtain news that male competitors could not get in order to keep employed during the Depression, Roosevelt held about 350 press conferences for women only during her White House years, coming in contact with almost all the WNPC members. Roosevelt herself became a member in 1938 on the basis of her daily syndicated, diary-like column, "My Day." She was proposed for membership by Fleeson and seconded by Black and Bess Furman, an Associated Press reporter who later moved to the *New York Times*.[42]

The club divided on the issue of allowing the President's wife to join. Some members thought it was wrong to admit a woman who did not earn her living by writing, even though Roosevelt earned a substantial sum from the column, which ran in hundreds of newspapers. Black, who had become the first woman to be hired by United Press because of Roosevelt's insistence that women only be assigned to cover her, was forced to deny "in all-inclusive detail and with final and definite emphasis that I am your ghost [writer] for 'My Day,'" she told the first lady.[43] Nine votes were cast against Roosevelt's admission, one of the few, if not the only time, when the club did not adhere to its strict requirements for membership.[44]

Roosevelt demonstrated her interest in the group in various ways. She annually invited its members to the Grid-Widow party she gave at the White House for women journalists and wives, who were not invited to the annual Gridiron Club dinner (which remained a stag affair until 1974 when women were admitted to the club). Roosevelt was a fixture at the WNPC's annual "stunt party,"—the group's version of a political show like the Gridiron performances.[45]

Stunt party activities were discontinued during World War II and then resumed until 1963, when the club decided to end them because they absorbed so much of the members' time. To stage them, the journalists devised elaborate dialogue, songs and costumes to satirize the Washington scene and invited outstanding figures in Washington to attend. Although humorous occasions, the stunt parties enhanced the professional stature of club members by giving them a showcase for political wisecracking and creativity. Over the years the audience grew in size and distinction to include presidents and their wives, as well as diplomats and members of Congress and the Cabinet.[46]

In later years Roosevelt was remembered by Furman, who became club president in 1945, as "a tall, distinguished, dramatic figure, who rose, year after year, from her seat at the head table . . . to reply to the ribbing she had just received in the dramatic skits of the club."[47] Although the stunt parties began in the Coolidge administration, Roosevelt was the first President's wife to attend them. She was so embarrassed by one skit at her initial stunt party in 1933 that she changed her plans to edit a magazine called "Babies, Just Babies." The skit poked fun at the inexperience of the new Franklin D. Roosevelt administration by opening with the following: "We are new to the business of running the show. We're babies, just babies, just babies." This mild ridicule influenced the first lady to cancel the magazine contract, according to her biographer.[48]

The first lady's patronage of the WNPC helped it to withstand the Depression, when some members struggled to find the money for the club events. In 1985 Lee Jaffee, correspondent for the *Wichita Beacon* in the 1930s, recalled when the WNPC's treasury had only $3.75. In those days paying $3.00 to attend a banquet was a hardship for some, she said.[49]

Outstanding women like Amelia Earhart, Ethel Barrymore and Rebecca West often spoke to the group, and sometimes guests, both male and female, appeared on an off-the-record basis. This led to friction over what could or could not appear in print as members sought to gain the maximum from their club activities by using them as the basis for news stories. In 1939 Black, as president, assured members that they could always write about the fact that a guest was there, who accompanied him or her, what clothing was worn, and "what impression" the speaker made.[50]

With male journalists in uniform, World War II enormously expanded opportunity for women to be hired in newspaper and government publicity jobs. Club programs boosted the war effort, featuring speeches by military and international leaders. Some members, like Ruth Cowan of the Associated Press, elected president in 1947, were war correspondents. As women covered beats ranging from the Pentagon to cooking, the WNPC drew new members.[51] The war also brought increased dependence on radio news, a fact recognized by the WNPC when it took in women broadcasters in 1944.[52]

By 1951 the WNPC had 335 members and a decade later more than 400, including most of the outstanding women journalists in the capital. But this number was only a fraction of the men who belonged to the National Press Club. In 1958, when it celebrated its golden anniversary, membership had grown from the original 192 to 4,673. Of this total, 3,703 were said by the club to be involved in newsgathering and transmitting, while the remainder included lobbyists and others interested in influencing the news.[53]

By this time the two clubs competed directly with each other. Luncheons and formal banquets of the WNPC, including annual dinners for members of Congress and inaugurations of club presidents, attracted the same famous figures who appeared at the National Press Club: Presidents Roosevelt, Truman, Eisenhower, Kennedy, Johnson and Nixon, as well as their wives, heads of foreign governments, ambassadors, visiting royalty, legislative leaders and candidates for high office. A merger of the groups seemed on the horizon, but it was not accomplished without a long struggle.

The Ending

During much of its existence the WNPC itself did not directly attack the sex discrimination that hampered women journalists, although a few prominent members did. In 1944, for example, Mary Hornaday, a *Christian Science Monitor* correspondent and former WNPC president, objected when women who belonged to the White House Correspondents' Association and paid the same dues as men were not allowed to attend the annual dinner. She also protested against the National Press Club ban on allowing women to "attend speeches given by officials to the press in the club's domain." But her protest was made as an individual, not as a representative of the club.[54]

Similarly, May Craig, a correspondent for Maine newspapers who was WNPC president in 1943, described herself as "hell fire on equal rights for women." Like Hornaday she protested against the all-male dinner of the White House Correspondents' Association, and in 1945 she finally won a fight to gain washroom facilities for women adjacent to the congressional press galleries. Yet she too waged her battles on an individual basis because the WNPC included some women who, at this point, did not think it "feminine" to directly seek equal rights.[55]

Following World War II the WNPC took a small step toward integration of the male and female press clubs. In 1946 it invited men for the first time to attend its annual dinner, at which President Truman was the guest of honor. Subsequently it opened its events to coverage by men. When Truman was honored, the club presented its first Woman of the Year award—to Lise Meitner, an atomic scientist.[56]

The WNPC swung back to a conventional

women's project in 1956 when it published a cookbook, "Who Says We Can't Cook!" This was followed by a sequel, "Second Helping," in 1962. The group continued to hold awards dinners for outstanding women until these events, like the stunt parties, were dropped as members turned their attention to issues involving equal access to the news.[57]

The question of admitting women to the National Press Club first arose in 1955 during a dispute over the application of a black journalist, Louis Lautier, a correspondent for the National Negro Press Association. His application came about the same time the WNPC took in its first black member, Alice A. Dunningan of the Associated Negro Press. Lautier said he wanted to join the National Press Club to attend luncheons at which world figures made speeches and answered questions. A minority of members opposed his application, but the majority voted for Lautier, contending the club was a professional, not a social, organization.[58]

Shortly thereafter 54 members of the National Press Club signed a petition to admit women. This movement expired quietly when the WNPC president, Elizabeth Carpenter, a *Houston Post* correspondent who later became press secretary to Lady Bird Johnson, told James J. Butler, sponsor of the petition, there was no substantial desire on the part of the women to become National Press Club members. At the same time an agreement was reached with the National Press Club to let "any member of the working press" cover luncheon addresses by newsworthy speakers. But newspaperwomen had to remain in the balcony overlooking the dining area and were not able to eat or drink.[59]

Carpenter's position reflected the opinion of WNPC members who thought it would not be dignified to join the National Press Club under the sponsorship of Butler because he had opposed the admittance of Lautier. Carpenter was quoted as saying, "we don't like being used by the Dixiecrats. . . . Why, our organization is much purer than the Press Club. We don't have morticians, patent attorneys and lobbyists on our rolls."[60]

Not surprisingly the balcony arrangement—which left the women at a decided disadvantage—did not work out well. In 1959 James C. Hagerty, press secretary to President Eisenhower, facetiously suggested a "summit meeting" between Helen Thomas of United Press International, WNPC president, and William H. Lawrence of the *New York Times*, who headed the National Press Club, "to blueprint a plan for an auditorium that has no balcony." His remark came after Soviet Premier Nikita S. Khrushchev insisted that the newswomen be allowed to eat with their male counterparts when he spoke at the National Press Club. Lawrence reluctantly agreed, saying "that's the way the Russians wanted it." After that event women were returned to the balcony, where space was limited and they could not hear well or ask questions.[61]

The WNPC grew increasingly militant during the Kennedy years. In 1962 newswomen sought support from President Kennedy in protest against relegation to the balcony during a speech by Indian Prime Minister Jawaharlal Nehru. Answering a question from Sarah McClendon, a correspondent for Texas newspapers, Kennedy commented at a press conference, "I will say that in my judgment, that when an official visitor comes to speak to the Press Club that all working reporters should be permitted in on a basis of equality." In response Bonnie Angelo, a *Time* magazine correspondent and WNPC president, said her organization's complaint was less with the National Press Club than the U.S. State Department for booking dignitaries "in a place that discriminates against women reporters." From this comment it appeared the women's group still was not willing to directly attack the National Press Club.[62]

The dispute intensified in 1963 when Elsie Carper, a *Washington Post* reporter, was elected president of the WNPC. Carper became incensed because Susanna McBee, another *Post* reporter, was taken off a civil rights story when she was not able to attend a male-only press conference at the National Press Club. Determined that women receive equal treatment with men in covering newsworthy appearances, Carper insisted that the WNPC bring pressure to bear on political figures to keep them from speaking at the National Press Club. Her stand was not approved by some of the WNPC members who thought "I wasn't lady-like enough," she recalled in 1974. "I took incredible abuse, but later some of my opponents said I had been right," she added.[63]

Carper had vivid recollections of a night in 1963 when she and Frances Lewine, an Associated Press reporter and former WNPC president, stood in the Western Union office in Washington sending cables to women members of the British Labor Party in Parliament. The cables asked the women to bring pressure on Harold Wilson, head of the party, not to speak at the National Press Club on a forthcoming trip to the United States. In response Wilson agreed to speak at the British Embassy instead.[64]

Finally, according to Carper, President Johnson, spurred by Elizabeth Carpenter, took action. At his direction the State Department informed the National Press Club that either women journalists must be permitted to sit beside men or visiting heads of state no longer would be scheduled there. At first the National Press Club wanted to escort women in through the back door, but "we refused to go," Carper said. The women insisted on entering through the front—just like the men.[65]

The early 1970s saw an end to the battle between the two press clubs, but also to the WNPC itself. In December 1970, the group voted to admit men and to change its name to the Washington Press Club. It soon elected two men to its governing body. In January 1971, by a vote of 227 to 56, the National Press Club decided to admit women and accepted applications from 24.[66]

Among the first women to join the National Press Club was Sarah McClendon, who wept for joy. She told a journalism student that she had worked in a twelfth-floor office in the National Press Club Building every night for 12 years but could not go to the thirteenth floor, the location of the club itself, to have a hamburger. "Honey, I can't tell you the snubs I've endured," she said. "It's taken me 27 years to travel one floor."[67]

McClendon recalled in 1985, "It had long been very obnoxious to me that I could not be a member." She said she had worked for a man who often went to the National Press Club and she was unable to reach him when she needed to. "The club desk was not cooperative . . . about calling men to the telephone when females called," she said, adding that men often gave orders not to be called, perhaps to escape their wives.[68]

Of more crucial importance was the fact that the press club permitted men to find out about jobs, McClendon continued. "When a popular male member would get out of work, he had but to go to the press club bar to get tips from his buddies about upcoming jobs." Women had no such opportunity to learn about openings.[69]

Conclusions

It took the WNPC over half a century to arrive at the point where its members were accepted into the National Press Club. Although the women did not always agree on the tactics to use against discrimination, the WNPC gave them a sense of identity as journalists until it was less strongly needed. As the Washington Press Club, it remained in existence for 15 years, claiming a greater professional purity than the National Press Club since the Washington Press Club refused to admit lobbyists and those with marginal claims to journalistic employment. Faced with lack of suitable clubhouse facilities, however, the Washington

Press Club, which then had 500 members, merged with the National Press Club in 1985. This came at a time when the National Press Club was seeking new members to help finance renovation of its building.[70]

The significance of the WNPC can be understood only in light of the discrimination and prejudice that surrounded women journalists during the years of the club's existence. They were barred from the National Press Club, an organization whose name showed that it was designed to be the inclusive organization for Washington reporters. Women journalists were not wanted there simply because they were women, just as they were not wanted in the Gridiron Club or at dinners of the White House Correspondents Association.

This reflected the fact that they were not welcome in the city rooms or other parts of news operations aside from women's and society departments. The suspicion of male journalists toward women was revealed by Delbert Clark, manager of the Washington bureau of the *New York Times,* when he wrote that the "peculiar merits" of women journalists included "readiness to employ any device, however unorthodox, to gain their ends."[71]

As firmly entrenched as discrimination was toward women journalists, it was essential that they have a social structure fostering development of their own professional competence and dignity. This was provided by the WNPC. In joining with other women to plan events that drew attention to themselves as journalists, the members of the WNPC showed that they were not willing to be isolated individuals fighting their way into a hostile occupation.

By fostering contacts with persons in the news through its stunt parties, programs and dinners, the club enabled members to increase their prestige and show that they could rival male reporters in gaining the attention of prominent people. It gave them a chance to practice leadership skills, enhance their knowledge of the capital's political climate, and recognize other women of achievement. Most of all, it enabled them to see themselves not as a submerged element, but as talented and valuable members of the journalistic field.

Endnotes

1. Michael Schudson, *Discovering the News: A Social History of American Newspapers* (New York: Basic Books, 1978), pp. 15–53.
2. Katherine Lanpher, "The Boys at the Club: An Examination of Press Clubs as an Aspect of the Occupational Culture of the Late 19th Century Journalist," unpublished paper presented to the History Division, Association for Education in Journalism annual convention, Athens, Ohio, July 1982, p. 5.
3. Theodora Penny Martin, *The Sound of Our Own Voices: 1860–1910* (Beacon Press: Boston, 1987), p. 48.
4. Burton J. Bledstein, *The Culture of Professionalism: The Middle Class and the Development of Higher Education In America* (New York: Norton & Co., 1976) p. 39.
5. Frank Luther Mott, *A History of American Magazines, 1885–1905,* vol. IV (Cambridge: Harvard University Press, 1957), p. 549.
6. Frank Luther Mott, *American Journalism: 1690–1960* (New York: Macmillan, 1962), p. 547.
7. Ibid., p. 599.
8. Marlon Marzolf, *Up From the Footnote* (New York: Hastings House, 1977), pp. 49–50.
9. Eliot Freidson, *Doctoring Together: A Study of Professional Social Control* (New York: Elsevier, 1975), p. 9.
10. John P. Cosgrove, ed., *shrdlu: An Affectionate Chronicle* (Washington, D.C.: National Press Club, 1958), p. 19.
11. Ibid., p. 20.
12. Mrs. J.C. Croly (Jennie June), *The History of the Woman's Club Movement in America* (New York: Henry G. Allen & Co., 1898), pp. 340–41. See also "The Women's National Press Association," *The New Cycle* bc, (organ of the General

Federation of Women's Clubs), October 1895, pp. 296–97.

13. Elizabeth S. Tilton, *The League of American Pen Women in the District of Columbia* (Washington, D.C.: District of Columbia Branch, League of American Pen Women, 1942), pp. 1, 4–6.
14. Cabell Phillips, ed., *Dateline: Washington: The Story of National Affairs Journalism in the Life and Times of the National Press Club* (Garden City, N.Y.: Doubleday & Co., 1949), p. 27.
15. Minute Book for 1921–24, Records of District of Columbia Federation of Women's Clubs, Columbia Historical Society (hereafter referred to as CHS), Washington, D.C., Box 2, p. 86.
16. Minute Book for 1928–30, Records of District of Columbia Federation of Women's Clubs, CHS, Box 2, p. 27.
17. Lonnelle Aikman, typed draft of first chapter for proposed book on the Women's National Press Club [1968], Box 23, Women's National Press Club files (hereafter referred to as WNPCF), National Press Club Archives, Washington, D.C. (hereafter referred to as NPCA), pp. 8–10, 16.
18. Carolyn Vance Bell, "Founding," typescript, 1968, Box 23, WNPCF, NPCA, pp. 4, 7.
19. Typed notes of interview with Alice Gram Robinson, March 29, 1968, Box 23, WNPCF, NPCA, p. 1.
20. Aikman, draft of first chapter, p. 16.
21. Christine Sadler, "The Poe Sisters," typescript, Box 26, WNPC, NPCA, p. 3.
22. Bell, "Founding," p. 8.
23. Typed copy of open letter from E.M. King, Cora Rigby, Caroline [sic] Vance Bell, Eleanor Taylor Marsh and Florence Brewer Boeckel, Box 23, Sept. 23, 1919, WNPCF, NPCA. (Robinson did not sign the initial letter.)
24. Ibid.
25. Aikman, draft of first chapter, p. 25.
26. Bell, "Founding," p. 8.
27. Winifred Mallon, "The Whole Truth, As Far As It Goes About Ourselves," typescript dated July 1937, Box 23, WNPCF, NPCA, p. 1.
28. Ibid., p. 4; Aikman, draft of first chapter, p. 33.
29. Mallon, "The Whole Truth," pp. 4–5.
30. Corinne Frazier Gillet, ed., typed manuscript for proposed book to be called *Pardon Our Petticoats: Annals of the Women's Press Club* [1961], Box 42, WNPCF, NPCA, p. 3.
31. Bell, "Founding," p. 3.
32. Aikman, typed draft, p. 34.
33. Membership qualifications as listed in 1924 directory, Box 32, WNPCFF, NPCA.
34. Ibid.
35. Ibid.
36. Notes from Lily Lykes Shepard for proposed book, [1968], Box 23, WNPCF, NPCA.
37. Ibid.
38. Gillett, typed manuscript, p. 32.
39. Katharine M. Brooks, "Some Recollections of the American Newspaper Women's Club," September, 1970, files of the American News Women's Club, Washington, D.C., pp. 1–2; see also F.B. Marbut, *News From the Capital: The Story of Washington Reporting* (Carbondale: Southern Illinois University Press, 1971, pp. 253–54.
40. Ishbel Ross, *Ladies of the Press* (New York: Harper & Brothers, 1936), p. 12.
41. Barbara Boardman, typed manuscript, "The 'B' Girls," [1968], Box 23, WNPCF, NPCA, p. 1.
42. Maurine H. Beasley, ed., *The White House Press Conferences of Eleanor Roosevelt* (New York: Garland Publishing, 1983), p. 1; Eleanor Roosevelt, *This I Remember* (New York: Harper & Brothers, 1949), pp. 102–03; Bess Furman, "Eleanor Roosevelt and the W.N.P.C." typed manuscript, 1968, Box 23, WNPCF, NPCA, p. 1.
43. Ruby Black to Eleanor Roosevelt, February 16, 1938, Ruby Black papers, now being processed at the Manuscript Division, Library of Congress, hereafter referred to as MD, LC.
44. Bess Furman diary, entry for Feb. 15, 1938, Box 1, Bess Furman papers, MC, LC.
45. Delbert Clark, *Washington Dateline* (New York: Frederick Stokes, 1941), p. 219.
46. Gillett, typed manuscript, p. 40.
47. Furman, "Eleanor Roosevelt and the W.N.P.C.," p. 2.
48. Joseph P. Lash, *Eleanor and Franklin* (New York: Signet, 1971), p. 494.

49. Telephone interview by the author with Lee Jaffee, September 12, 1985.
50. Open letter from Ruby A. Black to club members, December 27, 1939, Ruby Black papers, MD, LC.
51. Christine Sadler, "War Impetus" section, typewritten working outline of proposed WNPC book, May 14, 1968, Box 23, WNPCF, NPCA, p. 2.
52. Ruth Crane, typescript of suggested preface to radio-TV section of proposed WNPC book [1968], Box 23, WNPCF, NPCA, p. 1.
53. Cosgrove, *shrdlu: An Affectionate Chronicle,* p. 110.
54. Helen M. Staunton, "Mary Hornaday Protests Bars to Newswomen," clipping from *Editor & Publisher,* July 15, 1944, Box 23, WNPCF, NCPA.
55. "Mrs. Craig 'Hell Fire' on Women's Equality," clipping from *Editor & Publisher,* June 17, 1944, Box 23, WNPCF, NPCA.
56. Bess Furman, "The Change-Over Year," typescript of chapter for proposed WNPC book [1968], Box 23, WNPCF, NPCA, pp. 1, 5–7.
57. Typed outline of contents of scrapbooks [no dates], Box 23, WNPCF, NPCA, pp. 2–5.
58. Alice A. Dunnigan, typed recollection, Box 23, WNPCF, NPCA.
59. Eileen Summers, "WOMEN Say 'No Thanks' to Bid for Admission to Male Press Club," *Washington Post,* Feb 23, 1955, p. C1.
60. "Why Not Women?" *Newsweek,* February 28, 1955, p. 81.
61. "Hagerty Suggests a Summit," *Washington Post,* October 30, 1959, p. C1.
62. Marie Smith, "JFK Sharpens Blue Pencil," *Washington Post,* November 30, 1961, p. C1.
63. Personal Interviews by the author with Elsie Carper, September 1974, Washington, D.C.
64. Ibid.
65. Ibid.
66. Marzolf, *Up From the Footnote,* p. 104. For a chronology of events leading up to the admission of women into the National Press Club, see Kay Mills, *A Place in the News: From the Women's Pages to the Front Pages* (New York: Dodd, Mead & Co., 1988), pp. 93–104.
67. As quoted in Sonja Hilgren, "The Women in the Washington Press Corps," unpublished paper prepared in partial fulfillment of requirements for master's degree in journalism, University of Missouri, Columbia, 1972, p. 32.
68. Sarah McClendon, memorandum for the admissions committee, National Press Club event, October 22, 1985, honoring newswomen, NPCA, p. 2.
69. Ibid.
70. Anne Mariano, "The New National Press Building Proves Costly and Controversial," *Washington Post,* Business section, June 10, 1985, p. 1.
71. Clark, *Washington Dateline,* pp. 205–06.

The Role of the Foreign-Language Press in Migrant Integration

Jerzy Zubrzycki

1. Introduction: The Cultural Framework of the Process of Migration

Migration is all too frequently seen to be part and product of economic and political processes alone. It is often accepted that the processes of population growth, international mobility of labour, qualitative selection and adjustment of migrants—can be discussed solely in terms of the economic, demographic and political data that play a part in such phenomena. Such an approach is incomplete since it leaves out of account the very large area of intercultural relations between the host society and the migrants and between different nationalities involved in migration.

In studying trans-Atlantic migration in the nineteenth century, we might analyse the rhythm of *economic* growth in the principal sending countries of Europe and attempt to find a relationship between the course of migration and the changes in pace of American economic development. We might also relate the findings of such an economic analysis to a set of *demographic* data showing, as has been done by Brinley Thomas,[1] that outstanding secular upswings in trans-Atlantic migration occurred at times when the proportion of young people in the population of the sending countries was exceptionally high owing to changes in the birth rate.

The results of such a study would be of interest to students of select disciplines like economics and demography. There is, however, a large body of social sciences including, for instance, history, sociology, social psychology, criminology and social geography, which contribute special tools for the study of *cultural* factors affecting the volume and direction of international migrations. Emotional attachments to a community and to acquaintances, to a culture or language, to political and social institutions or to a way of life must be considered as factors inhibiting trans-Atlantic movement and affecting the adjustment of migrants in America. There is a whole range of topics which must be included in an analysis of trans-Atlantic migration if the study is to be comprehensive and if it is to contribute to the understanding of the process of migration. Such topics include firstly, the social history of the migrant family with special emphasis on persistence of family traditions, customs and names, the training of children before they go to school, family pastimes and mutual obligations and problems of the second generation. The second group of topics embraces all kinds of community activities such as the process of transplantation of certain institutions, sanctions relating to the retention of

[1] B. Thomas, *Migration and Economic Growth: A Study of Great Britain and the Atlantic Economy*, Cambridge, 1954.

the language, resistance of the churches, etc. Finally, analysis of the foreign-language press, records of migrant societies and personal reminiscences must be included in a comprehensive study. Without analysis of all these factors which, taken together, comprise the cultural framework of migration, settlement and adjustment, no study will be scientifically meaningful.

This paper considers one aspect of the cultural framework of the process of migration, namely the rôle of the foreign language press in the integration of migrants.[2] The subject can be approached in at least two ways. One method of approach involves an attempt to answer questions like "should the immigrant be cut off completely from his association with the language of his country of origin?," "should free circulation of foreign-language newspapers be allowed in countries of immigration?," or "will a liberal policy in this matter facilitate or hinder migrant integration?" The second approach is primarily based on analysis of available *empirical* evidence obtained from the principal countries of immigration and relating to the part actually played by the foreign-language press within the framework of cultural factors affecting migrant integration. In this paper both approaches will be used, but the second topic will be treated first.

II. The Social Function of the Foreign-Language Press

1. Natural history of the immigrant press

The history of the foreign-language press in modern times goes back to the period before the American War of Independence, to the foundation in Germantown, Pennsylvania, in 1739 by Christopher Sauer of a German paper entitled *Der Hochdeutsch-pennsylvanische Geschicht Schreiber, oder Sammlung wichtiger Nachrichten aus dem Natur- und Kirchen-Reich.* This paper, *Germantown Zeitung,* as it was later called, soon changed from a semi-annual publication to a quarterly, then to a monthly.[3] Other German papers soon followed in Philadelphia and by 1762 there were five papers published by the Palatinate Germans in Pennsylvania: two in Philadelphia, one in Germantown and two in Lancaster, the centre of the German farming community.[4]

The next in order of appearance in the United States was the Norwegian press. The first Norwegian paper in America was the *Nordlyset* which started publication in Muskego, Wisconsin, in 1847.[5] The publication of this paper ceased in 1852 when a new weekly the *Emigranten* appeared in its place. The latter paper had a distinguished record in the critical period of the Civil War when it rallied the Norwegian element on the side of the Union and campaigned for the abolition of slavery.[6] Several Swedish, Danish, Dutch and Swiss periodicals made their appearance in the "fifties" and early "sixties" of the nineteenth century.

The large-scale "new" immigration from Southern and Eastern Europe to America dates back to the fourth quarter of the nineteenth cen-

[2]By "integration of migrants" I mean a process of social change involving the host society and the migrants alike and aiming at an increasingly greater degree of participation by the migrants in the affairs of the country of adoption.

[3]A. B. Faust, *The German Element in the United States: with Special Reference to its Political, Moral, Social and Educational Influence,* New York, 1927, vol. II, p. 367.

[4]*Ibid,* p. 368.

[5]B. J. Hovde, "Norwegian Americans" in Francis J. Brown, and Joseph S. Roucek (Eds.), *One America: The History, Contributions and Present Problems of Our Racial and National Minorities,* New York, 1949, p. 56. It was no accident that the history of Norwegian journalism in America was inaugurated with a front-page translation of the Declaration of Independence.

[6]A. W. Anderson, *The Immigrant takes his Stand: The Norwegian-American Press and Public Affairs, 1847–1872.* Northfield, Minnesota, 1953, chapters iv and v.

tury. However, a number of short-lived newspapers published in the Italian, Polish, Czech, Hungarian and other East European languages were founded in the middle of the century by the political refugees fleeing from Europe after the revolutions of 1849. For example, the first Italian paper, *L'Eco d'Italia,* was founded in 1849 in New York City and catered to a small group of Italian revolutionaries who sought refuge in the United States. But the appearance of the first newspaper with large circulation was delayed till 1888 at the time when migration from Italy was becoming a mass movement. The paper was *Il Progresso Italo-Americano* which, to this day, is the leading Italian daily in North America.[7] The Hungarians, too, had a spate of short-lived papers in the early 'fifties of which the leading journal was the *Magyar Szamuzottck Lapja* (Bulletin of the Hungarian Exiles) founded in 1853. The first Hungarian-American newspaper really devoted to Hungarian-American life was the *Americai Magyar-Nemzetor* (American Guardian of the Nation) which was started in 1884.[8] None of the Polish political journals which were started in the fifties survived till 1878 when the Polish National Alliance, a leading organisation of Polish Americans, founded a weekly paper *Zgoda.*[9] The earliest Ukrainian paper was the *Alaska Herald and Sroboda* founded in 1868 in San Francisco by A. Honchurenko, a political exile. The first Ukrainian-American paper the *America* made its appearance in Skenandoah, Pennsylvania, in 1886.[10]

The origin of the foreign-language press in Canada (other than French-Canadian) goes back to the seventies of the last century though the first data relating to migrant newspapers were only published in the *Canadian Almanac* in 1905. Eighteen papers were then in existence published in four languages: German, Swedish, Danish and Icelandic. By 1911 the total had risen to 33 including a number of newly founded Ukrainian, Polish and Italian papers. In 1939 some 51 papers were published in 15 languages.[11]

The first foreign-language paper in Australia was the German journal *Die deutsche Post für die australischen Kolonien oder The German Australian Post,* which was founded in Adelaide in 1847. The publication of this paper was suspended in 1850 when a new journal the *Südaustralische Zeitung* was established. As a result of several amalgamations with smaller newspapers the *Südaustralische Zeitung* changed its title in 1875 to *Australische Zeitung* and was published weekly until March 1916. After a temporary suspension caused by World War I the paper was amalgamated with the *Queenslander Herald.*[12] The first Italian paper did not make its appearance until the beginning of the inter-war period; that was the *Voce d'Italia—Voice from Italy,* a bilingual weekly founded in Melbourne in 1918. But the great day of the migrant press dawned only around 1948 when, with the arrival of displaced persons from Europe, several new national groups hitherto almost completely unknown in Australia appeared on the stage. At the same time the existing national groups such as the Italians and the Greeks were greatly strengthened. In September 1955 some 70 periodicals in 28 languages were published in Australia.

Perhaps the most important single characteristic of the foreign-language press has been its high mortality. For example, in the U.S.A. between 1884 and 1920, 3,444 new papers were

[7]F. J. Brown, "Italian Americans," in Brown and Roucek (eds.) *op. cit.*, p. 265.

[8]E. Lengyel, *Americans from Hungary,* New York, 1948, chapter xiv.

[9]P. Fox, *The Poles in America,* New York, 1922, p. 99.

[10]W. Halich, *The Ukrainians in the United States,* Chicago, 1937, chapter viii.

[11]W. Kirkconnell, "The European-Canadians in their Press" in the Canadian Historical Association *Report of the Annual Meeting Held at London, May 1940,* Toronto, 1940, pp. 85–86.

[12]A. Lodewyckx, *Die Deutschen in Australien.* Schriften des Deutschen Auslands-Instituts Stuttgart, Stuttgart, 1932, pp. 182–85.

started and 3,186 discontinued. The peak of the development of the foreign-language press was reached during World War I when approximately 1,350 journals were reported using 36 different languages. By July 1948 the number had fallen to 973.[13]

The disappearance of a newspaper, however, often indicates the result of a merger. The German-language press in the U.S.A. is an outstanding example of the trend toward consolidation. Between 1900 and 1930 the number of German newspapers decreased by about two-thirds (from 750 to 250 periodicals). However, the position of the German-American press was strengthened during that period; in 1930 there were fewer but better organized German-language newspapers with a total circulation about equal to what it had been in 1900.[14] The reason why the circulation was sustained at its former level lay undoubtedly in the fact that there had occurred a substantial influx of German immigrants in the early twenties. In Canada where no such influx took place the total circulation of German periodicals was nearly halved between 1911 and 1931.[15] It appears that it takes a continuous immigration from a foreign country to support the newspapers in the foreign language, the tendency being for succeeding generations to prefer newspapers printed in the native language.

2. Contents of the foreign-language press

In a typical foreign-language newspaper space is allotted among five major divisions: news of the country of settlement, world news, home-country news, group life and interests, editorial features. Generally speaking conditions in the former homeland of a given immigrant group have much to do with the intensity of the nationalistic feelings reflected in its press and consequently in the allocation of space among the various topics. The late Robert E. Park in his classic book on the subject put this point in the following words:

> *"From the contents of the press it is possible to estimate the extent to which the immigrant peoples have actually taken root in the U.S.A. and accommodated themselves to the forms, conditions and concrete purposes of American life. If we represent the whole intellectual horizon of a language group by a circle we may characterise the outlook of the different immigrant areas, with reference to their interest and participation in American life, by the segments of the circle. For example the attitudes of the peoples we have called settlers—i.e. the Germans and Scandinavians—might be defined by a circle in which an area of 300 degrees represented interests in American life and an area of, perhaps, 60 degrees represented interests in the home country. On the other hand, the group of peoples already designated as exotic might be represented by a figure the converse of this, in which 60 degrees of the circle would represent interest in American life, and 300 degrees would represent interest in the home country."*[16]

The peoples whom Park describes as exotic include the Armenians, Turks, Chinese, Filipinos, Hindus and Japanese—all of whom, for various reasons, are more completely isolated or removed from contact and participation in American life than any other immigrant peoples. Between the two extremes—the settlers and the exotics—there are clearly many intermediate stages of integration reflected in the proportion of space devoted to home country interests as opposed to the news of the country of settlement.

[13]D. R. Taft and R. Robbins, *International Migrations: The Immigrant in the Modern World,* New York, 1955, p. 533.

[14]T. J. Woofter, *Races and Ethnic Groups in American Life,* N.Y., 1933, p. 216.

[15]Kirkconnell, *op. cit.,* p. 86.

[16]R. E. Park, *The Immigrant Press and its Control,* New York, 1922, p. 307.

In considering the foreign-language press in the U.S.A. it may be said that the newspapers of the older immigrant groups such as the German and the Scandinavian, almost from their inception were American newspapers printed in the German or Scandinavian languages. As to the "new" immigrants from Southern and Eastern Europe the outstanding change of the last three decades, since the imposition of quota restrictions in the early twenties, has been a stronger orientation toward America. The Czech press gives an outstanding illustration of this pro-American trend. The early Czech papers were strongly radical and anti-clerical and supported the cause of the national radicals in the former Austria-Hungary. The liberation of the Czech lands in 1918 considerably affected the attitude of the Czech press in the United States. In the early thirties the Czech press was described as "predominantly conservative with a distinct church background."[17] In 1933 there were a dozen pro-church publications to three radical journals.[18] "Americanization" of the foreign-language press is also illustrated by the increased use of press matter from American syndicates, including sporting news, feature stories, cartoons and comic strips. Finally, an increasing proportion of space is devoted to items in the English language.

A more recent example of a similar shift of editorial emphasis reflected in the allocation of space is provided by the Polish daily paper in London the *Dziennik Polski*. The paper was founded during the war by the exiled Polish Government in 1940 and has ever since remained an organ of the Polish exiles. During the post-war period, however, the paper ceased to be primarily a political journal and began to devote an increasing proportion of space not so much to news about Britain but rather to news from Polish camps, hostels and societies in the country. A comparative content analysis of this journal in 1946 and 1952 suggests strongly that the paper has shifted its emphasis away from political news items relating to Poland. In the 1946 sample of the paper 30.6% of the total space was taken by news items from Poland and about Poland compared with 18.1% in the 1952 sample. The proportion of space devoted to news from Polish societies and centres in Britain during the same period rose from 12.6 to 23.9%.[19]

3. Educating the migrant for citizenship

The principal function of the foreign-language press, has been to prepare migrants for good citizenship in the countries of settlement. The millions of migrants who crossed the Atlantic in the nineteenth and twentieth centuries could be reached far more effectively through their own languages than through English. They could not wait until they mastered the English language before learning anything about the country of their choice. They had to "acquire information about the customs, traditions and institutions of their adopted country, and about the political, economic and industrial organisation of America through the medium of their own native languages. The foreign-language press . . . has been an educational agency without equal among our immigrant population."[20]

Carl Schurz, that eminent American statesman of German birth, argued against the prejudice entertained by some people, that the publication of newspapers in any other language than English was an undesirable, if not positively dangerous, practice. He wrote:

> *"It is said that the foreign-language press prevents immigrants from learning the language of the country; that it fosters the cultivation of un-*

[17]Woofter *op. cit.*, p. 218.

[18]*Ibid.*

[19]J. Zubrzycki, *Polish Immigrants in Britain: A Study of Adjustment*. The Hague, 1956, pp. 139–141.

[20]W. C. Smith, *Americans in the Making*, New York, 1939, p. 191.

American principles, notions and habits, and that it thus stands in the way of the development of a sound American patriotism in those coming from foreign lands to make their home among us and to take part in the working of our free institutions. I think I may say without undue assumption that from personal contact and large opportunities of observation I have as much personal experience of the German-born population of the United States, its character, its aspirations and its American patriotism, as any person now living; and this experience enables me to affirm that the prejudice against the German-American press is groundless. On the contrary that press does the country a necessary and very important service. In the first place it fills a real and very urgent want. That want will exist as long as there is a large number of German-born citizens in this Republic. There will also be among them, especially persons of mature years, who arrived on American soil without any knowledge of the English language, who may be able to acquire enough of it to serve them in their daily work, but not enough to enable them to understand newspaper articles on political or similar subjects. Such persons must receive the necessary information about current events, questions to be considered and duties to be performed from journals published in the languages they understand or they will not have it all. The suppression of the German-American press would, therefore, be equivalent to the cultivation of political ignorance among a large and highly estimable class of citizens."[21]

The rôle of the foreign-language press as an educational agency is well illustrated by the following quotation from the reminiscences of another distinguished American citizen of foreign birth, Hans Mattson. At one stage of his career, Mattson published two Swedish weeklies, one in Minneapolis and one in Chicago, of which he wrote:

"My aim in this journalistic work was mainly to instruct and educate my countrymen in such matters as might promote their well-being and make them good American citizens. The Stats Tidning, *or at least a part of it, gradually became a kind of catechism on law and political economy, containing information under the heading "Questions and Answers." This was intended especially for the Swedish farmers in the state. If a farmer was in doubt as to his legal rights in the case of a road, a fence, the draining of a marsh, or wished to know how to cure a sick horse or other animal, or how he could get money sent from Sweden, or if he wished advice or information on any other question relating to everyday life, especially if he got into trouble of some kind, he would write to* Stats Tidning *for the desired information. Such letters were then printed in condensed form followed by short, clear, pointed answers and, so far, I have not heard of a single person being misled by those answers. On the other hand, I know that the public, and more especially the newcomers, reaped very great benefits from them. Few persons have any idea of how irksome and laborious this kind of journalism is, and at times I was on the point of giving it up in despair."*[22]

The foreign-language press in Australia is an interesting example of the part it can play in educating migrants for the fullest possible participation in the affairs of the country and ultimately for citizenship. Here foreign-language newspapers which until recently could only be published under special licence, may now be produced freely without official control. The policy appears to be as wise as it is liberal, for in most cases the migrant papers provide not only news of the home country but also news from Australia and news of the national group

[21]*The Reminiscences of Carl Schurz,* New York, 1907–17, vol. III, pp. 257–258, quoted by Edith Abbott, (Ed). *Historical Aspects of the Immigration Problem,* Chicago, 1926, 1–526.

[22]H. Mattson, *Reminiscences: The Story of an Emigrant,* St. Paul, 1891, quoted by W. C. Smith, *op. cit.,* p. 192.

in Australia. In this way the newspapers encourage the sense of belonging not only to the national group but also the wider Australian society.

Content analysis of several foreign-language newspapers with the largest circulation in Australia reveals how prominent is this tendency in the presentation of news and distribution of the newspaper space among the various items. For example, the leading Italian weekly *La Fiamma* devotes about one-tenth of its space to local Australian news in its weekly surveys covering each state separately. There is, of course, a tendency to publish only such items which are of interest to the local Italian communities, e.g. articles on the planned expansion of the cane sugar industry in Queensland or reports from the Murrumbidgee Irrigation Area referring to the abolition of the law which discriminated against Italians acquiring land. But the publication of such articles gives the readers a better introduction to Australia than straight news items which seemingly bear no relation to the problems faced by the Italian community.

That the paper takes its responsibilities to Australia seriously is illustrated by a recent reply of the Editor to an Italian migrant who asked whether he should apply for naturalisation. In reply the Editor urged the migrant to apply for naturalisation without delay. He then went on to point out that only Australian citizens have the right to vote without which the migrant

> *" . . . represents nothing but a statistical unit lacking the dynamic force, that power, that marvellous and amazing right of the citizen which consists in the intervention in the fundamental actions of the life of the country . . . in short in the government of the country. This is the meaning of "Democracy," this is the supreme right of citizenship in free countries, this is the goal to which every migrant should aspire who has chosen Australia as his place of residence . . . All Italians should understand that the important thing is to be able to take an effective part in the life of the country."*[23]

A consideration of the nature of the subjects which the foreign-language press treats editorially in America, Australia, Britain and in other countries, warrants the conclusion that the influence it radiates is a vital factor in the integration of migrants to the host societies. While sustaining some of the feelings which bind the migrant to his country of origin, the foreign-language press endeavours to inculcate an understanding and respect for the institutions of the country of settlement and to explain to its readers the significance of native customs. Above all the foreign-language press is a powerful factor in maintaining social cohesion of the immigrant group and providing the social controls which are indispensable in the prevention of such manifestations of personal disorganisation among migrants as delinquency and mental disorders arising from cultural isolation.

III. The Foreign-Language Press and the Policy of Migrant Integration

The existence of a foreign-language press in the main countries of immigration has not been without its abuses. Two main charges have been levelled against it: that it tends to transfer the partisan views and divisions of the country of origin to the new environment, and, secondly, that it might be used as an organ of propaganda of a nationalistic character by a foreign power.

The first charge is not a very serious one. It is true, of course, that the foreign-language press is often misused by editors who want to recreate, in the new environment, the minor political and social divisions of the country of origin. By keeping the immigrant in touch with the conflicts at home, it evokes nationalistic and particularistic tendencies. But all the evidence available to the present writer suggests that the continuation of opposing points of view and publicity given to certain ideological groups

[23]*La Fiamma*, Sydney, 31st August, 1956.

among the migrants is generally harmless enough. For one thing the foreign-language press is predominantly a *commercial* press which, if it is to survive, must cater for the everyday needs of the general public. On the other hand, what R. E. Park described as propagandist papers, have relatively small circulations and appeal only to select immigrants. Writing in 1922, he gave the following figures showing the ratio of circulation of commercial papers to all other papers for three language groups in the U.S.A.[24]

German 93%
Italian 83%
Polish 81%

The argument that the press might be used for fomenting hostile propaganda is a serious one. While most of the periodicals which the present author has surveyed have simply been good business propositions, serving profitably to integrate the social and religious life of their communities, there have been others that have been the definite instruments of alien policy. There are many examples of journals founded and subsidised by foreign powers to serve as vehicles for their propaganda. Mention must be made here of the Nazi and Fascist papers which were being published on the eve of World War II. In Canada the Nazi *Deutsche Zeitung für Canada* and the three Fascist papers *L'Italia Nuoua* (Montreal), *Il Balletino Italo-Canadese* (Toronto) and *L'Eco Italo-Canadese* (Vancouver) achieved notoriety for their insidious propaganda though they did not succeed in corrupting many Canadians of German or Italian stock.[25] The position in the United States was more serious because there the majority of the Italian-language publications and a sizeable proportion of the German-language newspapers owed their allegiance to the Axis Powers. Such periodicals as the Portland *Nachrichten* or the notorious *Deutscher Weekruf* and *Beobachter* together with the Fascist *Il Grido della Stirpe* preached hatred of the British, ridiculed American democracy as "sentimentalism" and opposed President Roosevelt's "lend-lease" policy.[26] In Australia, as Dr. Price has shown, the German paper *Die Brücke,* for some five years before the outbreak of the war, encouraged persons of German origin to adopt the Nazi attitude to "racial" problems.[27] Equally intrusive in their propaganda have been the Communist newspapers published in the various languages, e.g. *Glos Pracy (Polish)* and *Narodna Gazeta* (Ukrainian) in Canada, *Russky Golos* (Russian) and *Ludevy Dennik* (Slovak) in the U.S., and the Yugoslav weekly in Australia, *Napredak.* All these papers, whether controlled by Nazis, Fascists or Communists, have, at one time or another, been disseminating some very dangerous propaganda and disrupting not only the unity of the various ethnic groups but also acting as a disturbing element in the country of settlement. It seems doubtful, however, if their appeal has ever reached beyond relatively small nuclei of politically minded immigrants.

The abuses of the foreign-language press have engendered an attitude of caution in many countries of immigration since World War II. In Australia foreign newspapers had to be officially registered and obtain a special licence to publish. The publishers were obliged to print at least 25% of the text in English. Similarly in Canada foreign papers had to be registered.

But these restrictions were recently abolished in both countries and to-day foreign-language newspapers can be published without licence and time can be bought on commercial radio stations. The only vestige of government control in Canada is the practice of reviewing all foreign-language newspapers by the Citizenship Branch of the Department of Citizenship and Immigration. The purpose of this review is less to exercise control than to prepare a digest

[24]R. E. Park, *op. cit.*, p. 305.

[25]W. Kirkconnell, *op. cit.*, pp. 90–91.

[26]J. S. Roucek, "Foreign-Language Press in World War II," *Sociology and Social Research.* vol. xxvii, no. 6 (July–August 1943), pp. 462–471.

[27]C. A. Price, *German Settlers in South Australia.* Melbourne 1945, pp. 48–62.

of some of the more interesting items which is then distributed to all language groups. Some 150 papers published in approximately 25 languages are covered in this work.[28] An agency known as the Common Council for American Unity has supplied a similar service to the foreign-language press in the United States; formal licensing or other forms of direct control were introduced during World War II.[29]

The experience of Brazil provides an interesting object lesson, of a country in which all foreign-language publications were banned for eight years. It has always been a highly controversial matter in Brazil whether the existence of a minority press performs a useful function in bridging the cultural gap between the country of origin and Brazilian society. Most Luso-Brazilians would deny this and would assert that newspapers published in the languages of immigrant groups are a major obstacle to integration. For this reason the interdiction of the minority press by President Vargas in 1938 was supported by public opinion. This is how two eminent Brazilian social scientists describe the consequences of this action.

> *" . . . German, Italian, Japanese and even, in our own days, Greek newspapers have been established. What was not appreciated—and this helped to keep the immigrant still more isolated from the Brazilian scene—was that those papers, even written in the settlers' own tongues, were potentially excellent vehicles for acquainting their readers with, and integrating them into, Brazilian life. . . . Specifically, the initial phase of the immigrant's adjustment could have been eased by using the foreign language press to make him better acquainted with Brazil and its people and thus to enable him to understand them better. Instead we chose to isolate them and do nothing to prepare them for their contacts with the new country at the very stage—the initial phase of their residence—at which they were most receptive."*[30]

The example of Brazil serves as a useful reminder to those critics of the foreign-language press who choose to ignore the educational functions of this important medium of communication and emphasise only the abuses of a small fraction of this press. Cultural ties cannot suddenly be broken—they can only be gradually severed. To hasten this task is to court disaster and through a foreign-language press the merging of the two cultures is encouraged rather than prevented.

It might be fitting to close the present contribution by quoting the resolution on the minority press adopted by the Conference on the Cultural Integration of Immigrants at Havana in April 1956. The conference, convened by the United Nations Cultural, Educational and Scientific Organisation consisted of representatives of governments, inter-governmental agencies, and non-governmental organisations as well as social scientists and consultants, and included in its resolutions a recommendation that:

> *"the potentiality of a foreign-language press to operate, especially in respect of the first generation, in such a healthy and responsible manner as to retain association with the culture of the areas of origin, but at the same time to serve as a medium for extending knowledge of the culture of the country of settlement (and also of national and international affairs) should be recognized."*[31]

[28]"The Integration of Immigrants in Canada," a report prepared by the Canadian Department of Citizenship and Immigration, for the United Nations Educational, Scientific and Cultural Organisation (UNESCO), *Conference on the Cultural Integration of Immigrants,* Havana (Cuba), April 1956. Document no. UNESCO/SS/Mig. Conf. 12.

[29]Roucek, *op. cit.*

[30]Arthur H. Neiva and Manuel Diegues, Jr., "Cultural Assimilation of Immigrants in Brazil" in UNESCO, *op. cit.,* document no. UNESCO/SS/Mig. Conf. 13. For a description of some recent efforts to reorganise the minority press in the country see Emilo Willems, "Brazil" in Oscar Handlin (Ed.), *The Positive Contribution by Immigrants,* UNESCO, Paris 1955, p. 136.

[31]"Resolution and Recommendations" in UNESCO, *op. cit.,* document no. UNESCO/SS/Mig. Conf./43, Rev. 1.

Two Legendary Campaigns

Roland Marchand

No era provides such revealing insights into the cultural values of both producers and consumers of American advertising as the 1920s and 1930s, when admen not only claimed the status of professionals but also saw themselves as missionaries of modernity.

During the era, advertising came to focus less on the product that was for sale and more on the consumer who would do the buying. (An ad in the *Ladies' Home Journal* of the late 1920s assured each reader that "Elizabeth Arden is personally interested in you.") The scale and tempo of contemporary life left the average citizen anxious, advertisers saw, and they offered their products as palliatives. What made advertising "modern" was the advertisers' discovery of techniques for both responding to and exploiting the public's insecurities.

Advertisers regularly created detailed vignettes of social life to arouse empathy, envy, or guilt—with huge sums of money riding on their effectiveness. And since these ad agents worked with ingenuous self-assurance, they filled the trade press with gossip about their techniques. Their own enthusiastic naïveté and their facile assumptions about the masses they addressed make the ads of this era particularly revealing—about the men and women who wrote them, the consumers who responded to them, and the cultural anxieties they reflected.

On the following pages we will look at some of the more bumptious processes and the legendary successes of the age when advertising grew up.

During a single year in the early 1920s, major advertising campaigns rescued two fading products so successfully that the entire advertising industry had to ponder the lessons they offered in modern advertising technique.

Fleischmann's Yeast, the first of these advertising legends, had been "something merely to bake bread with—until Fleischmann advertisements said otherwise," the copywriter claimed. Prohibition had destroyed one sales outlet for yeast, and in the face of a steady decline in home baking, even Fleischmann's lofty characterization of its product as the "Soul of Bread" could not stem declining sales. Could a product with such specific functions be salvaged by promoting it for some new use?

Within a year, with the impetus supplied by its new agency, the J. Walter Thompson Company, Fleischmann's advertising had transformed yeast into a potent source of vitamins, a food to be eaten directly from the package. Two years later, when the market had become saturated by new vitamin products, Fleischmann's Yeast evolved once again, this time into a natural laxative. A prize contest brought in hundreds of testimonials for the product's newly advertised properties. From 153 of the winners, the agency gained permission to use their letters and "illustrate them in any way we saw fit."

Capturing the tempo of popular journalism, the J. Walter Thompson copywriters established a brash format for the Fleischmann campaign and placed their ads in the high-priced rotogravure sections. They injected as much human interest and eye appeal as possible by using multiple "candid" photographs and succinct, first-person testimony. Sometimes the ads so closely copied the layout of the magazine or newspaper that the reader might become thoroughly immersed in one before discovering that it was not an editorial feature.

By 1926 the Fleischmann Company had become one of the nation's ten largest magazine advertisers and a major purchaser of newspaper space. By the spring of 1926, sales had increased 130 percent over 1923, when the candid, man-in-the-street testimonials had begun.

When sales threatened to recede, the Thompson agency called doctors to the rescue. Authoritative physicians in white coats explained how the pressures of modern civilization had led to constipation and advised readers to eat half a cake of yeast three times a day to counteract "intestinal fatigue." "Fatigue is universal," one agency executive explained. "We simply have to credit it to the intestines, that's all." The agency dramatized the role of the intestines by superimposing bold diagrams of "where the trouble starts" over photographs of lovely young women. The American Medical Association was outraged and prohibited its members from testifying for Fleischmann. Undaunted, the agency turned for paid testimonials to European doctors, whose impressively unpronounceable names and prestigious hospital affiliations were most effective.

The success of Fleischmann's Yeast in the 1920s—in spite of the product's high price, its repulsive taste, and, according to the agency, "the almost complete absence of *quickly apparent* results"—seemed to confirm the power of advertising. One pleased copywriter reflected that advertising alone had increased sales, and had done so even though the home baking market had declined sharply.

The success of the Fleischmann campaign was overshadowed, however, by the even more spectacular story of Listerine. The profits of its manufacturer, the Lambert Pharmacal Company, mushroomed from approximately $100,000 per year in 1920 and 1921 to over $4,000,000 in 1927. Not surprisingly the company's strategy gave rise to a whole school of advertising practice.

Listerine was not a new product in 1920. For years it had been merchandised perfunctorily as a general antiseptic. Initially, the three men who transformed Listerine into the marvel of the advertising world—the copywriters Milton Feasley and Gordon Seagrove and the company president, Gerard B. Lambert—did not so much convert the product to a new use as induce the public to discover a new need. After a year of comparatively awkward ads for Listerine as a mouthwash, the copywriters hit upon a winning formula. The picture of a lovely girl introduced a story cryptically entitled "He Never Knew Why." The hero, a rising young businessman, was spurned by the "luminous" but "charmingly demure" girl of his dreams after a single romantic encounter. He seemed to have every advantage in life—wealth, good looks, charm—but he labored under one insurmountable handicap. He had "halitosis."

The term *halitosis* (exhumed from an old medical dictionary) had a scientific sound and took some of the coarseness out of a discussion of bad breath. The ads mimicked the tabloids' personal-interest stories and advice-to-the-lovelorn columns. As the advertising industry's journal *Printers' Ink* reflected in a tribute to Feasley: "He dealt more with humanity than with merchandise. He wrote advertising dramas rather than business announcements—dramas so common to everyday experience that every reader could easily fit himself into the plot as the hero or culprit of its action."

By 1926 *Printers' Ink* went so far as to eulogize Feasley for having transformed behavior patterns. He had "amplified the morning habits of our nicer citizenry—by making the morning mouthwash as important as the morning shower or the morning shave." But Gerard Lambert was not content to wed the fortunes of his product to *one* new habit. To maintain advertising momentum, he kept finding new uses for Listerine. Halitosis had hardly become an advertising byword before Lambert began to proclaim Listerine's virtues as a cure for dandruff. Between 1921 and 1929 the American public also learned the virtues of Listerine as an after-shave tonic, a cure for colds and sore throats, an astringent, and a deodorant: Lambert capitalized on the new fame of his product to market a Listerine toothpaste, which brought even greater financial returns. The Listerine advertising budget mounted from $100,000 in 1922 to $5,000,000 in 1928.

The financial feats of the Listerine campaign held the advertising trade enthralled. Phrases like "the halitosis style," "the halitosis appeal," and "the halitosis influence" became standard advertising jargon. Copywriters soon discovered and labeled over a hundred new diseases, including such transparent imitations as "bromodosis" (sweaty foot odors), "homotosis" (lack of attractive home furnishings), "acidosis" (sour stomach), and such inventive afflictions as "office hips," "ashtray breath," and "accelerator toe."

The promoters of Listerine were not the first to discover the sociodrama as an advertising technique—just as they had not pioneered the appeal to social shame or personal fear. In advertisements headlined "Within the Curve of a Woman's Arm," the deodorant Odo-ro-no had earlier confronted the threats to romance posed by underarm perspiration. But Listerine purchased larger space in a wider variety of publications. Its expanding appropriations and spectacular profits impressed the business community. The J. Walter Thompson Company summarized the new perception of proper advertising techniques in 1926: "To sell *goods* we must also sell *words*. In fact we have to go further: we must sell *life*."

The Low Road to High Profits

In January 1928 a young woman in the J. Walter Thompson advertising agency, who described herself as an "inexperienced but struggling enthusiast," challenged the recent trend of her own agency's advertising style. Why, she asked in the agency's confidential newsletter, had the recent layout and copy of the campaign for Fleischmann's Yeast "deteriorated . . . to such an extent that they have assumed the appearance of a *True Story Magazine* insertion?" Was it to appeal to the "minds of those morons . . . who daily dole out their 2 cents to secure the latest news not only unadulterated but graphically portrayed?" Had the agency lowered itself to producing "tabloid copy for tabloid readers"?

The agency's response, written by the experienced copywriter Gerald Carson, was immediate and devastating. In so skeptical an age, said Carson, people should welcome "any manifestation of idealism as precious, there is so little of it." Nevertheless, duty required the agency not to indulge its preferences but to advance the sale of Fleischmann's Yeast. This duty could be performed only with copy "comprehensible to the plain people." It might be more pleasant to "advertise exclusively to 'nice' people," but advertising success was "too dependent upon the franchise of the common people for us to cherish a purpose so aristocratic." Yes, by all means, "tabloid copy for tabloid minds."

Much the same debate over the characteristics and tastes of the audience for advertising regularly stirred the trade press. As the 1920s progressed, each of the various advertising media sought to capture its own definition of the audience in a pithy slogan. "Tell It to Sweeney," urged one American tabloid newspaper, the New York *Daily News*. "Sweeney," who might live in Brooklyn, Staten Island, the Bronx, or Upper Manhattan, and whose real name might be Muller, Cohen, Nelson, or Smith, read the *Daily News*. The wise advertiser would seek to tell his sales story to Sweeney. On the contrary, *Harper's Bazaar* urged advertisers to cultivate the "inner circle," the class with "the *most influential* purchasing power," which set the example for the rest of society. By making no "editorial concessions to the masses," *Harper's Bazaar* achieved the tone necessary for an effective appeal to this discriminating class. By the late 1920s scores of magazines and newspapers steadily harangued the advertising agent with similar slogans and arguments.

The private dialogue over style within the J. Walter Thompson agency and the clamorous competition of the media to define the optimum audience posed questions that never ceased to trouble the creative elite of advertising. What was the class structure of the buying public? What were its tastes and desires? How did the advertiser go about discovering them? Working in the rarefied atmosphere of an ad agency, how could one keep that audience and its tastes properly in focus?

To understand how inventive copywriters dealt with the problems of an inscrutable consumer audience, it is helpful to look at two phenomena of popular culture in the 1920s that fascinated advertising leaders: the tabloid newspaper and the confession magazine.

True Story Magazine and the *Daily News* first appeared within weeks of each other in May and June of 1919. *True Story* was the offspring of the magazine *Physical Culture,* published by the flamboyant strong man and health enthusiast Bernarr Macfadden. For several years Macfadden's wife, Mary, had been reading the letters and manuscripts that poured into the *Physical Culture* offices. In many of these, women brokenheartedly confided their romantic experiences. Mary Macfadden and other female co-workers became convinced that this was salable material. As one staff member remarked: "All the working girls go through the same love troubles. This one will be about themselves and *written* by themselves." For his new publication, therefore, Bernarr Macfadden adopted the first-person, confessional formula. *True Story* later touted its contents as the "first folk-literature since the days of the Bible." To illustrate the stories of girls gone astray, of jealous husbands intent on revenge, and of sublime love transformed to hatred, Macfadden broke away from the idealized art style of most magazine fiction and used photographs of models in menacing or sensuous poses.

Macfadden unflinchingly aimed *True Story* at an audience of young, working-class women. Insisting that the stories came from "common people," he tested any copy that sounded highbrow on the office elevator operator. Anything that puzzled him was rejected—a practice that provoked one irreverent staff member to compose his own underground confession story: "How I Was Demoted to Editor of *True Story* and Worked My Way Up to Elevator Man Again." Although it was not sold by subscription and carried a high newsstand price (twenty cents at first, compared with fifteen cents for the dominant *Ladies' Home Journal*), *True Story* soon found an impressive market. By 1924 it had pulled even with the reputable *Good Housekeeping* at a circulation of about 850,000. By 1927 it was challenging *Ladies' Home Journal* and *McCall's* for first place in national circulation among women's magazines with newsstand sales of over two million per issue.

True Story held fast to its astoundingly successful formula—women's personal, confessional accounts of temptations, love triangles, and tragic adventures. In the sociologist George Gerbner's epitome of the genre, the heroine of the confession, "buffeted by events she cannot understand," began a "headlong flight down the line of least resistance," which ended in "her inevitable sin." Punishment, physical or moral, was immediate and severe. Although *True Story* disavowed any intention to preach, every story proved a "powerful sermon."

Might the success of such a formula carry important lessons for advertising? In a series of sociological sermons to the trade, *True Story* ads proclaimed the magazine's discovery of the once down-trodden. *True Story* readers constituted a whole new market: the wives of skilled workmen, women who "can't comprehend the more sophisticated 'silk worm' magazines written for white collars." These women were not yet deafened by the "billion dollar din of repeated advertising." They were more likely to live in a modest frame house on Main Street than in a "palace on Lake Shore Drive," but they had plenty of money to spend on cars, radios, and appliances, as well as on soup, soap, and breakfast food.

At first, advertising agencies hesitated to buy space in *True Story,* despite its mounting circulation figures. Its tenor seemed incongruent with the copy they were producing for most of their clients. As late as 1926, with a circulation approaching two million, an issue of *True Story* often carried fewer than a dozen full-page or half-page ads for national advertisers. It still drew the bulk of its considerable advertising revenue from smaller ads for bust developers, weight reducers, cures for bunions or baldness, and moneymaking schemes.

By the beginning of 1928, however, when the principled young copywriter was bemoaning J. Walter Thompson's new "tabloid" style, *True Story* clearly had won many converts within the agencies. Here was a new *reading* public. Never mind how meager its vocabulary or narrow its interests; it could actually *read* advertisements, if properly written in the *True Story* style of "short words and shorter sentences," and could afford to buy the brands it chose. By 1928 products such as Fleischmann's Yeast, Kotex, Lux, Pond's, Jell-O, Pepsodent, Cutex, Lysol, Bayer, Wrigley, Camels, and the Cleanliness Institute's wares had joined *True Story's* roster of nationally advertised goods.

The idea of not only reaching the huge *True Story* audience but reaching it with advertisements in the *True Story* formula now began to take hold. The J. Walter Thompson agency, which was already placing ads for several clients in *True Story,* initiated seminars for its copywriters on the *True Story* approach. Gerald Carson opened up "whole new vistas" with a talk on "The Mental and Emotional Life of a Tabloid Reader."

The headlines of advertisements in *True Story* now began to echo the titles of its confessional stories: "Could She Be the Helen Brown I Used to Know?" (Golden Glint Shampoo); "Because I Confessed . . . I Found the Way to Happiness" (the Borden Company); "I Deceived My Husband and I'm Proud of It!" (the Postum Company); "Some Wives Do It, but I Wouldn't Dare" (Wheatena Corporation). The same confessional ads soon appeared in newspapers and in such staid women's magazines as *Good Housekeeping* and *Ladies' Home Journal.*

Meantime, the conception of a "tabloid audience" had gained even greater credibility from the prosperity of the tabloid newspapers themselves. *True Story* was a national magazine. But the *Daily News* gained its sensational success right in New York City, where no New York advertising agent could ignore it or its imitators. First introduced in 1919 as the *Illustrated Daily News,* in two years the *Daily News* was selling more copies than any other New York newspaper. By 1925 it approached a million in daily circulation, far surpassing any other daily in the United States. Tabloids had now appeared in eleven other American cities. In June 1924, William Randolph Hearst launched his own New York tabloid, the *Daily Mirror,* and Bernarr Macfadden joined the New York tabloid competition with *The Daily Graphic.*

The tabloids of the early 1920s—with their emphasis on sex, violence, and photographs—surpassed even *True Story* in their impact. The advertising agencies at first disdained them, but by early 1926 *Advertising and Selling Fortnightly* was noting that the tabloids were now "overriding the delicate sensibilities of advertisers and agents," convincing them no longer to "disdain to practice their art in terms of the lowest common denominator."

In its continuing "Tell It to Sweeney" campaign, the *Daily News* extolled the free-spending qualities of the newly prosperous common man, the "plutocrat in overalls." But it also boldly assured advertisers that its audience did not exclude the affluent. As the *News* succinctly put it: "Tell it to Sweeney; The Stuyvesants Will Understand."

Sizing up the Consumer

How, then, did the creative elite of American advertising in the 1920s and 1930s characterize its audience?

First, the consumer was a "she." As one ad in *Printers' Ink* succinctly put it, "The proper study of mankind is man . . . but the proper study of markets is *woman*." No facet of the advertiser-audience relationship held such consequence for advertising content as the perception by the overwhelmingly male advertising elite that it was engaged primarily in talking to masses of women.

Demographically, of course, women composed no more than a razor-thin majority of the nation's population, but contemporary statistics indicated that they—the family "purchasing agents"—did about 80 to 85 percent of the nation's retail buying.

Once the audience was understood to be overwhelmingly female, certain implications for copy content and selling appeal seemed evident. In a tone of scientific assurance, advertising leaders of the 1920s and 1930s asserted that women possessed a "well-authenticated greater emotionality" and a "natural inferiority complex." Since women were "certainly emotional," advertisements must be emotional. Since women were characterized by "inarticulate longings," advertisements should portray idealized visions rather than prosaic realities. Copy should be intimate and succinct, since "women will read anything which is broken into short paragraphs and personalized."

Although the articles in the quality women's magazines pictured their sophisticated readers as leading busy, diversified, action-packed lives, advertising agencies generally adopted a very different model of the typical woman consumer, one that owed more to the contemporary stereotypes of the *True Story* reader. "We must remember," wrote a *Printers' Ink* contributor, "that most American women lead rather monotonous and humdrum lives. . . ." The advertising pages, he argued, should become the "magical carpets on which they may ride out to love."

The second advertising man's assumption was about the consumer's level of intelligence. Army tests during World War I had recently startled Americans. New techniques of evaluation revealed that a shocking percentage of prospective inductees had not possessed the minimal level of intelligence to qualify for military service. Advertising writers followed these reports avidly and reminded their colleagues of the latest figure that had lodged in their memory: "Remember, the average citizen has the mentality of a child of twelve"—or "ten" or "thirteen."

The content of the popular press reinforced this image of an unintelligent public. Several advertising writers recalled that Arthur Brisbane, the editorial genius of the Hearst papers and the guiding spirit of the tabloid *Daily Mirror*, had posted a sign in the Hearst city rooms that read, "You *cannot* underestimate the intelligence of the American public."

Movie content, also, offered a measure of public intelligence. "We say Hollywood people are stupid, the pictures are stupid," reflected one agency representative. "What we are really saying is the great bulk of people are stupid." The Ruthrauff and Ryan advertising agency, flaunting its own success in following the example of "editors, movie directors, and popular novelists," instructed the trade in the deplorable but inescapable facts of life: "After all, men and women in the mass are apt to have incredibly shallow brain-pans. In infancy they are attracted by bright colors, glitter, and noise. And in adulthood they retain a surprisingly similar set of basic reactions."

A third assumption, closely related to the theory of the limited mental capacity of advertising's audience, was the assumption of public lethargy. "The mass mind is averse to effort," an experienced woman copywriter warned agency novices. "Women don't like to think too much when buying," added a contributor to *Advertising Age.* George Gallup, reporting on his polling information for the Young and Rubicam advertising agency, suggested that the success of the New York *Daily News* was related to the tendency of "whole legions of women to read only the headlines except in the case of a juicy crime story where their interest overcomes their mental inertia." The prolific advertising writer Kenneth Goode reminded the trade in *How to Turn People into Gold* that "man in the mass," except when caught up in emotion, "won't exert himself beyond the line of least resistance."

Advertising men associated consumer lethargy with weak-kneed conformity. The masses, the copywriters were convinced, never looked beyond the need for immediate gratification. They would greet with suspicion any invitation to differ from the crowd. Subtleties entirely escaped their "careless, uncomprehending mentality." They refused to respond to anything but the most blatantly sensational stimuli. In trying to capture a sense of the culture of the "people," a Ruthrauff and Ryan ad verbally panned across the advertising audience for a quick, cinematic impression: "Perspiring thousands at Coney Island. . . . Gaudy pennants. The crunch of peanut shells underfoot. Chewing gum. Mustard dripping from hot dogs. People struggling for a view of some queer freak in a side show. Red-faced men elbowing and crowding for a vicarious thrill of a cooch dancer . . . . Stopping for the shudder of gaping at a gory accident. . . . . Women tearing other women's clothing in the scramble at a bargain counter . . . huddling at a radio to hear a crooner drone Tin Pan Alley's latest potion of vapid sentimentality. . . . Waiting in line for hours to view the saccharine emotional displays of a movie idol. Taking a daily dose of culture from the comic strips."

The Man in the Picture

Unlike the varied ways in which women were depicted in advertising tableaux, men usually appeared in nondescript, standardized parts as husbands or businessmen. But their occupational roles were more varied than women's—an accurate reflection of social realities.

As doctors, dentists, or business executives, they might endorse the product; as truckers, deliverymen, house painters or gas-station attendants they entered the tableaux only when it was necessary to demonstrate the product's manufacture or use. But working-class men never appeared as consumers: an unspoken law decreed that the protagonist in every ad must be depicted as prosperous member of the middle class, dressed in a suit, tie, and hat or fashionable sporting togs.

When merchandising strategy did not call for a particular occupational function, the leading man tended to conform to a single stereotype: he was a businessman. Remedies for nerves, fatigue, and constipation regularly attributed such ills to the stress of business. Among the hundreds of thousands of advertisements that appeared during the 1920s and 1930s, I have yet to discover a single one in which the husband or the ambitious young man is defined as a factory worker, policeman, engineer, professor, architect, or government official, and only one in which he is a lawyer. Even such solid citizens as doctors and dentists appear only in their functional roles, duly proclaimed by a white coat—not as typical husbands.

Within the role of businessman, some slight differentiations emerged. Older men were likely to be cast as business executives. Young men were often salesmen, aspiring to the intermediate step on the business ladder of sales manager. When husbands telephoned their wives to prepare for an unexpected dinner guest, they always brought home either a "sales manager" or a "client." The spectrum of men's activities was described in one tableau in the phrase "wherever they may be, at their desks or on the golf course."

Ads also suggested that, in the struggle of business, the man had often lost "a bit of the sentiment that used to abide in his heart." He had been "shackled to his desk" and might even need to slacken his pace, get to know his wife and children again, and experience those softer sentiments preserved within the shelter of the home. But only for a brief respite. The competitive world of business helped make him a true man, and advertisers occasionally worried that the attempt to pretty him up for the collar ads and the nightclub scenes would sissify and weaken man's image, tailoring it too much to feminine tastes. Edgeworth Smoking Tobacco even suggested that the growing number of women smokers had effeminized cigarettes; men should respond by giving them up and turning to pipes. An Edgeworth ad proclaimed: "A man looks like a man when he smokes a pipe."

Color Sells

Although the notion that adding certain qualities of style or "fashion" to a product could enhance its value to the consumer is a very old one, the 1920s saw an enormous expansion of the range of goods merchandised on this basis. One obvious method of creating style was to introduce a choice of colors. But even this degree of novelty required the manufacturer to make a mental leap. He had to persuade himself that his product belonged to the realm of "fashion" goods.

The major breakthroughs in both color and design occurred between 1924 and 1928. After Willys-Overland pioneered with the colored "Red Bird" car in 1923, General Motors, with the new Duco synthetic lacquers, introduced multiple colors in its 1924 models with gratifying results. Meanwhile, Fisher Body ads accentuated the association between automobiles and high fashion. The Parker Pen Company had recently demonstrated that consumers would respond to the attraction of a bold terra-cotta red barrel on so mundane and utilitarian an instrument as a fountain pen. The Crane Company began offering booklets on color in the bathroom in 1925, and Hoosier Kitchen Cabinets cautiously tested the market for color in late 1924 by coming out with units in "French Gray." Meanwhile, academic psychologists analyzed color preferences—by sex and class, by the attention-getting power of certain colors, and by the "feeling-tone" of various color combinations. By 1927 a writer in *Printers' Ink* had enthroned color as the "sex appeal of business."

The evolution of Cannon and Martex towels in the 1920s illustrated how quickly tentative ventures into color and style could kindle the flame of aesthetic sensibility into the raging fire of a full-blown consumption ethic. In the early 1920s a towel was still a utilitarian staple, an accessory to the Saturday-night bath, and was available only in plain white.

But in 1924 the Cannon Manufacturing Company cautiously initiated consumer advertising, and by 1926 it was trading heavily on style. Cannon produced a "class" towel at four times the average retail price and introduced not only color but decorative designs. It employed a professional designer from Macy's to plan decorative motifs of whales, flamingos, dolphins, ships, and lighthouses. Meanwhile, Martex towels had already engaged René Clarke, an artist and designer with the Calkins and Holden advertising agency, to convert its plebian staples into images of exotic sensuality. Martex advertisements in those years displayed towels with feathery fronds and a band of clear blue water in a bathroom with a "sea-blue wall covering and green fish at the water spouts."

Cannon now escalated its merchandising drive. By 1928 it was subtly promoting increased bathing through advertisements that praised readers for their "wisdom" in adopting the habit of a bath a day. Ads even suggested more than one bath a day. They explained the benefits from such indulgence through a series of advice-laden "bathing recipes": "Because the first towel absorbs impurities from the skin it must never (under any circumstances) be used again before washing." The textile manufacturers were not alone in the color crusade to emancipate the bathroom from prim utilitarianism. By the late 1920s the Crane Company, the Kohler Company, and the American Sanitary Company were advertising color options in plumbing fixtures and tantalizing the public with luxurious full-color illustrations of model bathrooms. Freed from all connotations of shame and reticence, the bathroom rose to the status of a showplace of style and opulence. The American Radiator and Standard Sanitary Corporation dazzled readers with ornate depictions of its Roman-style bathroom with Pompeian motif and its neoclassic Pembroke Model in a Directoire setting. As early as 1927 a Cannon ad proclaimed that the "pistachio and orange" bathroom had supplanted older "plain vanilla affairs" in the public imagination.

The next color conquests took place in the kitchen, the bedroom, and the cellar. By the mid-1920s, color in low-cost kitchen items had been widely introduced. By 1928 the Hoosier Kitchen Cabinet Company was advertising the "new Hoosier Beauty" in such exotic tints as "Venetian green with Oriental red interior." Early in that same year *Printers' Ink* informed readers that the "humble gas range" was about to "blossom riotously in rainbow hues." Several electric refrigerators appeared in 1928 in "four intriguing colors." In the bedroom, advertisers found that the introduction of color and style could even increase consumption of items that usually were not visible. Sheets and pillowcases had previously been "bulk" goods, unbranded and undecorated. But the Pepperell Manufacturing Company brought out the Lady Pepperell line of color sheets and pillowcases in 1928, with an accompanying booklet describing "Personality Bedrooms" in which the sheets harmonized with a woman's complexion. The "daintiness of orchid," for instance, made it "particularly suitable for the 'feminine' type of woman, the woman with delicate, fair skin, small features, and a figure of slight proportions." It was suitable for "blue eyes, black eyes, and gray eyes—if the lashes are dark." Within three months competitors had announced their own colored lines.

The crowning achievement of advertising's emphasis on color, beauty, and style in the 1920s was its popularization of the idea of the ensemble. A passion for harmonies of color and style swept through one product area after another—including such unlikely items as galoshes, bedsprings, and automotive accessories—resulting by 1929 in a number of major merchandising successes.

Women's apparel led the way in the ensemble parade with the sale of purses, for instance, increasing fivefold between the start and end of the decade. In women's hosiery, so rapidly did shades and textures expand to enable precise matching with other elements of the clothing ensemble that the number of separate items produced by the Holeproof Hosiery Company grew from 480 in 1920 to 6,006 in 1927. A *Printers' Ink* writer noted in 1928 that expensive jewelry had largely given way to the preference of women for a large variety of rings, bracelets, and necklaces to harmonize with their various ensembles.

By 1930 advertisements for lipsticks, compacts, watches, and even cameras were promising color and style choices that would contribute to the harmony of the consumer's ensemble. Elgin advertised women's watches in several "Parisienne" styles. Each was designed by one of the "great couturiers of the Rue de la Paix to join your hat and your handbag, frock and flower, shoes and shingle, in composing the perfect *ensemble.*" Although the watch still had a functional value, its preeminent role was to provide the "fashionable touch that emphasizes your entire smartness as an exclamation point accents a sentence."

Meanwhile, the idea of the ensemble spread to the automobile, the kitchen, the bedroom, and the bathroom. With Corona's offer of a choice of six typewriter colors for "perfect harmony" with the user's environment, it even invaded "that little nook of a study where you write." The Ternstedt Company introduced the ensemble into automotive fashion with built-in "ensemble sets" of vanity and smoking cases. It urged consumers to notice how perfectly the paneling and the "theme design wrought into the metal" of the cases harmonized with each automobile's "interior color scheme and appointments." Du Pont, the manufacturer of Duco refinishing paint, beckoned the "gypsy-hearted motorist" to reflect on the changing natural hues of Indian summer. "Your car—it too can change its garment"; it could harmonize with the "golden orange of the hills or the soft gray of the fields." Hupmobile Motor Company went further. One of its advertisements asked: "Does the [car's] contour reflect the modern mode for restrained and governed grace? . . . Are the accessories placed where they accent the design as tellingly as the correct shoes, hat and handbag point a costume? . . . Are the metal trimmings chosen to touch the ensemble with brilliance as skillfully as you choose your jewels?"

Since women sometimes carried cameras as well as handbags, the Eastman Kodak Company reasoned, why should this additional accessory be allowed to disrupt the unity of the ensemble? In 1928 the company brought out the Vanity Kodak, a "highly ornamental and intensely personal" camera "designed to echo the color scheme of the particular costume." These came in five colored leathers—"Sea Gull (gray), Cockatoo (green), Redbreast (red), Bluebird (blue), and Jenny Wren (brown)."

Silverware might appear even less amenable than cameras to the new strategy of merchandising on the basis of color harmonies, but Oneida Ltd. remained undaunted. They introduced a line with colored handles to form a tasteful ensemble with other table accessories. The handles had the "translucent rose-red of rubies, the clear blue of sapphires, or the scintillant green of emeralds" and would blend with the silverware "in chords of color."

Reason might suggest that the rage for color ensembles could go no further. The B.V.D. Company perhaps reached the limit in urging a wife to "keep [her husband] decorative even in his underwear": "Make him a better boudoir decoration."

While the idea of the ensemble unquestionably appealed to advertising leaders on aesthetic grounds, its virtues as a merchandising strategy were at least equally attractive. In some industries the ensemble provided a welcome solution to the "bugaboo of market saturation, as *Printers' Ink* expressed it. For the woman who aspired to a stylish image, the purchase of a new dress now involved the additional purchase of matching shoes, hat, handbag, and color-coordinated hosiery and jewelry. She might even realize a need for new shades of underwear, makeup, lipstick, and fingernail polish as well. Once accepted, noted a writer in *Printers' Ink,* the prepackaged ensemble idea was a perfect tool for the smart retailer who "wants to sell a customer as much as he can in the shortest time with a minimum of floor and counter space."

The Parable of the First Impression

A flush of anticipation colored the cheeks of the beautiful young lady as her escort seated her at the elegant table. It was her first important dinner among the city's smart set. But as the butler served the first course, her excitement turned to terror. "From that row of gleaming silver on either side of her plate, which piece shall she pick up?" Suddenly she sensed that her chance of being invited to such an affair again—in fact, her whole future popularity—would be determined by this first impression of her "presence." As her social destiny hung in the balance, "she could feel every eye on her *hesitating hand.*"

Even if she passed the test of the "Hesitating Hand," a young lady was certain to encounter many other fateful first-impression judgments. In the episode of the "Open Door," she and her husband faced the greatest social crisis of their five-year marriage: they had taken the bold step of inviting the vice-president-in-charge-of-sales and his wife to dinner. For days the eager young wife planned the dinner menu. Her husband researched and rehearsed several topics for appropriate conversation. But both completely forgot about their tasteless front doorway, with its lack of beautifully designed woodwork. And neither realized how dreary and out-of-date the furniture they had purchased soon after their marriage had become. Thus, all their efforts at preparation came to naught, for their guests formed an indelible impression during "those few seconds" from the "touch of the bell" to their entrance into the living room.

Twenty years later, with the husband still third assistant for sales at the small branch office, they anxiously passed on to their children a hard-won bit of wisdom: "Your future may rest on what the Open Door reveals."

These dramas from advertisements of the late 1920s suggest the pathos with which copywriters could recount the popular parable of the First Impression. According to such tableaux, first impressions brought instantaneous success or failure. In a relatively mobile society, where business organizations loomed ever larger and people dealt far more often with strangers, the reasons one man gained a promotion or one woman suffered a social snub had become less explicable on grounds of long-standing favoritism or old family feuds. One might suspect that almost anything—especially a first impression—had made the crucial difference.

Sensing their power in these circumstances, advertisers made use of the parable of the First Impression. Often they modified the basic formula of the tableau slightly to fit their particular product. Clothing manufacturers stressed overall appearance; makers of gum, toothpaste, and toothbrushes promised a "magic road to popularity in that first winning smile." Williams Shaving Cream stressed that powerful initial impact of the "face that's fit" for the "double-quick march of business." All agreed that "it's the 'look' of you by which you are judged most often." One of the most important effects of preparing carefully for that crucial first impression, many ads suggested, was the sense of self-confidence it created. A lovely frock, washed in Lux, would enable any woman to overcome an inferiority complex and feel a "deep, sure, inner conviction of being charming," Dorothy Dix counseled readers of the *Ladies' Home Journal*. The House of Kuppenheimer confided to the up-and-coming young man that "someday your father may tell you how a certain famous letter *k* in his inner coat pocket . . . put confidence in his heart . . . the confidence born of good appearance. And so helped him land his first job."

The parable of the First Impression taught that these impressions were being formed constantly and almost instantaneously. Only because she was constantly prepared could the heroine of a Dr. West's toothbrush tableau pass the "Smile Test" during that moment when a handsome man picked her up from a fall off a speeding toboggan. A charming hostess who failed to obtain stylish new furnishings would henceforth be condemned to "lonely afternoons, dreary evenings" for being unprepared for acquaintances who called once out of courtesy but never came again. One ardent suitor completely destroyed the good impression he had built up over months "when she noticed a hint of B.O." as he knelt to pop the question. There was no appeal from such judgments; no way to escape the constant surveillance. The Cleanliness Institute of the Association of American Soap and Glycerine Producers counseled: "Everywhere we go the people we meet are sizing us up. Very quickly they decide whether we are, or are not, from nice homes."

Advertisers of home furnishings applied the "nice home" idea broadly. Johns Manville, for instance, argued that roofing shingles bespoke the "taste and standing of the family" and Sherwin-Williams cautioned that "many a man has been rated as lacking in community spirit . . . even as a business failure—merely because of a paint-starved house."

Advertisers of bathroom furnishings and fixtures boldly applied the parable of the First Impression to the innermost recesses of the home. If every room told a story, then this most hidden and intimate of rooms would clearly reveal family character. In "The Room You Do Not Show," discerning visitors would find a quick index to your standards and "beliefs on how a civilized person should live," a Kohler Company ad proclaimed.

The C. F. Church Manufacturing Company narrowed the focus ever further: "The bathroom, most of all, is a clue to the standards of the household and the most conspicuous thing in the bathroom is the toilet seat." Little wonder that the man in the Brunswick-Balke-Collender Company tableau, who had just learned of the impending visit of an influential business associate, thought first of the "old-fashioned wood toilet seat" as his mind's eye quickly scanned his house for social flaws.

No other medium of popular culture preached the parable of the First Impression with the insistence of advertising or accepted its validity so unquestioningly. Whereas movies and soap operas often provided vicarious experiences of triumphs over society's false accusations, advertisements emphasized the power, validity, and pervasiveness of the world's judgmental scrutiny. With headlines such as "When they look at YOUR FEET ON THE BEACH," "Suppose you could follow yourself up the street . . . What would you see?" and "more searching than your mirror . . . your husband's eyes," they encouraged the transformation of this scrutiny into self-accusation. Their cumulative effect was more likely to reinforce the readers' impression of being surrounded by a host of accusing eyes than to reassure them that new furniture, familiarity with good silverware, or a "face that's fit" would testify to their "innocence" and spare them social shame.

The Parable of the Unraised Hand

The Depression brought several new or little-used advertising parables into prominence. One of these was the parable of the Unraised Hand. The school classroom, which rarely had served as a setting for advertising tableaux in the 1920s, now came into wider use. Poignant scenes of the student's arrival home with a report card, or humiliating comparisons of report cards, also became more common. The most striking of these tableaux began to appear in 1933, when Post Bran Flakes presented a "Real Life Movie" of "The Strange Case of Mary Dodd." In the most heartrending scene of the "movie," little Mary sat listless with constipation while the other beaming children in the classroom eagerly raised their hands to answer the teacher's question. Later that year, General Foods (Postum) confided sadly to the reader, "A Dunce they called him . . . a sluggard," while depicting the scene in which a teacher gazed judgmentally down at a discouraged boy kept after school to work alone at his desk amid the deepening shadows of a deserted classroom.

Each parable of the Unraised Hand delivered a message that parents were guilty of neglect. The child was failing through no fault of his own; but his disadvantages could be easily removed by the proper parental purchases. In this respect, Depression versions of the parable of the Unraised Hand departed not a whit from precursors of the 1920s. What did change was the new emphasis on academic failure. In 1929 only one advertiser, Compton's Pictured Encyclopedia, had centered a general magazine campaign on possible failures in school examinations. Two other advertisers, Corona Typewriters and Quaker Oats, had given momentary attention to "slow" children and "distressing" report cards. But by 1933 a wide range of advertisers, from producers of breakfast cereals and vitamin supplements to pharmaceutical firms and toilet-paper manufacturers, were preaching the parable of the Unraised Hand.

Why this sudden emphasis on children's classroom performance? Advertising men during the Depression were fascinated with the topic of competitive struggle. Moreover, they may have perceived that many parents, frustrated in their own ambitions, had now fixed their aspirations and competitive anxieties on their children. And that poor boy, struggling in the ignominy of after-school detention, was not a natural "dunce"; only his parents' failure to substitute Postum for coffee had made him so.

Advertiser after advertiser found a sales argument in the parable of the Unraised Hand. A young student's mother in a Scott Paper Company ad confessed: "Mary was so fidgety she couldn't concentrate . . . I was shocked to find that harsh toilet tissue was the cause." The Eagle Pencil Company introduced parents vicariously to the terrible tensions of classroom competition: "Jim's in the 4th grade . . . How he does bear down on that pencil! He must hang on hard, for pencils will slip through chubby, damp fingers! 15 examples in 15 minutes . . . will he make it? You can help him pass his test . . . make sure he has a smooth pencil, with a strong lead that won't snap in the middle of 4 x 4 and upset him."

In the Post Bran Flakes version of the parable, the guilty mother played a particularly villainous role. While several of little Sally's schoolmates laughed mockingly at her report card, Sally's mother shrieked: "Sally Lennox! I'm *ashamed* of this report card. What will your father say?" Sally's mother *should* feel ashamed, the parable revealed, but for her *own* inattention in failing to recognize that Sally's real trouble was constipation. "Maybe you have a little girl like Sally," the company suggested, spreading the suspicion of guilt; "and perhaps, like Sally's mother, you have been unjust to her."

And so the message of the parable of the Unraised Hand continued to echo through the magazine pages with minor variations. In a tableau bluntly captioned "Here are the report cards of Two Boys," General Electric contrasted the A's of the son of "thoughtful parents" with the C's and D's of the boy who studied in poor light. Remington Rand, the typewriter maker, probed the pained conversation of two parents in "We tried to joke about it . . . But *was* Joe really dumb?"

The Parable of the Skinny Kid

Another closely related tableau gained remarkable momentum with the deepening of the Depression. Advertisements had previously touted various food and vitamin products as correctives for the underweight, but never had copywriters tortured mothers so frequently and unforgivingly for the sin of allowing their children to remain skinny as they did in the 1930s. Now a host of scrawny youngsters paraded before the consumer audience, each spindly leg and gaunt chest testifying to a mother's guilt.

No copywriters imbued the parable of the Skinny Kid with more power as a weapon of reproach and persuasion than those of the Ruthrauff and Ryan agency in ads for the milk supplement Cocomalt. Rejecting the warm, genteel tone of Cocomalt's previous sunlight-and-happy-healthy-children campaign, Ruthrauff and Ryan launched in the spring of 1931 an exposé of guilty mothers with such headlines as "Whose fault when children are frail?" and "People pitied my boy, he was so thin." Stark "slice-of-life" photographs and vivid conversational frankness marked the new Cocomalt style. One mother, stooping to pull up her boy's drooping sock, was "mortified"to hear one well-dressed woman on a nearby park bench comment to another, "That child looks half-starved."

The parable of the Skinny Kid explored new dimensions of social shame. Middle-class women have worried about their children's lack of weight at many other times, but in the view of advertisers their children's thinness made them most susceptible to persuasion through fears of social mortification during the Depression.

A Friendly Visit from Betty Crocker

In the January 1930 issue of *Better Homes and Gardens* the buoyant, chatty narrator of a Procter and Gamble advertisement related a heartwarming story. As a result of ads that had publicized her previous nineteen "actual visits to P and G homes," she was no longer a stranger to the average housewife. On her most recent visit to a randomly selected consumer, she had no sooner introduced herself than "Bobby's Mother" had "opened the door wide." "'Come in,' she invited smilingly, 'I've read every single P and G Naphtha story. And I've often wished on your trips that you could find me.'"

We may be tempted to dismiss this delightful modern fairy tale—in which the consumer longs to get to know better the advertiser of a cleaning product—as an archetypal copywriter's fantasy. But if we look at the record, we recognize this tableau as one of many signs that the new advertising had recognized another vacuum it might fill. From a variety of sources, advertising leaders perceived that people in the 1930s seemed to suffer from an insufficient sense of "the personal" in modern life. They hungered to be addressed as individuals. They even liked to "personalize" the products they used and to get advice about those products from people they felt they "knew." From Beatrice Fairfax to Dorothy Dix, newspaper advice-to-the-lovelorn columnists had attracted literally tons of mail from eager correspondents. And *True Story* and the tabloids were now demonstrating the popularity of "first-person" stories with which people could identify even more directly.

Of all the advertising outlets, however, it was radio that impressed advertising men most forcefully about the public craving for personal relationships through the mass media. Advertisers learned early that listeners formed attachments to radio personalities who were "guests" in their homes. Those who offered information and personal advice were bombarded with intimate letters. "Betty Crocker" had been invented in 1921 to sign company letters to housewives who responded to a contest with "questions that in more neighborly communities had been asked over the back fence." But it was radio that made Betty Crocker come alive. A 1925 experiment with the "chatty" style on the "Betty Crocker School of the Air" in Buffalo, according to the General Mills historian James Gray, attracted letters by the tens of thousands. Within a year, thirteen Betty Crockers were speaking over regional radio networks, offering friendly advice and reassurance. Eventually, Betty was signing replies to over four thousand letters a day.

Advertising leaders were impressed and astonished by both the number and the intimacy of the letters that poured in whenever a media personality like Betty Crocker, real or invented, invited personal communications. When Postum introduced the friendly adviser "Carrie Blanchard," this fictitious public confidante was soon receiving "more letters than a movie star."

By the end of the 1920s, advertising agencies were routinely creating fictitious confidantes and sponsoring helpful, personalized experts for their clients. There was "Ruth Miller" for Odo-ro-no, "Nurse Ellen J. Buckland" and "Mary Pauline Callender" for Kotex, "Marjorie Mills" for Lux, "Mary Dale Anthony" for S.O.S. scouring pads, "Aunt Ellen" for Griswold Cast Iron Cooking Utensils, "Helen Chase" for Camay, and more than a dozen others. Even the U.S. Bureau of Home Economics had its "Aunt Sammy" on radio. The J. Walter Thompson agency described the chatty column in the Libby ads by their Mary Hale Martin as "brimful of real 'heart interest.' " And advertisers made sure that those who wrote letters received "personally signed" replies from Mary Hale Martin, Aunt Ellen, or Helen Chase.

Advertising men often spoke of the outpouring of confidential correspondence with bemused contempt. They were amazed at the credulity of people and their eagerness to discuss their personal problems with invented commercial characters. But the confidantes sold goods, and young copywriters were urged to visualize the audience as "*one* person at a time" and to talk to each reader "just as you would if you were seated before a cheery log fire or chatting over tea cups." Scarcely anyone, either in the advertising trade or outside, objected to the illusion of human intimacy that such ads sought to create. Edward Bok, the crusading editor of the early-twentieth-century *Ladies' Home Journal,* had once campaigned zealously against the Lydia Pinkham ads for the fraud of soliciting personal letters to Mrs. Pinkham long after the company's founder had died. But no muckraker of the 1920s came forth to expose the "bored young men struggling for the feminine touch" who often wrote the copy for the fictitious public confidantes of the new advertising.

By the early 1930s the dulcet, friendly voices of commercial personalities were saturating the airwaves. Among the first celebrated radio confidantes were Don McNeill (of "The Breakfast Club") and the radio-show hostess Mary Margaret McBride. Advertisers noting the tons of mail that poured in to characters on the new radio soap operas eagerly recruited such personalities. In 1933 the Voice of Experience, a radio adviser on intimate problems, broke a record by eliciting more than sixty-five hundred letters on a single day. Another program, entitled "Your Lover," featured a male voice against the background of muted organ music in a virtual parody of the "one person at a time" approach: "Hello, young lady. Yes, I mean you. . . . It's grand to be with you. And it's sweet of you to let me have the thrill of talking to you. . . . Come over here near me—won't you. . . . Just for a minute let's forget everyone else in the world."

"Your Lover" also delivered the commercial message in the same intimate style. Trade journals like *Tide* might deplore the mawkish excesses of "Your Lover" and its willingness to play on the "sick day-dreams of . . . maladjusted women," but they also reported the heavy mail this program had inspired.

By the early 1930s advertisers had thoroughly accepted the public hunger for personalized communications, and advertising men were looking for new ways to apply the "personal touch." Advertising agencies convinced several company presidents to shed their dignity and become familiar friends to the public through "personalized . . . racy, man-to-man talks."

Given the rage for the personal touch, it was perhaps inevitable that advertising writers would eventually seek to "personalize" the product itself. "When all else fails I'm your best Friend," promised the protagonist of a Lucky Strike ad—the product itself. A Lucky was a "better friend than others," it promised the reader, because "in personal tragedies, minor or major, a Lucky stands you in good stead." *Printers' Ink* praised new techniques of bringing the ingredients of products to life by depicting them as "little characters with names," and trade-journal writers called on the advertising copywriters to find the "face" that lay embedded in every product.

Perhaps more than any other institution,

American advertising, although preeminently the spokesman for modernism and technological progress, tried to reassure an anxious public that society still operated on a comprehensible human scale in which people could expect their individual needs to be recognized and catered to.

Facing the Music

During the summer of 1931, an irreverent new magazine entitled *Ballyhoo* exploded like a bombshell on the advertising scene. An overnight financial success, this unlikely Depression phenomenon offered vivid evidence of a latent public skepticism of all advertising. Launched as a humor magazine, *Ballyhoo* relied for laughs entirely on lampoons of notorious advertisements. Its parody of Listerine toothpaste's what-you-can-buy-with-the-money-you-save campaign proclaimed the wonders of "Blisterine": "Buy yourself some false teeth with the money you save on toothpaste." In "How Georgie Cursed when Milktime Came," *Ballyhoo* lampooned the new Cocomalt style with a worried mother ad for Creme de Cocoa: "Georgie's weight has gone up a pound a week . . . since I began giving him milk this easy way. . . . You'll be surprised what Creme de Cocoa will do for your baby. It will darn near knock him outen his little bassinet!" Movie star "La Belle Zilch" kept her girlish figure by bathing "every fortnight" with "Lox Toilet Soap."

With ad copy of this character, the initial edition of *Ballyhoo* (August 1931) sold out the entire run of 150,000 copies in a few days. It simply burst into existence, an agency executive complained, "like some rank tropical flower." The September issue sold almost double that number—275,000 copies. October brought another sellout, this time of all 650,000 copies. Within five months *Ballyhoo* magazine, with a circulation of a million and a half, had become one of the most sensational new business enterprises to defy the Depression. The publisher began accepting paid ads at $3,750 a page but insisted that all adopt an appropriate satirical approach.

Ballyhoo also gained overnight success within the advertising trade. Everyone talked about it, joked about it, and shuddered a bit at its ultimate implications. "Anyone with two eyes in his head can see that the public is getting restive," warned H. A. Batten of N. W. Ayer and Son. *Advertising and Selling* sensed a growing public skepticism that regarded advertising as a "great joke." It was all right for advertising agents to enjoy private lampoons at their own expense, but quite a different story when the paying customers reacted to high-priced ads with a "coarse and disrespectful horse-laugh."

An even more disturbing symptom of rising public distrust of advertising emerged in the form of a fledging consumer movement. In 1927 the flustered advertising trade had reacted with a flurry of censure, ridicule, and counter-attack to Stuart Chase and F. J. Schlink's muckraking book, *Your Money's Worth*. Chase and Schlink had suggested that consumers create a test service to provide an objective source of information about products. Public response to the book encouraged them to expand their initial Consumers Club in White Plains, New York, into a national organization known as Consumers' Research. Its membership reached twelve thousand by 1930, and with the impetus of the Depression, membership doubled in 1931.

Meanwhile, other consumer-education organizations had emerged. A consumers' cooperative movement was expanding. In 1933 F. J. Schlink and Arthur Kallet published *1,000,000 Guinea Pigs*, a sensational account of the misleading advertising of drugs and cosmetics. The trade press erupted with furious denials. But some advertising leaders interpreted the incipient consumers' movement as a symptom of a public skepticism induced by the heavy-handed advertising of the early 1930s. Devoting its first page of copy to an unprecedented lead editorial, *Advertising and Selling* alerted readers that its

October 1931 article on the work of Consumers' Research had evoked more concerned responses than any article since a paid testimonials controversy of the late 1920s. The psychologist Henry Link reported survey results that indicated that only 4 to 5 percent of the public believed certain current advertising assertions. Even the most credible assertions convinced only 37 percent of those surveyed. *Printers' Ink Monthly* noted the growth of consumer councils and warned the smug creators of "misleading, vulgar advertising" that a "movement of this kind grows with the geometrical rapidity of a snow-ball."

By the mid-1930s the tiny new consumer organizations were inspiring fear in the advertising trade because they threatened to pursue their objectives through the new regulatory powers of the federal government. The Roosevelt administration proposed to extend the powers of the Food and Drug Administration to cover cosmetics and to regulate advertising as well as labeling. It also called for government-enforced grade labeling of food. What would happen to brand-name advertising, many advertising leaders wondered, if people were induced to base their buying decisions on a grading system defined by the government? Would it destroy all advertising that celebrated, by implication, the superiority of Jones's grade-A canned peaches over the grade-A peaches canned by Brown? And once the regulation of drug and cosmetic advertising began, would not other inhibiting forms of regulation follow?

As early as the fall of 1932, *Advertising and Selling* had begun to warn that such "pseudo-scientific" scare campaigns as the Scott Tissue ads, which dramatically warned of the dire results of using the arsenic-laden brands of toilet paper sold by competitors, were a "direct invitation to government regulation." The New Deal proposals for the expansion of FDA regulation inspired calls for preventive self-regulation within the industry. A contributor to *Advertising and Selling* warned that the 1934 elections would bring a new Congress and a "flood of social legislation which will place advertising on a hotter seat than it has ever been on before." In an editorial entitled "Let's Face the Music," *Printers' Ink* noted the growing number of dignified organizations now testifying to their skepticism of advertising before the Senate Commerce Committee. The specter of advancing government regulation provoked the editor to call upon "honest, intelligent, and high-minded advertisers" to silence the "fakers, charlatans, and crooks" of their trade.

The Golden Age was over. Never again would advertising be so uncritically accepted by the public or so unabashedly composed by the agencies.

Or would it?

"We may hear too much": American Sensibility and the Response to Radio, 1919–1924

Catherine L. Covert

I have always dodged this radio question," Chief Justice William Howard Taft is reported to have said during the early years of broadcasting. "Interpreting the law on this subject is something like trying to interpret the law of the occult. It seems like dealing with something supernatural. I want to put it off as long as possible."[1]

Taft could not be considered an innocent. His public life encompassed both the Radio Act of 1912 when he was president and the Radio Act of 1927 when he was chief justice. Yet here he expressed quite simply the bafflement many people felt when confronted with something so new, so incomprehensible as radio. All he could do was to reach for an old metaphor; invoking the "supernatural" was an ancient way of comprehending the new and making it accessible to the understanding.

This chapter focuses on such organizing ideas and images that Americans used to make sense—either intellectual or emotional sense out of what they saw and heard as they experienced radio's startling impact on sensibility after the Great War.[2]

Americans talked enthusiastically of the new radio in these years, borrowing prewar images of heroism and venture to describe their experiments with batteries and headsets. Most historians of radio have also focused primarily on the wonder, joy, and excitement radio produced.[3]

Barnouw would entitle an entire section of his first volume on radio history, "The Euphoria of 1922."[4] Radio did represent a remarkable expansion of powers over time and distance; "euphoria" was appropriate. But this heady sense was tinged by an uneasy impression that radio was also ominous and somehow foreboding. Some individuals could also, of course, project on any new cultural element all their dominant fears. Henry Ford's *Dearborn Independent* instantly saw in radio the frightful new weapon of Communists and Jews.[5] Such warnings are evidence to the extremes of sensibility in the period. Amid their din more contained voices sounded, those of observers who sensed the psychic costs this new technology was beginning to exact.

These pessimistic comments tended to be fleeting, atypical, and cloaked in denial of one sort or another. Nevertheless they were significant fore-runners of common apprehensions that would develop as electronic communications pervaded American life.[6]

One of the costs suffered in confronting such new technology—indeed in confronting anything new—was that of a sense of loss; loss of old behavior, old values, old relationships, old senses of the self. An argument can be advanced that such a loss resembled bereavement. The bereaved suffers not only the loss of the old but the meaninglessness of the new, and the grieving process can be successfully completed only by attaching the meanings of the lost object to the new. (Widows, for example, have to find some new person or activity which revives the old sense of themselves as valuable persons.)[7]

This process of assimilating the new to the old involved moving back and forth between the two, accommodating one to the other, until finally a synthesis was achieved. Only then could genuine new meaning evolve, and with it a new sensibility.

The people of the twenties experienced some such process of grief as they learned to attach old meanings to experience with new technology, reweaving patterns of imagination and behavior to encompass radio in the new fabric of their lives.[8]

This chapter focuses on a five-year transitional period, 1919–24, between the lifting of controls on amateur radio experimenters after World War I and David Sarnoff's proposal for a "chain" of high-powered stations across the country in 1924. In this period corporations fixed their hold on radio receiver manufacturing. They would shortly expand to control broadcasting, but the rationalizing effect of the networks and the radio legislation of 1927 were still to come. By 1922 some 500 transmitting stations had been set up under the auspices of such organizations as churches, newspapers, educational institutions, department stores, and equipment manufacturers. Programming was chaotic, built at first around speakers and performers who volunteered. Advertising developed only slowly; listening and transmitting were in a wildly experimental state. In this fluid period would be shaped the nature of radio impact on American sensibility.[9]

My primary sources for this study are selected from popular print media because I wish to argue that the press in this transitional time played a crucial conservative role in the process of confronting the new.[10] Serving as a cultural storehouse of images and metaphors, the press helped make it possible for people to imagine the new in terms of the old. This process took place with radio. Only after experiences with radio had been clothed with meaning according to old systems of images and explanations could this new technology become really "available to the imagination"—Fussell's phrase—on its own terms.[11]

Inherited Images

Leonard Smith, Jr., reporter for the *New York Times,* put on a pair of ear phones in 1922 and was "fascinated . . . awestruck" by "sounds that surely were never intended to be heard by a human being . . . noises that roar in the space between the worlds."[12]

"'What are those noises?' you ask the operator . . . He shrugs his shoulders. 'You know as much as I do,' he says."

The mysterious sounds proved difficult to describe. In mustering an analogy in order to domesticate the experience, Smith succeeded almost too well, comparing the "noises that roar in space" to the sound of frying eggs. Others found more trenchant analogies.

From deep in cultural memory came Taft's concept of the supernatural, primitive and powerful as an explanation of the unknown. Postwar readers appeared to conceive of radio most easily in images inherited from wireless. Some might carry in their imaginations the aura of the famous Kipling story published by *Scribner's* in 1902, a haunted thing about a night experimental wireless signals across England were blocked by transmissions from the beyond, the voice of the long-dead poet Keats.[13]

The two decades after the Kipling story had seen arguments among scientists and the laity as to whether electric "waves" relayed by wireless telegraphy provided evidence for the existence of thought "waves" relayed by telepathy.[14] In 1919 an essayist for *Harper's* sensed "something uncanny, something savoring of telepathy" in wireless, "something which did not obey the recognized laws that have been derived from experience in other fields" even though he promptly smothered such indiscretion in stolid arithmetic about sound waves.[15]

Almost all such excursions were immediately demystified by scientific explanation. These "magic powers," as Smith of the *New York Times* put it, had been "harnessed" by science.[16] The sentence would become a formula for science writers, a ritual transition from alluring "mystery" headlines to the more mundane account that followed.

Even the *Harper's* exercise had climaxed somewhat ambiguously, however, in speculation about voices from "spheres other than our own."[17] Such hearing of a disembodied voice was a shock to sensibility difficult to imagine a half-century later. But it struck ancient chords in the Protestant imagination, steeped in Old Testament imagery, resonating to the voice from the burning bush. Future movie makers and lyricists would apply old story to new technology, turning out film and song in which the voice from the radio was the voice of God.[18]

Much of the inherited language science used in discussing radio still bore religious or spiritual connotation. Mentions of the "ether" and the "heavens" had always invoked otherworldly associations.[19] And wireless shared its designation as a "medium" with the spiritualist practitioner, an individual of increasing prominence in the troubled years following the Great War.[20] A striking essay by W. H. Worrell appeared in the November 1922 issue of *Radio Broadcast,* a handsome new Doubleday publication whose contributors seemed particularly sensitive to the subtle implications of the new technology. Invoking radio as "apparently supernatural . . . affording a change from the regularity of nature and of average human experience," Worrell found that radio appeared to be "transmission and reception of pure form, without substance . . . This form, this exchange of thought, is constantly passing about us—*passing through us—from countless transmitting stations, at this very instant!*" Radio possessed all the fascination of a link between the physical and the spiritual; one felt at the threshold of fundamental truths.[21]

Adding lustre to this complex strand of associations was identification of wireless telephony with psychoanalysis, often linked in this period to the occult.[22] By 1922 the *New York Tribune* published a fantasy about a novelist who played golf while his unconscious dictated his latest work to his secretary by a mysterious kind of interpersonal radio.[23]

Altogether the experience of radio seemed to invoke a different sensibility. In contrast to the printing press or the motion picture, radio broadcasting "harks back to the primitive," said one *Scribner's* critic in 1923, "giving it new power as yet unmeasured."[24] In a period when fears rose and confidence in rationality grew increasingly fragile, the ancient comforts of the non-rational seemed appealing. Taft's intuitive remark floated on a strong under-current of the time.[25]

Contrary to this supernatural explanation, and existing in comfortable contradiction with it, was the quiet worldly experience of Americans with the telephone—as a direct connection between real human beings. In fact the new radiophone behaved in the American imagination as a sort of eccentric telephone without wires.

The old long-distance phone had moved signals dependably along wires between two people. Its primary purpose, as a turn-of-the-century telephone executive had assured his customers, had been to provide "confidential" conversations. Indeed a chief triumph for Angus S. Hibbard, general manager of the Chicago Telephone Company, had been to persuade late-Victorian businessmen that they were not "talking into a hole in the end of an iron arm," but "speaking into the ear of a man." Women had posed no such problem, Hibbard observed, being keen to "grasp the personality" of the invisible conversationalist, smiling and bowing into the telephone and even stopping to touch up their hair before taking a call in their own rooms. The whole effect had been that of intimate connection—private, personal, and direct.[26]

It seemed reasonable to expect that the new wireless telephony would also serve as a device for interpersonal communication. Veteran telephone users were affronted, then, to discover that radiophone signals connecting two people also radiated indiscriminately through the air, allowing other individuals with radiophones to listen or wantonly to interrupt. Writers spoke resentfully of "leakage of signals" into the hands of "unauthorized persons." The factor of "non-secrecy" was also deplored through the teens as a vital commercial defect. (The idea of deliberately using this unfortunate radiating quality to enable one person to communicate with many, i.e., to "broadcast," occurred only to a few before World War I. There seemed nothing in the technology to shape inevitably the mass form radio "broadcasting" would eventually take.[27])

At the same time the growing tribe of amateur experimenters shared the telephonic model, smirking about "eavesdropping" on others' signals. As late as 1923, radio fans would still talk of "listening in," language evoking the clandestine pleasures of the rural party line.[28]

When the American Telephone and Telegraph Company set out to exploit wireless telephony, it intended to facilitate private conversation from persons abroad, from moving vehicles, from ship to shore. Even its ground-breaking experiment of 1922 in setting up a station to send signals only one way, the famous Station WEAF, was conceived as a sort of open-ended telephone. Anyone who wanted to talk to the public could step up to the microphone and pay a toll for the time. Senders proved distressingly few, musical intervals had to be improvised, corporations began to buy time, and paid commercial "broadcasting" was willy-nilly under way.

The expectation of private communication between individuals died slowly as the idea of a medium controlled by institutions and broadcasting to masses came to dominate American consciousness.[29]

Radio also entered the national consciousness on a wave of fantasy about wireless operators. At hand were all the formulas lovingly compounded by writers over the years—romance, melodrama, heroism, self-sacrifice. "Never yet has a wireless operator failed in his duty to humanity on land or sea!"[30] There was a vital sense of connection, of responsibility.

Such images had crested on a wave of news stories about the operator on the liner "Carpathia" who clung to his key, speeding rescue to the sinking "Titanic" in 1912.[31] They surfaced in the enlistment propaganda of 1917. Whether the choice would be trench or radio shack, "You can be heroic and manly in either."[32] The "Romance of the Wireless" became almost a cliché in both headline and magazine title.

It was not surprising that the journalists assembling the first issue of the magazine *Radio Broadcast* in 1922 invoked that lovely sense of excitement in experimenting with radio, a pursuit endowed with a "romance" and a "spirit of adventure" that "no other branch of science enjoys!"[33]

The mention of science here invoked the notion of dominance. Images of power and control had frequently surfaced in both scientific journals and the magazines of lay science during the teens, reporting new dominion over trains, weather, crime, steamships, railroads, warfare, and indeed over time itself—all made possible by ever-expanding forays with radiotelephony.[34]

Thus when the amateur experimenter of the early twenties sat down in his garage, shack, or attic bedroom to assemble his mystifying array of wires, coils, and batteries, he could inhabit a world of excitement, drama, and power. He could choose to exert his will over time and distance. He could send his voice across the miles. In those precious hours of the imagination, there was symbolic expansion, aggression, responsibility, and action. "Manly" was indeed the word.

Transition

It is historically accurate for masculine terminology to have dominated the preceding paragraphs. Amateur radio was almost exclusively a male affair; a fraternal brotherhood pursued it.[35] Small boys bought parts and assembled crystal sets; fathers ventured into the complexities of the super-heterodyne. Mothers, sisters, daughters rarely participated. They were cast—at best—in popular periodical accounts on radio as mildly tolerant, so long as the venture did not intrude on their domain.[36]

In the early twenties articles began to appear in popular magazines describing devious ways of sneaking the radio apparatus into the living room. Females would object. There would be noise, mess, and battery acid on the rug. Therefore Mother must be lured from home and the radio installed in her absence. In some fashion the unreliable apparatus must be persuaded to emit enticing music as she was introduced back onto the scene. She would smile, and the battle would be won. In various forms this drama was re-enacted in contemporary print.[37] Radio appeared gradually to inhabit the living room, not the garage. Installed in a modishly designed cabinet, it was transformed from a laboratory apparatus into a piece of furniture. It began to be thought of as a family pastime, not a lone flight of the imagination. It meant listening, not transmitting; consuming, not creating. A once venturesome pursuit appeared to have become domesticated and passive.[38]

Indeed the notions of domestication and passivity would characterize much of the new imagery of radio listening. "Having my after-dinner coffee in the den," reflected one listener, "I couldn't help but think how comfortable I was, seated in my easy chair with the earphones in place." By 1924 a new symbolic triad of masculine satisfactions had emerged—radio, slippers, and cigar.[39]

There were many such expressions of delight over the new luxury and ease of access to distant events. But there was also dismay. The most cutting comments came from the cultists of true manhood. It was simply effete to lounge at home, listening to the ball game rather than shouting from the stands. Amateur radio experimenters also joined in the derision. Restricted by 1922 to transmitting on no more than a 200-meter wave length, amateurs saw themselves as an embattled elite of activists. Threatening them they saw a growing mass of sluggish "proletarians" who thought amateur signals interfered with living-room reception, a mass which could only listen, not transmit.[40] And keening from the edges of the battle were those critics who deplored radio as typical of all technology, transforming man into passive consumer or man into machine.[41]

Such loss of mastery and loss of connection were perhaps most effectively evoked by the magazine essayist, Bruce Bliven. In 1924 he made a fancied visit to the "Legion" family whose lives centered on radio. A once-dominant father now quails before a domineering wife—whose favorite radio listening is a fundamentalist preacher—and petulant children bent on the new jazz. Father will be banished to a portable in the basement if he persists in "debauching" himself with a prize fight. The teenage children commandeer the set, turn on jazz for dancing, and Father subsides with the rug rolled up over his feet.[42]

The sense of conflict between gain and loss expressed so vividly in this satire seems akin to the feelings of any loss. Journalism such as this gave imaginative shape to the ambivalence and anxiety occasioned by the new technology. Its phrases helped to crystalize the conflict between hope for the new and pain over loss of the old.

The New Ambiguities

Popular language about radio became more ambiguous as postwar Americans submitted to the electronic experience. That experience appeared subtly to be altering consciousness; gone was the old world of sight as primary vehicle of sensual data. One must be prepared to live alternatively and intensively in a world constructed only of sound. "For centuries the ear has played a secondary role," announced the *Dearborn Independent*. "The eye with the aid of the printed page, supplanted it. . . . With radio the ear comes back."[43]

To many, indeed, the ear now appeared supreme.[44] Its language dominated reports of the new radio-induced sensibility. In an April 1923 essay in *Scribner's*, O. E. McMeans reproduced the sensations of a new instantaneous experience of environment. By a "slight crooking of the finger" one could elicit a locomotive whistle in Georgia, a Kansas City siren, "My Old Kentucky Home" from Louisville, or the police gongs and crowd yells at the scene of a robbery-in-progress, reported by an announcer from a station window across the street. Even the early studio broadcast reproduced a complete aural environment with startling impact. One heard all too clearly the rustle of papers in the speaker's hand, the taking of breath between the singer's phrases, "every sound made or uttered while the switch is turned on."[45]

The experience was a new blind-man's bluff; the blind listener sat fascinated, wrapped completely in aural sensation, visual data replaced the eyes and imagination.[46] Earphones completed the sense of isolation. And yet one was not alone. Before long, predicted the *Literary Digest* in June of 1923, the radio would put every one on earth in the presence of every other, auditorily speaking.[47] The idea was staggering. This was not the old sound-world of the telephone with its sense of finite, personal exchange, nor yet the contrasting sound world of the phonograph with its impersonal performance available to all. Radio presented a new reality which transcended both—the immediate experience of the remote person or event, an experience in company with millions of others, yet strangely separate. Here were the ambiguities: the sense that one was participating, yet alone; in command, yet swept blindly along on the wave of sound. Prevalent images of mastery and connection, then, were punctuated by those suggesting intrusion into the intimate environment and alienation from social and personal relationship.

Extended Mastery Versus Intrusion

Prevailing descriptions of radio continued hearty and optimistic. The greatest new power seemed that of obliterating distance; the world appeared to shrink.[48] "DX fishing" became a ruling pastime; tuning in Cuba or California was the rage. For the Legion family it partook of a "sacrificial rite."[49] The new radio machine appeared also to be subtly altering consciousness; to some observers, listeners seemed to be developing a new imaginative mode. People had always envisioned themselves transported to distant vistas. Now listeners perceived the remote as though they had compelled it to appear in their own homes. "Pittsburgh and Newark are right here in the shack," exclaimed a correspondent from an Ontario mining camp.[50] The ability to command an experience to play itself out within one's own four walls was intoxicating—Melba singing next to one's own hearth, the Four Horsemen plunging through the door!

Having admitted radio and tuned to a station, however, one's sense of control weakened. Media language which presented radio's advent into the living room in sexual metaphor—male invasion of female space—also suggested invasion of personal boundaries for *all* members of a family—visual insult, aural trauma, perceptual disruption.[51]

The paraphernalia of radio, in the first place, was unaesthetic. Antennas were eyesores on rooftops. Lead-in wires dangled from fronts of houses. Inside, the necessary machinery seemed vulgar—so ironic, a box and a tangle of wires.[52]

The shock to hearing was even more universally observed. Articles and advertisements warned of "squawks, squeals, screams," and "enough howls and yells to make one think all Hell was let loose." In 1922, listeners were portrayed as victims of a hostile science.[53]

> *From the huge phonograph horn . . . comes a sudden shrill whistle which rises and falls, a terrific volume of noise battering at our ears . . . made by some far-off world as it flees shrieking in agony across the firmament. . . . In a moment this celestial caterwauling is shouldered aside, so to speak, by the Sextette [from* Lucia*] being sung in our very ears and evidently by giants a hundred feet tall. . . . Still, science has conquered, the music is there . . . brought down and hurled upon us from the horn.*

A sense of temporal disorientation, however, appeared the most significant source of distress. By the twenties, a sense of ever-accelerating time had been with Americans for a half-century. One had been able, however, to maintain a certain equilibrium, so long as time seemed a reliable linear flow.[54] Now, that vital sense of temporal continuity appeared threatened by radio's format—a succession of disparate elements, senselessly juxtaposed. One critic protested: "Busy as the average American is, he or she has not yet reached the point where either education or entertainment is absorbed in the five-minute installment plan. . .Yet the originators of the present style in radio programs multiply [the five-minute period] indefinitely."[55]

The jumble now included bands, orchestras, national rites, and public functions interspersed mindlessly with "explanations" by announcers. Radio broadcasting provided "the biggest crazy-quilt of audition" ever perceived by human ear. "Crazy-quilt"—a seemingly homely metaphor from the pioneer past—could also hint at fragmentation, disjunction, and consciousness pushed to the edges of sanity.

Modern science had split the older order into a thousand fragments, asserted sociologist E. C. Lindeman in a perceptive *New Republic* essay on radio. Increases in stimuli might result in increased difficulty in integrating behavior. "We may hear . . . too much for our capacities for experience." The stress seemed related to what the German sociologist, George Simmel, had called in 1903 the development of "urban perception." He had spoken of the "intensification of nervous stimulation" stemming from swift change of stimuli. Impressions from more regular experience "use up, so to speak, less consciousness than does the rapid crowding of changing images, the unexpectedness of onrushing impressions." In 1913, such discontinuity had been specifically associated with the new electronic experience by the Italian futurist, F. T. Marinetti, as he invoked the "confused medley of sensations and impressions" characteristic of what he called the "wireless imagination." Here then was a profound challenge to traditional consciousness posed by the new technology—the disruption of a sense of linear flow, of continuity, of unbroken time at one's command.[56]

To the modernist sensibility of the twenties, the "unexpected" in radio montage appeared a venture in surrealism, the method of *Ulysses* or *The Wasteland*. The sense of disconnection for the "modern" man would be forcefully put by Walter Lippmann in 1929, asserting that press, radio, and film compelled attention to elements "detached from their backgrounds, their causes, and their consequences . . . having no beginning, no middle, and no end, mere flashes of publicity playing fitfully on a dark tangle of circumstances."[57]

The disconcerting mosaic of radio did resemble the older make-up of the newspaper, to which citizens were accustomed.[58] And yet the visual mosaic of the newspaper seemed more under control than the temporal mosaic of radio. Once tuned to a particular station, radio provided a flow of impression like time itself which, as Bergson had said, permitted no repetition, no return. The radio listener was indeed helpless, concluded *Radio Broadcast* in 1922. "You turn on your switches and wait . . . . It may be a selection from 'Aida,' wonderfully executed, or it may be nothing but a scratchy, cracked phonograph record. You have nothing to say about it."[59]

"The newspaper can be read at one's convenience," asserted one radio reviewer, "it can be read to suit one's moods or interests, and selectivity therefore is at one's command. Radio's output must be caught at the hour it is scheduled, and if the auditor misses a few words, effectiveness is lost because it is not possible to go back."[60] Priority and rate of attention, reprise, and scanning—all had passed to others' control.

Accommodating both visual and auditory stimuli simultaneously appeared intolerable. Now the evening paper received short shrift, said one academic critic. Who could read while a loud speaker poured out the latest jazz?[61]

Such irritability over disruption of the newspaper ritual was amplified in a wave of periodical comment, comparing the impacts of newspaper and radio on society and the self.[62] Advantages were properly chronicled, but there remained a lingering sense of dis-ease. Americans had heavily invested themselves in the experience with newspaper; newspapers reflected not only exterior reality but the self. "We see ourselves in our newspapers," reflected one critic. "We *are* our newspapers."[63] Radio, with its raucous form, its demand for new behavior, and its seemingly erratic reflections of experience, meant a sharp break with the past. It appeared to threaten a traditional identification, an anchoring of self in what had been continuous relationship to a stable form.[64]

The importance of radio was scarcely to be overestimated, concluded the Dutch historian, Johan Huizinga, on visiting America in 1926. Farm families and invalids could share through radio some of the life of the city. "But no one who listens to it any longer chooses for himself the stuff upon which his mind feeds." Radio compelled a strong but "superficial" exercise of attention, "completely excluding reflection, or what I might call reflective assimilation." Huizinga's American colleagues amplified the observation, blaming radio for a national decay in concentration and predicting standardization of the American mind.[65]

One conflict thus emerging in the early twenties opposed a new sense of mastery to a newly discerned loss of control. On the one hand was the ability to command the remote event to occur within one's own hearing; on the other, the consequent threat to personal boundaries and familiar patterns of sensibility.

With the advent of the radio age, the optimistic predicted the strengthening of international ties, enhancement of the democratic process, and the revival of the family. The magical new electric tie would surely bind. In conflict with such expectations came reports of individual alienation from social and personal involvement, an alienation which appeared to be encouraged by peculiar aspects of the process, content, and form of the new technology.

Though some could see in radio a potential for new social control over immigrants, criminals, and other non-conformists, a striking aspect of radio *process* seemed more apt to separate the ordinary individual from customary forms of authority.[66] Traditional mediators were circumvented. Children listened secretly at night under the covers, headphones over their ears, eluding parental authority. Women savored the forbidden male environment of the prize fight. Voters heard candidates without the filter of a partisan press.

Churchmen and politicians began to bewail lack of participation in their rites as individuals sensed the insulation radio could provide against community surveillance. "Why go to your parish church," came the ironic query from the Episcopal bishop, "when you can sit at ease in your parlor and hear a capable choir . . . a magnetic preacher?"[67]

The implications of this new escape from others' expectations appealed to the media columnists. As Heywood Broun remarked, one could listen to a sermon on the radio, throw in a few cuss words, and smoke a cigar all at the same time. If one disagreed with a political speaker, pointed out Mark Sullivan, no need to tip-toe, embarrassed, out of the auditorium. One just turned the dial.[68]

Oddly enough, however, freedom also meant loneliness. There came over individuals a new and strange sense, that of being one of an atomized mass. A distinctive impact of radio, said Eunice Fuller Barnard, lay in the unique position of auditors who were "of an audience, yet each alone in it." Though one addressed a million people at once, "he can count on no group response; his voice reaches them not as a mass but as isolated units. They do not, they cannot react on him or each other. He cannot sense their feeling. There is no mutuality, no give and take. . . . The listeners do not have to declare themselves. . . . They hear him practically alone."[69]

Radio could indeed separate one from all social activity. He was not going to the political meeting that night, a Middletown businessman told an interviewer in 1924, and he turned to his radio instead "for an evening's diversion." (More intimate connection was subject to the same strain. Most powerful symbol of interpersonal alienation was the "radio divorce," new to the headlines. One partner appeared to withdraw behind a wall of sound, leaving the spouse no recourse but the courts.[70]

The *process* of radio broadcasting was not the only alienating factor; some of its more unconventional *content* appeared to threaten traditional moral and political beliefs as well. The Tudors' sixteenth-century concern for the spread of sedition and heresy via the new technology of print was echoed four centuries later by those who viewed radio content as detrimental to government and dangerous to the immortal soul.

In the grip of paranoia over alien religious and political expression, the *Dearborn Independent* warned of Communist ideas beamed to innocent farm youth by "organized Jewry" from a radio station on the Sears, Roebuck building in Chicago. Borrowing the language of the Great War, the *Independent* saw radio as a new "poison gas." Liberals poked fun at such extremes. ("See grandmother being converted to Socialism as she knits of an evening with her earphones on.") But the problem remained, implicit in radio's most remarkable quality, the obliteration of time. No longer could an encounter with strange experience be delayed by its conversion into newsprint, while its language was tidied and its moral or political dangers removed. Now the listener was instantly present and vulnerable at the event.[71]

The *Chicago Tribune* polled readers on its proposal to broadcast the sordid Leopold-Loeb trial in 1924, and implied that the shock would be discreetly cushioned by an approximation of the old editing process. "Sensation there will be," asserted the *Tribune,* "but no filth. The censor will be as discriminating with his push button as are the editors of the *Tribune* with their copy pencils. . . . Broadcasting of the trial will be as clean as the *Tribune.*" Readers by the thousands voted against the promised "superlative experiment." Immediate exposure to such content was too threatening to the sensibilities; instant editing would not do. In Chicago, at least, time between such an event and its comprehension would stretch out for a comforting few more years.[72]

Probably the most intriguing questions were posed in connection with radio *form.* Could a reproduction provide an authentic experience of communication between individuals? Was the real, once reproduced, still real? Some observers saw in the adulation poured out on radio personalities a form of pseudo-encounter. Little Howard Legion, aged 8, did not suspect that the Uncle Charlie who told him bedtime stories was merely "pushing his personality through the ether at some thousands of children whom he has never seen, will never see, and cares rather less than nothing for."[73] More poignant must have been the plight of the hypothetical listener to a broadcast communion service who wondered whether the ritual was binding. Were the body and the blood truly hers?[74] "The presence of the original is the prerequisite to the concept of authenticity," the critic Walter Benjamin would declare on entering this debate, which ranged through the new technologies and across continents during the period. Reproduction, he said, would destroy both the uniqueness and the aura of the original.[75]

Perhaps a similar sense of inauthenticity, of lack of meaning, moved young Edmund Wilson to describe in his journal the "empty sonority," the "hollow yowling" of radio. The year was 1925, the same year T. S. Eliot published "The Hollow Men."[76]

Resolution and Transcendence

As Americans of the early twenties gave up their complete dependence on newspapers and wireless in order to cope with radio, they experienced an inevitable sense of loss—loss of the feelings of mastery and connection attached to the old means of communication. Print journalism seemed to reflect and respond to the ambiguity of a process like that of grief—providing familiar metaphors and analogies to make these contradictory new experiences more understandable. There were the images of romance and conquest that belonged to confidence, but also the crazy quilts and poison gas of fear and defensiveness.

Though this conflict appeared unresolved by the mid-twenties, a complex psychological process also seemed to be under way in which individuals were devising ways to barricade themselves against radio. Only gradually would they allow the barricade to become a kind of semi-porous membrane, admitting desired aspects of the new radio-mediated world and rejecting others. This transcendent process would involve development of a new sensibility appropriate to an electronic environment, and its beginnings would be seen by 1924.[77]

In that year the *New York Times* reviewed the first American edition of *Beyond the Pleasure Principle.* In it the Viennese philosopher Sigmund Freud advanced speculatively the idea of consciousness as a "little fragment of living substance" threatened by a world charged with powerful energies. To avoid destruction, the organism developed what Freud called "a stimulus shield" allowing some stimuli to penetrate but excluding others. *Times* reviewer Mary Keyt Isham was reminded of the child's notion of a caterpillar, "all skin and squash." The skin was the rind against excessive stimuli; the squash, the inner consciousness.[78]

Freud intended to illustrate psychic process, but his language resembled that of others speculating on the problem of overwhelming stimuli in modern life. From Berlin two decades before, Simmel had suggested the "increased awareness" developed by the urban dweller to protect against environmental threat. And Walter Benjamin had specifically invoked Freud's stimulus shield in discussion of the "training" to which communications technology—newspaper or film—subjected the human sensorium.[79]

In his 1924 essay on radio Lindeman applied the model of the "postponed or delayed response to stimuli" specifically to the radio listener. Such secondary modes of communication as radio, he said, might well produce an environment so artificial that human adjustment would become impossible. Therefore their value depended on man's capacity to "control and appropriate" the resulting stimulus.[80]

In the first years of the decade, Americans

seemed far from control. A great proportion were caught up in an infatuation with novelties of sound and distance. Those others who resisted engulfment by the new technology seemed to defend themselves either by denial or retreat. The usual prescription was to turn the switch. "If you have a radio," Will Rogers advised during the 1924 presidential campaign, "now is the time to get it out of fix." (Intellectuals, of course, had never taken up radio in the first place. They had not as yet, said one observer, come to grips with the typewriter.[81])

Some took aggressive action, advising stations to stop broadcasting when the supply of quality material ran out. Others talked censorship or legislation. A few took direct action. Secretary of State Charles Evans Hughes was entertaining distinguished guests in his own home when, in their full hearing on his own radio, a news commentator sharply criticized his State Department policy. The angry Hughes protested directly to the president of AT&T, owners of the offending station. The contract of the commentator, Hans von Kaltenborn, was not renewed.[82]

A bleak passivity, however, seemed more characteristic of the modernist reaction represented by Bliven, who sardonically predicted the world of 1930 in which "there will be only one orchestra left on earth, giving nightly world-wide concerts; when all the universities will be combined into one super-institution conducting courses by radio for students in Zanzibar, Kamchatka, and Oskaloosa; when instead of newspapers, trained orators will dictate the news of the world day and night . . . when every person will be instantly accessible day or night to all the bores he knows . . . when the last vestiges of privacy, solitude, and contemplation will have vanished into limbo."[83]

Such reactions—denial, rage, cynical despair—resembled the classic reactions to grief. Now came also, however, tangible indications of the fulfillment of Lindeman's prescription for adjustment to altered environment.

Looking back on the scene from 1931, the historian Frederick Lewis Allen would recollect that around 1923 people had begun to take their radio sets for granted, as background for a newer craze, Mah Jong. His recollection was faulty; radio was still very much in the foreground in 1923. What is significant in Lewis' statement is its embodiment of the consciousness that would develop by 1931 when radio would indeed have become psychically assimilated, a state which could be projected back onto the people of the early twenties.[84]

Perceptions and actions were reorganized around what once had been strange; as early as 1924 one writer could describe his habit, "to punctuate my space bar, as I typewrite, to whatever tempo radio sets for me."[85]

More importantly, an occasional observer perceived a new exercise of individual initiative. It became apparent that listeners, ventured one columnist, were no longer spellbound by a mediocre and haphazard succession of performers. A number now listened with discrimination, added another, instead of "swallowing all that they hear, whole and without thought."[86] Such individuals neither listened passively nor tuned out. They continued to engage with the new form. More selective reactions began to emerge—wariness, choice, control.

It would be impossible to recapture the old consciousness, so structured by the linear patterning and delayed timing of print. The new electric sensibility would range far more widely, but less contemplatively. It would accommodate the discontinuous more easily, but concentrate less effectively. It would extend relationships, but pursue them in less depth.

The unity of mankind was not to be sought in machines, Lindeman suggested in 1924, but in the human personality.[87] The way would be "complicated, difficult and conducive to sober reflection." An implication was there for an age troubled by dehumanizing forces: technology need not be destiny. Even in the face of such forces, the individual might reassert something of the old sense of communion and command, tempered by regret for what had gone. Such would be the kind of meaning and comfort future generations must find.

Endnotes

1. C. C. Dill. *Radio Law* (Washington, D. C.: National Law Book Co., 1938), pp. 1, 2.
2. This essay uses "sensibility" to mean association and interaction of feeling and thought. Of major influence in shaping my thought have been Wolfgang Schivelbusch, *The Railway Journey: Trains and Travel in the 19th Century* (New York: Urizen Books, 1979), and Marshall McLuhan, *Understanding Media: The Extensions of Man* (New York: 1964), both indispensable to study of sensibility in relation to technology. For particularly useful comment, I thank Michael Barkun, Seymour Fisher, and Andre Fontaine.
3. "Era of Expansion" is the title Gleason L. Archer gave to this early period in his classic work, *History of Radio to 1926* (New York: American Historical Society, 1938). By 1922 there were an estimated 600,000 "receiving stations," of which 678 were commercial. The overwhelming mood was astonishment and pleasure; as late as 1925, radio fan letters expressed primarily "enthusiastic surprise." "The March of Radio," *Radio Broadcast* (June 1922): 95; *New York Times,* 13 October 1925.
4. Erik Barnouw, *A Tower in Babel: A History of Broadcasting in the United States* (New York: Oxford University Press, 1966) 1:91. The separation of transmitting from receiving equipment, mass marketing of receiving equipment, and growth of "broadcasting" stations made living room listening possible for the general public in the early twenties. See also J. Fred MacDonald, *Don't Touch That Dial!* (Chicago: Nelson-Hall, 1979), pp. 1–23, and Philip T. Rosen, *The Modern Stentors: Radio Broadcasters and the Federal Government, 1920–1934* (Westport, Conn.: Greenwood Press, 1980), pp. 1–14.
5. "Shall the Youth of America be Exploited? A Brand of Communism Which Aims at Control of Junior Farm Centers," *Dearborn Independent,* 6 September 1924, p. 10.
6. The literature on culture and electronic technology is vast. See, for example, James Carey and John J. Quirk, "The Mythos of the Electronic Revolution," *American Scholar* 39 (Spring, Summer 1970): 219–41, 395–424. Harold A. Innis, *The Bias of Communications,* 2nd ed. (Toronto: University of Toronto Press, 1964); Barry N. Schwarz, ed., *Human Connection and the New Media* (Englewood Cliffs, N.J.: Prentice-Hall, 1973), and Raymond Williams, *Television: Technology and Cultural Form* (New York: Schocken Books, 1975).
7. "The working out of a severe bereavement represents . . . a general principle of adaption to change . . . Change [involves] the need to re-establish continuity, to work out an interpretation of oneself, and the world which preserves, despite estrangement, the thread of meaning. . . . The outcome of social changes, too, may depend on the management of the process of transition." Peter Maris, *Loss and Change* (New York: Pantheon, 1974), pp. 38, 42
8. The language of the indexers to mass media—those of morgue-keepers for newspaper clippings or indexers to periodicals—is clues to the categories for organizing experience, which are available at any one time to culture. The *Readers' Guide* filed articles about wireless telephony under "WIRELESS"—a category indicating the loss of something, i.e., wires, until 1915. That year a new category, RADIO, merited one entry. By 1922 all extracts about wireless were indexed under RADIO. The absence of wires as an organizing idea had been transcended by the presence of a new object, radio.
9. Barnouw, *Tower in Babel,* pp. 75–188
10. Five sources have been particularly fruitful for comment on radio with regard to culture: the *New Republic* and the *New York Times,* appropriate to an urban, educated readership; the *Scientific American,* for a national audience of relatively sophisticated readers; *Radio Broadcast,* which appealed across class and geographic lines to a readership including children and the poor, and *Dearborn Independent,* calculated to suit small-town and rural Midwesterners.
11. Paul Fussell, *The Great-War and Modern Memory* (New York: Oxford University Press, 1975), pp.

74 and 137–39; also D. H. Hirsch, *Validity in Interpretation* (New Haven: Yale University Press, 1967), pp. 105.

12. "Broadcasting to Millions," *New York Times,* 19 February 1922.

13. Rudyard Kipling, "Wireless," *Scribner's Magazine* 32 (August 1902): 129–43. Kipling had a firm hold on the electronic imagination of the era. To Bruce Bliven in 1922 the radio control switchboard with instruments, dials, and handles evoked the ray and its vigilant slave in Kipling's "With the Night Mail." See Bliven's "The Ether Will Now Oblige," *The New Republic,* 15 February 1922, p. 328.

14. "The Analogy between Wireless Telegraphy and Waves from Brain to Brain," *Current Opinion* 57 (October 1914): 253.

15. Buckner Speed, "Voices of the Universe," *Harper's* 138 (April 1919): 613.

16. "Broadcasting to Millions," *New York Times,* 19 February 1922.

17. Speed, "Voices of the Universe," p. 615.

18. Before the advent of the microphone and radio, a disembodied voice figured in the human imagination most dramatically as the voice of God. Electronic technology made the voice an imaginable *thing* in its own right, separate from its bodily connection; see Schivelbusch, *Railway Journey,* p. 54. In the film, "The Next Voice You Hear" (1950), God would speak on the radio. The gospel song, "Turn Your Radio On," Barnaby Records, X30809, implored hearers to "listen to the Master's radio."

19. Scientific debates about wireless were marked by dispute as to the composition and function and indeed the very existence of the ether. See for example, the subhead to the article on brainwaves, "Subtlety of the Wave in the Ether," *Current Opinion* 57 (October 1914): 253; "Sir Oliver Defends the Ether," *Literary Digest,* 2 December 1922, p. 28.

20. "Spiritualism" was a substantial index category in the *New York Times* after the war. See R. Laurence Moore, *In Search of White Crows: Spiritualism, Parapsychology, and American Culture* (New York: Oxford University Press, 1977), p. 175. During the same years Edison was developing a "spiritual communications machine"; see Matthew Josephson, *Edison: A Biography* (New York: McGraw-Hill, 1959), p. 439.

21. W. H. Worrell, "Do Brains or Dollars Operate Your Set?" *Radio Broadcast* 2 (November 1922): 70.

22. This association was best preserved in the amber of the Dewey Decimal System which shelved Freud next to works on ghosts, spooks, and witches.

23. "Hitching the Wireless to Your Subconscious Mind," *New York Tribune,* 21 May 1922.

24. Orange Edward McMeans, "The Great Audience Invisible," *Scribner's Magazine* 72 (April 1923): 410.

25. Gilbert K. Chesterton in 1921 lectured in New York on "The Revolt Against Reason," discussing Christian Science, jazz, spiritualism, psychoanalysis, and associated phenomena: "Calls Psychoanalysis a Rival to Jazz," *New York Times,* 28 March 1921. See also Michael Schudson, *Discovering the News: A Social History of American Newspapers* (New York: Basic Books, 1978), pp. 126–27.

26. Angus S. Hibbard, "How to Use a Telephone," *Saturday Evening Post,* n.d., in Ray Brosseau, ed., *Looking Forward: Life in the Twentieth Century as Predicted in the Pages of American Magazines from 1895 to 1905* (New York: American Heritage Press, 1970), p. 81.

27. "The Persistent Mysteries of Wireless Telegraphy and Telephony," *Current Literature* 49 (December 1910): 636. See also William Peck Banning, *Commercial Broadcasting Pioneer: The WEAF Experiment, 1922–1926* (Cambridge, Mass.: Harvard University Press, 1946), pp. 41–61; David Sarnoff, writing his famous "Radio Music Box" memo in 1916, was among those who broke out of the telephonic model. His superiors at American Marconi ignored his suggestion. Eugene Lyons, *David Sarnoff* (New York: Pyramid, 1967), pp. 87–89; Laurence Bergreen, *Look Now, Pay Later: The Rise of Network Broadcasting* (Garden City, N.Y.: Doubleday, 1980), pp. 20–22.

28. "'Listening In,' Our New National Pastime," *American Review of Reviews,* 19 January 1923, p. 52.

29. *New York Times,* 22 February 1922.

30. "75,000 American Boys Have This Enthusiasm," *American Magazine* 81 (June 1916): 104.

31. Guglielmo Marconi, "Wireless and the 'Titanic,'" *World's Work* 24 (June 1912): 225.

32. "Work for Wireless Amateurs," *Literary Digest,* 18 August 1917.

33. "Adventures in Radio," *Radio Broadcast* 1 (May 1922): 72–3. This article featured radio as a leading factor in the lives of gun-runners, smugglers, revolutionists, and international spies.

34. "Floods and Wireless," *Technological World* 23 (August 1915): 806–807; "How Wireless Helps the Mariner," *Scientific American,* 13 April 1918, p. 340; "Time by Wireless," *Harper's Weekly,* 28 June 1913, p. 19.

35. Making one's own crystal set became almost a ritual passage to manhood. See "Almost a Soldier is the Boy Who Understands Wireless Nowadays," *Woman's Home Companion* 43 (October 1916): 32. Women who assembled sets were so rare as to merit special articles: "How Two Girls Made a Receiving Radiophone," *Literary Digest,* 10 June 1922, p. 29.

36. "The first-class scout who . . . calls me 'dad,' worked manfully with me while we wound our coil of nights in the kitchen. . . . The good wife and scout-mother grew tired of our fussing around in the kitchen, so we retreated to the attic and kept on winding coils." McMeans, "Eavesdropping on the World," pp. 226–27.

37. A. R. Pinci, "This Is Radio-Casting Station 'H-O-M-E,'" *Dearborn Independent,* 20 September 1924, p. 4. For feminine response see Alice R. Bourke, "O Woe! Radio," *Radio Broadcast* 2 (December 1922): 107: "Of course I am the boss, but it . . . is handy in many ways to let him think he is the Great Voice around this radio-devastated remainder of What Was."

38. The feminization of male experience with radio was exquisitely represented by an interior decorator's proposal for a special radio room. "Of masculine character, obviously," the room would be "developed" in the attic, that old male redoubt, with floors in two shades of slate, tinted plaster walls and chairs in dark blue corduroy. Alwyn T. Covell, "Decorating the Radio Room: A New Thought for the House in Town or Country Where 'Listening In' Is Getting to be One Serious Pastime," *House and Garden* 44 (August 1923): 50–1.

39. Ford A. Carpenter, "First Experiences of A Radio Broadcaster," *Atlantic Monthly* 132 (September 1923): 388.

40. "The Long Arm of Radio," *Current Opinion* 72 (May 1922): 684; "The March of Radio: Too Many Cooks Are Spoiling Our Broth," *Radio Broadcast* 2 (November 1922): 3; "Is The Radio Amateur Doomed?" *Literary Digest,* 2 December 1922, p. 28; Carl Dreher, "Is the Broadcast Listener at Fault?" *Radio Broadcast* 4 (March 1924): 424–25.

41. Some writers of the period saw passivity everywhere. They attributed it to a malign technology and to the growth of consumerism. Men were groveling before the machine, said Waldo Frank, because they had not the "consciousness" to master it; "The Machine and Metaphysics," *The New Republic,* 18 November 1925, pp. 330–31; Johan Huizinga bewailed the disappearance of "the active man, as embodiment of enterprise," in the wake of technological expansion, *America: A Dutch Historian's Vision from Afar and Near* (New York: Harper & Row, 1972), p. 234; Charles and Mary Beard ambivalently evoked masses listening "passively" to manufactured music, but also to a radio which permitted "buyers" to choose their music, in *The Rise of American Civilization* (1927; New York: Macmillan, 1930), p. 785.

42. Bilven, "The Legion Family and the Radio," *Century* (October 1924): 811–18.

43. "Radio To Supplant Press That Exploits It?" *Dearborn Independent,* 3 June 1922, p. 8.

44. The "presumed superiority of the radio over the newspaper," based on the assumption that "the sense of seeing is inferior to the sense of hearing," was hotly debated in a decade when psychology focused on comparative effects of sensual stimuli; e.g., E. C. Lindeman, "Radio Fallacies," *New Republic,* 19 March 1924, p. 228.

45. McMeans, "Great Audience Invisible."

46. *Ibid.,* p. 411.

47. "Wanted, A Radio Language," *Literary Digest,* 23 June 1923, p. 24.

48. Radio's ability to annihilate the time was frequently expressed in spatial metaphor. A tiny, dispirited globe was overshadowed in a *Chicago Daily News* cartoon by a gigantic radio listener, remarking, "Well, Well! Isn't he a cute little fellow?" The caption: GETTING SMALLER EVERY DAY; *Literary Digest*, 17 June 1922.
49. Bliven, "The Legion Family," pp. 814.
50. "A Wireless in Every Home," *Radio Broadcast* 1 (June 1922): 110.
51. The sense of physical invasion comes in a news account of a couple terrified by sounds of burglars apparently counting the family silver. The counting, it developed, came from a new radio, broadcasting setting-up exercises in the next room. *New York Times*, 3 August 1924.
52. Bliven, "The Legion Family," pp. 815; for some critics the machine created its own esthetic, to others it represented sheer vulgarity, the result of a desire for consumer goods. See Lewis Mumford, *American Taste* (San Francisco: Westgate, 1929), pp. 16–22, 27–31, 34; on life style in a machine age, see Warren Susman, *Culture and Commitment, 1929–1945* (New York: George Braziller, 1973), pp. 4–8.
53. *Radio Broadcast* (April 1923): 525; Bliven, "The Ether Will Now Oblige," p. 328.
54. Americans had always been people in a hurry. By the early years of the twentieth century, linear time itself seemed under seige—there was the relative time of the physicists, the simultaneity of the Cubists, and the rediscovery of "primitive" time by the anthropologists.
55. "Broadcasting or Outcasting," *Dearborn Independent*, 13 June 1925, p. 13.
56. Lindeman, "Radio Fallacies," pp. 227–28; Georg Simmel, "The Metropolis and Mental Life," in *The Sociology of Georg Simmel*, ed. Kurt H. Wolff (New York: The Free Press, 1950), p. 410; F. T. Marinetti, "Wireless Imagination and Words at Liberty: The New Futurist Manifesto," *Poetry and Drama* 1 (September 1913): 322.
57. Walter Lippmann, *Preface to Morals* (New York: Macmillan, 1929), p. 64.
58. McLuhan, *Understanding Media*, p. 188.
59. Review of *Time and Free Will: An Essay on the Immediate Data of Consciousness*, by Henri Bergson, *The Nation*, 24 November 1910, p. 499; *Radio Broadcast* 1 (May 1922): 1.
60. "The Lure of the World's Aerial Theater," *Dearborn Independent*, 30 August 1924, p. 3.
61. E. M. Johnson, "The Utilization of the Social Sciences," *The Journalism Bulletin* 4 (1927): 32.
62. See, for example, "Radio to Supplant Press," p. 8; McMeans, "Eavesdropping," p. 226; Eunice Fuller Barnard, "Radio Politics," *New Republic*, 19 March 1924, p. 91; "The Future of Radio," *New Republic*, 8 October 1924, p. 135; Mark Sullivan, "Will Radio Make the People the Government?" *Radio Broadcast* 6 (November 1924): 24–25.
63. Thomas L. Masson, "Well, What's All This About the Newspaper?" *Dearborn Independent*, 18 October 1924, p. 2.
64. The problem of relating the self to radio often surfaced in fantasy; authors imagined themselves as incorporating radio's powers or *as* radio. The zenith of the form probably came in *Argosy's* 1924 story in which the protagonist transmitted *himself* to Venus. Ralph Milne Farley, *The Radio Man* (Los Angeles: Fantasy, 1948).
65. Huizinga, *America*, p. 235; Jennie Irene Mix, "Is Radio Standardizing the American Mind?" *Radio Broadcast* 6 (November 1924): 49–50.
66. "Ether Waves Versus Crime Waves," *Literary Digest*, 7 October 1922, p. 25. J. M. McKibbin, Jr., "The New Way to Make Americans," *Radio Broadcast* 2 (January 1923); 238–39.
67. "The Effect of Broadcasting on the Churches," *Radio Broadcast* 2 (October 1923): 273.
68. "Listening In On The Radio," *New York Times*, 3 August 1924; Sullivan, "Will Radio Make the People the Government?" p. 23.
69. Barnard, "Radio Politics," p. 92.
70. Robert S. Lynd and Helen Merrell Lynd, *Middletown: A Study in American Culture* (1929; New York: Harcourt, Brace, 1956), p. 416; "Wife Leaves Radio Fan: Judge Says She's Right," *New York Times*, 10 February 1924.
71. "Shall the Youth of America . . . ?" p. 10; "The *Tribune* Gets A Fast One," *Dearborn Independent*, 16 August 1924, p. 8; Barnard, "Radio Politics," p. 92.

72. Hal Higdon, *The Crime of the Century: The Leopold and Loeb Case* (New York: Putnam's, 1975), pp. 158–59, p. 167.

73. "The Legion Family," p. 812.

74. "Holy Communion by Radio," *Radio Broadcast* 5 (July 1924): 221–22.

75. Walter Benjamin, *Illuminations*, ed. Hannah Arendt (New York: Schocken, 1969), pp. 220–21.

76. Edmund Wilson, *The Twenties: From Notebooks and Diaries of the Period*, ed. Leon Edel (New York: Farrar, Straus and Giroux, 1975), p. 213. The sense of meaninglessness evoked by the content of electronic media would appear in 1961 in an echo of Eliot, the description of TV as "vast wasteland." Barnouw, *Tube of Plenty: The Evolution of American Television* (New York: Oxford University Press, 1975), pp. 299–300.

77. The structure of the following argument owes much to Schivelbusch, *Railway Journey*, pp. 152–60.

78. *The Standard Edition of the Complete Psychological Works of Sigmund Freud* (London: Hogarth Press, 1955–66) 12: 24–33; Mary Keyt Isham, "Freud's Imagination Flooding Wide and Obscure Areas," *New York Times*, 7 September 1924.

79. Wolf, *Sociology of Georg Simmel*, pp. 410–11; Benjamin, *Illuminations*, pp. 160–63; 175.

80. Lindeman, "Radio Fallacies," p. 228.

81. "Will Rogers, Humorist, . . ." *Radio Broadcast* 6 (November 1924): 39; Bliven, "The Legion Family," p. 811.

82. "And the sooner some stations curtail their programs, and go in for silent days and nights, the better." Pinci, "Broadcasting or Outcasting," p. 14; H. V. Kaltenborn, *Fifty Fabulous Years, 1900–1950* (New York: Putnam's, 1950), pp. 112–13.

83. Bliven, "The Ether Will Now Oblige," p. 328. Some historians would characterize such a reaction as Bliven's as "desperately resisting" mechanized culture, accepting alienation as the survival price. Evidence indicates, however, that a number of ordinary individuals, neither alienated nor despairing, found means to assert their own autonomy against mechanization of communication. Henry F. May, "Shifting Perspectives on the 1920's," *Mississippi Valley Historical Review* 43 (December 1954): 404.

84. Frederick Lewis Allen, *Only Yesterday* (1931; New York: Bantam Books, 1946), p. 101.

85. Pinci, "Station H-O-M-E," p. 4.

86. Edgar White Burrill, "Broadcasting the World's Best Literature," *Radio Broadcast* 2 (November 1922): 54; Mix, "Is Radio Standardizing?" p. 50.

87. Lindeman, "Radio Fallacies," p. 228.

The Public Debate About Broadcasting in the Twenties: An Interpretive History

Mary S. Mander

Preface

This paper is an analysis of the public debate regarding broadcasting prior to the passage of the Radio Act of 1927. The evidence which provides the basis of the argument posed here is comprised of the private papers of Herbert Hoover, then Secretary of Commerce, the *Congressional Record,* hearings before House and Senate Committees, articles which appeared in the popular and trade press, and related material in legal and scholarly journals. The intent of the ensuing analysis is not to rehash the factual, legal or technological history of broadcasting. That already has been done by, among others, Erik Barnouw and Asa Briggs. Rather, the intent here is to delineate the ways in which the people of the time dealt with the future of a new technology and to suggest some reasons for their conceptualization of broadcasting and its future in certain ways.

My reading of the debate is not intended as a definitive, conclusive or even comprehensive analysis. Nor do I wish to suggest a shallow stimulus-response conception of social policy—that is, that people think certain ways and their thinking automatically is incorporated into public policy. I merely am trying to examine the capacity of a model or metaphor to influence the ways in which certain people conceptualized the future of broadcasting. Thus the arguments raised here are best seen as cultural interpretations of oral and written data. This paper is an analysis of the "picture" people shared of the "way things are" or will be. Moreover, it is only one of a number of possible interpretations.

The Emergence of Radio

In the 1920s there was some uncertainty about radio's social role, its economic base and its ultimate destiny. In this respect it was no different from communications technologies preceding it. There is, in fact, a remarkable similarity among predictions, hopes and beliefs enunciated by people about the telegraph, the railroad and the telephone as well as the radio.[1] Yet, what made radio different from these other communications technologies was its phenomenal growth. Within a few years of its birth in 1920, broadcasting had penetrated America with what seemed like a stunning suddenness. The remarkable growth of the industry augmented a feeling that this new art had become a power "boundless for pos-

[1]See Asa Briggs, "Predication and Control: Historical Perspectives," pp. 73–87 in *Mass Communications,* ed., K. J. McGarry (Hamden: Linnet Books, 1972); *The Social Impact of the Telephone;* ed. Ithiel de Sola Pool (Boston: MIT Press, 1977); Carolyn Marvin, "The Electrical Imagination" (Ph.D. diss., University of Illinois, 1979).

sibilities for good or evil."[2] Figures supplied by both the industry and the US Government Census Bureau confirmed the belief held by many that something stupendous was happening.[3]

Despite the general elation felt about broadcasting, at the same time a feeling of ambivalence about the invention permeated the views entertained not only by the farmer's wife in South Dakota or the journalist in New York City, but also by the people who were "in charge" of the regulation and growth of the new industry. In regard to the issue of who should do the broadcasting, the solution to the problem of the federal government versus private ownership was couched in negative terms. On the right hand was Scylla in the form of socialism, and on the left hand was Charybdis in the form of trusts.

Early Regulation

The first flower of regulatory government or regulatory capitalism originated in the Interstate Commerce Act of 1887, passed to divest the railroads of economic power attained through pooling.[4] To many people of the time, entrenched in the laissez-faire economics of Adam Smith and the laws of Spencer's social Darwinism, regulatory government was contrary to human nature and to a basic morality common to civilized nations. To others the Act represented the triumph of democracy in the struggle against the power-abusing trusts.[5] However perceived, the government's attempt to regulate the rails represented the first step toward the setting up of independent regulatory commissions to guide the US economy. From the 1880s to the 1980s, antitrust has remained an instrument to achieve economic well-being for the country. Curiously enough, however, the federal government never has been willing to either completely use or completely abandon regulation.[6] In the case of radio, it was a question of "steering the legislative ship between the Scylla of too much regulation and the Charybdis of the grasping selfishness of private monopoly."[7]

Although regulatory fence-sitting provides a context for understanding the early ambivalence toward ownership of the air, the important connection between 19th century government regulation and broadcasting is that those early attempts to regulate provided a transportation model for then Secretary of Commerce Herbert Hoover, his colleagues, members of the House and Senate, and the men working in the industry. The significance of this point, simply put, is that broadcasting since its inception has been conceptualized and then regulated in terms of transportation, rather than as a symbol-producing, culture-maintaining medium.

Models and metaphors establish categories of what is possible or what is impossible. Model is defined here as an example which is used for comparison; metaphor is something spoken of

[2]"Radio—The New Social Force," *Outlook* 136:465–67 (19 March 1924).

[3]See a press bulletin issued by the Census Bureau quoted in "The Growth of Radio," *The Literary Digest* 91:29 (20 November 1926); see also Allan Harding, "What Radio has Done and What It will Do Next," *American Magazine* 101:46–7 (March 1926); "The Long Arm of Radio Is Reaching Everywhere," *Current Opinion* 72:684–87 (May 1922); J. George Frederick, "Radio—A New Industrial Giant," *The American Review of Reviews* 71:167–70 (February 1925); "About the Radio Round-Table: Opinions of Radio Leaders Regarding the Past, Present, and Future of Broadcasting," *Scientific American* 127:378–79 (December 1922); "'Listening In', Our New National Pastime," *Journal of Broadcasting* 5:238–40 (Summer 1961). Reprinted from *Review of Reviews* (January 1924).

[4]For an excellent review of historical interpretations of this act, see Albro Martin, "The Troubled Subject of Railroad Regulation in the Gilded Age—A Reappraisal," *Journal of American History* 61:339–71 (September 1974).

[5]David M. Chalmers, *Neither Socialism nor Monopoly; Theodore Roosevelt and the Decision to Regulate the Railroads* (Philadelphia: J.B. Lippincott, 1976), pp. 7–17.

[6]*Ibid.*, p. 10.

[7]US Congress, Senate: *Congressional Record*, 69th Congress, 1st session, 1926, p. 12335.

as if it were something else. In the 1920s three models and metaphors were used to conceptualize the issues surrounding broadcasting and to envision the future of the new invention: transportation, public utilities and the newspaper press. At once, a cautionary note must be introduced: These categories have been superimposed on the data; however, in the discourse concerning the future of broadcasting, these models and metaphors are very much entangled. Thus, in the discussion of the public utilities model, for example, reference may be made to a transportation metaphor. To avoid repetition it is left to the reader to recognize these cross-over references.

The Transportation Model

In the 1920s the men who met in Washington to discuss the future of broadcasting had difficulty formulating ideas about radio's future. They used the transportation model to make sense of the chaos connected to the new art. Hoover, for example, was the "traffic cop" whose main job it was to police the air waves and to relieve the "congested lanes of ether."[8] Hoover himself explained his policy of granting licenses to all comers, instead of limiting access to a privileged few, in terms riddled with transportation metaphors. The following is a representative example:

> *. . . if we place a limit on the number of those who can use ether, then the possession of a license becomes commercially valuable, and, in a sense, a monopoly. Suppose, for instance, that we were to limit the* number of vessels which could navigate the Hudson river *[sic]. A large commercial advantage would attach to the privilege and we would have on our hands a monopoly, with all of its attendant evils.*[9] (Italics added)

In the House of Representatives, Congressman White of Maine argued that the physical limitations of the airwaves made it imperative that a law be passed, that there be "regulation governing the use of air paths and that traffic policemen enforce these laws. . . ."[10] The analogy he drew upon was the control of traffic in the streets and cities of the United States.[11]

In both chambers of Congress, the search for a legal analogy by which to frame new laws regarding broadcasting rested on the existing laws governing the waterways. Senator Bruce thus argued:

> *We all know that any private rights which may exist in the public waters of the United States are subject to the power of the Federal Government to regulate navigation and commerce. It seems to me that that is a subject which supplies a legal analogy, so far as this bill is concerned.*[12]

The elusive and enigmatic character of the ether was pinned down with images of the thorough-

[8]Examples abound, but the following are representative: "Hoover on the Ether's 'Howls and Growls'," *Literary Digest* 87:35 (19 December 1925); *To Regulate Radio Communication*, Hearings, Committee on Merchant Marine and Fisheries, House of Representatives, 69th Congress, 1st Session, H.R. 5589, 1926, pp. 18, 65, 91, 127; "Radio—Its Influence and Growth," Address on Stations WRC, WJZ and WGY, by Secretary of Commerce Hoover, 12 September 1925; "Radio Talk by Secretary Hoover," Washington, DC, 26 March 1924; George K. Burgess, Director of the Bureau of Standards, Memo for the Secretary of Commerce, Subject: Discussion of Possibilities of Radio, in *Herbert Hoover Papers*, Commerce Papers—Radio—Correspondence, Press Releases (West Branch: Herbert Hoover Presidential Library); *New York Times* "Hoover to Advise on Radio Control," 10 February 1922; Clipping in *Hoover Papers*. Hereafter all references to Hoover, unless otherwise noted, will be drawn from this collection.

[9]Interview for *Cleveland Plain Dealer*, by Harry A. Mount, n.d., *Hoover Papers*.

[10]US Congress, House: *Congressional Record*, 67th Congress, 4th Session, 1923, p. 2330, cf. 2331.

[11]*Ibid.*

[12]US Congress, Senate: *Congressional Record*, 68th Congress, 1st Session, 1924, p. 5736; cf. US Congress, House: *Congressional Record*, 67th Congress, 4th Session, pp. 2350 and 2351.

fare: it had boundaries, rights of way and its users were bound to follow the rules of the road.[13] Rules of the road were necessary partly because spectrum space was scarce. That scarcity likewise is thought of in terms of transportation: "It is as though we have too few tracks to accommodate our trains, or not enough streets for our automobiles, or too little ocean for our ships."[14]

This view of communication in terms of transportation originated during the period of exploration and discovery in the 15th century, when navigation from the Old World to the New World represented a profound belief in the pursuit of freedom.[15] As decades and then centuries passed, communication was coextensive with transportation until the invention of the telegraph. Twentieth-century mass communications research is permeated with transportation-like concepts. Communication is thought of as both a process and a technology whereby information and ideas are sent from one locus to another. Audience research conducted both in universities and in the broadcast industry rested on this assumption. In other words, the literature indicates industrial metaphors were used to conceptualize communication acts. Professor Lasswell summarized this model in his now famous phrase: "Who said what, to whom and with what effect." Wilbur Schramm's explanation of how communication works is likewise a transportation-like model: Source-Signal-Destination.[16]

Besides the fact that early communications technologies were transportation technologies, both steamships and trains were equipped with the wireless before the birth of broadcasting.[17] The Department of Commerce perfected the use of radio as a compass for some ships at sea, which made dependence on the accuracy of clocks less necessary. Ships could determine their longitude through radio signals sent at a given time from a particular place, e.g., New York. The signals could then compare to the time of day calculated by astronomical observations. Thus it should come as no surprise that transportation technologies, in bequeathing their terminology to electronic technologies, have left an indelible imprint on it.[18]

However, the primary reason behind the tendency to conceptualize broadcasting and communication in terms of transportation was the importance of precedent in the law. Judge Stephen B. Davis, in an article concerning the air, remarked that the tendency in making legislation is to look up some old law and follow its ideas as far as possible:

> *Since most of the radio apparatus was then on board of ships, it was natural to look in that direction for hints for the new law [law of 1912].*

[13]Interview with *Cleveland Plain Dealer, Hoover Papers;* Address by Herbert Hoover, Secretary of Commerce, by radio to Convention of National Electric Light Association at Atlantic City, 12 May 1924.

[14]Judge Stephen B. Davis, "The Law of the Air," in *The Radio Industry: The Story of Its Development* (Chicago: A. W. Shaw, 1928), 162, cf. 180.

[15]Professor James W. Carey has examined the transmission versus the cultural view of communication in his elegant essay, "A Cultural Approach to Communications," *Communication* 2:1–22 (1975); see also Raymond Williams, *Culture and Society* (New York: Harper and Row, 1966), pp. 295–338; and Daniel Czitrom, *Media and the American Mind: From Morse to McLuhan* (Chapel Hill: University of North Carolina Press, 1982).

[16]Wilbur Schramm, "How Communications Works," in *The Process and Effects of Mass Communication,* ed. Wilbur Schramm (Urbana: University of Illinois Press, 1965), pp. 3–26.

[17]See *To Regulate Radio Communication,* p. 18 (see note 8); L. B. Foley, "New Ideas in Radio-Communication," *The Engineering Magazine: An Industrial Review* 59:253–59 (May 1915); Herbert Hoover, "Masonic Review and Radio Broadcast," c. August 1922; Cf. Memorandum for the Secretary of Commerce, Subject: Discussion of the Possibilities of Radio, 8 March 1924. The auto industry also provided a model for cooperative pooling of patents and cross-licensing. See John K. Barnes, "Cooperative Competition," *Radio Broadcast* 2:516–20 (April 1923).

[18]See statement by Secretary Hoover at Hearing Before the Committee on the Merchant Marine and Fisheries on H. R. 7357, "To Regulate Radio Communication, and for Other Purposes," 11 March 1924, mimeo, *Hoover Papers;* see also the untitled draft on the use of radio for the determination of longitude, *Hoover Papers,* 12 June 1924.

The license plan there found was consequently adopted, and since the Bureau of Navigation had control of ship licenses and was part of the Department of Commerce, it was equally natural to provide that the new radio licenses be issued by the Secretary of Commerce.[19]

Although a vessel was required to have a federal license, the requirement was little more than a registration statute. In other words, it was a method by which the federal government could keep track of ships which were entitled to fly the national flag.[20] Because some ships had wireless sets, the licensing of broadcasting was based partly on licensing precedents from transportation.

Secondly, further precedent for the regulation of radio was found in the regulation of the rails, the telegraph and the telephone. The locus of federal over state power in regulating radio rested on the commerce clause of the US Constitution. This point is significant because the commerce clause provided an over-arching model by which broadcasting's future was envisaged: a market model. "Market model" is not meant to suggest some precise, preordained, inelastic market of the 1920s isomorphic with the marketplace (real or imagined) of the 1980s. "Market model" as it is used here, implies a way of seeing the "real world" primarily in terms of trade, economics and commodities. An alternative view might have posited "the real world" in terms of beauty, education, art, culture—or even the post office, a more mundane version actually referred to in the debate, although very briefly. In other words, this refers not to the real world but to ways of *conceptualizing* the real world, and then guiding public policy formation along those lines of conceptualization.

From 1923 on, the debate in Congress regarding radio law centered in part on the issue of jurisdiction.[21] Some members of Congress were concerned with what they termed ever-diminishing state's rights, an ever growing federal government and a resulting centralization. If, for practical reasons, states had to concede their jurisdiction rights in radio communication, the argument ran, then the legitimacy of federal control resided in the commerce clause. As one senator articulated it: "If it is true that the ether is the inalienable possession of the people of the United States or of the Government, it must be by virtue of no other constitutional provision of any sort of which I am aware."[22]

The commerce clause was the main source of federal jurisdiction over previous communications technologies. The private rights regarding public waters of the United States, for example, were subject to the federal government, in order to regulate commerce.[23] The precedent on the waterways provided a legal analogy for framers of radio law, an analogy which was further reinforced by the passage of the Air Commerce Act of 1926 to regulate air traffic.[24]

In addition, technologically radio was the sidekick of the telegraph and was used originally to supplement the older invention. Regulation of the telegraph made the inclusion of radio inevitable.[25] Although questions concern-

[19]Davis, *ibid.*, p. 165.

[20]*Ibid.*

[21]US Congress, House: *Congressional Record,* 67th Congress, 4th Session, 1923, pp. 2331, 2338, 2343, 2346–47, 2792; US Congress, Senate: *Congressional Record,* 68th Congress, 1st Session, 1924, p. 5736f; US Congress, House: *Congressional Record,* 69th Congress, 1st Session, 1926, p. 5586; US Congress, Senate: *Congressional Record,* 69th Congress, 1st Session, 1926, pp. 12338, 12352–53, 12502–03.

[22]Senator Bruce, US Congress, Senate: *Congressional Record,* 68th Congress, 1st Session, 1924, p. 5736.

[23]*Ibid.*

[24]See US Congress, House: *Congressional Record,* 67th Congress, 1st Session, 1921, 2915; Joseph P. Chamberlain, "The Radio Act of 1927," *ABA Journal* 13:343–47 (June 1927); *ABA Journal* 13:368–70 (July 1927), cf. Davis, *ibid.*, p. 157: "The law of the air, by which we really mean the law regulating the use of space over and above the earth's surface, is interesting and novel and important and still in the development state, but it belongs more in the field of aviation than in that of radio communication."

[25]The Radio and Interstate Commerce," *Michigan Law Review* 26:919–21 (June 1928).

ing the applicability of regulation to broadcast entertainment and information arose, as early as 1910 legal briefs affirmed the applicability of the commerce clause to communication via the ether.[26] Thus, conceptions of the social use and development of radio, for good or ill, were tied to a market model derived from the regulation of transportation technologies.

The Public Utilities Model

Clearly, the precedent set in the 19th century with the passage of the Interstate Commerce Act left an indelible mark on broadcast regulation, and hence on the social uses of broadcasting. The rights of Congress to regulate radio and later television, as a consequence of the 19th century experience, were connected to the common carrier notion and thus the public utility concept came into play. As Congressman Davis of Tennessee noted, in reference to a proposed amendment which would require radio license applicants to file written contracts or statements of oral contracts between the applicant and any other radio or wire utility:

> *The fact of the matter is that a railroad common carrier cannot enter into a contract of any consequence with another common carrier without first submitting the contract to the Interstate Commerce Commission and obtaining their approval. Why should we treat these people differently? It has already been stated, and I have stated it in my minority views that the Interstate Commerce Commission has been given certain jurisdiction over wireless utilities, as well as wire utilities, but they have never exercised it.*[27]

Those who supported the notion that radio ought to be declared a public utility often pointed to the disposition of current licenses, i.e., the number of radio stations operated by the government and by public institutions. *Radio,* a popular magazine published in San Francisco, argued that the broadcasting of information, especially addresses by the President, would soon become as much a necessity of life as good roads.[28] Some enthusiasts pointed to the possible extinction of the market for receiving sets to underscore the advantage of declaring radio a public utility. Broadcasting was financed by manufacturers of sets, but once the market was saturated, where would the money to finance radio come from? The public utility character of broadcasting, this argument ran, is connected to the very real possibility that broadcasting might die of hasty consumption. In order to ensure the buyer of the radio set continued broadcasting service, broadcasting ought to be declared a public utility and financed accordingly. Finally, there were arguments echoing Hoover's philosophy: monopolistic control of radio was against national policy, and if declared a public utility, radio could be regulated and operated much like the post office or public school system. Arguments against establishing radio as a public utility, on the other hand, rested on a belief that radio was *not* a necessity, not an essential service and need not be operated by a monopoly—as public utilities by definition do.[29]

[26]*Ibid.;* see also Frank Kahn, "Economic Regulation of Broadcasting as a Utility," *Journal of Broadcasting* 7:97–112 (Spring 1963), who quotes Harry Frease, *A Political Paradox* (Philadelphia: John C. Winston, 1934), p. 78: "Commerce, in its simplest signification, means an exchange of goods; but in the advancement of society, labor, transportation, intelligence, care, and various mediums of exchange become commodities and enter into commerce." This quote was attributed to a judge writing in 1824; Frease's source is V Peters Condensed Reports 562 in connection with the first commerce case to come before the Supreme Court: *Gibbons v. Ogden* (9 Wheat. 1); see p. 71 of *A Political Paradox;* see also "Application of the Commerce Clause to the Intangible," *Pennsylvania Law Review* 58: 411, 414, cited in "Radio," *Michigan Law Review, ibid.,* 920. See note 25.

[27]US Congress, House: *Congressional Record,* 69th Congress, 1st Session, 1926, p. 5557.

[28]Walter Kaempffert, "The Progress of Radio Broadcasting," *The American Review of Reviews* 66:303–04 (September 1922).

[29]Bruce Bliven, "How Radio is Remaking the World," *Century Magazine* 108:149 (June 1924); "Broadcasting Is Not

The phrase, "public interest, convenience or necessity," was used in many state statutes governing public utilities and was incorporated eventually into the Radio Act of 1927. But belief that radio ought to be conducted in the public interest goes back at least as far as the first radio conference in 1922.[30]

Although the public interest phrase applied to broadcasting has become something of a cliche, analysis of the debate surrounding regulation discloses that its meaning often was connected to various concepts and goals: to the disposition of traffic on the high seas, to the issue of control of the airwaves and to the concept of political democracy. The meaning of public convenience is at once the most obvious and the most obscure. It is obvious because we all understand what convenience means, especially when it is connected to public utilities, i.e., the convenience of indoor plumbing. It is obscure because it does not seem to apply to broadcasting. As far as broadcasting regulation goes, the original use of the term may have had to do with the location and movement of ships at sea. In 1912, when the Radio Act was passed, people feared that ships could not find each other or the shore. Stress was put on calling waves to establish contact. Once ships were in communication, they were free to roam about the ether on whatever channel was *convenient.* When broadcasting arrived on the scene, the congestion of the spectrum called for a reversal of the practice, lest interference make actual communication impossible.[31] By 1924, convenience seems to be extended to the concept of comfort and happiness of the members of the audience. In a debate regarding a federal tax on sets, for example, Senator Copeland argued against levying a tax on radio sets because broadcasting gave people "a knowledge of health, of the chemistry of the soil, of the weather, of marketing, of literature and of music."[32]

Regulation also was viewed in terms of the public interest. In an interview with *Radio News,* Hoover commented that radio was a public concern and should be considered from the standpoint of public interest "to the same extent and upon the basis of the same general principles as other . . . public utilities."[33] Public interest was equated with service to the listener, and that service became the basis for the privilege of broadcasting. RCA, in a letter to the Committee on Merchant Marine and Fisheries, summed up its beliefs in terms of service: "radio [is] calculated to afford the most good and the best radio service to the greatest number."[34]

Contrary to the intent of the law of 1912, the new radio law was based on the right of the people to public service, a right "superior to the right of any individual to use the ether."[35] This service, moreover, was not conceived solely in terms of commercial interests. Rather it was believed that the future development of broad-

a Public Utility," *Radio Broadcast* 9:375–76 (September 1926); "Fourteen Years Without a Change in Radio Legislation," *Radio Broadcast* 9:371f (September 1926).

[30]"Is Radio Only a Passing Fad?" *The Literary Digest* (3 June 1922), pp. 31–32; see also the Report of Department of Commerce Conference on Radio Telephony, (17 February, 1922); Frederick W. Ford, "The Meaning of the 'Public Interest, Convenience or Necessity'," *Journal of Broadcasting* 5:205–218 (Summer 1961); *Second Annual Report of the Federal Radio Commission* (Washington, DC: US Government Printing Office, 1928), pp. 166–70.

[31]See Address by Herbert Hoover, Secretary of Commerce before the International Radiotelegraph Conference, Washington, DC, 4 October 1927, especially pp. 3–4; Ford, *ibid.*, pp. 206–08; cf. *To Regulate Radio Communication,* p. 27; (see note 8).

[32]US Congress, Senate: *Congressional Record,* 68th Congress, 1st Session, 1924, p. 7699.

[33]Interview with Herbert Hoover, by J. R. Winters, published in *Radio News* (October 1924), mimeo in *Hoover Papers,* see p. 4 for this comment; Ford, *ibid.*, p. 208; interview for *Cleveland Plain Dealer,* by Harry A. Mount, n.d., *Hoover Papers;* Herbert Hoover to Wallace H. White, 4 December 1924, p. 2, especially; cf. US Congress, House: *Congressional Record,* 69th Congress, 1st Session, 1926, pp. 5484, 12452.

[34]*To Amend the Radio Act of 1912,* Hearings, Committee on Merchant Marine and Fisheries, House of Representatives, 67th Congress, 4th Session, 1923, p. 60

[35]US Congress, House: *Congressional Record,* 69th Congress, 1st Session, 1926, p. 54709.

casting ought to be done with a view to the social and economic good of the people.[36] Judge Davis, in response to Senator Dill's suggestion that wave lengths be limited in the interest of set makers, remarked, "I look at it from the standpoint of how many stations do we really need to efficiently serve the American Public. To give them all of the broadcasting that they want, all of the diversity on broadcasting that they desire. I look at it from the viewpoint of the listener and not from the viewpoint of the individual who may desire to broadcast."[37] The test was not whether an individual businessman desired to get into broadcasting for profit, but whether the public would be served by his doing so.[38]

The inherent difficulty of treating broadcasting as if it were a public utility was recognized in the Senate debate in 1926. The following exchange between Senators Caraway and McKellar underscores the problem caused when radio is viewed as a utility, but it also demonstrates that the right to use and dispose of private property was entangled in the problem of regulating broadcasting (this principle will be examined later):

Mr. Caraway: I want to ask the Senator by what principle of justice he would give the commission the right to take one's property and exercise jurisdiction over it?

Mr. McKellar: The amendment provides that if he sells it to one, he must sell to all alike.

Mr. Caraway: Why should he do that? If a man has a horse, he has the right to sell it wherever he pleases.

Mr. McKellar: The Senator knows this same principle applied to those who have electricity to sell in the form of power.

Mr. Caraway: Oh, that is an entirely different matter.

Mr. McKellar: No; it is exactly the same thing. One sells light and the other sells sound.

Mr. Caraway: The Senator thinks there is no difference between brains and electricity?[39]

Thus, people were taking stands both pro and con on radio conceived as a public utility. Herbert Hoover in hearings before Congress argued that radio never should be considered merely a business carried on for private gain, private advertisement or "idle" entertainment. Instead he proposed that radio "is a public concern impressed with public trust and ought to be considered primarily from the standpoint of public interest to the same extent as public utilities."[40]

At the same time, the question of public utility seemed to be connected to the concept of natural monopoly. Davis believed that radio was a natural monopoly to the extent that it would cost two stations to operate from the same point as much as it would cost one.[41] "Natural Monopoly" engendered concerns for political freedom, moreover, for it was held that any other kind of monopoly would affect press censorship. "It would be in principle the same as though the entire press of the country was controlled."[42] The other side of this debate, a minority side, can be found in a letter to Senator Bingham:

[36]US Congress, Senate: *Congressional Record,* 69th Congress, 1st Session, 1926, p. 21358.

[37]*Radio Control,* Hearings, Committee on Interstate Commerce, US Senate, 69th Congress, 1st Session, 1926, p. 30; for emphasis on diversity as the standard, see also *Jurisdiction of Radio Commission,* Hearings, Committee on the Merchant Marine and Fisheries, House of Representatives, 70th Congress, 1st Session, 1927, p. 55.

[38]Davis, *ibid.,* p. 173.

[39]US Congress, Senate: *Congressional Record,* 69th Congress, 1st Session, 1926, p. 12506.

[40]US Congress, House: *Congressional Record,* 69th Congress, 1st Session, 1926, p. 12452; Hoover's remarks are quoted in the text of a speech broadcast by Congressman Davis on WRC radio; cf. pp. 5483, 5578.

[41]US Congress, House: *Congressional Record,* 67th Congress, 1st Session, 1921, p. 2919.

[42]Telegram, Herbert Hoover to E. E. Plummer, 10 March 1924; cf. text of a letter from W. G. Cowles to Hiram Hingham, 18 May 1926, in US Congress, Senate: *Congressional Record,* 69th Congress, 1st Session, 1926, p. 12500.

The fact remains that if the common carrier clause in the Dill bill becomes law, stations will be compelled to give their time and undertake the expense of broadcasting anything which some crank may offer. Bolshevist propaganda will have a better chance in this country than ever before.[43]

However, while some expressed doubt about allowing certain political parties access to the airwaves, Representative Luther A. Johnson in the House was pointing out the importance of nondiscrimination against political parties or candidates for office. Again, his precedent was Section 10051 of the US Compiled Statutes, a law governing a public utility: the telegraph; all telegraph companies, according to the law, must "provide equal facilities to all without discrimination in favor of or against any person, company, or corporation whatsoever, either as to rates or as to service."[44]

Finally under questioning from members of the Committee on Interstate Commerce, Judge Davis became reluctant to compare broadcasting to public utilities lest the rates charged to advertisers fall under federal regulation. Instead he chose to compare the practice of varying advertising rates to the custom prevailing in the newspaper world: "A newspaper of large circulation or a magazine of large circulation can get a greater rate per line than a newspaper or magazine of small circulation. . . ."[45] This brings us to the third model predominating discourse on broadcasting in the 1920s: the press.

The Newspaper Model

In the case of the public utilities, at one level the arguments which arose were economic in nature: how to finance radio broadcasting. At a second level the argument became a political one: if declared a public utility then all parties would have equal access to the airwaves. The same pattern can be found in the discourse which focuses on broadcasting's resemblance to the newspaper press. In terms of the press model, the story of broadcasting, dubbed "the magazine of the air,"[46] is the story of one medium solving its economic problems by patterning itself after another medium, the newspaper.[47] As in the case of public utilities, at one level the issue was primarily economic, e.g., advertising rates. At a second level, the economic issue was bolstered by a political and intellectual one. Testifying before Congress, Mr. Herbert Smith of the National Carbon Company (manufacturer of Eveready batteries) noted that the comparison of radio with the newspaper was "a correct one": "Here we have a new art of communication that has burst on us within a very few years. It is an avenue of spreading intelligence and matters of interest that parallels the newspaper and magazine."[48]

Hoover also turned to the press associations and used them as models of interconnection and financing. With the cost of programming rising, he thought it was only a matter of time before stations would band together into an organization similar to the press associations to bear mutually the costs of carrying national programs and events of importance." . . . Just as the local newspaper could hardly serve its community adequately except with the assistance of press associations, and feature syndicates, so even in a large measure, the individual broadcasting stations are assisted by network operation."[49]

[43]W. G. Cowles to Bingham, reprinted in *ibid.*, cf. US Congress, Senate: *Congressional Record*, 69th Congress, 1st Session, 1926, p. 12502.

[44]US Congress, House: *Congressional Record*, 69th Congress, 1st Session, 1926, p. 5559.

[45]*Radio Control*, p. 92, (see note 37).

[46]Merlin H. Aylesworth, "The National Magazine of the Air," in *The Radio Industry, ibid.*, p. 242.

[47]*Ibid.*; see also *To Regulate Radio Communication, ibid.*, pp. 32, 34, (see note 8).

[48]*To Regulate Radio Communication, ibid.*, p. 84, (see note 8).

[49]Dr. Alfred N. Goldsmith, "Analysis of Network Broadcasting," paper presented before the Mid-Winter Meeting of the National Electrical Manufacturers Association, 29 November 1927, *Hoover Papers;* for remarks made by Hoover

Before advertising rates and their regulation became a concern, another economic issue attached to radio had to do with the transoceanic radio news service between the US and points in the Far East. Of special interest was the low-cost press service provided by the Navy to US businesses who wished to send news to the Orient. At bottom, the fear of newspaper owners and some Congressmen was that the Navy would try to retain private radio business by charging rates so low that private businesses could not compete. In other words, the Navy was suspected of attempting to build a government monopoly.[50] What began as an economic argument again became a political one. Private ownership, it was argued, would (1) ensure that the news was "independently and truthfully edited and free from government control";[51] and would (2) be a means of disseminating American news values, i.e., "propoganda-free news," and by extension, political and social values to peoples in the Orient.[52]

While the press was a model for regulating broadcasting in the early days, by 1924 it seems to have become a metaphor for freedom. In the Senate, Dill argued that to tax radio sets to subsidize broadcasting would be tantamount to taxing the nation's newspapers. He elaborated, "Just as firmly as I believe that the press ought to be kept free and that speech ought to be kept free, I believe the right to use radio ought to be kept free, because I believe it will eventually be a greater blessing than the free press has been in this country."[53]

The question of subsidy was closely related to another issue in early broadcast regulation: the power of monopolies. Again, the press was used as a model, but in this case it was a question of the limitations of two different technologies. In the House, Representative Johnson of Texas proposed:

> *If every newspaper in the United States could be purchased by some trust or combination, independent and competing newspapers could be established. But if the broadcasting stations, which are necessarily limited in number, can be acquired, or even a majority of high-powered stations owned and controlled by a trust, then the public will be helpless to establish others, unless the government protects them in this right. Freedom of the air will be impossible if the government either licenses or permits monopoly ownership of radio sending stations.*[54]

In the 1920s, then, the question of who is to use the airwaves was connected at least in part, to the notion of intellectual liberty and initiative. Before the United States entered the First World War, the Secretary of the Navy had urged the federal government to take control of radio communication as a matter of national defense. Convinced that only national control would eliminate certain problems in radio, the Navy asked the government to purchase all commercial stations. At once a hue and cry arose from owners of commercial companies,

---

see "Secretary Hoover Reviews Radio Situation," Press Release, 8 February 1925, *ibid.;* Arthur Sears Henning, "Hoover Sees End of Jazz in Radio," *Chicago Tribune* (22 December 1924), clipping in *Hoover Papers.*

[50]US Congress, Senate: *Congressional Record,* 66th Congress, 2nd Session, 1920, pp. 4112–16; see especially the editorials from the *Sacramento Bee* and the remarks of Senator King.

[51]*Ibid.,* p. 4113.

[52]*Ibid.,* cf. US Congress, House: *Congressional Record,* 67th Congress, 1st Session, 1921, p. 2915. After radio systems were returned to private owners, the government was not allowed, by provision of the law of 1912, to render service to the public if a private radio station was within 100 miles of the naval station. When private stations were unable to render adequate press service, Congress sought to address the problem to ensure that the American reader received adequate foreign news, and the foreign reader receive "full accounts of American activities," US Congress, House: *Congressional Record,* 67th Congress, 1st Session, 1921, p. 2920.

[53]US Congress, Senate: *Congressional Record,* 68th Congress, 1st Session, 1924, p. 7700; cf. US Congress, House: *Congressional Record,* 69th Congress, 1st Session, 1926, pp. 5484, 5488.

[54]US Congress, House: *Congressional Record,* 69th Congress, 1st Session, 1926, p. 12503; cf. Davis, *ibid.,* p. 187.

who believed that once the government got a foot in the door she would never leave. The businessmen operating commerical stations insisted that the campaign run by the Navy in the name of national security was designed for government ownership of all communications lines in the country. With the military in complete economic control of radio, "the air we breathe," the argument contended, "is no longer free."[55] Control of the airwaves and political freedom went hand in hand.

The question of monopoly and its attendant evils, however, was raised in large part in connection with the corporate pooling of patents. Concerns were voiced that "the powerful, the wanton, and the willful violations of the spirit and purpose of the law"[56] might give RCA and others an advantage in the burgeoning industry. Cross-licensing in and of itself was not so much the issue as the extent to which it was executed in radio and the consequences of pooling practices. For example, in hearings before the Committee on the Merchant Marine and Fisheries, it was said that a station in the South got nowhere in its effort to get a better wavelength until it joined the NBC chain of the "powerful RCA."[57] Hoover himself had said time and again that any monopoly given in radio would be the equivalent of giving exclusive right of navigation on one of the nation's rivers. The public interest demanded diversified ownership, the argument ran; monopoly emphatically was not in accordance with either public interest or with "the genius of our society."[58] The conflict, then, was between two very American principles: opposition to monopoly and a profound belief in the right of the individual to own and dispose of his/her private property.

In its response to the public attack on the illegality of the radio trust, RCA and others defended themselves by saying that they were a patriotic institution organized at the request of the US government.[59] Their protests, however, received little sympathy. In this case the rights of independent companies, it was argued, had been contravened and the general public had been exploited.[60]

In the question of monopoly ownership the prevailing economic concerns likewise evolved into political ones:

> *If the strong arm of the law does not prevent monopoly ownership and make discrimination by such stations illegal, American thought will be largely at the mercy of those who operate these stations. For publicity is the most powerful weapon that can be wielded in a Republic, and when such a weapon is placed in the hands of one, or a single selfish group is permitted to either tacitly or otherwise acquire ownership and dominate these broadcasting stations throughout*

[55]"Government Control of the Wireless," *Literary Digest* 54:336 (10 February 1917); "Is Government Ownership of Wireless Intended?" *Scientific American* 116:116 (3 February 1917); for corroboration of these early arguments against government control, the situation in Europe, especially France, was viewed as proof positive that real democracy and government control of the wireless were mutually exclusive. See *Radio Broadcast* 6 (February 1925); cf. "Hoover's Suggestions for New Radio Regulation," *Radio Broadcast* 6:890–92 (March 1925).

[56]US Congress, House: *Congressional Record,* 67th Congress, 4th Session, 1923, p. 2786; see also US Congress, Senate: *Congressional Record,* 67th Congress, 2nd Session, 1922, p. 8400; US Congress, House: *Congressional Record,* 67th Congress, 4th Session, 1923, pp. 2782; 2334, 2341–42; US Congress, Senate: *Congressional Record,* 69th Congress, 1st Session, 1926, p. 12616; US Congress, House: *Congressional Record,* 69th Congress, 1st Session, 1926, p. 5585.

[57]*Jurisdiction of Radio Commission, ibid.*, p. 58, (see note 37).

[58]"Broadcasting and the Public Interest," *The Independent* 112:172, 3865 (25 May 1924); cf. "Secretary Hoover Reviews Radio Situation," 8 February 1925, clipping in *Hoover Papers;* Statement by Secretary Hoover before the Committee on Merchant Marine and Fisheries, 11 March 1924, mimeo, *Hoover Papers;* Grover A. Whalen, "Radio Control," *The Nation* 119:90–1 (23 July 1924).

[59]*Jurisdiction of Radio Commission, ibid.*, p. 277, see note 37; for a counter argument see W. L. Chenery, "The Monopolies of 1924, II; The Radio Monopoly," *The Independent* 113:158, 3877 (13 September 1924).

[60]Oswald F. Schuette, Executive Secretary of the Radio Protective Association, *Jurisdiction,* 277; cf. remarks of Davis, US Congress, House: *Congressional Record,* 69th Congress, 1st Session, 1926, pp. 5482, 5483.

the country, then woe be to those who dare differ with them.[61]

The survival of political democracy itself was staked on proper regulation of "the young giant that would rule the future."[62] If broadcasting were placed into the hands of a few, it was thought, then political and religious propaganda would result.[63] Senator Howell of Nebraska noted: "We are all familiar with the results of propaganda, its dangers and its advantages, and the question which we are called upon to settle now is how the public may enjoy the advantages of broadcasting and avoid the dangers that may result therefrom."[64] Or, as the Secretary of the Chicago Federation of Labor Radio Broadcasting Association, asked: "A monopoly of the air is already here. Is it wise to build up so colossal a *political* power?"[65] (Italics added.)

After the passage of the 1927 law, the question of monopoly arose again, but this time in reference to the new Federal Radio Commission. Only if the FRC were staffed by both political parties, the argument ran, could the interests of democracy be furthered:

You are dealing with what is going to be the most powerful political instrument of the future. We are dealing with something that enters and can enter into every home in this country, in respect to matters along social, religious, educational or any other lines, and the people are spending hundreds of millions of dollars for radio apparatus and other people are wanting to use the apparatus and service and they ought not to have to invariably go to the monopoly.[66]

Thus the newspaper press, rooted in private ownership, provided broadcasting an example of diversity in terms of ownership and its consequent contribution to the marketplace of ideas.

In the 1920s, moreover, some people connected to broadcasting saw radio as a kind of paperless newspaper, an aerial edition. Interconnected broadcast stations were called newspapers of the air and national magazines of entertainment and information. Although some critics were beginning to predict the demise of the printed newspaper, others insisted that radio was not a rival to the press, but a supplement.[67]

Connected to the concept of the radio as newspaper was the democratic function of the press: keeping the body politic informed so that it might carry out its civic duties. David Sarnoff saw radio as "the bar at which great causes will be pleaded for the verdict of public opinion."[68] He and others believed the same principles of freedom guiding the newspaper press applied equally to broadcasting. The only test of admission to the broadcast forum was the public interest, free of racial and political bias.[69]

As a "splendidly sprawling bulletin board,"[70] reminiscent of the bulletin boards used in the 19th century by the newspaper press, radio was seen as a new kind of public forum. It wo[illegible]

[61]Rep. Johnson, *ibid.*, 5558.

[62]US Congress, House: *Congressional Record*, 67th Congress, 4th Session, 1923, p. 2341.

[63]See editorial, reprinted in US Congress, Senate: *Congressional Record*, 69th Congress, 1st Session, 1926, p. 12501; remarks of Senator Blease, p. 12508; *ibid.*, House, pp. 5500, 5579, 12452; for arguments concerning the international political questions see *ibid.*, pp. 5489, 5494.

[64]*Ibid.*, p. 12503.

[65]*Ibid.*, p. 5487; see also p. 5489.

[66]*Ibid.*, p. 5487; see also *To Amend the Radio Act*, p. 59 (see note 34); *To Regulate Radio Communication*, *ibid.*, p. 26 see note 8; cf. 67–68 for international radio communication.

[67]James C. Young, "Is the Radio Newspaper Next?" *Radio Broadcast* 7:575–80 (September 1925); Earl Reeves, "The New Business of Broadcasting," *American Review of Reviews* 72:529–32 (November 1925); "Why Broadcasting Offers No Real Competition to the Newspapers," *Radio Broadcast* 10:146–47 (December 1926); cf. Marc A. Rose, "Radio or Newspaper—Can Both Survive?" *The Nation* 119:699–700 (24 December 1924); Silas Bent, "Radio Steals the Press' Thunder," *The Independent* 119:33–34, 48 (9 July 1927); Winfield Barton, "What Broadcasting does for the Newspaper," *Radio Broadcast* 4:344–46 (February 1924); James H. Collins, "Giving Folks What They Want by Radio," *Saturday Evening Post* 196:10–11, 102, 107, 109 (17 May 1924).

[68]David Sarnoff, "Uncensored and Uncontrolled," *The Nation* 115:90 (23 July 1924); also see, "Radio—the New Social Force," *ibid.*, p. 465.

[69]Sarnoff, *ibid.*, p. 90.

[70]Rose, *ibid.*, p. 700.

provide for the nation what the New England Town Meeting provided the small isolated communities of early America. Radio had the advantage over the newspaper, moreover, because it reached the illiterate as well as the literate, the comic strip readers as well as the readers of the editorial page.[71]

Conclusion

In this paper I have tried to show how people dealt with the future of broadcasting prior to the passage of the Radio Act of 1927. An analysis of public discourse, both oral and written, shows that three models and metaphors were used to conceptualize the use and development of radio: transportation, public utilities and the newspaper press. The over-arching model, rooted in the regulation of transport industries, was a market model, since the right to regulate broadcasting rested on the commerce clause. Thus from its inception broadcasting was not regulated as a symbol-producing, culture-maintaining medium, the purpose of which was art, intellectual exchange and the maintenance of a public sphere or community. Instead a market model prevailed. This way of visualizing the real world assumes a neutral society in which each individual is free to pursue his/her own interests and his/her own advantage as a natural right. [72] Thus, the political freedom that such a society supposes is used to underscore the market interests of a minority of that society. Raymond Williams suggests a connection between a market model and a way of looking at members of a society, not as community or public, but as masses.[73] As he so eloquently suggests:

> *If our purpose is art, education, the giving of information or opinion, our interpretation (of society) will be in terms of the rational interested being. If, on the other hand, our purpose is manipulation—the persuasion of a large number of people to act, feel, think, know, in certain ways—the convenient formula will be that of the masses.*[74]

Thus, what appears on the surface to be a harmless, neutral way of directing the future of broadcasting, is at a subterranean level quite the opposite.

Lastly, many people of the 1920s believed that control of the airwaves had political consequences for the future of democracy. Thus economic interests were legitimated by arguments concerning political democracy, intellectual liberty and initiative. In their recent analysis of radio, Higgins and Moss argue that from the time of this early victory by powerful manufacturing interests, broadcasting has been impregnated with the spirit of commerce and the ethos of consumption.[75] Although public service does enter into the debate concerning the future of broadcasting, it does so in reference to radio as a public utility. However, as the reader will recall, there was disagreement over the suitability of the model's application to broadcasting. Regarding radio in terms of transportation or the press went unquestioned or unexamined. Thus, the habits of industrial capitalism, a form of government in which commerce takes precedent over the social well-being of the community, made it unavoidable that economics determine the future use and social development of broadcasting in the United States.

[71]Bent, *ibid.*, p. 33; M. H. Aylesworth, "Radio's Accomplishment: The Part It May Play in National and International Affairs," *Century Magazine* 118:214–21 (June 1929).

[72]Williams, *ibid.*, p. 325.

[73]*Ibid.*, pp. 297–300.

[74]*Ibid.*, p. 303.

[75]C. S. Higgins and P. D. Moss, *Sounds Real: Radio In Everyday Life* (St. Lucia and New York: University of Queensland Press, 1982), p. 80.

VI

Free Speech Issues in the Twentieth Century

In 1791, the framers of the Constitution voted to add to this important document ten amendments, or the Bill of Rights. These amendments granted a variety of civil liberties, including freedom of expression, to citizens of the new nation. Historical evaluation of press freedom in the eighteenth century has focused on the relationship of the press to the government, analyzing the levels of freedom experienced by the colonial press and studying the origins of the Bill of Rights. Studies usually emphasized the role of legislative actions and seditious libel prosecutions before and after the Revolution. Some scholars also have considered the effects of economic constraints on self-censorship and the role of public opinion in silencing opposing views.

Although the nineteenth century witnessed technological developments that caused the press to be identified more clearly with corporate business than with individuals, the concept of protection for the individual prevailed. State courts did prosecute newspaper publishers—primarily in the traditional areas of libel and contempt—but the Supreme Court heard no cases that required development of First Amendment theory. Nevertheless, freedom of expression was restricted as southern state legislatures and public violence curtailed the voices of those who supported the abolition of slavery. In addition, the postmaster general by precipitous action further restricted the free flow of information. With the Civil War, issues of censorship faced editors in both North and South. Looking back, scholars also concern themselves with the censorship effects of corporate development and ask questions about what that meant for diversity of information.

Legal actions mushroomed in the twentieth century. Some concerns in traditional areas—seditious libel—were reflected in the sedition cases of the teens, as radicals faced prosecution for unpopular "anarchist" thought. But the definition of free expression and claims to its privileges expanded. The introduction of conscription for the first time since the Civil War, combined with a new interest in political theory sparked by the Bolshevik Revolution, produced a collision between authority and libertarian values.[1] This tension continued through the 1930s as America's intellectuals questioned whether the political system was functioning in a country where one-third of the work force was unemployed; in subsequent decades fears of communism and fascism created a climate of suspicion of those outside the mainstream, and an atmosphere conducive to suppression. Such suppression was not always imposed from outside the industry; but leaders within it often sought ways to avoid public opposition and/or government regulation, or colluded in varying ways with government to avoid prosecution.

Further complicating the twentieth-century picture has been the development of broadcasting and the subsequent regulatory apparatus that has sprung up around the industry. From the early 1920s, when it became apparent that the broadcast industry needed, at the very least, a "traffic cop" to police the airwaves to avoid the total chaos caused by overlapping use of frequencies, critics have debated the necessity and wisdom of the extensive governmental regulation that was created. According to regulation supporters, the doctrine of "scarcity" of airwaves required a "trusteeship" model, in which broadcast regulators merely leased airwaves belonging to the public and operated them in the public "interest, convenience and necessity."

The passage of the Radio Act of 1927 and the Federal Communications Act of 1934 created administrative agencies with power to determine who would broadcast across the limited channels available. Some argued that these pieces of legislation were not passed—as proclaimed—to ensure that broadcasting would operate in the public interest, but to preserve the rights and privileges of private commercial broadcasters. The Federal Communications Commission, created by the 1934 act, has exercised its powers differently as the composition of the commission has changed under different administrations.[2] In 1941, for example, the Commission ruled that editorializing was not in the public interest, but by 1949 it had changed its mind to allow broadcast licensees to broadcast opinion. Although the FCC was relatively passive during the 1950s, during the next two decades its activist approach mirrored some of the activism occurring in society. During the 1960s and 1970s the FCC instituted regular procedures to ascertain community needs and to broaden content to address the needs of minorities and women, and citizens were granted the right to challenge license renewals.

In "Franklin Roosevelt, His Administration, and the Communications Act of 1934," the selection here that deals with broadcast regulation, Robert W. McChesney evaluates the public debate about regulation that occurred between 1927 and 1934. He argues that the adoption of the Federal Communications Act of 1934 was not necessarily a natural sequel to the adoption of the Radio Act of 1927 but that government, in collusion with private commercial interests, worked hard to ensure there would be no extended public debate over the fundamental structure of the broadcasting system. The 1927 act, McChesney argues, solidified the position of the private operators, making it more difficult for educational and other noncommercial groups to obtain licenses and broadcast freely. This article, therefore, challenges the idea that the legislation of 1927 and 1934 was adopted to protect the airwaves and ensure action in the public interest. Public interest, in McChesney's interpretation, was defined as the public interest of the corporate, commercial world.

The motion picture industry also maneuvered around the spectre of government regulation. Gregory Black argues in "Hollywood Censored: The Production Code Administration and the Hollywood Film Industry, 1930–1940" that the film industry, by attempting to avoid government regulation through self-censorship by the Motion Picture Producers and Distributors of America (MPPDA), essentially excluded many controversial social and political themes from film. Reform groups of the early twentieth century regarded films as a threat to traditional values, and by 1911 those groups were demanding film censorship. State and municipal boards were created to police movies, and the 1915 Supreme Court ruling in *Mutual Film Corporation* v. *Ohio* excluded film from the protection of free speech clauses of federal and state constitutions.

Print media were not exempt from government pressure. Patrick S. Washburn's article, "J. Edgar Hoover and the Black Press in World War II," focuses on the pressure exerted on a minority press during wartime. J. Edgar Hoover, the iron ruler of the Federal Bureau of Investigation, began scrutinizing the black press as early as 1919, in conjunction with investigations of subversive activities. Hoover feared that black editors would encourage blacks to riot or to join with Communist organizations to undermine the U.S. government. During the early months of World War II, FBI officials regularly visited black editors, chiding them for articles about discrimination that the FBI believed hampered the war effort. Washburn describes a 1941 meeting between John Sengstacke and Attorney General Francis Biddle, in which the black editor promised increased cooperation if Biddle would ensure access to high government officials. Although Hoover persevered in his investigations of the black press, Biddle and other Justice Department officials effectively blocked indictments of it during the war.

In "Institutional Paralysis in the Press: The Cold War in Washington State," Gerald J. Baldasty and Betty Houchin Winfield discuss a more subtle form of of censorship, one that arises from institutional procedure and ritual. They argue that during the post–World War II communist scare the practice of collecting information from institutional sources precluded a balanced account of a state legislative inquiry into alleged communist activity at a state's premier public institution, the University of Washington. The concern about institutional constraints of the media reflects a concern about the increasing power of the media in the corporate power elite structure of the postwar world. In this corporate milieu, the Supreme Court has become a more active interpreter of the First Amendment, attempting to balance the traditional individual rights with corporate and social rights.

In addition to political and economic tensions, the complex marketplace forces of the twentieth century have generated an expanding legal war over control of the marketplace of ideas, writes historian Richard Schwarzlose. Schwarzlose's exhaustive study of free expression over several centuries is too long to be reprinted here, but he notes that the "twentieth-century combatants—principally media institutions, on the one hand, and a mixture of private individuals, citizen action groups, domestic governments, and public officials on the other hand—all claim a piece of the First Amendment free speech and free press clause as their sword or shield." Schwarzlose further notes that the Supreme Court has settled on an "ad hoc balancing" test to weigh free expression against competing social values but has failed to develop a consistent theory of the First Amendment.[3]

Furthermore, in recent years scholars have argued that the doctrine of scarcity, the underlying presumption on which broadcast regulation was based, has disappeared. The advent of multiple cable channels theoretically could provide diversity without the massive regulatory apparatus that was at least partly dismantled during the 1980s. Nevertheless, others recognize that citizen involvement may diminish with deregulation, which eliminated many provisions of the activist years, although it leaves in place some regulations regarding political and commercial speech.

Endnotes

1. Donald M. Gillmor, Jerome A. Barron, Todd F. Simon and Herbert A. Terry, *Mass Communication Law: Cases and Comment* (New York: West Publishing Co., 1990), 9.
2. James L. Baughman, *Television's Guardians: The FCC and the Politics of Programming, 1958–1967* (Knoxville: University of Tennessee Press, 1985).
3. Richard Schwarzlose, "The Marketplace of Ideas: A Measure of Free Expression," *Journalism Monographs* 122: (August 1990): 30.

Franklin Roosevelt, His Administration, and the Communications Act of 1934

Robert W. McChesney

The period between the passage of the Radio Act of 1927 and the Communications Act of 1934 was a critical one in broadcast history. It was only *after* 1927 that the shape of the private and commercial broadcasting system that subsequently dominated American radio (and television) emerged in full-force. This development generated the rapid creation of a diverse group of persons and organizations that opposed the private and commercial domination of the airwaves and sought to have Congress address the situation through the passage of reform legislation. Unlike the period preceding 1927, this highly charged context provided the backdrop in which the Communications Act of 1934 was drafted and passed.

In the debate over broadcast policy, President Franklin D. Roosevelt and his administration played a pivotal role. Roosevelt was not *the* dominant figure in the formulation of radio policy in 1933 and 1934. Indeed, several other public figures, including Senator Clarence C, Dill, Democrat of Washington, took a far more active role in radio affairs and deservedly play a larger role in broadcasting history than Roosevelt. Nevertheless, Roosevelt did play a central role in determining the shape of the legislation that emerged, and, furthermore, his decision to ignore the concerns of the reformers and maintain the private commercial status quo was decisive. Roosevelt alone had whatever opportunity may have existed to arrest the private and commercial domination of the American airwaves. He elected not to exercise that prerogative, and the private structure and control of the American broadcasting system has been beyond fundamental public political debate ever since.

The preponderance of scholarship in broadcast history has concentrated upon the period before 1927 and the Radio Act of 1927 as the decisive era and legislation for the future development of American radio and television. The period from 1927 to 1934 and the Communications Act of 1934, on the other hand, have been generally overlooked despite the fact that the 1934 act provided the permanent basis for the regulation and structure of American broadcasting. Since the 1934 act essentially re-enacted the Radio Act of 1927, its construction and passage have been seemingly deemed as little more than a footnote to the "real debate" over American broadcast policy which transpired in the 1920's. Furthermore, most broadcast history scholarship has regarded the Radio Act of 1927 to be, as one scholar put it, " . . . a progressive victory . . . passed in the best interest of the citizenry."[1]

[1]Donald G. Godfrey, "Senator Dill and the 1927 Radio Act," *Journal of Broadcasting* 23 (1978): 485. Until rather recently this has been the dominant school of thought in broadcast history scholarship. Thus Sydney Head would observe that the Radio Act of 1927 revealed a "remarkable soundness" because it has "withstood the test of time and

Insofar as the Communications Act of 1934 reenacted the 1927 Radio Act, when scholars have assessed it, they have generally discussed it in the same lofty and flattering terms.[2]

Given these dominant themes in broadcast history scholarship, it is not surprising that historians generally have overlooked the role of President Franklin D. Roosevelt and that of his administration. If one assumes that the Radio Act of 1927 was the really significant piece of legislation, then Roosevelt clearly played no important role. Furthermore, even if one concentrates on the history of the Communications Act of 1934, Roosevelt tends to be ignored, as he usually avoided public pronouncements on the matter and conducted his affairs in the area of broadcast regulation and reform through a number of presidential aides and congressmen. He remained behind the scenes and avoided anything that smacked of controversy. On the surface, Roosevelt appears barely to have considered the issue of broadcast regulation and legislation.

attacks from every imaginable source." (Sydney W. Head, *Broadcasting in America* [Boston: 1956], 134.)

More recent scholarship has discovered that much of the so-called greatness of the 1927 Act was based less on hard research than on the belief that the status quo of American broadcasting was so outstanding that any legislation which had authorized it could only be exemplary as well. This scholarship has cut through the rhetoric of the commercial broadcasting industry and taken a far more critical stance toward both the Radio Act of 1927 and the Communications Act of 1934. For some excellent examples see: Philip T. Rosen, *The Modern Stentors; Radio Broadcasters and the Federal Government 1920–1934* (Westport, Conn., 1980); George H. Gibson, *Public Broadcasting; The Role of the Federal Government, 1919–1976* (New York, 1977); and Erick Barnouw, *A Tower in Babel* (New York, 1966) and *The Golden Web* (New York, 1968).

[2]Thus Walter B. Emery notes regarding the Communications Act of 1934: "The national policy which the Act embodies was conceived in terms of the democratic concepts and values. . . ." He terms it the "Magna Charta for broadcasting" which accentuated unparalleled freedom in the "good society." (Walter B. Emery, "Broadcasting Rights and Responsibilities in Democratic Society," *The Centennial Review* 8(1964): 312.)

Key Developments in American Radio, 1927–1933

While considerable debate transpired over how best to organize and regulate American broadcasting prior to the passage of the Radio Act of 1927, little of it dealt with the implications of a fully private commercial system dominated by two enormous national networks. In the mid 1920's there were some 200 licensed non-profit radio stations, of which approximately one half were affiliated with colleges or universities.[3] Virtually all discussion prior to 1927 anticipated a continued major presence for non-profit broadcasting. Secretary of Commerce Herbert Hoover was adamant about the need to protect and preserve independent educational stations. The role of commercial advertising as the sole means of support for the industry also was far from sacrosanct prior to 1927. Hoover, for example, was extremely critical of the excesses and implications of commercial advertising at both the third and the fourth National Radio Conferences.

If the public debate and the discussion among the concerned parties tended to concentrate on issues that seem tangential to the dominant trend toward the private commercial domination of the airwaves, the congressional debate over the Radio Act of 1927 was even less significant. Most congressmen had not the slightest understanding of the technology or the meaning of the legislation. The legislation was rushed through after a Federal appeals court, in late 1926, had ruled that the selective issuance of broadcast licenses was unconstitutional. In just a few months some 200 new broadcasters entered the industry, and the airwaves became a mass of chaos.[4] In addition, the committee

[3]S.E. Frost, Jr., *Education's Own Stations* (Chicago: 1937), 1–5; *Digest of Hearings, Federal Communications Commission Broadcast Division, under Sec. 307(c) of the "Communications Act of 1934" October 1–20, November 7–12, 1934* (Washington D.C.: 1935), 180–249. [Hereafter *FCC Digest*]

[4]For a discussion of this period see Marvin R. Bensman,

hearings and the floor debate avoided any discussion that addressed the central issues of how the emerging broadcast industry was to be organized, structured, controlled, and supported in the broadest sense of these terms.

Indeed, one of the two authors of the Radio Act of 1927, Senator C. C. Dill, intended to keep controversial issues out of the congressional debate. His reasoning was that the newly formed Federal Radio Commission (FRC) should be left on its own to determine how best to regulate the airwaves and allocate the limited number of broadcast channels among the contending applicants in the "public interest, convenience and necessity."[5] This phrase had been included, if for no other reason, to ensure the statute's constitutionality.[6] The FRC was established as a temporary body; its purpose was to bring order to the airwaves and to reduce the number of broadcasters. In 1928 the FRC instituted a general reallocation of the air frequencies—General Order No.40—which, in effect, favored private commercial broadcasters over non-profit and non-commercial broadcasters.

Broadcasting was transformed between 1927 and 1933 in a manner that made the experience of the early and mid-1920s fade quickly into the past. The two networks, the National Broadcasting Company (NBC) and the Columbia Broadcasting System (CBS), scarcely existed in 1927 and failed to merit political consideration. By 1933 they were affiliated with thirty percent of all U.S. radio stations, and they dominated the airwaves.[7] The business community hardly paused to observe the Great Depression in its hurry to place advertisements over the air. As Philip Rosen has observed, the Radio Act of 1927 permitted commercial broadcasters to go on a "prosperous, almost triumphant expansion."[8]

On the other hand, the number of non-profit stations plummeted during the reign of the FRC. During the seven years after the passage of the Radio Act of 1927, 188 non-profit broadcasters discontinued operations while only a handful of new ones were licensed. By 1934 this left only sixty-five non-profit broadcasters, thirty-five of which were affiliated with educational institutions.[9] Indeed by 1934 it was estimated that non-profit broadcasters accounted for only two percent of the total airtime.[10] To no small extent the policies of the FRC drove them off the air. Furthermore, the commercial broadcasters tended to pursue aggressively, with great success, the channels the non-profit broadcasters occupied.

However, it would be inappropriate to locate the demise of educational and non-profit broadcasting solely in the actions of the FRC. In simple economic terms, the non-profit broadcasters were never under the illusion that they could compete on an equal footing with the commercial broadcasters. Displaced educational and non-profit broadcasters argued emphatically that in 1927 Congress had assured then that the Radio Act had been loosely framed and that the FRC was intended to *favor* their cause in its interpretation of the "public interest, convenience

"The Zenith-WJAZ Case and the Chaos of 1926–27," *Journal of Broadcasting* 14 (Fall 1970): 423–440.

[5]Senator Clarence C. Dill, who was one of the co-authors of the 1927 Radio Act, argued that: "Congress would find it extremely difficult, if not impossible, to legislate on all the situations and conditions that develop from time to time. For this reason, the radio law granted the Federal Radio Commission, which it established, extremely broad powers." (Clarence C. Dill, "Safe-Guarding the Ether—The American Way," *Congressional Digest*, August–September 1933, 196.)

[6]See Louis G. Caldwell, "The Standard of Public Interest, Convenience or Necessity as Used in the Radio Act of 1927," *Air Law Review* 1 (July 1930): 295–330.

[7]Figures cited in Christopher H. Sterling, *Electronic Media, a Guide to Trends in Broadcasting and Newer Technologies 1920–1983* (New York: 1984), 12.

[8]Rosen, *Stentors*, 12. Barnouw has noted that in the brief period between 1927 and 1933, "almost all forms of enterprise that would dominate radio and television in decades to come had taken shape." (Barnouw, *Tower*, 270.)

[9]*FCC Digest*, 180–249.

[10]*Congressional Record*, 78 (May 15, 1934): 8830–8834.

and necessity."[11] FRC members, on the other hand, denied the constant charges that they were insensitive to the concerns of the non-profit broadcasters. They simply argued that the legislation was tightly worded and *forced* them to allocate licenses as they did.[12] The FRC member most sympathetic to autonomous educational broadcasting, Ira Robinson, candidly informed disgruntled educators in 1930 that their only recourse was to demand that Congress change the law.[13] Most FRC members simply told the educators that they should learn to use the airtime the commercial broadcasters offered them and not be so concerned about maintaining their own channels. Non-profit broadcasters quickly came to despise the FRC, and it was generally held in low regard in Washington. Its second General Counsel, Bethuel M. Webster, Jr., quit in disgust in 1929 and would characterize the FRC as an institution of "unparalleled mediocrity and ineptitude."[14] The only interested parties that seemed satisfied with the FRC and its administration of the Radio Act of 1927 were the two networks and the commercial broadcasters.

Displaced non-profit broadcasters formed the foundation of the movement which came to oppose the private and commercial domination of American radio between 1927 and 1933. While religious and labor broadcasters played an important role, educators were clearly the most significant component of this opposition movement. Under the aegis of Commissioner of Education William J. Cooper, nine of the leading national educational organizations formed the National Committee of Education By Radio (NCER) in 1930 to promote and preserve non-profit and non-commercial broadcasting stations. The NCER was mandated in its charter to lobby Congress to pass a law requiring that fifteen percent of the channels be reserved for non-profit educational broadcasters. The NCER was predicated on the principle that it was impossible to expect commercial broadcasters to provide adequate educational or cultural programming. In virtually all of their arguments, the educators stressed that the private censorship of commercial broadcasters, and especially the two major networks, undermined the traditional notion of free speech. The NCER had a full-time staff of three, published a monthly newsletter, and provided a relentless critique of the private and commercial domination of American radio throughout the early 1930s. The chairman of NCER, Joy Elmer Morgan, also edited the *Journal of the National Education Association*.

A number of intellectuals began to consider the full implications of a private commercial radio system during this period as well; their observations were also quite critical of the

[11]During the committee hearings concerning the Radio Act of 1927 educators pushed for Congress to mandate that the new FRC *favor* educational and non-profit broadcasters in the allocation of air channels. They were told that such a mandate was unnecessary as it was implicit in the term "public interest," convenience and necessity. "See the testimony of Father Harney in the *Hearings before the Committee on Interstate Commerce United States Senate 73rd Session on S. 2910 1934* (Washington D.C.: 1934), March 13, 1934, 186. [Hereafter *Senate Hearings 1934*] Also see Gibson, *Public Broadcasting*, 8.

[12]In 1931 the Chairman of the FRC, Charles McKinley Saltzman, argued that: "The Commission wishes to help the cause of education and the plans of educators, but it can do so only in accordance with the provisions of the law that prescribes its powers." Saltzman's interpretation of the Radio Act of 1927 was not that it was the vague yet powerful instrument Senator Dill claimed he had written but, rather, that the FRC's powers, "limitations, and functions" were "prescribed in considerable detail." See Charles McKinley Saltzman, "Commercial Broadcasting and Education." In *Radio and Education; Proceedings of the First Assembly of the National Advisory Council on Radio in Education, 1931*, edited by Levering Tyson, (Chicago: 1931), 26. (Hereafter *Radio and Education 1931*)

[13]Ira R. Robinson, "Who Owns Radio?" In *Education on the Air; First Yearbook of the Institute for Education by Radio*, Edited by Josephine H. MacLatchy (Columbus: 1930), 16–17.

[14]Bethuel M. Webster, Jr., "Notes on the policy of the Administration with Reference to the Control of Communications," *Air Law Review* 5 (April 1934): 108. Also, interview of Mr. Webster by the author, February 18, 1987.

status quo. This group included figures such as Bruce Bliven, James Rorty, Norman Thomas, John Dewey, William A. Orton, and Jerome Davis. Indeed, Joy Elmer Morgan was not far from the truth in 1933 when he argued that it was impossible to find any intellectual in favor of the status quo unless the person was receiving either money or broadcast time from a commercial broadcaster.[15] The American Civil Liberties Union (ACLU) even formed a Radio Committee in 1933 to address its alarm at the restrictions to free speech "inherent in the American system of broadcasting."[16] Many of the criticisms and concerns raised by these thinkers anticipated much of the serious media criticism of today. Nevertheless, the vast majority of the American people had little exposure to the ideas of these scholars or groups like the NCER. The major networks and the National Association of Broadcasters (NAB), on the other hand, were far more successful in their efforts to legitimize the status quo.

Yet, while the opposition movement may have been long on compelling arguments, it was short on political acumen. The various elements of the opposition movement rarely coordinated their activities. Some reformers sought a fixed percentage of the airwaves for non-profit broadcasters, other called for the establishment of a non-commercial government network to supplement the commercial broadcasters, and yet others had their own specific models for a reconstructed broadcasting system. The question of whether or not non-profit broadcasting should also be non-commercial proved to be a divisive issue for the opposition. The NCER and the ACLU were opposed to commercialism on principle while many labor and religious broadcasters argued that it was a necessary source of revenues. After several futile attempts to pass legislation assuring that fifteen percent of the airwaves be set aside for educational broadcasters, NCER decided to push instead for an independent (i.e., non-FRC) study of radio that would recommend fundamental changes in the structure of American broadcasting; it was certain that any independent study could *only* recommend radical changes in American broadcasting. The NCER stuck to this platform in 1934 even as another reformer, Father John B. Harney of New York, managed to get a measure to the floor of the Senate calling for twenty-five percent of the airwaves to be set aside for non-profit broadcasting. In addition, the ACLU Radio Committee also removed itself from this key debate in 1934 after it determined that its own radio reform package had no hope of passage.

Despite this lack of political sophistication, the arguments of the reformers, if not their specific remedies, found many sympathetic ears on Capitol Hill. By 1932 the NCER and some other reformers were able to generate considerable support for some sort of measures to restrict advertising and bolster educational broadcasting.[17] The Senate finally passed a resolution which called for the FRC to make a prompt study which was to address, among other things, whether advertising should be eliminated or reduced, whether government-owned stations were a viable option, and whether educational programming could be left safely to voluntary contributions of the commercial broadcasters. The FRC response, titled *Commercial Radio Advertising*, was based entirely on the response of commercial broadcasters to a questionnaire sent out by the FRC which did not

[15]Joy Elmer Morgan, "The New American Plan for Radio." In *A Debate Handbook on Radio Control and Operation*, edited by Bower Aly and Gerald D. Shively (Columbia, Mo.: 1933), 82.

[16]Roger Baldwin to Harris K. Randall, April 4, 1933, American Civil Liberties Union Manuscripts, Princeton University, Princeton, New Jersey, 1931–1933, Volume 513. [Hereafter ACLU Mss]

[17]One study described this as a "Major movement . . . under way in the Senate" and deemed the educators as largely responsible for its existence. See Carl J. Friedrich and Jeannette Sayre, *The Development of the Control of Advertising on the Air* (New York: 1940), 14.

solicit any input from the NCER or the other reform organizations. The report was a resounding defense of the status quo. It left NCER disgusted with what it considered a white-wash. The commercial broadcasters and their allies in Congress, to the contrary, were quite satisfied. The momentum for reform had been successfully defused for the time being.

Between 1928 and 1933 Congress was unable to agree on permanent legislation for the regulation of broadcasting and communications in general. When Franklin Roosevelt assumed the presidency in March 1933, opposition to the status quo was still intense if somewhat demoralized by the lack of progress on Capitol Hill; the commercial broadcasters themselves were alarmed by the threat of reform and the NAB was constantly sounding the alarm to its membership.[18] Yet, they were rapidly consolidating their hold over the industry. By now the airwaves had been stabilized from the drastic restructuring of 1928–32, and the commercial broadcasters were in favor of a permanent body to replace the FRC. In early 1933 the NAB generated funds from member stations for "war plans" to fight off "attacks by unfriendly groups" and to "speed up the movement toward a thoroughly stabilized broadcasting industry."[19] The outcome of the conflict would determine the basic structure and the essence of American broadcasting into the last decades of the century.

President Roosevelt: Preliminary Observations

Before providing a chronological examination of the key events regarding President Roosevelt and radio legislation, a few preliminary observations are necessary. From the outset Roosevelt never revealed much inclination to make any fundamental reform in the structure of American broadcasting. In his rare public pronouncements, he was vague and generally supportive of the status quo.[20] He did not even pay lip service to the criticism surrounding commercial radio; he merely ignored it.[21] Most of his efforts regarding communications legislation were conducted through two of his assistant secre-

[18]The NAB was continually waving the red flag of reform to its membership in its weekly newsletter during these years. It characterized the Wagner-Hatfield amendment as bringing "to a head the campaign against the present broadcasting set-up which has been smoldering in Congress for several years." From "Wagner Amendment Up Next Week," *NAB Reports*, May 5, 1934, 618. One proponent of the status quo argued that the commercial broadcasters needed to engage in a "public relations" campaign or "run the risk of government ownership" due to the "growing dissatisfaction" of the American people toward commercial radio. See F. X. W., "Will American Broadcasting Become Classified and Regulated as a Public Utility?" *Public Utilities Fortnightly* 10 (August 4, 1932): 155.

[19]Sol Taishoff, "War Plans Laid to Protect Broadcasting," *Broadcasting*, March 1, 1933, 5. The Standing Committee on Communications of the American Bar Association noted a sharp decrease in the number of contested license hearings by 1932. By this point the airwaves, by and large, were allocated along the lines where they would remain thereafter. See "Report of the Standing Committee on Communications." In *Report of the Fifty-Fifth Annual Meeting of the American Bar Association, 1932* (Baltimore: 1932), 452.

[20]Roosevelt's rare public pronouncements tended to be to industry groups at their annual conventions. For example, in a message to the Radio Manufacturers of America in 1934 Roosevelt stated: "In cooperation with the government, radio has been conducted as a public agency. It has met the requirements of the letter and spirit of the law that it functions for 'public convenience and necessity.' " He used the type of terminology that lent itself to multiple interpretations: "To permit radio to become a medium for selfish propaganda of any character would be shamefully and wrongfully to abuse a great agent of public service." ("Keep Radio Free, Roosevelt Urges," New York *Times*, June 14, 1934, 21.) This is a statement to which Joy Elmer Morgan and Henry A. Bellows, the chief lobbyist for the NAB and a vice-president of CBS, could both whole-heartedly agree insofar as they each had entirely differing notions of "selfish propaganda."

[21]Roosevelt only mentioned radio policy during this period in one instance during his many presidential press conferences, and then it was only in the vaguest of senses. See *Complete Presidential Press Conferences of Franklin D. Roosevelt Volumes 1–2* (New York: 1972), 541–543.

taries, Stephen Early and Marvin H. McIntyre, as well as another aide, Louis M. Howe.

The president took much of his counsel on radio matters from Senator Dill, who was chairman of the Senate Interstate Commerce Committee that was responsible for handling all legislation concerning broadcasting. *Broadcasting* regarded him as "unquestionably" having "the most influential voice in federal radio control of any figure in public life."[22] Although eclectic in his criticism of broadcast regulation, Dill was vehemently opposed to any reform of the status quo. Given his power and his status as Congress' recognized "expert" on radio, by 1933 or 1934 most elements of the opposition movement had little hope of getting reform legislation to the floor of the Senate.[23]

Rosen has argued that Roosevelt was concerned mostly with establishing a new Democratic-staffed regulatory commission especially when it became clear that Hoover's appointments would not resign. He also argues that Roosevelt desired to maintain cordial relations with the commercial broadcasting industry. This would "ensure his ready access to the airwaves."[24] Considering Roosevelt's legitimate concerns regarding his treatment by the largely Republican newspaper industry, this is certainly a powerful argument. Furthermore, the commercial broadcasters were not to be dealt with lightly. Even those associated with the New Deal who favored a restructuring of radio recognized the immense task involved. One noted: "Radio is credited with one of the strongest of the swarming lobbies in Washington—one with substance behind it. Members of Congress are dominated by tactics which are constantly under the direction of private interests."[25] Roosevelt was probably in no hurry to take on an uphill battle with the radio industry when the fruits of an unlikely victory did not promise much immediate political payback and when the cost of a defeat or even a protracted victory could be immense.

Thus, there is a marked similarity between the program for broadcasting which the White House generated in 1933 and 1934 and the one the commercial broadcasting industry desired. The commercial broadcasters had two essential goals. First, they wanted to maintain the status quo in radio; as for legislation, their ideal was to re-enact the Radio Act of 1927 and the Federal Radio Commission on a permanent basis under new titles.[26] Second, they wanted to make certain that no debate over the basic structure of the American broadcasting system take place in Congress. They felt far more comfortable with their fate in the hands of regulators than those of elected officials.[27] The two networks cultivated a healthy relationship with Roosevelt and they encouraged him to utilize their airwaves whenever he pleased, which he did some fifty-one times in his first year in office. This was significantly greater than the record of Herbert Hoover for any year he was in office.[28]

[22]Martin Codel, "Dill and Davis Seen Powers in Radio Rule Under Roosevelt," *Broadcasting*, Nov. 15, 1932, 8.

[23]In correspondence in late 1933 representatives of NCER and the ACLU agreed that Senator Dill was a "weak sister" who would provide the reform effort no assistance. Roger Baldwin to Tracy Tyler, Oct. 24, 1933; Tracy Tyler to Roger Baldwin, Oct. 26, 1933, ACLU Mss, 1933, Volume 599.

[24]Rosen, *Stentors*, 174.

[25]Eddie Dowling, "Radio Needs a Revolution," *Forum* 91 (February 1934): 69. Dowling was a theatrical producer from New York who had been active in Roosevelt's 1932 presidential campaign.

[26]The commercial broadcasters were unabashed in their praise of the 1927 Radio Act. As Henry A. Bellows told a Senate Committee hearing on the subject in 1934: "Almost everyone recognizes that, despite minor effects, the Radio Act of 1927, as amended, and the court decisions under it, have established a solid basis for Government regulation of radio." (*Senate Hearings 1934*, March 10, 1934, 53–55.) Bellows also stressed this point in a letter to White House aide Stephen Early in February of 1934. (Bellows to Early, Feb. 28, 1934, Franklin Delano Roosevelt Manuscripts, Franklin D. Roosevelt Presidential Library, Hyde Park, New York, OF 859a, 1933–1945.) (Hereafter FDR Mss)

[27]This point is developed in Rosen, *Stentors*, 173, 174.

[28]"F.D.R.'s Radio Record," *Broadcasting*, March 15, 1934, 8.

Nevertheless, the opposition movement wished to associate itself with Roosevelt and the New Deal and attempted to interpret his lack of public comment as a sign of support. Reformers never questioned Roosevelt's sympathies, at least not in their public pronouncements, throughout this entire period, although they had reason to be suspicious. In late 1933 the NCER and the ACLU Radio Committee, in the only instance they worked together, convinced the noted economist and New Deal Democrat Adolph A. Berle to use his influence to get Roosevelt to support the legislation calling for an independent and comprehensive study of broadcasting. Berle was unsuccessful, and both the NCER and the ACLU gave up hope of getting the bill passed in 1934.[29] This faith in Roosevelt may have reflected a degree of sophistication as much as it did naivete. Certainly no reform of radio was conceivable without, at the very least, the tacit support of the White House.

In addition, the opposition movement had considerable evidence that there was significant dissatisfaction with the status quo in radio within the administration ranks. Eddle Dowling, an actor who was in charge of the Stage, Screen and Radio Division of the Democratic Campaign Committee in 1932, emerged as a vocal critic of network, commercial radio and urged breaking up the two networks and establishing a number of smaller networks on a regional basis. He was almost nominated for a position on the FRC in early 1934 but Roosevelt placed him in another position.[30] Dowling did manage to convey his ideas in radio to White House staffers, but they let it out quickly that his proposals were "not being considered seriously in any fashion."[31] Another opponent was Dr. Arthur Morgan, the chairman of the Tennessee Valley Authority (TVA), who in a speech in May 1934 stated that radio as well as newspaper and motion pictures "should not be operated for profit . . . they should be operated as social services and not for commercial profit just as are the public schools."[32]

Most of the Roosevelt Administration opponents to the status quo were in positions far away from the FRC or any place where broadcast policy decisions were being made. Two exceptions were James H. Hanley and Josephus Daniels. Hanley was a protege of Arthur R. Mullen, who had been the floor leader for Roosevelt at the 1932 Democratic convention. Roosevelt appointed Hanley to the FRC in 1933 to pay back Mullen, whereupon Hanley developed, quite unexpectedly, into what one trade publication characterized as an irresponsible radio "radical."[33] Hanley became the one FRC member who regularly defended nonprofit broadcasters and, in a press release commemorating his first anniversary on the FRC, attacked the status quo and called for setting "aside a liberal number of channels for the exclusive use of educators and educational institutions." Hanley's views were applauded by the reformers but repudiated by administration officials and the balance of the FRC.[34]

Roosevelt's close personal friendship with Josephus Daniels provided him with an oppor-

[29]Assorted letters between Tracy Tyler and Roger Baldwin, November-December 1933, ACLU Mss, 1933, Volume 599. When Berle Reported Roosevelt's lack of interest, Baldwin would conclude: "The bill is therefore dead." From Baldwin to Webster, Jan. 13, 1934, ACLU Mss, 1934, Volume 699.

[30]"Starbuck's Job Sought By Eddie Dowling, et al, As End of Term Nears," *Broadcasting*, Jan. 1, 1934, 16.

[31]"President Ignores Dowling Proposals," *Broadcasting*, March 1, 1934, 15.

[32]Arthur E. Morgan, "Radio as a Cultural Agency in Sparsely Settled Regions and Remote Areas." In *Radio as a Cultural Agency; Proceedings of a National Conference on the Use of Radio as a Cultural Agency in a Democracy*, Edited by Tracy F. Tyler (Washington D.C.: 1934), 81.

[33]Sol Taishoff, "Fate of FCC Measure Hangs in Balance," *Broadcasting*, June 1, 1934, 6.

[34]Hanley Criticism of Broadcasting Setup Denied by Administration, Colleagues," *Broadcasting*, May 1, 1934, 22; Sol Taishoff, "Powerful Lobby Threatens Radio Structure," *Broadcasting*, May 15, 1934, 5, 6.

tunity to become acquainted with arguments for the full nationalization of broadcasting. Roosevelt had served under Daniels when Daniels had been responsible for administrating radio as Secretary of the Navy during the Wilson administration. At that time Daniels had suggested that the U.S. government own and operate every radio station in the nation. Roosevelt appointed Daniels to be Ambassador to Mexico in 1933, and the two of them maintained contact with each other. Daniels never lost his interest in radio, and the issue appears frequently in his correspondence to Roosevelt. Roosevelt asked Daniels to represent the United States at the North American Radio Conference in Mexico City in 1933.[35]

Daniels never abandoned his belief that broadcasting and indeed the entire realm of communications should be nationalized. In January 1935 he wrote Roosevelt:

> *I understand that a movement is on foot in Washington to make a monopoly of all communications—telegraph, telephone, radio and cable. I am in favor of this if the monopoly is owned and controlled by the government, but strongly opposed to it if it is to be privately owned and operated. In time of war, we must take over communications. The government should own and control them all the time. There is no more reason why other communications should be privately owned than the mails. Radio and telephone are as important parts of communication as the mail was when Benjamin Franklin was Postmaster General.*

However, Daniels was not ignorant of the political fallout such a proposal would engender:

> *I am not suggesting that at this time you should propose this plan. You have too many other plans that must be carried out now to justify you in digging up more snakes than you can promptly, and the controllers of the telegraph and telephone and radio and cable are powerful.*[36]

Yet despite Daniels' repeated professions on behalf of nationalized radio to Roosevelt, his actual activity on behalf of radio reform was nonexistent. He had no contact with any of the reform groups or any awareness of their activities. His letters to Roosevelt reveal an ignorance of the relevant events transpiring on Capital Hill. Daniels' major contact in Washington was a naval officer named Stanford C. Hooper who was a proponent of private radio but feared foreign ownership for national security reasons. Nevertheless, his close friendship with Roosevelt provided him an audience that any other reformer would envy and none would ever approach.

The Roosevelt Administration and Radio Policy, 1933–34

In May 1933 Secretary of Commerce Daniel Roper concluded a study that proposed a reorganization of his department. The report suggested that a separate study of communications be conducted and, furthermore, that all the communications regulatory functions be shifted from the Interstate Commerce Commission (ICC) and the FRC to the Department of Commerce.[37] Even before his inauguration, Roosevelt announced plans to introduce legislation which would consolidate all the communications regulatory bodies into one large commission. Legislation was proposed to that effect, but by the summer of 1933 it became clear that it would suffer the same fate as the

[35]Daniels wrote to Roosevelt with his analysis of the situation. (Daniels to Roosevelt, July 12, 1933, FDR Mss, OF 136, 1933.)

[36]Daniels to Roosevelt, Jan. 15, 1935, FDR Mss, PPF 86, 1935.

[37]"Report of the Committee on Reorganization of the Department of Commerce," May 2, 1933, Department of Commerce manuscripts, National Archives, Washington D.C., NARG 40, General Correspondence, File 80553. (Hereafter Commerce Mss)

earlier attempts at comprehensive and permanent legislation. Then, in late July, Roosevelt submitted a personal letter he had received from Josephus Daniels, calling for the government ownership and control of broadcasting, to Secretary Roper and requested that Roper appoint a committee to study the matter.[38] Roper appointed a committee of four under the direction of former FRC Chairman Charles McKinley Saltzman.

On September 8 this committee submitted an eight-page single-spaced report to the president which described in no uncertain terms the impracticality of government ownership of communications. The report stressed the fundamental soundness of the Radio Act of 1927 and the regulatory system which emerged out of it.[39] The report also emphasized the immense opposition that would fight an effort to eliminate private broadcasting—particularly the commercial broadcasters and newspapers which "after losing much advertising revenue due to radio advertising are becoming interested in owning radio stations." The report then asked: "Under the present unfortunate economic conditions, is the time ripe to incur the opposition that would arise?" the report concluded by calling for the consolidation of all communications regulatory functions under one government department. Yet the report was also critical of the lack of planning that had characterized the development of broadcasting and communications regulation. Thus, it also called for the establishment of a group to make "a careful survey of existing facilities and consolidations with a view to the formation of a national communication policy."[40]

[38]Roper to Roosevelt, Aug. 15, 1935, Commerce Mss, NARG 40, General Correspondence, File 80553/13-D.

[39]Rosen, *Stentors*, 176.

[40]"Report of a Committee on Communications Appointed by the Secretary of Commerce," Sept. 8, 1933, National Bureau of Standards Manuscripts, National Archives, Washington, D.C., NARG 167, J. Howard Delinger File, 1933.

Roosevelt responded to this report by advising Roper to assemble an interdepartmental committee to "make a study for me of the entire communications situation."[41] He also advised Roper to consult with the FRC regarding Daniels' ideas about government ownership.[42] Nothing ever came of this. In September and October Roper gradually assembled representatives from eleven federal agencies and departments for weekly meetings to study the matter of communications regulation and policy. Senator Dill and Representative Sam Rayburn, the chairman of the respective congressional committees that considered communications legislation, were ostensibly on this "Roper Committee," but they were never able to attend. There is some question as to Roper's level of involvement as well.[43] The Roper Committee met in secrecy during the fall and did not solicit any public testimony. Roper would justify this secrecy by explaining that the committee was conducting a "study," not an "investigation," and therefore had not sought the opinions of "outsiders." According to Roper, these "outsiders" would have their opportunity to provide input on the legislation during the upcoming congressional committee hearings.[44] Nevertheless, despite the efforts to keep the activities of the Roper Committee out of the public eye, neither the commercial broadcasters nor the reformers could be kept at bay. As early as April, the NAB

[41]Roosevelt's directive instructed Roper " . . . to organize an interdepartmental committee to make a study for me of the entire communications situation in the fall of 1933." From *Study of Communications by an Interdepartmental Committee, Letter from the President of the United States to the Chairman of the Committee on Interstate Commerce Transmitting a Memorandum from the Secretary of Commerce Relative to a Study of Communications by a Interdepartmental Committee* (Washington D.C.: 1934). (Hereafter *Roper Report*)

[42]Roosevelt to Roper, Sept., 12, 1933, FDR Mss, OF 3, X Refs 1933.

[43]Dill to Roper, Jan. 9, 1934, FDR Mss, OF 859a, 1935–1945; Webster, "Notes," 109–110.

[44]"Control Board Planned for All Communications; With Mergers Permitted," New York *Times*, Dec. 14, 1933, 1.

expressed alarm to Roosevelt at the rumor that the Department of Commerce was considering "drastic changes" in the "the method of administering the Radio Act of 1927."[45] However, by autumn the concerns of the commercial broadcasters had been allayed. In December, when the contents of the Roper Committee's impending report were leaked to the press to gauge the response, *Variety* noted that "probably few changes in the 1927 Radio Act will take place."[46] *The New York Times* reported that "there was little fear of government ownership of communications."[47]

The secrecy of the Roper Committee had been shattered by Drew Pearson and Robert S. Allen in their "Daily Washington Merry-Go-Round" column of November 30. The column began:

A secret move is on foot to perpetuate the present monopoly which the big broadcasting companies have on choice wave lengths. It is being worked out behind closed doors by the so-called Roper radio committee. Appointed by the Secretary of Commerce originally to bring a new deal for radio, the committee is actually working to continue the old deal. . . . . What they are trying to do is get their report adopted by the White House before the general public knows about it, before opposition can develop.[48]

This column was the first that the NCER had heard of the Roper Committee. Tracy Tyler of the NCER wrote Secretary Roper on December 5 to express his concern that the Roper Committee was attempting to "crystallize the system" before there was a "thorough-going impartial Congressional study of radio broadcasting." Both Roper and Saltzman wrote Tyler to assure him that he was misinformed and that his concerns would be brought before the Roper Committee.[49]

By this time, however, the committee had already sent its report, which came to be known as the Roper Report, to the president. In addition, Roosevelt received a "minority report" from the one member of the Roper Committee who dissented with the manner in which the proceedings had transpired. This was Naval Captain Stanford C. Hooper, who, as was mentioned above, was a friend and associate of Josephus Daniels. Although Hooper was no advocate of government ownership, he shared Daniels' great interest in radio and the belief that it merited serious attention by the Federal government.

In his minority report, Hooper expressed his displeasure with the superficial examination the Roper Committee had made of the question of broadcasting:

. . . the subject of regulation of radio broadcasting, mentioned so prominently in the directive to the committee, and of such great importance to the communication facilities of the nation, has not been considered by the committee, although their report recommends regulation of the communication service of the country, without excluding broadcasting, *by a single body. The minority member feels that any study of Federal relationship to communications is incomplete unless a thorough study of radio broadcasting has been included.*

Hooper also disagreed with the notion that the "real" study of broadcasting could or should be left to the FRC or the to-be-created supra-communications regulatory agency. He wrote:

My experience in government affairs has convinced me that if the large companies in an in-

[45]McCosker to Roosevelt, April 12, 1933, Commerce Mss, NARG 40, General Correspondence, File 80553/13-D.

[46]"Communications Mergers," *Variety*, Dec. 19, 1933, 38.

[47]New York *Times*, Dec. 14, 1933, 2.

[48]"Daily Washington Merry-Go-Round," Nov. 30, 1933, Commerce Mss, NAEG 40, General Correspondence, File 80553/13-G.

[49]Tyler to Roper, Dec. 5, 1933; Roper to Tyler, Dec. 8, 1933; Saltzman to Tyler, Dec. 11, 1933; Davis to Dickinson, Dec. 12, 1933, Commerce Mss, NARG 40, General correspondence, File 80553/13-G.

> *dustry wish to attain a common end they will eventually succeed unless the laws passed by Congress are such as to provide adequate barriers. With clever executives and high-priced lawyers, the Government administrators have little chance in the long run to resist such pressure, due to the ever-changing personnel in the Government, regardless of the unquestioned faithfulness of these employees. Consequently, I believe that unlimited discretion should not be given to any regulatory body, on matters of broad policy, especially to the extent of authorizing departure from anti-trust and other natural laws under which the public is protected.*[50]

In early January Roosevelt met with Roper, Dill, and Rayburn to discuss "the whole matter of communications."[51] The question of how to characterize the Roper Committee's study of broadcasting loomed large. The Roper Report which was released to the public in late January, stated that "the problems of broadcasting are not being considered in this study."[52] The report was all of fourteen pages long; it barely mentioned radio. Nevertheless, as Hooper had pointed out in his minority report, the report did include radio broadcasting in its conclusions. It suggested the continuation of private ownership and operation as well as the regulation of all communications industries by one new agency.

As one might imagine, those interested in reforming the structure of radio were not impressed with the report. James Rorty lashed out at it for ignoring and postponing the formulation of a sound policy regarding broadcasting. In an article in *The Nation*, he termed it "mumbing, evasive and futile."[53] The sharpest attack came from Bethuel M. Webster, Jr., who had served as General Counsel for the FRC in its early years and was active on the radio committees of both the American Bar Association (ABA) and the ACLU. After terming both the Roper Report and the Administration's efforts in regard to communications policy as "inept," he observed:

> *In fact, it appears on analysis that the Administration has no program or policy at all, except to consolidate communications control, and that it had not and apparently will not come to grips with the really vital questions which must be solved before the country has a sound communications policy.*

Webster derided the absurdity of the Roper Committee's closed meetings and its rejection of any expert testimony. He concluded that anyone who had read

> *. . . almost any report prepared by almost any committee or commission which had taken the trouble, with the assistance of specialists, to gather and organize the facts and to formulate statesmanlike conclusions and recommendations, will blush at the sight of the Roper Report.*[54]

The matter of conducting a distinct study of radio broadcasting did not disappear with the release of the Roper Report. On January 25, 1934, Roper sent the following letter to Roosevelt:

> *I feel that inadequate attention was given to the subject of broadcasting in the study recently made by our interdepartmental committee. Broadcasting should have special consideration in the light of its importance for educational social entertainment and commercial advertising.*
>
> *Would you think it advisable to have a committee pursue this matter? If you approve, such a committee could well consist of a representa-*

[50]Comments on Report of Majority Members of Committee and Discussion of Position of Minority Member, FDR Mss, OF 859a, 1933–1945.

[51]Roosevelt to Roper, Jan. 8, 1934, FDR Mss, OF 3, Jan.-Feb. 1934.

[52]"Wash. Omits Radio From Fed. Control of Communications," *Variety*, Jan. 30, 1934, 37.

[53]James Rorty, "Order on the Air," *The Nation*, May 9, 1934, 529.

[54]Webster, Jr., "Notes," 108, 117.

tive of the State Department, The Bureau of Education in the Interior Department and Secretary of the Radio Commission.

Roosevelt had the letter returned to Roper with an "OK" written in his handwriting.[55] On February 7 Roper called a press conference and announced that Roosevelt approved of his forming a committee to study broadcasting.[56]

During February, plans were developed for this "Federal Committee to Study Radio Broadcasting." The initial plan recognized the controversial nature of the topic and recommended that various organizations and individuals be invited to submit briefs on the matter but that no hearings he held.[57] Representatives of the NCER wrote to Roper on several occasions to offer their input and to plead for a thorough and independent study of radio.[58]

The plans for the study were quietly dropped in late February. Dill and Rayburn convinced Roosevelt and Roper that the study was unnecessary and that it would take so long that it would be impossible to get communications legislation passed in the current session. The broadcasting industry made its displeasure with the proposed study known as well, particularly when it became clear that "anti-broadcasting groups" intended to use the proposed study as an opportunity to present their case.[59] The Commerce Department informed interested parties that the committee had been terminated and "this matter, for the time being, will be entirely handled by the Congress."[60]

During February Dill and Rayburn drafted the legislation in frequent consultation with Roosevelt and White House aides.[61] They hoped to stem any potential opposition to the proposed legislation by authorizing the to-be-created communications commission to make a thorough study of communications on its own and report back to Congress with any suggestions for legislative reform the following year. Dill commented, "If we leave out the controversial matters the bill can be passed at this session." In addition he argued:

It is far wiser to let the proposed commission have the power to make studies than to have Congress legislate on intricate and complex aspects of the communications program at this time.[62]

In late February Dill and Rayburn each introduced their respective bills to the Senate and the House. President Roosevelt issued a formal statement to Congress announcing his support of the legislation and urging its passage. He also reiterated Dill's argument:

The new body [the proposed communications commission] should, in addition, be given full power to investigate and study the business of existing companies and make recommendations to the Congress for additional legislation at the next session.[63]

The advocates of non-profit broadcasting were unenthusiastic about postponing any fundamental discussion of American radio and transferring it to another regulatory commission. In March of 1934 the Senate Interstate Commerce Committee took up its hearings on

[55]Roper to Roosevelt, January 25, 1934, FDR Mss, OF 3, X Refs 1934.

[56]Sol Taishoff, "Roosevelt Demands Communications Bill," *Broadcasting*, Feb. 15, 1934, 6.

[57]Koon to Roper, Feb. 21, 1934, Commerce Mss, NARG 40, General Correspondence, File 80553/13-D.

[58]Roper to Tyler, Feb. 15, 1934; Tyler to Roper, Feb. 12, 1934; Kerlin to Morgan, Feb. 26, 1934, Commerce Mss, NARG 40, General Correspondence, File 80553/13-D.

[59]"Broadcasting Survey Postponed," *NAB Reports*, Feb. 24, 1934.

[60]Roper to Hohenstein, March 6, 1934, Commerce Mss, NARG 40, General Correspondence, File 80553/13-G.

[61]*Variety*, Feb. 13, 1934, 1; Assorted Memos between Dill, Rayburn, Roosevelt and McIntyre, FDR Mss, OF 859, 1933–1945.

[62]"Roosevelt Approves Communications Board to Rule Radio, Telephone, Telegraph, Cable," New York *Times*, Feb. 10, 1934, 12.

[63]"Asks Body to Rule Wires and Radio," New York *Times*, Feb. 27, 1934, 1.

the proposed legislation. The vast majority of the nineteen witnesses were either corporate executives, representatives of industry groups, or government officials. Only five dealt with broadcasting, and only one of those presented a critical view of the status quo. Indeed, a 331-page report on communications companies which had been prepared for Congress by Walter Splawn of the Interstate Commission recommended the passage of the legislation and maintenance of the status quo in broadcasting, yet devoted only twelve pages to the topic of broadcasting, in which simply the stations and their owner were listed. Splawn indicated a "fuller report on broadcasting" would be forthcoming.[64] The dissenting voice was that of Father John B. Harney, who represented the Paulist Fathers of New York City which operated station WLWL in New York City. During the course of the station's continual battles with the FRC and several commercial broadcasters which had successfully taken most of WLWL's airtime, Harney had become a fiery advocate of preserving and expanding the role of non-profit broadcasting.

Harney proposed that the legislation include an amendment which would nullify all radio broadcast licenses within ninety days and require a complete reallocation of the airwaves with a minimum of twenty-five percent of the channels to be distributed to non-profit and educational broadcasters. Senator Dill attempted to impress upon Harney his idea of having the newly formed communications commission study the matter and make recommendations the following year. Harney argued that given the track record of the FRC it was impossible to put any faith in a regulatory agency and that it was the duty of Congress to specifically direct the newly formed communications commission in the matter.[65]

The committee rejected Harney's amendment. Nevertheless, Harney had considerable support in the Senate; and Senators Robert Wagner, Democrat of New York, and Henry Hatfield, Republican of West Virginia, introduced a slightly revised version of his amendment, now termed the Wagner-Hatfield amendment, to the Senate in April. Perhaps sensing impending problems, Dill had the committee insert a passage into the bill specifically instructing the new commission to study the Harney proposal and then to report back to Congress in early 1935 with its recommendations. This would become Section 307(c) of the Communications Act of 1934. Indeed, Father Harney and the Paulist Fathers coordinated a nationwide campaign to generate support for the Wagner-Hatfield amendment. They managed to obtain some 60,000 signatures on petitions in just a few weeks, largely through Catholic organizations, in support of the measure.[66] FRC member Hanley announced his support, which was immediately repudiated by the White House and the balance of the FRC, and even representatives of organized labor lobbied on behalf of the amendment.[67]

By early May *Variety* noted that the sentiment on Capitol Hill was that the Wagner-Hatfield amendment stood "better than a 50–50 chance of being adopted" and that the NAB was "in panic checking off names of Senators and trying to pull wires and get votes."[68] Indeed, the NAB and the networks launched an extravagant

[64]"Radio Submerged at Capitol Hearings," *Broadcasting*, April 15, 1934, 11. The author can find no indication that Splawn ever completed this "further study" of broadcasting, at least within the time frame for the enactment of legislation.

[65]*Senate Hearings 1934*, March 15, 1934, 186–190.

[66]United States Senate Interstate Commerce Committee Papers, National Archives, Washington, D.C., Sen-J28, tray 155.

[67]*Broadcasting*, May 1, 1934, 22; *Broadcasting*, May 15, 1934, 5, 6; "Labor Aids Bill for Free Radio," *Federation News*, April 7, 1934, 6; "Labor Toils for Radio Freedom," *Federation News*, May 26, 1934, 1.

[68]"Air Enemies Unite Forces," *Variety*, May 8, 1934, 37, 45.

counter-offensive in early May; as Henry Bellows of the NAB put it, passage of the Wagner-Hatfield amendment "obviously would have destroyed the whole structure of broadcasting in America."[69] The campaign was successful. By May 12 the NAB would confidently inform its membership that the Wagner-Hatfield would be defeated "overwhelmingly."[70] Indeed, the radio lobby elected to force a vote on the amendment rather than have it sent back to committee, in order, as an NBC vice-president put it, "to dispose of this matter for all time."[71]

The Wagner-Hatfield amendment reached the floor on May 15, 1934. Senator Dill led the floor fight against the amendment, and it was voted down 42–23. The same day his bill was passed on the voice vote without any floor debate. A key reason for the defeat of the Wagner-Hatfield amendment was the inclusion of what would become Section 307(c) in Dill's bill. The president avoided taking a public position on the Wagner-Hatfield amendment and merely stressed the need to get some sort of communications legislation through Congress in the current session.[72] Rosen has argued that the White House played a critical behind-the-scenes role in defeating the Wagner-Hatfield amendment: "Quick action from the Roosevelt administration overwhelmed its opposition."[73] With little fanfare, the House passed the bill two weeks later, and President Roosevelt signed the Communications Act of 1934 into law of June 18.

The trade publication *Broadcasting* regarded the passage of the Communications Act as a victory for the industry contingent upon whom Roosevelt would appoint to the newly formed FCC.[74] These concerns were soon erased when Roosevelt announced his appointees on June 30. Two members of the old FRC were retained on the new FCC: Chairman Eugene O. Sykes and Vice-Chairman Thad H. Brown. Hanley, the radio "radical," was not carried over. Sykes, Brown, and newcomer Hampson Gary of Texas were appointed to the FCC's new Broadcasting Division, which would be responsible for all broadcast regularity matters. At its first meeting on July 11, the new FCC voted to "retain the status quo insofar as broadcasting regulation is concerned" and to move "cautiously" toward any reform.[75] Broadcasting greeted these developments with satisfaction and noted:

> *Any fears harbored by those in broadcasting that an immediate upheaval of radio might result from the new FCC are dispelled with the organization of that agency into divisions. The Broadcasting Division . . . is a conservative group. It can be expected to carry on the basic policies of the old Radio Commission, for, indeed, two of its members were on the former agency.*[76]

The victory for the continuation of the status quo still faced one final obstacle: the hearings on whether a fixed percentage of air channels should be set aside to non-profit groups as required by Section 307(c) of the Communications Act. The Broadcasting Division, at its first meeting announced that these hearings would be held in October. There was little suspense as to the outcome. At the annual NAB national convention in September, both Gary and Brown made it clear that they would not tamper with the private commercial broadcasting structure.[77]

[69]Henry Bellows, "Report," *NAB Reports*, Nov. 15, 1934, 618.

[70]"Senate to Pass Dill Bill," *NAB Reports*, May 12, 1934, 387.

[71]Frank Russell to Merlin Aylesworth, May 11, 1934, National Broadcasting Company Papers, Wisconsin Historical Society, Madison, WI, Box 90, Folder 53.

[72]*Variety*, May 8, 1934, 45.

[73]Rosen, *Stentors*, 177.

[74]Sol Taishoff, "FCC Replaces Radio Commission July 1."

[75]Sol Taishoff, "Radio Status Quo as FCC Convenes," *Broadcasting*, Aug. 1, 1934, 5.

[76]"Three-Man Control," *Broadcasting*, Aug. 1, 1934, 22.

[77]Gary assured the broadcaster that they had nothing to fear from the upcoming hearings: "Nothing revolutionary is in view. Naturally, we will bend every effort to improve the

Sykes was a long-time advocate of the status quo. Nevertheless, the NAB organized the pro-industry case with the same resolve that typified their legislative efforts. Father Harney, convinced of the impossibility of an impartial hearing, decided not to testify on behalf of the fixed-percentage principle. The ACLU publicity director argued that the hearings were "called simply to satisfy the squawks of educators" and that they were a "set-up for the broadcaster."[78] Ironically, the NCER, which had never lobbied on behalf of the Wagner-Hatfield amendment, agreed to organize the "pro-fixed percentage" side of the hearings.

The reformers were granted the first ten days of October to present their case. The industry was permitted the next week to make its rebuttal. The Roosevelt Administration stayed abreast of the proceedings; Gary sent his own summaries of the two cases to White House aide Stephen Early.[79] In contrast to the well rehearsed industry position which emphasized the merits of the status quo and the tremendous commitment of the commercial broadcasters to educational and cultural programming, the pro-fixed percentage forces appeared disorganized and even contradictory.

Despite the strength of the pro-industry position, a potentially serious crisis emerged when the Broadcasting Division began accepting testimony from representatives of government agencies in late October. On October 19, quite unexpectedly, Dr. Floyd W. Reeves, the official representative of the Tennessee Valley Authority (TVA), issued a sharply worded critique of the limitations of commercial broadcasting. Furthermore, he called for the establishment of a federally owned and operated network to supplement the commercial networks and to be managed and supported in a manner similar to the British Broadcasting Corporation (BBC).[80] Joy Elmer Morgan of the NCER, who had seen his side being battered during the hearings, immediately seized the initiative and interpreted Reeves' testimony as an indication of the New Deal position on radio. On October 26 he sent the text of Reeves' testimony to a number of people and encouraged them to notify the FCC of their support for the TVA proposal. The FCC would receive several hundred letters—many of considerable length and thought—endorsing Reeves' TVA proposal over the following few weeks.[81]

The day after Reeves' testimony, journalists contacted the White House asking if it represented the administration's or even the TVA's position on radio. White House aide M. H. McIntyre had several inquiries on the matter and in a memo to Stephen Early noted that "the broadcasters themselves seem very perturbed." Early immediately contacted Dr. Arthur Morgan, chairman of the TVA, and told him to

existing set-up for the benefit of the public's reception and for your benefit." Brown was also reassuring in his comments to the broadcasters: "It is our steadfast desire to vest in the broadcaster all powers of control properly belonging to him. It is rightly your job, and you are the ones properly qualified to do the job of directing broadcasting for the benefit of and to protect the rights of millions of American listeners." ("Government Interference Fear Groundless, Say Commissioners," *Broadcasting*, Oct. 1, 1934, 18.)

[78]Clifton Read, "Memorandum for Member of the Radio Committee," Sept. 12, 1934, ACLU Mss, 1934, Volume 699.

[79]Gary to Early, October 1934, FDR Mss, OF 1059, Sept.-Dec. 1934.

[80]Reeves' comments reflected much of prevalent sentiment of the reformers toward commercial radio: "There should be an opportunity for people to hear a reasonable amount of educational and cultural broadcasting free from advertising. It should not be forgotten that freedom of speech needs to be safeguarded not only from interference by political forces but also from interference by commercial forces. This cannot be accomplished with all or almost all of the radio channels operated under commercial ownership." (Cited in "Tennessee Valley Authority Urges Chain," *Education by Radio*, Oct. 25, 1934, 45.)

The New York *Times* described this unexpected testimony by Reeves as the "only fly in the ointment for the broadcasters in their case against the educators. ("A 5-Point Plan For Radio," New York *Times*, Oct. 28, 1934, section 9, 11.)

[81]These letters can be found in Federal Communications Commission Manuscripts, National Archives, Suitland, Md., NARG 173, Box 497, File 201–4. [Hereafter FCC Mss]

withdraw Reeves' statement and replace it with one that rejected government ownership of radio.[82] Morgan complied on October 23 in a telegram to the FCC.

The NAB immediately insisted that Morgan's telegram repudiated Reeves' testimony and therefore rendered it irrelevant and forgettable. They attacked Joy Elmer Morgan for attempting to continue to capitalize on it. Joy Morgan, on the other hand, argued that it was the NAB that was, in fact, misinterpreting Dr. Morgan. He noted that at the NCER conference earlier in the year, Dr. Morgan had delivered a ringing denunciation of the private ownership of any of the mass media. Unfortunately for Joy Morgan, the media and the FCC accepted the NAB interpretation of the events. Indeed, the FCC wrote to each of the persons who had written on behalf of the TVA proposal to inform them that since the TVA had formally withdrawn the proposal, the FCC could no longer consider the proposition of a government network.[83] In addition, Dr. Morgan remained silent and made no effort to clarify his position on Joy Elmer Morgan's behalf.

The incident was soon forgotten, and the Broadcasting Division hearings concluded the following month. To the surprise of no one, in January 1935 the FCC recommended to Congress that the status quo was performing adequately and that any fixed allocation of channels to non-profit broadcasters was unnecessary. The reform movement rapidly dissolved. Only the ACLU continued to push for substantive reform legislation that challenged the private, commercial control of the airwaves. By 1938 it dispensed with these unsuccessful efforts and noted in an internal memo: "The big broadcasting chains are very strong with the administration. . . . The whole radio picture looks very sad."[84] The era of legitimate public debate over the structure and control of American broadcasting was formally over; the era of debate over manipulation of the status quo through regulation and social responsibility theorizing had begun.

Some Concluding Observations

Three critical and closely related points emerge from this study. First, the period from 1927–1934 warrants considerably greater attention by broadcasting historians than it generally had been accorded. The Radio Act of 1927 hardly mandated the corporate commercial status quo of broadcasting nor was it the result of strenuous public debate which anticipated what was to follow. The seven years after 1927 are so important because it was only then that the contours and attributes of the private commercial system became apparent. People had an opportunity to see the future and to react accordingly.

Much of the scholarship heretofore has seemingly accepted that the private commercial basis of broadcasting was entrenched by the mid 1920's and that the following decade, at best, simply records the gradual recognition of this fact. This seems overly deterministic. Granted, as this article had argued, the commercial broadcasters were operating from a position of considerable strength in the 1930's. Nevertheless, there was significant dissatisfaction with the status quo. Indeed, only recently have scholars begun to appreciate the extent of this dissatisfaction with the private commercial domination of the airwaves.[85] The opposition included

[82]Early memo, McIntyre Memo, Oct. 20, 1934, Oct. 22, 1934, FDR Mss, OF 136, 1934. *Broadcasting* wrote that Arthur E. Morgan's telegram was "promptly interpreted in political circles" as a move by the Roosevelt administration to "squelch the whole incident" and make it absolutely clear that the New Deal had no interest in government ownership of radio stations. (Sol Taishoff, "Class Wave Plan Overwhelmingly Opposed," *Broadcasting*, Nov. 1, 1934, 5.)

[83]FCC Mss, NARG 173, Box 497, File 201–4.

[84]Hazel Rice to Henry Eckstein, Dec. 22, 1937, ACLU Mss, Volume 1011.

[85]For a recent example see Susan Smulyan, " 'And Now

educators, religious figures, intellectuals, labor, civil libertarians, traditional Republicans, and numerous reform-minded New Dealers.

Second, while the Communications Act of 1934 becomes more important in this context, this does not imply that its passage signified a public ratification of the status quo. To some extent this can be attributed to factors that lie outside the scope of this article. Most important, the legislation was drafted during the depths of the Great Depression when Congress and the public were most concerned with the pressing need for economic recovery. Indeed, the legislation was lost among the seemingly countless reform proposals of the New Deal. And even if attention was given to the communications legislation, the focus tended as much to be on those aspects of the bill which dealt with the other communications industries as on radio.

To a larger extent, however, this lack of debate was the result of the conscious efforts of the commercial broadcasters and their allies in Washington, D.C., to continually postpone, eliminate, and defuse any possibility of a public examination of the American radio system. During 1933–1934 the reformers were continually frustrated by the ineffectual Roper Committee, the disbanded Federal Committee hearings, the intentionally ineffectual Congressional committee hearings, and the pre-determined FCC hearings. The only window of opportunity was the two-hour debate over the Wagner-Hatfield amendment which many reformers failed to take seriously and for which the pro-industry forces were able to overwhelm the reformers with their greater political strength. The industry forces showed no inclination to include the American people in the debate over radio; and, indeed, the vast majority of the population never had the slightest idea about what was transpiring in the spring of 1934 or its implications for American society.[86] This does not mean that the American people were necessarily opposed to the status quo; indeed, one could marshal an argument to the contrary. The point is, quite simply, that the commercial broadcasters and their allies were opposed even to granting the public the knowledge that there were alternatives to the status quo or that the public had a right to recreate the system if it so desired. In sum, it would not be unfair to conclude that there has never been a viable public debate in the United States over the fundamental control and structure of its broadcasting services.

Indeed, the Communications Act of 1934 was clearly a resounding triumph for the large corporations that dominated American broadcasting and a mortal blow to the opposition movement. In 1934 the challenge of the status quo did not come from the enemies of democracy or proponents of totalitarianism. Whatever the faults and limitations of the opposition movement its members were genuinely propelled by a desire to see radio opened up to a wider spectrum of voices and to see it held under firm popular control. This notion that the Communications Act of 1934 represents some sort of victory for the "public interest" is only credible if one accepts that the public interest is identical with the interest of the major private networks and advertisers. This "public interest" thesis may have been so prevalent in the past because the opposition movement has been largely ignored

a Word from Our Sponsors . . . ': Commercialization of American Broadcast Radio, 1920–1934" (Ph.D. dissertation, Yale University, 1985). See chapter five.

[86]Obviously, if people had no notion that any alternative to the status quo was possible, then the status quo was safe from any life-threatening attacks. Indeed since 1934 the notion that the American broadcasting system is ingrained into the essence of our society and is unalterable has become a largely unquestioned supposition. Thus in a 1945 study of American attitudes toward radio, Paul Lazarsfeld noted that people seem to accept the commercial structure of American broadcasting. He added, however, that: "People have little information on the subject, they have obviously given it little thought." Paul F. Lazarsfeld, *The People Look at Radio* (Chapel Hill: 1946), 89.

or trivialized and the rhetoric of the commercial broadcasters has been taken at face value.

Finally, President Roosevelt's role in broadcast history merits greater recognition. It is understandable that he had no interest in engaging the commercial broadcasters in a political battle. However, had he done so he may well have been able to generate considerable popular support. The fact that the Wagner-Hatfield amendment got as far as it did, with only the ad hoc campaign put together by a small Catholic order behind it and with hardly a trace of coverage in the mass media, may indicate that the range of possible action was greater than the traditional view had countenanced.

Had Roosevelt supported a fixed allocation of channels to non-profit broadcasters or some sort of national non-commercial network along the lines of the BBC, it would hardly have guaranteed success. Indeed, a measure along these lines still may have faced defeat. However, his decision not to challenge the status quo clearly sounded the death knell for the reform movement. One does not sense that Roosevelt has particularly strong convictions with regard to how best to structure American broadcasting. Yet, the notion that he may not have been especially interested in broadcast policy is almost beside the point: his few actions set the tone for his administration, and the policy was to avoid antagonizing the big commercial broadcasters. Even if we posit that Roosevelt was stridently in favor of the status quo on an intellectual level, he nevertheless was willing to sacrifice the last and only opportunity the public would have to debate the merits of its broadcasting services for what would appear to be the sake of short-term political gain. While this is understandable and pardonable on one level, in the long run it may have proven to be a very high price to pay for American society.

Hollywood Censored: The Production Code Administration and the Hollywood Film Industry, 1930–1940

Gregory D. Black

In July 1934 an editorial in *The Commonweal*, a semiofficial organ of the Catholic church, declared that the "muck merchants" of Hollywood, that "fortress of filth" that had been destroying the moral fiber of the American people, had finally been brought to its knees by the Catholic church and its Legion of Decency. In less than a year the church had recruited millions of Americans of all religious denominations to pledge not to attend "immoral" movies. With a national depression already threatening Hollywood's financial stability, movie czar Will Hays, head of the Motion Picture Producers and Distributors of American (MPPDA), accepted the terms of surrender dictated by the church and its legions.

The truce struck between Hays and the Most Reverend John T. McNicholas, Archbishop of Cincinnati, and written and negotiated by Martin Quigley, publisher of *The Motion Picture Herald*, signaled a turning point in a 30-year battle among religious leaders, women's groups, civic organizations, municipal and state censorship boards, and the motion picture industry over the content of Hollywood films.[1] The victory took the form of a new agency inside the MPPDA, the industry's trade association. The Catholics demanded that Hays create a Production Code Administration (PCA) to enforce the censorship code adopted by the industry in 1930. The code, written by a Catholic priest, had not, in the opinion of the church, been enforced. The church demanded, and Hays agreed, that a staunch lay Catholic, namely Joseph I. Breen, would head the PCA and interpret the code.

To guarantee that Breen would have enforcement powers, the agreement forced every studio to submit scripts to the PCA before production. The studios agreed that no production would begin without script approval and that no film would be distributed without a PCA seal of approval. The MPPDA was given power to levy a $25,000 fine against any violator.

But that was not all. The church demanded that Hollywood permanently withdraw from circulation films it viewed as "immoral" and that local theater owners be empowered to cancel any film currently in circulation if they judged it to be "immoral." The industry promptly withdrew a score of films, including Mae West's SHE DONE HIM WRONG (Paramount, 1933), THE STORY OF TEMPLE DRAKE (Paramount, 1933) (adapted from William Faulkner's *Sanctuary*), and Frank Borzage's filmed version of Ernest Hemingway's A FAREWELL TO ARMS (Paramount, 1932). Finally, the church demanded that any appeal of

PCA decisions be resolved not by a jury of Hollywood producers, as in the past, but by Will Hays in New York.

The PCA, created to mollify religious critics and to disarm proponents of federal censorship, exercised a strong, often dominating influence on movie content for more than two decades. From 1934 until the mid-1950s Breen and his staff closely scrutinized every Hollywood script for offensive social, political, and sexual themes. Although the initial intent was to protect the public from sexual improprieties, Breen was determined to eliminate controversial subjects from the screen to maximize the worldwide appeal of Hollywood films. In the process he imposed on film producers and filmgoers a rigidly conservative view of politics and morality. As film historian Robert Sklar has observed, Breen and the code virtually "cut the movies off from many of the most important moral and social themes of the contemporary world."[2]

Unfortunately most film history is written as if the code and the PCA did not exist. An understanding of Hollywood requires an appreciation of how self-censorship functioned in the studio production system. The fate of two productions from early 1934, Mae West's BELLE OF THE NINETIES (Paramount, 1934) and Ernst Lubitsch's THE MERRY WIDOW (MGM, 1934) illustrate the PCA's moral strictures. Two films that contained no moral violations, Walter Wanger's THE PRESIDENT VANISHES (Paramount, 1934) and Warner Bros. production of BLACK FURY (Warner Bros., 1935), were nevertheless considered "dangerous" by Breen and Hays and show how the PCA prevented films from making serious social or political comment.[3]

By 1934 films had become a collaborative, corporate art form. The industry had come a long way from its beginning as a provider of cheap entertainment for urban immigrants at the turn of the century. Films quickly evolved into a form of mass entertainment that attracted viewers from every segment of American society. Box office success, it turned out, frequently resulted from sexually titillating themes and from stories that seemed to glorify gangsters and social deviants. This in turn brought increasing demands for regulation. Pennsylvania established the first state board for film censorship in 1911, and Ohio and Kansas followed in 1913. By 1915 a host of municipal and state censorship boards had been created to impose local community standards of morality on films by censoring films before their exhibition. The film industry challenged the legality of "prior censorship" in 1915. In a landmark decision that was to influence the content of films until the 1950s, the Supreme Court upheld the right of prior censorship by local communities when it ruled in *Mutual Film Corporation v. Ohio* that movies were not protected under freedom of speech provisions of either the state or federal constitutions.

By the mid-1920s eight states and more than 200 municipalities had enacted censorship boards. There was no real consistency: Pennsylvania was the most strict, Kansas the most pristine (the latter limiting screen kissing to a few seconds and banning scenes of smoking and drinking). The common denominator was that all the censorship boards were committed to eliminating portraits of changing moral standards, limiting scenes of crime (which they believed to be responsible for an increase in juvenile delinquency), and avoiding as much as possible any screen portrayal of civil strife, labor-management discord, or government corruption and injustice. The screen, these moral guardians held, was not a proper forum for discussing delicate sexual issues or for social or political commentary.

Nor was this view of films limited to the United States. By the end of the 1920s every European nation had established a national censorship board, as had most Asian and Latin and South American nations. Committed to protecting fledgling national film industries, foreign censorship boards often established strict quotas for American films and were quick to censor gangster films, films that were an affront to local customs, or those deemed likely to disturb the public peace. As the industry faced its third decade, it confronted a morass of worldwide censorship.

In the early 1920s the industry was rocked by a series of sensational scandals about the private lives of its stars, the most famous being the scandal involving Fatty Arbuckle. The dual forces of scandal and censorship forced the industry to unite under a common banner, the MPPDA. In 1922 industry leaders chose as their first president Will H. Hays, a prominent Republican politician and architect of Warren Harding's presidential victory. He symbolized the veritable puritan in Babylon. Teetotaler and elder in the Presbyterian church, Hays saw it as his mission to bring a Jewish-dominated film industry the respectability of mainstream middle America. Hays was, according to one screen writer, "the visible sign of invisible grace."[4]

A front man for the industry, Hays served as the lightning rod for public complaints. Promoted by press agents as the movie czar, Hays was in fact no more than an employee of the moguls. As a public relations agent, he was an unqualified success; as a censor or regulator of movie content during the 1920s, he was a failure. Rejecting the notion of censorship by government, Hays embraced a system of industry self-regulation. In 1924 he introduced "The Formula," a series of rules designed to prevent "objectionable" plays and novels from being produced as films. Hays' formula did manage to keep some material off the screen, but he was dependent on voluntary compliance by the studios. A steady stream of "modern" films increased criticism of the industry. In 1927, the year in which sound first accompanied images on the silver screen, Hays created the Studio Relations Committee (SRC). Under the direction of Colonel Jason Joy, the SRC codified the most common demands of the municipal and state censorship boards into a single working document informally known as the "Don'ts and Be Carefuls." This document prohibited, among other things, profanity, nudity, drug trafficking, and white slavery in films and urged producers to exercise good taste in presenting such adult themes as criminal behavior, sexual relations, and violence.[5] Still the studios interpreted these guidelines according to their own taste, however, and still the antimovie lobby fulminated and grew ever larger and more threatening.

Although reformers had favored cooperation with Hays in 1922, by the end of the decade they were convinced that Hays was ineffective and that federal intervention was necessary to control Hollywood. Until the early 1930s the opponents of Hollywood had been primarily an alliance of Protestant ministers and women's organizations. As traditional guardians of public morality, they claimed that Hollywood was directly responsible for the dramatic changes that had taken place in American society in the past three decades. Alarmed at an increasing divorce rate, a rise in juvenile delinquency, and a general flaunting of traditional values by young men and women, the ministers held the movies directly responsible for what they saw as America's moral collapse. The Reverend William H. Short, executive director of the Motion Picture Research Council, attacked excessive sex and crime in films as being destructive to the moral fiber of American youth. Canon William Sheafe Chase, rector of Christ Protestant Episcopal Church in Brooklyn and director of the Federal Motion Picture Council in America, was the national spokesman for federal censorship of movies. In his *Catechism on Motion Pictures*, he condemned the "Hebrew" owners and producers as vile corrupters of American morals and demanded federal intervention. Protestant publications such as *The Christian Century* and *The Churchman* denounced Hollywood throughout the decade. The ministers and the women's organizations considered themselves "experts" on obscenity. They could not define it, but they knew it when they saw it. In this case anything they saw on the screen that offended their sense of propriety, whether it was social, political, or moral in nature, was defined as obscene and had to be banned.

In 1926 Chase, Short, and more than 200 representatives of women's organizations descended on Washington to demand federal regulation of the movies. Testifying before the House Committee on Education, Chase branded the movies a "threat to world civilization." He denounced the industry's financial practice of block-booking, which forced theater owners to rent films not individually by title but in a block. This film rental practice, Chase testified, forced local theater owners to play films unacceptable to their communities and made local control ineffective. Only the federal government, Chase claimed, was powerful enough to control Hollywood.[6] In their rabid testimony Chase and his supporters blamed the movies for all the social ills of America, but they also demanded censorship of the press as well as of the movies. In so doing they exposed themselves as narrow bigots and failed to stir Congress.[7]

If these moral guardians were upset by silent cinema, they were infuriated when films began to talk. The talkie opened up new dramatic possibilities, and the movies became more popular than ever. Now sexy starlets could rationalize their immoral behavior; criminals using hip slang could brag about flaunting law and order; and politicians could talk about bribery and corruption. Film dialogue could and did challenge conventional norms. In 1928 the New York censorship board cut more than 4000 scenes from the more than 600 films submitted, and Chicago censors sliced more than 6000 scenes. But even as the censors were snipping away at a furious pace, audiences were flocking to the theaters. In 1922 the average weekly attendance at movie theaters in the United States stood at 40 million. By 1928 it had leaped to 65 million and by 1930 had reached the staggering figure of 90 million.

Hays faced the delicate problem of how to satisfy increasingly restrictive municipal and state censorship boards and calm civic and religious organizations without destroying the popularity of the movies. From 1922 to 1934 Hays searched for a formula that would give him authority over film content, undercut the vocal opposition to the movies, and at the same time attract the largest possible audience to movies.

The Catholic church, before 1930, played no part in the controversy over film content. Church leaders and lay activists consistently lobbied against Protestant efforts to pass censorship laws. Accepting entertainment as a feature of modern life, the church neither banned members from attendance nor restricted Sunday viewing. By 1930, however, a small group of Catholic laymen and priests was becoming more and more uncomfortable with what it perceived as the declining moral quality of films. Martin Quigley, a staunch lay Catholic and owner and publisher of the industry trade journal *The Motion Picture Herald*, took the first steps toward Catholic involvement. An advocate for theater owners, Quigley opposed government censorship and argued that block-booking was in the financial interests of small theater owners because it reduced the overall price they had to pay for individual films. Yet he shared the conviction of other reformers that movies were becoming "immoral" and was further convinced that movies had to avoid social, political, and economic subjects or face strict government censorship. To Quigley, movies had to be "harmless entertainment."

Convinced that the industry could regulate itself through the Hays office, Quigley began to think about a new code of behavior for the movie industry in the summer of 1929. Acting on the advice of his priest Father FitzGeorge Dinneen, who was a friend and confidant of Cardinal George W. Mundelein of Chicago, Quigley invited Father Daniel Lord, a Jesuit from St. Louis, to work with them.[8]

Lord was a professor of dramatics at St. Louis

University and editor of the widely read *The Queen's Work,* which preached morality and ethics to Catholic youth. As a boy, Lord wrote in his autobiography, he had been overwhelmed by D.W. Griffith's THE BIRTH OF A NATION (Epoch, 1915). He left the theater convinced that he had seen a new medium of communication powerful enough to "change our whole attitude toward life, civilization, and established customs." As a young priest he was selected to work as technical adviser to Cecil B. DeMille in THE KING OF KINGS (Pathé, 1927). When Quigley invited him to think about a new moral code for the industry, he leapt at the opportunity.[9]

Joseph I. Breen was another major figure in this small group of aroused Catholics. An active lay Catholic, Breen had been the press relations chief for the 1926 Eucharistic Congress in Chicago, where he was also public relations director of the Peabody Coal Company. Invited by Quigley to work with the group, Breen was to emerge in 1934 as the director of the PCA.[10]

For several months Quigley, Breen, Lord, Father Dinneen, and Father Wilfred Parsons, editor of the influential Catholic publication *America*, exchanged ideas about a code of behavior for the movies. They all agreed that government censorship could not ensure "moral" films. They believed that the only way to ensure that films were morally and politically correct was to intervene in their production. If films were made correctly in the first place, there would be no need for government censorship. After studying the various state and municipal censorship codes, the Hays office's "Don'ts and Be Carefuls," and the objections of Protestant reformers, Daniel Lord took on the task of writing a new movie code. What emerged is a fascinating combination of Catholic theology, conservative politics, and pop psychology that was to control the content of Hollywood films for the next two decades.[11]

Although the code is most often discussed as a document that prohibited nudity, required married couples to sleep in twin beds, and effectively ruined the movie career of that saucy favorite Mae West, its authors intended it to control much more. Lord and his colleagues shared a common objective with Protestant film reformers: They all wanted entertainment films to emphasize that the church, the government, and the family were the cornerstones of an orderly society and that success and happiness resulted from respecting and working in this system. They believed that entertainment films should reinforce religious teachings that deviant behavior, whether criminal or sexual, costs violators the love and comforts of home, the intimacy of family, the solace of religion, and the protection of law. In short, they believed films should be twentieth century morality plays that illustrated proper behavior to the masses.

As Lord put it, Hollywood films were first and foremost "entertainment for the multitudes" and as such carried a "special *Moral Responsibility*" requisite of no other medium of entertainment or communication. Their universal popularity, cutting across social, political, and economic classes and penetrating communities from the most sophisticated to the most remote, meant that filmmakers could not be permitted the same freedom of expression allowed to producers of legitimate theater, authors of books, or even editors of newspapers.[12]

Movies had to be more restricted, Lord believed, because they were persuasively and indiscriminately seductive. Although audiences of books, plays, and even newspapers were self-selective, the movies had universal appeal. Hollywood's films, its picture palaces, and its beautiful and glamorous stars combined to create an ultimate fantasy. In the late 1920s, when sound was combined with visually striking images, a sensation was created that Lord believed would be irresistible to the impressionable minds of children, the uneducated, the immature, and the unsophisticated. These very groups, Lord believed, represented a large majority of the national film audience. It was because this massive film audience was incapable of distinguishing between fantasy and reality—or so Lord and the film reformers believed—that self-regulation or control was necessary.

Therefore, the basic premise behind the code was that "no picture should lower the moral standards of those who see it." Recognizing that evil and sin were a legitimate part of drama, the code stressed that no film should create a feeling of "sympathy" for the criminal, the adulterer, the immoralist, or the corrupter. No film should be so constructed as to "leave the question of right or wrong in doubt." Films must uphold, not question or challenge, the basic value of society. The sanctity of the home and marriage must be upheld. The concept of basic law must not be "belittled or ridiculed." Courts must be shown as just and fair, police as honest and efficient, and government as protective of all people. If corruption were a necessary part of any plot, it had to be restricted: a judge could be corrupt but not the court system; a policeman could be brutal but not the police force. Interestingly, Lord's code stated that "crime *need not always be punished, as long as the audience is made to know that it is wrong.*" What Lord wanted films to do was to illustrate clearly to audiences that "evil is wrong" and that "good is right."[13]

Quigley immediately took Lord's draft to Hays and began agitating for industry adoption. Quigley's strategy was to combine economic threat and moral pressure. He and Father Dinneen convinced Cardinal George Mundelein of Chicago to "sponsor" the code and to use his influence with the investment firm of Halsey-Stuart, a major industry investor, to pressure the industry to accept it. In a series of meetings in December 1929 and January 1930 with Cardinal Mundelein, Harold S. Stuart, Quigley, Lord, industry leaders, and members of the Hays office, the basic tenants of the code were accepted.

With the dramatic stock market crash only a few weeks behind them film corporation heads in New York were jittery, and Hays convinced them that the code would be good for business. It might quiet demands for federal censorship and undercut the campaign to eliminate block-booking. It remained for Hays to convince Hollywood producers that the code made good sense from an entertainment, as well as an economic, point of view. With the full support of the corporate offices in New York, Hays set off for Los Angeles to "peddle a script" for movie behavior.[14]

Hays found the producers less than enthusiastic over the tone and content of Lord's code. A small group of producers, MGM's head of production Irving Thalberg, studio boss Jack Warner of Warner Bros., production head B. P. Schulberg of Paramount, and Sol Wurtzel of Fox, offered a counterproposal.[15] The producers rejected Lord's basic argument that the movies had to be more restrictive in presenting material than other art forms. They maintained that films were simply "one vast reflection of every image in the stream of contemporary life." In their view, audiences supported movies that they liked and stayed away from those that they did not. No other guidelines were needed, it seemed to them, to determine what audiences would accept. The advent of sound, in their view, brought a wider, not more restrictive, latitude in subject matter to the movies. The addition of screen dialogue, they held, would allow actors and actresses to "speak delicately and exactly" on sensitive subjects that could not be portrayed in silent films. Therefore, the producers countered, the talkies should be able to use "any book, or play or title which had gained wide attention."[16]

The two documents could not have been any farther apart. From the producer's perspective Lord's code, representing reformers of all ilks, asked them to present a utopian view of life that denied reality. But Daniel Lord, convinced that the screen was undermining church teachings and destroying family life, wanted a partnership of the industry, church, and state that would advocate a fair, moral, and orderly society. Lord admitted that the world's imperfections were the stuff of good drama, but he saw no reason why films should not show simple and direct solutions to complex moral, political, economic, and philosophical issues. The producers countered that film was no different from any other means of entertainment and required no special restrictions. The American people, they argued, were the real censors, and the box office was their ballot box.

The fascinating aspect of this conflict is that Lord's position, backed by Hays, the Catholic church, and the financial backers of the industry, was adopted almost without a whimper. Why the industry would adopt a code that, if interpreted literally, would cut out important social, political, and economic themes and turn movies into defenders of the status quo remains a question. Why would the industry, enjoying an all-time high of 90 million paid admissions per week, agree to such severe restrictions on content and form?

There are several possibilities. One is that Will Hays wanted to extend his influence from New York to Hollywood. Since his appointment in 1922, Hays had little control over the Hollywood studios. This lack of control kept him in continual hot water with the reformers. When Quigley first approached Hays with Lord's code, Hays was supportive. He recognized immediately that this Catholic plan did not ask for federal intervention, demand outside censorship, or attack the financial cornerstone of the industry, block-booking. It placed movie regulation squarely in the Hays office, just where Will Hays believed it belonged. Furthermore, acceptance of the code by the industry might actually undercut the various religious reform groups. By accepting the Catholic code, Hays prevented, at least temporarily, a Catholic-Protestant antifilm coalition.

Adopting the code also made good economic sense. Although the industry was booming at the box office, the financial structure of the industry was always fragile. Any major interruption in the cash flow from the box office or from the bankers could bring the movie house of cards tumbling down. With American Catholics making up around twenty percent of the population, and with that population being heavily concentrated in America's largest cities, the industry was especially sensitive to Catholic opinion. The industry likewise needed a steady flow of loans to finance its more than 500 features a year. Catholic threats to pressure bankers, combined with their implied threat of box office pressure, were not lost on Hays or the corporate headquarters in New York.

From the producer's point of view, the industry had lived and prospered with codes since 1911. The various efforts of Hays and the municipal and state censorship boards had been irritating but not destructive. Further, it should be noted that many also believed that Lord was basically right. Perhaps there was too much sex, too much crime, too much drinking, too much corruption, too much violence, and too little good taste in films. Furthermore, few people in Hollywood believed that the code meant exactly what it said. Even if it did, the producers insisted on one provision that gave them, not Hays, the final say over film content: If any studio felt that the Hays office interpreted the code improperly, a "jury" of producers, not MPPDA officials, would decide whether or not the offending scene would be cut. With that understanding, the code was formally adopted by the industry on March 31, 1930.[17]

Hays gave the task of enforcing the code to Jason Joy and the SRC in Hollywood. Producers submitted scripts to Joy, who served as chief censor until 1932, and then to Dr. James Wingate, who served until the Legion of Decency crisis in 1934. Both men attempted to alter films to make them consistent with the code, but both experienced major problems.

Although industry leaders gloated in 1930 that the movies were "depression proof," a serious box office downturn started in 1931. Within a year theater attendance plunged from 90 million to 60 million per week in 1930. The studios responded in typical fashion: They tried to lure fans back into the theater with sensational movies. The crisis was so severe that by 1932 several studios faced bankruptcy, and as a frustrated Joy told Hays " . . . with box-office figures down, with high pressure being employed back home [New York corporate offices] to spur the studios to get more cash, it was almost inevitable that sex . . . should be seized upon."[18]

Thus despite the code themes of sex, crime, and politics appeared in the movies with increasing frankness. Marlene Dietrich seduced an aging professor in DER BLAUE ENGEL (UFA, 1930) and bedded a gangster in BLONDE VENUS (Paramount, 1932). Greta Garbo, rejected by her lover, turned openly to prostitution in SUSAN LENOX, HER FALL AND RISE (MGM, 1931). In POSSESSED (MGM, 1931) Joan Crawford rose from a poor factory worker to a life of luxury as the mistress of an ambitious politician. Joy challenged MGM producer Irving Thalberg over this last production, but Thalberg argued that because there was no nudity in the film and because the subject was handled in "good taste" there was no violation of the code. Joy admitted to Hays that there was little he could do to force Thalberg to make changes because, in his view, a jury would most certainly rule for Thalberg.[19]

In 1932 Mae West emerged in Hollywood as the woman who best epitomized the sexual revolution of the past decade. West was kept by no man, did not need nudity to suggest sexuality, and both delighted and infuriated moviegoers with the way in which she flaunted tradition. As a stage performer in 1926, her Broadway production of *Sex* brought notoriety and a ten-day jail sentence for obscenity. Undeterred by what she considered bluenose repression, she followed with another smash hit, *Diamond Lil*. Hays immediately branded it unsuitable as a subject for a film. Nevertheless, in 1932 Paramount Studios, fighting off bankruptcy and desperate for a hit, brought West to Hollywood. In a special ruling the MPPDA Board of Directors gave Paramount permission to film *Diamond Lil* as a story that the studio released under the title SHE DONE HIM WRONG. Audiences loved West's humor, and within months she was starring again in I'M NO ANGEL (Paramount, 1933). By 1934 more than 46 million people had seen the two films.

James Wingate, who had just replaced Jason Joy as chief censor, found little to object to in either film. When he saw SHE DONE HIM WRONG at an audience preview he told Hays that he found nothing really offensive in the film and that "the audience loved" it. Although he realized that some people would object to the "general low tone," Wingate took it for what it was—a comedy. When paramount submitted the script of I'M NO ANGEL, Wingate found no objection and later told studio authorities that he "enjoyed the picture as a piece of entertainment."[20]

The critics agreed. West was, observed *The New Republic*, "the most honest and outrageous and lovable vulgarity that ever was seen on the screen." To the *New Orleans Tribune* West was a performer who "has caught the trick of satirizing the flamboyant creatures she impersonates. That imperils the morals of nobody but the humorless." Even Christian publications found West amusing. From the bible belt, the *Christian of Kansas City* wrote that "women are more tickled at Mae West than men are, because it is the picture of woman triumphant, ruthlessly and unscrupulously triumphant over poor, blundering, simpleminded men."[21]

Although West received approval from industry censors, accolades from the critics, and adoration from millions, moral guardians contended that she represented a total collapse of moral standards. When Lord saw SHE DONE HIM WRONG, he was horrified. He wrote to Hays that he had written the code to prevent just such films. When Hays responded that fans and critics alike had praised the film, Lord demanded that Catholic youth boycott it. While a Mae West craze swept the nation, a groundswell among women's clubs and civic and religious organizations protested the screening of her films. SHE DONE HIM WRONG was banned in Atlanta; in Haverhill, Massachusetts the town clergy denounced West as "demoralizing, disgusting, suggestive and indecent."[22]

Along with West the popularity of the gangster films illustrated the problems of enforcing the code. In the early 1930s a series of flashy gangsters—Edward G. Robinson in LITTLE CAESAR (Warner Bros., 1930), James Cagney in THE PUBLIC ENEMY (Warner Bros., 1931), and Paul Muni in SCARFACE (UA, 1932)—murdered their way to the top of the gang world. Penetrating the dangerous, but seductive, urban underworld, movie gangsters spoke colorfully, their guns barked out their own form of law, and their cars, squealing around corners at breathtaking speed, epitomized life in the fast lane. In an era of depression, their reward was money, admiring friends, fancy clothes, and even fancier women. They flaunted the traditions of hard work, sacrifice, and respect for institutions of authority. Robinson, Cagney, and Muni dominated each of these films, and despite the fact that their characters were killed in the last reel reformers believed that each film violated the code by creating "sympathy" for the criminal or taught the methods of successful crime to impressionable youth.

The films cut to the center of the controversy over what was acceptable on the screen. LITTLE CAESAR began production before the code was adopted, and therefore no script was submitted. When public protests flooded the Hays office, Joy was forced to pay admission to a local Los Angeles theater to see the film. He told Hays that the "audience loved the film" and that he had no objections. When Joy saw the script for THE PUBLIC ENEMY he judged it to be a marvelous combination of contemporary realism with a strong "moral lesson" that crime does not pay. Identifying the root of the problem of censorship, he wrote that censors, in his view, should not be "small, narrow, picayunish" individuals who remove the details and fail to see the overall impact of the film. If this happened, the code would destroy the industry or the industry the code because producers would have no room to create serious drama. "We are sure," he wrote, "that it was never intended that censorship should be destructive . . . but rather that its duty should be a constructive one of influencing the quality of the final impression left on the minds of audiences by the whole."[23]

The problems that Joy and Wingate faced were immense. To be sure, Joy found the gangster films to be violent but, in their overall tone, anticrime and infused with the strong moral lesson that the criminal was the enemy of society and always paid for his crimes in the end. Wingate, fully realizing that Mae West made any attempt at censorship look foolish and being quite aware that she could turn the most innocent-sounding dialogue in a script into blatant sexual innuendo, took her for what she was: a comic, a satirist poking fun at, in Joy's terms, the small, narrow, and picayunish. Although Joy and Wingate each fought with producers to eliminate violence, to cut overt sexuality, and to tame critical views of American life, neither believed that films had to be so restrictive as to eliminate the gangster, the adulterer, or the comic from the screen.

Others did, however. Lord, invited to Los Angeles to evaluate the effectiveness of the code after one year of operation, praised Joy's efforts but condemned the industry for drifting into subject areas that were "fundamentally dangerous" no matter "how delicate or clean the treatment." He urged the industry to move away from stories of "degenerates" and instead to fill the silver screen with uplifting stories of "business, industry, and commerce." He urged Hays to replace stories of gangsters and kept women with the biographies of American heroes such as Lindbergh, sports figures such as Babe Ruth or Bobby Jones, or political leaders such as Al Smith. The code that he had written in 1930, he told Hays, was not a document open to liberal interpretation. Unlike Jason Joy, Lord found no moral lessons in films about gangsters and kept women and, by 1933, was appalled by the sexual humor of Mae West.[24]

From his position in Los Angeles, Joseph Breen confirmed what many already felt: that "nobody out here cares a damn for the Code or any of its provisions." In frustration he wrote Father Wilfred Parsons that, in his opinion, Hays had sold them all "a first class bill of goods when he put over the Code on us." It may be that Hays thought "these lousy Jews out here would abide by the Code's provisions but if he did he should be censured for his lack of proper knowledge of the breed." The only standard of ethics understood in Hollywood was the box office, Breen told Parson. Breen was convinced that if they were to be successful in reforming the industry it would have to be through box office pressure.[25] Quigley agreed with Breen that effective reform required economic pressure, but in his view the code failed because Cardinal Mundelein and the Catholic church had failed to maintain pressure on the industry to uphold the code.[26]

By the beginning of 1933 all three men conceded that the code was not working. At the same time more than 40 national organizations had passed resolutions condemning the film industry and were demanding federal control and the elimination of block-booking. To make matters worse, in the spring a sensational book published by Henry James Forman, *Our Movie-Made Children*, openly accused movies of corrupting the nation's youth. Forman's book was a summary of nine other publications, each written by respected academics under the sponsorship of the Payne Fund. Although the academics had been careful to avoid making sweeping generalizations and stressed that films influenced individuals on different levels, Forman boldly charged that 72 percent of all movies were unfit for children and were "helping to shape a race of criminals." *Our Movie-Made Children* was a sensational indictment of the movie industry and became a national best seller. Forman toured the country denouncing the movies. The Payne Fund studies, and especially Forman's summary of them, provided movie reformers with seemingly irrefutable evidence that the content of films was damaging and had to be controlled.[27] From the editorial pages came a torrent of concern, and the nation's pulpits reigned indignant with demand for action. The Hays office was stunned by the publications and made feeble and ineffective attempts to refute the findings.

Sensing that Hays and the industry were now vulnerable to outside pressure, Quigley lobbied for increased Catholic involvement. His opening came with the announcement that the newly appointed apostolic delegate, Monsignor Amleto Giovanni Cicognani, would deliver a speech to the Catholic charities in New York. Meeting with Quigley only days before his speech, Cicognani agreed to incorporate into his speech a draft statement that Quigley had written calling for Catholic action against the movies. "What a massacre of innocence of youth is taking place hour by hour," said Cicognani. "Catholics are called by God, the Pope, the Bishops, and the priests to a united and vigorous campaign for the purification of the cinema, which has become a deadly menace to morals."[28]

The speech kicked off the Legion of Decency campaign, which succeeded beyond Quigley's wildest dreams. Taking the speech as a papal directive, the American bishops formed an Episcopal Committee on Motion Pictures and appointed John McNicholas as chairman. Joining McNicholas were Bishop John Cantwell of Los Angeles, Bishop John Noll of Fort Wayne, and Bishop Hugh Boyle of Pittsburgh, who under guidance from Quigley adopted a three-part plan to (1) create a pressure group; (2) boycott offensive films; and (3) support self-regulation and conformity with the production code.[29]

"Purify Hollywood or destroy Hollywood," demanded Bishop Joseph Schrembs of Cleveland. Fifty thousands of his faithful, including Mayor Harry Davis and the papal delegate Cicognani, roared their approval of his declaration of war against Hollywood at a Legion of Decency rally in Cleveland's Municipal Stadium. The campaign swept the country. In a matter of a few months the legion counted more than 3 million pledges, and by the end of the year more than 7 million people of all religious denominations had joined the movement.[30]

Although Quigley was delighted with the reaction to the campaign, he was concerned about the direction. Father Lord, for example, had begun his own campaign. Lord published a "black list" of films to be avoided by Catholics and asked all readers of the *Queen's Work* to write letters of protest to the studios. He wrote a booklet, *The Movies Betray America,* in which he called for boycotts and an end to block-booking. Lord's idea of the publication of "white lists" of good films and "black lists" of bad films caught on; in Boston, Philadelphia, Detroit, and Chicago local church authorities began local boycotts against the industry, and wildcat boycotts broke out across the country.[31]

In Quigley's view the situation was out of control and, ultimately, would embarrass the champions of decency. He feared, first of all, that Catholics could not sustain national boycotts over the long term. He was convinced that the emphasis on "black lists" would bring added publicity, and increased attendance, to immoral movies. He saw inconsistency when Chicago condemned films that other areas found to be suitable for children. He was fearful that local boycotts would undercut support for reform among theater owners. He was even more fearful that a new Mae West movie would be released at the height of the decency campaign (IT AIN'T NO SIN was in production) and, in part because of the campaign, become a smash hit. If all or any of those things happened, Quigley feared that the opportunity to clean up the movies would be lost.

Quigley and Joseph Breen went to McNicholas with an alternative plan: to allow Joseph Breen to enforce the code by incorporating a "voice for morality" in each film that dealt with sin, to allow theater owners to cancel ten percent of each block on moral grounds to pacify the anti-block-booking groups, to eliminate the "jury" system, to remove certain offensive films from circulation, and to attach a PCA seal to every film released after July 1934.[32]

The alternative offered by Quigley and Breen was attractive to McNicholas because it took him out of the movie business. He realized that the Catholic church could not regulate film content. The best he could hope for was to influence the general tone of the movies. Will Hays also endorsed Quigley's ideas. He recognized that Quigley offered a formula to mute criticism from the community and yet retain internal control over production and issues that appealed to the mass audience. Quigley's alternative to ad hoc "black lists" and boycotts was the subject of the letters exchanged by Hays and McNicholas in August 1934. After the exchange, Hays announced that the PCA would be under the direction of Joseph Breen.[33]

Breen had been working for Hays in Los Angeles since 1931. In late 1933, Hays appointed Breen to the staff of the SRC. Although he was technically an assistant to James Wingate, Breen was effectively placed in control of Hollywood operations. When Breen was announced as the new director of the PCA he was well known to the Hollywood studios. In appearance Breen was a moral reformer placed in power by the Catholic church, a man with a mission determined to clean up what he saw as "filth" in the industry. But he was also an employee of the industry, a vital part of the studio production system. His job was not to prevent films from being made but to infuse entertainment films with a strong sense of moral value.

He fully realized that the very studios that paid his salary were determined to challenge his authority, and he also knew that his power base—the Catholic church—was badly split. Quigley, McNicholas, and the bishop's committee favored cooperation, whereas Dinneen and Lord along with Catholics in Chicago, Boston, New York, and Philadelphia advocated confrontation and boycott. As Breen attacked the piles of film scripts, moral purists and reformers, both Protestant and Catholic, withheld judgment until his labor yielded fruit.

Could Breen succeed in enforcing the code with enough strictness to keep the antimovie lobby under control without reducing Hollywood's multimillion dollar fantasy world to pabulum? Would the producers accept the opinions of a journalist and public relations man turned moral reformer? Most important, would the public accept its entertainment infused with a strong dose of Catholic morality?

One of Breen's first actions as head of the PCA was to write a new definition of "moral compensating values" for the movies. This document is vital to understanding Breen's overlordship of the PCA. Breen went further than even Daniel Lord in advocating film as a vehicle to promote proper social and political behavior. Every film, according to Breen, must now contain "sufficient good" to compensate for any evil that might be depicted. Films that had crime or sin as a major part of the plot must contain "compensating moral value" to justify the subject matter. To Breen this meant that these films must have a good character who spoke as a voice for morality, a character who clearly told the criminals or sinner that he or she was wrong. Each film must contain a stern moral lesson: regeneration, suffering, and punishment. He urged that wherever possible stars, not stringers, should play the characters who represented good. In building respect for the law, Breen held that the existing code was a "full mandate to enforce respect for all *law* and all *lawful* authority. Nothing "subversive of the fundamental law of the land" could be shown in a movie. "Communistic propaganda is banned from the screen," he said. The screen was to promote "social spirit" and "patriotism" and not confuse audiences with a "cynical contempt for conventions" nor too vivid a recreation of the "realism of problems" encountered in life.[34]

Breen and his staff looked at each script with an eye toward its impact on "industry policy." This category was reserved for those films that, although technically within the code, were judged by Breen or Hays to be "dangerous" to the well-being of the industry. Undefined to allow as much latitude as possible, "industry policy" was invoked on those scripts that touched on social or political themes. Fearing loss of valuable markets, both domestic and international, the PCA used the code to limit studios in their selection and presentation of social criticism.

Moral guardians believed that no one was more in need of "compensating moral values" than Mae West. Martin Quigley was embarrassed when his *Motion Picture Herald* declared West one of the box office champions of 1933. Her popularity was as strong in small-town rural America as it was in the so-called sophisticated urban areas. The experience of D. W. Fiske, owner-manager of the Fiske Theater in Oak Grove, Louisiana, best summed up the uniqueness of West: "Did the best business of the year" (with I'M NO ANGEL). "Whether they like her or not they all come out to see her. The church people clamor for clean pictures, but they all come out to see Mae West and stay away from the clean sweet pictures. . . ."[35]

While Quigley and Breen worked toward strengthening the enforcement of the production code, and while the Legion of Decency's boycott movement steam-rolled across the nation during the spring of 1934, Paramount studios was producing a new Mae West vehicle. IT AIN'T NO SIN became a test case for Breen, Hays, and the PCA.

The basic plot was vintage West. The film is set in the 1890s, and West plays the role of Ruby Carter, a St. Louis riverboat queen. Her boyfriend is Tiger Kid, an ex-con and up-and-coming prize fighter. Ruby is hired by New Orleans gambler Ace Lamont as the headline act in his establishment, The Sensation House, and is soon the toast of New Orleans. When one of her many admirers asks her whether she is in New Orleans for good, Ruby replies "I expect to be here, but not for good."[36]

When the first script arrived from Paramount, Breen pulled his entire staff into a day-long conference to pore over the material line by line. Unlike his predecessor James Wingate, he was shocked by the script and told Paramount that he was "compelled to reject in toto" the project. His objections were not a matter of cleaning up some bits of dialogue, Breen wrote, because in his view the script was a "vulgar and highly offensive yarn" and was "a glorification of prostitution and violent crime without any compensating moral values of any kind." The character West was to play, Breen wrote, "displays all the habits and practices of a prostitute, aids in the operation of a dishonest gambling house, drugs a prizefighter, robs her employer, deliberately sets fire to his premises, and, in the end, goes off scot free in the company with her illicit lover who is a self-confessed criminal, a thief, and a murderer." He declared the script to be in total violation of the code.[37]

Breen's letter sent officials at Paramount, where production had already begun, into a panic. They assured Breen that he was "unnecessarily alarmed" over "a harmless comedy." Breen refused to budge and rejected revised scripts submitted in February and March. Paramount chose to ignore Breen and went forward with production. They submitted a completed film to Breen in June 1934, and he rejected it. He informed Paramount president Adolph Zukor that the "low moral tone" of the film was especially "dangerous when viewed in light of the industry's present position with the public." Privately he wrote to Hays that the studio heads "sneer" and "belittle" industry critics and were determined to produce pictures "without any counsel, guidance or reference" from their New York offices or the Hays office.[38]

The battle lines were drawn. In Hollywood the studios were determined to make films without interference. In New York the corporate heads were not so sure. The real power in the film industry was in New York, not Hollywood. The corporate offices allowed studio heads a great deal of freedom as long as box office revenues produced a steady stream of profits. But these were trying times, and corporate leaders were uneasy. When Paramount erected huge billboards on Broadway advertising IT AIN'T NO SIN, Catholic priests countered with placards announcing "IT IS." The rapidly changing atmosphere was troublesome, and New York officials ordered the studios to tone down publicity on the film to avoid problems with "women's clubs" and "hinterland censors."[39] Hays continued to pressure Zukor and finally convinced the mogul that the studio could have West, but only in a tightly restricted format. New York instructed Hollywood to cooperate with Breen. Mae West would be given an infusion of "compensating moral value." Breen demanded that the studio delete all references to Ruby's past as a prostitute, remove all references to her boyfriend Tiger Kid as an ex-con, remove scenes detailing a "five day affair" between Ruby and Tiger Kid, remove scenes of Ruby stealing jewels from her employer, remove any suggestion that Ruby and her employer were having an affair, and end the film with Ruby and Tiger Kid getting married.[40]

In its new version, Ruby is a famous entertainer who is showered with jewels by her admirers, a "woman with a big heart" who spurns every advance by Ace Lamont. When her maid asks her what type of man she should have, Ruby replies "a single one." Rather than setting a fire to cover up a murder, Ruby calls the fire department and says (presumably to the audience) "I've done all I can." Tiger Kid now emerges on the screen as "an ambitious prizefighter" who is tricked into stealing Ruby's jewels by Ace and who accidentally kills the villain in a fair fight. He refuses to run away, telling Ruby that he must stay and face the police or be forever hounded by them. Ace Lamont now emerges as the villain who plans the robbery, is responsible for burning his own building to escape paying off his bets, and pays for his crimes with his death. In the grand finale Ruby and Tiger accept traditional values by taking marriage vows. But even in the marriage scene West got in another one-liner. When a member of the wedding party tells Ruby that he is the best man, she pauses, looks him over, and deadpans "Oh no you're not."

Despite the one-liners, Breen believed that these changes infused a sense of compensating moral value into the film. He did not attempt to remove every sexual innuendo from the script, although he insisted that West appear as a "good character" and Tiger Kid as a bit of a dupe and that all criminal activity center on Ace Lamont. With this accomplished, he issued PCA Seal Number 136 to IT AIN'T NO SIN. The film was approved as re-edited in Kansas and many other sensitive states but was unexpectedly rejected in total by New York and placed on the condemned list by the Chicago Legion of Decency.

Breen and Hays were crushed. They knew that if they could not guarantee that PCA-approved films would be given complete access to domestic markets they were doomed. Paramount was furious with Hays. Breen was summoned to New York, where he and Hays met privately with New York censors. They explained in detail the changes that they had forced on the studio and stressed to New York officials that if they rejected the film all that had been accomplished by the Legion of Decency and the creation of the PCA would be lost. IT AIN'T NO SIN, they emphasized, had begun production before the creation of the PCA. It was the last of the old breed. Breen told New York censors that he was determined to clean up Hollywood, and Hays pledged his full support. New York relented but insisted that the film be given a new title. In September New York approved BELLE OF THE NINETIES, and the film opened on Broadway without interference from local priests.[41]

Although these changes did not please everyone, Breen worked quietly behind the scenes to let Catholic leaders know what he had done. Paramount did its part by having West grant a rare interview in which she stated her willingness to clean up her act. "I'm trying to do my best to comply with their wishes," she said. "If they thought I was a little too frank, I want to do as they suggest." And she did. Her next film, GOIN' TO TOWN (Paramount, 1935) was endorsed by the Legion of Decency, and Breen found the film to be devoid of "fundamentally questionable material" and "highly amusing." Predictably, perhaps, it was a box office bust.[42]

Mae West was an obvious target for the censors, but few would have guessed that a lighthearted MGM comedy starring Jeannette MacDonald and Maurice Chevalier would cause a major internal crisis in the film industry. Directed by Ernst Lubitsch, a master at portraying sex as a frivolous game played by the idle rich, THE MERRY WIDOW was based on Franz Lehar's 1905 operetta. The setting is the mythical kingdom of Marshovia, 52 percent of which is owned by an immensely wealthy widow. Unable to find a husband, the widow leaves for Paris. Her departure represents an economic crisis for the tiny kingdom, and the king commands Captain Danilo, the kingdom's greatest lover, to woo her back to Marshovia. Around this slender plot Lubitsch wound satirical wit, elaborate costumes, dancing, singing, and a heavy dose of comedy.[43]

When the script arrived at the PCA, it caused little concern. Breen advised the studio to eliminate all close-up shots of a Paris "can-can" dance and to tone down a few scenes that seemed a bit risqué. The PCA issued a seal of approval to the film in September 1934.[44]

THE MERRY WIDOW was approved by every state censorship board, including New York's. In October MGM held a gala premier at the Astor Theater in New York City. While overhead blue arc lights streamed up and down Broadway, mounted policemen worked to control a huge crowd that had gathered outside the theater for a glimpse of some of their favorite Hollywood stars. Attending the premier were two industry men who drew little attention from the thousands of movie fans that October evening. When Will Hays and Martin Quigley settled into their seats, they were unprepared for MGM's version of THE MERRY WIDOW.

As the film unfolds on the screen, the kingdom of Marshovia is seen to be preoccupied with sex. The king (George Barbier) is a bumbling fool, and the queen (Una Merkel) spends her leisure time inviting a series of lovers to her bedchamber. When the king accidentally discovers Captain Danilo (Maurice Chevalier) in the queen's boudoir, he orders Danilo to Paris to woo the widow Sonia (Jeannette MacDonald) back to Marshovia or be sentenced as a traitor. In Paris, and determined to have one last fling before taking up his diplomatic duties, Danilo goes to Maxim's where he is well known by the host of "ladies" who help customers spend money and drink champagne. Dinner at Maxim's is always served in private chambers, where the ladies can entertain the customers. Unknown to Danilo, Sonia is also at Maxim's, pretending to be one of the ladies of the evening. Naturally Danilo and Sonia fall in love, but Sonia soon discovers that Danilo has been ordered to romance her and refuses to see him.

A failure, Danilo is brought back to Marshovia to stand trial. At the trial all the beautiful women of the kingdom swoon over Danilo and are distraught at the thought of losing him. Even Sonia returns to testify in his behalf. He did his duty, she tells the court: He lied, he deceived, he cheated. When Danilo professes true love for Sonia, he tells the court that he should be hanged because he could have any woman but is willing to marry only one. The men in the courtroom break into wild applause. The women sigh. In the grand finale, the lovers are locked in jail overnight. In a royal conspiracy the king orders a Gypsy orchestra to play romantic music outside the cell while a constant supply of champagne is slipped into the room. The combination works its effect, and at the right moment a minister appears and quickly marries the couple. Marshovia is saved.

The tiny kingdom may have been saved, but Quigley was outraged and Hays shocked by the flaunting of traditional values. How, they both wondered, could Breen possibly have approved this film? Quigley cornered Hays in the lobby; something had to be done to THE MERRY WIDOW before it was released nationwide. Hays fully agreed.[45]

"The jig is up," Quigley told Breen, if this film was allowed to play without further censoring. If MGM was allowed to produce this type of film "while a campaign is on," Quigley wrote, how could he "assume the attitude, with McNicholas and others, that things are going generally in the right direction?" He viewed the film as an "industry double-cross" and specifically faulted MGM's Irving Thalberg, who "deliberately introduced a lot of filth" into a charming operetta. If no changes were made, Quigley told Breen, he would immediately withdraw his support from the reform movement.[46]

Hays was equally concerned. He contacted MGM corporate officials in New York and expressed his concerns over "several suggestive sequences." He telephoned the PCA office and confirmed that the film had indeed been approved and then summoned Breen to New York. The long train ride from Los Angeles to New York must have been difficult for Breen. With scenes from THE MERRY WIDOW playing in his head and the thought of losing his

$35,000-a-year job, he admitted to Hays that the film as it stood was "not the light, gay frivolous operetta" but a "typical French farce that is definitely bawdy and offensively—in spots—suggestive." After sternly lecturing Breen Hays took him to MGM headquarters, where they previewed the film with Legion of Decency representatives Father Wilfred Parsons, editor of *America*, and Pat Scanlan, editor of the Catholic *Brooklyn Tablet*, along with MGM representatives. Hays left, and the group worked until 2:00 A.M. agreeing on additional cuts that would make THE MERRY WIDOW decent.[47]

The basic problem was Danilo's preoccupation with sex. The small group of censors decided that Danilo was not "a carefree, happy-go-lucky fellow" but an "immoral person." If his character were changed it would "make him a more attractive character to the mass audiences" who were in their view "less sophisticated" than the Broadway audiences currently enjoying the film. Thirteen new cuts were proposed to effect this change. Grouped together, they centered on removing the "coxsman" view of Danilo, eliminating the impression of Maxim's as a "whore house," and cutting or trimming a scene of Sonia "partially undressed."[48]

The problem now was how to get the cuts into the film that had already been distributed throughout the country and was ready for general release. Hays called Irving Thalberg, and although there is no record of the conversation Hays noted that it was "a long one." Given the pressure from New York, Thalberg agreed to the revisions. MGM wired all their distribution offices with instructions to make the required cuts before all play dates. Hays, Breen, and Father Parsons previewed the film once again in New York to ensure that the cuts had indeed been made. On November 1, Will Hays declared THE MERRY WIDOW fit for American audiences to see.[49]

Films dealing with social and political topics were subjected to similar restructuring. Falling under the guidelines of "industry policy," Breen and Hays watched with great alarm for scripts that dealt with contemporary issues. Fearing critical reaction from state censorship boards, which were as sensitive to political commentary as they were to expressions of sexual immorality, both men were determined not to allow "social issues" films to damage foreign or domestic markets. Citing "industry policy," they used the code and the threat of external censorship to force producers into providing "harmless entertainment."

A major test came in September 1934, when independent producer Walter Wanger submitted a script for THE PRESIDENT VANISHES. Wanger and Hays had clashed over another political film a year earlier. In 1933 Wanger had combined forces with newspaper magnate and Cosmopolitan Productions boss William Randolph Hearst to produce one of the most bizarre films in Hollywood history, GABRIEL OVER THE WHITE HOUSE (MGM, 1933). The film, intended by Hearst as a tribute to newly elected Franklin D. Roosevelt, called for the establishment of a benevolent dictatorship to solve the economic crisis facing America. When Hays saw the film he was dumbfounded. He called an emergency meeting of the MPPDA Board of Directors and forced them to watch the film. Why, he demanded to know, with the nation seemingly ready for radical solutions to the economic crisis, with the Republican Party humiliated in a national election, with Wall Street in shambles, and with the film industry sinking into a sea of red ink, would the industry produce a film calling for martial law and fascism? The next day Hays ordered GABRIEL OVER THE WHITE HOUSE back to the studio for a political reorientation. Despite the fact that more than $30,000 was spent on retakes, GABRIEL OVER THE WHITE HOUSE played to American audiences with most of its original message intact. "Fascism Over Hollywood," screamed the *Nation* in its review. A disgruntled Hays warned each studio that he would no longer tolerate code violations. If the studios refused to cooperate, Hays vowed to begin enforcing the code from New York.[50]

In the midst of the legion crisis Wanger proposed THE PRESIDENT VANISHES, a melodrama that featured a group of greedy American businessmen who conspire to lure America into a world war. Although the industrial "fat cats" publicly speak of patriotism, they speak with scorn for the principles of democratic government. The traditional political parties are befuddled. Only the American Communist party urges workers not to be fooled into dying for capitalist profits, but the public is easily duped into demanding war. The president views this as folly but is helpless to stop the hysterical demands of the public. As Congress is about to pass a declaration of war, the president arranges for his own kidnapping. With attention being switched to finding the president, the conspirators begin bickering among themselves. Given time to come to its senses the public changes its view, and the president emerges from hiding and promises "Not one American boy will be sent to foreign soil to leave his blood there as a security for loans." The plot is uncovered, and democracy is restored.

Wanger envisioned an antiwar film that clearly took advantage of the public perception that munitionmakers and bankers had tricked Americans into World War I. As an antiwar film THE PRESIDENT VANISHES paled in comparison to ALL QUIET ON THE WESTERN FRONT (Universal, 1930), yet Breen was concerned about the script from the moment it arrived at the PCA. In a series of meetings and letters, he warned the producer not to characterize the vice president as a "drunkard" or a tool of a "gluttonous group of capitalists." He also worried about Wanger's descriptions of the conspirators: Andrew Cullen, a steel magnate; Martin Drew, a banker who supports the Grey Shirts; Hartley Grinnell, a newspaper owner who controls public opinion; George Milton, an oil man; and United States Senator Joseph Corcoran, a pawn in the hands of the conspirators.

From the standpoint of "industry policy," Breen wrote "I . . . question the advisability of your designating the heavies as representatives" of American industry. He suggested that Wanger could resolve the problem by making the "heavies" represent "a combination representing international munitions men with an international viewpoint." In his view this "should cut down on the criticism." Perhaps Breen believed the conspiracy thesis of America's entry into World War I. For whatever reason, he approved Wanger's script with only a few changes and gave a seal of approval to the film.[51]

When Hays saw the film in New York he was furious. He told Breen to withdraw the seal of approval because in his view the film was "communist propaganda, subversive in its portrait of American government, contrary to the accepted principles of established law and order, and perhaps treasonable." Hays specifically wanted the following lines of a Communist during a street rally removed: "Fellow workers . . . it's the workers' blood they are after . . . so that the capitalistic bloodsuckers can grow rich . . . join the Communist Party." He ordered Breen to renew negotiations with Wanger and arranged an emergency meeting with the Board of Trustees and Paramount's Adolph Zukor.[52]

Hays made his position clear. First he established who was in charge. He told Breen that Breen was to act "as programmed"; that is, he would tell Wanger what had to be done to the film. He was not to negotiate with the producer but to instruct him on the exact nature of the changes required. He pressured Zukor not to distribute the film until the required changes were made and told him "the screen has no right . . . to present a distorted picture which condemns the banking industry per se as warmongers, which presents the Communist Party as the leading protagonist . . . and which indicated such banality and corruption in our government and political machinery, that even the

Secret Service of the nation cannot be trusted to protect the President of the United States." His suspicions were confirmed when *Newsweek* reported that "preview audiences noticed that certain characters resembled Andrew Mellon, John D. Rockefeller, and William Randolph Hearst."[53]

Although Hays was often accused of never going to the movies, he saw THE PRESIDENT VANISHES in his office several times. He disliked the film and insisted that no amount of editing could eliminate all his objections. Yet Hays was in a difficult position because Breen had given Wanger a seal, and the producer was threatening a legal action if the film were withdrawn. Therefore, Hays agreed to allow the film to play if the line about "capitalistic bloodsuckers" was removed and if several other cuts were made to tone down the film. Wanger agreed, and the film was released.

Nevertheless, Wanger was determined to challenge the authority of Breen and Hays. In an interview in *Newsweek*, he told reporters "Hays ought to take over the censorship of the comic strips." Wanger refused to make any changes and released a print of the film to Pennsylvania with the "bloodsuckers" line intact, hoping that the state would pass it and embarrass Hays. When Pennsylvania censors indignantly demanded that the offending scene be removed, the Hays office discovered the subterfuge. Hays was furious, especially when he was told that it was done with "the knowledge" of Paramount officials in Hollywood. Zukor, subjected to another lecture by Hays, gave his personal assurances that only the approved prints would be distributed.[54]

THE PRESIDENT VANISHES, with its anti-war, anti-big business tone, was precisely the type of film that Hays, and the Catholic bishops, did not want the industry to make. Determined to be more strict with the studios, Breen and Hays did not have to wait long for another sensitive political topic to be proposed. Warner Bros. submitted a script for BLACK FURY, which dealt with labor problems in the coal industry, in the fall of 1934. Violence, poverty, and despair were the prevailing characteristics of the coalfields of America. Led by John L. Lewis, workers fought for basic rights and dignity in the most conservative industry in America. The subject matter, often front page news, was ripe for dramatization on the screen. But any view of America's coal industry would have to be presented in the strict constraints set by the PCA.

When the script arrived at the PCA, Breen and his staff were disturbed. Although BLACK FURY contained no violations of the code dealing with sexual immorality, it did raise controversial political issues. The first script clearly blamed the mine owner for the miserable working conditions that forced the workers into a strike. The owner reacted typically: He hired scabs and a private police force of thugs to protect his property. The police ruled with terror. Breen worried that this portrait, no matter how close to reality, would cause problems for Hollywood.

Citing "industry policy," Breen asked Warner Bros. to alter the film. He offered the studio a solution: to eliminate the critique of the mineowners and the idea of class struggle in the coal fields by presenting a humane mine owner and a conservative, legitimate union tricked into an unwanted and unnecessary strike by evil labor agitators. Breen suggested that the studio insert several lines of dialogue into the film that would state the conditions in the industry, although not perfect, were constantly improving. The legitimate union representative should state clearly that conditions are "reasonable . . . and acceptable."[55]

It was also vital to present the company president in a more positive manner. Breen suggested that several speeches be inserted into the script that would indicate to the audience that the owner was forced to hire strike breakers "very much against his will" to protect the investments of stockholders. He was further to state clearly to the private police force that under no circumstances were they to use violence against his workers. This would allow all the violence necessary for dramatic purposes to be the responsibility of the private police force. By virtue of these changes, BLACK FURY could dramatize a violent strike and workers being dispossessed. The responsibility for these conditions would not be placed on American business or American labor but rather on a police force of "thugs" run by a dishonest owner.[56]

Breen kept Hays informed of these discussions with the studio and assured him that Warner Bros. was cooperating fully. Hays was delighted with the rewriting, which he told Breen was "progressing in exactly the proper way." The film that emerged on the screen was not the film that Warner Bros. had originally proposed. Yet Warner Bros. did manage, within the restrictions imposed, to illustrate many of the hardships of life in the mines. Although the mineshafts in the film look big enough for a good game of basketball, it is clear that the miners work hard for little pay. They live in neat little houses, but those houses are owned by the company, not the workers. Nevertheless, the point for Breen and Hays was that BLACK FURY did not place blame on industry or labor for the strike. BLACK FURY was not a social critique of American management or labor. The proof of that was that Breen's version of life in America's coalfields was endorsed by both the National Coal Association and John L. Lewis' United Mine Workers.[57]

Throughout the rest of the decade Breen and Hays worked together to reconstruct political and social films. When MGM submitted a script based on Sinclair Lewis' *It Can't Happen Here*, Breen branded the script "inflammatory" and demanded so many changes that MGM backed out of the project. The studio ran into similar problems with Fritz Lang's FURY (MGM, 1936). Lang, who fled Nazi Germany in 1933, soon discovered that censorship existed in America. Lang proposed a powerful antilynching film. When Breen read the first script he informed MGM that FURY could not deal with racial prejudice, criticize Southern law enforcement officials, or be "a travesty of justice" story. After several rewrites, Breen accepted the script. The results were obvious to film critic Otis Ferguson, who wrote the *New Republic* that FURY was "a desperate attempt to make love, lynching and the Hays office come out even." The movie code was at work, Ferguson noted, when the movie had the Southern sheriff stand "like Jesus Christ with a rifle" in front of his jail while the mob pelts him with stones.[58]

Breen was unconcerned with the view of the movie critics. He wrote to Hays in early 1937 that there was a "definite trend away from serious drama." He told his boss that he saw "no indication, anywhere, of any plans to produce pictures dealing with . . . social or sociological questions." Even Shakespeare, he told Hays, "seems to be dead on his own doornail." Breen's control over content was complete. The PCA report for 1937 is telling. In that year the PCA drafted 6477 official opinions; examined 379 books, short stories, and plays for their suitability for the screen; inspected 2584 scripts; and viewed 1489 films. In addition they had 1478 private meetings with writers, directors, and producers.[59] By the end of the decade Breen's power was so entrenched that John Steinbeck's powerful critique of the American system, *The Grapes of Wrath*, could be brought to the screen without a whimper. With the politics having been written out in the script, Breen told Hays that the film was a modern day "covered wagon" epic. Like the pioneers, Breen saw the Joads going west in search of a better life, and although conditions depicted in the film were "shocking" they were all counterbalanced by "good images" and, most important, by an "uplifting ending."[60]

As long as the industry was determined to reach the largest possible market it was susceptible to economic blackmail, whether it came in the form of a Legion of Decency, state censorship boards, American businessmen, or foreign governments. The goal of Hays, Breen, Lord, the Catholic church, and the entire movie reform movement was to eliminate controversial subjects and ideas from the screen. Yet as the *Nation* complained, if the movies were not allowed to "interpret morals, manners, economics, or politics," what was left? The lowest common denominator was the answer.[61]

Worth M. Tippy, director of the Federal Council of Churches, who had been active in the film reform movement for years and had favored the Legion of Decency movement, was convinced by 1935 that Hays and the PCA were being too restrictive. PCA regulations would not allow a "notable and wholesome film" such as Fritz Lang's M (Nero Films, 1931) or I AM A FUGITIVE FROM A CHAIN GANG (Warner Bros., 1932) to come to the screen. Was that the purpose of self-regulation, he asked? Further, he believed that the current enforcement of the code was "too preoccupied with sex." There was no room under the current administration to allow the cinema its rightful place in portraying the "moral standards which are emerging out of the present social ferment, and especially of the new concept of industrial and political responsibility." Hollywood had the right, Tippy wrote, to "portray vested evils and entrenched privileges in their true light" but could not do so under the current code.[62]

To do so would have required the industry to challenge various antimovie groups and perhaps to sacrifice some markets, domestic and international, or to limit attendance at certain films to adults to make serious films deal with with serious topics. The industry chose instead to bow to the censors, to cooperate with the Legion of Decency movement, and to restrict films to the limiting formula established by the PCA. The formula was established and enforced not to protect the public from the industry but to protect the industry from the public. Although the studios sometimes fought for greater freedom of expression on the screen, the PCA remained the dominating force in determining screen content until the late 1940s and early 1950s, when a combination of factors—the rise of television with a parallel box office collapse, the effective deregulation of the industry by the federal government, a Supreme Court ruling granting freedom of expression to films, a determination by independent producers to challenge the authority of the PCA, and the impact of foreign films produced without PCA guidance—eliminated the PCA formula from the screen.

While it existed, the PCA formula was applied to some 20,000 films. Each script that came to the PCA office was different, and Breen and his staff negotiated each film with the studio that offered it. Although there are exceptions, and although sweeping generalizations blur the complexities, it seems clear that the goal of the PCA was to have each film clearly identify evil, make sin and crime appear as deviant behavior, have strong character "stars" play roles representing good, and dilute political and social comment. Convinced that films could educate, the purpose of the code and the PCA was to use popular entertainment films to reinforce conservative moral and political values.

Endnotes

1. "Hollywood Wins a Truce," *The Commonweal*, July 20, 1934, 295; "Rules Set for Cancelling Film," *Motion Picture Herald*, July 14, 1934, 10. For films removed from circulation, see Breen to Hays, Feb. 20, 1935, DR. MONICA, Production Code Administration Files, Margaret Herrick Library, Academy of Motion Picture Arts and Sci-

ences, Beverly Hills, Calif. (hereafter cited as PCA Files). For the agreement between Hays and McNicholas, see Hays to McNicholas, August 10, 1934 and McNicholas to Hays, August 14, 1934, box 47, Will Hays Papers, Indiana State Historical Society, Indianapolis, Ind. (hereafter cited as Hays Papers). For Quigley/Lord as author of the agreement (Joseph Breen also drafted part of it), see Wilfred Parsons to M. J. Ahern, August 10, 1934, box D-204, Wilfred Parsons Papers, Georgetown University, Washington, D.C. (hereafter cited as Parsons Papers).

2. Robert Sklar, *Movie Made America: A Cultural History of American Movies* (New York: Vintage, 1975), 173–74.

3. A recent exception is Lea Jacobs, "Industry Self-Regulation and the Problem of Textual Determination," *The Velvet Light Trap*, Spring 1989, 4–15.

4. "The Hays Office," *Fortune*, Dec., 1936, 68–70.

5. Garth Jowett, *Film: The Democratic Art* (Boston: Little Brown, 1976), 237–40.

6. For a typical statement, see William H. Short, "Block-Booking Must Go!" *Parents Magazine*, April 1934, 13. For a counteropinion, See Howard M. LeSourd, "Block-Booking—Cause or Camouflage?" *Literary Digest*, June 9, 1934, 28.

7. House Committee on Education, *Hearings, Proposed Federal Motion Picture Commission*, H. Rep. 4094 and H. Rep. 6233, 69th Cong. 1st Sess., 1926.

8. Daniel Lord, *Played By Ear* (Chicago: Loyola University Press, 1955), 285–90.

9. Ibid., 273–76; 285–91.

10. J.P. McEvoy, "The Back of Me Hand to You," *Saturday Evening Post*, December 24, 1938, 8–9; "The Catholic Movie Censorship," *New Republic*, October 5, 1938, 233.

11. The details of the controversy are beyond the scope of this paper. Quigley campaigned for 20 years to have the credit for the code bestowed upon him. At one point he softened his feud with Breen and asked for a formal letter from the PCA director crediting him with authorship (see Breen to Quigley, June 19, 1937, box C-81, Parsons Papers). The debate really heated up when Lord's autobiography was published shortly after his death. The debate simply represents the deep levels of disagreement over the direction of the entire movement. In 1929, when relations were friendly and perhaps more accurate, Quigley wrote to Lord "I have received this morning your final draft of our code." Only a few minor changes were made in the document approved by the industry. There is little doubt that Quigley contributed many ideas that were incorporated into the code, but Lord wrote it. See Quigley to Lord, November 26, 1929, Daniel Lord Papers, Jesuit Province Archives, St. Louis, Mo. (hereafter cited as Lord Papers).

12. Several drafts of the code are in the Lord Papers. The code has been printed in various film books. For an excellent discussion see Jowett, *Film: The Democratic Art*, 240–43; 468–72.

13. "Suggested Code To Govern the Production of Motion Pictures," n.d., Lord Papers.

14. Will Hays, *The Memoirs of Will H. Hays* (Garden City: Doubleday, 1955), 440.

15. "General Principles To Govern the Preparation of a Revised Code of Ethics for Talking Pictures," n.d., Lord Papers. The copy of the document in the Lord papers has "Irving Thalberg" written on it. Whether this means that Thalberg wrote the document or merely presented it to the meeting is unclear. There are no known records of the meeting, but it is clear that the producers had a view of the movies and their role in society that differed radically from Lord's.

16. Ibid.

17. For accounts of the various meetings, see Quigley to Lord, January 3, 1930, January 10, 1930, February 17, 1930, February 24, 1930, February 28, 1930, March 1, 1930 and Lord to Mundelein February 14, 1930, Lord Papers; Lord, *Played By Ear*, 298–304; Hays, *Memoirs*, 439–43.

18. Joy to Hays, December 15, 1931, POSSESSED, PCA Files.

19. Ibid.

20. Wingate to [A. M.] Botsford, September 18, 1933, I'M NO ANGEL, PCA Files.

21. Wingate to [Harold] Hurley, January 11, 1933, SHE DONE HIM WRONG and Wingate to Botsford, September 18, 1933, I'M NO ANGEL,

PCA Files; *New Republic*, October 24, 1934, 31; *New Orleans Tribune*, January 4, 1934; Stark Young, "Angels and Ministers of Grace," *New Republic*, November 29, 1933, 73–76.

22. K. L. Russell to Hays; November 17, 1933, box 33, Hays Papers; Hays to Lord, February 28, 1933, Lord Papers.

23. Gerald Peary, *Little Caesar* (Madison: University of Wisconsin Press 1981), 21–28 for the controversy over that film; Joy to McKenzie, January 30, 1931, Joy to Wingate, February 5, 1931, LITTLE CAESAR, PCA Files. The PCA File for SCARFACE has been lost, but Joy visited every state censorship board except Kansas' to negotiate with the state censors for the release of the film. He was successful and in so doing added fuel to the arguments of those who believed that the Hays office was not enforcing the code. The SCARFACE controversy brought additional demands for the elimination of the industry practice of block-booking. By 1932 Protestant religious groups centered their demands for industry reform on block-booking or federal censorship, believing that Hollywood would never reform and that local communities had to have the right to reject films that they judged harmful. For a summary of newspaper editorials against gangster films, see "Protests against Gangster Films, 1931," box 42, Hays Papers.

24. Daniel Lord, "The Code—One Year Later," April 23, 1981, box 42, Hays Papers.

25. Breen to Parsons, October 10, 1932, box C-9, Parson Papers. Breen's rabid anti-Semitism is present in a large number of letters that he sent to Lord, Parsons, Dinneen, and Quigley. It is unclear whether or not they shared his beliefs. In return correspondence they make no mention of his anti-Semitic views, neither statements agreeing with him nor statements taking him to task for his obvious racism. Lord, who published *Dare We Hate the Jews* (St. Louis: The Queen's Work) in 1939, would seem an unlikely anti-Semitic. Nevertheless, anti-Semitism was an issue in the campaign against the movies, and Jewish domination of the movie industry was often given as a reason for "indecent films."

26. Quigley to Parsons, August 27, 1934, box C-76, Parsons Papers.

27. Henry James Forman, *Our Movie-Made Children* (New York: Macmillan, 1933).

28. Parsons to Maguire, June 22, 1934 and Parsons to M. J. Ahern, August 10, 1934, box D-202/203, Parsons Papers.

29. Paul W. Facey, *The Legion of Decency: A Sociological Analysis of the Emergence and Development of a Pressure Group* (New York: Arno, 1974), 45.

30. *Cleveland Plain Dealer*, June 18, 1934; F.W. Allport to Hays, "Catholic Action," May 29, 1934, box 46, Hays Papers. Allport provided Hays with weekly updates on the activities of the Catholic church throughout the legion campaign. The reports detailed the internal problems that the Catholics had.

31. Lord to Hays, May 26, 1934, Lord Papers. See also Lord to Parsons, August 30, 1934, box D-204 and Parsons to Lord, September 13, 1934, box C-50, Parsons Papers, Daniel Lord, *Movies Betray America* (St. Louis: The Queen's Work, 1934).

32. Films such as A FAREWELL TO ARMS [Paramount, 1933], BABY FACE [Warner Brothers, 1933], THE STORY OF TEMPLE DRAKE [Paramount, 1933], SONG OF SONGS [Paramount, 1933], SHE DONE HIM WRONG, I'M NO ANGEL, DR. MONICA [Warner Brothers, 1934], GEORGE WHITE'S SCANDALS [Fox, 1934], and SO THIS IS AFRICA [Columbia, 1933] were withdrawn from circulation and not given a PCA seal as part of the agreement.

33. McNicholas to Dinneen, March 3, 1934, Quigley to Parsons, March 17, 1934, and Quigley to McNicholas, March 20, 1934, box C-76, Parsons Papers. The Cincinnati agreement set off an incredible fight in the church. Cardinal Mundelein was furious that the publicity over the agreement failed to give him proper credit for beginning the code in the first place. He refused to speak to Quigley and encouraged Lord and Father Dinneen to publish "black lists" and to boycott films. Dinneen and Lord both accused Quigley and Breen of selling out the Legion of Decency movement and of substituting the PCA seal as the standard of morality. The two priests maintained that neither Quigley nor Breen could represent the Catholic church and that they both had economic interests in a healthy movie industry that

influenced their decisions. See Dinneen to Lord, June 27, 1934, box C-50, Parsons to McNicholas, March 24, 1934, box C-50, and Lord to Parsons, August 30, 1934, box D-204, Parsons Papers.

34. "Compensating Moral Values," June 13, 1934, box 47, Hays Papers.

35. Quigley's *Motion Picture Herald* regularly published brief reactions to films from small-town theater owners and managers. The purpose was to let small-town theater owners know how films draw in markets similar to theirs. Although there were complaints about too much sex in films from these owners, they all praised Mae West as good entertainment and an even better box office draw in small towns. The reformers who attacked block-booking hoped that freeing local owners from this rental practice would solve their problems, but there is no evidence that it would have hurt any Mae West film. It is noteworthy that these evaluations were taken at the height of the Legion of Decency movement, and they illustrate why Quigley was fearful of an uncensored West film being released during the campaign. See *Motion Picture Herald*, July 29, 1933, January 20, 1934, February 24, 1934, March 17, 1934.

36. James Rorty, "It Ain't No Sin," *Nation*, August 1, 1934, 124–27.

37. Breen to Botsford, February 23, 1934, Breen to Files, March 6, 1934, and Breen to Botsford, March 7, 1934, BELLE OF THE NINETIES, PCA Files.

38. Breen to Hays, June 2, 1934, Breen to John Hammond, June 2, 1934, and Breen to Zukor, June 4, 1934, BELLE OF THE NINETIES, PCA Files.

39. *Variety*, October 3, 1933. Paramount directed that the advertising referring to West's line "Come up and see me" be presented "as an invitation to tea."

40. "Memo Conference at Paramount," *Variety*, June 6, 1934.

41. "Memo to Files," *Variety*, June 13, 1934. During this controversy Paramount requested that the PCA not release any details of the changes made in the film. The PCA agreed.

42. *Los Angeles Herald*, June 29, 1934; Breen to Hammell, December 19, 1934, January 16, 1935, January 25, 1935, April 1, 1935, GOIN' TO TOWN, PCA Files.

43. *Literary Digest*, October 27, 1934, 34; A. Slide, *Selected Film Criticism, 1931–1941* (1982), 151.

44. Breen to Louis B. Mayer, March 29, 1934, "Memo MGM Conference," August 11, 1934, and Breen to Mayer, September 25, 1934, THE MERRY WIDOW, PCA Files.

45. Quigley to Breen, October 12, 1934, box D-205, Parsons Papers; "Memorandum by WWH," November 1, 1934, box 47, Hays Papers.

46. Quigley to Breen, October 12, 1934, box D-205, Parsons Papers.

47. "Memorandum by WWH," November 1, 1934, box 47, Hays Papers.

48. Breen to Hays, October 22, 1934, THE MERRY WIDOW, PCA Files.

49. Thalberg to Hays, October 26, 1934, THE MERRY WIDOW, PCA Files; "Memorandum by WHH," November 1, 1934, box 47, Hays Papers.

50. The film was to be released by MGM; see Wingate to Thalberg, 8 February 1933, Hays to Files, March 6 and 7, 1933, Hays to Wingate, March 11, 1933, GABRIEL OVER THE WHITE HOUSE, PCA Files, "Facism Over Hollywood," *Nation*, April 26, 1933, 482–83. The most complete account of the production history of the film is in Robert L. McConnell, "The Genesis and Ideology of *Gabriel Over the White House*," *Cinema Journal*, Spring 1976, 7–726. McConnell did not have access to the PCA Files; see Hays to Mr. — — —, March 7, 1933, Lord Papers (a copy was sent to all studios). In July Hays named titles: He told MGM that BOMBSHELL [MGM, 1933], DANCING LADY [MGM, 1933], and HOLLYWOOD PARTY [MGM, 1934] violated the code. Paramount was warned that I'M NO ANGEL, DESIGN FOR LIVING [Paramount, 1933], and DUCK SOUP [Paramount, 1933] were in violation. RKO was told to correct ANN VICKERS [RKO, 1933], OF HUMAN BONDAGE [RKO, 1934], and PRELUDE FOR LOVE [RKO, 1933].

51. Breen to The General (Hays), September 14, 1934, Breen to Wanger, September 19, 1934, and September 20, 1934, and Breen to Hays,

November 9, 1934, THE PRESIDENT VANISHES, PCA Files.

52. Hays to Maurice McKenzie, November 21, 1934 and Breen to Wanger, November 21, 1934, THE PRESIDENT VANISHES, PCA Files.

53. *Newsweek*, December 15, 1934; Hays to Zukor, November 23, 1934, THE PRESIDENT VANISHES, PCA Files.

54. *Newsweek*, December 15, 1934; Breen to Hays, January 31, 1935, THE PRESIDENT VANISHES, PCA Files.

55. Breen to Jack Warner, September 12, 1934, BLACK FURY, PCA Files.

56. Ibid.

57. Hays to Breen, September 12, 1934, BLACK FURY, PCA Files.

58. Breen to Warner, June 18, 1936, BLACK FURY, PCA Files; Breen to Mayer, January 27, 1936, BLACK FURY, PCA Files; "Hollywood's Half a Loaf," *New Republic* June 10, 1936, 130.

59. Elizabeth Yetman, "The Catholic Movie Censorship," *New Republic*, October 5, 1938, 234.

60. Breen to Hays, February 27, 1937, BLACK LEGION, PCA Files.

61. "The Movie Boycott," *Nation*, July 11, 1934, 34.

62. Tippy to Quigley, March 20, 1935, box C-77, Parsons Papers. There is no record of a reply from Quigley.

J. Edgar Hoover and the Black Press in World War II

Patrick S. Washburn

The Federal Bureau of Investigation has been one of the 20th Century's most powerful and feared government agencies, primarily because of its vast investigations. While little still is known about most of those investigations, they unquestionably have included publications and journalists who dared to criticize the government or express dissident views. Such persons received little sympathy from J. Edgar Hoover, an extreme patriot who directed the FBI with an iron hand from 1924 until 1972.

In this collision between journalists and the government, Hoover occasionally found his power checked unexpectedly and significantly. An excellent example was his World War II attempt to obtain a sedition indictment of the emerging and highly critical black press. A story hidden in government documents for over 40 years, it involved a protracted struggle between Hoover and Attorney General Francis Biddle as well as other Justice Department officials. The result was a small but important First Amendment victory.

"Radicalism And Sedition Among Negroes"

Hoover's drive to indict the black press in World War II had its origins in 1919. Following nine anarchist explosions on June 2, he was named head of the Justice Department's newly created General Intelligence Division (GID), which was ordered to study "subversive activities."[1] With Hoover providing the impetus, the GID moved at a dizzying pace, preparing biographies on 450,000 radicals in a year and a half.[2] Among those investigated were authors, publishers and editors as the GID made regular checks of 625 radical newspapers, including 251 considered ultraradical.[3]

Black publications, many of which complained continually about discrimination and other injustices such as lynchings, were among those watched closely.[4] Hoover noted in September 1919, for example, that both *The Crisis*, the magazine of the National Association for the Advancement of Colored People, and *The Messenger*, a socialist publication, "are well known to me." He said that "if possible something should be done to the editors of these publications as they are beyond doubt exciting negro [sic] elements in this country to riot and to the committing of outrages of all sorts" with numerous racial complaints.[5]

However, Hoover was stymied because both the Espionage Act and the Sedition Act, passed in 1917 and 1918 respectively, applied solely to wartime sedition. Therefore, he and Attorney General A. Mitchell Palmer began pressing for a peacetime sedition act, which had not existed since the Alien and Sedition Acts of 1798 to 1801. To emphasize the need for such an act, reports on the connection between communism and blacks were sent to the Senate in November 1919 and the House in June 1920.[6] The 1919 report, titled "Radicalism and Sedition Among Negroes As Reflected in Their Publications," contained the following:

> *Among the most salient points to be noted in the present attitude of the Negro leaders are . . . the identification of the Negro with such radical organizations as the I. W. W. and an outspoken advocacy of the Bolsheviki or Soviet doctrine. . . . The Negro is "seeing red," and it is the prime objective of the leading publications to induce a like quality of vision upon the part of their readers.*[7]

The report claimed "the number of restrained and conservative [black] publications is relatively negligible." As evidence, the GID sent Congress numerous objectionable black press articles.[8]

The reports helped stimulate extensive congressional activity. Seventy House and Senate proposals were combined into the Graham-Sterling Bill, which provided fines and/or imprisonment for those who sought to overthrow or destroy the government.[9] The public became alarmed, however, when Oliver Wendell Holmes, Samuel Gompers and Zechariah Chafee spoke out against the bill, and the House Rules Committee reported out unfavorably on it. Thus, no action was taken.[10]

Although Hoover was unsuccessful, the importance of 1919–21 in determining his World War II actions cannot be overemphasized. In Hoover's mind, the black press was troublesome, even un-American, and the passage of time would not erase that belief.

Furthermore, once the government's investigation of the black press began, it was not about to end. Documentary evidence strongly suggests, and in some cases confirms, that the Bureau of Investigation (which was renamed the FBI in the 1930s) studied black publications continuously between the two wars. Reasons for this investigation included attempts by Communists and the Japanese to enlist black support[11] and indirect encouragement from Franklin D. Roosevelt, who early in his presidency requested information on all subversive groups, particularly Communists.[12]

Still another reason was the black press' growing criticism of discrimination. The Army, which confined blacks to four units, was a particular target of the black press, which in 1938 began a campaign to open up that branch of the military and escalated the drive into 1942. Other criticism centered around blacks being unable to join the Marines, Coast Guard or Air Corps, and only being messboys in the Navy. In civilian life, blacks resented oppressive poll taxes, educational and job discrimination, police violence against them, and lynchings.[13]

As a result of this criticism, FBI agents visited the Pittsburgh *Courier*, the country's largest black newspaper, in 1940. The visit was precipitated by articles on black attempts to vote in the South, which the agents complained were "holding America up to ridicule."[14]

In the same year, the FBI received a complaint that the Chicago *Defender* contained "propaganda" which "might hinder the Government in securing registrations from negroes [sic] who come within the draft age." Hoover forwarded the paper to the Justice Department, which informed him that no federal statute had been violated.[15] In another 1941 example, Hoover had the Pittsburgh *Courier* investigated following War Department complaints. After several months, Hoover informed the Army that no evidence indicated the paper was engaged "in questionable activities with reference to the national defense program."[16]

Unofficial Censorship

Shortly after the bombing of Pearl Harbor, Hoover sought his first sedition indictment of the black press, which was then represented by over 200 newspapers with a circulation of about 1.3 million.[17] It involved the Afro-American chain of five East Coast newspapers, which on December 30, 1941, ran comments by five Richmond blacks hypothesizing on what Japan's attitude would be toward blacks if it won the war. "The colored races as a whole would benefit," said a printer, echoing the comments of two others. "This would be the first step in the darker races coming back into their own."[18]

On January 30, Hoover asked Wendell Berge, head of the Justice Department's Criminal Division, if the article violated federal statutes.[19] Berge replied that it was permissible because the comments were "mere expressions of individual opinion as to the possible course of future events" and not "false statements." "Clear" evidence also was lacking, he continued, that the statements were designed to harm the armed forces or affect recruiting or enlistment, all of which were covered by the Espionage Act. Nevertheless, Berge encouraged an investigation of the chain's ownership as well as of the "character and pertinent activities" of its editors to see if there was a tie-in with "hostile or subversive sources."[20] This resulted in an extensive FBI investigation of the chain throughout the war.

Meanwhile, the FBI began exercising unofficial censorship by openly subscribing to black newspapers and visiting those which it felt were hurting the war effort with frequent articles on discrimination. P.B. Young Sr., publisher of the Norfolk *Journal and Guide*, recalled that it was "a rare day" when the FBI did not visit a black paper early in the war.[21]

The first known visit was on January 27, 1942, when an FBI agent saw Atlanta *Daily World* columnist Cliff MacKay. The agent asked if the paper had received any Japanese news releases, or if the Communist Party had attempted to influence the *World* editorially. MacKay, whom the agent described as "very cooperative," said that neither had occurred.[22] Then, on March 27, the black Birmingham *World* ran a MacKay column criticizing Hoover for having no black FBI agents.[23] Hoover wrote editor Emory O. Jackson that it was "grossly" inaccurate and "a slander in my opinion upon the many loyal, patriotic Negro members of this Bureau."[24] Jackson used Hoover's letter in the *World* and said he would like to discuss its contents in several weeks when he would be in Washington.[25]

In an April 23 meeting, an FBI agent criticized MacKay and told Jackson that "certain subversive forces were seeking to use the Negro press to stir up disunity." Possibly out of fear, the editor admitted that the column should not have run and agreed that it was important for the country to "stick together" because of the war.[26] Hoover wrote Jackson after he returned to Birmingham, thanking him for understanding the FBI's viewpoint and saying that several local agents had been instructed to "communicate" with him.[27] This obviously was a ploy to keep the *World* in line.

On July 1, an agent again visited MacKay in Atlanta on an undisclosed matter.[28] MacKay promptly lashed out angrily in a column:

> *One gathers after the conversation [with the agent] that some white people would like to read "sedition" and "subversive activity" into the determination of Negroes to achieve democracy here at the same time they are called upon to fight for its preservation abroad.*
>
> *Nothing could be further from the truth, as these FBI agents were told on both occasions of their visits. The Negro, in fact, is the most American of all Americans. He has proved this over and over again. He has no split loyalties, no ties with other countries, no relatives "across the pond." He is all American, first, last and always.*[29]

The Pittsburgh *Courier*, which was visited by FBI agents at least once in the war's first six and a half months, also reacted angrily. "This sort of thing is an obvious effort to cow the Negro press into soft-peddling its criticism and ending its forthright exposure of the outrageous discrimination to which Negroes have been subjected," said a March 14 editorial.[30]

Then, in May, William O. Walker, publisher of the Cleveland *Call and Post*, revealed that a black newspaperman in Texas had written him that "the FBI has frightened all of the Negro editors in the southland." Walker suggested that "the papers in the northern and more liberal states are going to have to assist those in the South to resist intimidation."[31]

Meanwhile, Hoover was seeking further Justice Department opinions on the black press. On May 30, he sent Berge 10 March, April and May issues of the Baltimore *Afro-American* which he considered seditious.[32] He followed this up in July by forwarding four issues of the Oklahoma City *Black Dispatch*. In the latter paper, Hoover pointed out articles that complained about black soldiers riding 24 hours on trains without food and being fed in Oklahoma City in "dirty, filthy, Jim Crow" kitchens located in the rear of white restaurants. He also noted an editorial that concluded with the recommendation that all men should be equal instead of only one race being granted "special dispensation to inherit happiness."[33] Berge replied that none of the issues had violated the Espionage Act. Even so, Hoover told his Baltimore agent to continue forwarding possibly seditious material because the Justice Department wanted to review it.[34]

Biddle and Sengstacke

A Washington meeting in mid-June affected FBI attempts to indict the black press. It resulted in part from a May 22 Cabinet meeting at which black morale problems were discussed. Roosevelt told Attorney General Francis Biddle to talk to black editors "to see what could be done about preventing their subversive language."[35]

At the same time, black editors, concerned about being suppressed, were seeking out high government officials. Not only were they apprehensive from open visits from FBI agents and critical comments by government officials, but rumors abounded.[36] The Pittsburgh *Courier's* Billy Rowe, for example, recalled hearing that some papers might lose their second-class mailing permits or even be shut down. He did not believe such talk. "The government was powerful enough that if it wanted to, it would have been able to do these things," he said. "But I didn't see any evidence of anything being done. So, I figured it was just rumors started by groups who hated blacks, like the Ku Klux Klan."[37]

But other black editors and publishers were unsure. Therefore, in mid-June, Chicago *Defender* publisher John Sengstacke sought a meeting with Attorney General Biddle, who was one of the high government officials most sympathetic to blacks. When he had been sworn in as attorney general in September 1941, a number of blacks had backed him vigorously as a "friend of the colored people of America." Such support was deserved. Not only had he championed the work of the Justice Department's civil liberties unit upon joining the agency in January 1940, but he prosecuted some Detroit whites in 1942 for preventing blacks from moving into the federally supported Sojourner Truth housing project.[38]

Despite all of this, Biddle quickly let Sengstacke know this was not a low-key chat. When the publisher was ushered into a Justice Department conference room, he found copies of numerous black newspapers, including the *Defender*, the Pittsburgh *Courier* and the Baltimore *Afro-American*. Each carried headlines about early April clashes in New Jersey and Alabama between black soldiers and whites which had left three people dead and several injured. Without mincing words, Biddle said such articles were a disservice to the war effort, and if the black papers did not change their tone, he was "going to shut them all up" for being seditious.[39]

Sengstacke, who was as tough as Biddle, countered that the black press was not hurting the war effort and he noted it had been fighting race prejudice for over 100 years. Nor was the fight about to end. Sengstacke took a hard line with Biddle: "You have the power to close us down, so if you want to close us, go ahead and attempt it." Despite such an unpromising start, they worked out a compromise in the next hour. Biddle promised Sengstacke that the Justice Department would not indict any black publisher for sedition. In turn, Sengstacke said the black press would be "glad" to cooperate with the war effort if allowed more access to high government officials, many of whom were refusing interviews with black reporters or not allowing them into press conferences.[40]

While it is not known whether Hoover was informed about Biddle's decision, documents show that he continued to seek an indictment. Between November 1942 and July 1943, he sent Berge the *People's Voice*, a black New York paper, the Pittsburgh *Courier* and papers in the Afro-American chain, inquiring if they had violated the Espionage Act. They contained such items as an editorial cartoon of a black soldier, who was meant to represent 450,000 black servicemen, with heavy chains on his wrists to symbolize the way blacks were hampered from fighting in the war. Another issue had a letter from a black corporal, who cited a number of alleged instances of Army discrimination and called for a government investigation. In each case, Berge replied that the papers were within the law.[41]

"Survey of Racial Conditions"

In September 1943 Hoover mounted his major wartime attack on the black press, and blacks in general, in a 714-page "Survey of Racial Conditions in the United States." Consisting of material gathered over more than two years from 53 FBI field offices, the report was compiled "to determine why particular Negroes or groups of Negroes or Negro organizations have evidenced sentiments for other 'dark races' (mainly Japanese) or by what forces they were influenced to adopt in certain instances un-American ideologies."[42] It stressed that the FBI felt some black publications were hurting the war effort:

> *Sources of information have volunteered the opinion that the Negro press is a strong provocator of discontent among Negroes. It is claimed that its general tone is not at all, in many instances, informative or helpful to its own race. It is said that more space is devoted to alleged instances of discrimination or mistreatment of Negroes than there is to matters which are educational or helpful. The claim is that the sensational is foremost while true reportorial material is sidetracked.*[43]

The FBI criticized 43 publications for causing problems with their inflammatory articles and headlines. Thirteen of them had alleged Communists on their editorial staffs or employees who maintained contacts with Communists, according to the FBI, or they ran articles that followed the Communist Party line.[44] In addition, five publications were cited for running pro-Japanese material.[45]

Thirty pages of the report specifically examined seven black newspapers.[46] The detailed information foreshadowed what would become commonplace in the McCarthy era. While there were no claims of illegal activity, the FBI suggested that six of the papers were causing massive discontent among blacks and, in numerous instances, had communist connections or were running pro-communist propaganda. This implied that the papers were un-American and possibly should be suppressed.

Of course, the survey may have been inaccurate or misleading. Knowing that Hoover was concerned about Communists and blacks, some FBI agents may have reported what they felt would please him. Furthermore, the report's information may have been selected from the FBI's files with the intention of making some black publications appear seditious. Unfortunately, in 1943, as today, outsiders did not have open access to the FBI's files, and the survey's objectivity may never be determined.[47]

The material on the seven newspapers included the following:

Baltimore Afro-American. The FBI noted that the paper had numerous "Communist connections." A former staff member, for example, recently had been named administrative secretary of the National Negro Congress, "a Communist influenced organization." In addition, the Communist Party and the Young Communist League had run an announcement on September 19, 1942, congratulating the paper on its 50th anniversary.

The paper's city editor also had expressed appreciation for the Communist Party's campaign to allow blacks to become telephone operators and bus drivers in the Baltimore area. "The city editor made it clear that in the future the *Afro-American* newspaper would be glad to print any other information concerning these or related programs which the Communist Party might sponsor," the report said.[48]

Amsterdam Star-News. The only one of the seven newspapers not criticized, it was included to show the difference between its editorial practices and those of the *People's Voice,* which competed with it for New York's black circulation. The FBI noted that the *Star-News* was "comparatively conservative" and had criticized communism several times.[49]

People's Voice. In contrast, the FBI described this paper as "a very helpful transmission belt for the Communist Party." Not only were its editorials and articles considered pro-communist, but the FBI said its well-known publisher, Adam Clayton Powell, had been "affiliated" with numerous pro-communist individuals and groups. Furthermore, the survey pointed out that Max Yergan, who was prominent in several communist groups, recently had contributed at least $3,000 to the paper, resulting in his name appearing in its "publication block."[50]

Oklahoma City Black Dispatch. Editor Roscoe Dungee, while not a Communist, was reported to be "sympathetic with the Communist cause to such an extent that he has allowed his name to be used by many Communist front organizations and is said to have used his talent as a speaker in appearing at meetings of these groups." The FBI also pointed out that the paper apparently did "considerable" printing for the state's Communist Party and had carried a pro-communist editorial on October 10, 1942. "We shall have to report that we personally do have [a] Communistic leaning," a *Black Dispatch* writer had said, since "Communism believes in social equality and so does this writer."[51]

Chicago Defender. The FBI reported that two of the paper's employees had been attending local Communist Party meetings, where they sat on the platform and made speeches. While numerous people with communist connections also wrote articles for the paper, the FBI admitted that the paper's editorials strongly supported the war effort even though they also militantly attacked inequality. For example, on April 4, 1942, the paper reported that some black soldiers had been killed in Little Rock and commented that this proved "that in the South the uniform of the United States has no respect if the wearer is a Negro.[52]

Michigan Chronicle. According to the FBI, the paper's editor was active in the National Student League, a communist-front organization, during his college years. Although he had not joined a similar group since then, sources said he still believed "sincerely" in communism, and they emphasized that the *Chronicle's* editorials had followed the Communist Party line for years. Furthermore, the editor had attended the

Communist Party's state convention in March 1943. The FBI also noted that a number of the paper's other editors and columnists had belonged to communist organizations or currently were members.[53]

Pittsburgh Courier. Although no communist connections were noted, the survey stressed the frequent use of both pro-Japanese and anti-Japanese articles. On January 10, 1942, for example, columnist George Schuyler had written that blacks would not be worse off if the Japanese won. Then, on March 28, 1942, he praised the Japanese for "their cleanliness, their courtesy, their ingenuity, and their efficiency." The FBI specifically pointed out that this column contained no anti-Japanese material. In contrast, Executive Editor Percival Prattis wrote on May 16, 1942, that he preferred white Southerners to the Japanese.[54]

No Support From Above

Hoover probably hoped such revelations would result in black press indictments. He sent the survey to the White House, but no documents show that Roosevelt urged any action, if indeed he even read the report. Such a reaction was predictable. The president rarely became involved in black problems because of the political risks.[55]

Without the president's support, that left only Attorney General Biddle, and no evidence indicates that he commented on the survey either. That was equally nonsurprising considering his well-known support of blacks and the black press.[56] "The Negro press throughout the country, although they very properly protest, and passionately, against the wrongs done to members of their race, are loyal to their government and are all out for the war," Biddle said in a speech on February 12, 1943.[57] That may have been his only public statement about the black press, but it indicated his likely response to the report seven months later.

Furthermore, the Supreme Court's decision in Dunne v. United States on November 22, 1943, eliminated any faint hope of success held by Hoover. The case involved 18 Minneapolis Trotskyites, who had published, sold and distributed material advocating a violent overthrow of the government. Biddle, believing sedition statutes were "unnecessary and harmful," had approved the prosecution to test the constitutionality of the Smith Act. He had done so reluctantly, feeling that the 3,000-member Trotskyite group "by no conceivable stretch of the liberal imagination could have been said to constitute any 'clear and present danger' to the government."[58] Confident that the Supreme Court would overturn the convictions, he was shocked when it refused to hear the case, letting the convictions stand. As a result, Biddle was criticized heavily by the American Civil Liberties Union and his liberal friends.[59] Thus, it would have been inconceivable for him to have approved a black press indictment.

Meanwhile, Hoover was rebuffed again when he sought to attack a black paper. On October 11, 1943, he sent Assistant Attorney General Tom C. Clark a June 19 Chicago *Defender* column that criticized blacks' treatment in Army camps. The columnist wrote: "Mainly, their [the black soldiers'] bitterness adds up to—'I [would] just as soon die fightin' for democracy right here in Georgia, as go all the way to Africa or Australia. Kill a cracker in Mississippi or in Germany, what's the difference!' " Noting that the column apparently referred to a gun battle between black and white soldiers at two Georgia camps, Hoover asked if such material violated the Espionage Act.[60]

Clark replied that the column was legal. Furthermore, in the fall of 1943, the Justice Department discontinued weekly summaries of black press articles. This was yet another sign that it had concluded sedition prosecutions of the black press were inadvisable.[61]

More Refusals to Prosecute

Nevertheless, Hoover continued collecting black press material and pushing for an indictment. In February 1944, he sent Clark a 17-page report on material appearing in the Afro-American chain of papers during the preceding November and December. The report emphasized articles "describing alleged brutal treatment of Negro soldiers in U.S. Army camps."[62]

Three months later, Hoover attacked the Pittsburgh *Courier* for a Schuyler column which criticized Roosevelt and other government officials for allowing segregation and discrimination to continue in the armed services. "Indeed, one sometimes asks whether they [government officials] are not fighting the Negro harder than they are fighting the Germans and the Japanese," wrote Schuyler. "Certainly many German and Japanese prisoners are being treated better than some of the Negroes wearing the uniform of Uncle Sam."[63] On both occasions, Clark refused to allow a prosecution.[64]

Hoover's final hopes of a black press indictment ended on December 9, 1944, after he had sent Clark a 24-page report pointing out that the Afro-American chain was still running critical articles about the armed services. He wanted to know if the FBI's investigation of the chain, which had begun in 1941, should continue. After noting that none of the material violated federal statutes, Clark recommended halting the investigation because of a June 12 Supreme Court ruling.[65]

It involved Elmer Hartzel, who had been convicted of violating the Espionage Act by writing and distributing three pamphlets in 1942. The pamphlets not only called upon the country to abandon its allies and turn the war into a racial conflict, but they questioned Roosevelt's integrity and patriotism. In reversing the decision, Supreme Court Justice Frank Murphy said there had been insufficient evidence for a jury to determine "beyond a reasonable doubt" that Hartzel had meant to bring about insubordination, disloyalty or mutiny in the armed services. "An American citizen has the right to discuss these matters either by temperate reasoning or by immoderate and vicious invective without running afoul of the Espionage Act of 1917," said Murphy.[66]

Following that setback, Hoover sought only one more wartime indictment of the black press. That occurred on February 22, 1945, when he complained to Clark about the Pittsburgh *Courier*. Hoover reported that three officials of the federal War Manpower Commission had told the FBI that the newspaper had used "confidential" agency information to attack the WMC for supposedly "condoning" black discrimination by Pittsburgh-area companies with defense contracts. Because the article contained confidential WMC material on a national defense matter, Hoover wondered if the newspaper could be charged with espionage.[67]

Clark was not sympathetic, telling Hoover that "prosecutive action" under any federal statute was unwarranted.[68] Thus, despite all of his information, Hoover was effectively controlled by the Justice Department for the final time.

Conclusions

It is tempting to believe that Hoover's persistent attempts to obtain a black press indictment in World War II were racially motivated. After all, he was a well-known racist. "J. Edgar Hoover, who has steadfastly refused to include Negroes among his 4,800 special agents, has a long record of hostility to Negroes," *The Nation* noted in July 1943.[69] Similarly, William C. Sullivan, one of his assistants, found that Hoover definitely "disliked" blacks.[70] Historians agree. Sanford J. Unger, who labeled him "prejudiced and narrowminded, overtly biased against black people," traced Hoover's intolerance to his Old South attitude.[71] Still another historian, David J. Garrow, pointed out that Hoover's racism was "widely documented."[72]

But such an explanation is simplistic. While Hoover's racist views cannot be ignored, he unquestionably had valid reasons to investigate the black press from his earliest days as a Justice Department administrator. The nation was in the throes of a "Red Scare" when he took over the General Intelligence Division in 1919, and some black publications were not only critical of the government but socialist-oriented. In such an atmosphere, it was easy to believe that disenchanted blacks were an easy target for Bolshevik propaganda, which made the black press potentially dangerous because of its influence with readers.

Furthermore, Roosevelt indirectly contributed to the FBI's black press investigations by granting Hoover immense investigatory powers in the 1930s.[73] Given such freedom, and the continual push by Communists and Japanese to attract black support, Hoover was drawn naturally to the black press. It criticized the government heavily, which suggested that Communist and Japanese propaganda efforts might be successful.

Much of the black press also encouraged Hoover by openly praising Russia and by showing little fear of communism.[74] In October 1941, for example, columnist Ralph Matthews of the Baltimore *Afro-American* criticized the United States and England for getting rich by exploiting people, "especially the darker races." In contrast, he pointed out that Russia had tried to "perfect a way of life for her own people which will spread out the good things of life to the greatest number instead of to a chosen few."[75]

In addition, black journalists and Communists had continual contacts.[76] Ironically, these often were unavoidable. Two former Pittsburgh *Courier* reporters, Frank Bolden and Billy Rowe, recalled that Communist press agents constantly sought out black journalists in the 1930s and 1940s.[77] Such contacts were noted by watchful FBI agents and described to Hoover, who had a consuming desire to destroy communism.

Finally, for much of 1942, the United States was not sure it could win the war. But the black press, instead of patriotically toning down, continued to be critical and hint that this might not be "the good war" that much of the country was proclaiming it to be. The government understandably viewed such criticism as detrimental to morale. Blacks made up 10 percent of the population and no one was sure the United States could win if they refused to fight.[78]

There also was concern that the press' criticism would cause blacks to become fifth columnists.[79] In such a situation, Hoover's investigations, even his attempts to indict the black press for sedition, can be seen as a logical wartime safeguard against a possible internal threat. And it was unlikely that such investigations would have ended in the latter half of 1942 as the black press toned down and the United States swung over to the military offensive. There was a war to be won, Hoover had an important role to play, and he was determined to do his job.

So, the war was fought and no indictments occurred. In 1947, publisher P.B. Young Sr., of the Norfolk *Journal and Guide*, one of the country's major black newspapers, recalled the FBI's investigation of the black press during World War II. He boasted of the result:

> *The fact that years of watching and distilling of every line, every word printed in the Negro press that could by any process of reasoning have been classified as treasonable brought not one single arrest, not one single act of suppression, constituted irrefutable proof of the undiminished patriotism of the American Negro at a time when efforts to sabotage our war effort were quite general in other circles.*[80]

Young was only partially correct. Black journalists' loyalty certainly played a role in their lack of arrests and the non-suppression of their publications. But the deciding factor for Hoover and the FBI, in terms of the black press, was the unwavering constitutional views of Attorney General Biddle and the Justice Department.

Endnotes

1. Fred J. Cook, *The FBI Nobody Knows* (New York: Macmillan, 1964), p. 89.
2. Ibid., pp. 94–95.
3. Max Lowenthal, *The Federal Bureau of Investigation* (New York: William Sloan Associates, 1950), p. 91; Stanley Coben, *A. Mitchell Palmer: Politician* (New York: Columbia University Press, 1963), p. 207.
4. Lowenthal, *The Federal Bureau of Investigation*, pp. 120–29.
5. Memorandum, J.E. Hoover to Mr. Fisher, September 10, 1919, record group 60, file 9-12-725, National Archives, Washington, D.C.
6. Lowenthal, *The Federal Bureau of Investigation*, p. 120.
7. Hank Messick, *John Edgar Hoover* (New York: David McKay, 1972), p. 14.
8. Lowenthal, *The Federal Bureau of Investigation*, p. 121.
9. Robert K. Murray, *Red Scare: A Study in National Hysteria, 1919–1920* (Minneapolis: University of Minnesota Press, 1955), pp. 178, 230–31.
10. Ibid., pp. 244–46.
11. Patrick S. Washburn, *A Question of Sedition* (New York: Oxford University Press, 1986), pp. 32–33.
12. Don Whitehead, *The FBI Story: A Report to the People* (New York: Random House, 1956), pp. 157–58, 161–62.
13. Lee Finkle, *Forum for Protest* (Cranbury, N.J.: Associated University Presses, 1975), pp. 61, 131–47; Patrick S. Washburn, "The *Pittsburgh Courier*'s Double V Campaign in 1942," *American Journalism* 3, no. 2 (1986): 74.
14. Interview with Frank Bolden, January 14, 1983.
15. J.E. Clegg to Director, Federal Bureau of Investigation, September 30, 1940; Memorandum, John Edgar Hoover to Lawrence M.C. Smith, October 10, 1940; Memorandum, Hugh A. Fisher to J. Edgar Hoover, November 7, 1940. All are in file 100-122319, Federal Bureau of Investigation, Washington, D.C.
16. Special Agent Report, Federal Bureau of Investigation, October 21, 1941; John Edgar Hoover to Assistant Chief of Staff, G-2, November 29, 1941. Both are in file 100-31159, Federal Bureau of Investigation.
17. Circulation figures for the black press are somewhat difficult to establish because they were not reported every year and, when they were reported, some papers refused to give out figures. According to the best available data, the black press had a circulation of 600,000 when Roosevelt entered office in 1933. This more than doubled to 1,276,000 by 1940 and reached 1,808,060 by the end of World War II. Finkle, *Forum for Protest* pp. 51–54; U.S. Department of Commerce, *Negro Newspapers and Periodicals in the United States: 1940*, Negro Statistical Bulletin, no. 1, May 1941, p. 1; Arnold M. Rose, *The Negro's Morale: Group Identification and Protest* (Minneapolis: University of Minnesota Press, 1949), pp. 104–05.
18. "The Inquiring Reporter," *Baltimore Afro-American*, December 20, 1941, p. 4.
19. Memorandum, John Edgar Hoover to Wendell Berge, January 30, 1942, file 100-63963, Federal Bureau of Investigation.
20. Memorandum, Wendell Berge to J. Edgar Hoover, February 5, 1942, file 100-63963, Federal Bureau of Investigation.
21. Robert Durr, *The Negro Press: Its Character, Development and Function* (Jackson: Mississippi Division, Southern Regional Council, 1947), pp. 2–3.
22. F.R. Hammack to Director, Federal Bureau of Investigation, September 4, 1942, file 94-8-1399-7, Federal Bureau of Investigation.
23. Cliff MacKay, "A Note to Mr. Hoover," *Birmingham World*, March 27, 1942.
24. John Edgar Hoover to Emory O. Jackson, April 10, 1942, file 94-8-1399, Federal Bureau of Investigation.
25. Emory O. Jackson to J. Edgar Hoover, April 20, 1942, file 94-8-1399, Federal Bureau of Investigation.
26. Memorandum, L.B. Nichols to Mr. Tolson, April 24, 1942, file 94-8-1399, Federal Bureau of Investigation.
27. J. Edgar Hoover to Emory O. Jackson, April 29, 1942, file 94-3-1399, Federal Bureau of investigation.
28. Cliff MacKay, "Now Just Who is Subversive?" *Birmingham World*, July 10, 1942.

29. Ibid.
30. "Cowing the Negro Press," *Pittsburgh Courier*, March 14, 1942, p. 6.
31. "Publishers to Answer Pegler Challenge," *Chicago Defender*, May 30, 1942, p. 5.
32. Memorandum, J. Edgar Hoover to Wendell Berge, May 30, file 100-63963, Federal Bureau of Investigation.
33. Memoranda, J. Edgar Hoover to Wendell Berge, July 7, July 10, July 17, and July 18, 1942, file 100-20076, Federal Bureau of Investigation.
34. Memoranda, Wendell Berge to Director, Federal Bureau of Investigation, June 24 and July 25, 1942; and John Edgar Hoover to Special Agent in Charge, Baltimore, July 6, 1942. All are in files 100-63963 and 100-20076, Federal Bureau of Investigation.
35. Private typewritten notes, Francis Biddle, "May 22, 1942," Francis Biddle papers, Cabinet Meetings, January-June 1942 folder, Roosevelt Library, Hyde Park, N.Y.
36. Interviews with Billy Rowe, January 3, 1983, and James E. Alsbrook, April 18, 1984.
37. Interview, Billy Rowe, January 3, 1983.
38. Francis Biddle, *In Brief Authority* (Garden City, N.Y.: Doubleday, 1962), pp. 166, 169; Clinch Calkins, "Wartime Attorney General," *Survey Graphic*, October 1942, p. 423.
39. Interviews with John H. Sengstacke, April 21, 1983, and September 15, 1983. The only document mentioning the meeting between Sengstacke and Biddle is C.W.H., "Memorandum for the Office Files: The Chicago Defender," June 26, 1942, record group 28, file no 103777-E, case no. E-128, National Archives.
40. Ibid.
41. Memoranda, John Edgar Hoover to Wendell Berge, November 24, 1942, and March 26, April 12, May 3, May 29, June 8 and July 1, 1943; Memoranda, Wendell Berge to Director, Federal Bureau of Investigation, December 7, 1942, and April 30, June 12, July 12 and August 23, 1943; E.E. Conroy to Director, FBI, March 18, 1943. All are in files 100-51230 and 100-63963, Federal Bureau of Investigation.
42. Federal Bureau of Investigation, "Survey of Racial Conditions in the United States," undated, p. 1, OF 10B, No. 2420, Justice Dept. FBI, Reports folder, Roosevelt Library. A letter which was sent with the report to the White House indicates that it was completed in September 1943.
43. Ibid., p. 430.
44. The 13 publications were: Baltimore *Afro-American, California Eagle* (Los Angeles), Chicago *Defender, Colorado Statesman* (Denver), *The Crisis* (New York), Denver *Star*, Kansas City *Call*, Los Angeles *Sentinel, Michigan Chronicle* (Detroit), Oklahoma City *Black Dispatch, Opportunity* (New York), *People's Voice* (New York), and *Racial Digest* (Detroit).
45. The five publications were: Cincinnati *Union, The Crisis, Moorish Voice* (Prince George, Va.), *Pacific Topics* (Chicago) and Pittsburgh *Courier*.
46. Federal Bureau of Investigation, "Survey of Racial Conditions in the United States," pp. 433–42.
47. Historian Eric Foner has warned researchers about the dangers of blindly using FBI documents. "Reports of intelligence agents and paid informers cannot be taken at face value," he wrote. "More often than not, investigating agents revealed their own prejudices and preconceptions more accurately than . . . reality." Eric Foner, "Roots of Black Power," *New York Times Book Review*, February 5, 1984, p. 25.
48. Federal Bureau of Investigation, "Survey of Racial Conditions in the United States," pp. 433–42.
49. Ibid., p. 443.
50. Ibid., p. 443–44.
51. Ibid., p. 445–547.
52. Ibid., p. 448–51.
53. Ibid., p. 451–53.
54. Ibid., pp. 545–59. In connection with the Pittsburgh *Courier*'s pro-Japanese activities, the FBI reported that Schuyler apparently had been invited to visit Japan in 1938 or 1939 and had written several pro-Japanese articles upon his return. At the same time, it said columnist J.A. Rogers had been entertained by Japanese officers in Ethiopia and allegedly had promised "favorable publicity" for Japan when he returned to the United States.
55. Nathan Miller, *FDR: An Intimate History* (Garden City, N.Y.: Doubleday, 1983), p. 360; James Mac-

Gregor Burns, *Roosevelt: The Soldier of Freedom* (New York: Harcourt, Brace, Jovanovich, 1970), p. 472: Neil A. Wynn, *The Afro-American and the Second World War* (London: Paul Elek, 1976), pp. 109–13..

56. Blacks particularly were impressed with Biddle's support of Arthur W. Mitchell, a black congressman who filed a complaint with the Interstate Commerce Commission when in 1937 he was forced to move from a Pullman car to a segregated coach when his train passed into Arkansas. The case went to the Supreme Court in 1941 and Biddle wrote a memorandum supporting Mitchell's right of equal and nonseparate travel means. Biddle, *In Brief Authority*, pp. 152–53, 166, 169.
57. "Biddle Lauds Race Press As Loyal to U.S.," *Amsterdam Star-News*, February 20, 1943, p. 1..
58. Biddle, *In Brief Authority*, pp. 151–52.
59. Ibid.
60. Memorandum, John Edgar Hoover to Tom Clark, October 11, 1943, file 100-122319, Federal Bureau of Investigation.
61. Tom C. Clark to Director, Federal Bureau of Investigation, November 9, 1943; J. Edgar Hoover to Tom C. Clark, December16, 1943; Tom C. Clark to Director, Federal Bureau of Investigation, January 1, 1944. All are in file 100-122319, Federal Bureau of Investigation.
62. Federal Bureau of Investigation Report, December 31, 1943; J. Edgar Hoover to Tom C. Clark, February 2, 1944. Both are in file 100-63963, Federal Bureau of Investigation.
63. Tom C. Clark to Director, Federal Bureau of Investigation, May 24, 1944, file 100-31159, Federal Bureau of Investigation.
64. Memorandum, Tom C. Clark to Director, Federal Bureau of Investigation, February 23, 1944, file 100-63963; Tom C. Clark to Director, Federal Bureau of Investigation, May 24, 1944, file 100-31159. Both are at the Federal Bureau of Investigation.
65. Federal Bureau of Investigation Report, November 10, 1944; John Edgar Hoover to Tom C. Clark, November 29, 1944; and Tom C. Clark to Director, Federal Bureau of Investigation, December 9, 1944. All are in file 100-63963, Federal Bureau of Investigation. It is not known why Clark took six months to conclude that the Hartzel decision made further investigations of the Afro-American chain unnecessary.
66. Hartzel v. United States, 322 U.S. 680 (1944).
67. John Edgar Hoover to Tom C. Clark, February 22, 1945, file 100-31159-204, Justice Department, Washington, D.C.
68. Tom C. Clark to Director, Federal Bureau of Investigation, March 1, 1945, file 146-7-64-354, Justice Department.
69. XXX (pseud.), "Washington Gestapo," *The Nation*, July 24, 1943, pp. 94–95.
70. Bill Brown and William C. Sullivan, *The Bureau: My Thirty Years in Hoover's FBI* (New York: W.W. Norton, 1979), pp. 268–69.
71. Sanford J. Ungar, *FBI* (Boston: Little, Brown, 1975), pp. 255–56, 328.
72. David J. Garrow, *The FBI and Martin Luther King, Jr.: From "Solo" to Memphis* (New York: W.W. Norton, 1981), p. 153.
73. Washburn, *A Question of Sedition*, pp. 168–69.
74. Finkle, *Forum for Protest*, p. 201.
75. Ralph Matthews, "The Big Parade," *Baltimore Afro-American*, October 11, 1941, p. 4.
76. In July 1941, a black Military Intelligence agent reported that "Japanese and Communist press agents are releasing news in all available negro [sic] publications and in some cases, Communists or Communist sympathizers are employed on the editorial staffs of these papers." Sherman Miles to J. Edgar Hoover, July 11, 1941, record group 165, MID 10110-2452-1174, box 3085, National Archives. Also see Washburn *A Question of Sedition*, pp. 176–77.
77. Interviews with Billy Rowe, January 3, 1983, and Frank Bolden, January 14, 1983.
78. Washburn, *A Question of Sedition*, pp. 100–06.
79. Louis Martin, "Fifth Column Among Negroes," *Opportunity*, December 1942, pp. 358–60.
80. Durr, *The Negro Press*, pp. 2–3.

Institutional Paralysis in the Press: The Cold War in Washington State

Gerald J. Baldasty and Betty Houchin Winfield

During World War II and the ensuing Cold War, scholars turned their attention to the function and responsibilities of the press. The products of these studies include the 1947 report of the Commission on Freedom of the press (the Hutchins Commission), Lasswell's 1948 article on structure and function of communication and Siebert's classical propositions on press freedom and societal stress, in 1952.[1] All followed the Hutchins Commission's contention that the media should provide a "truthful, comprehensive and intelligent account of the day's events in a context which gives them meaning."[2] Lasswell stressed that the press was operating in a dangerous world where "ideological conflict" could result in internal national disruption or even world war.[3] Siebert quoted the Hutchins Commission's report:

> *The citizen, as a participant in government has an obligation to inform himself on the merits of current issues and on the qualifications of candidates for public office. Out of this grows the proposition that it is the duty of the press and of other media of mass communication to inform the citizen and to make available to him such materials as will enable him to arrive at sound and rational conclusions.*[4]

This project, as a study of the press in the late 1940s and based on the major ideas of these scholars, examines newspaper coverage of the Washington State Committee on Un-American Activities investigation of alleged Communist infiltration at the University of Washington.

The research centered around this general question:

To what extent did the press, during a period of societal stress, such as the Cold War, provide a truthful and comprehensive account of the day's events in a context which gives them meaning?

Historical background: Communism and Washington State. Many Washingtonians had been concerned about the Communist menace for years before the Cold War. The fight between "good" citizens and the "Reds" was integral to West Coast labor history, particularly during the Seattle General Strike of 1919, the Everett massacre trial, the 1934 waterfront strike and the

[1]Commission on Freedom of the Press, *A Free and Responsible Press* (Chicago: University of Chicago, 1947); William E. Hocking, *Freedom of the Press—A Frame-Work of Principle* (Chicago: University of Chicago Press, 1947); Harold D. Lasswell, "The Structure and Function of Communication in Society," found in *The Process and Effects of Mass Communication*, Wilbur Schramm and Donald F. Roberts, eds. (Urbana: University of Illinois Press, 1971 ed.), pp. 84–99; Frederick S. Siebert, *Freedom and the Press in England, 1476–1776* (Urbana: University of Illinois Press, 1952).

[2]*A Free and Responsible Press*, p. 21.

[3]Lasswell, *op. cit.*, p. 92.

[4]Siebert, *op. cit.*, p. 12.

1936 Newspaper Guild strike at the Seattle *Post Intelligencer*.[5] The Communist Party in the Pacific Northwest grew from a few members in 1932 to nearly 6,000 by 1936.[6] Seattle was the important center for the Party, and Mayor John F. Dore continually provided newspaper headlines about the "communist menace" in the city.[7]

The state legislature was concerned, as well, about Communists, and a front page article in the Dec. 13, 1946 Seattle *Post Intelligencer* disclosed that a coalition of state Democrats and Republicans planned a "state Red probe." A fact-finding committee "with full powers of subpoena" would probe the "undercover operation of Communists," particularly "the infiltration into the state's educational institutions." Reporter Fred Niendorff quoted Republican Senator Harry Wall:

> *It is common knowledge in many quarters . . . that the Communists have infiltrated the University of Washington campus and that their supporters have found important places on the faculty. . . . As a matter of fact, there is abundant evidence to show that besides their infiltration into labor unions and political organizations, the Communists are trying everything in the book to reach American Youth through the schools.*[8]

Senator Thomas Bienz also charged that the University of Washington was a haven for Communist subversion:

> *There isn't a student who has attended this University who has not been taught subversive activities and when they come home it is very hard for parents to change their minds. I have reports that show definitely that five professors teach subversive activities at the school and other reports that the number is as high as thirty. . . .*[9]

Senator Bienz urged an investigation into activities which "undermine the stability of our American institutions; confuse and mislead the people. . . ."[10] The legislature concurred, and seven of its members were appointed to the Committee on Un-American Activities. The Chairman, Representative Albert Canwell, announced that his committee would "investigate" Communist infiltration at the University of Washington in July, 1948.[11]

The Committee began by charging that 150 members of the university faculty were Communists or Communist sympathizers. During the klieglight hearings in Seattle's National Guard Armory with the state patrol for protection, the committee attempted to substantiate its accusations with local and imported witnesses and refused to allow the accused or their lawyers a chance to cross-examine the witnesses. Six university faculty members admitted past membership in the Communist Party. Three others refused to answer questions about affiliations, and another two, who had been named as Communists, denied that they had ever been members. Four others who were also accused of Communist Party membership refused to answer questions.[12]

When the committee gave its final report to

[5]Roger Sale, *Seattle, Past and Present* (Seattle: University of Washington Press, 1976), pp. 124, 126, 129–31; Murray Morgan, *Skid Road, An Informal Portrait of Seattle* (New York: Ballantine Books, 1960 ed.), pp. 210–14; William E. Ames and Roger A. Simpson, *Unionism or Hearst, The Post Intelligencer Strike of 1936* (Seattle: Pacific Northwest Labor History Association, 1978), pp. 89–90.

[6]Ames and Simpson, *op. cit.*, pp. 144–45.

[7]Vern Countryman, "Washington, The Canwell Committee," in *The States and Subversion*, Walter Gellhorn, ed. (Ithaca: Cornell University Press, 1952), p. 282.

[8]Fred Niendorff, "Demo–G.O.P. Coalition Plans State Red Probe," *Post Intelligencer*, December 13, 1946, p. 1.

[9]Countryman, *op. cit.*

[10]*Second Report of Un-American Activities in Washington State* (State of Washington, 1948), p. v: Countryman, *Un-American Activities in the State of Washington*, p. 22.

[11]Countryman, *op. cit*, pp. 285–287. The Committee also investigated the Washington Pension Fund in hearings during January, 1948. Examination of the press coverage of these January hearings will be included in a larger study.

[12]*Ibid.*, pp. 308–09, 311–17. See *Second Report, Un-American Activities*, pp. 328–85, 346.

the 1949 legislature, it urged further investigations into the university, citing "proof" of Communist infiltration. The legislature was not convinced, however, and refused.[13]

Methods

The following newspapers were examined for July 1948 (the hearings lasted from July 19 through 21; news articles during the month were examined to analyze coverage related to the hearings): *The Spokesman-Review* (Spokane); the *Post Intelligencer* and the *Times* (Seattle); and the *News Tribune* (Tacoma). These four papers were the state's leading daily newspapers. Also included were two Puget Sound dailies, the *Sun* (Bremerton) and the *Daily Olympian* (Olympia). Total circulation of these newspapers was 705,188; the state's population was 2.3 million in the 1950 census.

Based on secondary sources, we suspected that the press was unbalanced in its reporting of the Canwell Committee—that it prominently carried charges of Communist infiltration at the University while ignoring or minimizing rebuttals from accused faculty members. Hence, we measured three categories of coverage: direction, placement and source.

I. *Direction.* First, all sentences in news articles were coded[14] according to whether the sentence was negative, neutral or positive toward the accused faculty.

In coding the statements pertaining to the subpoenaed faculty, we used the following scheme:

1) Negative sentences were those that linked one of the accused faculty to a) the Communist Party, b) other Un-American activities (*e.g.* the U.S. Attorney General's list of front organizations) or c) implied or stated assertion that the faculty member was a fellow traveller. Negative sentences also included charges linking educators with Communism.

2) Positive statements were those absolving the accused faculty of any Un-American activity, praising the faculty or upholding academic freedom or freedom of belief.

3) Neutral statements were those which were neither negative or positive, such as "the meeting convened at 10 a.m."

II. *Placement.* The placement of the sentences was also coded, according to page (page one or inside pages). This measure was designed to mark any glaringly obvious tendency to segregate negative or positive stories to one part of the paper.

III. *Source.* Each attributed sentence was coded by source: Canwell, committee members, accused faculty, witnesses (for or against faculty), university administration or students. Only sentences clearly attributed to a particular source were coded; others were assigned to the general category "other." The purpose of this procedure was to avoid guesswork in coding which would produce inflated estimates of source orientation. We hypothesized that balanced or fair coverage would show no marked favoritism in sources used.

Findings

The Washington state press showed little sympathy for the accused faculty. Indeed, the press coverage of the Canwell Committee hearings was predominantly negative to the 11 accused professors.

1. *Direction.* A majority of *all* sentences, in *all* newspapers studied, were hostile to the sub-

[13]*Second Report, Un-American Activities*, pp. iii, iv; Countryman, "Washington, The Canwell Committee," pp. 324–25.

[14]For the present study, the two authors did all coding. The authors examined ten articles in the Seattle *Post Intelligencer* for all categories (direction, placement, and source). Reliability figures were 91% for direction, 98% for placement and 93% for source.

Table 1 *Direction of News Coverage*

	Negative	Positive	Neutral	
Seattle *Post-Intelligencer*	62.1	22.7	15.2	(N = 1069)
Seattle *Times*	62.8	18.8	18.4	(N = 927)
Tacoma *News-Tribune*	72.9	19.9	7.2	(N = 431)
Spokesman-Review	78.1	14.3	7.6	(N = 288)
Olympian	92.5	6.7	.8	(N = 133)
Bremerton *Sun*	91.8	6.2	2.0	(N = 147)

poenaed faculty (see Table 1). The *Spokesman-Review* dispatched writer Ashley Holden to Seattle to cover the hearings. During the week of the public investigation, the newspaper endorsed the committee in an editorial, "They Walk Softly: Carry Big Stick," and praised the "calm, untheatrical investigation that is thorough to the last degree," with an addition:

> *The reaction to the Canwell committee in leftist circles of the state verges on hysteria. The fact is good evidence of the havoc that the quiet, purposeful work of the committee is bringing to the Anti-American community.*[15]

When some audience members at the hearings booed Canwell, Holden dismissed them as"university students and communist sympathizers."[16] Holden also quoted at length one witness who characterized Professor Joseph Butterworth, an accused Communist, as a "character who looked like he came from skid-road, a fellow who needed a bath."[17] Holden praised the leading anti-faculty witness George Hewitt as the "most eloquent witness so far."[18] The *Post Intelligencer* included feature articles during the hearings, such as the one on July 21, 1948, entitled, "Why Educators Join Reds is a Matter for Psychiatrists."

In contrast to the *Spokesman-Review* and the *Post Intelligencer*, the Seattle *Times* attempted to be fair. The *Times* printed a variety of attacks from persons who opposed the committee, and reporter Edwin Guthman parenthetically corrected one witness after quoting his erroneous testimony.[19] Later, Guthman exposed the committee's heavy-handed tactics, especially in the case of Professor Melvin Rader, and won the 1950 Pulitzer Prize for national reporting of the Canwell hearings.[20] Despite this effort to be fair, even in 1948, the *Times*'s reporting did not differ substantially from that of other papers studied. The *Post Intelligencer* and the *Review* seemed more outspokenly suspicious or accusatory of the university, yet the *Times* coverage was equally negative (see Table 1).

II. *Placement.* The vast majority of negative statements appeared on the front page. Sentences favorable to the university generally were on the inside pages, while those attacking the accused faculty were on the front page (see Table 2).

On July 24, 1948, front page headlines in the *Post Intelligencer* included:

> Son Became Red at U,
> Attorney Tells Canwell Probe

On the bottom of page 2, that same day, however, came this headline:

> Dr. Melvin Rader Flatly Denies to Probers
> He Was Ever Red.

[15]*Spokesman-Review*, July 21, 1948.
[16]*Ibid.*
[17]*Spokesman-Review*, July 23, 1948.
[18]*Ibid.*

[19]Seattle *Times*, July 21, 1948.
[20]Countryman, *op. cit.*, pp. 331–35, 342.

Table 2 *Placement*
(Four Major State Daily Newspapers: Percentages)

	Page One			Inside Pages		
	Negative	Positive	Neutral	Negative	Positive	Neutral
Seattle *Post-Intelligencer*	33.6	4.1	4.0	28.6	18.6	11.1 (N = 1069)
Seattle *Times*	34.7	6.6	7.3	28.0	12.3	11.0 (N = 927)
Spokesman-Review	53.1	1.4	3.5	25.0	12.8	42 (N = 288)
Tacoma *News Tribune*	54.3	6.7	1.4	18.6	13.2	5.8 (N = 431)

Table 3 *Placement*
Page 1 Coverage (in percentages)

	P1	Times	TNT	S-R	DO	BS
Negative	80.4	71.4	83.0	90.0	76.0	89.0
Positive	9.9	13.3	17.0	2.9	12.0	7.5
Neutral	9.7	15.3	10.00	7.1	12.0	3.5
	(N = 446)	(N = 451)	(N = 269)	(N = 167)	(N = 102	(N = 133)

Table 4 *Sources of News Articles*

	Accused Faculty	Canwell Committee, Anti-Faculty Witnesses	Not Attributed
Seattle *Post-Intelligencer*	27.7	56.6	18.3 (N = 1069)
Seattle *Times*	24.9	67.0	8.1 (N = 927)
Tacoma *News Tribune*	12.5	85.1	2.4 (N = 431)
Spokesman-Review	11.8	57.6	30.6 (N = 288)

When front pages are considered without reference to inside pages, the placement measurement becomes more dramatic. (See Table 3.) Again, the Seattle *Times* did not differ from the other state papers, despite Guthman's coverage.

III. *Source*. Consistently, the Washington state newspapers relied on a very small number of sources, the vast preponderance of which were hostile to the accused faculty members. The sources used were those most likely to produce hostile statements toward the accused faculty. In the *Post Intelligencer*, 65% of all negative sentences came from hostile witnesses or from the Canwell committee itself; in the *Times*, 80% (N=604); 68.8% in the *Spokesman-Review* (N=250), and in the *Tacoma News Tribune* 47% (N=445). Accused faculty members generally were ignored *unless* testifying during the proceedings (see Table 4).

The press was dependent upon Canwell, his committee and its star witnesses for information. As an arm of the state legislature, the Canwell committee and its witnesses were an official institution. Canwell, for example, gladly gave interviews to reporters, and thus appeared frequently in stories. The accused, disorganized faculty lacked such official or institutional status; even the university administration did not counter the committee's charges against the faculty. Prepared press statements by the accused faculty were not printed in state newspapers.[21]

The nature of the hearings may have naturally led to a greater emphasis on anti-faculty statements. However, outside the hearing room, reporters generally still interviewed Canwell but not the accused faculty members.[22]

Discussion

The three measures (direction, placement and source) used here provide the basis for serious questioning about newspaper coverage, and cast doubt on the ability of the press to provide a "true and meaningful" account of the day's events. The first two measures could be in part expected due to the deep anxiety and post war fears of 1948. The charges of Communist infiltration were serious; reporters, editors and publishers were products of an environment burdened with the Cold War and a very real fear of Communism.

Clearly, there was little sympathy for the accused faculty. Some papers even editorially praised the work of the Canwell committee. They all used large headlines and placement at the top of the first page to report the Canwell committee's charges; rebuttals were rare and when they did appear, they were relegated to inside pages. The implications of such coverage are worthy of note. Allen Reitman in *The Pulse of Freedom*, summarized the problem of the Cold War era well:

> *The responsibility of the print media in helping create the McCarthy monster has been amply documented. Hindsight merely adds to the observation that the page-one publicity given these wild charges undoubtedly inflamed public feeling and provoked that era's easy acceptance of gross violations of free speech and due process.*[23]

The measure of source orientation provides an interesting aspect of this study. Even the Seattle *Times*, which two years later won a Pulitzer Prize award for championing those faculty unfairly accused, did not fare much differently from newspapers which stridently accused the faculty. Source orientation appears to be an important—if not the most important—determinant of news. The measures used here cannot fully trace the causal link between source orientation and news, but these measures raise this issue of source determination quite dramatically.

News became what the source said it was. Walter Lippmann wrote, in *Public Opinion*:

> *News is not a mirror of social conditions, but the report of an aspect that has obtruded itself . . . (events) do not take shape until somebody publicly in the etymological meaning of the word, makes an issue of them.*[24]

If the source is hostile, as was the case with the investigation by the Canwell committee, the

[21]For example, see Melvin Rader, *False Witness* (Seattle: University of Washington Press, 1969), pp. 64–5. Rader read a statement that he and his wife had prepared discounting Hewitt's testimony. The *P.I.* alone among the state newspapers examined carried the statement and then at the bottom of the inside page. See *Post-Intelligencer*, July 24, 1948.

[22]Coverage during the hearing, but during recesses, etc. (outside actual testimony) depended primarily on Canwell and his committee. Fifty-one percent of the *Post-Intelligencer*'s coverage came from Canwell or the anti-faculty witnesses during these recesses, and only 20% from the accused faculty members (N equals 122). In the *Times*, 79.2% came from the committee or the anti-faculty witnesses, while 20.8% came from the accused faculty (N equals 53).

[23]Allen Reitman, ed., *The Pulse of Freedom: American Liberties 1920–1970's* (New York: N.W. Norton and Co., Inc., 1975), p. 312.

[24]Walter Lippmann, *Public Opinion* (New York: The Free Press, division of MacMillan Publishing Co., 1949 copy of 1922 edition), pp. 215–16.

news is determined by forces well beyond the reporter's attempts to give a "truthful, comprehensive and intelligent account of the day's events in a context which gives them meaning."

Such paralysis may stem, in part, from the institutional nature of the press. Lippmann suggested that institutional methods for gathering news were functionally necessary:

> *Without standardization, without stereotypes, without routine judgments, without a fairly ruthless disregard of subtlety, the editor would soon die of excitement. . . . The thing could not be managed at all without systemization.*[25]

Such standardization and systemization included, in part, source orientation. Such standardization includes a preference for such official sources as members of the Canwell committee and its witnesses.

Conclusions

A generation before the Canwell hearings, Robert E. Park wrote, "We don't know much about the newspaper."[26] In the late 1940s, the functions of the newspaper in society still intrigued such scholars as Lasswell, Siebert and the members of the Hutchins Commission. In those times of political stress, the press did not provide a sympathetic or even a neutral hearing for the accused faculty members. Balanced reports may have been victims of the very real and widespread fears of the Cold War. But more importantly, the institutional, systematic method of collecting news—from sources—and particularly from institutional sources, may be the antithesis of a full and meaningful report, at least at times of crisis. The report of charges, albeit sensational ones, is not a full and meaningful account of the day's events without some consideration for rebuttal or clarification.

The press, according to the Hutchins Commission, "must be free for making its contribution to the maintenance and development of a free society. This implies that the press must also be accountable. It must be accountable to society for meeting the public need and for maintaining the rights of citizens and the almost forgotten rights of speakers who have no press. It must know that its faults and errors have ceased to be private vagaries and have become public dangers."[27]

[25] *Ibid.*, p. 222.

[26] Robert E. Park, Ernest Burgess and Roderick D. McKenzie, *The City* (Chicago: University of Chicago Press, 1967 reprint), p. 83.

[27] *Commission on Freedom of the Press*, pp. 18–19.

VII

Politics, Economics, and Professionalism in a Postwar World

By the end of the 1950s, television was the dominant form of mass media, pervading all aspects of American life. In the mid-1950s books began referring to the decade as "The Age of Television."[1] While only one-third of American homes had television in 1953, nearly 90 percent had televisions by 1960. From the June 1953 televised coronation of Queen Elizabeth II to the Army-McCarthy hearings of 1954 and election campaigns of 1956 and 1960, television viewers selected from a variety of special-event news coverage and developing entertainment programming.

Television did not, of course, replace the print media, but the expanding technology that seemed so attractive to Americans gave the print media reason to revamp their formats in the face of grave competition. From the beginning, television was controversial. While radio had sparked debate about intrusiveness versus mastery, television seemed more mesmerizing and more intrusive. Educators, politicians, and journalists debated its effects. Would it enhance or destroy the political process? Would it lower morals? Would the business aspects of the huge industry insidiously invade interpretation of news?

By the end of the 1950s, media were big business. As television survived its last government freeze on technology at the end of 1952, the networks struggled to fill empty broadcast hours by developing programming that would entice a wide audience of viewers and advertisers. CBS and NBC dominated the ratings, but ABC gained some additional recognition by the end of the decade. By the beginning of the 1970s newspaper groups or chains accounted for one-half the nation's dailies and two-thirds of its circulation. The intimate connection of big media business and government evoked concerns similar to those expressed during the late nineteenth century about the interplay between business and politics and set the stage for questions about entertainment content and coverage of political affairs. Although newspapers represented big business in much the same way as television did, more attention focused on television because of the connection of parent industries to the military-industrial complex and because of its pervasive influence in American life through entertainment as well as news production. Critics questioned whether network ownership by defense-contracting parent companies and the interlocking responsibilities of network and newspaper executives altered either the approach to or the content of coverage of such issues as civil rights and the Vietnam War.[2] Increasingly, critics questioned whether television entertainment content served to preserve the parent industries' status quo. Oddly enough, just as these critics concerned themselves with the conservative influence of television, others criticized the media in general for opposing authority and challenging government decision-making.

The early days of television provoked optimistic predictions about the medium's impact on mass culture. In 1953, NBC's president Sylvester L. Weaver, Jr., described programs that "serve the grand design of television, which is to create an aristocracy of the people, the proletariat of privilege, the Athenian masses—to make the average man the uncommon man."[3] By the end of the decade Weaver and his grand design had been replaced at NBC. In 1961, Newton Minow, speaking to the National Association of Broadcasters, reflected the pessimism of the decade, "I invite you," he said, "to sit down in front of your television set when your station goes on the air and stay there without a book, magazine, newspaper, profit-and-loss sheet or rating book to distract you—and keep your eyes glued to that set until the station signs off. I can assure you that you will observe a vast wasteland."[4]

In "Television in the 'Golden Age': An Entrepreneurial Experiment," the selection here that describes what some refer to as the "Golden Age of Television," James L. Baughman describes the market forces at work that first created, then ended, an era of innovation. Television at first adapted much of its programming from successful radio series; the motion picture industry resisted all overtures, pinning its hopes on pay television that would grant the movie industry more control over use of films than the networks would guarantee. In addition, live anthologies combined with spectaculars, and innovative news programs such as Ed Murrow's "See It Now," provided exceptional fare for early television. Between 1956 and 1958, however, many of the live shows were canceled and replaced with situation comedies, crime series, and quiz shows. At the end of the decade Murrow decried the "decadence, escapism and insulation" of television content. Baughman concludes that competition between networks during the early years of the decade, the challenge to defeat the threat of pay television, and the need to program for a new medium promoted the development of superior programming. By 1958 the market was nearly saturated, growth rates of advertising were leveling off, and the industry decided to contain costs rather than spend lavishly on expensive programming.

Just as the "golden age of television" was declining, television news was becoming institutionalized in the evening news format. The reassuring Walter Cronkite became CBS's anchor, replacing World War II's more controversial commentators, although the fifteen minutes of news provided did little to encourage in-depth coverage. In 1963, the same year that the United States committed 12,000 advisers and $400 million in assistance to Vietnam, NBC and CBS extended the news program to thirty minutes. This was the first war in which the United States suffered defeat, and the television camera went to cover it. It was widely believed, wrote Michael Mandelbaum, that the coverage was the cause of the defeat.[5] Richard Nixon, writing his memoirs, blamed the media for creating a "serious demoralization of the home front, raising the question of whether America would ever again be able to fight an enemy abroad with unity and strength of purpose at home."[6] Mandelbaum argued that television had little to do with the war but it was possible that the recognition that many citizens opposed the war did have an effect. "The United States lost the war in Vietnam because the American public was not willing to pay the cost of winning, or avoiding losing. The people's decision that the war was not worth these costs had nothing to do with the fact that they learned about it from television. Whether it was based on the fact that many of their fellow citizens were vehemently opposed to the war, which they also learned from television, is difficult to say. It is possible that it was not. It is possible that the public would have reached the same judgment in the same way over the same period of time—that is, that the war would have followed the course it did—even if the cathode ray tube had never been invented."[7]

In "The Media, the War in Vietnam, and Political Support: A Critique of the Thesis of an Oppositional Media," the selection on Vietnam, Daniel C. Hallin states clearly that his purpose is to counter the thesis that media during the 1960s and 1970s shifted toward "an oppositional relation to political authority." He points out that a decline of public confidence in American institutions has been documented for the period, but that despite this decline Americans continued to express a high level of faith in the system. Testing his thesis about media coverage and political culture, Hallin examines a sample of newscasts between 1965 and 1973, arguing that television coverage was quite favorable to administration policy before the Tet offensive of 1968 but that it grew considerably less favorable after that point. Although journalists were indeed more willing to be critical in the late 1960s and 1970s than they had been in early 1961 when the *New York Times* agreed to suppress stories of the Bay of Pigs invasion, Hallin claims that no substantial change in journalistic ideology took place. The "professional ideology of objective journalism and the intimate institutional connection between the media and government which characterized American journalism before the turbulence of the sixties and seventies both persisted more or less unchanged," Hallin argues.

Hallin also rejects the idea that coverage reflected society, arguing that increased negative coverage cannot be attributed to a change in the course of events. Rather, he notes, the change must be explained as a "reflection of and a response to a collapse of consensus—especially elite consensus—on foreign policy." As an establishment institution, Hallin contends, television reported the lack of consensus about the war as it moved from the sphere of the illegitimate to the sphere of legitimate controversy. When only antiwar activists protested the war, television responded gingerly, but when authority figures such as congressmen and businessmen joined the protest, television increasingly covered oppositional viewpoints that reflected the breakdown of consensus.

James Boylan, whose article "Declarations of Independence" appears here, does not agree that institutional ideology remained the same throughout the period, at least for print media. Boylan's account covers more than a study of Vietnam news and reflects his knowledge of reporters and the news business. It is a study from within, rather than without, and therefore provides interesting nuances about changes in the newsroom while also being subject to the biases that can produce. Boylan argues that newspaper journalism in the 1950s was mired "in a creed of impenetrable smug." It was a press that had spoken out only timidly and sporadically against Joseph McCarthy's anticommunism purge and that had cooperated with the government to keep major stories secret, such as that of the Bay of Pigs. It is surprising, writes Boylan, that by the 1960s the press was able to view itself "as an apparently potent, apparently adversary press." Boylan attributes the shift to changes in leadership at several of the nation's elite newspapers, a change that emphasized reporting over editing and encouraged "allegiance to standards considered superior to those of the organization and its parochial limitations."

Boylan dates the changes in reporting on Vietnam to 1961, several years before Hallin begins his study. With the arrival of the *New York Times*'s correspondent Homer Bigart in Vietnam, press coverage became more critical, according to Boylan, and he recalls President John F. Kennedy's 1963 attempt to remove another *Times* reporter, David Halberstam. These reporters came to reject the idea, notes Boylan, "that they were in any sense part of the American 'team' in Vietnam." Analyses of journalists of the period support Boylan's arguments that reporters prided themselves on a high degree of autonomy and rejected at least some of the ideology of objective journalism.[8]

With the end of the Vietnam War in the early 1970s and increasing criticism of government and media institutions, reporter power declined under efforts by editors to regain credibility. By 1982 journalists indicated they felt significantly less autonomy in their jobs and had less freedom to determine the emphasis of their stories than they had in 1971.[9]

Endnotes

1. See Leo Bogart, *The Age of Television*. See also Christopher Sterling and John Kittross, who entitle a chapter "The Age of Television (1952–1960)" in *Stay Tuned: A Concise History of American Broadcasting*, 2d ed. (Belmont Calif.: Wadsworth, 1990).
2. See Herbert Schiller, *Mass Communications and the American Empire* (New York: Augustus M. Kelley, Publishers, 1969).
3. Sylvester Weaver, "Television 1953: The Case for the Networks," *Television Magazine* 10 (January): 17; address by Weaver, June 15, 1953, Broadcast Pioneers Library, Washington, D.C., File 179, p. 16, cited in Baughman, reprinted here.
4. Newton N. Minow to NAB Convention, 1961, cited in Christopher Sterling and John Kittross, 316.
5. Michael Mandelbaum, "Vietnam: The Television War," *Daedalus* 3:4 (Fall 1982): 157.
6. Richard Nixon, *The Memoirs* (New York: Grosset & Dunlap, 1978), p. 350, cited in Daniel Hallin, *The Uncensored War: The Media and Vietnam* (New York: Oxford University Press, 1986), 3.

7. Mandelbaum, 167.
8. See John W. C. Johnstone, Edward J. Slawski, and William W. Bowman, *The News People: A Sociological Portrait of American Journalists and Their Work* (Urbana: University of Illinois Press, 1976).
9. See David Weaver and G. Cleveland Wilhoit, *American Journalists* (Bloomington: Indiana University Press, 1986).

Television in the "Golden Age": An Entrepreneurial Experiment

James L. Baughman

In recent years historians have begun to include mass culture among those areas considered worthy of research and analysis. For generations, "cultural history" denoted intellectual or literary history, the lives and thought of great writers and thinkers in discourse with each other, and not those communicating with the masses. Although James Gordon Bennett was far more likely to be read in the 1840s than Ralph Waldo Emerson, the study of the transcendentalist was much more likely to be regarded as a legitimate scholarly exercise; Bennett's life, until recently, was left to amateurs who had, to be generous, little sense of historical scholarship. Similarly, weighty digressions on Henry Adams were far more common among historians of the late nineteenth century than discussions of Joseph Pulitzer and William Randolph Hearst, even though these publishers reached many more contemporaries than Adams and his Lafayette Square circle.[1]

Yet it is precisely the size of the audience that Pulitzer and others reached that may lead historians into difficulty. Although few historians claim so much for the life of the mind as Perry Miller and others did a generation ago, students of mass communications may commit their own heresy. The very popularity of the works they analyze can cause them to infer too much. A specific film or broadcast program, they may argue, "mirrors" American values at a given point, when, in fact, it may say far more about the operators of a medium than their audience.[2]

[1]Daniel W. Howe, "Descendants of Perry Miller," *American Quarterly* 34 (Spring 1982): 91; Gene Wise, " 'Paradigm Dramas' in American Studies: A Cultural and Institutional History of the Movement," *ibid.* 31 (Bibliographic Issue, 1979): 306–07, 314; Jennifer Tebbe, "Print and American Culture, *ibid.* 32 (Bibliographical Issue, 1980): 259–79; Robert Sklar, review of *The Manipulators*, by Robert Sobel, *Journal of American History* 64 (September 1977); 44; Thomas Cripps, review of *Television Fraud*, by Kent Anderson, *ibid.* 66 (March 1980): 988; Garth S. Jowett, "Toward a History of Communication," *Journalism History* 2 (Summer 1975): 35; Alan Havig, "Radio and American Life," *Reviews in American History* 8 (September 1980): 403; Raymond Williams, "Culture is Ordinary," in Norman Mackenzie et al., *Conviction* (New York, 1959), 74–92; Elizabeth L. Eisenstein, *The Printing Press as an Agent of Change*, 2 vols., (New York, 1979), 1:25–39; Michael Kammen, letter to *New York Times Book Review*, 18 March 1979, 40, and introduction to *The Past Before Us: Contemporary Historical Writing in the United States* (Ithaca, 1980), 41–42; Arthur M. Schlesinger, Jr., "Foreword," to John E. O'Connor and Martin A. Jackson, eds., *American History/American Film: Interpreting the Hollywood Image* (New York, 1979); Stephen J. Whitfield, "The Eggheads and the Fatheads," *Change*, April 1978, 66.

[2]Works utilizing the mirror theory abound. See Kathryn Weibel, *Mirror, Mirror: Images of Women Reflected in Popular Culture* (New York, 1977); O'Connor and Jackson, *passim*; Havig, 405–06; J. Fred MacDonald, *Don't Touch That Dial! Radio Programming in American Life, 1920–1960* (Chicago, 1979), x; Louis Galambos, *The Public Image of Big Business in America, 1880–1940* (Baltimore, 1975); Richard L. Merritt, *Symbols of American Community, 1735–1775* (New Haven,

Indeed, much of the content of the American mass media has related not to consumer preference but to managerial imperatives. Various production factors and costs along with the state of technology have bound the mass communicator in deciding what material could be offered. This is not to say that the popular preference has been irrelevant, or that Say's Law truly applied to the penny presses of the 1830s and to the radio soap operas of the 1930s. Rather, it is only to caution students of mass culture. Before too much is made of an individual presentation, management's reasons for rendering such fare as opposed to other types must be appreciated.[3] On the other hand, though the exploration of separate programs can be laden with difficulties, an entire era or period in mass communication history can be "explained" in part by recognizing the objectives of and obstacles to the mass communicator.[4]

A case in point is the first decade of American television. Between 1948 and 1958, network programmers experimented with new ways of informing and entertaining while adapting from older media more traditional fare. For many viewers, critics, and participants, TV's first ten years seemed "a Golden Age." "These are great days," NBC President Sylvester L. Weaver, Jr. remarked in 1953 of the newest medium. He described programs that "serve the grand design of television, which is to create an aristocracy of the people, the proletariat of privilege, the Athenian masses—to make the average man the uncommon man."[5] Weaver and others encouraged innovative forms of entertainment that created a sense of optimism about the possibilities of mass culture. In the middle Fifties, observed Erik Barnouw, "Things were happening in television. There was a sense of exploration and achievement."[6]

Although the new medium included programs panned at the time and quickly forgotten (*Trash? or Treasure!, Your Hit Parade*), strung together with awkwardly managed commercials, there were self-conscious attempts to create new and higher forms of entertainment.[7] TV's "dramatic anthology" offered live and original teleplays, with a different cast and setting each week. Most of these originated from New York, the center of the nation's theater and, arguably, of its culture. Chicago's network-owned stations produced for regional and national distribution a range of programs graced with a spe-

1966); Michael Wood, *America in the Movies* (New York, 1975). A variation of the "mirror theory" is the application of Gramsci's theory of cultural hegemony, which assumes the autonomy of the mass media manager over content. See Douglas Kellner, "Network Television and American Society: Introduction to a Critical Theory of Television," *Theory and Society* 10 (1981) 31–62; T.J. Jackson Lears, "From Salvation to Self-Realization: Advertising and the Therapeutic Roots of the Consumer Culture, 1880–1930," in Richard Fox and Lears, eds., *The Culture of Consumption: Critical Essays in American History 1880–1980* (New York, 1983), 3–38.

[3]David Paul Nord, "An Economic Perspective on Formula in Popular Culture," *Journal of American Culture* 3 (Spring 1980): 17–28; Raymond Williams, *Television: Technology and Cultural Form* (New York, 1975), chap. 1; Williams, "The Press and Popular Culture: An Historical Perspective," in George Boyce et al., eds., *Newspaper History: From the Seventeenth Century to the Present Day* (London, 1978), 41–50.

[4]For similar efforts see Stephen Botein, "Printers and the American Revolution," in Bernard Bailyn and John B. Hench, eds., *The Press and the American Revolution* (Worcester, 1980) 59–98; Philip Elliott, "Professional Ideology and Organizational Change: The Journalist Since 1800," in Boyce et al., 172–91.

[5]Weaver, "Television 1953: The Case for the Networks," *Television Magazine* 10, January 1953, 17; address by Weaver, 15 June 1953, Broadcast Pioneers Library [or BPL], Washington, D.C. File 179: 16.

[6]Docket 12782, vol. 14, *Proc.*, vol. 36, p. 5332, vol. 16, *Proc.*, vol. 43, pp. 6499, 6500, Federal Communications Commission Records, Commission Dockets Room. See also Gore Vidal, "Writing Plays for Television," *New World Writing* 10 (1956), reprinted in *Homage to Daniel Shays* (New York, 1972), 27–33; Robert Saudek, "The Coming Breakthrough," *Television Magazine* 12, October 1955, 34–35, 89; Hubbell Robinson, address, 18 May 1966, Robinson Papers, State Historical Society of Wisconsin.

[7]William E. Leuchtenburg, *The Troubled Feast*, rev. ed. (Boston, 1979), 114; Charles C. Alexander, *Holding the Line: The Eisenhower Era, 1952–1961* (Bloomington, 1975), 138; Douglas T. Miller and Marion Nowak, *The Fifties: The Way We Really Were* (Garden City, N.Y., 1977), chap. 13.

cial, wry "Chicago style." Such series as *Kukla, Fran, and Ollie* and *Dave Garroway and Friends* enjoyed fine critical reception. First NBC, then CBS, promoted "spectaculars"—special programs of 90 to 120 minutes—that came over live and consisted of original or adapted work. On NBC, Mary Martin played *Peter Pan* and Laurence Olivier's feature film, *Richard III*, premiered on television before its release to American motion picture houses.

Finally, the networks offered public affairs programming that combined the visual impact of the newsreel and photograph with the immediacy of radio news. In 1951 and again in 1954, controversial congressional committee hearings, telecast live, gave millions their first look at their national legislature. CBS's *See It Now* and NBC's *The Today Show* put the world in the living room, with the latter program altering many early morning rituals. Commenting on the informational program *Omnibus*, choreographer Agnes de Mille spoke of "my own realization that nowhere else in the world could I go to find this."[8]

Crime series like *Dragnet* and *Mr. District Attorney* and situation comedies like *I Love Lucy* and *Beulah* flourished, yet there was also space on the schedule, whether in evening prime time or on Sunday afternoons, for other types of fare. These, in turn, often possessed certain production "values" that added to the uniqueness of TV's first decade. Television relied heavily on live programming, originally weekly dramas, entertainment from Chicago and New York, extended coverage of congressional hearings, and long, costly, live spectaculars of dramatic and music hall fare. Like many radio-TV critics, Jack Gould of *The New York Times* abhorred much of what passed for programming in the 1950s. But the appearance of live drama and informational programming helped to reconcile him to the newest medium. "Television will always be a medium of compromise," he wrote in May, 1955. "It's the nature of the beast. It must appeal to the largest audience it can get. This may put good minority programs [appealing to small audiences] at bad hours. But the overall effect of television on the country has been beneficial.[9]

By the end of the 1950s, most of what had distinguished early television had all but disappeared. Programs like *Omnibus* and *See It Now* left the air; congressional hearings were no longer aired extensively. Although the amount of news programming did rise after the 1958–59 season, the networks invested most time and money into short evening newscasts.[10] The networks also sharply reduced the number of spectaculars and dramatic anthologies, while the surviving ones originated not live from New York but on film from Hollywood. More of the schedule, all told, went to those program types already on the air—situation comedies and action melodramas—most with a standard cost and setting.[11] Little room remained by 1959 for that which could not be quickly constructed on a studio assembly line.

Rather than mourn the passing of a Golden Age, however, or take a mirror to its programming, it is worth asking why between 1948 and 1958 an American commercial mass medium had bothered to commit such creative and financial resources in the first place. Network radio in the late 1940s had not been a large artis-

[8]Quoted in Walter Kerr, *The Decline of Pleasure* (New York, 1962), 5.

[9]*New York Times*, 17 May 1955. See also Jay Nelson Tuck, New York *Post*, 11 April 1956; David Manning White, "What's Happening to Mass Culture," *Saturday Review* 39, 3 November 1956, 11–13.

[10]See programming data in Lawrence W. Lichty and Malachi C. Topping, eds., *American Broadcasting* (New York, 1975), 436ff. See also Raymond L. Carroll, "Economic Influences on Commercial Network Television Documentary Scheduling," *Journal of Broadcasting* 23 (Fall, 1979): 411–25.

[11]Joseph R. Dominick and Millard C. Pearce, "Trends in Network Prime-Time Programming," *Journal of Communication* 26 (Winter 1976): 70–80; Richard Austin Smith, "TV: The Light That Failed," *Fortune* 58, December 1958, 78–81.

tic repository.[12] Few contemporaries then likened that medium, as one anthology writer did TV in 1956, to "Athens in the days when the entire city would come to watch a new play by Aristophanes."[13]

Much of TV's more ambitious programming in the early Fifties, some have incorrectly maintained, merely reflected an upper-class bias in television set ownership. Because the well-to-do were supposedly the most likely to own a set, programs like *Goodyear Theatre* served this disproportionately upper-class audience.[14] Data on set ownership, however, belies this contention. Except for the first two years, TV set ownership was not highly correlated with income. But geography was a factor. People in less-populous areas in the West and South were among the last to have television service, but mainly due to their distance from TV stations. Otherwise, most Americans bought sets eagerly, often before their communities had adequate reception. One survey of New Brunswick indicated that only ministers and college professors resisted the TV boom. Indeed, in some neighborhoods TV became so popular that some status-conscious residents, forced to put off the purchase of a first TV set, had antennas installed atop their homes so to seem part of the enveloping trend.[15]

The upper-class audience argument similarly suffers when TV's history is compared to radio's. Broadcast historians agree that radio enjoyed a "Golden Age" of dramatic and informational programming in the late 1930s.[16] That epoch occurred, however, precisely when most Americans had finally secured their first radio receivers. Into the middle 1930s, up to one-third of all American households, many in rural areas without electrification, had lacked a set.[17]

A somewhat different reason offered for TV's early distinctiveness concerned the magnanimity of the network's managers. The more romantic interpreters of television's past contend that industry leaders initially held to a standard of service characterized by the airing of not only less profitable informational programming, but by creative risk-taking in entertainment as well. Over time, the temptations of advertisers corrupted these same individuals, who came to look increasingly for maximum ratings and revenues at the expense of many "golden age" programs. "Bill Paley became a more and more mercantile figure," observes

[12]Charles C. Alexander, *Nationalism in American Thought, 1930–1945* (Chicago, 1969), 212–13; Arthur Wertheim, *Radio Comedy* (New York, 1979), 380–81.

[13]Docket 12782, vol. 14, *Proc.*, vol. 36, p. 5376, vol. 38, p. 5832. For a critical analysis of the anthologies see Kenneth Hey, "*Marty*: Aesthetics vs. Medium in Early Television Drama," in John E. O'Connor, ed., *American History/American Television* (New York, 1983), 95–133.

[14]Les Brown, *Television: The Business Behind the Box* (New York, 1971), 154; Russ Wetzsteon, "Get Television Out of Hollywood," *Channels of Communication* 2, September-October 1982, 43.

[15]Leo Bogart, *The Age of Television*, rev. ed. (New York, 1958), chap. 1; William Zinsser, "Out Where the Tall Antennas Grow," *Harper's* 212, April 1956, 36–37; Thomas F. Dernburg, "Consumer Response to Innovation," in Dernburg et al., *Studies in Household Economic Behavior* (New Haven, 1958), 1–50; Alfred Oxenfeldt, "A Dynamic Element in Consumption: The TV Industry," in Lincoln H. Clark, ed., *Consumer Behavior: Research on Consumer Reactions* (New York, 1958), 420–41; Charles A. Siepmann, *Radio, Television and Society* (New York, 1950), 337–39; Groucho Marx to Fred Allen, 20 March 1950, Box 1, Marx Papers, Library of Congress; Wilbur Schramm et al., *Television in the Lives of Our Children* (Stanford, 1961), chap. 1; Edward R. McDonagh, "Television and the Family," *Sociology and Social Research* 35, November-December 1950, 121; Bernard B. Smith, "Television: There Ought to be a Law," *Harper's* 197, September 1948, 35; Charles E. Swanson and R.D. Jones, "Television Owning and Its Correlates," *Journal of Applied Psychology* 35 (October 1951): 352–57.

[16]MacDonald, 53–55; Alexander, *Nationalism in American Thought*, 95–98; Erik Barnouw, *A History of Broadcasting in the United States*, 3 vols. (1965–70), 2: 55–154; David H. Culbert, *News for Everyman: Radio and Foreign Affairs in Thirties America* (Westport, Conn., 1976), chap. 1; John Houseman, *Run-Through: A Memoir* (New York, 1972), 359–71.

[17]MacDonald, 60–61; Alexander, *Nationalism in American Thought*, 94; William E. Leuchtenburg, *Franklin D. Roosevelt and the New Deal* (New York, 1963), 157–58.

one popular writer of CBS's owner. "Superprofit negated quality."[18]

Yet television's managers *always* set their schedules with the goal of larger profits and markets. The men responsible for the great radio ratings war of 1947–1950—what one contemporary termed "one of the greatest fights for leadership industry has experienced for many years."[19]—did not become altruists with television between 1950 and 1958. Rather, a set of entrepreneurial imperatives (and not high-mindedness) first created and then closed the Golden Age of Television.

At the outset television's executives were beset by a number of problems, the answers to which helped to give a golden cast to early TV. Each of these difficulties tended to relate to a natural quest for a steady supply of programming that would assure vast audiences and substantial advertisers. The availability of sources for programming between 1948 and 1958 left the networks more at the mercy of Broadway than Sunset Boulevard. Furthermore, advertisers' demands for time, as well as the networks' determination to curb the sponsors' powers over that programming which they did air, brought a different alignment. Finally, rivalries between networks that before 1948 in radio or after 1958 in television might foster more of the same, encouraged more diverse and unusual programming in TV's first decade.[20]

The initial and overriding concern of all networks was to have a large quantity of programming. This was a formidable task given the background of the industry's leaders. With the advent of TV, two companies, CBS and NBC, dominated broadcasting with far more stations for affiliates and capital for programs.[21] These entities combined produced some 160 hours of programming. Yet virtually all of the managers of the then four networks—including the weak Du Mont and ABC chains—had worked only in radio. Their experience had been in the programming of sound, not of sight. "The demand for low-cost film productions made especially for television," remarked an United Artists executive in January, 1949, "is unquestionable."[22]

Nevertheless, early TV borrowed from radio more than from any other medium. Established radio players and programs simply changed frequencies. Fulton J. Sheen, Jack Benny, George Burns, Gracie Allen, and Arthur Godfrey had developed their program formats and style over radio.[23] *Amateur Hour, Sky King, Truth or Conse-*

[18]David Halberstam, "CBS: The Power and the Profits," *Atlantic* 237, January 1976, 38, 44; *idem., The Powers That Be* (New York, 1979), *passim*; Alexander Kendrick, *Prime Time: The Life of Edward R. Murrow* (Boston, 1969), 412–25, 513–15, chap. 11.

[19]George M. Burbach to Joseph Pulitzer, II, memorandum, 20 June 1949, Box 109, Pulitzer Papers, Library of Congress.

[20]Two studies, one of the NBC News Division and the other of managerial practices generally, have helped to shape the analysis of management that follows. Edward Jay Epstein, *News from Nowhere: Television and the News* (New York, 1973); E.A.G. Robinson, *The Structure of Competitive Industry* (Cambridge, 1931).

[21]In 1955, Du Mont ceased network operations. ABC remained a competitor, though still at some distance from the Big Two. That year, 11.2 percent of all TV stations were affiliated with ABC compared to 33.8 percent for Columbia and 46 percent for NBC. In gross time sales to advertisers, ABC held a 12.6 percent share to CBS's 46.5 and NBC's 40.2 percent. House Committee on Interstate and Foreign Commerce, *Network Broadcasting:* Report No. 1297, 85th Cong., 2d. sess., 1958, 203–05; Columbia Broadcasting System, *Network Practices* (New York, 1956), 96; Christopher H. Sterling and John M. Kittross, *Stay Tuned* (Belmont, Calif., 1978), 515.

[22]John Mitchell to William Roach, memorandum, 11 January 1949, Mitchell to Paul Lazarus, Jr., draft of memoranda, 12 September 1948, Record Group 2, Box 52, United Artists Papers, State Historical Society of Wisconsin; notes of interview with Hubbell Robinson, n.d., "TV Notebook," Box 63, Martin Mayer Papers, Columbia University; Robinson, "Television Faces Life," *Esquire* 43, January 1955, 56.

[23]Radio Daily, *The 1948 Radio Annual* (New York, 1948), 961–91; Wertheim, 390–95; *The 1952 Radio Annual* (New York, 1952), 1237–264; Rudolf Arnheim, "The World of the Daytime Serial," in Paul F. Lazarsfeld and Frank N. Stanton, eds., *Radio Research, 1942–1943* (New York, 1944), 34–107; Max Wylie, ed., *Best Broadcasts of 1939–40* (New York, 1940), 111–30, 169–84, 185–202; Ben Gross, *I Looked and I Listened;*

quences, *The Lone Ranger*, *Sergeant Preston*, *Death Valley Days*, *Our Miss Brooks*, *Ozzie and Harriet*, *Gunsmoke*, and *The Life of Riley* all began on radio. *Lux Radio Theater* became *Lux Video Theatre*. In January of 1951, ABC President Robert Kintner wrote that TV "has copied radio, its older brother, in countless ways."[24]

One of radio's legacies was that programming should be aired live. From the earliest days of network radio, producers had assumed that viewers preferred live originations. Part of radio's initial allure had been the simultaneous transmissions of events and entertainment. Moreover, a 1929 Federal Radio Commission rule required stations to announce any recorded program as a "transcription,"[25] which came to have a negative connotation. Columbia discarded one of its most popular radio players, Bing Crosby, when the self-conscious crooner demanded that his performances be taped and edited before broadcast.[26] Seeking to buy the hard-pressed American Broadcasting Company, Leonard Goldenson of United Paramount Theatres told the FCC in March, 1952, "I think the real vitality in the future of television is in live television."[27]

In June, 1953, eighty-two percent of all network programming came over live, and rose to eighty-seven percent two years later.[28] Slip-ups might occur, participants acknowledged, but "the live hour or ninety minute dramatic hour," TV writer Rod Sterling contended, "has a feeling of theatre, a spontaneity and an immediacy that a filmed show can never hope to duplicate."[29] "Useful as film may be," commented Frank Stanton of CBS in March, 1958, "it is the live quality, the sense of seeing the actual event or performance taking place before your eyes, that is the real magic of television. To confine television largely to film is to confine its excitement, scope, and impact."[30] One television critic recalled of the early years, "It was the most exciting period in the history of television, mainly because it was live."[31]

As in the days of radio, early television aired some programs from Chicago as well as from New York and Hollywood.[32] Initially, Chicago's television originations had more to do with technical problems than with broadcast tradition. Before direct connections could be made between a network and its affiliates for simultaneous transmission, AT&T had to lay a special coaxial cable. Until then, stations in Chicago and in middle western, far western, and southern markets had to produce a higher percentage of their own programs.[33] In most areas, this exercise in localism elicited little critical atten-

Informal Recollections of Radio and TV (New York, 1954), 124, 161–62; Bart Andrews, *The Story of I Love Lucy* (New York, 1977), 29.

24Robert Kintner, "The Main Entrance," *Variety*, 3 January 1951, 98; *New York Times*, 19 October 1952; handwritten notes from meeting with CBS executive officers, 6 October 1958, 2–3, FCC Office of Network Study, Box 15, GSA Invoice No. 72-A-1986, FCC Records; Dan Wakefield, "The Fabulous Sweat Box," *Nation* 184, 30 March 1957, 270; William S. Paley, *As It Happened: A Memoir* (New York, 1979), 23lff; Docket 12782, vol. 11, *Proc.*, vol. 23, 4292–93; *Business Week*, 10 March 1956, 80; New York *Herald Tribune TV-Radio Magazine*, 18 October 1958, 9–10.

25FRC General Order 78, 5 December 1929, cited in C. Joseph Pusateri, *Enterprise in Radio: WWL and the Business of Broadcasting in America* (Washington, 1980), 82; Judith C. Waller, *Radio: The Fifth Estate* (Cambridge, Mass., 1944), chap. 10; E.P.J. Shurick, *The First Quarter Century of American Broadcasting* (Kansas City, 1946), 172–74; NBC, *Responsibility: A Working Manual of NBC Program Policies* (New York, 1948), 22.

26Wertheim, 275.

27Docket 10031, vol. 12, Proc., vol. 44, p. 6866 FCC Records, National Archives.

28*Broadcasting Yearbook 1963* (Washington, D.C., 1963), 20.

29Rod Serling, "TV in the Can vs. TV in the Flesh," *New York Times Magazine*, 24 November 1957, 54; *New York Times*, 24 July 1981.

30Docket 12258, *Proc.*, p. 255, FCC Records, Box 8, GSA Invoice No. 72-A-1986.

31Kay Gardella, New York *Daily News*, 20 August 1980.

32In 1944, for example, NBC produced programs from Omaha, Canada, Chicago, Hollywood, Washington and Hartford. FCC, *Public Service Responsibilities of Broadcast Licensees* (1946), 8–9.

33The live network product in those areas came late on film. "Kinescoped quiz and panel shows caused Dallas girl to remark, 'Why do those New York women run around in strapless ballgowns in broad daylight?' " *Variety*, 7 January 1953, 97.

tion. But Chicago's greater cultural resources helped stations there to meet the challenge better than most. Indeed, the networks picked up some of the Second City programs, meant at first only for local consumption, for national telecasting. The curator of the Lincoln Park Zoo, Marlin Perkins, hosted *Zoo Parade*. The Chicago *Tribune*'s station, WGN, produced *Down You Go*, a quiz program moderated by Professor Bergen Evans of Northwestern University, later telecast by Du Mont and ABC. In 1950, Chicago's WNBQ provided NBC six hours of national network programming per week, including *Kukla, Fran, and Ollie* and *Mr. Wizard*, children's programs that won national air time and critical applause.[34] Critics spoke of a "Chicago touch," a creative, detached, and continually bemused style quite apart from that of New York or southern California.[35] Other cities had their local TV personalities and programs absorbed by the national networks,[36] but Chicago offered the most. Irv Kupcinet, Second City columnist and occasional performer, boasted in January, 1951, "There are more important television experiments being conducted in Chicago than anywhere else in the country."[37]

Far more than the Second City, early television looked to Hollywood and the motion picture industry as an obvious source for programs. Most film companies, however, avoided any arrangement with the networks. Motion picture makers regarded TV as the enemy, a rival for the entertainment dollar. For some six years Jack Warner not only refused to deal with the new competition, but banned TV sets from the Warner Brothers lot. Harry Cohn of Columbia Pictures and Robert Kintner of ABC literally exchanged blows over Cohn's unwillingness to provide series for Kintner's network.[38] Many feature films, including all of those released after 1948, were not available for use on TV.[39]

Some movie executives waited for the spread of pay television systems.[40] Tested by Paramount, RKO, and Zenith in 1951, these processes transmitted programming after users inserted coins in a box (an NBC attorney called them "slot machines") atop their sets.[41] Producer Sam Goldwyn declared in November, 1952 that "pay TV is where the wedding between motion pictures and television will come." One pay television promoter wrote in February, 1954, "I am sure that you have well in mind the potentialities of showing over Subscriber-Vision some of the all-time top grossers."[42]

Hollywood's gamble on pay television forced

[34]Notebook, WBKB, Balaban & Katz Television Theatre, n.d., c. 1949, includes descriptions of Chicago TV originations, copy in Box 10 of Sterling Quinlan Papers, Boston University; Anthony Michael Maltese, "A Descriptive Study of Children's Programming on Major American Television Networks From 1950 Through 1964," (Ph.D. diss., Ohio University, 1967) 162–65; Joel Sternberg, "Television Town," *Chicago History* 4 (Summer, 1975): 108–17.

[35]Harriet Van Horne, "The Chicago Touch," *Theatre Arts* 35 (July, 1951), 36–39; John Crosby, New York *Herald Tribune*, 6 January 1952; Maltese, 152–55; Ted Mills to Robert E. Lee, 1 March 1962, Docket 14546, vol. 1, and *Proc.*, vol. 1, pp. 144, 175, FCC Records, NA.

[36]Fireman, ed., 92; House Select Committee on Small Business, *Activities of Regulatory and Enforcement Agencies Relating to Small Business*, Hearings, 1966, 89th Cong., 2d sess., 588; Vincent Terrace, *The Complete Encyclopedia of Television Programs 1947–1976*, 2 vols. (South Brunswick, N.J., 1976), 1: 52, 17–18.

[37]*Variety*, 10 January 1951, 26, 42; *ibid.*, 27 May 1953, 32–33; Robert Lewis Shayon, "Toynbee TV and Chicago," *Christian Science Monitor*, 3 June 1950.

[38]Tino Balio, *United Artists: The Company Built By the Stars* (Madison, 1976), 224; Erik Barnouw, 2:61–62; notes of interview with Robert Kintner, n.d., "TV Notebook," Mayer Papers.

[39]Gerald Mast, *A Short History of the Movies*, 2d ed. (Indianapolis, 1976), 326.

[40]*New York Times*, 19 February 1954; Robert Sklar, *Movie-Made America: A Cultural History of American Movies* (New York, 1975), 277–78.

[41]NBC, "Comments," 6 June 1955, 8, 18, Docket 11279, FCC Records, NA; John Chamberlain, "Pay-As-You-See TV?" *Barron's*, 2 May 1955, 3, 23–24; *Newsweek*, 11 January 1954, 74–75; Bogart, 310–316; Robert Denton to James P. Hagerty, 16 February 1954, General Files 129-A-2, Box 1003, Dwight D. Eisenhower Papers, Eisenhower Library; King Vidor, *A Tree is a Tree* (New York, 1953), 282–83.

[42]Arthur Levy to Matthew Fox, 19 February 1954, James M. Landis Papers, Library of Congress; New York *Herald Tribune*, 6 November 1952; NBC, "Comments," 10.

the networks to seek alternative sources for programming. New York, with its reservoir of available talent in the legitimate theater and night clubs, was the most obvious starting point. Hence, NBC and CBS each hired New York-based producers, writers, and actors for dramatic anthologies.[43] Catskill resort comedians like Sid Caesar and Milton Berle, the latter a child of vaudeville, dominated the new medium's comedy hours. "The straight vaudeville act," Jack Gould of *The New York Times* contended in April, 1949, "is widely employed in television."[44]

In other instances, the need to fill time led to experimentation. Stuck with two early morning hours in 1950, a Philadelphia station hired a Trenton radio and newspaper humorist, Ernie Kovacs, to produce something in an entertaining fashion. Kovacs developed a wildly unpredictable program telecast live and full of unexpected gags, trick camera angles, and surrealistic effects.[45]

NBC resourcefully overcame the early morning gap in 1952 with *The Today Show*. With television offering little that was not adapted from another medium, *Today* amounted to sheer innovation on Pat Weaver's part. In his Radio City offices, Weaver planned a program that combined newscasts with a range of informational features, with Dave Garroway of Chicago's NBC station as host.[46] *The Today Show* not only attracted set owners who had been non-viewers of TV in the morning, but altered their daily routine as well. In January of 1953, *Variety* reported people moving their breakfast tables into their living rooms, where their sets were, to catch the show. To view *Today* while eating his toast, one man cut a hole in his kitchen wall; others utilized mirrors to observe the program. One woman brushed her hair more than she had before Garroway and his chimp co-host, J. Fred Muggs, came on the air. Such trends caught advertisers' attention; a Weaver aide noted that in August, 1954, *Today* had grossed larger revenues than *Gone with the Wind*.[47]

Two other NBC programs modeled after *Today* in their length and unusual air time soon followed. For later in the morning, Weaver introduced *Home*, and in 1954, after repeated pleas from NBC affiliates, came *The Tonight Show*, running from 11:15 P.M. (eastern time). The creation of *Tonight*, *Home*, and *Today* could be regarded, then, as a reaction to the pressure of time, unfilled hours that gave license to one programmer's imagination.[48]

In the evening, Weaver and NBC faced not an excess of time, but a shortage of stars. In the mid-1940s, the NBC radio network had the greatest collection of popular performers of any broadcast chain. With variety and comedy programs built around these players, NBC's ratings led the field. But between 1947 and 1950, Paley of CBS lured away all but one member (Bob Hope) of NBC's galaxy; Jack Benny, Red Skelton, Amos 'n' Andy, among others, quit NBC for Columbia.[49] The exodus of these stars gave

[43]New York *Daily News*, 23 August 1981; Paddy Chayefsky, *Television Plays* (New York, 1955), introduction; Richard M. Levine, "Live from New York, It's 'Playhouse 90' " *American Film*, 7 December 1981, 62–64.

[44]*New York Times*, 24 April 1979; Milton Berle and Haskel Frankel, *Milton Berle* (New York, 1974), chap. 22; Berle, interview, *The Tonight Show*, NBC, 24 March 1978; New York *Herald Tribune*, 5 December 1979; Wertheim, 388–89, 391; *idem.*, "The Rise and Fall of Milton Berle," in O'Connor, 58–59, 60, 62, 64, 66, 67.

[45]David Walley, *Nothing in Moderation* (New York, 1975), chap. 3; James L. Baughman, "Ernie Kovacs," John A. Garraty, ed., *Dictionary of American Biography, Supplement, 1961–1965* (New York, 1981), 442–43; New York *Herald Tribune*, 6 November 1957.

[46]Max Wilk, *The Golden Age of Television: Notes from the Survivors* (New York, 1976), 196ff; Robert Metz, *The Today Show* (Chicago, 1977), 24ff.

[47]*Variety*, 21 January 1953, 38, 58; Richard A. R. Pinkham address, 31 August 1954, BPL File 337, 3.

[48]Comments of member of NBC Affiliates Committee, Docket 12285, *Proc.*, pp. 2821–822, 2832, Pinkham address, 31 August 1954, *passim*.

[49]*Time*, 10 January 1949, 51; *ibid.*, 21 February 1949, 46; *Newsweek*, 31 January 1949, 49; Paley, 191lff; interview with

CBS the radio ratings leadership. Most of these performers successfully made the transition from radio to TV, leaving NBC desperate to prevent Columbia from capturing the largest TV audience. Weaver and NBC had to rely on novel types of programs rather than established personalities. In contrast to CBS's weekly comedy series featuring a well-known personality, NBC offered the expensive and specially-scheduled spectacular.

Rather than admit that his programming philosophy resulted from Paley's raid, Weaver tried to promote NBC's emphasis on the new and the expensive as the likely pattern of television entertainment. Such fare, he maintained, was well worth the risks to advertisers. "My money is on flexibility, novelty of pattern," he said in June, 1953. "Only through program innovation [and] specialized programming," he remarked in April, 1954, "can we be sure that [television] is not depressed to a toy status, a feeder of pale carbon copies."[50]

CBS tried unavailingly to resist such arguments. The regularly scheduled comedy or dramatic program with the same cast and setting, Columbia executives contended, encouraged a weekly viewing habit. TV watchers would ritualistically return to CBS every Sunday or Monday night. "If it isn't a regular show," Stanton said, "it's not television."[51] The popularity of some of Weaver's initiatives, however, forced CBS's hand. In March, 1955, *Peter Pan* overwhelmed Captain Hook and the normally impregnable Burns and Allen, Arthur Godfrey, and Lucille Ball comedies. To remain competitive with NBC, Columbia had to schedule some spectaculars after the 1954–55 season. "The CBS-TV network, which has long been content to go along with such 'safe' week-in-week-out entries as 'I Love Lucy,' 'Our Miss Brooks,' and 'Meet Millie,' " wrote a Boston critic, "finally is waking up to the necessity of varying its nightly line-ups with occasional splurges of big and unique entertainment."[52]

Still, more than CBS's reliance on former NBC stars and regular series accounted for Weaver's spectaculars. Costing far more than filmed weekly series,[53] the live specials could be justified as on-air promotions of RCA's latest and most expensive living room commodity, color TV. Since the late 1940s, RCA, NBC's parent corporation, had gambled millions on a color TV transmission system, and by 1954 the corporation was ready to promote color TV sets. President Eisenhower and every Federal Communications Commissioner received a free color TV set from RCA.[54] When rebroadcasting for Christmas 1954 *Amahl and the Night Visitors* (an opera NBC had originally commissioned and telecast in 1951), the network aired the special in color, with the first part of Act One stressing subdued pastels, grey, brown, and green. When the three kings came into Amahl's shabby home, the color arrangement changed to reflect brilliant scarlets, blues, and golds.[55] Always one for

Paley, *Broadcasting* (31 May 1976), 35 (19 September 1977), p. 108; *Forbes* (15 January 1964), p. 21; *New York Times*, 30 January 1949; memorandum, George M. Burbach to Joseph Pulitzer II, 22 May 1950, Pulitzer Papers, Box 112; *Fortune* (July, 1953), p. 79.

[50]Thomas Whiteside, "The Communicator," *New Yorker* 29, 23 October 1954, 64, 66; Weaver addresses, 15 June 1953, 8, 12–14, 23 April 1954, 8–9, BPL File 179.

[51]*Business Week*, 10 March 1956, 80; *ibid.*, 16 February 1957, 92.

[52]Anthony La Camera, *Boston Advertiser*, 20 March 1955, clipping in NBC Papers, Box 169, State Historical Society of Wisconsin; *New York Times*, 22 May 1955, 10 June 1956; Weaver Address, 31 January 1955, 12, BPL File 179.

[53]NBC's *Mayerling* was the most expensive of the spectaculars, costing $500,000 or more than ten times the cost of one episode of a half-hour series. *Business Week*, 16 February 1957, 90; *Fortune*, July 1953, 164; Gilbert Seldes, "The Lessons of 'Mayerling,' " *Saturday Review* 40, 2 March 1957, 27.

[54]James Hagerty to Dwight D. Eisenhower, 10 December 1953, with notation from HEW, 18 December 1953, Box 914, Official File 250-A, Eisenhower Papers; David A. Frier, *Conflict of Interest in the Eisenhower Administration* (Ames, 1969), 150, 153, 156.

[55]Richard A. R. Pinkham, address, 1 February 1955, 11, BPL File 337.

hyperbole, Weaver proclaimed the color telecast "the birth of another revolution."[56]

Columbia wanted no part of Weaver's revolution. CBS had entered TV manufacturing by acquiring the Hytron Radio and Electronics Corporation in 1950. Columbia engineers, however, had been unable to develop a color TV receiver that could obtain both black and white and color signals; RCA color sets could. Paley and his staff had to acknowledge bitterly after a March, 1955 test that RCA TV cameras also transmitted signals better than did CBS equipment. CBS could not compete with RCA in the marketing of color transmitters or sets and lacked NBC's incentive to produce extravagant programs in color.[57] Moreover, Hytron was generally proving a failure in diversification, and Columbia could not expect that division's revenues to compensate for losses in broadcasting. Most of CBS's earnings still came directly from broadcasting transactions, whereas NBC's losses could be recovered from RCA's other operations.[58] Although Columbia followed Weaver's lead by presenting some spectaculars of its own, it telecast far less in color. For one month in 1956, NBC offered 80 hours of color programs to CBS's eight.[59]

In color telecasting, Weaver had more than RCA color set sales in mind: he wished to discourage potential new entrants in national broadcasting. RCA's great rival in TV set manufacture, Zenith, advocated a pay TV system by claiming extraordinary benefits in programming. Live New York stage productions, opera, championship heavyweight fights, and recent feature films could all be telecast on television with a pay system to cover the added costs of such fare. "Free" TV, Zenith maintained, could never bring expensive and diverse programming to viewers. "Many talented and prominent stars, producers, and writers have so far refused to work for television," a Zenith spokesman asserted in June, 1955, "either because television does not offer enough money, or because they believe that the current limitations of television programming will not give them a sufficient or satisfactory outlet for their artistic talents." Pay television, however, can "offer unique and high quality programs which are beyond the economic reach of the producers of advertising-sponsored programs."[60] Earlier, Zenith's chief executive officer had declared, "There is nothing wrong with television that money won't cure"[61] And many accepted Zenith's logic—a subscription process would bring better programs. "Fee TV," wrote a Wash-

[56]Weaver, address, 23 April 1954, 3, BPL File 179; *Business Week*, 21 August 1955, 41, 43; notes of interview with executives of NBC, Office of Network Study, 5 January 1956, 6 January 1956, 37–38, Box 13, GSA invoice no. 72-A-1986, FCC Records; interview with Michael Dann, 14 June 1979, Whiteside, 23 October 1954, 67.

[57]Joan Simpson Burns, *The Awkward Embrace: The Creative Artist and the Institution in America* (New York, 1975), 87–90; Paley, 182–85, 199, 208, 221–22; *Forbes*, 1 October 1956, 16. See also Charles Kirshner, "The Color Television Controversy," *University of Pittsburgh Law Review* 13 (Fall, 1951): 64–84.

[58]*Fortune*, July 1953, 80, 164. The CBS and RCA annual reports for the 1950s were also consulted. NBC accounted for between 20 and 30 percent of RCA's revenues.

[59]*Forbes*, 1 October 1956, 18; *ibid.*, 15 January 1965, 25; Walter Guzzardi, Jr., "R.C.A: The General Never Got Butterflies," *Fortune*, October 1962, 105.

[60]Zenith, "Comments," 9 June 1955, 30, 37–38, Docket 11279. See also *Newsweek*, 28 February 1955, 71, 72; McDonald Statement in Zenith press release, 6 June 1955, copy in Andrew F. Schoeppel Papers, Kansas State Historical Society; Richard Hammer, "Zenith Bucks the Trend," *Fortune*, December, 1960, 133; *New York Times*, 19 June 1955; *Time*, February 1954, 64; House Committee on Interstate and Foreign Commerce, *Subscription Television*, Hearings, 85th Cong., 2d sess., 1958, 199ff, 272, 277; Morris L. Ernst to Emanuel Celler, 13 January 1958, Box 512, Celler Papers, Library of Congress; *See It Now* telecast, 14 June 1955, transcript in *ibid.*

[61]E.F. McDonald, *Colliers*, 29 June 1946, 80, quoted in NBC, "Comments," 18, Docket 11279. McDonald's decision for Pay TV predated World War II. See his essay, "Television: An Economic Riddle," Des Moines *Register Tribune*, 12 October 1941, copy in James Lawrence Fly Papers, Columbia University; McDonald to Zenith shareholders, 29 October 1939, copy in Box 102, NBC Papers; *Wall Street Journal*, 31 March 1955.

ington *Star* TV critic, "should give us a superior product."[62]

RCA and NBC fought Zenith with programming. While Zenith and others petitioned the FCC for the use of channels for subscription system tests, NBC engaged heavily in the live and costly fare that Zenith said only its process could give America. NBC representatives before the FCC cited *Peter Pan* as an example of what "Free TV" could provide the great audience. To counter the arguments of pay TV forces that recent feature films would come to a home screen only with a coin meter, NBC presented Olivier's *Richard III* in March, 1955, prior to its release to America's movie theaters. In June, *Variety* observed:

> *NBC-TV appears intent on killing "the toll-tv scare" all by itself. With the fee-see system fronting, among other show biz values, for first-run films, the web is on the move to frustrate these objectives by buffo presentation of high-budget celluloid, even if it loses several millions in the process.*[63]

Both Weaver and Paley sought to manipulate the schedule to check another and more apparent power: advertisers. Since the early days of radio, sponsors had exercised enormous power over programming. Advertisers or their agents owned a program and contracted with stars, and, hence, often decided not only the program that network carried but the large and small matters of production. Weaver and Paley, as experienced radio men, sought to lessen advertisers' leverage and achieve a vertical integration of the industry. "I was very stubborn about it," Paley recalled. "I just knew that eventually we had to have control of our own medium, have more to say about it than we had."[64]

First Weaver, then Paley, blocked advertisers' positions and enhanced their own by promoting longer, more expensive programs. Instead of fifteen or thirty minute segments with one sponsor, NBC arranged for sixty to 120 minute shows that a single underwriter was hard-pressed to afford. Rather than suffer an exclusive advertiser meddling in a presentation, the networks offered programs like *Today* or the spectacular or two or more potential sponsors who could dictate little about a telecast because each only shared the costs. Weaver termed his scheme, first tried with *Today* in 1952, the "magazine" format for the purchase of air time. The network, not the underwriter, initiated programs and retained control by dividing sponsors.[65] Weaver recognized what publishers from James Gordon Bennett to Edward Bok had proven: If the medium proved popular enough, advertisers seeking large audiences had no choice but to deal with the communicator.[66] Commenting on Weaver's strategy, a grateful North Carolina station manager wrote in February, 1955, "If Pat had done nothing more than latch on to the three words—Today, Home, and Tonight—he would have earned his salt."[67] One year later, CBS began *Playhouse 90*, a live anthology series

[62]Washington *Star*, 13 March 1955, 1 May 1955. See also Irving Kolodin, "Whose Money Talks?" *Saturday Review* 38, 30 April 1955, 39.

[63]*Variety*, 27 June 1955, 1; NBC, "Comments," 5–6, Docket 11279, notes of interview with NBC executives, 15–16.

[64]*Broadcasting*, 31 May 1976, 34; *Business Week*, 21 August 1954, 41; MacDonald, 32–34.

[65]Weaver, "Television, 1953"; memorandum, Weaver to NBC Sales Staff, 11 October 1954, Box 142, NBC Papers; Whiteside, 23 October 1954, 68; Martin Mayer, "Television's Lords of Creation," *Harper's* 213, November 1956, 27; *Variety*, 18 February 1953, 27; *Business Week*, 21 August 1954, 40; "*Today*: The Future Pattern of TV Advertising," *Television Magazine* 9, October 1952, 18–19; *ibid.* 10, January 1953, 17; *ibid.* 11, January 1954, 21.

[66]James L. Crouthamel, "The Newspaper Revolution in New York, 1830–1860," *New York History* 45 (April 1964): 106–07; Edward Bok, *The Americanization of Edward Bok* (New York, 1923), 164.

[67]B.T. Whitmire to Sydney H. Eiges, 7 February 1955, Box 169, NBC Papers.

of 90 minutes to be sponsored by more than one advertiser.[68]

In some instances, advertisers fostered the Golden Age by not seeking time. In the early years of the medium, the networks could not sell every evening hour. Few advertising agencies, for example, sought the 10:30 to 11:30 P.M. (eastern) time segment,[69] and all four networks had some evening periods when no programming at all appeared. On Tuesdays at 10:30 in the 1951–52 season, Columbia offered *Roller Derby*, only to abandon that enterprise after one season; CBS affiliates had to fill the time. A year later, with the slot still vacant, the network moved Murrow's *See It Now* from Sunday afternoons to evening prime time. Nothing else was available, and carrying the program promised goodwill among the newsman's influential admirers.[70] *See It Now* had a sponsor (though, revealingly, not initially),[71] yet the program cost the network far more to produce than Alcoa paid. Although the decision to air *See It Now* in the evening had thus been a calculated one, based on goodwill and unfilled air time, the idea that Columbia's managers acted out of idealism about the medium nonetheless gained currency. "Bill Paley's got a conscience," one contemporary observed, "and he cares about more than making money."[72]

Nothing better illustrates the role of unsold time in shaping the programming of early TV than the airing of congressional hearings in 1951 and 1954. Although widely observed, the televised Kefauver and Army-McCarthy Senate committee sessions were actually carried by only two of the four networks, ABC and Du Mont. These chains presented the hearings, as CBS did *See It Now*, because of the dearth of ready alternatives to a gangster's testimony or Joseph Welch's theatrics. Neither Du Mont nor ABC had much programming scheduled for the daytime hours, while both NBC and Columbia did. Moreover, AT&T, whose cables connected the networks' stations, charged all four systems the same rate and for a full day and evening, whether they transmitted or not. Du Mont and ABC, in other words, had already paid the phone company to telecast something, and Senators Kefauver and McCarthy, like Murrow, were better television than a blank screen.[73]

Some advertisers, in buying time, made their own contribution to the Golden Age. Among the medium's earliest underwriters were "institutional" advertisers, those selling a company rather than a specific product; all were large enough to be subject to the whims of the Antitrust Division. Uneasy then about the future of their oligopolies, Alcoa and U.S. Steel executives sought to improve their companies' images, especially with upper-class opinion leaders thought to be viewers of *See It Now* or *U.S. Steel Hour*. Alcoa took *See It Now*, a company general manager recalled, "to create the proper corporate image; an adult and as elite as possible [an] audience was sought." And never did Alcoa interfere with *See It Now*'s productions.[74]

[68]Memorandum re. interview with representatives of CBS, 6–9 October 1958, 47, GSA 72-A-1986, Box 16, Office of Network Study, FCC Records.

[69]Docket 12782, vol. 2, *Proc.*, vol. 6 p. 856. See also Joseph Turow, "Television Sponsorship Forms and Program Subject Matter," *Journal of Broadcasting* 24 (Summer 1980): 388, 392.

[70]James L. Baughman, "*See It Now* and TV's Golden Age, 1951–58," *Journal of Popular Culture* 15 (Autumn 1981): 106–15.

[71]Kendrick, 341.

[72]Unnamed source quoted in Charles Wertenbaker, "The World on His Back," *New Yorker* 29, 26 December 1953, 30, 32.

[73]Statement of Richard Salant before subcommittee on rules, Senate Committee on Rules and Administration, 4 August 1954, 15, copy in General Files 129-A-21, Box 1003, Eisenhower Papers; *New York Times*, 21 October 1956; *ibid.*, 24 October 1965; Milton Viorst, "The Rise and Fall of Robert Kintner," *The Washingtonian* 2, June 1967, 36. See also *Broadcasting*, 4 February 1957, 50.

[74]Summary of interview with Tod Hunt, Alcoa general manager, 23 August 1961, Box 5, GSA 72-A-1986, Office of Network Study, FCC Records; *New York Times*, 13 May 1955; Docket 12782, vol. 15, *Proc.*, vol. 40, pp. 6146, 6154, 6157–58; memoranda, Carroll P. Newton to Bruce Barton, 9 June 1950, 13 September 1950, 24 October 1950, 7 October 1952,

Nor did such sponsors as U.S. Steel disrupt the making of the anthologies they paid for.[75]

By the late 1950s, however, the market for TV time had changed to the disadvantage of the institutional advertiser. The demand for air time rose so steeply that institutional advertisers began to lose bidding wars to product advertisers like General Foods. Always underwriting some evening hours filled usually with popular weekly series, the product advertisers were prepared after 1956 to increase their participation in television if the networks provided them with more programs and larger audiences. "The advertiser and his agency," acknowledged a CBS vice president in mid-1958, "are finally concerned with the program and the time they occupy."[76]

Then, too, the rising cost of television time alone caused some institutional advertisers to curtail or end their buying of huge blocks of TV time. To celebrate its fiftieth anniversary in June, 1953, Ford had bought 120 minutes of evening prime time for a simulcast on both NBC and Columbia, the first TV spectacular. Four years later, to promote a new automobile, the Edsel, Ford sought the same arrangement only to settle for sixty minutes on one network. A Ford advertising agent complained of "preemptive costs."[77]

Factors stimulating the presentation of spectaculars no longer loomed over the medium's managers. By 1959, the threat of Zenith's Pay TV proposal had been turned back by congressional and consumer resistance.[78] Americans also frustrated RCA by refraining from purchasing color televisions in sufficient numbers to justify the extravagance of the live spectacular. In New Brunswick, New Jersey, the site of a famous ten-year "Videotown" survey of consumers, 0.4 percent of all homes in 1958 had color TV receivers.[79]

The national networks in the late Fifties had, in effect, reached a point where they had to consolidate gains and minimize losses. The diffusion of television had been so rapid that by late 1958 just under ninety percent of all homes had a set.[80] New audiences need not be won. Nor were growth rates in advertising sales rising after 1955 and 1956 at the pre-1955 velocity.[81] Costs had to be contained.

Industry competition by the late 1950s encouraged standardization. By the fall season of

---

11 June 1954, Boxes 80, 81, Barton Papers, State Historical Society of Wisconsin.

[75]Docket 12782, vol. 14, *Proc.*, vol. 36, p. 5389, vol. 38, p. 5846, Paddy Chayefsky, *Television Plays* (New York, 1955), xi; Rod Serling to Harry M. Scoble, 10 March 1958, Box 7, Serling Papers, State Historical Society of Wisconsin; Serling to Stan Optowski, 26 April 1960, Box 11, *ibid.*

The sponsors' benevolent role is acknowledged in John O'Toole, review of *The Sponsor*, by Erik Barnouw, *Federal Communications Law Journal* 31 (Winter 1978): 181; Barnouw, *The Sponsor: Notes on a Modern Potentate* (New York, 1978), 51–52; Ross Wetzsteon, "The Importance of Being Ernie," *Village Voice*, 25 April 1977, 39; Ashbrook P. Bryant, "Historical and Social Aspects of Concentration of Program Control in Television," *Law and Contemporary Problems* 34 (Summer 1969): 621; Robert Eck, "The Real Masters of Television," *Harper's* 234, March 1967, 45–52.

[76]Hubbell Robinson, "TV's Myopia of the Wide Screen," *Esquire* 50, July 1958, 24. See also Robert Alan Aurthur et al., *The Relation of the Writer to Television* (New York, 1960), 203; Docket 12782, vol. 14, *Proc.*, vol. 36, p. 5369; memorandum, Jack Elliott to Bruce Barton, 18 April 1956, Box 76, Barton Papers; notes from interview with Weaver, c. 1958, Mayer Papers, Box 66, *ibid.*

[77]Notes of interview with John B. Simpson, c. 1958, Box 19, Mayer Papers. See also Robert W. Crandall, "The Economic Effect of Television Network Program 'Ownership,' " *Journal of Law and Economics* 14 (October 1971): 395; transcript of interview with Weaver, 8 June 1958, "The Mike Wallace Show," copy in Fund for the Republic Papers, Princeton University.

[78]Robert W. Horton, *To Pay or Not to Pay: A Report on Subscription Television* (New York, 1960) is the best account of Pay TV's problems in the late 1950s. See also Jack Gould, *New York Times*, 2 March 1958; *Wall Street Journal*, 6 February 1958.

[79]Cunningham & Walsh, Inc., *Videotown* (New York, 1958), 12. See also Guzzardi, 103.

[80]U.S. Department of Commerce, *Statistical Abstract of the United States 1959* (Washington, 1959), 520, 825.

[81]Annual increases in network time sales to advertisers between 1952 and 1956 ranged from 19 to 41 percent. Be-

1956, CBS's emphasis on the weekly series had clearly bested Weaver's experimentalism. *Peter Pan* had proved to be an exception. Just as Stanton had predicted, the majority of viewers preferred regularity. Columbia commanded larger daytime and evening shares of the audience than NBC.[82] Furthermore, by the 1956–57 season, ABC had begun to emerge as a rival. ABC relied heavily on filmed, action adventure detective and western dramas modeled after the old "B" movies. These series attracted large enough audiences to dispel the notion that the public preferred live, over filmed, programming.[83]

By then both NBC and Hollywood had undergone a change of heart regarding the home screen. In September of 1956, General Sarnoff dismissed Weaver and soon thereafter replaced him with Robert Kintner. A past president of ABC, Kintner firmly believed in the cheaper, filmed series. While still at ABC, he had helped to break the Hollywood boycott in 1954 and 1955 by persuading Walt Disney and Warner Brothers to enter TV production.[84] "Why go to the movies," Sam Goldwyn cracked late in 1955, "when you can stay home and see nothing worse?"[85] Warners, one studio official noted, was soon "turning out the equivalent of one feature picture a day—eight solid hours of film a week—for TV."[86] Others joined in such production and in selling off their theatrical films previously unavailable to stations and networks.[87] "The studios have learned a lesson," *Advertising Age* reported in January, 1959, "Television is a highly profitable and steady source of income to major film studios and it causes year-round predictable employment."[88]

The rise of the Hollywood Series came at the expense of the live anthology drama. Almost immediately after taking over from Weaver, Kintner removed virtually all of NBC's anthologies.[89] Both he and his counterpart at Columbia abandoned the anthology form. By the season of 1958–59, some seventy-six percent of all the networks' anthologies had left the air.[90] Those few remaining were made in Hollywood, filmed or taped, and relied almost entirely on

tween 1956 and 1961, increments fell between 2 and 8 percent. *Broadcasting Yearbook 1964* (Washington, D.C., 1964), 27.

[82]CBS memorandum George Bristol to all TV network salesmen, 14 February 1956, Box 140, NBC Papers; *Forbes*, 1 October 1956, 16.

[83]James Lewis Baughman, "ABC and the Destruction of American Television, 1953–1961," in *Business and Economic History*, 2nd series, vol. 12 (1983) 56–73; notes of interview with Frederick W. Ford, c. February 1962, Box 124, Dwight MacDonald Papers, Yale University; memorandum, Ashbrook Bryant to Newton N. Minow, 19 June 1962, Box 26, Minow Papers, State Historical Society of Wisconsin; Martin Mayer, "ABC: Portrait of a Network," *Show* 1, October 1961, 59; Patrick D. Hazard, "Out of the Sewer and Into the Sky," *New Republic*, 26 October 1959, 23; memorandum, L.P.B. Emerson to John S. Cross, 18 January 1962, Box 53, E. William Henry Papers, State Historical Society of Wisconsin.

[84]American Broadcasting-United Paramount Theaters, *Annual Report 1954*, 17, 21; *ibid.*, 1955, 15, 16; *Variety*, 31 March 1954, 41; *New York Times*, 12 April 1955.

[85]Quoted in Milton Lehman, "TV's Colossal Hassle," *Saturday Evening Post*, 29 October 1955, 28.

[86]Dwight Whitney, "The Producer Assembles His Products," *TV Guide*, 31 October 1959, 22.

[87]Gerald Mast, 326; Balio, 239; *Business Week*, 26 March 1955, 45; *Sponsor*, 20 August 1956, 1; *ibid.*, 3 September 1956, 1.

[88]*Advertising Age*, 12 January 1959, 72. See also Lawrence L. Murray, "Complacency, Competition and Cooperation: The Film Industry Responds to the Challenge of Television," *Journal of Popular Film* 6 (1977): 66–68.

[89]Minutes, NBC Television Affiliates Executive Committee Meeting, 13 May 1956, Box 140, NBC Papers, Marie Torre, *Don't Quote Me* (Garden City, N.Y., 1965), 133–34; *Business Week*, 29 June 1956, 108, 114; *ibid.*, 31 January 1959, 42–43; San Francisco *Chronicle*, 1 October 1958. See also the novel by a Kintner underling, David Levy, *The Chameleons* (New York, 1964). The novel's mercurial network president is Kintner.

[90]Calculation based on all dramatic anthologies listed in Tim Brooks and Earle Marsh, *The Complete Directory to Prime Time Network TV Shows, 1946–present* (New York, 1979). Not counted were "genre" anthologies (westerns, mysteries) like *Alfred Hitchcock* or *Zane Grey Theater*. See also House, *Small Business*, 496–98, 505, 596–97; *New York Times*, 1 March 1957; *Variety*, 7 November 1962, 20; *Business Week*, 29 June 1957, 198–214; Docket 12782, vol. 2, *Proc.*, vol. 6, pp. 855–56.

tried and true adaptations. In December, 1951, NBC had commissioned Gian-Carlo Menotti to write an original opera for *The Hallmark Hall of Fame*. By the decade's end, Hallmark remained an occasional NBC offering, but one that avoided such artistic risks by telecasting plays already performed on Broadway like *Victoria Regina*.[91] "We have run into a situation," complained one writer in 1960, "where practically all of our dramatic [anthology] shows have disappeared."[92]

Fewer programs originated in New York, and virtually none in Chicago. In early 1959, NBC forbade Jerry Lewis from originating a program in the Second City.[93] The percentage of live programming on all three networks dropped markedly. Between June, 1953 and June, 1958 the rate of live telecasts slipped from 81.5 to 69.7 percent. *The New York Times* noted in July, 1957 that TV "for better or worse clearly seems to be moving to a philosophy of film."[94]

By the later 1950s, TV had been standardized by marketplace forces which, ironically, earlier in the decade had stimulated differences rather than similarities. The challenge of programming for a new medium, discouraging pay TV rivals, and promoting the sales of expensive color sets had fired Weaver's imagination, when, in 1956, he spoke of the newest medium as an instrument of mass enlightenment, capable of creating "an all-people elite."[95] But new managerial imperatives ended Weaver's career in television along with those of many creative producers and writers dedicated to the possibilities of elevating mass culture in postwar America.

All told, what had gone on the air in the Fifties was determined not so much by what was popular as by what was possible. An unusual set of circumstances between 1948 and 1958 encouraged experimentation, a reliance on legitimate theater rather than the B-movie. Thus the shape of early television said less about the American mind of the Fifties than it did about the entrepreneurial environment of a new and struggling enterprise.

[91]Arthur Shulman and Roger Youman, *The Golden Age of Television* (New York, 1966), 164; *Television Age*, 6 April 1959, 32–33, 70; Fairfax M. Cone, *With All Its Faults* (Boston, 1969), 210, 212–15; *TV Guide*, 7 November 1959, A-2; Docket 12782, vol. 14, *Proc.*, vol. 36, p. 5331.

[92]Aurthur et al., 29; Docket 12782, vol. 14, *Proc.*, 5374.

[93]Chicago *Sun-Times*, 13 February 1959. See also Robert Lewis Shayon, "Chicago's Local TV Corpse," *Saturday Review* 43, 11 October 1958, 32; Paul H. Douglas to David Sarnoff, 16 October 1958, Box 277, Douglas Papers, Chicago Historical Society; John Crosby to Eric Sevareid, c. February 1959, Box A-6, Sevareid Papers, Library of Congress.

[94]*New York Times*, 14 July 1957; *Broadcasting Yearbook 1963*, 20.

[95]Address, 19 January 1956, Series B, Box 1, NBC Papers. On Weaver's ouster, see *Business Week*, 27 June 1964, 146; *New York Times*, 8 September 1956.

The Media, the War in Vietnam, and Political Support: A Critique of the Thesis of an Oppositional Media

Daniel C. Hallin

Since the late 1960s the thesis has been put forward repeatedly in academic and public discourse that the American news media have been transformed from a relatively passive and conservative institution into an institution of opposition to political authority. This transformation, accordingly, is in large part responsible for the well-documented decline of public confidence in political institutions (Miller, 1974; Lipset and Schneider, 1983) and, more generally, for a weakening of political authority. "The most notable new source of national power in 1970, as compared to 1950, was the national media," writes Huntington (1975, pp. 98–99). "In the 1960s the network organizations, as one analyst put it, became 'a highly creditable, never-tiring political opposition, a maverick third party which never need face the sobering experience of governing.'"[1]

The State of the Evidence

The most important empirically backed statement of this thesis is Michael Robinson's "Public Affairs Television and the Growth of Political Malaise" (1976). Robinson presented data to show that people who relied primarily on television for information about public affairs (like most proponents of the oppositional media thesis, Robinson considers television a particularly important source of delegitimizing news coverage) tended to be more cynical about political institutions and more doubting of their own political capacity than those who utilized other media. These differences, according to Robinson, could not be explained by the low educational level of those who depended on television; it was reduced but not eliminated by a control for education. The explanation, therefore, had to lie in the content of television news: "events are frequently conveyed by television news through an inferential structure that often injects a negativistic, contentious or anti-institutional bias. These biases . . . evoke images of American politics and social life which are inordinately sinister and despairing" (p. 430).

Robinson's study, however, has a critical flaw. It is based on the association between political attitudes (efficacy and trust in government) and self-reports of media habits (reliance on television as opposed to other media), and it contains no measure of what according to Robinson's theory is the real independent variable: the content of television news.[2]

[1]Huntington is quoting from Robinson (1975). Other statements of this perspective include Clarke (1974), Ladd and Hadley (1975), and Rothman (1979).

[2]There are other problems with Robinson's study as well, some discussed in Miller et al. (1976, 1979). Robinson

A stronger test of the link between critical news coverage and declining support for political authority is Miller, Erbring, and Goldenberg's "Type-Set Politics: Impact of Newspapers on Public Confidence" (1979). In 1974 the CBS National Election Study included a content analysis of the front-page articles appearing in newspapers collected from the areas surveyed. This made it possible for the authors to assess directly the association between news content and the political attitudes of those exposed to it. The association proved substantial. News content varied considerably from paper to paper, and those whose newspapers contained more criticism of political authorities and institutions tended to score lower in indices measuring trust in government and, to a lesser degree, political efficacy. This finding persevered in the face of numerous controls. The authors concluded that there was a "significant relationship between negatively critical media content and evaluations of government" (p. 78).

Here, however, we run up against the basic limitations of the media effects paradigm, with its focus on the link between news content and individual attitudes. Establishing that critical news content does indeed affect popular attitudes toward government only takes us one step toward resolving the larger issue of the role of the media in the legitimation or delegitimation of political authority, and therefore whether they can be seen, in Huntington's terms, as institutions of political opposition. Two crucial questions remain unanswered.

The first is the question of aggregate news content, which becomes essential as soon as we attempt to move from statements about the link between content and individual attitudes to statements about the impact of the media on public opinion at the aggregate level. Given that critical news coverage leads to critical attitudes —and favorable content to favorable attitudes; i.e., that Miller, Goldenberg, and Erbring could have stated their conclusion in the opposite way: "There exists a significant relationship between positive media content and evaluations of government"—we need to know how much of news content, overall, is favorable and how much unfavorable to political authority.

Miller, Erbring, and Goldenberg do, in fact, provide interesting evidence on aggregate news content. The papers in their sample contained more criticism of political authority than praise, but more neutral content than either of these: 31 percent of the stories contained criticism, 6 percent praise, and 63 percent were neutral. Their data also showed that most criticism was directed at individuals rather than at institutions and that most came from other political authorities rather than from journalists—both very significant findings, as we shall see below. But theirs was not primarily a study of news content, and Miller, Goldenberg, and Erbring are limited in the conclusions they can draw about the political messages to which the American public is generally exposed. Most important, that analysis was confined to a relatively brief and unusual period of time, the denouement of the Watergate affair in the middle of 1974. It thus contains no information about changes in news content over time, which is clearly important for assessing claims about the role of the media in a secular decline of public confidence.

The second question concerns the process by which news content is produced—the functioning of the media as institutions, the constraints under which they operate, their relations with other political institutions, and so on. Does a high level of negative news content, for exam-

used reliance on television as opposed to other media as a surrogate measure of exposure to television content. But in 1974, when a direct measure of television exposure was available in the CPS Election Study, it was not associated with lower levels of political trust or efficacy. Robinson's article also contains an experimental study of the impact of the CBS documentary *The Selling of the Pentagon* on subjects' political attitudes. *The Selling of the Pentagon*, however, cannot be taken as representative of television content in general; and in any case Robinson's data show only slight effects.

ple, reflect an ideology of adversary journalism? Or does it simply reflect policy failures and conflicts between elites, faithfully recorded by an essentially apolitical news media? Certainly in the two cases our assessment of the media's role in the overall process of opinion formation would be very different.

Methodology

This study addresses the relatively neglected questions of shifts in news content over time and the functioning of the media as political institutions.[3] On the basis of a content analysis of television coverage of the war in Vietnam, it offers a critique of the thesis that the American news media shifted toward an oppositional stance during the Vietnam period, and a reinterpretation of their changing relation to political authority.

Vietnam and television are both obvious choices for a case study of this sort. Vietnam was the most extensively covered and the most controversial news story of the period from 1960–64 through 1976, during which the bulk of the decline of public confidence in American political institutions took place. The argument that the media were in large part the cause of that decline is essentially a historical one, and in that sense this study is less subject to the problems of generalizability that often limit the value of case studies. The argument made by Robinson, Huntington, and other proponents of the oppositional media thesis is not that the media have always played a delegitimizing role (though Robinson, perhaps, can be taken to imply that television is by its nature destructive of political support); it is that they began to play this role sometime during the middle or late 1960s. And for such a hypothesis Vietnam is clearly a critical case. It is, moreover, television which these researchers have generally singled out as the most important source of delegitimizing news coverage.

The data which follow are based on a stratified random sample of 779 television broadcasts from the period beginning 20 August 1965 and ending with the cease-fire on 27 January 1973. The analysis begins in August 1965, because archives of television news are not available before that date (the Vanderbilt Television News Archive was established in August of 1968). All material after that date is taken from Vanderbilt. Interestingly, it is possible to extend this analysis back to 1965 only because the Defense Department, alarmed by the now famous report by CBS correspondent Morley Safer which showed the Marines burning peasant huts with cigarette lighters, began filming news coverage relevant to military activities in August of that year. This material is now in the National Archives. It is unfortunately not as complete as the Vanderbilt collection is, at least for weekday news. It omits an unknown amount of coverage less directly related to the military, including some coverage of domestic debate, the actions of civilian policymakers, and the diplomatic and political sides of the war. When there is reason to believe these omissions might bias figures presented here, this will be noted.[4]

[3]Two studies which address the content question (though not over time) and which offer critiques of the thesis of media opposition to authority are Pride and Richards (1974, 1975). There are a host of other studies, not necessarily in political science nor directly addressed to the oppositional media thesis which bear on these questions and will be cited as this analysis progresses.

[4]Eight, ten, or twelve dates were selected randomly from each month during this period, and for each date one network broadcast was then selected randomly. The National Archives material was sampled more heavily (ten dates per month) because, in part due to the limitations of the Pentagon's archiving, certain types of stories occur in it relatively rarely. The 1968 campaign period was also sampled heavily to permit separate analysis. All data presented below are weighted to correct for these sampling differen-

The argument will proceed as follows. On the surface, the pattern of change in television content seems consistent with the thesis of an increasingly oppositional news media. The data suggest a dramatic shift from one-sidedly favorable coverage of U.S. policy in the early years—before the 1968 Tet offensive—to substantially more critical coverage after Tet. This change, moreover, cannot be dismissed as a mere reflection of the actual course of events. In some cases the increase in negative content clearly has no relation to changes actually taking place in Vietnam. So one must conclude that the media were indeed applying different journalistic standards in the latter part of the war.

When we probe more deeply, however, the thesis of an oppositional media begins to fall apart. The evidence does not suggest any dramatic shift in the basic ideology and news-gathering routines of American journalism. The routines of objective journalism—routines which are incompatible with an actively oppositional conception of the journalists' role—seem to have persisted more or less unchanged throughout the Vietnam period. The media continued, in particular, to rely heavily on official information and to avoid passing explicit judgment on official policy and statements. Data will also be presented which suggest that the media were not inclined to favor opponents of administration policy, and it will be argued that critical coverage in the latter part of the war did not extend to the political system or to basic consensus beliefs.

The concluding section presents a model for explaining changes in the level of critical coverage, emphasizing the response of an objective media to the degree of consensus or dissensus that prevails particularly among political elites.

ces. The three networks did not differ greatly in their coverage of the Vietnam War, and they are combined in the analysis which follows. More detailed information on the content analysis is given in Hallin, 1980.

News Content: The Growth of Critical Coverage

The following four tables illustrate the shift in Vietnam coverage from a balance quite favorable to administration policy prior to the Tet offensive to a considerably less favorable balance after Tet.[5] Table 1 gives a summary of journalists' editorial and interpretive comments on the news. It includes all statements by journalists which offered explicit opinions on the war (commentaries included), drew explicit conclusions about controversial issues (e.g., a conclusion that one side or the other was winning), or used strong evaluative language (words like "butchery" or "massacre") without attribution. I shall return to this table on a number of occasions. Presently, it is enough to observe that the figures show a shift from a heavily favorable balance (by a ratio of 4–1, though the Ns for this period are small) before Tet, to an unfavorable balance of more than two to one.

Tables 2 and 3 chart the development of two important themes in news coverage which were

[5]A word about statistical significance. Many cells in the tables which follow have small *N*s, and for that reason the data should be interpreted cautiously, particularly given the limitations of the National Archive sample. Nevertheless, most of the comparisons cited in the text are statistically significant. Take as an example the first column of table 1. The 4–1 favorable ratio in journalists' editorial comments on the administration during the pre-Tet period is significant at a level of better than .03 (if the null hypothesis is a balanced 50–50 ratio); for the 2–1 unfavorable ratio in the post-Tet period, $p < .001$, and for the difference over time (eliminating the Tet period), $p < .001$ ($x^2_{1df} = 12.83$). *N*s for the Tet period are clearly too small for statistical inference; data for this period are presented separately for illustrative purposes, and because that period is too distinctive to be lumped with either of the others. *N*s for the pre-Tet period, incidentally, are so much smaller than those for the post-Tet for three reasons: (1) the pre-Tet period is shorter; (2) there were fewer news stories, in part because the war was not as important a domestic issue; and (3) the National Archives collection does not include every story.

Table 1 *Direction of Television Journalists' Editorial Comments on Major Actors of the Vietnam War (percentages down)*

	Favorability to Action or Policy of:			
Period	Adminis-tration, Supporters	South Vietnam Govt.	Dove Critics of War	North Vietnam, NLF
Pre-Tet				
Favorable	11	2	0	0
Comment or Interpretation	78.6%	50.0	0.0	0.0
Unfavorable	3	2	2	20
	21.4	50.0	100.0	100.0
Tet				
Favorable	0	0	0	2
	0.0	0.0	0.0	40.0
Unfavorable	6	3	3	3
	100.0	100.0	100.0	60.0
Post-Tet				
Favorable	23	17	7	10
	28.8	29.8	31.8	25.6
Unfavorable	57	40	15	29
	71.3	70.2	68.2	74.4

Note: Pre-Tet period is 20 Aug. 1965–30 Jan. 1968 (about thirty-six months); Tet, 31 Jan.–31 March 1968 (three months); post-Tet, 1 April 1968–26 Jan. 1973 (about fifty-one months).

Table 2 *Positive and Negative References to Democracy in South Vietnam*

	Positive References	Negative References
Prior to Tet Offensive	4.5	6.0
Tet Offensive	0.0	0.5
After Tet Offensive	3.5	37.0

Note: Figures are raw frequencies. For dates and relative lengths of periods see note to table 1.

Table 3 *Positive and Negative References to Morale of U.S. Troops*

	Positive References	Negative References
Prior to Tet Offensive	4.0	0.0
Tet Offensive	0.0	1.0
After Tet Offensive	2.5	14.5

Note: Figures are raw frequencies. For dates and relative lengths of periods see note to table 1.

lightly covered early in the war but reflected unfavorably on administration policy after 1968. These tables, in contrast to table 1, take into account not only comments made directly by journalists, but also comments attributed to others and the subject of the stories themselves. Table 2, for instance, gives a count of positive and negative references concerning the status of democracy in South Vietnam. A reporter's observation that the South Vietnamese regime was unpopular would appear in this table as a negative reference, as would a report on antigovernment demonstrations. A report on administration statements lauding South Vietnamese democracy would appear as a positive reference. When a relevant statement or event is the major subject of a story, it is scored as one reference; when it is mentioned but is not the major subject, it is scored as half a reference. The table shows that negative references to South Vietnamese democracy increased by an order of magnitude after 1968. Table 3 shows a more modest but still substantial increase in negative references to the morale of U.S. troops. These figures reflect primarily an increase in stories about drug use, attacks on officers, protests by soldiers, and refusals to follow orders.

Table 4, finally, shows how often representatives of different points of view on the war appeared on television. Briefly summarized, the table suggests that spokesmen for administration policy were heavily predominant during

Table 4 *People Speaking or Quoted by Reporters in Television Coverage of Vietnam*

	Prior to Tet Offensive	Tet Offensive	After Tet Offensive	Total
Administration Representatives, Supporters[a]	59 26.3%	4 13.8	250 28.4	310 27.5
South Vietnamese, Laotian, Cambodian Govt. Officials	8 3.6	0 0.0	33 3.8	41 3.6
Critics of Administration Policy[b]	10 4.5	7 27.6	230 26.1	247 21.9
North Vietnamese, NLF, Officials	4 1.8	1 3.4	35 4.0	41 3.6
American Officers and GIs in the Field[c]	110 49.1	11 41.4	152 17.3	273 24.2
Others	34 15.2	4 13.8	179 20.3	216 19.1
Total	224 100.0	26 100.0	880 100.0	1128 100.0

[a] Includes domestic but not foreign supporters of administration policy.
[b] Includes both "doves" and "hawks," though most are "doves." Includes only domestic critics of administration policy.
[c] Also includes lower-level civilian officials, e.g., pacification advisors.
Note: Figures—including frequencies—may not add to totals because of rounding. Frequencies are rounded because of weighting (see note 4 in the text).

the early period, while after Tet there was relative parity between the administration and its critics.[6]

Similar patterns emerge for many dimensions of news content. Before Tet, for example, of those military operations reported on television in which some conclusion was offered as to who had won or lost, 62 percent were reported as victories for the U.S. and its allies, 28 percent as defeats, 2 percent as stalemates. After Tet the figures were 44 percent victories, 32 percent defeats, and 24 percent stalemates. Before Tet positive assessments of the overall military situation in Vietnam outnumbered negative assessments by ten to one in television coverage; it must have been difficult for the average viewer even to conceive of the possibility of a U.S. defeat. After Tet positive and negative assessments were roughly balanced.

It could of course be argued that the increase in negative news had nothing to do with any change in the media, but simply reflected the evident failure of U.S. policy and the growth of domestic opposition. This is the mirror theory of news—a theory cherished by news people themselves. And there is a good deal of truth to it. The data summarized in table 3, for instance, which show an increase in the coverage of morale problems among U.S. troops, more or less parallel the actual figures for fragging incidents (attacks on officers) and insubordination convictions.[7] Table 4 similarly reflects the spread of public and congressional opposition to the war.

But this explanation cannot be carried too far. Consider table 2, which shows a massive increase in negative coverage of the South Vietnamese political system. Did the South Vietnamese regime suffer a dramatic loss of public support between, say, 1966 and 1970? Not at all; indeed, 1966 was a year of intense political strife in South Vietnam, more intense than anything that occurred after 1968. In this case it was clearly the selection of news—rather than South Vietnamese politics—which was changing.

Objective Journalism

On the surface then, Vietnam seems to confirm the thesis of a shift in American journalism toward an oppositional stance: news content became substantially more critical as the war went on, and the pattern of change cannot be explained away as a simple reflection of the course of events. But as soon as one begins to probe beneath the surface of news content, to explore the production of news as well as the ideology and organization of American journalism, the thesis of an oppositional media begins to unravel.

It is true that during the Vietnam period journalists became more inclined to report information critical of official policy. Any history of journalism in this period and any journalist's memoir will confirm this. In 1961 the *New York Times*, showing the typical caution with which the media approached any story related to national security in the early sixties, suppressed on its own initiative information on the impending Bay of Pigs invasion which was public knowledge in Miami and Guatemala; in 1971 the *Times* was willing to defy threats of criminal prosecution to publish the *Pentagon Papers* (cf. Salisbury, 1980). But there were certain basic elements of the structure and ideology of American journalism which persisted more or less unchanged through the Vietnam period, and which make it very hard to sustain the thesis of an actively oppositional news media.

Most important here is the continuing impor-

[6]Figures for both administration representatives and domestic opponents are probably biased downward for the Tet and pre-Tet periods by the limitations of the National Archives data. See Hallin, 1980, p. 50.

[7]Reported fragging incidents rose from 126 in 1969, the first year data were kept, to 333 in 1971; insubordination convictions from 82 in 1968 to 152 in 1970 (Lewey, 1978, pp. 156–67).

tance of the professional ideology of objective journalism. What is most striking about the modern American news media, if one compares them with the media of other historical periods or other countries, is their commitment to a model of journalism which requires disengagement from active political involvement and assigns to the journalist the relatively passive role of transmitting information to the public. Studies of the socialization and professional ideology of the modern American journalist have consistently confirmed the centrality of the ideal of a politically neutral press (e.g., Cohen, 1963; Tuchman, 1972; Gans, 1979), as have analyses of news content. Miller, Goldenberg, and Erbring found that even at the height of the Watergate affair most news stories were neutral toward political authority. Studies of campaign coverage have generally found rough but consistent balance in coverage of the major candidates (e.g., Graber, 1980; Hofstetter, 1976).

Did the rise of critical news coverage during the later years of Vietnam represent a break with the tradition of objective journalism, a return perhaps to something resembling the partisanship of the nineteenth century press?[8] That is not what the data on television coverage suggest.

It will be useful here to reconsider table 1, which shows the shifting balance of journalists' editorial comments on the war. The table seems to indicate that journalists held strong and very imbalanced opinions about the war, though very different opinions in different periods. And the table may well reflect accurately journalists' personal attitudes toward U.S. policy in Vietnam. But those attitudes were expressed infrequently: table 1 represents a small proportion of news content. When commentaries are excluded, only 8 percent of all Vietnam stories contained explicit comments by journalists reflecting favorably or unfavorably on major actors: most coverage fit the traditional "who, what, when, where" model of objective journalism. This percentage changed over the course of the war, but only to a limited extent: from 5.9 percent in the pre-Tet period it shot up to 20 percent during the offensive, and then settled back to an average of 9.8 percent for the post-Tet period.

It is worth adding here a few words about the rise of what has come to be called investigative journalism. In the wake of Watergate there has been revival of interest in the muckraking tradition, which can be seen as the major rival to the principle of objectivity in the value system of American journalism. How extensive this revival has actually been in the post-Watergate period is beyond the scope of this study. But it is important to observe that investigative journalism played a very small role in Vietnam coverage. None of the major news stories which can be considered especially damaging to the administration resulted primarily from initiatives taken by the media.[9] The Tet offensive simply erupted under the noses of the journalists. The *Pentagon Papers* were leaked unsolicited by a disgruntled official. My Lai was not discovered by the major media until the story was broken by an independent reporter. The secret bombing of Cambodia did not become a major story until it was investigated by Congress. The revival of the muckraking tradition was essentially a post-Watergate phenomenon,

[8]On the decline of partisan journalism in the United States see Schudson, 1978. Newspapers in the nineteenth century were often vitriolic in their denunciation of political authorities whom they opposed. Toqueville (1969, p. 182) begins his discussion of the American press by quoting the first newspaper encountered, which denounced Andrew Jackson as a "heartless despot."

[9]An important exception was Harrison Salisbury's trip to North Vietnam for the *New York Times* in 1966. Walter Cronkite's call for negotiations in a CBS special following the Tet offensive, though not an instance of investigative journalism, was also an important exception in that it represented a departure from the normal practice of avoiding political stands.

which means that it occurred after most of the decline of public confidence in American political institutions had already occurred.

To stress the professional ideology of objective journalism is not to imply that the news is literally objective or neutral. News content is of course shaped by many factors which can create a political slant irrespective of journalists' commitment to objectivity. That commitment does, however, have important consequences, one of which is that it generally inhibits the journalist from taking sides openly and actively on controversial political issues. The persistence of this ideology through the Vietnam period (when it was challenged, for a time, by the idea of advocacy journalism) is eloquent testimony to its centrality in the value system of American journalism.

The Use of Official Sources

The damage to the thesis of an oppositional media becomes increasingly severe as we probe more deeply into the newsgathering procedures of American journalism. Once it is accepted that the task of journalism is to provide the public not with opinion but with information, the crucial journalistic choice becomes the choice of sources. And the American journalist in the twentieth century has solved this problem by relying primarily on official sources. Studies of American journalism in the 1950s and early 1960s, when the consolidation of objective journalism was first being noted by observers of the press, were essentially unanimous in identifying as the most prominent characteristic of the newsgathering procedures the intimate connection between the media and political authority. The whole organization of journalism, centering around a beat system which located journalists at the points where official information was released, was geared toward covering the affairs and perspectives of government. In practice, therefore, the function of objective journalism was generally to transmit to the public the government's perspective on the world. There was, as Bernard Cohen observed in a 1963 study of foreign affairs coverage, an irony in this:

> *The more "neutral" the press is—that is, the more it tries faithfully to transmit a record of "what transpires" (including therein the policy statements of officials) and the more constrained it feels about making judgements on the meaning or importance of "what transpires"—the more easily it lends itself to the uses of others, and particularly to public officials whom reporters have come to regard as prime sources of news merely by virtue of their positions in government.* (Cohen, 1963, p. 28)

How much had newsgathering procedures changed by the latter part of the Vietnam War? Again, surface appearances are deceptive. Table 4, which gives a count of the kinds of people who appeared or whose statements were cited in television coverage, shows a substantial increase in the number of opponents of administration policy represented. This would seem to indicate a diversification of sources. But when these data are broken down it becomes clear that they mask an important element of continuity.

The evidence does not suggest that the reporters in Saigon and Washington who covered the basic news of the Vietnam War did their work much differently in 1973 than in 1963. What happened instead is that a new issue arose alongside the basic Vietnam story: the story of domestic dissent. As domestic conflict increased, television reported the rising tide of dissent, and opponents of the war became increasingly visible in the news. The news from the field and from executive branch beats in Washington—from which the hard news of the war was primarily covered—continued to reflect a heavy predominance of official sources. This can be seen in table 5, which presents the

Table 5 *People Speaking or Quoted by Reporters in Television Coverage of Vietnam, Domestic Stories Excluded*

	Prior to Tet Offensive	Tet Offensive	After Tet Offensive	Total
Administration Representatives, Supporters[a]	48 26.2%	3 18.8	145 32.4	195
South Vietnamese, Laotian, Cambodian Govt. Officials	8 4.4	0 0.0	33 7.4	41
Critics of Administration Policy[b]	1 0.5	0 0.0	16 3.6	17
North Vietnamese, NLF, Officials	4 2.2	1 6.2	34 7.6	40
American Officers and GIs in the Field[c]	101 55.2	11 68.8	143 32.0	255
Others	22 12.0	1 6.2	75 16.8	96
Total	183 100.0	16 100.0	447 100.0	644 100.0

[a] Includes domestic but not foreign supporters of administration policy.
[b] Includes both "doves" and "hawks," though most are "doves." Includes only domestic critics of administration.
[c] Also includes lower-level civilian officials, e.g., pacification advisors.
Note: Figures—including frequencies—may not add to totals because of rounding. Frequencies are rounded because of weighting (see note 4 in the text).

same data as table 4, but excludes from the analysis all purely domestic stories, primarily stories about the conflict on the home front.[10] These findings are supported by other studies of news coverage during the latter period of the Vietnam War. Leon Sigal, for instance, found in a study of *Washington Post* and *New York Times* coverage in 1969 that 72 percent of the sources used in stories with Washington datelines were U.S. government officials, as were 54 percent of the sources used in Saigon stories (Sigal, 1973).

One way to summarize the contrast between tables 4 and 5 is to say that administration representatives and their opponents appeared in different kinds of television stories: dissenters appeared in stories primarily about dissent itself, while official spokespeople appeared in stories which reported the actual news of the war. This may seem at first glance an obvious

[10]Figures for administration representatives may be biased downward for the pre-Tet and Tet periods due to the limitations of the National Archives sample. Officers and GIs in the field were clearly another important part of television coverage. About 45 percent of this category were officers, upon whom journalists relied to explain particular events and also, as with pilots commenting on the air war, to explain the rationale behind certain aspects of policy. Officers were thus another important official source. Enlisted men were generally presented describing their own feelings or experiences, although occasionally they were asked their opinions about the war or about domestic dissent.

and trivial finding. But it is more significant than it appears. Stories on domestic dissent, first, often did not give opponents of administration policy any real opportunity to present alternative interpretations of the news. A large proportion of these stories focused on the issue of domestic dissent itself: the prospects for legislative opposition, the tactics of the demonstrations and how many people were attending them, whether violence would occur, and how order would be restored (cf. Gitlin, 1980; Paletz and Dunn, 1969–70). Opponents of administration policy would appear in these stories to explain and justify themselves, not to discuss the war in Vietnam. Only about 40 percent of all stories on domestic debate contained any substantive discussion of the war, and often this was extremely brief. Even to the extent that domestic critics did appear in stories that contained discussion of policy issues (this happened most often in reports on congressional hearings), critics and officials appeared in essentially different roles. Critics were shown giving their opinions about a political issue. Officials were shown defending their policies against criticism, but they also appeared in the authoritative and nonpolitical role of providing the basic information about events in Vietnam and explaining those events to the public.

This reliance on officials for authoritative information has several implications. First, it suggests that administration spokesmen were likely to have been taken more seriously by the news audience than their critics. One of the basic findings of the long tradition of media effects research is that a communicator presented in a nonpolitical, information-providing role has higher credibility than one presented as an exponent of partisan opinions (Hovland, Janis, and Kelly, 1953). Second, it means that when the administration decided to exploit fully its ability to initiate news, it was often very successful; even in the skeptical context of the post-Tet period. For example, the key element in the Nixon administration's efforts to sell its Vietnam policy to the American public was Vietnamization—the replacing of American with Vietnamese troops. The data in table 6 suggest that the initiation of Vietnamization not only put the South Vietnamese armed forces on the news agenda, but also resulted in a continued preponderance of favorable references to their performance, despite the generally more critical tone of coverage in the latter part of the war. These favorable references were largely the result of what Boorstin (1962) has called "pseudo-events": statements by U.S. officials, ceremonies turning over U.S. bases to the South Vietnamese, etc. which, because they represented official policy, were considered mandatory news stories.

Finally, the practice of turning to officials as the primary source of authoritative information is an important symbolic recognition of their legitimacy: it is an affirmation both of their claim to superior knowledge ("trust us—we have access to information you don't have") and of their right to be considered representative of the community as a whole and thus above politics. The right to be considered the primary source of authoritative information about world events should probably be considered a central component of the legitimacy of modern political institutions, comparable in a secular age to the right of the Church in medieval Europe to interpret the scriptures (cf. Paletz et al., 1971).

Two further sets of figures illustrate the persistence of journalistic respect for official sources. It was not simply the use of official sources which, according to analysts like Cohen, gave officials so much influence over news content. It was the fact that the norms of objective journalism required the journalist to pass on official information without comment on its accuracy or relevance. Did these restraints also persist through the Vietnam period? The fact that only 8 percent of the stories sampled contained explicit commentary by journalists suggests that they did. And when

Table 6 *Positive and Negative References to Performance of South Vietnamese Armed Forces, before and after Vietnamization*

	Positive References	Negative References
Prior to Vietnamization	11.5	3.0
After Vietnamization	40.5	14.5

Note: For purposes of this table the beginning of Vietnamization is dated 7 June 1969, the day before the Midway conference at which Nixon announced his first withdrawal of U.S. troops. Figures are raw frequencies. The two periods are about equal in length, forty-six and forty-four months, respectively.

Table 7 *Frequency of Editorial Comments in Television Coverage of Major Actors of the Vietnam War*

	Number of Editorial Comments	Comments per Hour of Coverage
Coverage of U.S. Policy, Activity	99	5.07
Coverage of Opposition to Admin. Policy	27	6.52
Coverage of South Vietnamese Government	63	15.92
Coverage of North Vietnam, NLF	65	37.55

Note: Amount of time devoted to activities of various actors must be estimated, since many television stories deal with several actors at a time. Estimates used here are based on Hallin, 1980, appendix II.

that figure is disaggregated, it becomes clear that it very much overstates the willingness of journalists to comment on official policy and statements. The data in table 7 indicate that commentary was substantially less common in coverage of the U.S. executive than in coverage of other political actors relative to the amount of time devoted to each.

Data on the frequency of news reports questioning the accuracy of official statements tell a similar tale. Fourteen and one-half such references turned up in the sample for the post-Tet period (with the half references, again, scored when the theme was not the primary subject of the story, and all references to inaccuracy or dishonesty of official statements counted, whether made by journalists or attributed to others). To put this figure in perspective, it can be estimated that a faithful viewer who watched the evening news every night would have seen an average of about one such reference a month—considerably more, no doubt, than a viewer would have seen before Tet (only three references occurred in the pre-Tet sample), but not a figure that suggests journalists were going out of their way to question official information, or even to air such questions raised by others. Of those 14.5 references only 3.5 involved charges of deliberate efforts to mislead the public.

Coverage of the Opposition

If the media had become an oppositional institution during the later years of the Vietnam war, it is reasonable to assume that they would have given relatively favorable coverage to other opponents of administration policy. But here again the data do not square with the thesis of an oppositional media.

The media did give increasing coverage to the opposition as the war went on. But this coverage was not particularly favorable. As shown in table 1, journalists' interpretive comments were unfavorable to domestic opponents of the war by roughly two to one in the latter part of the war, approximately the same ratio that prevailed in coverage of administration policy. A count of all statements about the antiwar movement presented on television, including both journalists' and attributed comments, yields a similar two to one negative ratio for the post-Tet period—forty-eight unfavorable comments, twenty-five favorable. Whatever tendency there may have been for journalists to become more skeptical of administration policy, it does not seem to have been translated into sympathetic coverage of the opposition.

Coverage of "The System"

It is important to note, finally, that the increase in critical coverage during the latter part of the Vietnam War did not involve coverage critical of the political system in any meaningful sense of that term. Just as critical coverage during the immediate post-Watergate period, as measured by Miller, Goldenberg, and Erbring, was directed at particular incumbents rather than at the system or its major institutions,[11] critical coverage in Vietnam reporting was directed at the administration and its policies. For the most part, the political system was simply not an issue in Vietnam coverage, which, like most news coverage, focused on what journalists call hard news—news of specific events, policies, and personalities. When the political system—or important consensus beliefs, like the belief that American foreign policy is motivated by a concern with democracy—did become an issue in the news, coverage was generally of a legitimating character. Journalists reporting on the antiwar movement, for example, often distinguished between those who, in the phrase of the day, "worked within the system" and those who did not, and made clear their preference for the former. Journalists also made a special point on certain particularly delegitimizing occasions (the Tet offensive and the evacuation of Saigon in 1975) to stress that the motives of U.S. policy had been good.[12] This finding parallels the evidence from public opinion surveys: despite their loss of confidence in the conduct of government during the sixties and seventies, the American public continued to express a high level of faith in the system (Citrin, 1974; Sniderman et al., 1975).

Conclusion: Objective Journalism and Political Support

The case of Vietnam, in short, does not support the thesis that the American news media shifted to an oppositional role during the 1960s and 1970s. There was, to be sure, a very substantial turn toward more critical coverage of U.S. policy in Vietnam. But it is hard to argue that journalists began to take on an actively op-

[11]McLeod et al., 1977, found that those who followed Watergate in newspapers were more likely than those who did not to blame Nixon rather than the system. See also Paletz and Entman, 1981.

[12]Thus Cronkite's famous commentary following the Tet offensive (27 February 1968) included both a call for de-escalation of the war and an affirmation that its intent—to "defend democracy"—had been honorable, whatever the outcome.

positional role; the professional ideology of objective journalism and the intimate institutional connection between the media and government which characterized American journalism before the turbulence of the sixties and seventies both persisted more or less unchanged.

That conclusion made, however, we are left with an important problem of how to account for the substantial change in news content over the course of the Vietnam War. The puzzle is the more acute as we have already rejected the most obvious alternative explanation: the mirror theory that changing news content reflected a changing course of events.

As paradoxical as it may seem, the explanation for the media's changing level of support for political authority during the Vietnam War lies in their constant commitment to the ideology and the routines of objective journalism. Tom Wicker of the *New York Times*, referring to the early 1960s, once observed that "objective journalism almost always favors Establishment positions and exists not least to avoid offense to them" (1978, pp. 36–37). He was, as we shall see, essentially correct. But from the point of view of a particular administration and its policies, objective journalism can cut both ways politically. A form of journalism which aims to provide the public with a neutral record of events and which, at the same time, relies primarily on government officials to describe and explain those events obviously has the potential to wind up as a mirror not of reality, but of the version of reality government officials would like to present to the public. At the same time, objective journalism involves a commitment to the political independence of the journalist and to the representation of conflicting points of view. The journalist's relation to political authority is thus not settled in any definite way by the professional norms and practices of objective journalism. It is on the contrary something of a paradox for the journalist, and it is resolved in different ways depending on political circumstances.

Consider the early period of the Vietnam War, when coverage was by most measures heavily favorable to administration policy. How could coverage so imbalanced be reconciled with a conception of journalism which requires neutrality and balance on controversial issues? The onesided character of news coverage in this period is not hard to understand if one simply keeps in mind that Vietnam was not yet a particularly controversial issue within the mainstream of American politics. There were debates in Congress over certain tactical questions—whether the military should have greater freedom in selecting bombing targets, whether enough was being done on the political and diplomatic fronts, and so on. But on the broad outlines of U.S. policy there was still relatively little disagreement among the major actors of American politics. To reflect the official viewpoint did not seem in this context to violate the norms of objective journalism: it did not seem to involve taking sides on a controversial issue.

This consensus, of course, did not last forever. Its erosion became serious politically, by most accounts, about the middle of 1967, and was accelerated by the Tet offensive (Schandler, 1977). Given this change in the parameters of political debate it is perfectly reasonable to expect that the media, without abandoning objective journalism for some more activist and anti-establishment conception of their role, would produce a far higher quantity of critical news coverage. Here, then, is an explanation for the change in Vietnam coverage that seems to fit nicely both with the data on news content and with our knowledge of the institutional relations between the media and political authority: *the change seems best explained as a reflection of and a response to a collapse of consensus—especially of elite consensus—on foreign policy.* One journalist expressed it this way:

> *As protest moved from the left groups, the antiwar groups, into the pulpits, into the Senate—with Fulbright, Gruening and others—as it be-*

came a majority opinion, it naturally picked up coverage. And then naturally the tone of the coverage changed. Because we're an Establishment institution, and whenever your natural constituency changes, then naturally you will too. (Max Frankel, quoted in Gitlin, 1980, p. 205)

It is useful to imagine the journalist's world as divided into three regions, each of which involves the application of different journalistic standards. The first can be called the sphere of consensus. This is the region of motherhood and apple pie; in its bounds lie those social objects not regarded by journalists and by most of the society as controversial. Within this region journalists do not feel compelled to present opposing views, and indeed often feel it their responsibility to act as advocates or ceremonial protectors of consensus values. The discussion of patriotism that marked coverage of the homecoming of the hostages after the recent Iranian crisis is a good example. So is the journalists' defense of the motives of U.S. policy in Vietnam. Within this region the media play an essentially conservative, legitimizing role; here the case for a Gramscian model of the media as maintainers of the hegemony of a dominant political ideology is strong.

Beyond the sphere of consensus lies what can be called the sphere of legitimate controversy. This is the region where objective journalism reigns supreme: here neutrality and balance are the prime journalistic virtues. Election coverage best exemplifies the journalistic standards of this region.

Beyond the sphere of legitimate controversy lie those political actors and views which journalists and the political mainstream of the society reject as unworthy of being heard. It is, for example, written into the FCC's Fairness Doctrine that "[it is not] the Commission's intention to make time available to Communists or to the Communist viewpoints" (quoted in Epstein, 1974, p. 64). Here neutrality once again falls away and the media become, to borrow a phrase from Parson (1951), a "boundary-maintaining mechanism": they play the role of exposing, condemning, or excluding from the public agenda those who violate or challenge consensus values (cf. Gans, 1979), and uphold the consensus distinction between legitimate and illegitimate political activity. The antiwar movement was treated in this way during the early years of the Vietnam period; so were the North Vietnamese and the Viet Cong, except during a brief period when peace talks were near completion (Hallin, 1980).

All of these spheres, of course, have internal gradations, and the boundaries between them are fuzzy. Within the sphere of legitimate controversy, for instance, the practice of objective journalism varies considerably. Near the border of the sphere of consensus journalists practice the kind of objective journalism that involves a straight recitation of official statements; farther out in the sphere of controversy they become more willing to balance official statements with reactions from the opposition or with independent investigations of controversial issues.

Using this framework the major changes in Vietnam coverage can easily be summarized. First, the opposition to the war expanded, moving from the political fringes of the society into its mainstream—into the electoral and legislative arenas, which lie within the sphere of legitimate controversy. As this occurred the normal procedures of objective journalism produced increasing coverage of oppositional viewpoints; when a presidential candidate comes out against the war, as occurred for the first time at the New Hampshire primary in 1968, the opposition becomes not only a respectable but an obligatory subject for news coverage. The reader may recall that Miller, Goldenberg, and Erbring found most criticism of political authorities reported in post-Watergate newspaper coverage to be criticism of one political authority by another—of Congress by the president and vice versa. (For all the drama of investigative journalism it is unlikely that the Watergate story would have gone very far if Congress had been controlled by the Republicans.) Similarly, the data on television coverage of Vietnam show 49 percent of all domestic criticism of administration policy attributed to other public officials, compared with 16 percent which came from reporters in commentaries and interpretive comments, and 35 percent from all other sources, including antiwar activists, citizens in the street, and soldiers in the field.

Second, the sphere of consensus contracted while the sphere of legitimate controversy expanded. Not only did the media report the growing debate over the war, they were also affected by it. As the parameters of political debate changed, so did the behavior of the media: stories that previously had been reported within a consensus framework came to be reported as controversies; subjects and points of view that had been beyond the pale in the early years came to be treated as legitimate news stories. Neither the institutional structure nor the professional ideology of the media had changed substantially, but in a changed political environment these could have very different implications for the reporting of the news. The media did not shift to an oppositional role in relation to American foreign policy during the Vietnam War, but they did start to treat foreign policy as a political issue to a greater extent than they had in the early sixties. This meant that the journalistic standards they applied were less favorable to administration policymakers.

In short, then, the case of Vietnam suggests that whether the media tend to be supporting or critical of government policies depends on the degree of consensus those policies enjoy, particularly within the political establishment. In a limited sense, the mirror analogy is correct (cf. Tuchman, 1978). News content may not mirror the facts, but the media, as institutions, do reflect the prevailing pattern of political debate: when consensus is strong, they tend to stay within the limits of political discussion it defines; when it begins to break down, coverage becomes increasingly critical and diverse in the viewpoints it represents, and increasingly difficult for officials to control (cf. Gitlin, 1980, ch. 10). This does not necessarily imply that the media's role is purely passive or unimportant. It seems likely, on the contrary—though the question of media impact is beyond the scope of this study—that the media not only reflect but strengthen prevailing political trends, serving in a time of consensus as consensus-maintaining institutions and contributing, when consensus breaks down to a certain point, to an accelerating expansion of the bounds of political debate. If this interpretation is correct, however, the media are clearly intervening and not—as the oppositional media thesis implies—independent variables in the process by which political support is generated or broken down. One must therefore look to other factors besides the structure and ideology of the media for the more basic causes of the current crisis of confidence in American politics.

References

Boorstin, Daniel J. (1962). *The Image*. New York: Atheneum.

Citrin, Jack (1974). "Comment: The Political Relevance of Trust in Government." *American Political Science Review* 68: 973–88.

Clarke, Peter B. (1974). "The Opinion Machine: Intellectuals, the Mass Media, and American Government." In Harry M. Clor (ed.), *Mass Media and American Democracy*. Chicago: Rand McNally.

Cohen, Bernard C. (1963). *The Press and Foreign Policy*. Princeton: Princeton University Press.

Epstein, Edward Jay (1974). *News from Nowhere*. New York: Vintage.

Gans, Herbert J. (1979). *Deciding What's News*. New York: Pantheon.

Gitlin, Todd (1980). *The Whole World Is Watching: Mass Media in the Making and Unmaking of the New Left*. Berkeley: University of California Press.

Graber, Doris A. (1980). *Mass Media in American Politics*. Washington, D.C.: Congressional Quarterly Press.

Hallin, Daniel C. (1980). *The Mass Media and the Crisis in American Politics: The Case of Vietnam*. Ph.D. dissertation. University of California, Berkeley. Oxford University Press, forthcoming.

Hofstetter, C. Richard (1976). *Bias in the News: Network Television Coverage of the 1972 Election Campaign*. Columbus: Ohio State University Press.

Hovland, Carl I., Irving L. Janis, and Harold H. Kelly (1953). *Communication and Persuasion*. New Haven: Yale University Press.

Huntington, Samuel J. (1975). "The United States." In Michel J. Crozier, Samuel P. Huntington, and Joji Watanuki, *The Crisis of Democracy*. New York: New York University Press.

______ (1981). *American Politics: The Promise of Disharmony*. Cambridge: Harvard University Press.

Klapper, Joseph T. (1960). *The Effects of Mass Communication*. Glencoe, IL: Free Press.

Ladd, Everett C., Jr., with Charles D. Hadley (1975). *Transformations of the American Party System*. New York: Norton.

Lewey, Guenter (1978). *America in Vietnam*. New York: Oxford.

Lipset, Seymour Martin, and William Schneider (1983). *The Confidence Gap*. New York: Free Press.

McLeod, Jack, Jane D. Brown, Lee B. Becker, and Dean A. Zieke (1977). "Decline and Fall at the White House; A Longitudinal Analysis of Communication Effects." *Communication Research* 4: 3–22.

Miller, Arthur H. (1974). "Political Issues and Trust in Government, 1964–1970." *American Political Science Review* 68: 951–72.

Miller, Arthur H., Lutz Erbring, and Edie N. Goldenberg (1976). "Type-set Politics: Impact of Newspapers on Issue Salience and Public Confidence." Paper presented at the annual meeting of the American Political Science Association, Chicago.

______ (1979). "Type-set Politics: Impact of Newspapers on Public Confidence." *American Political Science Review* 73: 67–84.

Paletz, David N., and Robert Dunn (1969–70). "Press Coverage of Civil Disorders: A Case Study of Winston-Salem, 1967." *Public Opinion Quarterly* 33: 328–45.

Paletz, David, and Robert Entman (1981). *Media Power Politics*. New York: Free Press.

Paletz, David N., Peggy Reichert, and Barbara McIntyre (1971). "How the Media Support Local Government Authority." *Public Opinion Quarterly*. 35: 80–92.

Parsons, Talcott (1951). *The Social System*. New York: Free Press.

Pride, Richard A., and Barbara Richards (1974). "Denigration of Authority? Television News Coverage of the Student Movement." *Journal of Politics* 36: 637–60.

______ (1975). "The Denigration of Political Authority in Television News: The Ecology Issue." *Western Political Quarterly* 28: 635–45.

Robinson, Michael J. (1975). "American Political Legitimacy in an Age of Electronic Journalism." In Douglass Cater and Richard Adler (eds.), *Television as a Social Force*. New York: Praeger.

______ (1976). "Public Affairs Television and the Growth of Political Malaise: The Case of 'The Selling of the Pentagon.'" *American Political Science Review* 70: 409–32.

Rothman, Stanley (1979). "The Mass Media in Post-Industrial Society." In Seymour Martin Lipset (ed.), *The Third Century*. Chicago: University of Chicago Press.

Salisbury, Harrison E. (1980). *Without Fear or Favor*. New York: Ballantine.

Schandler, Herbert Y. (1977). *The Unmaking of a President: Lyndon Johnson and Vietnam*. Princeton: Princeton University Press.

Schudson, Michael (1978). *Discovering the News*. New York: Basic Books.

Sigal, Leon V. (1973). *Reporters and Officials*. Lexington, MA: D.C. Heath.

Sniderman, Paul M., W. Russell Neuman, Jack Citrin, Herbert McClosky, and J. Merrill Shanks (1975). "Stability of Support for the Political System: The Initial Impact of Watergate." *American Politics Quarterly* 3: 437–57.

Toqueville, Alexis de (1969). *Democracy in America*. Garden City, NY: Doubleday.

Tuchman, Gaye (1972). "Objectivity as a Strategic Ritual: An Examination of Newsmen's Notions of Objectivity." *American Journal of Sociology* 77: 660–79.

______ (1978). *Making News*. New York: Free Press.

Wicker, Tom (1978). *On Press*. New York: Viking.

Declarations of Independence

James Boylan

Back in the early 1950s, when the sixty-four of us huddled over spavined wooden desks at Columbia's Graduate School of Journalism,* we were not given to understand that journalism was a privileged or even a very desirable calling. That we were in a *graduate* school of journalism proved to be only an ambiguous sign of status, for the curriculum was irretrievably aimed at dissipating dreams of glory. The regimen resembled that of my army basic of four years before, both in the insistence on unquestioning acceptance of authority and in the scorn for matters intellectual. We learned a good deal about the terminology and practices of afternoon newspapers and the wire services, using classic exercises dating in some cases from the 1930s; about news leads and feature leads; about counting headlines and about timing radio news broadcasts. The students who ranked highest in these endeavors tended to be those who had already learned these same things on the job and were attending Columbia as a finishing school.

When our mentor and guide urged us, "Be a pro," we understood the term to mean nothing very grand: don't get flustered; don't screw up the process; do it the way it's always been done. The lesson of being a pro was underlined in our inspirational project for the year, an essay contest sponsored by the American Newspaper Publishers Association, which claimed to be seeking fresh ideas about how to improve American newspapers. We wrote our essays, and some of us sent them in. We were not entirely startled when the prize went to a porcine young man from, I think, Boston University, who averred that, given the opportunity, he would change nothing about American newspapers because they were already so close to perfection.

Nor were we much burdened by frills. We each produced a "crusade," the kind of series churned out many times yearly by the feature aces of the *New York World-Telegram;* we would hardly have dared to call it investigative reporting. Our law course had no airy talk about the First Amendment; instead, E. Douglas Hamilton led us through a semester of old-fashioned libel, just enough butcher-sues-press-for-silly-error stuff to keep us from getting future employers in trouble. As for history, we were assigned to produce chapter drafts of a group-book (never published) about former Pulitzer Prize winners. Illustrious forebears who had not won Pulitzers, such as Benjamin Franklin, Horace Greeley, or Ida Tarbell, remained unmentioned. The little that we learned about Joseph Pulitzer himself was ingested by happenstance when we were assembled in the lobby of the journalism building to hear Mayor Impellitteri dedicate a plaque in the lobby bearing the founder's words: "Our Republic and its press will rise or fall together. . . . "

*Our class included only eight women, the survivors of an admissions policy that deemed women poor employment prospects and thus mercifully shielded them from disappointment.

Stirrings Below Decks

If we had taken that proposition seriously, we would have had to conclude that the Republic was destined to fall, or at least to stumble. The Graduate School of Journalism of that day I have come to regard as a faithful replica of the side of American journalism—primarily newspaper journalism—that was mired in a creed of impenetrable smug. For a journalist to criticize a newspaper, any newspaper, was, in the terminology often applied, to foul one's own nest; for an outsider to do it, as did the Commission on Freedom of the Press (Hutchins Commission) in 1947, smacked of subversion. To suggest further that journalists might have individual rights (aside from ordinary employee rights, which publishers had grudgingly yielded at the insistence of the Supreme Court) would simply not have occurred to anyone. Had they read it more carefully before cursing it, publishers would have agreed heartily with the conclusion of the Hutchins Commission that the "writer works for an employer, and the employer, not the writer, takes the responsibility. . . . The effective organization of writers on professional lines is . . . almost impossible."

To many of us viewing it from the underside in the 1950s, the journalism business seemed dead in the water, a reasonably enjoyable occupation offering the opportunity to live frugally for a time before moving, if one were to judge by the alumni association of the Columbia school, into public relations or banking. A professor hired out to the Ford Foundation wrote of journalism that "the glamour and magic of the craft have leaked out of it. . . . Three or four decades ago, the newspaperman was appealingly raffish—at once a bum who drank too much and a knight errant who charged unafraid at social injustice, succored the weak, and crossed lances with the powerful and arrogant." The professor, the late David Boroff, wrote with more cultural than historical accuracy; reporters perhaps thought of themselves and their unsanitary newsrooms as raffish, but they had never been given a long leash for seeking social justice. Further, it was the Great Depression that had drained the "glamour and magic" from the newspaper "game"—the romantic myth that had succored (or suckered) previous generations. With the founding of the American Newspaper Guild in 1933, journalists had opted for pay over romance, but in the 1950s not many had worked their way far enough past insecurity to be caught up in the newer romance of professionalism.

Even in the 1950s, though, there were stirrings below decks. The journalist-sociologist Warren Breed's classic study, "Social Control in the Newsroom" (1955), unveiled the struggle: newsrooms were becoming bureaucracies and tacit but firm bureaucratic pressures were bringing neophytes into line with policy, thus assuring that news would continue to be produced in the manner that the organization preferred. (I remember that, on reading Breed's article for the first time, I understood better the initiation experience at Columbia.) Breed also found that there was a kind of permanent newsroom underground, which caucused, in normal times, in the bar across the street. It had been the previous generation of that underground that had created the early Newspaper Guild in its own image—outspoken, socially concerned, broke, and all but powerless. By 1955, Breed noted, the Guild, which had long since become a union of newspaper employees rather than of journalists alone, no longer served as a focus of resistance. Opposition to newsroom practices that were seen as illegitimate—favoritism, blacklisting, arbitrary management interventions—were combated more by subversion than by defiance. Or, as Breed put it bluntly in 1955: "There is no evidence available that a group of staffers has ever 'ganged up' on policy."

Most discouraging for anyone contemplating the rise and fall of the Republic was evidence that, when summoned to great tasks, the journalism of the 1950s had proved far from adequate. As yea-sayer to power, journalism had proved a fine vehicle for negotiating the tricky ice floes of the Cold War, when former enemies swiftly became staunch friends and vice versa. But it had not proved that it could move upstream against a political current, and the tide in the 1950s was running with the new Red Scare, personified in Senator Joe McCarthy. Journalism's one recognized elite, the Washington press corps, failed to meet the test, in the basic journalistic sense of offering an account that could stand even rough historical scrutiny. Rather than challenging McCarthy, for four years the capital's chief news suppliers, the (then) three wire services, feasted from McCarthy's abattoir.

Commonly, this failure—and it was a journalistic as well as a political failure—has been attributed to McCarthy's devilishly clever manipulation of the dogmas of objective journalism of the sort we were taught at Columbia—the official quote, the "go with what you've got." In light of later experiences, it seems clearer now that over the long run even objective journalism disseminates mainly what its managers see as legitimate, and that McCarthy was a news diet of choice. Almost to the end the press remained more accomplice than adversary, despite nitpicking by what McCarthy would have called the "comsymp" press, led by *The Washington Post*. The serious challenges to McCarthy—the Edward R. Murrow broadcast of March 9, 1954, is the one that has entered memory—came late, only when McCarthy's exit chute, greased at last by the Eisenhower administration, was clearly visible.

Such an experience is, for an institution, a little like a serious illness. There may be recurrences: *The New York Times* buckled and fired employees under pressure of a post-McCarthy senatorial investigation of communism in the New York press. But after recovery there may be a kind of immunity. The failure to respond more actively to McCarthyism, or more accurately the embarrassment rising from failure, remained ever after a reference point, invoked in other contexts: the Bay of Pigs, Vietnam, the Pentagon Papers, Watergate. The great surprise, in retrospect, is the speed with which the bedraggled, victimized press of the 1950s came to see itself as an apparently potent, apparently adversary press in the 1960s.

Part of the change was generational. The early 1960s brought changes in management at a string of national news organizations: Otis Chandler, the young heir, took over the disreputable old *Los Angeles Times* in 1960 and began to overhaul it. In 1963, Arthur Ochs Sulzberger, fourth in a family succession that had started at the turn of the century, became publisher at *The New York Times* and appointed A. M. Rosenthal metropolitan editor, the first step in Rosenthal's rise to the top of the *Times*'s news operation. The doomed Philip Graham, publisher of *The Washington Post*, acquired *Newsweek* and with it Benjamin C. Bradlee, who in 1965 was named editor at the *Post* by Graham's widow and successor, Katharine.

Such changes may have opened the way to a new ethos in newsrooms. Before 1960, most news operations, although no longer so madly authoritarian as in the old days, remained under firm institutional control: that is, the news agenda and style reflected almost entirely what the organization, working through editors and the copy desk, wanted. A prototype was *The New York Times*, where "desk" people had traditionally carried greater authority than reporters.

In general, these new managements—and specifically that at the *Times*—shifted toward greater emphasis on reporting, less on editing, allowing reporters to look on themselves as the true professionals, overcoming at last the petty standards imposed by the desk. Being a pro came to mean more than being a good soldier; it meant allegiance to standards considered superior to those of the organization and its parochial limitations. It is certainly no coincidence that every one of what are commonly cited as the critical episodes in press confrontations with official power in this era developed to a great degree from actions of reporters in the field. Reporters, given new scope, were repeatedly able to test management oratory about press freedom, to place acute political questions before the press establishment, and gradually to change the ideology of press-government relations. As early as 1960, Melvin J. Lasky, an editor of *Encounter* magazine, professed to see that the power of the press was devolving from the press lord onto the reporter: he predicted the emergence of a "reportocracy."

Breaching the Covenant

Through the Cold War years, powerful taboos of national security obstructed journalism. The U-2 affair—the capture by the Soviets in 1960 of the pilot of an American spy plane, in which Washington proved to be considerably less truthful than Moscow—marked a change in climate. A deception that the press might have excused a decade before, it now condemned. A. J. Liebling remarked in *The New Yorker* that he foresaw "a less blind acquiescence in Papa-knows-best national policy in the future."

Reporters encountered other taboos—and precipitated major controversies—in their attempts to cover the Cuban revolution. In 1957, Herbert Matthews, an old-fashioned war-loving correspondent for *The New York Times*, found the guerrilla Fidel Castro, who had been proclaimed dead by the Batista government, alive and well in the Sierra Maestra. By 1961, after Castro had taken power and had been widely identified (by Matthews, among others) as a communist, Matthews had been attacked by a congressional committee, had received stacks of hate mail, and had been reviled in *Time* magazine as a kind of Rasputin. Worse, his employer silently concluded that Matthews had made a serious political mistake in giving publicity to Castro and quarantined him for the rest of his career. Even after he died, his name continued to be used as a symbol of the journalist who should have left well enough alone.

In 1960 and 1961, the press became entangled in the project that eventually became known to history as the Bay of Pigs. The significance of that incident may not in retrospect be the commonly cited one—that the country's leading newspaper humiliated itself by bending to mild government pressure. Rather, the Bay of Pigs demonstrated that reporters could legitimately disclose secret actions of their government. It is sometimes forgotten now that the invasion of Cuba sponsored by the Central Intelligence Agency, far from being a well-kept secret, leaked out at an increasing rate for months before the disastrous event itself. Although the government initially managed to suppress articles in *The Miami Herald* and *The New Republic*, the *Herald* itself and many other publications eventually carried stories on the preparations. That great latter-day watchdog, *The Washington Post*, chose to be part of the cover-up.

The *Times*, which played a passive role at first, was eventually forced into the arena by the aggressive Tad Szulc (whose arrival in any Latin American country, folklore said, caused the existing government to start looking over its shoulder for a coup). Szulc moved in on the invasion story on his own and made the newspaper face the choice of printing what he had found or suppressing it. Influenced by James Reston, head of the Washington bureau, who may or may not have been in communication with the White House, the *Times* did neither: it tampered with (rather than suppressed or buried, contrary to common recollection) the text of Szulc's story to remove hints of an "imminent" invasion. For their pains, the *Times*'s editors were tossed a sop a year later by President Kennedy, who told them privately he wished they had printed the whole story. Such an *in camera* comment, of course, scarcely overrode Kennedy's officially declared desire that editors should subject themselves to self-censorship on national security matters.

Even this minor intervention in the news process remained seared in the memories of those involved, so much so that five years later the managing editor of the *Times* restated the whole matter before an international press body and his newspaper printed his text. In essence, E. Clifton Daniel acknowledged that the *Times* had erred in altering its news process for national security considerations defined only by the government, and implied that it would not do so again. The press critic Paul H. Weaver has put an epochal interpretation on the matter: Daniel, he says, was announcing "that an important article in the informal covenant between press and government was being renegotiated, if not unilaterally repudiated."

Vietnam: The First Phase

If indeed the period of automatic deference was ending, the change had been not by fiat but in the field, primarily in Vietnam. Here the challenge to reporting was more consistently demanding than in the Bay of Pigs episode. There was already in place a policy of uncritical support of Ngo Dinh Diem's client government, which had benefited since 1955 from a glossy American public-relations operation (exposed in Robert Scheer's classic 1965 pamphlet, *How the United States Got Involved in Vietnam*) carried out by Madison Avenue consultants, Roman Catholic functionaries, big-name committees, and—as cheerleaders—the magazines of Henry R. Luce, who always took a special interest in managing the Far East.

Until 1961, almost the only critical coverage from Vietnam had been foreign-aid exposés, a staple of conservative newspapers, but a profound alteration began with a simple change of assignment. In 1961, *The New York Times*, aware that a new guerrilla war was under way in South Vietnam, sent its best war correspondent, Homer Bigart, to Saigon. Bigart, then fifty-four years old, was far different in temperament from Matthews; he had won two Pulitzer Prizes covering wars, but he hated war; even more, he hated pretense. His student and successor, David Halberstam, later wrote of him: "To be with him was to have one's own doubts about management confirmed. . . . Bigart's sense of institutions, what they did to good men, was very good, and far ahead of the times."

Bigart did not win a Pulitzer in Vietnam (that honor went to Halberstam), but he gained the fame of legend as the mentor of a whole class of Vietnam correspondents who emulated his insistence on reporting demonstrable fact, his skepticism of official p.r., his lack of confidence in the whole enterprise. He left after a year, having inspired the first of many secret communications between Saigon and Washington complaining about the unfriendliness of American correspondents. The pioneers who remained included Halberstam; Malcolm Browne, Peter Arnett, and photographer Horst Faas of The Associated Press; Neil Sheehan of United Press International and later of *The New York Times*; Peter Kalischer of CBS; Charles Mohr of *Time*; François Sully of *Newsweek* (soon expelled by the Diem government); Beverly Deepe of *The Christian Science Monitor*; and Merton Perry, who had three employers in his eight-year tour.

This crew and those who joined them soon found themselves playing in a big league. With Washington's interest in Vietnam rapidly intensifying, they had to report on two developments that neither the American government nor their home offices wanted to hear about: that the guerrilla war was not going well and that the Diem government was not only an autocracy but an autocracy in collapse.

This time, the *Times*, for one, met the test: by the fall of 1963, what Halberstam was reporting was earning him the Matthews treatment in

Hearst newspapers. In October 1963, President Kennedy, at a White House meeting with the paper's new publisher, Arthur Ochs Sulzberger, said that perhaps Halberstam was ripe for another assignment since he was (JFK used journalists' jargon deftly, as always) "too close to the story, too involved." Just such an official hint to Sulzberger's father in 1954 had removed a *Times* correspondent, Sydney Gruson, from Guatemala shortly before the CIA coup there. But the junior Sulzberger merely responded that he did not believe that Halberstam was too involved; Halberstam, in fact, was kept on beyond his scheduled recall to make the point clear.

It was a different matter entirely at *Time*, where Henry Luce was still in control. New York editing softened a Charles Mohr cover story on Madame Nhu, the force behind South Vietnam's presidential throne. Later, a story filed by Mohr and Perry started: "The war in Vietnam is being lost." Headquarters suppressed it in favor of something optimistic written thousands of miles from the scene. Moreover, within a month the *Time* press department printed two attacks on the Saigon correspondents. Perry resigned and went over to *Newsweek*, where he stayed until his death in 1970; Mohr moved to the *Times*. *Time* magazine remained manic on South Vietnam. In 1965 it hailed the American escalation as "the right war in the right place at the right time."

The temerity of the Vietnam correspondents showed they had come to view their work as different from that of war correspondents of World War II or even of Korea. They had come to reject the idea that they were in any sense part of the American "team" in Vietnam. Halberstam stated the new view flatly: "The job of the reporters in Vietnam was to report the news, whether or not the news was good for America." Equally important, they rejected the notion that their reporting should provide aid and comfort to their employers' views.

Critics charged then and later that this new attitude reflected a kind of naive, rosy-cheeked, radical romanticism, sympathetic to any revolution anywhere. Others saw the self-aggrandizement of careerists. Neither impulse, it appears in retrospect, was as dominant as a simple commitment to getting the story right, to providing an account that would stand the scrutiny of history. In 1965, Halberstam invoked that standard when he wrote (more prophetically than he could have known): ". . . if nothing else, we would have been prevented from sending tranquilizing stories to our papers by a vision of the day when the Vietcong walked into Saigon and *Time* righteously demanded to know where those naive reporters were now who had been telling the world that all was going well with the war in Vietnam."

New Journalisms

In April 1965, *New York*, the Sunday magazine of the *New York Herald Tribune*, published two bizarre articles by Tom Wolfe, a Ph.D. in American Studies who had been cutting a swath with a supercharged, superpunctuated style of cultural reportage. Wolfe's two pieces ridiculed *The New Yorker* magazine, and it is not clear, even today, whether, as he wrote later, he intended them as a jape or whether they were merely wildly erroneous. In any case, Wolfe stirred a minor scandal, for *The New Yorker* was not only synonymous with reputability but had indeed been the leader in the kind of literary reporting of which Wolfe's was an offshoot. Predictably, supporters of *The New Yorker* swarmed all over him. The columnist Joseph Alsop denounced Wolfe as, of all things, a leftist. In a long article for *The New York Review of Books*, Dwight Macdonald coined for Wolfe's work the term "parajournalism"—"the factual authority of journalism and the atmospheric license of fiction." Only near the end of the controversy did Pete Hamill apparently attach to the style the name that clung to it ever after: "New Journalism."

Gradually, Wolfe and his peers came to appear less revolutionary and the New Journalism became recognizable as a fresh phrase of literary—primarily magazine—journalism, notable for extended reporting devoted primarily to penetrating and understanding subcultures. In the setting of its time, the controversy was astringent, waking up the establishment to the presence of those who were going to disregard the rules and make trouble. The best of the New Journalists, in fact, were reviving the nineteenth-century concept of the journalist as interpreter, advocate, and critic rather than as merely the processor and translator of the words of the powerful. For much of the managerial side of journalism, however, the individuality this suggested was a distinctly unwelcome trend, suggesting as it did lack of control, lack of reliability, and youth. "New Journalism" became and remained over the years an epithet covering a multitude of sins—subjectivity, advocacy, news-faking, fictionalization, everything short of indictable fraud.

In actuality, the New Journalists tended not to get too close to the political heat of the 1960s. That was left to a corps of what amounted to domestic war correspondents, who infused journalism with a new social drama. They started in the civil-rights revolution in the South and worked their way through the whole gamut of turbulence. Although Harrison Salisbury was writing about the *New York Times* staff in *Without Fear or Favor* (1980), he could have been paying tribute to the whole corps when he praised "the cadre of a skilled, physically courageous, battle-trained staff which would go on to cover . . . the street conflicts in the northern Civil Rights struggle, the campus violence, the Vietnam demonstrations. . . ."

The appearance of the New Journalists and the battalion of reporters of social conflict (neither of which were confined, by the latter middle years of the 1960s, to the conventional press) transmitted a signal that journalism had turned around, that it was no longer a dead end, "a sort of dark corridor where only screw-ups went," as Halberstam once remarked. One clue could be found in the journalism schools: just about the time that Boroff's study declared them dead, their enrollments rebounded (long before any stimulus that could be attributed to Watergate). It appeared that journalism had begun to attract aspirants who, a few years before, had been going into other fields. Although Gay Talese, in *The Kingdom and the Power* (1969), found even the *Times*'s reporting staff still to be "dominated by men from the lower middle class," there was a feeling in the 1960s that more Ivied types, with more ambitious ideas, were moving in.

It was one of the oldest practitioners, Walter Lippmann, seventy-five years old in 1965, who signaled the arrival of the new generation. Lippmann, who four decades before had helped enunciate a new standard of objectivity for the press, now issued a new call for the independence of the journalist. In a notable address to the International Press Institute in London on May 27, 1965, Lippmann claimed that journalism was at last becoming a profession, an intellectual discipline. He set forth a standard that justified and reinforced what reporters had been doing in fact:

> *This growing professionalism is, I believe, the most radical innovation since the press became free of government control and censorship. For it introduces into the conscience of the working journalist a commitment to seek the truth which is independent of and superior to all his other commitments—his commitment to publish newspapers that will sell, his commitment to his political party, his commitment even to promote the policies of his government.*

He warned sternly that the new power and affluence of journalism carried hazards:

> *As the press becomes securely free because it is increasingly indispensable in a great society, the crude forms of corruption which belonged to the*

infancy of journalism tend to give way to the temptations of maturity and power. It is with these temptations that the modern journalist has to wrestle, and the unending conflicts between his duty to seek the truth and his human desire to get on in the world are the inner drama of the modern journalist's experience. . . . The most important forms of corruption in the modern journalist's world are the many guises and disguises of social climbing on the pyramids of power. . . .

In the same spring of 1965, Lippmann himself faced a test of his own incorruptibility. This was the era of the "credibility gap," a term evidently coined by a copy editor at the *Herald Tribune* for a story about the Johnson administration's fluctuating rationales for intervention in the Dominican Republic. The term was readily translatable to Vietnam, where Johnson, since the Tonkin Gulf resolution of 1964 (itself a failure of journalistic and legislative curiosity), had been engaged in Americanizing the war while insisting that policy had not changed. Johnson and his staff tried to co-op Lippmann by pretending to seek his advice. When Lippmann realized that Johnson wanted only flattery, he cut off the relationship, and over the next two years became more and more biting in his criticism of Vietnam policy. The White House retaliated with private and public derogation of Lippmann's record. His biographer, Ronald Steel, writes of "the snide remarks about his age and judgment, the embarrassed encounters at his club when old acquaintances nodded curtly or averted their eyes, the all-pervasive climate of intellectual fratricide and vendetta."

But Lippmann held firm. He had already made his plans for leaving Washington, and he took pains to assert that LBJ was not driving him out of town. His valedictory was serene: "A long life in journalism convinced me many presidents ago that there should be a large air space between a journalist and the head of a state. I would have carved on the portals of the National Press Club, 'Put not your trust in princes. . . .' "

Vietnam: The Roads to Tet

The Americanization of the Vietnam conflict raised a whole new set of issues in Saigon. Critics moved from questioning reporters' journalism to attacking their personal character. When Morley Safer of CBS reported on August 5, 1965, the burning by Marines of huts at the village of Cam Ne, the administration hinted that Safer's foreign birth (Canada) had affected the way he reported the story. In the fall of 1966, General S.L.A. Marshall, a widely published military analyst, charged correspondents with laziness, cowardice,* and lack of enthusiasm for things military: "The war is being covered primarily for all bleeding hearts. . . . "

It was no surprise that the first American reporter to visit the enemy capital underwent similar treatment. Late in 1966, Harrison Salisbury of *The New York Times* was granted a visa for a trip to Hanoi, and filed his first story, detailing damage from American bombing, on Christmas Eve. The Pentagon reluctantly conceded for the first time that American planes had hit civilian areas, but days later, speaking through the friendly *Washington Post*, it charged Salisbury with being a dupe—SALISBURY'S CASUALTIES TALLIED WITH VIET REDS'—because he had not attributed civilian casualty figures. Free-swinging attacks on Salisbury by other journalists led I.F. Stone, whose *I.F. Stone's Weekly* was for years the conscience of the capital press, to write that Salisbury had "evoked as mean, petty, and unworthy a reaction as I have ever seen in the press corps." Nonetheless, he had performed the service of enforcing candor

*Peter Braestrup dedicates his study of coverage of the Tet offensive, *Big Story* (1977), to fifty-two foreign journalists killed or missing in the conflict in Southeast Asia.

by extending coverage to include not only the bombardier but the bombed. This was in healthy contrast to what Michael J. Arlen of *The New Yorker* called the glamorization on the television networks of the air war ("The Bombs Below Go Pop-Pop-Pop").

Eventually, all roads led to Tet—that is, to some critical determination of who was telling the truth about the war. As the conflict swelled along its indeterminate course, correspondents tried harder to relate what they believed to be the truth of the matter—that the enterprise was headed toward no good end. Eventually, in August 1967, R.W. Apple, Jr., of the *Times* even dared to use the dread word "stalemate."

The startling North Vietnamese offensive at the end of January 1968, with its dramatic incursion into the grounds of the American embassy in Saigon, crystallized the issue of judgment. Tet had vast historical consequences, finally tipping the balance in the Washington establishment toward those who wanted to cut the losses; and for journalists it remained ever after the touchstone of Vietnam reporting. Those critical of Vietnam journalism still charge that correspondents, willing to believe the worst, monstrously misreported what happened at Tet as a defeat, when it was, by all military criteria, a victory. As late as 1985, the issue was the subject of a long libel struggle between the American commanding general and CBS.

In his mammoth study of Tet coverage, *Big Story* (1977), Peter Braestrup concluded that the character of the Tet battles had been misrepresented, partly because of circumstances that, he said, played upon journalism's weaknesses. But he also suggested that the character of journalists had been at fault—that Tet had inspired "the first show of the more volatile journalistic style . . . that has become so popular since the late 1960s. With this style came an often mindless readiness to seek out conflict, to believe the worst of the government or of authority in general, and on that basis to divide up the actors on any issue into the 'good' and the 'bad.' " He did not buttress this criticism with examples, perhaps because it was impossible to do so. Nonetheless, this motif has run through the years of criticism of Tet reporting—that journalists reported a defeat because that was what they preferred.

Even granting that initial reporting of Tet may have overemphasized disaster, this alone could hardly account for the unexpected shift back home. There dawned one of those mysterious moments of press agreement, the kind of thing that makes paranoids believe that a grand conspiratorial directorate must meet in a skyscraper somewhere and issue instructions to the media. A similar moment had occurred in the spring of 1954, when it became legitimate to oppose McCarthy openly. Now it was all right, at last, to sell out the war. Osborn Elliott, then managing editor of *Newsweek*, recalled that there had been division in his shop on Vietnam but abruptly, after Tet, "common ground began to form among us."

Most dramatically, Walter Cronkite—one of the few public voices in a position to compete with that of the president—returned from a visit to Vietnam and on February 27, 1968, discarded neutrality for a personal declaration that he believed that the United States must promptly negotiate its way out. From that point, criticism of war policies had an easier time gaining prominence in the news.

Despite this change of posture, the most memorable piece of investigative reporting to come out of the war had to fight its way into the press. More than a year after Tet, Seymour M. Hersh, then a free-lance investigative reporter, got a tip that a Lieutenant Calley was awaiting court-martial. Tracking down lawyers, Army officials, and Calley himself, he soon had a story: an American army unit had killed civilians at a village that became known to the world as My Lai. Hersh offered the story to *Life* and *Look*; both rejected it. Finally it broke into the press via syndication by the Dispatch News Service, an organization all but created for the occasion.

In November 1969, twenty months after the event, the American public learned another unpleasant truth about the war.

The Press Defiant

For Saigon reporters, Tet had represented a kind of vindication, for at last their home offices had concurred in their skeptical view of the war. But one more dramatic confirmation remained, evidence that over the course of American involvement in Vietnam the government, much more than the press, had been misleading. The Pentagon Papers provided a means to substantiate Charles Mohr's later judgment: "Not only ultimately, but also at each major milestone of the war, the weight of serious reporting corresponds quite closely to the historical record."

A curious combination of circumstances led to the existence and publication of the papers: Secretary of Defense McNamara's decision to create a historical record of the war; the chance selection of Daniel Ellsberg, hawk-turned-dove, as the courier to whom this record was entrusted; Ellsberg's futile efforts to get the material released officially; his reading of Neil Sheehan's extraordinary article on war crimes, which appeared in *The New York Times Book Review*; and, finally, Sheehan's receiving the documents. Once Sheehan had given the papers to the *Times*, there occurred the most extraordinary circumstance of all—the willingness of *The New York Times* to keep and prepare covertly for publication government documents clearly marked as secret.

Certainly, the publication of the documents, with accompanying narrative, starting on June 13, 1971, represented a further change in the old rules of deference to national security. In the debate that preceded publication, the journalists noted lawyers' frantic warnings and resolved to proceed anyway. Reston, his attitude a measure of how much the climate had changed since the Bay of Pigs, led the pro-publication side. While concerned with possible retaliation by the government, the debates were devoid of any talk of committing a political act; at least, the political was rationalized into the journalistic cover story of merely printing the news. Yet what could be more political than, in effect, seeking to show that the whole Vietnam exercise since the early 1960s had been based on publicly misstated premises? There were those who hoped and believed that publication would bring the war to a standstill; as journalists, they hardly dared say so.

Their hopes were doomed to disappointment. During the two weeks that publication was stopped—with a prior restraint of a kind never before imposed on an American newspaper—attention shifted to the legal battles and never returned fully to the substance of the secret documents. By the time the Supreme Court ruled in favor of the *Times*, a decision in which only three of the justices upheld the First Amendment with any enthusiasm, the Pentagon Papers had entered history as a case rather than as an exposé.

More striking in retrospect than that ambivalent decision was the astonishing response of other newspapers. Once restraint had been clamped on the *Times*, *The Washington Post*, freshly supplied with documents, began publication, only to be halted. Then it was *The Boston Globe*, the *Chicago Sun-Times*, the *Los Angeles Times*, the *St. Louis Post-Dispatch*, and *The Christian Science Monitor*—much of the nation's quality press joining instantly in what the Nixon administration had charged was lawbreaking. The Justice Department scurried about, trying to stop up all the holes, but of course failed in the end. (Network television, which also had a chance to participate, declined.)

The Pentagon Papers marked a high tide in institutional defiance, a response conditioned without doubt by the unique tensions of the moment, the widespread desperation to do something about the war. But it left a permanent residue in the emergence of a high-blown new ideology about the role of the press in relation to government. The germ of this new claim could be found in Justice Potter Stewart's assertion that the First Amendment had provided protection for the press as an institution so that it could serve as a watchdog or check on the constitutional branches of government. Journalists began to take more seriously what had previously been the rather informal notion of performing as a fourth branch of government, and Salisbury even claimed that publication of the Pentagon Papers had meant that the *Times* had "quite literally become that Fourth Estate, that fourth co-equal branch of government."

To Stewart's idea of a protected institutional press, journalism's ideologues added the idea of a First Amendment that was absolute. To support this claim they constructed a kind of pseudo-history that Fred Friendly, former president of CBS News and now a professor and commentator on press law, described as "making a dazzling leap from John Peter Zenger and the Alien and Sedition Acts to the Pentagon Papers . . . , treating the intervening two centuries as though they had produced only a series of . . . court decisions upholding the freedoms and privileges of the press." In the setting of the early 1970s, with plentiful real examples of government hostility to the press at hand, journalists equipped with this doctrine saw even mildly adverse developments, such as qualified court decisions, as repression.

The Newsroom Mutiny

The late 1960s and early 1970s were an era of anti-organizational discontents. What Gay Talese wrote of *The New York Times* was representative of many newsrooms—that there was "frustration in working for a place so large, so solvent and sure—a fact factory where the workers realize the too-apparent truth: they are replaceable." News staffers had little voice in determining the nature of their work; they were seldom asked for their ideas or listened to when they volunteered them. In particular, many reporters, witnessing the turbulence beyond the newsroom, found that their organizations were responding too slowly or not at all to the social and political crises of the Vietnam years; the magazines and the underground press seemed to get closer to the heart of things. Often, disaffection was expressed simply by leaving. Such departures usually did not alarm news organizations, which had always run on high turnover and an oversupply of labor. But even the *Times* must have found it disconcerting when it lost a parade of talent, including most of its crew of civil-rights reporters, as well as Halberstam.

Among those who stayed in the mainstream press there rose a new dissident movement, quite unlike anything seen before in the news business. Certainly there had been union organizing in newsrooms, but, as Breed had remarked, staff members had never ganged up on policy. Early activism took the form of violating the organizational taboo against politics: small numbers of journalists signed ads, wore buttons or armbands opposing the war, and even marched. But the focus soon began to shift to a general reappraisal of the individual journalist's place within the organization and a critique of the organization itself—of the standards of noninvolvement it imposed, of its supposed role in upholding established power, of the legitimacy of its least-examined premise, objectivity. Ron Dorfman, a Chicago reporter, commented: "Our 'objective' reporting is like the 'objective' scholarship of social scientists who study the powerless on behalf of the powerful, but never the powerful on behalf of the powerless." The movement contended that journalists literally had a right to autonomy—the right to determine the nature of their work without, as Lippmann implied, commercial, political, or even patriotic hindrance.

The underground ferment burst out abruptly in Chicago in the wake of the street theater of the Democratic convention of August 1968, that maelstrom of police and demonstrators into which journalists were dragged willy-nilly and, many of them, professionally radicalized. Afterward, a core of thirty-five met at Riccardo's restaurant to plan their next move. What they decided on was, of all things, a journalism review.

Why "journalism review"? The term had been around for nearly a decade, applied first to an annual publication issued by the University of Montana. The *Columbia Journalism Review*, issued by my old journalism school, which I served first as managing editor and then as editor, had been published since 1961. Thus the name had a certain recognizability, but it was clear that the Chicago group did not have in mind the Columbia model, which was viewed, not without justice, as being somewhat managerial in tone.

The Chicago founders wanted to create something completely different—a vehicle in which working journalists could criticize management and its policies.* This was indeed a fresh departure, a million light-years from the assumptions of the 1950s about the proper role of the employee-journalist and particularly the younger journalist. But it worked. From its first issue in October 1968, the *Chicago Journalism Review* was a lively, wide-ranging forum of critical discussion of the Chicago and national press, presented in a clean newsletter format often adorned by Bill Mauldin drawings.

The *Chicago Journalism Review* inspired a string of local reviews, which were run on volunteer help and were similarly impecunious and fragile. Philadelphia, St. Louis, Providence, Hartford-Springfield, Dallas, Houston, Baltimore, the Twin Cities, San Francisco, and southern California all eventually had such reviews.

Chicago outlasted all but one or two. (Washington finally got its own long after most of the others were dead.) Like any volunteer effort, they tended to stumble as initial enthusiasm declined, but often managements took steps to hasten the end. The Philadelphia *Evening Bulletin* forbade its staff to have anything to do with the local review. A trial issue of an Atlanta review, published in the *Columbia Journalism Review*, cost one participant his job on the *Journal-Constitution*. A mimeographed *AP Review* lasted but two issues, the second of which revealed that the AP had suppressed Peter Arnett's references to looting by American soldiers during the 1970 Cambodian incursion.

Although the Chicago effort was the pioneer, the journalism review that took charge of the young dissident movement was *More*, founded in New York in 1971 by Richard Pollak and others. Not only did the publication tap a stable of vigorous young writers, such as Halberstam and J. Anthony Lukas, but it displayed a certain chic missing in other reviews—for example, in its corporate name, Rosebud Associates (cf. *Citizen Kane*).

More arrived at a propitious moment, when the original dissidence had flowered into what was called, in 1960s style, the "reporter-power" movement. Pollak's editorials helped to formulate a national program, and the A. J. Liebling Counter-Conventions, scheduled by *More* opposite the ANPA's spring fertility dance and named for the critic who had dissected those gatherings from time to time, became rallies for the new cultures of journalism.

The call to the first counter-convention, in 1972, stated the premises of reporter power succinctly: "The journalist is one of the nation's most foolishly wasted resources. In city rooms and television newsrooms across the country, thousands of men and women capable of giving their communities the kind of enlightened, tough-minded reporting they deserve are daily demeaned by the feckless institutions for which they work. And thousands more leave or refuse to enter the profession every year because of a

*In general, writers on local journalism reviews were not expected to write about their own employers. Such a policy not only prevented a direct conflict of interest but kept the staffer's head from getting too far under the guillotine.

system that still rewards stenography and discourages enterprise. . . . " After the successful 1972 event in New York, attended by 3,000, a committee met to formulate a platform. It was as general as, say, the American Society of Newspaper Editors' unenforced "Canons of Journalism," yet it represented a fresh departure, an alteration of previous understandings, claiming that "journalists must be as free from censorship and arbitrary interference by management as management is free from censorship and interference by government."

It is possible that by the time this declaration was issued the newsroom movement had already crested. Although *More* dismissed The Newspaper Guild as hopeless, in fact the reformers often found that the collective-bargaining process, available only through the Guild, was the sole avenue to contractually protected reporter power. The Guild was not unsympathetic; it supported "a more direct voice in the product" and greater protection for the integrity of the individual's work and by-line. But it shunned the most foreign seeming and radical-sounding of reporter-power proposals, borrowed from such newspapers as *Le Monde* of France—a veto over change in ownership and the election of editors. Somehow, not much reporter power ended up in contracts. In Chicago, where the most intensive effort was made, the proposals were gradually pushed off the bargaining table by both sides. The one place where the effort endured was in Minneapolis, where the "underground church" at the *Minneapolis Tribune* developed, with management encouragement, a staff consultative body of some influence.

The newsroom-democracy movement produced its list of martyrs, mostly reporters who violated the taboo against fouling one's own nest. Three reporters were dismissed for attending and writing for outside publications about the counter-convention. Donald Drake of *The Philadelphia Inquirer* was demoted for writing an article in the *Philadelphia Journalism Review* titled "I Was a Whore for the Press"; *PJR*'s editors eventually counted up seven such casualties among eight founders. Four of five *Houston Chronicle* reporters on the masthead of the first issue of the *Houston Journalism Review* were gone within weeks, via firing or forced resignation. David Deitch of *The Boston Globe*, who had campaigned for worker (not merely reporter) control was fired for writing an article in *The Real Paper*, a weekly that allegedly competed with the *Globe*.

In each of these cases, the commonsensical view was that the employer had had extreme provocation and that the employee had been disloyal. At the same time, managements seemed in each case to be seeking to disregard the message that these journalists were conveying at such great risk to their careers. That rationale was well stated in the evanescent *AP Review*: "We seek change not because we are dissidents or militants—although some of us may be—but because we are journalists." The general management response to such assertions was that the contagion of wanting change had to be stamped out by strenuous measures before it could spread.

There was one more critique of news organizations: that they, like so many other employers that prided themselves on running pure meritocracies, discriminated in favor of those who belonged to the same group—white and male—from which management was drawn. Although most employers had given up overt forms of discrimination, the Kerner Commission report of 1968 found that the minority status in the newsroom was not much improved over the 1950s, when a Guild survey had found 38 blacks among 75,000 newspaper editorial employees. The commission inspired many expressions of good intent and eventually the minority component in newspaper newsrooms rose to 4 percent or so. But somehow many minority trainees never made it onto staff and most minority staff members never made it into positions of authority.

Women had less trouble being hired but just as much difficulty in rising. They were not usually paid as much as men, even when they did comparable work, with comparable seniority. Even when they escaped the pink-collar ghettos of "women's" news, they were considered primarily qualified as "soft" news reporters or for copy editing (which, being repetitive and fussy, was thought of as being like housework). In 1971, a year after the modern feminist movement got fully under way, the Associated Press Managing Editors Association maintained that women had no aptitude for executive roles and that, should they inadvertently be stuck in an executive role, their duty was "to make a man *feel* like the boss."

Minority and women's caucuses opened a new front of the anti-organizational campaign. The state and federal civil-rights legislation of the era, capped by the passage of the federal Equal Employment Opportunity Act of 1972, gave these groups new powers to call their employers into court. A successful early sortie took place at *Newsweek*, where women (as at *Time*) were largely segregated into the corps of fact-checkers. Over the next years there was concerted action, followed by lawsuits, by women or minorities or both at major organizations—the AP, *The New York Times*, NBC, *Reader's Digest*. No such suit ever came to trial and most were settled on terms of limited employer commitment over a limited time. As in the reporter-power movement, journalists risked their careers—in many cases without hope of personal gain.

Muckrakers Rampant

"Today, the question is not whether muckraking is being done, but whether anything *except* muckraking is being done." So, hyperbolically, the critic Jay Martin described the scene in 1970—the wave of exposures ranging from Hersh's My Lai story, through Ralph Nader's industrial investigations, through the underground press, to all-exposé magazines such as *Ramparts* and *Scanlan's*. The impulse to expose had deep roots, extending, the sociologist Herbert Gans has asserted, back into the Progressive era. But whereas the old muckrakers exposed the system so as to repair it, the new style was apocalyptic, implying both despair and desperate solutions.

Investigative reporters extended their scope not only to existing institutions but to the new dissidence: civil-rights and black-power agitation, radical student uprisings, peace activism, the drug culture. Such reporting demanded confidentiality, but even as reporters sought to protect their sources, prosecutors became more intent on forcing them to disclose their information. The most significant case was that of Earl Caldwell of *The New York Times*, who refused to discuss his Black Panther coverage before a grand jury. Yoked with two other culprits, Caldwell lost his case before the Supreme Court, which said, between the lines, that society could do without Caldwell's type of reporting.

Increasingly, the new muckraking focused intensively on national, presidential, bureaucratic government. This was truly the work of journalism as a Fourth Branch, devoted less to reporting on society as a whole than on the misdeeds of the Executive. Anthony Smith commented: "There is an assumed permanent relationship between journalism and political bureaucratic power comparable to that between a law-enforcement agency and the criminal classes."

The ground was prepared for the investigation of the ultimate in bureaucracy run amok—Watergate. What might have been called the "investigative culture" pointed toward a task never before essayed by American journalists—indicting a president. Conceivably, only the Nixon administration could have been so vulnerable. For one thing, perhaps no other administration had had so much to hide. For another, the administration hurt itself by fixing on the press as a mortal foe. It placed four dozen journalists on its secret "enemies" list and sent the vice-president around the country in 1969 and 1970 to attack the national media.

In the summer of 1972 Bob Woodward and Carl Bernstein, young *Washington Post* practitioners who had had no part in the feuding with the administration, got themselves into the Watergate story, having no initial idea of its dimensions or implications. Although their work has been dismissed by Edward Jay Epstein as a mere replay of leaks of a case developed by government investigators, it is clear from their own durable account, *All the President's Men*, that Woodstein in fact worked very hard to assemble facts that government did not want assembled.

Moreover, they and their editors presented Watergate in the only mode that could have survived the hostile scrutiny of the White House and won serious attention in the long run from an indifferent public—the neutral-sounding journalese of the investigative reporter. The major break came on October 10, 1972, with a story that announced that "the Watergate bugging incident stemmed from a massive campaign of political spying and sabotage conducted on behalf of President Nixon's reelection and directed by officials of the White House and the Committee for the Re-Election of the President. . . . " This even Epstein conceded to be investigative reporting.

For a time the dam held, and then Watergate exposures tumbled forth as other national media sought to catch up with the *Post*: Seymour Hersh's disclosure in the *Times* on January 14, 1973, of payments to the Watergate burglars; *Time*'s revelation of the first "White House horror"—the wiretaps on journalists and officials in 1969 following disclosure of the secret bombing of Cambodia; the stories in *Newsweek* in May 1973 on the damaging information emanating from the White House insider and informant, John Dean. In addition, the networks, notably NBC, undertook investigations that contributed to the resignation of Agnew. Finally, starting in May 1973, the Senate hearings began—and, as Timothy Crouse remarked in *Rolling Stone*, "put the Good Housekeeping Seal of Approval on the scandal, made it credible, and largely took over the investigation from the always-suspect press." The process of toppling the Nixon administration took about a year thereafter.

What had journalists wrought? Had they in effect killed the king? Some, such as the professional maverick Nicholas von Hoffman, looked back and found Watergate the nadir of press performance: "It wasn't journalism; it was lynching. Not only were the pretentious canons of the trade chucked overboard; so were fairness and common sense."

The only turn of events that could be called a mob action was another consensus of the kind that had moved press opinion on McCarthy and Tet. The consensus on Nixon appeared after the "Saturday-night massacre" (the firing of special prosecutor Archibald Cox and the resignation of his superiors) on October 20, 1973, when major newspapers and national magazines, as well as network commentators, began to call, almost in unison, for Nixon's resignation.

But the charge of lynching is more commonly applied to the behavior of reporters. Certainly there was deep antagonism toward Nixon, and it cropped up repeatedly during his late news conferences. But, as in Vietnam, what was actually published stood up well against the historical record; the repeated threats of the administration to take libel action did not materialize, and it was the White House, not the press, that chronically had to correct the record. If an adversary journalism was to exist in America, if only for a moment, this had been the right moment.

Attack from the Right

Even secure in the knowledge of having been mostly right, the press felt a chill. The problem was not revanchism; there seemed to be no impulse to punish the press for bringing down Nixon. But a longer-term trend was running by the mid-1970s, a flow of comment that pictured modern journalism as a usurper—much more visible than in the past, more powerful, and somehow alien. Although a certain amount of this criticism was aimed at the institutions of the press—notably the New York and Washington newspapers, the networks, and the newsmagazines—most was directed at journalists themselves. Journalists, it was alleged, were out of control and out of line with dominant social values; they had come to constitute a separate and subversive class. The effort to bring them back under control proceeded on three fronts: that of the external, largely conservative, critique; that of management-oriented public relations; and that of internal restrictions.

The conservative critique had begun to form long before Watergate. Edith Efron's *The News Twisters* (1971) became a bible for those who believed that television news carried an indelible liberal bias. Agnew added the idea that journalists exercised illegitimate political power. In 1971, Daniel P. Moynihan, then a subcabinet official in the Nixon administration, elaborated in *Commentary* an already commonplace idea that journalists now made up an elite drawn, he proposed metaphorically, from the *Harvard Crimson* and the *Columbia Daily Spectator*. They were, he charged, the charter members of the adversary culture, devoting their careers to promoting "attitudes genuinely hostile to American society and American government." Although the details of such a proposition tended to collapse under scrutiny, it had at least the germ of support in the fact that journalists had come to talk a good game about themselves as professionals; and a profession is, by definition, an elite.

Such critics as Irving Kristol focused on what they saw as the derangement of journalism's relationship with government. Writing in 1975, Kristol bemoaned the loss of deference, "the single most significant change that has occurred in journalism in our lifetime." He complained: "Not only do journalists no longer concede the government any prior claim to defining the news, they do not see government as having any right at all to have this point of view fully and fairly presented. . . . Instead, journalists today insist that *their* point of view is what defines 'the news.' " This was accurate enough; the question was whether it was a fault.

The most incisive of these analyses was the one that Paul H. Weaver wrote for the spring 1974 issue of *The Public Interest*. He attacked persistently adversary journalism as a kind of heresy posing as a tradition. At its extreme, Weaver contended, the movement placed journalists' rights—notably confidentiality—above the law. Down the road he could see America rent by a Europeanized, politicized journalism; he urged journalists to return to the ways of objective cohabitation with government.

Weaver and others portrayed this apparent change in the operating basis of journalism as alarming; but the more alarming possibility was that the basic change had been in the opposite direction. Ben H. Bagdikian, successor as national press critic to Liebling, raked over coverage of the 1972 campaign and found that, in effect, Agnewism had triumphed. Far from being adversarial, the behavior of most news organizations had represented "a tragic time of reversal of the lessons of the 1950s and 1960s," which had "moved the American news system closer to becoming a propaganda arm of the administration in power." Joseph P. Lyford, writing at about the same time, presented the case even more forcefully:

> *. . . the Cold War and Vietnam have institutionalized a system for the massive production by private and public bureaucracies of something that might be called "supernews"—the type of news that results from a mixing of censorship, propaganda, and "public information."*

Journalists, Lyford maintained, had but puny power to counter the voice of the Executive. To those who pointed to the Watergate controversy as a contradiction of his thesis of "a growing symbiosis" between government and the press, Lyford responded: "What most of the news media want is a return to the days when things went smoothly."

The Managers Regroup

Lyford was on target. Nixon had hardly left the White House when journalism's own managers—led by *The Washington Post*'s publisher, Katharine Graham—suggested that a period of less aggressiveness was in order. The managerial network had already set in motion public relations measures designed to temper the conservative critique and to reduce public anxiety about journalism. Inevitably, these measures took the form of controlling, or seeming to control, the activities of employees.

On the macro level, a national press council took shape, fertilized by the example of the British press council and recommended by the Hutchins Commission in 1947. A consortium sponsored by the Twentieth Century Fund issued a prospectus in November 1972 and the National News Council—an unofficial, quasi-judicial body devoted to receiving, investigating, and opining on complaints—began to function in the following year.

From the start, the council had to struggle. It was chronically short of funds, even after it began to accept contributions from the organizations it was monitoring. A key newspaper, *The New York Times,* denounced the council as backdoor opening to government controls. The journalism review *More* fixed on it as a basically managerial solution and thus antithetical to its program of reform. (By contrast, the *Columbia Journalism Review* published reports of council decisions for four years.) In the end, the council persisted for eleven years. After its demise, its unrealized possibilities were paid a kind of tribute by General William C. Westmoreland, who said after his protracted libel battle with CBS that such disputes ought to be resolved in some kind of news council; he had apparently never heard of the one that was in existence when he sued.

The same technique of handling complaints microscopically was transferred to the local level by creation of the newspaper ombudsman or reader representative. The concept was first floated by A. H. Raskin in *The New York Times* (which has itself always shunned an ombudsman like poison) and was first adopted, in Louisville, in 1967.

The essentially managerial character of the ombudsman was not always clear in the public-relations fluff that portrayed the individual (usually a senior journalist in the organization) as an independent representative of the public interest. Ben Bagdikian's struggle with the position at *The Washington Post* made this clearer. Bagdikian raised hackles with his first column, which dealt with the "Metro Seven"— black reporters at the *Post* who demanded reform of the newspaper's hiring and promotion systems. Then, in a panel at Harvard on April 6, 1972, he said something that the executive editor, Bradlee, interpreted as favoring a black boycott of the *Post*, and there was an angry parting of the ways. The *Post*, however, continued to be the leading exponent of ombudsmanship, and over the years it was joined by as many as three dozen like-minded newspapers.

In the same era, journalism's interlocking public-relations directorate raised the unassailable banner of ethics to keep journalists from stirring up unfavorable publicity. Three major national organizations—the American Society of Newspaper Editors, the Associated Press Managing Editors, and Sigma Delta Chi/Society of Professional Journalists—all rewrote their codes of principles between 1973 and 1975, each implicitly condemning misbehavior by individual journalists, but offering not a word on individual journalists' rights, inside the organization or out.

Codes at particular news organizations were cut from the same pattern, but with more specificity. Employees were to refrain from any activity that might embarrass the employer, from political involvement to—and this indicated the changing status of journalists—investments that might create a conflict of interest. Moreover, management was to be the sole judge of propriety—a proposition upheld in a National Labor Relations Board decision in 1975. Diane Woodstock, president of a Guild local in Wisconsin, stated correctly that the issue was "the power of the management to control the staff versus the power of the staff to control its work and its privacy." The management position was stated, with unintended bluntness, in a National News Council report asserting that under such codes reporters "are not forfeiting their rights; they are temporarily suspending the exercise of some of them."

Although such codes did not directly restrict the newsroom-democracy campaign, they were a symptom of reasserted managerial control. In that light, the reporter-power movement began to look less like a revolution than a last stand against bureaucratization, accelerated in these years by the widespread adoption of the perfect bureaucratic tool, the newsroom computer—a system permitting not only easier tracking of work product and worker, but also the shifting of technical, clerical, and production functions onto journalists. Only a year after the buoyant 1972 counterconvention, *More* found that the reform movement had lost momentum—that the "redistribution of power seems to spook those who ought to be most interested in it"; two years later, it conceded that most journalists "accept management control as a given." Reporter power became the concern of a minority, or rather of a minority of the concerned minority.

Rank-and-file disenchantment may have risen in part from a realization that reporter power might not mean much more democracy. A Harvard specialist in organizational behavior, Chris Argyris, gained access to *The New York Times* for a time in the early 1970s, during the efflorescence there of reporter-power activity. The *Times* news operation, Argyris noted (in *Behind the Front Page,* 1974), was already run by former reporters; those who wanted to gain power were much like those already in power—"authoritarian, individualistic, and competitive."

Moreover, there was a disconcerting note of social unconcern in the reporter-power platform. Peter Dreier, who studied the Chicago reporter-power movement, attributed its collapse in part to its failure to develop bases in the community. Indeed, some journalists came to regard the public as enemy number one, their chief responsibility being to live up to the expectations of their peers and the abstractions of their profession. "Professionals," James Carey remarked in 1978, "are privileged to live in a morally less ambiguous universe than the rest of us."

Order Restored

It is impossible to tell when a whiff of Pulitzer Prize began to waft through *The Washington Post* in connection with Janet Cooke's story about an eight-year-old black heroin addict—no later, certainly, than the time it was published on September 28, 1980, under the headline JIMMY'S WORLD. In the account later offered by the *Post* ombudsman, it is clear that in the process that permitted the fabrication, Cooke, a neophyte reporter, was less important than her powerful organizational sponsors. The attacks by Washington officials on the story and the *Post*'s indignant defense of its right to conceal its sources seemed only to enhance the story's prize value. It was soon shipped off to the Pulitzer factory, where its quasi-realism, luminous detail, and implied sense of moral concern struck the jury and the advisory board as representing the very best in journalism (and, of course, it arrived under the best of aegises, that of the heroes of Watergate). On April 13, 1981, it received a Pulitzer. Within two days, anomalies appeared, first in Janet Cooke's résumé, then in the story itself, and the *Post* was compelled to return the prize.

Almost at once it became clear that the significance of the matter within the journalism community extended far beyond the circumstances that it involved the Pulitzer Prizes and *The Washington Post,* although these certainly gave it initial prominence. The incident mobilized the whole journalistic counterreformation, for it crystallized among those whom the critic David Eason has dubbed the "conventionalists" everything that had gone awry in journalism over the previous two decades. Eason wrote: "The predominant thrust of this commentary—so predominant that few alternative conceptualizations were published—was that journalism had lost its way in the 1960s and 70s and that it needed to turn away from these new practices and reconnect with the better traditions of its history." In short, these commentators were ready to evoke an imagined past of tough-minded (and dead) city editors as a replacement for the uncomfortable present—somebody along the lines, say, of Walter Burns of *The Front Page.*

Editors even tried to put this romantic notion into practice. There was for a time a hot pursuit of news-fakers, and *The New York Times,* the New York *Daily News,* and the AP each had its petty embarrassment. A poll conducted a year later for the ASNE revealed that editors on nearly 30 percent of the responding newspapers claimed to have tightened controls to reporters—mostly over use of anonymous sources—as a result of the episode. Tellingly, four out of five respondents still said they considered it important for their newspaper to compete for prizes.

Yet it has long been clear that unwritten newsroom policies are more important than the written, and the unwritten rules that were in effect by 1982 mocked the notion that journalism could turn the clock back to an imaginary time. Stephen Hess, in *The Washington Reporters* (1981), observed that real-life editors, "not caring very much, not knowing very much, being too busy, deferring to experts, wanting to retain morale," exerted little control over the output of reporters.

At first glance, such an analysis might have made it sound as if reporter power had triumphed in the long run, that reporters at last had the autonomy envisioned in the 1970s. Yet any working reporter knew instinctively that it was not true. Certainly, as Hess observed, most stories were developed on reporter initiative and were left largely intact on the way to publication, but there were still rules guiding the work. A reporter still knew that a news story demanded a certain approach and political placement. Any major violation would, of course, result in nonpublication and eventually, perhaps, in nonemployment.

How could reporters be free and confined at the same time? One student of the problem, John Soloski of the University of Iowa, has concluded that the standards of professionalism, which were the symbols of rebellion in the 1950s, have been transmuted into a system of control: "The value of news professionalism for the news organization is that it establishes norms of conduct making it unnecessary for the news organization to arbitrarily establish elaborate rules and regulations for news staffers." What had once been the reporters' weapon against the parochialism of the organization had become the organization's weapon against their autonomy.

This was indeed a balance point in the equilibrium that returned to newsrooms after the disruptions of the 1970s. Hess saw it as a specific bargain: although reporters have less supervisory authority than employees of comparable rank in other fields, they have the quasi-professional prerogative of not having specific managerial judgments imposed on their work. He hardly needed to add that they also have careers in a sense not known to previous journalistic generations—salaries extending at the major institutions toward the upper reaches of five figures (and well beyond in television), as well as the comforts of professional prestige and social status. "This is a trade-off," Hess wrote, "that seems to satisfy both management and labor."*

This truce also embodies a condition of near-stability in the composition of the news staff. Despite the affirmative-action lawsuits that once threatened to force change, and even the sharing of authority, the hiring and promotion of women and minorities has remained at a level that poses little challenge to the dominant culture of the newsroom (with a few exceptions, such as the Gannett Company, which carries out its affirmative-action programs with a corporate thoroughness worthy of the country's biggest newspaper publisher). Authority is shared, not primarily with those who first defined themselves as discriminated against, but with those successors among women and minority journalists who are willing to accept the terms of those now in charge.

In the historical setting, this new stability can be seen as the result of the long transition of the newsroom from a quasi-industrial shop, with direct and arbitrary controls, to the invisible controls of a mature bureaucracy, more enlightened than the restrictions that Breed depicted but, in the end, equally protective of the stability of the institution. Such stability plays an important role in fitting otherwise anomalous news operations into the diffuse conglomerates that have become their economic base. Corporate managements need not tinker with a news operation so long as it sells papers and attracts advertisers; news is simply a consumer product of certifiable quality.

*Conditions in many smaller organizations, it must be noted, have not risen far above the level of the 1950s. Employers hold salaries down to secretarial levels and gouge employees by denying them overtime pay or by using their services on an hourly basis without making them employees, thus denying them benefits.

The New Age of Deference

There remained at the end of the 1970s one more major item on the agenda of journalism—to reach some kind of new understanding with power. A specific call for a truce came in May 1982 from Michael J. O'Neill of the New York *Daily News*, who spoke as the retiring president of the American Society of Newspaper Editors. "We should make peace with the government," he said. "We should not be its enemy. . . . We are supposed to be the observers, not the participants—the neutral party, not the permanent political opposition." He added: "We should cure ourselves of our adversarial mindset. The adversarial culture is a disease attacking the nation's vital organs." Disavowing, as it did by implication, what many in journalism considered its major achievements of the previous twenty years, this proposition hardly met universal approval. Benjamin Bradlee of *The Washington Post*, for one, responded that making such a peace with the government was "a pact with the devil." Yet O'Neill's speech had wide appeal, proposing as it did a return to deference and release from the stresses of being a watchdog.

In fact, a truce with government was already setting in, but not necessarily on the cozy terms that O'Neill envisioned. Neither side really acknowledged the arrangement, for the national press still lived by the slogans of adversariality, and the government still complained regularly about press irresponsibility.

But government appeared at last to realize that it did not need to engage in the paranoid feuding of the Johnson and Nixon periods, and there have been no further grand confrontations of the type of the Pentagon Papers or Watergate. For its part, the press no longer automatically lines up against government pleas for secrecy. When in 1979 Carter's Justice Department tried to suppress an article about the technology of the H-bomb in *The Progressive* magazine, *The Washington Post* advised *The Progressive* to back down, since no major social interest was involved.

Moreover, press behavior has become more cautious politically. One telling incident occurred in 1982, when *The New York Times* again had a foreign corespondent in hot water—this time Raymond Bonner, for his coverage of a village massacre in El Salvador by government forces. The assault on Bonner (and on Alma Guillermoprieto of *The Washington Post*) was couched in familiar terms: a long editorial in *The Wall Street Journal* ranged through the roster of the deluded and disloyal, starting with John Reed and working through Herbert Matthews and David Halberstam (Halberstam, being alive, defended himself ably), Janet Cooke, and finally Bonner. Accuracy in Media (the long-lived scourge of the liberal press) joined in by saying that Bonner was part of a "propaganda war favoring the Marxist guerrillas in El Salvador." Six months later, the *Times* withdrew Bonner, suggesting that he had had insufficient experience, and he soon left the newspaper. Before long, the paper hired—not exactly as a replacement—Shirley Christian of *The Miami Herald*, who had criticized as dupes the reporters who had covered the Sandinista revolution in Nicaragua and was publishing an anti-Sandinista book. Curiously, where Bonner's politicization had pointed him toward an exit, Christian's had not hurt her at all.

This sequence may have said less about the *Times* specifically—although it certainly said *something*—than about the increasingly restricted political setting in which all the national press was operating. Starting with the seizure of the Teheran embassy late in 1979 and the Russian occupation of Afghanistan the press had both reported and joined what George Kennan called the greatest "militarization of thought and discourse" since World War II. Roger Morris wrote in 1980: "American opinion this winter bristled with a strident, frustrated chauvinism—and, from sea to shining sea, American journalism bristled with it." In such episodes and in repeated international terrorist incidents, the press, led by television, played the patriot, obsessively focusing on crisis and suggesting that America, not individuals, had been held hostage. At the same time, the press thus cannily painted itself as being as loyalist as the jingo in the street.

Grenada brought home to journalists their new impotence. An invasion in 1983 of a puny antagonist, on grounds at least partly fabricated, was widely accepted as a major American victory. The press chose to complain less about the flaws in policy than about the Pentagon's refusal to let reporters ride in with the troops, and was rebuked by public indifference to its pleas. There followed self-examination and vows to take new steps to restore "credibility"—journalism's public-relations term of last resort.

Grenada was a clinching instance in the rise and triumph of "supernews"—the concept invented a decade before by Joseph Lyford but now carried to Orwellian lengths that he had perhaps not envisioned. The supernews of the Reagan era—that is, the official voice that renders all countering voices impotent—has been augmented by three characteristics. First, it has little competition from within government, for the administration has done its best, by legal action and retaliation, to shut off the important flow of information that is trivializingly called "leaks." Second, and more important, the official voice is now so persistent that it outlasts non-Executive voices, including the only occasionally adversarial voice of the press. Finally, supernews is so dominant and clear that it seems always to be saying much more than it actually tells—for example, claims of success in the raid on Libya in the spring of 1986 were made before Washington could have known the actual results.

The standard that provided incentive for coverage of Vietnam and Watergate, that of journalism that could stand the test of history, has been placed in jeopardy by supernews. In

Central America, American journalists have exposed serious shortcomings in American policies and clients, but over the years the government has successfully overcome such details and has won its main points, to the extent that by 1986 official premises—that, for example, a government in Central America constitutes a major security threat to the United States—underlay many news stories. Such assumptions were effectively tested by reporting from Vietnam; in the case of Central America, by contrast, supernews has made it possible for official policy to triumph over mere fact.

Neither journalists nor their critics would necessarily agree that the journalism of 1986 is at a dead end. After all, in comparison with their status in the 1950s, journalists are immensely more visible, more endowed with the trappings of power, more secure in status and economic expectations. They can view this current period, if they so choose, as one of healthy consolidation for themselves and their institutions, the inevitable sequel to insurgency.

Moreover, they can argue, the present arrangements may be merely a pause, while the generation that first took over in the 1960s, its managers now contemplating retirement, tidies up its work. At last report, Homer Bigart, approaching eighty, was living as a gentleman in retirement in New Hampshire; and even the Young Turk, David Halberstam, has passed fifty. The group of new managers that came in early in the 1960s—of which A. M. Rosenthal has been the most eminent—have been stepping down one by one.

Similarly, the shaking-out of news institutions that has proceeded in the background in these past decades can be looked on as a kind of corporate rationalization of the field. Certainly it has left behind much-mourned institutions—the *New York Herald Tribune, The Washington Star*, the *Chicago Daily News*, the Philadelphia *Bulletin*, to name a few. (It has erected few new ones—Gannett's *U.S.A. Today* is the only major new newspaper—in their place.) The three wire services of the 1950s have been reduced to two, or, arguably, one and a half; the three networks have been augmented only by a scrawny public broadcasting arm and a cable news service. The three newsmagazines are just the same titles as thirty years ago. What has changed is that each of these institutions (except the AP and public broadcasting) and almost every major newspaper is now part of a larger corporate structure, itself a bureaucracy in a society in which bureaucracies are the major institutions.

This once-insurgent generation can begin now to look back and contemplate how well it has fared in the struggle that Walter Lippmann predicted more than two decades ago: "the unending conflicts between [the] duty to seek the truth and [the] human desire to get on in the world." Many journalists (and journalistic institutions), if they are in a self-congratulatory mood, can say plausibly that they have both sought truth and gotten on, and that in fact getting on has enabled them to seek the truth more freely. Yet at the same time they may have lost that quintessential sense of being outside, of being below the salt, that made them at least intermittently effective critics of society and polity. And they have certainly yet to demonstrate that they are immune, in Lippmann's words, to "the most important forms of corruption in the modern journalist's world . . . the many guises and disguises of social climbing on the pyramids of power."

Index

A

B

C

D

N

Q

R

S

T

U

V

W

Y

Z